Advances in Theory and Practice of Emerging Markets

Series Editor
Yogesh K. Dwivedi
EMaRC, School of Management
Swansea University Bay Campus
Swansea, UK

Emerging Markets (EMs) exhibit a number of unique characteristics (i.e. unique challenges and opportunities) in terms of socio-economic, demographic, cultural, political, and regulatory. Examples of such unique challenges and opportunities includes diversity and fragmentation of markets, differential market growth rate in terms of urban vs rural, evolution of institutions, political instability, distinct cultural heritage, inherent corruption, and unusual technological diffusion trends. Unique characteristics of EMs makes this context different from developed countries, causing implications for both theory and practice. It necessitates substantial adaptations of theories developed and approaches employed in the Western world for investigating problems specific to such markets. As such, doing research in the EMs context for establishing new conceptual and theoretical paradigms from multidisciplinary perspectives is vital for making the global economy more equitable and sustainable.

This book series aims to publish scholarly work from a variety of disciplines (for example, information systems, electronic government, marketing, digital and social media marketing international business, human resources, public administration, entrepreneurship, operations and supply chain management, health care management, finance, accounting, economics, innovation, science policy, built environment, energy production and consumption, agriculture extension and management, biodiversity conservation and management, sustainable development) focusing on the issues prominent in Emerging Markets such as India, China, Brazil, Russia and South Africa in a book series.

The series will strive to publish conceptual, theoretical, and empirical works relating to the contexts of Emerging Markets. This series will contain four sub-series including: monographs, handbooks, edited volumes, and text books. The Research Monographs and Handbooks sections will focus on the state-of-the-art of both established and emerging topics specifically in the contexts of Emerging markets. Doctoral research produced from the institutions based in one of the EMs countries would also be considered for publication in the monograph category of the series. Monographs will be considered both in the form of relatively shorter pieces and traditional more extended works. This series would also encourage and invite academics and researchers to publish text books specific to EMs context.

More information about this series at https://www.springer.com/series/15802

Richard Boateng • Sheena Lovia Boateng
Thomas Anning-Dorson
Longe Olumide Babatope
Editors

Digital Innovations, Business and Society in Africa

New Frontiers and a Shared Strategic Vision

Springer

Editors
Richard Boateng
University of Ghana Business School
Accra, Ghana

Sheena Lovia Boateng
University of Ghana Business School
Accra, Ghana

Thomas Anning-Dorson
University of the Witwatersrand
Johannesburg, South Africa

Longe Olumide Babatope
American University of Nigeria
Yola, Nigeria

ISSN 2522-5006 ISSN 2522-5014 (electronic)
Advances in Theory and Practice of Emerging Markets
ISBN 978-3-030-77986-3 ISBN 978-3-030-77987-0 (eBook)
https://doi.org/10.1007/978-3-030-77987-0

This Springer imprint is published by the registered company Springer Nature Switzerland AG
The registered company address is: Gewerbestrasse 11, 6330 Cham, Switzerland

To the current and next generation of scholars, researchers, practitioners, policymakers, and students in Africa and beyond.

Foreword by Helen Inseng Duh

Africa is alive and active in digital innovations and use. But is the African story well told about its digital innovations and use? The answer is an emphatic NO! How much do we know about the numerous digital innovations available for use – and influencing business and society in Africa? I dare to say very little! There hasn't been a comprehensive book attempting to document Africa's digital innovations and how the innovations shape business and society in the continent. A point worthy of note is that Africa's Internet and mobile phone penetration rate is faster than that of any other continent.

Additionally, the uptake of digital innovations on the continent has seen quantum leaps in the past few years. The level of online and digital activities within the continent is fast catching up with the rest of the world. Africa has become a massive market for developing and testing as well as an expansion market for all kinds of digital products and services. Consumption of digital innovation in different sectors rises year on year. Therefore, Africa's story about digital innovations, their uses, and the value creation for businesses and society needs to be told more comprehensively.

This book portrays the African story of digital innovations, their uses, and value creation across businesses and society in several captivating chapters. In its three enriching parts (i.e., digital innovation and value creation, digital disruption and transformation, and digital innovation and development), this book is invaluable to everyone; academics, business executives, entrepreneurs, public sector officials, healthcare practitioners, social workers, and human development officers interested in population displacement and human geography. Through its intriguing and encompassing chapters, this comprehensive book offers insightful lessons to both businesses and the general society. The book creates a nexus of knowledge that relies on the deep insight of African experts and researchers across different countries and disciplines, which makes the book a multidisciplinary compendium on digital innovation and consumption in the African continent.

From the knowledge-enriching journey the book takes you, there would be a clear articulation of how far and fast the African continent is going with digital innovations. This book enlightens us on the use and what works through the success stories and lessons. These would empower for greater digital innovations and attract profitable investments for the advancement of the African society we dream of. From the rich contents of this book, the route for Africa's development – be it healthcare, agriculture, commerce, communication, education, supply chain, etc. – will be assured. Enjoy your reading, and we wish you a wonderful learning experience as you journey through the pages of this enriching book.

Head, School of Business Sciences Helen Inseng Duh
University of the Witwatersrand,
Johannesburg, South Africa

Foreword by Muesser C. Nat

The basis for digital innovation has been to enhance business strategy and understand organizational processes and systems in order to improve efficiency. Digital innovations continue to facilitate this objective. In today's digital ecosystem, digital innovations largely inspire new strategy. Current digital innovations like virtual reality, cloud services, social media, and IoTs provide businesses with different capabilities to inspire strategy. For example, (a) endless collaborative opportunities, (b) massive data for new insights, (c) globalization, and (d) digital economy. Embracing digital innovations inspires the means of identifying new customer value propositions achieved by the reengineering of existing services or processes with digital technology.

Technology available to drive digital innovation is readily available, and almost all organizations irrespective of size or value can readily access and deploy them. Thus, digital technology today is no longer a source of market barrier or competitive advantage. Anyhow an organization applies or deploys a technology can be carbon copied. In other words, deploying digital technologies alone may only raise the competitive barrier of the baseline expectations for products or services for an enhanced consumer experience.

Therefore, if deploying digital technologies cannot create a competitive advantage, then innovatively using them to achieve new value propositions is the source of advantage. Businesses in this case need to innovate with new strategies, ideas, processes, and skills to deliver services or products consistent with new value propositions of consumers. This is not easy to achieve. The fact that organizations must rapidly innovate and excel in their core business functions makes it a huge task. These two objectives are almost opposed to each other. Rapid innovation thrives on agile teams supported by business and digital technology components. Operational excellence is largely supported by large enterprise systems with well-streamlined processes. While innovation is more about trial and error during learning, operational excellence emphasizes process optimization.

As a result, many organizations in their quest to digitally innovate have found it a 'zigzagging' and cumbersome journey. In my study of digital innovation and organizational transformation, no organization has fully completed this journey. This notwithstanding, new discoveries continue to emerge on how organizations are progressing on this path.

This book particularly captures principles and best practices for digital innovation. The contributions herein offer valuable insights into what works and does not. It is an insightful starting point. The journey of digital innovation may be long but very rewarding. Many extraordinary visions will be fulfilled to improve consumer experience. We hope you find valuable insights and tips to help any organization digitally innovate effectively as you review this book.

Director, School of Applied Sciences Muesser C. Nat
Head, Department of Management Information Systems
Cyprus International University
Nicosia, Cyprus

Testimonials

This book is a long-needed inquiry into how Africa is responding to new and emerging digital innovations through various entrepreneurial activities. A 'must read' across disciplines and sectors for entrepreneurs, policymakers, academics, and students.

Chris Mahony
CEO, Peloria Insights

This book is designed for entrepreneurs, policymakers, governmental and non-governmental organizations, business professionals, academics, researchers, and students seeking current research on how Africa is responding to the new and emerging digital innovations through various entrepreneurial and societal activities. An entertaining and insightful read.

Daniel Marfo
Senior Vice President, Zipline International

Digital innovations are shaping the different areas of business and global development. Therefore, it is paramount that organizations evolve to realize the digital value and benefits presented by the digital revolution. This book presents well-structured, industry-relevant and academically sound cases with tangible results. This book is an excellent source of inspiration and insight for every practitioner who cares about digital innovations.

Asst. Prof. Dr. Tuğberk Kaya
Cyprus International University
Northern Cyprus

Digital innovation has pushed aftown beyond the borders of Ghana to countries like Nigeria, South Africa, just to mention a few, faster than I imagined. Payment integrations amongst other integrations into business platforms like aftown have proven that Africa has experienced enormous growth taking into consideration the impact of digitalization on music sales in African. This book confirms the immeasurable evidence that digital innovation has brought Africa closer to the technological world, and indeed has come to stay.

Jefferson Seneadza
Founder & Head of Technology, aftown
Ghana, Nigeria, South Africa

This book makes an important contribution to understanding the social and economic dynamics of the African continent. Because of these features, it is a book that appeals to policymakers in addition to academics, students, and the business world.

İpek Akad, Ph.D.
Department of Economics, Bitlis Eren University, Turkey

Preface

For African enterprises, entrepreneurs, and governments to take full advantage of new digital opportunities, we need a shared strategic understanding of where we are, what we have, and what we may need to have for the future. This book presents this shared strategic vision to help coordinate future actions of African enterprises, entrepreneurs, consumers/citizens, and governments in using new and emerging digital technologies.

Our idea behind editing this book is to present a contemporary reference that tells Africa's story in the digital economy and its response to new and emerging technologies. Considering existing institutional challenges and the birth of new ones, including the COVID-19 pandemic, we aim at showcasing how consumers/citizens, entrepreneurs, researchers, organizations, institutions, and governments are leveraging new and emerging digital innovations to disrupt and transform value creation and service delivery in Africa. For this book, we gathered 17 contributions on new directions for Africa in the use of new and emerging digital technologies. The contributions span thematic areas such as online pharmaceutical marketing, influencer marketing, smart cities, the COVID-19 pandemic and digital platform consumption, COVID-19 and small and medium-sized enterprises, artificial intelligence and forecasting Internally Displaced People (IDP), fairness and digital platforms, drones and health care, and mobiles payments. The contributions detail new strategies, best practices, and lessons from the successes and failures in addressing challenges and leveraging new and emerging technologies appropriately for the good of Africa. Further, future research directions, guidelines, and recommendations for practice and policy are provided for researchers, practitioners, policymakers, teachers, and students.

The contributions presented in this book are grouped into three major blocks, representing thematic areas of concern. Part I contains contributions to digital innovation and value creation. The six contributions report on e-commerce and globalization with implications for Africa, the use of drones in healthcare in Africa, digital value and entrepreneurial behavior in Africa, mobile payments and micro-business activities in Ghana, and defining effective twitter message characteristics to aid in creating value in communication among interest groups and organizations in Africa.

The first contribution highlights that despite two decades of research on e-commerce, Africa has yet to make a substantial contribution from the perspective of globalization. Such a contribution may stem from the regional level or cross-national studies which examine the adoption and use of new technologies in e-commerce, the comparative review of national policies, and the use of globalization theories in e-commerce research in Africa. Considering Africa's diverse differences in technology readiness, and our rich patterns of communication (offline and online), there is room for a unique contribution from Africa. The contributions of drones in healthcare and mobile payment and micro-business activities tend to provide such new perspectives from Africa. Drones and mobile payments demonstrate how technology equips African institutions, businesses, and society to work collectively to address or navigate institutional and structural weaknesses. For example, quick delivery time for drones, healthcare facilities in remote areas, and the late arrival of medical supplies were identified as the most important factors and conditions facilitating drones' implementation for healthcare delivery. There is, therefore, an opportunity to save lives and preserve the needed human capacity in remote areas in Africa. The other contribution also echoes that mobile payments enhance the performance and potential sustenance of micro-businesses. It is in this same light that the contribution on digital value and entrepreneurial behavior established that across the 54 African states, digital value generated from technology adoption facilitates entrepreneurial behavior (SME start-up). These measures to eliminate or reduce technology adoption barriers should be a national agenda to spur entrepreneurial behavior in Africa. Then again, the final contribution in Part I of the book examines the characteristics underlying highly effective messages of 123 Interest Group Organizations (IGOs) in Africa. Largely, highly effective messages reveal an average of 9 verbs and 3.5 nouns per message. An average of 37 words per message and 13.5 words per sentence. They also possess an informal tone and are written in a direct style. Hence, to draw desirable engagement reactions in the form of increased dissemination and comments from Twitter audiences, African IGOs may need to follow these and other recommended guidelines.

Part II represents contributions related to digital disruption and transformation. Two of the five contributions take on emerging trends – influencer marketing and online pharmaceutical marketing – which should be of interest to African researchers, practitioners, and students. Though key knowledge gaps exist for future research, both areas of research require a theoretically driven, multidisciplinary, and multi-actor approach (academia, industry, government, and civil society) to create a unique and contextually relevant voice for Africa. They also add that only a very limited number of countries from Africa, like South Africa, are contributing to these areas of research, and as such, cross-national and regional studies are required to foster collaboration and to create that contextually relevant voice for Africa. The remaining contributions provide a review of business models of e-logistics platforms in Sub-Saharan Africa, a case report on digital strategies for surviving COVID-19 pandemic in an SME, and an examination of digital platforms' consumption during the COVID-19 pandemic among university students in South Africa and Ghana. The contributions on business models and digital strategies tend to highlight that platform business owners and SMEs leveraging digital innovations should focus on strategies that will build and enhance the digital ecosystem (interactions and value accrued by participants connected via the digital platform). The latter contribution in Part II adds that the problematic use of digital platforms in the height of the COVID-19 pandemic led to myriad consequences, including *mental health complications (depression and frustration), health complications and impaired social life functions, and emotional instability (despair and mood swings)*. Unfortunately, institutional and national post-COVID interventions were often silent on these issues. The authors propose a model and recommendations on the use of self-regulation as a technology use reduction mechanism.

Finally, Part III covers contributions related to emerging perspectives on digital innovations and development. Two of the six contributions review literature on fairness in the platform economy and the dimensions and issues in smart city research. Future research directions and guidelines are provided with respect to these contemporary themes. Concerning fairness on platform economy, the contribution emphasizes the need to shift the focus of research, practice, and policy from discussions revolving around digital platforms and resources that facilitate platform work to issues related to discrimination, bias, inequality, and equity in engaging in the platform economy. The latter issues have the potential of threatening the sustainability and the 'good' of digital platforms. Concerning Africa, though some studies are emerging, there is a need for regional analysis or comparative studies across countries, examining the forms of platform injustice, the role of labor unions and other worker associations, and the effects of platforms on traditional providers of services. Concerning smart city research, the contribution suggests that smart cities are multidimensional, comprising governmental, socioeconomic, and environmental factors, each with unique dynamics and a degree of context sensitivity. Hence, both practitioner and academic measures to implement or create smart communities and cities should adopt a multidimensional and multi-actor approach. Two other contributions draw on artificial intelligence and machine learning techniques to forecast the movements of Internally Displaced People (IDP) in Congo and to examine patterns of morbidity and mortality among countries in Africa in relation to COVID-19. Both contributions establish new ways of tackling development challenges and shaping development practices. For example, in forecasting the movements of IDPs, UNHCR reports that ineffective protection monitoring mechanisms currently cause a delay or a failure of service delivery to forcibly displaced persons, which could be mitigated by building and leveraging an early warning system. The authors, therefore, propose an approach that could be used to predict not only IDP flows but also refugee flows, expanding the use of machine learning for social good. The remaining contributions present a regional analysis of the impact of ICTs on human development, and the IS competencies required by organizations in Sub-Saharan Africa. Concerning ICTs and human development, the contributions findings suggested that using ICT alone does not adequately support development. Africa has different dynamics than other continents. African countries have fallen behind the world in keeping up with these technologies due to fundamental problems they need to solve, such as education, health, and food. The use of ICTs in three sectors agriculture, health, and education is the most effective way for Africa to achieve its sustainable development goals. Concerning IS competencies, the contribution identified that competencies that tend to matter for African organizations include the *ability to collaborate and work in teams, monitor technology trends, and innovate by exploiting an emerging method or technology; the ability to be flexible and adapt to change, manage IS projects and programs, apply broadly used project management tools and techniques, and demonstrate an understanding of the specific business or domain processes; the ability to effectively make decisions; and the ability to negotiate with internal and external stakeholders*. Though this knowledge is useful for this comparatively less-researched area, future research needs to focus on identifying the competencies of different categories of IS professionals in different countries to facilitate a broader comparison in ascertaining the dominant and enduring competencies across geographical areas, countries, and industries as well as across time to inform hiring, training, and IS education.

We want to thank the contributors for supporting this book's compilation and dedicating much time and effort to aiding the double-blind review process. These contributors span more than 15 universities and research institutions across Cyprus, Finland, Japan, Ghana, Kenya, Nicaragua, Nigeria, South Africa, Turkey, the United Kingdom, and the United States of America. We can confidently say that this book demonstrates how African and non-African academics and practitioners can effectively collaborate for the good of our beloved continent. There are at least five contributions that feature collaborations between authors from three to five different countries across Africa and beyond. This is laudable, and we are proud that this book has created the platform for such a nexus of knowledge. The contributions in this book create a shared strategic understanding of what works in Africa and how Africa and other interested stakeholders can take advantage of its success stories.

Finally, and most importantly, we thank Prof. Yogesh Dwivedi, the Series Editor of *Advances in Theory and Practice of Emerging Markets*, and Shobha Karuppiah and Nitza Jones-Sepulveda from Springer for continuously supporting us in managing the overall book project from the publisher's side.

We hope you will enjoy reading the book and applying the new directions and shared vision communicated by these diverse contributions. We invite you to contact us for questions, feedback, and discussions.

Accra, Ghana — Richard Boateng
Sheena Lovia Boateng
Johannesburg, South Africa — Thomas Anning-Dorson
Yola, Nigeria — Longe Olumide Babatope

Contents

Contributors

Bryan Acheampong University of Ghana Business School, Accra, Ghana

Eunice Yeboah Afeti University of Ghana Business School, Accra, Ghana

Richard O. Agjei University of Central Nicaragua Medical Center, Managua, Nicaragua

Divine Q. Agozie Cyprus International University, Haspolat, Cyprus

İpek Akad Bitlis Eren University, Bitlis, Turkey

Kunikazu Akao International Organization for Migration, Freetown, Sierra Leone

Toluwalase Janet Akingbade Kogi State University, Anyigba, Nigeria

Samuel Anim-Yeboah Kwame Nkrumah University of Science and Technology, Kumasi, Ghana

Patrick Annan-Noonoo University of Ghana Business School, Accra, Ghana

Thomas Anning-Dorson University of the Witwatersrand, Johannesburg, South Africa

Eric Ansong Wisconsin International University College, Accra, Ghana

Richard Apau Kwame Nkrumah University of Science and Technology, Kumasi, Ghana

Donald Douglas Atsa'am University of the Free State, Bloemfontein, South Africa

Longe Olumide Babatope American University of Nigeria, Yola, Ghana

Oluwafemi Samson Balogun University of Eastern Finland, Kuopio, Finland

Kobina A. Benson Cyprus International University, Haspolat, Cyprus

Emmanuel Koree Boakye University of Ghana Business School, Accra, Ghana

Richard Boateng University of Ghana Business School, Accra, Ghana

Sheena Lovia Boateng University of Ghana Business School, Accra, Ghana

Joseph Budu Ghana Institute of Management and Public Administration, Accra, Ghana

Oluwaseun Alexander Dada University of Helsinki, Helsinki, Finland

Olayinka David-West Pan-Atlantic University, Lagos, Nigeria

Samuel Nii Odoi Devine Presbyterian University College, Abetifi-Kwahu, Ghana

Paul Owusu Donkor University of Ghana School of Pharmacy, Accra, Ghana

Sam A. Edu Cyprus International University, Haspolat, Cyprus

Edward Entee University of Ghana Business School, Accra, Ghana

Hikaru Hirose Peace Tech Foundation, Tokyo, Japan

Tsuyoshi Kano University of Michigan, Ann Arbor, MI, USA

Mark-Oliver Kevor Presbyterian University College, Abetifi-Kwahu, Ghana

Megumi Kiriha NTT Data, Tokyo, Japan

Naoki Kojima Link and Motivation, Tokyo, Japan

Emmanuel Awuni Kolog University of Ghana Business School, Accra, Ghana

Muesser C. Nat Cyprus International University, Haspolat, Cyprus

Chihiro Noda ICT for Development, Tokyo, Japan

Makafui Nyamadi University of Ghana Business School, Accra, Ghana

Ayaka Oishi Peloria Insights, Washington, DC, USA

Temidayo Oluwatosin Omotehinwa Centre for Multidisciplinary Research and Innovation, Abuja, Nigeria

Oseyenbhin S. Osemeahon Cyprus International University, Haspolat, Cyprus

Acheampong Owusu University of Ghana Business School, Accra, Ghana

Obed Kwame Adzaku Penu University of Ghana Business School, Accra, Ghana

Mansah Preko University of Ghana Business School, Accra, Ghana

Takuya Sasaki Koei Research & Consulting Inc., Tokyo, Japan

Patrick Shabaya Strathmore University, Nairobi, Kenya

Kenji Tajima Koei Research & Consulting Inc., Tokyo, Japan

Kentaro Takahira Kyoto University, Kyoto, Japan

Jumpei Takami Pasco Corporation, Tokyo, Japan

Tomonori Takeuchi ICT for Development, Tokyo, Japan

Takeshi Teshima The University of Tokyo, Tokyo, Japan

Pitso Tsibolane University of Cape Town, Cape Town, South Africa

Charles Turkson University of Kent, Kent, UK

Shigeki Yamanaka Actit Inc., Tokyo, Japan

Part I
Digital Innovation and Value Creation

Chapter 1
E-Commerce and Globalization: A Bibliometric Review of 24 Years of Research

Obed Kwame Adzaku Penu, Richard Boateng, and Longe Olumide Babatope

Abstract E-commerce is replacing traditional forms of doing business, as business owners are gradually moving from brick-and-mortar structures to online platforms and customers no longer have to visit physical business outlets to transact. The purpose of this research is to examine research on e-commerce (also known as electronic commerce) and globalization using bibliometric analysis. In all, 625 Scopus-indexed journal articles and conferences papers were analyzed. The results revealed that though conference papers were not the primary source of citations for researchers in that field of research, they were sources with the most publications. Also, contributions to research in the area mostly originated from Asia (China) and North America (the USA), while countries in Africa barely made any contribution to the research area. The results of the analysis found a potential research opportunity in e-commerce research due to the emerging new technologies such as social media and sectors of application or adoption such as the SME sector. This may change the direction of future research in e-commerce, especially for developing regions such as Africa where research on the area is dearth.

Keywords E-commerce · Globalization · Bibliometric analysis · Africa

---

O. K. A. Penu · R. Boateng (✉)
University of Ghana Business School, Legon, Accra, Ghana
e-mail: okapenu@st.ug.edu.gh; richboateng@ug.edu.gh

L. O. Babatope
American University of Nigeria, Yola, Nigeria
e-mail: longeolumide@fulbrightmail.org

R. Boateng et al. (eds.), *Digital Innovations, Business and Society in Africa*, Advances in Theory and Practice of Emerging Markets,
https://doi.org/10.1007/978-3-030-77987-0_1

1.1 Introduction

The integration of the Internet in business trade has become a key factor in business trade information management transcending geographical boundaries and turning the world into a single market trade (He & Wang, 2019). This phenomenon has traditionally been referred to as globalization (Malhotra, 2016; Dubreuil, 2002). Globalization refers to the process of cross-border (country/regional) integration arising from the exchange of world views, products, services, and other aspects of culture (Mirmiran, 2015). With the development of the global economy, new ways are emerging of engaging in trade through an accelerated means of making payment for goods and services among entities in different geographical regions or countries (Terzi, 2011; Bhati et al., 2017). "Marketers have optimally utilized IT particularly internet and mobile applications to make their business global" (Malhotra, 2016, p. 45). The cornerstone of this business model is the term referred to as "e-commerce" which is a major contributing factor in globalization and has generated further interdependence of economic and cultural activities beyond geographical boundaries (Gibbs et al., 2003; Mirmiran, 2015). Huang (2017) defines e-commerce as "the buying and selling of products and services online and it refers to the use of the internet to conduct commerce" (p.171). It can also be defined as "the application of information and communications technologies to capture, processes, store, and communicate business information" (Boateng et al., 2008, p. 564), maintaining business relationships and performing business transactions by the use of telecommunication platforms (Zwass, 1996). It "draws on technologies such as mobile commerce, electronic funds transfer, supply chain management, internet marketing, online transaction processing, electronic data interchange (EDI), inventory management systems, and automated data collection systems" (Mirmiran, 2015, p. 2). Notable examples of e-commerce platforms with origins in developed economies include "Amazon" (USA), "Asos" (UK), "eBay" (USA), and "Alibaba" (China) and in developing economies include the likes of "Kilimall" (Kenya), "Bidorbuy" (South Africa), "Konga" (Nigeria), and "Tonaton" (Ghana), among others.

E-commerce has been integrated into different sectors of the world's economies, which greatly affects the way of life, especially the way of doing business (Boateng et al., 2008). According to Dubreuil (2002), e-commerce generally provides an acceptable avenue for businesses and consumers to engage and maintain a stable commercial relationship. In the field of supply chain, for example, electronic commerce is widely influencing the running and scheduling of product orders in the supply chain process (Almajali et al., 2016). Also in retail, for example, e-commerce has contributed to global exposure of goods and services by encouraging both standardization and variety within an increasingly competitive industry (Nisar & Prabhakar, 2017; Weinstein & Standifird, 2010; Albataineh & Qusef, 2020). For many of these businesses, e-commerce provides an opportunity to increase their marketing and sales, expand market share, and make business decisions (Globerman et al., 2001). SMEs in particular have been one of the beneficiaries and adopters of e-commerce (Jardim-Goncalves & Grilo, 2010; Bo et al., 2010; Rowe et al., 2012).

Through mobile-enabled trade websites, they can diffuse and assert themselves in the global economy (Kabanda, 2011). For example, with e-commerce, transaction and operational cost can be minimized through efficient marketing campaigns, reducing the possibility of human error (Xiaowei et al., 2011; Wahyuni et al., 2020), and "lowering coordination costs associated with distance" (Forman et al., 2005, p.11). Processes done via paper work are also reduced in various work activities such as distribution and delivery of goods and services (Wahyuni et al., 2020). Coupled with the convenience of making secured payments, online e-commerce platforms are more appealing to consumers as they prefer to shop in the virtual marketplace rather than via physical marketplaces (Albataineh & Qusef, 2020).

Due to the expected change of economic structure of nations as a result of e-commerce and globalization, the subject or topic has received some considerable level of research attention (Babenko et al., 2019; Boateng et al., 2009). However, most studies regarding e-commerce have been empirical, with many of these studies focusing on customer expectations and experience regarding e-commerce platforms (e.g., Ali & Bharadwaj, 2010; Terzi, 2016; Vakulenko et al., 2019) as well as organization and business perspective (e.g., Lin et al., 2010; Ueasangkomsate, 2015; Deng & Wang, 2016; Nurhadi & Purnomo, 2018; Gregory et al., 2019). Empirical studies on e-commerce are of significant value, but they only project one aspect of research regarding the topic; there is arguably an absence of research that takes stock of the quantum and maturity of studies that focus on e-commerce and globalization.

In taking stock of these studies, this paper is drawn into the debate on the impact and sources of studies on various topics and research fields (e.g., Merediz-Solà & Bariviera, 2019; Koseoglu et al., 2016; Alonso et al., 2018; Guo et al., 2020; Dhamija & Bag, 2020). The closest attempt to bibliometric studies on e-commerce is the study by Cui et al. (2018). Their study, however, is characterized by some limitations. First, they focus on the subject of only "e-commerce" and only six e-commerce journals from 1999 to 2016 as sources of scientific publication for their analysis, thus being limited in terms of the number of scientific publications that can be extracted and analyzed. Therefore, this study fills these gaps by exploring studies that discuss the subject of "e-commerce and globalization," a focus which is different from Cui et al. (2018) who focus on the subject of only "e-commerce." Further, we use a much larger database for the collection of papers and expand the timespan of the publications. Specifically, the purpose of this study is to identify the trend and characteristics (influential authors, sources, countries and institutions, as well as keywords most often used) regarding e-commerce and globalization in the literature. Additionally, the main methodological and theoretical approaches in the most cited documents are identified.

Having introduced the paper, the remainder of this paper is structured as follows: The initial section presents the gaps in the literature that this study seeks to address. Next is a section that describes the bibliometric methodology used in this study. This is followed by a section that analyzes and discusses the results of the study, followed by a section that puts a spotlight on Africa and its future research prospects in the area of study. The last section concludes this study and makes recommendations for future research.

1.2 Existing Research Limitations to Be Addressed in This Study

Bibliometric analysis is a powerful means of quantitatively taking stock of research done in a particular field through the use of tools and techniques (Zupic & Čater, 2015). Through bibliometrics, the scientific outputs of countries/regions, journal authors to institutes can be measured to guide other researchers with similar new interest in their next course of actions regarding a particular field of research (Koseoglu et al., 2016; Khiste & Paithankar, 2017). This approach (bibliometrics) is particularly useful in meeting the objectives of this study because it enables scientific knowledge through the use of mathematical, statistical, and visualization tools to generalize research patterns and trends in the research topic (Tran et al., 2019).

Though there have been a considerable number of studies done regarding e-commerce, most of these studies have arguably been deficient in performing a holistic bibliometric review. First, as earlier indicated in the introduction, most of these studies have generally been empirical (e.g., Chang & Graham, 2012; Liao et al., 2011; Ahmad et al., 2015; Jones et al., 2013). Second, attempts have been made by some scholars to review the literature on these empirical studies. However, such studies have been systematic (e.g., Kareen et al., 2018; Giuffrida et al., 2017). In the view of Mallett et al. (2012), systematic studies are often restricted to literature that is familiar to the author; hence, the same studies are cited repetitively and this introduces biases to the literate that are reviewed. Therefore, systematic literature review approaches for the lack of tendency to account for all, if not a considerable amount of, research done in a particular field. Third, even though some studies come close to quantitatively take stock of scientific output to rank and classify the literature in the field of e-commerce, they have some drawbacks: One such drawback is seen in the paper by Cui et al. (2018), on "Knowledge mapping of social commerce research: a visual analysis using CiteSpace." Their study focuses on the general subject of "e-commerce" and also on only six e-commerce journal outlets as the source of scientific publications for the papers that were used in the analysis of their study, published from 1999 to 2016. Hence, there is a deficiency in what the true level of research output on the topic is, as there are many journals out there other than the six e-commerce journals that are churning out e-commerce research outputs that were not captured in the study (Mou et al., 2019). Also, while these studies (e.g., Cui et al., 2018; Mou et al., 2019) look at the total citation counts of papers, other aspects were not included. That is to say, these papers lack a comprehensive analysis. For example, there is a lack of discussion on the h-index that measures the impact of authors (Hirsch, 2005; Merigó et al., 2017). Unlike those studies, the analysis in this study does not only consider the total citations as a measure of the impact of an author. As indicated by Hirsch (2005), and corroborated by Liao et al. (2019), measuring the impact of an author with only total citations rather than the h-index is questionable, as the h-index is a critical factor in bibliometric studies, given that it is "influenced by the number of papers and the frequency of citations at the same time" (Liao et al., 2019, p. 224), and not just the total number of citations, thereby providing a more justifiable means of comprehensively evaluating the scientific outputs and academic influence of scholars. In contrast to the above drawbacks seen on other studies, this paper provides a comprehensive and holistic bibliometric study on research done on e-commerce and globalization.

Furthermore, unlike in the studies by Cui et al. (2018), and Mou et al. (2019), that focused on e-commerce in general, this study focuses on e-commerce and globalization "as the booming of cross-border e-commerce continues to draw attention from governments and policymakers to propel the further growth of international trade" (Wang & Lee, 2017, p. 2; Gibbs et al., 2003), and other researchers in like manner are giving the subject area some considerable level of attention (Babenko et al., 2019; Savrul et al., 2014).

1.3 Methodology

Bibliometric analysis is a powerful and unbiased approach to examining the patterns and future trends regarding a particular research topic and to contribute to research (Mayr & Scharnhorst, 2015; Cobo et al., 2015; Martínez et al., 2015). It has been used to examine the level of research done in diverse fields such as information technology and business analytics (e.g., Ardito et al., 2019; Muhuri et al., 2019), education technology (e.g., Chen et al., 2019; Hashim et al., 2018), supply chain and finance (e.g., Xu et al., 2018; Martínez-Climent et al., 2018), project management (e.g., Ng & Chai, 2015), agriculture (e.g., Raparelli & Bajocco, 2019; Liu et al., 2019), and healthcare and medicine (Verma & Gustafsson, 2020; Guo et al., 2020), among others. In this study, it is used to examine the characteristics of e-commerce and globalization articles to date.

1.3.1 Search String Selection

To identify the search strings, relevant keywords were examined. The opinions of coauthors of this study who are both academic experts in e-commerce were also sought before arriving at the final string of keywords. According to Xu et al. (2018), views from experts and academics are acceptable in the selection of keywords for bibliometric studies. The search strings used were "e-commerce" **or** "electronic commerce" **or** "electronic business" **or** "e-business" **or** "ecommerce" **or** "Internet commerce" **or** "Internet business" **and** "globalization" **or** "global village" **or** "global economy."

1.3.2 Databases and Search Protocol

The search was performed in the Scopus database following inclusion and exclusion criteria. The search options provided in the database were used. The search tags were used on the titles, abstracts, and keywords. To explore the magnitude of work done on the topic, the search range was left open to get all published work in the area. The criteria used to retrieve the papers are summarized in the inclusion and exclusion criteria section.

1.3.2.1 Inclusion and Exclusion Criteria

For a paper to be included the title, abstract or keywords must mention an issue regarding e-commerce and globalization **or** any of the string of keywords used. As such, the search was carried out on the titles, abstracts, and keywords of the articles (Zupic & Čater, 2015). Further, the articles were manually screened by scanning through the titles, abstracts, keywords, and introductions to ensure their relevance and applicability to the study. This manual screening process lasted for 2 weeks. An average of 50 papers were screened daily. Additionally, the language of the publications was limited to the English language, so papers were excluded if they were not written in English. Also, to be included, papers must be journal articles or conference papers only. This led to the removal of books, book chapters, reviews, surveys, and notes. Only journal articles and conference papers were considered because they are usually subjected to peer review by the scientific community (Durieux & Gevenois, 2010) and serve as reliable and top-quality mediums for researchers to communicate their research ideas and findings (Martí-Parreño et al., 2016). Table 1.1 provides a breakdown of stages in arriving at the final number of papers used for the analysis in this study.

1.3.3 Data Analysis

The 625 articles deemed fit for use were extracted from the Scopus database and saved as a comma separated value (CSV) document containing author names, article titles, journal names, language used, document types, abstracts, and reference lists. This information is invaluable for bibliometric analysis (Shah et al., 2019).

Table 1.1 Stages in arriving at the final number of papers for the analysis

In Initial search (titles, abstracts, and keywords)	Number of papers removed after filtering to include only journal articles and conference papers published in English	Number of papers removed after manual screening of titles, abstracts, and introductions	Final number of papers used
763	108	30	625

The CSV document was imported into R-Studio, and the most influential authors, articles, journals, references, research documents, institutions, and countries were extracted. Also, the CSV file was imported into VOSviewer to generate the network maps (van Eck & Waltman, 2010).

1.4 Results and Discussion

Having discussed the methods we applied in our study, this section presents the results of the finding in this study. Table 1.2 provides an overview of the contents of the data. The table indicates that publication on the topic began in 1996 and continues to receive attention from researchers as of August 2020. The composition of the papers is comprised of 316 journal articles and 309 conference papers.

1.4.1 The Trend in the Yearly Publication

The results as shown in Fig. 1.1 indicate that the indexing of articles on e-commerce and globalization in the Scopus database has so far been over 24 years (1996–2020). The results further show that the number of papers increased dramatically from 2 papers a year in 1996–1997 to 53 and 52 papers in 2010–2011, albeit with a hiatus in growth rate in the early 2000s. In 2012, the number of papers dropped suddenly from 52 to 22 papers and remained at about 20 papers per year until 2018 and 2019 when publication increased to 35 and 43 papers, respectively. As of August 2020, the number of publications was half the number recorded in 2019.

This trend witnessed in the yearly publications of literature on the topic is an indication that the field has attracted the interest of the scientific community throughout the years, with the most productive years being between 2008 and 2011. The years 2008 and 2009 were the most productive. However, over the time that research has been published, one of the critical points has been between 1996 and 2001, where the initial attention to research on the topic began. The inference from these findings in that the steady rise in the number of publications over the initial 5-year period (1996–2001) is a result of the emergence of electronic payment

Table 1.2 Overview of data extracted

Description	Results
Main information about data	
Timespan	1996:2020
Document types	
Articles	316
Conference papers	309
Total number of paper in this study	625

Fig. 1.1 Trend in yearly publication

systems to replace conventional payment systems. In the USA, for example, by the year 2000, e-commerce had begun to penetrate the agriculture sector, as well as other parts of the world, with farmers in the USA buying or selling agricultural products via e-commerce platforms (Fritz et al., 2004).

1.4.2 Characteristics of Publications

This section presents characteristics of the scholarly publications on e-commerce and globalization from the bibliometric point of view as per the objectives set out in the introduction of this study. For the avoidance of doubt, this study seeks to identify the trends in characteristics (impactful authors, influential sources, countries and institutions, as well as keywords mostly used) regarding e-commerce and globalization in literature.

1.4.2.1 Most Impactful Authors

Based on the data extracted, the top 10 most active authors are presented in Table 1.3. "Li L" tops the list as the most impactful author with publications comprising number of publications (NP) of 4, total citations (TC) of 22, and an h-index of 2. The author h-index refers to the number of publications of the author that received "h" or more citations each, while the other publications have not more than h citations each. Providing an example with "Li L," the author's h-index of 2 means among all

Table 1.3 Top 10 most active authors

Author	NP	TC	h_index	g_index	m_index
Li L	4	22	2	4	0.118
Forman C	3	40	2	3	0.111
Jardim-Goncalves R	3	62	2	3	0.154
Kurnia S	3	10	2	3	0.105
Li S	3	4	2	2	0.143
Standing C	3	11	2	3	0.143
Andrews J	2	14	2	2	0.133
Gereffi G	2	282	2	2	0.100
Gunasekaran A	2	431	2	2	0.125
Gupta H	2	8	2	2	0.200

publications by the author, two of these publications have received at least two citations each. Even though authors like "Forman C" and "Jardim-Goncalves R" also have the same h-index but higher TCs, their g- and m-indexes as well as NC are less than that of "Li L." Thus, the h-index is an impactful assessment that combines both quantity (number of papers) and an approximation of quality (impact, or citations to these papers) and not just having a high number of publications or just a high number of citations (Hirsch, 2005). Again, citing an example of "Gunasekaran A" who has total citations that are 12 times the citations that have been received by "Li L," the latter is more productive with a higher number of publications than that of "Gunasekaran A."

Though "Lil" was impactful, based on the general parameters as seen in Table 1.3, "Gunasekaran A" had been cited much more often by authors. The significant number of citations received by "Gunasekaran A," whose two publications focused on the development of e-commerce frameworks and models (Gunasekaran & Ngai, 2005), as well as a literature review on some of the reported case experiences of e-commerce in the global economy (Gunasekaran & Kobu, 2007), suggests an interest by researchers in the field of research development, their arguments in model development and in seminal literature reviews that point out new frontiers of research in the area. Further, an author such as "Gereffi G", whose two publications also received a significantly higher number of citations than "Lil" (see Table 1.3) and focused on business-to-business (B2B) as well as business-to-consumer (B2C) transactions in the global economy (Gereffi, 2001a, b), points to an interest by researchers in publications regarding the emergence of the Internet in heralding a new age of digital globalization.

The cooperative pattern of the leading collaborative authors (coauthorship) is shown in Fig. 1.2. Nodes of the same color belong to a cluster and a node represents an author. The larger the size of the node, the more papers the author has published with other authors in the network. As seen in Fig. 1.2, there are five clusters with two major nodes in the network. The largest nodes being "Yang Y" (largest blue node) and "Lil L" (largest purple node) are the authors with the most collaboration on papers regarding e-commerce and globalization. These two authors have the

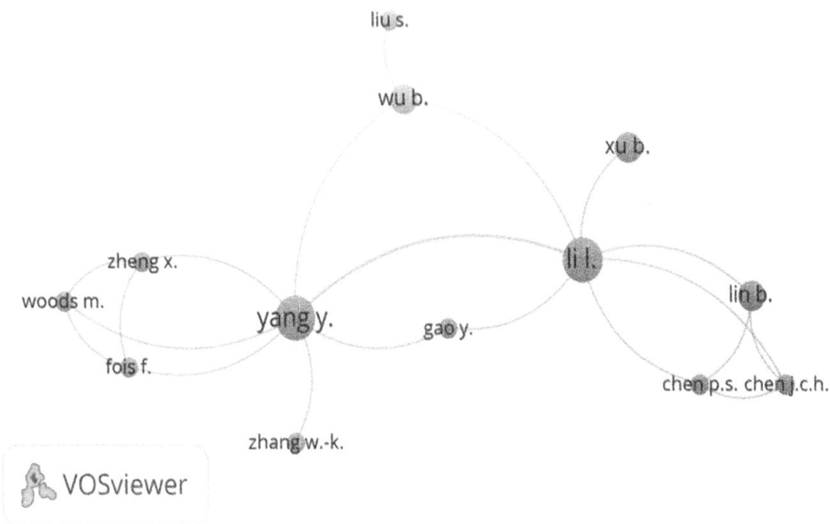

Fig. 1.2 Network of the leading collaborating authors (coauthorship)

same linkages (seven linkages) and total link strength (total link strength of 8). The total link strength indicates the number of publications in which the author occurs, and the linkages refers to the number of nodes that the author is connected to (Van Eck & Waltman, 2013). The two major clusters are the largest because they are linked to more authors in the network as compared to the yellow, red, and green clusters which have relatively fewer links to other nodes in the network. The purple node (Yang Y), for example, has seven major linkages with a total link strength of 8 in the network as compared to the largest yellow node (Wu B) which has three linkages with a total link strength of 3. Figure 1.2 also shows that "Li L," for example, is not only productive (as seen in Table 1.3) as an independent writer but writes by collaborating with other authors in the research space on e-commerce and globalization; the authors that collaborate most with "Lil L" are "Xu B" and "Gao Y."

Also, from the nature of the names of the leading collaborators, one can infer that these authors are of Asian origin. As asserted by Liao et al. (2019), "many factors can influence collaboration, such as geographical location, language, and scientific research exchange" (p .235). Hence the visibility of these collaborations among these authors can be a result of the similar languages used by the authors as well as their closeness in terms of geographical proximity.

1.4.2.2 Most Cited Author Documents

Table 1.4 shows the top 10 most cited author documents or articles. It can be noted from the table that the document (specific paper) titled "Environment and Policy Factors Shaping Global E-Commerce Diffusion: A Cross-country Comparison"

Table 1.4 Top 10 most cited author documents

Author	Title	Source	Total citation
Gibbs et al. (2003)	Environment and Policy Factors Shaping Global E-Commerce Diffusion: A Cross-country Comparison	*Information Society*	215
Jardim-Goncalves and Grilo (2010)	SOA4BIM: Putting the Building and Construction Industry in the Single European Information Space	*Automation in Construction*	56
Morris et al. (2004)	Supplier Parks in the Automotive Industry	*Supply Chain Management: An International Journal*	43
Forman et al. (2005)	Geographic Location and the Diffusion of Internet Technology	*Electronic Commerce Research and Applications*	38
Ali and Bharadwaj (2010)	Factor Analysis Approach of Decision Making in Indian E-Banking: A Value-Adding Consumer's Perspective	*International Journal of Business Innovation and Research*	19
Chen et al. (2004)	Logistics Management in China: A Case Study of Haier	*Human Systems Management*	18
Shi et al. (2013)	Leveraging Social Grouping for Trust Building in Foreign Electronic Commerce Firms: An Exploratory Study	*International Journal of Information Management*	12
Chen et al. (2010)	A Knowledge-Commercialised Business Model for Collaborative Innovation Environments	*International Journal of Computer Integrated Manufacturing*	12
Benisch et al. (2006)	Cmieux: Adaptive Strategies for Competitive Supply Chain Trading	*Proceedings of the ACM Conference on Electronic Commerce*	8
Kurnia and Johnston (2002)	A Review of Approaches to EC-Enabled IOS Adoption Studies	*Proceedings of the Annual Hawaii International Conference on System Sciences*	6

(Gibbs et al., 2003) published in *Information Society* was the most cited paper with a total citation of 215. Followed by the paper titled "SOA4BIM: Putting the Building and Construction Industry in the Single European Information Space" (Jardim-Goncalves & Grilo, 2010) published in *Automation in Construction* was the second most cited paper with a total citation of 56. The third leading document on the list is titled "Supplier Parks in the Automotive Industry" (Morris et al., 2004) published in *Supply Chain Management: An International Journal* with a total citation of 43.

It is worth indicating that the most cited paper, which received over 215 citations, is about 3 times more the second most cited document. The paper examines the critical global, environmental, and policy factors that act as determinants of e-commerce diffusion based on the cases of ten countries (i.e., Brazil, China, Denmark, France, Germany, Mexico, Japan, Singapore, Taiwan, and the USA). It finds that B2B e-commerce seems to be driven by global forces, whereas B2C seems to be more of a local phenomenon. This significant number of citations received by the document suggests an interest by other authors in research regarding e-commerce diffusion, especially considering that the study was done with an assessment of several countries.

It is also worth noting that as many as three out of ten authors (i.e., "Jardim-Goncalves, R"; "Forman, C"; and "Kurnia, S") in Table 1.3 can be found on Table 1.4. This is an indication that not just individual authors are being cited, but the documents produced by authors among the leading authors are getting a lot of attention by scholars in the research field.

A look into the ten top-cited papers reveals that the main methodological and theoretical approaches used when researching on e-commerce and globalization point to an interest in conceptual models and frameworks (used in 80% of the analyzed papers). Researchers seem to be less interested in using a qualitative (10%) and a computational analysis research approach (10%). The prominence of a conceptual research approach translates into the use of conceptual models in 80% of the papers, which makes the identification of conceptual models as the dominant theoretical approach used by research on the topic as was found in this study not surprising.

Nevertheless, papers that adopt known theories represent 10% of the papers suggesting a need for the adoption of known theories in the field. Table 1.5 shows the type of methodology and theoretical approaches used in the top 10 most cited documents.

1.4.2.3 Most Influential Sources

The sources that are influential on the topic of e-commerce and globalization are shown in Table 1.6. These sources are composed of journal and conference sources. Conference sources have been prefixed in the table with double asterisks (**). These sources were ranked, based on the total number of publications (NP) and total citations (TC) received. The top 3 sources on the list are the *2011 2nd International Conference on Artificial Intelligence, Management Science and Electronic Commerce, AIMSEC 2011 – Proceedings* (16 publications), followed by *ACM*

Table 1.5 Methodology and theoretical approaches in the top 10 most cited documents

Methods		Number	Percentage
Empirical	Qualitative	1	10%
	Quantitative	3	30%
Nonempirical	Review/conceptual	5	50%
	Computational analysis	1	10%
Theory adoptions			
Conceptual model/framework		8	80%
Theory		1	10%
No model/framework/theory		1	10%

Table 1.6 First 20 most influential sources

Source	NP	TC
***2011 2nd International Conference on Artificial Intelligence, Management Science and Electronic Commerce, AIMSEC 2011 – Proceedings*	16	2
***ACM International Conference Proceeding Series*	16	20
***Proceedings of the International Conference on E-Business and E-Government, ICEE 2010*	14	5
***Proceedings of the International Conference on Electronic Business (ICEB)*	11	0
***2011 International Conference on E-Business and E-Government, ICEE 2011 – Proceedings*	7	1
First Monday	4	2
**IC4E 2010 – 2010 International Conference on E-Education, E-Business, E-Management and E-Learning*	4	0
Journal of Advanced Oxidation Technologies	4	0
***PACIS 2008 – 12th Pacific Asia Conference on Information Systems: Leveraging ICT for Resilient Organizations and Sustainable Growth in the Asia Pacific Region*	4	2
***Proceedings – International Workshop on Database and Expert Systems Applications, Dexa*	4	10
Electronic Commerce Research and Applications	3	136
Indian Journal of Marketing	3	13
Information Technology Journal	3	13
International Journal of Business and Globalisation	3	4
International Journal of Business Information Systems	3	29
International Journal of Computer Integrated Manufacturing	3	49
International Journal of Innovative Technology and Exploring Engineering	3	5
International Journal of Recent Technology and Engineering	3	3
International Journal of Services, Technology and Management	3	25
International Journal of Supply Chain Management	3	2

International Conference Proceeding Series (also 16 publication), then followed by *Proceedings of the International Conference on E-Business and E-Government, ICEE 2010* (14 publications). Even though the two leading conference sources have the same number of publications, on the score of citation, *ACM International Conference Proceeding Series* is the most dominant as it has more citations (about eight times more) than that of the *2011 2nd International Conference on Artificial Intelligence, Management Science and Electronic Commerce, AIMSEC 2011 – Proceedings.*

However, journal articles were the most cited sources despite the relatively lower number of publications in these sources as compared to the conference sources which had a relatively higher number of publications. The top 3 most cited sources as seen in Table 1.6 are the *Electronic Commerce Research and Applications* (136 citations), followed by *International Journal of Computer Integrated Manufacturing* (49 citations) and *International Journal of Business Information Systems* (29 citations). Specifically, *Electronic Commerce Research and Applications* which is the most cited journal focuses on multidisciplinary research on technology, theory, and applications for the development of electronic commerce.

Looking at the statistics that emerged from the findings, it is clear that although research on the topic appealed to both journal and conference sources (outlets), conference sources had the most publications as compared to journal sources. This is particularly not surprising as conference papers undergo less scrutiny as compared to journal sources. Juxtaposing it to the reasons for the lack of citations in conference sources, the inference can be made to the rather less strict measures in conference submissions and review process which makes conference source or outlets the preferred places for researchers to publish their papers. However, they cited less from such sources and would rather turn to cite from journal sources. In fact, for most conferences, the maximum number of words is 5000, and pages not more than 10, with some conferences restricting the maximum number of pages to 5 in the case of short papers, as compared to journal sources which mostly require between 7,000 and 10,000 words and undergo stricter review processes.

1.4.2.4 Countries and Institutions

The top 10 most productive countries are listed in Table 1.7. These are the countries that have paid the most attention to e-commerce and related research aspects. China, the USA, and the UK stand out as the leading three countries above all others with the highest number of contributors; China has 109 articles, followed by the USA with 59 articles and the UK with 17 articles.

The table further indicates that, regionally, the majority of the leading countries (60%) were from Asia, suggesting a high interest by these countries in research on e-commerce and globalization. Specifically, China is identified as the major facilitator for research in e-commerce and globalization. The conference paper by Ma (2020) on the "Development of Cross-border E-commerce Based on Big Data Analysis" is an example of a conference paper emanating from China. Also, the journal article by Li and Huang (2019) on "Subsidy Strategy of Pharmaceutical

Table 1.7 Top 10 most productive countries

Country	Region	Articles
China	East Asia	109
USA	North America	59
UK	Europe	17
India	South Asia	13
S. Korea	East Asia	11
Australia	Oceania	8
Canada	North America	8
Japan	East Asia	7
Iran	Western Asia	6
Malaysia	Southeast Asia	6

E-commerce Platform Based on the Two-Sided Market Theory" was one of the studies in the Chinese category.

In terms of country collaborations as seen in Table 1.8, the three leading pairs of countries that are collaborating are China and the USA (ten collaborations) followed by China and Hong Kong (seven collaborations) and then by the USA and Canada (five collaborations). A geographical representation of the country collaborations is provided in Fig. 1.3. This indicates there are a lot more collaborations happening among countries located in Asia (e.g., China, Hong Kong), North America (e.g., the USA and Canada), and Europe/Oceania (e.g., the UK, Italy, Australia, and New Zealand). Therefore, these countries have widespread cooperation with other countries when it comes to research on the topic. Highlighting further on the level of multiregional or multicountry collaborations, most of the country collaborations were seen to be coming from collaborations between Asia and North America. An example is a study by Bin et al. (2003) on "Cultural Differences in E-commerce: A Comparison Between the USA and China." Another example is the collaborations between the USA and Hong Kong highlighted by Kong Koh et al. (2012) where they explore the "Trust Across Borders: Buyer-Supplier Trust in Global Business-to-Business E-commerce."

The institutions leading the research on the topic are listed in Table 1.9. Among these 10 institutions, the leading ones are Carnegie Mellon University (seven papers) followed by California State University, Islamic Azad University, and Tsinghua University (six papers each) and then Jiangxi University of Finance and Economics, Universiti Utara Malaysia, University of California, University of Hong Kong, and Wuhan University of Technology (five papers each). Notably, many of these institutions are located in China, a finding that corroborates the findings in Table 1.7 with China as the country with the most articles.

One of the papers from the Carnegie Mellon University, located in the USA, which leads in terms of authors' institutional affiliations is the study by Forman et al. (2005) on "Geographic Location and the Diffusion of Internet Technology."

Table 1.8 Top 10 country collaborations

From	To	Frequency
China	USA	10
China	Hong Kong	7
USA	Canada	5
UK	China	4
S. Korea	USA	3
USA	Italy	3
Australia	New Zealand	2
China	Germany	2
China	Malaysia	2
S. Korea	China	2

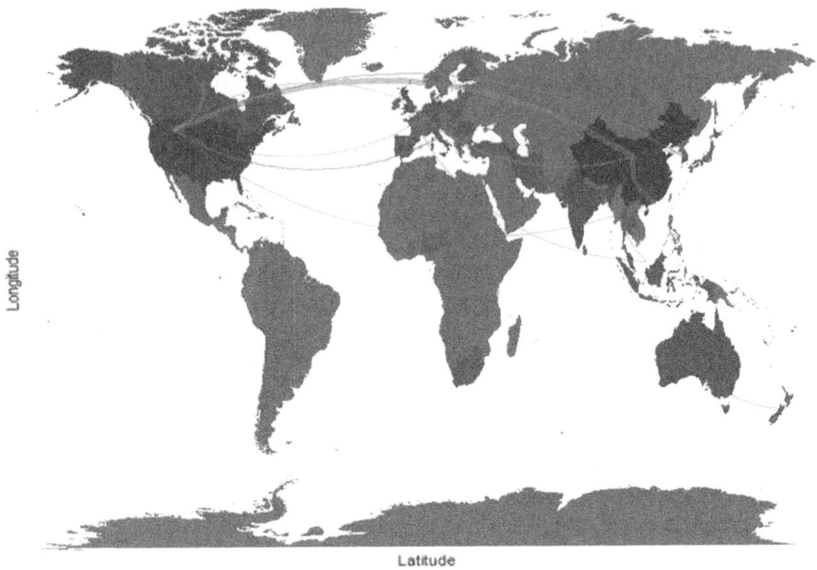

Fig. 1.3 Geographic representation of country collaborations

Table 1.9 Top 10 institutions

Affiliations	Country	Number of articles
Carnegie Mellon University	USA	7
California State University	USA	6
Islamic Azad University	Iran	6
Tsinghua University	China	6
Jiangxi University of Finance and Economics	China	5
Universiti Utara Malaysia	Malaysia	5
University of California	USA	5
University of Hong Kong	China	5
Wuhan University of Technology	China	5
Bina Nusantara University	Indonesia	4

1.4.2.5 Keywords

Table 1.10 presents the ten leading keywords that emerged from the publications, while a network of keywords is presented in Fig. 1.4 to show the relationship between author keywords used in the published papers. To have a comprehensive keyword collection, one modification was applied. Thus, keywords with the same meaning were combined; as such, words like "e-commerce" and "electronic commerce" were combined to acquire a consolidated frequency of words. Secondly, spelling variations such as "globalisation" and "globalization" were combined.

Table 1.10 Top 10 keywords of publications

Words	Occurrences
E-commerce	141
Globalization	73
E-business	38
Internet	31
Supply chain management	23
Supply chain	19
ICT	11
Information technology	11
Strategy	11
Knowledge management	10

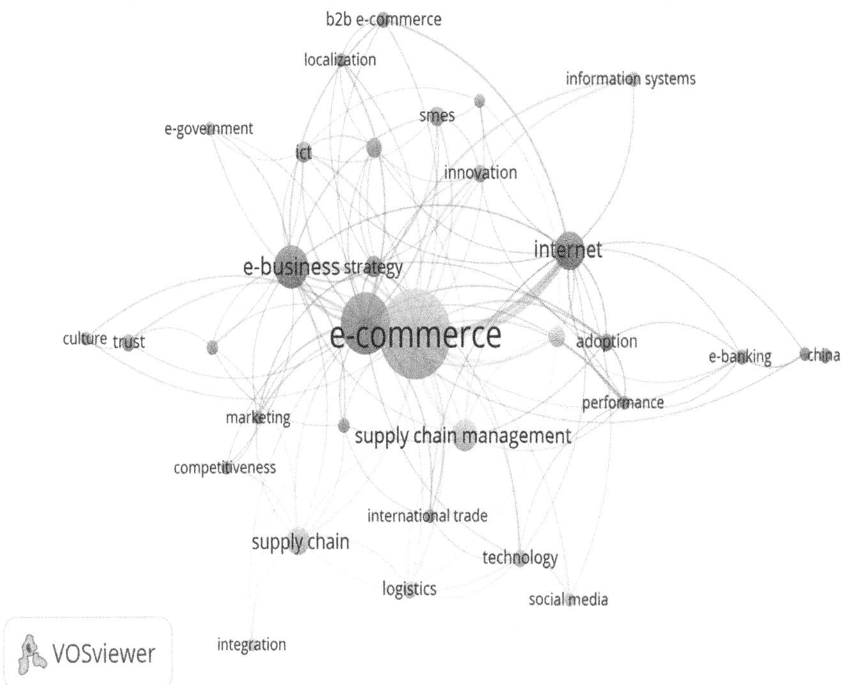

Fig. 1.4 Map of keyword co-occurrence

In Fig. 1.4, each node represents a keyword, and nodes of the same color form a cluster. The size of a node indicates the number of publications that have the corresponding term in their keywords. The more nodes are close to each other, the more they co-occur in the papers. In this case, the keywords were grouped into ten clusters, of which four are of significance in size and clustering. These four significant clusters are yellow, purple, blue, and red clusters. The yellow cluster covers terms related to e-commerce, supply chain, supply chain management, integration, and logistics. The purple clusters consist of words regarding globalization, culture, and trust. The blue cluster is related to e-business, marketing, competitiveness, and strategy, while the red cluster is more focused on the Internet, adoption, performance, and e-banking.

The overlay visualization of keywords is shown in Fig. 1.5. The inference that can be made from Fig. 1.5 (as seen emerging in yellow from 2014) is that e-commerce research is moving toward "social media"-related e-commerce platforms, trust for such platforms, and their applications within SMEs. The occurrence of the keywords in the field indicates that to date, much of the e-commerce and globalization research has had keywords centering on e-commerce, supply chain, and supply chain management. Given that people trade online or use electronic marketplaces to request the supply of goods and services (Dubreuil, 2002), the emergence and clustering of such words is not surprising. Additionally, there have been words such as globalization, culture, and trust, as well as e-business, marketing, competitiveness, and strategy, which are credible from the findings as many businesses and individuals who use e-commerce platforms do so to break geographical boundaries and enhance cross-border trade (He & Wang, 2019), are concerned about trust (Shi et al., 2013) and security issues regarding the platforms (Bhati et al., 2017; Bartolini et al., 2017) to have a competitive advantage (Wahyuni et al., 2020; Albataineh & Qusef, 2020) especially for business, and also, more importantly, need to strategize (Li et al., 2020; Wang et al., 2020) to adopt and use such platforms. It is also worth noting that keywords in the studies also touch on the technologies used to facilitate

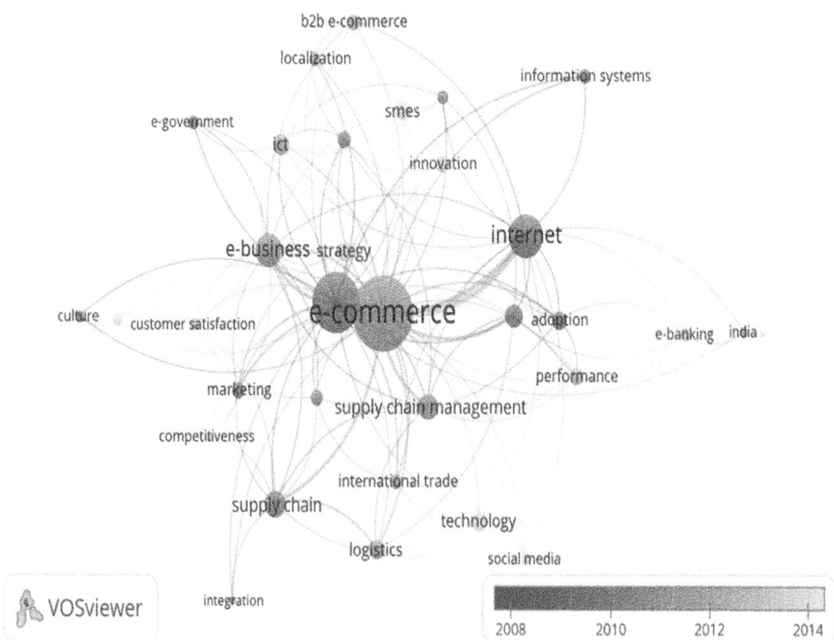

Fig. 1.5 Overlay visualization of keyword co-occurrence

e-commerce use (e.g., Internet, ICT, information technology, information systems, and innovations) (Kabanda & Brown, 2017; Kurnia et al., 2015). However, as seen in the visualization overlays, the trend in the use of keywords in the field of e-commerce between 2008 and 2012 has shifted away from words such as "e-commerce, supply chain, and technology". It, however, has shifted to words such as "social media," "trust," "innovation," and "SMEs." For such words to be emerging, post-2012 all through to 2014 points to the shift in how social media have become a key platform for businesses to engage in e-commerce or e-business. Also, SMEs are seen to be one of the focuses for discussions regarding e-commerce (Anim-Yeboah et al., 2020; Sombultawee, 2020), probably because most SMEs may not have the resources and logistics to run fully fledged traditional brick-and-mortar businesses, hence having resorted to e-commerce platforms. With these words emerging, one can expect to have more studies surrounding these words, especially how new "innovations" can help micro- to medium-scale enterprises thrive and remain competitive in their quest to supply goods and services globally.

1.5 Spotlight on Africa

Findings from this bibliometric analysis show a lack of research from African countries and their institutions. Out of the 625 publications on ecommerce and globalization, no papers were identified to have been spearheaded by researchers from Africa or lead researchers affiliated to institutions in Africa. It is important to reiterate that the country and institutional productions in bibliometric studies are determined by the first author's affiliation (Cristino et al., 2018).

Following in the path of the ten most cited papers on e-commerce and globalization, there are a number of research gaps that could be explored by researchers in Africa and their institutions to make up the research deficit that has characterized the research area of "e-commerce and globalization" in the region of Africa. Table 1.11 provides a summary of possible future study directions that researchers in Africa could explore.

1.6 Conclusions

This study uses a bibliometric analysis to examine 24 years of e-commerce and globalization research. Considering the purpose and nature of this study, bibliometrics is a powerful and useful tool for reviewing and investigating extant literature in a given field or topic (Mayr & Scharnhorst, 2015; Cobo et al., 2015). Various aspects including the most impactful authors and collaborators; most influential journals and cited documents, countries, and institutions; and the most occurring and emerging research keywords were discussed. Comparing the rationale for this study to existing ones, this current study provides a bibliometric review of studies beyond a

Table 1.11 Summary of future study directions for researchers in Africa

Theme	Possible questions	Further reading
Policy and regulations for e-commerce adoption	1. What global and national policies affect the adoption of e-commerce across countries in Africa? 2. How do global and national policies influence the types of e-commerce platform adoption (i.e., B2B, B2C, C2C)?	Gibbs et al. (2003) and Forman et al. (2005)
Drivers and barriers to e-commerce adoption	1. What are the predominant e-commerce platforms adopted across countries in Africa? 2. What are the enablers and constraints of e-commerce adoption across countries in Africa? 3. How do factors such as location, labor cost, or other endowments impact e-commerce adoption and the types of e-commerce platforms adopted in African countries?	Gibbs et al. (2003) and Jardim-Goncalves and Grilo (2010)
Industry adoption of e-commerce	1. What factors account for the adoption of e-commerce across different industries in Africa? 2. Which industries/firms in Africa are adopting e-commerce platforms? 3. What is the role of firm size in the adoption of e-commerce platforms in Africa?	Gibbs et al. (2003) and Morris et al. (2004)
Theorization and conceptualization of e-commerce adoption	1. What are the key global, environmental, and policy factors that act as determinants of e-commerce diffusion in Africa? 2. What globalization theories (e.g., the *global village theory for diffusion* and *urban density theory*) can be adopted to study e-commerce and globalization within the context of Africa?	Morris et al. (2004) and Jardim-Goncalves and Grilo (2010)
E-commerce adoption implications	1. What is the impact of e-commerce on managerial decisions of business/firms in the African subregion? 2. What is the role of e-commerce technology developers and service providers in lowering coordination costs associated with e-commerce adoption among businesses/firms in African countries?	Forman et al. (2005) and Ali and Bharadwaj (2010)
Trust and security issues in e-commerce adoption	1. What security concerns impact customer confidence to adopt e-commerce platforms in Africa? 2. What are the differences in customer and company levels of trust for foreign and local e-commerce platforms in Africa?	Shi et al. (2013)

focus on only six e-commerce journals. Also, this study is done to examine papers that have been published within the specific context of e-commerce (i.e., e-commerce and globalization) unlike existing bibliometric studies (e.g., Cui et al., 2018; Mou et al., 2019) that have focused on the general concept of e-commerce despite the level of attention given by researchers in the specific area of e-commerce and globalization (Babenko et al., 2019; Savrul et al., 2014).

Research on the topic has attracted the interest of the scientific community throughout the years, with the most productive years being between 2008 and 2011, suggesting the need for more research in the area. As found in this study, research themes have largely bordered on e-commerce within the context of supply chain, supply chain management, and logistics, with the emerging themes being a focus on "social media"-related e-commerce platforms, trust for such platforms, and their applications within SMEs.

Further, from an author and source perspective, it was found that taking into consideration factors such as m-index and g-index, "Li L" was the most impactful author, though the author had a relatively lower number of citations. Citations were dominated by "Gunasekaran A" who performed a seminal literature review on case experiences in the field of e-commerce and globalization and "Gereffi G" who has focused a lot of the research attention on e-commerce and globalization toward business-to-business (B2B) as well as business-to-consumer (B2C) transactions in the global economy.

Also, an analysis of the source impact reveals the majority of research was published conference sources as compared to journal sources. However, journal sources emerged as the most cited sources. Geographically, the USA and China remain most influential in this research area. This is further strengthened by the ties in their collaborations on papers, as the majority of the papers were done between authors in Asia (China) and North America (USA). Countries and institutions in regions such as Africa, the Middle East, and East Europe barely made contributions to research on e-commerce and globalization; hence, attention to research within the context of these regions will be worthwhile.

The results of this study are useful in providing a number of benefits for e-commerce practitioners and researchers. First, the results can help new researchers to find the leading journals involved in high-quality papers. Through this, authors and researchers can be guided on leading journals and sources to cite from and to submit their manuscripts to high-quality publications. Second, it will benefit researchers by emphasizing the leading authors, countries, and institutions that are spearheading research on the topic. This can help researchers to find the most impactful authors, countries, and institutions in a field and hence seek future collaborations or academic exchanges. Third, the results of this study can help scholars to find the most relevant key topics and future research directions in e-commerce and globalization, to engage in further research or extend their research interests. Contextually, future studies can also explore how developing countries, especially those in Africa, can leverage the studies of e-commerce and globalization in developed economies.

1.6.1 Study Limitations and Other Possible Explanations

This study is constrained by some limitations; firstly, in terms of the study design, we only focused on journal articles and conference papers that have been published in academic journals and conference proceedings indexed in Scopus. Also, considering that the authors of this paper are only proficient in English, the study was limited to only papers published in English, which may skew the findings in favor of Anglo-Saxon countries. Also, it is important to realize that bibliometric studies/software do not consider self-citation bias. We, therefore, consider this as one of the limitations of bibliometric studies that our study inherits—in essence, self-citation bias is rarely discussed in bibliometric studies. Further, using only English-based papers has the propensity of reducing the international visibility of the research. Finally, the nature of the results that come from bibliometric studies is usually silent on methods used and theoretical approaches used in undertaking the studies, though we have tried to touch on these with regard to the top 10 most cited author documents. Hence it will be prudent to undertake further research to contextualize the results of this study which will provide deeper insights into the type of theoretical and methodological approaches being used in the studies that have been done. Despite these limitations, the results are seen to reflect the general trends that exist on research regarding e-commerce and globalization.

References

Ahmad, S. Z., Abu Bakar, A. R., Faziharudean, T. M., & Mohamad Zaki, K. A. (2015). An empirical study of factors affecting e-commerce adoption among small-and medium-sized enterprises in a developing country: Evidence from Malaysia. *Information Technology for Development, 21*(4), 555–572.

Albataineh, A., & Qusef, A. (2020, April). Why companies in Jordan should adopt e-business solutions? In *2020 11th international conference on information and communication systems (ICICS)* (pp. 272–276). IEEE.

Ali, S. S., & Bharadwaj, R. K. (2010). Factor analysis approach of decision making in Indian E-banking: A value adding consumer's perspective. *International Journal of Business Innovation and Research, 4*(4), 298–320.

Almajali, D., Mansour, K., & Maqableh, M. (2016). The impact of electronic supply chain management usage on firm's performance. *International Journal of Communications, Network and System Sciences, 9*(6), 280–293.

Alonso, J. M., Castiello, C., & Mencar, C. (2018, June). A bibliometric analysis of the explainable artificial intelligence research field. In *International conference on information processing and management of uncertainty in knowledge-based systems* (pp. 3–15). Springer.

Anim-Yeboah, S., Boateng, R., Odoom, R., & Kolog, E. A. (2020). Digital transformation process and the capability and capacity implications for small and medium enterprises. *International Journal of E-Entrepreneurship and Innovation (IJEEI), 10*(2), 26–44.

Ardito, L., Scuotto, V., Del Giudice, M., & Petruzzelli, A. M. (2019). A bibliometric analysis of research on Big Data analytics for business and management. *Management Decision, 57*(8), 1993–2009.

Babenko, V., Kulczyk, Z., Perevozova, I., Syniavska, O., & Davydova, O. (2019). Factors of Development of International e-Commerce in the Context of Globalization. *CEUR Workshop Proceedings, 2422*, 345.
Bartolini, D. N., Benavente-Peces, C., & Ahrens, A. (2017, July). Risk assessment and verification of insurability. In *PECCS* (pp. 105–108). IEEE.
Benisch, M., Sardinha, A., Andrews, J., & Sadeh, N. (2006, August). CMieux: Adaptive strategies for competitive supply chain trading. In *Proceedings of the 8th international conference on electronic commerce: The new e-commerce: Innovations for conquering current barriers, obstacles and limitations to conducting successful business on the internet* (pp. 47–58). ACM.
Bhati, A., Thu, Y. T., Woon, S. K. H., Phuong, L. L., & Lynn, M. M. (2017). E-commerce usage and user perspectives in Myanmar: An exploratory study. *Advanced Science Letters, 23*(1), 519–523.
Bin, Q., Chen, S. J., & Sun, S. Q. (2003). Cultural differences in e-commerce: A comparison between the US and China. *Journal of Global Information Management (JGIM), 11*(2), 48–55.
Bo, W., Yufen, W., & Lishi, H. (2010, May). The application of electronic business in transnational operations of small and medium enterprises. In *2010 International conference on e-business and e-government* (pp. 384–387). IEEE.
Boateng, R., Heeks, R., Molla, A., & Hinson, R. (2008). E-commerce and socio-economic development: Conceptualizing the link. *Internet Research, 18*(5), 562–594.
Boateng, R., Molla, A., & Heeks, R. (2009). E-Commerce in developing economies: A review of theoretical frameworks and approaches. In *Emerging markets and e-commerce in developing economies* (pp. 1–56). IGI Global.
Chang, K. P., & Graham, G. (2012). E-business strategy in supply chain collaboration: An empirical study of B2B e-commerce project in Taiwan. *International Journal of Electronic Business Management, 10*(2), 101–112.
Chen, J. C., Lin, B., Li, L., & Chen, P. S. (2004). Logistics management in China: A case study of Haier. *Human Systems Management, 23*(1), 15–27.
Chen, T. Y., Tsaih, D., & Chen, Y. M. (2010). A knowledge-commercialised business model for collaborative innovation environments. *International Journal of Computer Integrated Manufacturing, 23*(6), 543–564.
Chen, X., Yu, G., Cheng, G., & Hao, T. (2019). Research topics, author profiles, and collaboration networks in the top-ranked journal on educational technology over the past 40 years: A bibliometric analysis. *Journal of Computers in Education, 6*(4), 563–585.
Cobo, M. J., Martínez, M. Á., Gutiérrez-Salcedo, M., Fujita, H., & Herrera-Viedma, E. (2015). 25 years at knowledge-based systems: A bibliometric analysis. *Knowledge-Based Systems, 80*, 3–13.
Cristino, T. M., Neto, A. F., & Costa, A. F. B. (2018). Energy efficiency in buildings: analysis of scientific literature and identification of data analysis techniques from a bibliometric study. *Scientometrics, 114*(3), 1275–1326.
Cui, Y., Mou, J., & Liu, Y. (2018). Knowledge mapping of social commerce research: A visual analysis using CiteSpace. *Electronic Commerce Research, 18*(4), 837–868.
Deng, Z., & Wang, Z. (2016). Early-mover advantages at cross-border business-to-business e-commerce portals. *Journal of Business Research, 69*(12), 6002–6011.
Dhamija, P., & Bag, S. (2020). Role of artificial intelligence in operations environment: A review and bibliometric analysis. *The TQM Journal, 32*(4), 869–896.
Dubreuil, E. (2002, August). Mastering e-commerce and globalization. In *IFIP World Computer Congress, TC 11* (pp. 281–291). Springer.
Durieux, V., & Gevenois, P. A. (2010). Bibliometric indicators: Quality measurements of scientific publication. *Radiology, 255*(2), 342–351.
Forman, C., Goldfarb, A., & Greenstein, S. (2005). Geographic location and the diffusion of Internet technology. *Electronic Commerce Research and Applications, 4*(1), 1–13.

Fritz, M., Hausen, T., & Schiefer, G. (2004). Developments and development directions of electronic trade platforms in US and European agri-food markets: Impact on sector organization. *International Food and Agribusiness Management Review, 7*(1), 1–21.

Gereffi, G. (2001a). Shifting governance structures in global commodity chains, with special reference to the internet. *American Behavioral Scientist, 44*(10), 1616–1637.

Gereffi, G. (2001b). Beyond the producer-driven/buyer-driven dichotomy the evolution of global value chains in the internet era. *IDS Bulletin, 32*(3), 30–40.

Gibbs, J., Kraemer, K. L., & Dedrick, J. (2003). Environment and policy factors shaping global e-commerce diffusion: A cross-country comparison. *The Information Society, 19*(1), 5–18.

Giufrida, M., Mangiaracina, R., Perego, A., & Tumino, A. (2017). Cross-border B2C e-commerce to Greater China and the role of logistics: A literature review. *International Journal of Physical Distribution and Logistics Management, 47*(9), 772–795.

Globerman, S., Roehl, T. W., & Standifird, S. (2001). Globalization and electronic commerce: Inferences from retail brokering. *Journal of International Business Studies, 32*(4), 749–768.

Gregory, G. D., Ngo, L. V., & Karavdic, M. (2019). Developing e-commerce marketing capabilities and efficiencies for enhanced performance in business-to-business export ventures. *Industrial Marketing Management, 78*, 146–157.

Gunasekaran, A., & Kobu, B. (2007). Performance measures and metrics in logistics and supply chain management: A review of recent literature (1995–2004) for research and applications. *International Journal of Production Research, 45*(12), 2819–2840.

Gunasekaran, A., & Ngai, E. W. T. (2005). E-commerce in Hong Kong: An empirical perspective and analysis. *Internet Research, 15*(2), 141–159.

Guo, Y., Hao, Z., Zhao, S., Gong, J., & Yang, F. (2020). Artificial Intelligence in Health Care: Bibliometric Analysis. *Journal of Medical Internet Research, 22*(7), e18228.

Hashim, K. F., Rashid, A., & Atalla, S. (2018). Social media for teaching and learning within higher education institution: A bibliometric analysis of the literature (2008–2018). *International Journal of Interactive Mobile Technologies (iJIM), 12*(7), 4–19.

He, Y., & Wang, J. (2019). A panel analysis on the cross border e-commerce trade: Evidence from ASEAN Countries. *Journal of Asian Finance, Economics and Business, 6*(2), 95–104.

Hirsch, J. E. (2005). An index to quantify an individual's scientific research output. *Proceedings of the National academy of Sciences, 102*(46), 16569–16572.

Huang, R. (2017). Ecommerce in rural areas and environmental sustainability: The Last-Mile Delivery (2017). *WHICEB 2017 Proceedings*. 50

Jardim-Goncalves, R., & Grilo, A. (2010). SOA4BIM: Putting the building and construction industry in the Single European Information Space. *Automation in Construction, 19*(4), 388–397.

Jones, P., Packham, G., Beckinsale, M., Jahanshahi, A. A., Zhang, S. X., & Brem, A. (2013). E-commerce for SMEs: Empirical insights from three countries. *Journal of Small Business and Enterprise Development, 20*(4), 849–865.

Kabanda, S. (2011). E-commerce institutionalization is not for us: SMEs perception of e-commerce in Tanzania. *The African Journal of Information Systems, 3*(1), 1–16.

Kabanda, S., & Brown, I. (2017). A structuration analysis of Small and Medium Enterprise (SME) adoption of E-Commerce: The case of Tanzania. *Telematics and Informatics, 34*(4), 118–132.

Kareen, P., Purwandari, B., Wilarso, I., & Pratama, M. O. (2018, August). E-commerce adoption in SME: A systematic review. In *2018 6th International conference on cyber and IT service management (CITSM)* (pp. 1–7). IEEE.

Khiste, G. P., & Paithankar, R. R. (2017). Analysis of Bibliometric term in Scopus. *International Journal of Library Science and Information Management (IJLSIM), 3*(3), 81–88.

Koh, T. K., Fichman, M., & Kraut, R. E. (2012). Trust across borders: Buyer-supplier trust in global Business-to-Business e-commerce. *Journal of the Association for Information SYSTEMS, 13*(11), 886–922.

Koseoglu, M. A., Rahimi, R., Okumus, F., & Liu, J. (2016). Bibliometric studies in tourism. *Annals of Tourism Research, 61*, 180–198.

Kurnia, S., Choudrie, J., Mahbubur, R. M., & Alzougool, B. (2015). E-commerce technology adoption: A Malaysian grocery SME retail sector study. *Journal of Business Research, 68*(9), 1906–1918.

Kurnia, S., & Johnston, R. B. (2002, January). A review of approaches to EC-enabled IOS adoption studies. In *Proceedings of the 35th annual Hawaii international conference on system sciences* (p. 10). IEEE.

Li, C., Chu, M., Zhou, C., & Zhao, L. (2020). Two-period discount pricing strategies for an e-commerce platform with strategic consumers. *Computers and Industrial Engineering, 147*, 106640.

Li, C., & Huang, Z. (2019). Subsidy strategy of pharmaceutical e-commerce platform based on two-sided market theory. *PloS One, 14*(10), e0224369.

Liao, H., Tang, M., Li, Z., & Lev, B. (2019). Bibliometric analysis for highly cited papers in operations research and management science from 2008 to 2017 based on essential science indicators. *Omega, 88*, 223–236.

Liao, J., Jiang, Z., Chen, Z. (2011, November). Cultural barriers against electronic businesses in globalization. In *2011 international conference on information management, innovation management and industrial engineering* 2: 407–410. IEEE.

Lin, C., Liu, Y. C., Feng-Chia, L., Jalleh, G., Huang, Y. A., & Jhuang, Z. R. (2010, January). B2B e-commerce adoption and implementation constraints and critical success factors in the healthcare organizations. In *Proceedings of the 4th international conference on uniquitous information management and communication* (pp. 1–10). ACM Digital Library.

Liu, W., Wang, J., Li, C., Chen, B., & Sun, Y. (2019). Using bibliometric analysis to understand the recent progress in agroecosystem services research. *Ecological Economics, 156*, 293–305.

Ma, H. (2020, March). Development of cross-border e-commerce based on big data analysis. In *International conference on application of intelligent systems in multi-modal information analytics* (pp. 84–89). Springer.

Malhotra, P. (2016). Globalization and E-commerce in India: Issues and Challenges. *International Journal of Information Systems and Software Engineering for Big Companies (IJISEBC), 3*(1), 44–52.

Mallett, R., Hagen-Zanker, J., Slater, R., & Duvendack, M. (2012). The benefits and challenges of using systematic reviews in international development research. *Journal of Development Effectiveness, 4*(3), 445–455.

Martínez, M. A., Cobo, M. J., Herrera, M., & Herrera-Viedma, E. (2015). Analyzing the scientific evolution of social work using science mapping. *Research on Social Work Practice, 25*(2), 257–277.

Martínez-Climent, C., Zorio-Grima, A., & Ribeiro-Soriano, D. (2018). Financial return crowdfunding: Literature review and bibliometric analysis. *International Entrepreneurship and Management Journal, 14*(3), 527–553.

Martí-Parreño, J., Méndez-Ibáñez, E., & Alonso-Arroyo, A. (2016). The use of gamification in education: A bibliometric and text mining analysis. *Journal of Computer Assisted Learning, 32*(6), 663–676.

Mayr, P., & Scharnhorst, A. (2015). Combining bibliometrics and information retrieval: Preface. *Scientometrics, 102*(3), 2191–2192.

Merediz-Solà, I., & Bariviera, A. F. (2019). A bibliometric analysis of bitcoin scientific production. *Research in International Business and Finance, 50*, 294–305.

Merigó, J. M., Blanco-Mesa, F., Gil-Lafuente, A. M., & Yager, R. R. (2017). Thirty years of the International Journal of Intelligent Systems: A bibliometric review. *International Journal of Intelligent Systems, 32*(5), 526–554.

Mirmiran, S. F. (2015). The study of relationship between globalization strategies and e-commerce implementation in Iran. In *9TH international conference on e-business with focus on: E-commerce approach*. Available at https://www.academia.edu/19630258/IEEE_Conference_Paper_Template. Accessed 23 Dec 2020.

Morris, D., Donnelly, T., & Donnelly, T. (2004). Supplier parks in the automotive industry. *Supply Chain Management: An International Journal, 9*(2), 129–133.
Mou, J., Cui, Y., & Kurcz, K. (2019). Bibliometric and visualized analysis of research on major e-commerce journals using Citespace. *Journal of Electronic Commerce Research, 20*(4), 219–237.
Muhuri, P. K., Shukla, A. K., & Abraham, A. (2019). Industry 4.0: A bibliometric analysis and detailed overview. *Engineering Applications of Artificial Intelligence, 78*, 218–235.
Ng, J. J., & Chai, K. H. (2015, December). A bibliometric analysis of project management research. In *2015 IEEE international conference on industrial engineering and engineering management (IEEM)* (pp. 976–980). IEEE.
Nisar, T. M., & Prabhakar, G. (2017). What factors determine e-satisfaction and consumer spending in e-commerce retailing? *Journal of Retailing and Consumer Services, 39*, 135–144.
Nurhadi, N., & Purnomo, M. (2018). Predicting e-commerce adoption in small hotel: The role of technology-organisation-environment framework. *International Journal of Business Information Systems, 29*(3), 324–341.
Raparelli, E., & Bajocco, S. (2019). A bibliometric analysis on the use of unmanned aerial vehicles in agricultural and forestry studies. *International Journal of Remote Sensing, 40*(24), 9070–9083.
Rowe, F., Truex, D., & Huynh, M. Q. (2012). An empirical study of determinants of e-commerce adoption in SMEs in Vietnam: An economy in transition. *Journal of Global Information Management (JGIM), 20*(3), 23–54.
Savrul, M., Incekara, A., & Sener, S. (2014). The potential of e-commerce for SMEs in a globalizing business environment. *Procedia-Social and Behavioral Sciences, 150*, 35–45.
Shah, S. H. H., Lei, S., Ali, M., Doronin, D., & Hussain, S. T. (2019). Prosumption: Bibliometric analysis using HistCite and VOSviewer. *Kybernetes, 49*(3), 1020–1045.
Shi, Y., Sia, C. L., & Chen, H. (2013). Leveraging social grouping for trust building in foreign electronic commerce firms: An exploratory study. *International Journal of Information Management, 33*(3), 419–428.
Sombultawee, K. (2020). Antecedents and consequences of e-commerce adoption for SMEs. *Kasetsart Journal of Social Sciences, 41*(2), 256–261.
Terzi, N. (2011). The impact of e-commerce on international trade and employment. *Procedia-Social and Behavioral Sciences, 24*, 745–753.
Terzi, N. (2016). The impact of e-commerce on international trade and employment. In *Encyclopedia of e-commerce development, implementation, and management* (pp. 2271–2287). IGI Global.
Tran, B. X., McIntyre, R. S., Latkin, C. A., Phan, H. T., Vu, G. T., Nguyen, H. L. T., ... & Ho, R. (2019). The current research landscape on the artificial intelligence application in the management of depressive disorders: a bibliometric analysis. *International journal of environmental research and public health, 16*(12), 1–16.
Ueasangkomsate, P. (2015). Adoption e-commerce for export market of small and medium enterprises in Thailand. *Procedia-Social and Behavioral Sciences, 207*, 111–120.
Vakulenko, Y., Shams, P., Hellström, D., & Hjort, K. (2019). Service innovation in e-commerce last mile delivery: Mapping the e-customer journey. *Journal of Business Research, 101*, 461–468.
Van Eck, N. J., & Waltman, L. (2010). Software survey: VOSviewer, a computer program for bibliometric mapping. *Scientometrics, 84*(2), 523–538.
Van Eck NJ, Waltman L (2013) VOSviewer manual. : Univeristeit Leiden, 1(1):1–53.
Verma, S., & Gustafsson, A. (2020). Investigating the emerging COVID-19 research trends in the field of business and management: A bibliometric analysis approach. *Journal of Business Research, 118*, 253–261.
Wahyuni, S., Widodo, J., Zulianto, M., Islami, N. N. (2020, May). The analysis of e-commerce utilization in Micro, Small and Medium Enterprises (MSMEs) at Jember. In *IOP conference series: Earth and environmental science, 485*(1), 012037. IOP Publishing.
Wang, Y., & Lee, S. H. (2017). The effect of cross-border e-commerce on China's international trade: An empirical study based on transaction cost analysis. *Sustainability, 9*(11), 1–13.

Wang, Y., Lei, L., Zhang, D., & Lee, L. H. (2020). Towards delivery-as-a-service: Effective neighborhood search strategies for integrated delivery optimization of E-commerce and static O2O parcels. *Transportation Research Part B: Methodological, 139*, 38–63.

Weinstein, M., & Standifird, S. S. (2010). The advent of the internet and the on-line book trade: The role of managerial cognition and the liabilities of experience. *Academy of Strategic Management Journal, 9*(1), 15.

Xiaowei, J., Qi, S., & Yanfeng, G. (2011). New approaches to the green economy of China in the multiple crises. *Energy Procedia, 5*, 1365–1370.

Xu, X., Chen, X., Jia, F., Brown, S., Gong, Y., & Xu, Y. (2018). Supply chain finance: A systematic literature review and bibliometric analysis. *International Journal of Production Economics, 204*, 160–173.

Zupic, I., & Čater, T. (2015). Bibliometric methods in management and organization. *Organizational Research Methods, 18*(3), 429–472.

Zwass, V. (1996). Electronic commerce: Structures and issues. *International Journal of Electronic Commerce, 1*(1), 3–23.

Obed Kwame Adzaku Penu is a PhD student in information systems at the University of Ghana. He holds an MPhil in Management Information Systems from the same University. Obed is also a Teaching and Research Assistant at the Operations and Management Information Systems (OMIS) Department, University of Ghana Business School (UGBS). He also has work experience as a software tester and documentation writer. His research interests is in the sharing/platform economy, digitalization (enterprise IS/IT implementation and usage), e-learning, artificial intelligence, business analytics, and information systems security. He can be reached at okapenu@st.ug.edu.gh.

Richard Boateng is a Professor of information systems at the University of Ghana Business School (UGBS). Richard's experience covers the digital economy, cloud computing, e-learning, information and communication technologies (ICT) for development, electronic governance, social media, electronic business, gender and technology, mobile commerce, and mobile health at the national, industrial, organizational, and community levels. His papers have been published in or are forthcoming in the *International Journal of Information Management*, *Internet Research*, *Qualitative Market Research: An International Journal*, and many others. Richard can be reached at richboateng@ug.edu.gh.

Professor Longe Olumide Babatope is Professor and Chair of the Department of Information Systems at the American University of Nigeria (AUan), Yola, Nigeria. Prior to joining the services of AUN, he was the Dean of the Caleb University Business School and also the Dean of Student Affairs and Deputy Dean of School of Postgraduate Studies at Caleb University, Lagos, Nigeria. A recipient of several national and international awards and recognitions, he is an alumnus Fulbright Scholar, Google Scholar, MacArthur Scholar, and an alumnus MIT Scholar. His current research focuses on management information systems security and social and enterprise informatics (using ubiquitous computing and social theories to aid management decision-making processes). He is also involved in cybercriminality profiling for identifying causation, assisting apprehension, and providing treatments for cybercrime cases. He can be reached at longeolumide@fulbrightmail.org.

Chapter 2
Drones in the Digital Transformation of Healthcare Delivery in Africa

Samuel Anim-Yeboah, Richard Apau, and Mansah Preko

Abstract Healthcare in Africa faces many challenges with the growing problem of diseases. However, most of the healthcare challenges confronting Africa are expected to be overcome with digital technologies. Recently, drones are increasingly being used to transport blood and medical supplies to remote and underserved communities in some African countries. However, academics are yet to catch up with empirical research on the impact of drones' use on healthcare. Considering the paucity of research in this domain, this chapter investigates the drivers, conditions, and factors that facilitate the implementation and use of drone systems for healthcare delivery through the Delone and Mclean Information Systems Success Model lens. A survey was conducted with a questionnaire to gather responses from 298 individuals who are the staff of healthcare facilities and zipline drone operation centers in Ghana and Rwanda. The data were analyzed using partial least squares structural equation modeling (PLS-SEM). The results indicate that information quality, system quality, service quality, user satisfaction, and perceived financial cost were confirmed as drone technology adoption drivers for healthcare. The use of drones has also substantially impacted healthcare delivery. Also, quick delivery time for drones, healthcare facilities in remote areas, and late arrival of medical supplies were identified as the most important factors and conditions facilitating drones' implementation for healthcare delivery. It is recommended that governments in Africa consider the rapid adoption and deployment of medical drone technology to

S. Anim-Yeboah (✉)
Department of Pharmacy Practice, Kwame Nkrumah University of Science and Technology, Kumasi, Ghana
e-mail: ssanim-yeboah@st.ug.edu.gh

R. Apau
Department of Computer Science, Kwame Nkrumah University of Science and Technology, Kumasi, Ghana
e-mail: rapau@st.knust.edu.gh

M. Preko
Department of Operations & MIS, University of Ghana Business School, Accra, Ghana
e-mail: mpreko@st.ug.edu.gh

R. Boateng et al. (eds.), *Digital Innovations, Business and Society in Africa*, Advances in Theory and Practice of Emerging Markets,
https://doi.org/10.1007/978-3-030-77987-0_2

save lives in remote hard to reach areas. Future studies should explore the barriers and challenges that confront medical drone usage.

Keywords Drone · Healthcare delivery · Digital transformation · Medical supply · IS Success Model · Africa

2.1 Introduction

Several of the Millennium Development Goals (MDGs) endorsed by the United Nations (UN) in 2001 concern various health issues (Wagstaff & Claeson, 2004). Many of these health-related goals are also focused on healthcare delivery. Yet, achieving these goals has been a significant challenge for most countries, especially those in the developing world. Studies, including Wagstaff and Claeson (2004), attribute these challenges to factors such as the lack of resources, inadequate budget, the paucity of strategies, lack of commitment, and ultimately, the absence of appropriate technologies to facilitate healthcare delivery. Through the health-related Sustainable Development Goals (SDGs) and Universal Health Coverage (UHC), there have been calls for innovative strategies to support healthcare delivery in Africa (Ibeneme et al., 2020; Wynn & Jones, 2019). In the wake of these, technological innovation, particularly the use of digital technologies, has been commended as a vehicle for achieving most of the health-related Millennium Development Goals (Wynn & Jones, 2019). The use of digital technologies in service robots has been established to have improved the service sector and impacted both employees and customers (Lu et al., 2020).

Despite the preceding, one of the things that remain a significant challenge in delivering healthcare involves the supply chain of medicines, i.e., getting medicines at the right place and at the right time. Since emergency health services require emergency supplies, and the accuracy of delivery targets is essential in the healthcare delivery process, the aspect of supply chain efficiency and effectiveness that calls for drones' use in medical delivery becomes eminent. Drone technology can ensure accurate and timely medical supplies to even the very remote and rugged access areas (Scott & Scott, 2017). Just as mobile phones helped most developing countries spring ahead with personal communication technologies, drones can overtake traditional transportation infrastructure (Scott & Scott, 2017).

Drones can solve most of the supply chain challenges that behoove developing countries, improve logistical efficiency, and eliminate barriers that prevent medicines from reaching remote and underserved populations (Clarke, 2014). However, the technology limits transporting only one item per trip and may require recharging or swapping its batteries afterward (Boukoberine et al., 2019). Hence, drones may not replace conventional delivery modes and vehicles, especially when high volumes are required. Yet, for small parcels and emergency deliveries, drones can play significant roles in their delivery.

The timely delivery of urgently required healthcare products such as medications, vaccines, and blood is significant in the health sector. However, sites needing such deliveries are usually difficult or near impossible to access due to poor road infrastructure, long distance, ineffective or insufficient vehicles, traffic congestion, bad weather, disasters, etc. Since drones can fly overhead and overcome inaccessible roads and significant transportation challenges, innovative organizations and countries have begun to employ drones for healthcare delivery. Lately, drones are increasingly being used to transport blood and medical supplies to remote and underserved communities in some African countries.

Although the use of drones in the delivery of medical supplies has become topical, the academic literature on the subject is limited, and the few available have focused on parcel delivery (Scott & Scott, 2017). The use of drones in the context of healthcare is very pertinent and cannot be overemphasized. However, academics are yet to catch up with case studies and empirical research on drones' use in medical delivery (Lu et al., 2020). Moreover, the health, social, and economic impact of drones' usage in medical delivery has not been assessed much (Kellermann et al., 2020; Sandbrook, 2015).

Therefore, this chapter seeks to address this research gap by investigating the drivers and factors facilitating drones' use for medical delivery and its health, social, and economic impacts. The following questions would be considered to achieve this purpose: What drives and motivates drones' use for medical supply delivery in Africa (RQ1)? What conditions and factors facilitate the implementation of drone delivery systems for healthcare (RQ2)? How does the use of drones for healthcare delivery impact the healthcare systems, societies, and economies of the communities and nations being served (RQ3)?

The study's objectives would be explored through the theoretical lens of the DeLone and McLean Information Systems Success Model (DMISSM), as well as conceptualizations from extant literature on drivers and impacts of digital transformation. A quantitative methodology approach will be used to investigate the research objectives through a survey of the medical drone delivery implementation in Ghana and Rwanda. This book chapter sections are structured as follows: Sect. 2.1 covers the introduction, and Sect. 2.2 presents insights into drone use and applications with a focus on delivery and healthcare. Section 2.3 presents the theoretical underpinnings of the study, while Sect. 2.4 presents the methodology used. The study's empirical findings are presented and discussed in Sect. 2.5, with conclusions and recommendations in Sect. 2.6.

2.2 Drone Use and Application in Healthcare

The use of drones in healthcare delivery has been touted as one of the most useful endeavors in healthcare emergency supplies, including vaccines, blood samples, and medicine (Agatz et al., 2015; Hügler et al., 2018; Lin et al., 2018; Preimesberger,

2016). There is also the potential for drones to carry other medical devices, such as oxygen masks.

Autonomous drones have been utilized to deliver medicines to remote locations where good and adequate roads are lacking (Raptopoulos, 2013). Matternet drones delivered medicines in Haiti and the Dominican Republic following the 2010 earthquake (Choi-Fitzpatrick et al., 2016). Similar feats were achieved in New Guinea and Switzerland by Matternet in collaboration with Doctors without Borders and UNICEF (French, 2015). Drones from Matternet can carry 1 to 2 kilograms of items and transport them to about 10 km in about 20 min (D'Andrea, 2014).

DHL Parcel service developed three generations of drones called Parcelcopter for medical delivery in Germany (Scott & Scott, 2017). The first generation delivered blood samples over 1 km across the Rhine River at Bonn. The second-generation drones also delivered medicines and other emergency materials over 12 km to Juist across the open sea for 3 months in 2014. Moreover, the third-generation Parcelcopter delivered over 130 parcels of emergency medicines or sporting goods to Bavarian Alpine villages (Agatz et al., 2015; Wagstaff & Claeson, 2004). In the USA, drones were used to drop medical supplies to a health clinic in rural Southwest Virginia as the first approved Federal Aviation Administration drone service (Pepitone, 2015). Flirtey drones delivered the prescription items in about 3 min instead of the usual 90 min along a winding, bumpy road 35 miles away. The Dutch prototype ambulance drones were also used to deliver defibrillators (Prigg, 2014).

For instance, in the African context, Zipline has also developed drone systems to deliver blood and vaccines to clinics and hospitals in Rwanda and Ghana's remote locations. When vaccines and blood are needed urgently, drone delivery would not be hindered by bad roads (Khazan, 2016; Preimesberger, 2016; Tilley, 2016). Zipline drones are made to launch from a nest or launchpad, and before the launch, the delivery package (blood, medicine, or vaccines) is inserted together with a new battery. The delivery process involves dropping the package with a paper parachute at the destination based on programmed GPS location. After the delivery, the drone uses the same route and GPS navigation to return to the nest. Zipline drones weigh between 1 and 1.5 kg and can fly about 70 km in 30 min. Their route is tracked, monitored, and controlled with a tablet app. With the faster drone response, a patient's chance of survival could increase to 80% against 8% for traditional emergency services (Prigg, 2014).

Drone use has not been without challenges and concerns. There have been widespread concerns with the use of drones. Some consider it as a nuisance, particularly where it is used to spy on or attack people. Some believe that drones for delivery could be shot down for package stealing (Welch, 2015). Commercial drone use has been restricted or banned in some aviation authorities' jurisdiction because of possible collisions in airline airspace and regular aircraft interference. The restrictions of drone use for commercialization in some jurisdictions have been of much concern to businesses and industries considering its delivery potential (Welch, 2015). Meanwhile, drone use has been disparaged for insufficient regulation, security, privacy, safety concerns, abuse, and misuse (Clarke, 2014; Welch, 2015). Besides, there have been a few instances where drone deliveries have failed, thereby fueling the concerns of using drones for medical delivery (Varnholt, 2016).

2.3 Theoretical Underpinning and Hypothesis

2.3.1 The Theory

The updated and modified DeLone and McLean Information Systems Success Model (DMISSM), a popular framework for measuring the complex dependent variable in IS research, is used as the underpinning theory for this study. The DMISSM was initially propounded in 1992 by William H. DeLone and Ephraim R. McLean based on the review and integration of about 180 research studies in information systems (IS) (DeLone & McLean, 1992). The outcome factors were initially determined as "individual impact" and "organizational impact" (DeLone & McLean, 1992). It was later revised after a decade, following critiques and feedback from other scholars, resulting in what is now known as the updated DeLone and McLean Information Systems Success Model (DeLone & McLean, 2003). Subsequently, the two separate individual and organization impacts were considered as "net benefits" (DeLone & McLean, 2003).

The original DeLone and McLean IS Success Model (1992) and the updated DeLone and McLean IS Success Model (2003) have been beneficial models for measuring and understanding IS success factors. However, a careful review of the outcome measures of success as "net benefits" obviously implied that outcomes were expected to be only positives since the word "benefit" has an affirmative implication. Hence, the term was later changed in 2016 to "net impacts" in an updated, modified model to appreciate the possibility of having both positive and negative outcomes in an IS implementation (DeLone & McLean, 2016).

Therefore, this study employs the updated and modified DeLone and McLean Information Systems Success Model, illustrated in Fig. 2.1, as its theoretical lens to investigate the drivers and factors facilitating drones' use for medical delivery and the associated health, social, and economic impacts.

The variables used in the updated and modified model (Fig. 2.1) are the *quality dimensions* of system quality, information quality, and service quality. The quality dimensions influence the *use dimensions* of intention to use, use, and user satisfaction, which results in the *outcome dimension* of net impacts (DeLone & McLean, 2016). *Net impacts* focuses on the extent to which an IS contributes (or does not contribute) to the success of industries, organizations, groups, and individuals. These include improved profits, improved decision-making, improved productivity, market efficiency, consumer welfare, economic development, increased sales, and cost reductions, among others. Hence, these net impacts can be either positive or negative, depending on the outcome's nature, either favorable or unfavorable. In this conceptualization, it is assumed that there could be feedback loops to "intention to

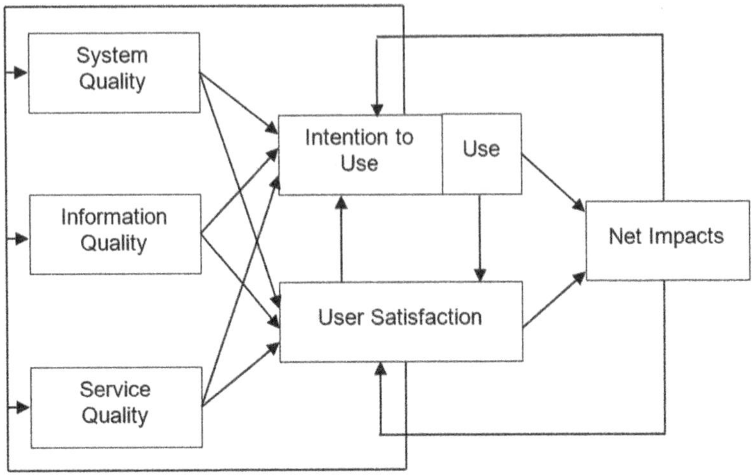

Fig. 2.1 The updated and modified DeLone and McLean Information Systems Success Model (DeLone & McLean, 2016)

use or use" and "user satisfaction" after achieving the net impacts positively or negatively. It thereby causes reiteration of more (or less) "use" and greater (or lesser) "user satisfaction" depending on whether the impact is positive or negative (DeLone & McLean, 2016).

By applying this model, we would appreciate the possibility of having both positive and negative impacts of using drones to deliver emergency supplies in Africa's healthcare industry. This assessment is imperative because drone applications have been touted as a worthwhile endeavor in healthcare emergency supplies (Hügler et al., 2018; Lin et al., 2018; Preimesberger, 2016). Meanwhile, the African continent has also been notably reported as being confronted with a myriad of challenges regarding IS implementations in its healthcare industry (Preko et al., 2020; Olu et al., 2019). These challenges are mainly known to arise from the lack of requisite governance framework, institutional capacity, and funding (Preko et al., 2020; Olu et al., 2019).

Hence, assessing the net impacts of applying this novel technology amid those unfavorable circumstances is a good starting point for determining its overall success and a way forward for its future. In this study, the DMISSM has been extended to include relevant constructs comprising perceived financial cost and organizational considerations. In the healthcare sector's digital transformation, the cost is considered an essential predictor of information system adoption. Similarly, organization enablers and inhibitors affect the successful implementation of IS in most sectors, including healthcare. Table 2.1 summarizes the definitions of the constructs and their sources from the literature.

Table 2.1 Construct definition and sources

Construct	Definition	Source
Information quality (INFOQUAL)	The desirable characteristics of the system outputs	DeLone and McLean (2016)
System quality (SYSQUAL)	The desirable characteristics of the information system	DeLone and McLean (2016)
Service quality (SERVQUAL)	The quality of support that system users receive from the IS organization and IT support personnel	DeLone and McLean (2016)
Intention to use/use (IU/SU)	The degree and way employees and customers utilize the capabilities of the information system	DeLone and McLean (2016)
User satisfaction (USERSAT)	The users' level of satisfaction with reports, websites, and support services	DeLone and McLean (2016)
Perceived financial cost (PFC)	Users' cognitive trade-off between the monetary cost of using the technology and the perceived benefits	Venkatesh et al. (2012)
Organizational consideration (ORGCON)	The belief that there are organizational facilitating conditions, events, and processes that serve either as enablers or inhibitors to the successful implementation of information systems (drone delivery system)	New (proposed by authors)
Net system impacts (DSYSB)	The extent to which the information system contributes to the success of individuals, organization, and nations	DeLone and McLean (2016)

2.3.2 *The Hypothesis*

2.3.2.1 Information Quality

The *information quality* concentrates on the system outputs with desirable characteristics, like management reports. The factors include relevance, accuracy, understandability, completeness, conciseness, timely, and usability (DeLone & McLean, 2016). The use of drones in the healthcare industry has impacted healthcare facilities' information systems (Amukele et al., 2017). Eichleay et al. (2019) argued that the quality of the information provided by drone transportation systems influences medics' reliance on such technology for healthcare delivery. Logistics information systems, health information systems, and monitoring and evaluation systems of hospitals have been substantially impacted by drones' introduction (Eichleay et al., 2019). Medical personnel working in remote areas have been satisfied with the quality of information drone technology provides (McCall, 2019), hence their continuous usage. Therefore, it is hypothesized that:

H1a: Information quality of drones' delivery system positively influences intention to use/system use.

H1b: Information quality of drones' delivery system positively influences user satisfaction.

2.3.2.2 System Quality

The *system quality* considers IS's desirable characteristics, including the ease of use, system reliability, system flexibility, ease of learning, and the features of sophistication, intuitiveness, flexibility, and response times. Moreover, drones can gather real-time data cost-effectively, deliver payloads, and have initiated a rapid revolution in the healthcare sector (Rosser et al., 2018). In many parts of the world, particularly in developing countries where access to healthcare is a challenge, drone technology has contributed to the rapid supply of medical equipment and drugs to remote areas (Gangwal et al., 2019). Conditions such as traffic congestions in cities, the poor road network in rural communities, and lack of reliable network facilities in rural areas have contributed to the use of drones in many African countries (Gangwal et al., 2019). The reliability and flexibility of the drone system are envisaged to drive the healthcare sector's adoption. Hence, it is hypothesized that:

H2a: System quality of drones' delivery system positively influences intention to use/system use.

H2b: System quality of drones' delivery system positively influences user satisfaction.

2.3.2.3 Service Quality

The *service quality* considers the quality of support that system users receive from the IS organization and information technology (IT) support personnel. Service quality includes accuracy, responsiveness, reliability, empathy, and technical competence of the IT support staff (DeLone & McLean, 2016). According to Jeyabalan et al. (2020), people raised concerns such as privacy, security, and safety of drones' system as the reasons for not using the technology for medical supply, and, if these concerns are addressed, they will adopt the technology. Also, lack of resources, including human resources and competent staff, and technical challenges in drone implementation affect drones' adoption in healthcare (Jeyabalan et al., 2020). Therefore, putting in place facilitating conditions such as competent drone operators could drive drone usage for healthcare delivery. Hence, it is hypothesized that:

H3a: Service quality of drones' delivery system positively influences intention to use/system use.

H3b: Service quality of drones' delivery system positively influences user satisfaction.

2.3.2.4 Perceived Financial Cost

Perceived financial cost is considered positive when technology benefits are perceived to be greater than the cost of using it. Consumers are more likely to adopt services at a reasonable cost. A pivotal relationship has also been established between price and novel technology adoption (Venkatesh et al., 2012). Eichleay et al. (2019) identified cost as a significant factor influencing drones' implementation within the health sector. If the cost of transporting medical supplies through drone technology is perceived to be low, compared to the traditional mode of transport, adoption will be increased considerably. Therefore, we hypothesized that:

H4: Perceived financial cost of drones' delivery system positively influences intention to use/system use.

2.3.2.5 Organizational Consideration

There are enablers or inhibitors at the organizational level that affect the successful implementation of information systems. In the health sector, implementing drones for medical supply requires safety assurance and bureaucratic decision processes. These events and processes become discouraging in adopting such technology. As McCall (2019) observes, if governments in sub-Saharan African countries are ambitious and willing, drones could be heavily used to provide healthcare to the people. This observation means that even if all conditions are favorable for adopting drones, specific events and processes at the organization affect the decision to use or not to use. Hence, we hypothesized that:

H5: Organizational considerations have effects to intention to use/use of drones' delivery system.

2.3.2.6 Intention to Use/Use

Intention to use and use considers the extent and manner in which organizational employees and clients utilize the information system's capabilities. This utilization includes the extent of use, nature of use, frequency of use, appropriateness of use, the amount of use, and purpose of use (DeLone & McLean, 2016). Drone technology has contributed significantly to medical professionals' work within the healthcare sector (Rosser et al., 2018). The direct benefits of drones have derived the satisfaction of healthcare providers and stakeholders alike. Braun et al. (2019) assert that drones' use for medical supply has positively impacted healthcare delivery. We, therefore, hypothesized that:

H6a: Intention to use/use of drones' delivery system positively influences user satisfaction.

H6b: Intention to use/use of drones' delivery system positively influences the drone's system benefits (impacts).

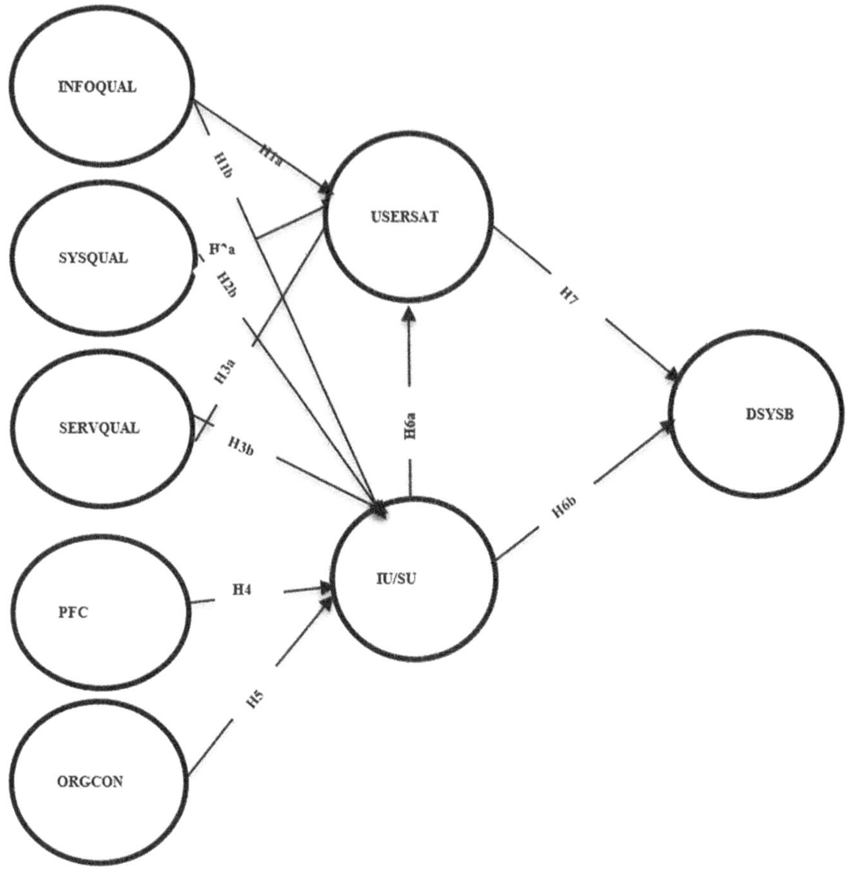

Fig. 2.2 Proposed hypothesized conceptual framework for the study

2.3.2.7 User Satisfaction

User satisfaction looks at the users' level of satisfaction with reports and support services. As already mentioned, drones have directly impacted medical professionals' work and have ultimately had a substantial positive impact on people's healthcare delivery. This presupposes that, as drones' user satisfaction increases, technology usage will be sustained, thereby driving positive benefits. Therefore, it is hypothesized that:

H7: Satisfaction of the drones' delivery system positively influences the drone's system benefits (impacts).

Figure 2.2 represents the hypothesized framework for the study.

2.4 Methodology

The survey research design for cross-sectional data was adopted for this study rather than longitudinal in terms of time horizon. Since this study seeks to test hypotheses related to the applicability of modified DeLone and McLean Model of Information Systems Success Model (DMISSM) on the drone delivery system, the deductive approach was considered suitable (Saunders et al., 2009). Questionnaires were used as the means of data collection, which consisted of three parts. The first part asked questions on respondents' demographic characteristics. The second part was on drivers and the impact of drones on healthcare. The third part bordered on the conditions and factors that facilitate the implementation of drone technology for healthcare. The questionnaire adopted a five-point Likert scale with ranges of (1 = strongly disagree, 2 = disagree, 3 = neither disagree nor agree, 4 = agree, 5 = strongly agree) to measure the constructs.

Consequently, links to an English-based survey questionnaire designed with Google Forms were sent to conveniently sample individual respondents via email. The questionnaire did not gather data that could link or identify respondents to ensure confidentiality and anonymity. Besides relevant demographics, opinions on information quality, system quality, service quality, intention to use, perceived financial cost, organizational considerations, and user satisfaction were asked. Responses to the questionnaire were voluntary, and no financial reward was offered. Partial least squares structural equation modeling (PLS-SEM) was used to analyze the collected data. This study's approach for the data analysis was appropriate because it is resilient to multivariate distribution errors. Furthermore, it is very efficient for approximating the relationships among latent variables (Hair et al., 2019). The approach was justified as the Cronbach's alpha reliability thresholds for the question items were all above 0.7 as required by Bagozzi et al. (1991).

2.5 Results

2.5.1 *Descriptive Analysis*

The collected data were screened to detect duplicate responses and missing data. Table 2.2 shows that missing data for all the 32 indicators is zero, indicating that all the 298 respondents answered all the questions accurately. Since there were no missing data and duplicate response, further data treatment was not required; hence the same data could be used for the final data analysis. The initial model consisted of 8 constructs (information quality, system quality, service quality, intention to use/system use, perceived financial cost, organizational consideration, user satisfaction, and net drone system benefit) and 32 indicators. Out of the eight (8) constructs, INFOQUAL, SYSQUAL, SERVQUAL, and IU/SU were measured using five (5) items each, whereas PFC, ORGCON, USERSAT, and DSYSB were also measured using three (3) items each.

Table 2.2 Results showing the test of normality

Items	Missing	Min	Max	Mean	Standard deviation	Kurtosis	Skewness
INFOQUAL1	0	3	5	4.143	0.639	−0.600	−0.135
INFOQUAL2	0	3	5	4.286	0.547	−0.522	0.036
INFOQUAL3	0	3	5	3.595	0.726	−0.708	0.792
INFOQUAL4	0	2	5	4.381	0.754	0.724	−1.095
INFOQUAL5	0	2	5	3.786	1.186	−1.253	−0.525
SYSQUAL1	0	2	5	3.643	0.840	−0.668	0.027
SYSQUAL2	0	2	5	3.762	0.921	−1.227	0.123
SYSQUAL3	0	2	5	3.667	1.228	−1.485	−0.350
SYSQUAL4	0	3	5	3.952	0.785	−1.377	0.084
SYSQUAL5	0	3	5	4.524	0.626	−0.117	−0.967
SERVQUAL1	0	3	5	4.214	0.513	−0.033	0.260
SERVQUAL2	0	3	5	4.048	0.844	−1.597	−0.091
SERVQUAL3	0	3	5	4.357	0.570	−0.721	−0.198
SERVQUAL4	0	3	5	4.452	0.697	−0.471	−0.889
SERVQUAL5	0	3	5	3.952	0.722	−1.079	0.072
IU/SU1	0	3	5	4.714	0.547	2.259	−1.789
IU/SU2	0	3	5	4.429	0.583	−0.700	−0.443
IU/SU3	0	2	5	4.310	0.740	0.586	−0.922
IU/SU4	0	2	5	4.000	0.724	−0.030	−0.379
IU/SU5	0	3	5	4.429	0.728	−0.626	−0.864
PFC1	0	3	5	4.024	0.636	−0.516	−0.020
PFC2	0	1	5	4.071	0.936	3.125	−1.544
PFC3	0	1	5	3.619	0.950	0.975	−1.015
ORGCON1	0	3	5	4.786	0.513	3.347	−2.382
ORGCON2	0	2	5	3.976	0.801	0.567	−0.794
ORGCON3	0	3	5	4.810	0.449	3.104	−2.340
USERSAT1	0	3	5	4.571	0.583	0.018	−1.005
USERSAT2	0	3	5	4.333	0.604	−0.648	−0.313
USERSAT3	0	3	5	4.357	0.570	−0.721	−0.198
DSYSB1	0	3	5	4.405	0.657	−0.601	−0.658
DSYSB2	0	2	5	4.738	0.620	3.031	−2.776
DSYSB3	0	3	5	4.762	0.569	3.165	−2.295

For all the items, the mean value ranges from 3.595 (INFOQUAL3) to 4.810 (ORGCON3). This mean value means that all items' mean value was above 3, indicating a generally positive response by respondents toward the constructs under consideration. The test of normality was conducted for further analysis to ensure data accuracy. The partial least squares (PLS) analysis portrays absolute kurtosis values range from 0.018 (USERSAT1) to 3.347 (ORGCON1), and the absolute skewness values also range from 0.020 (PFC1) to 2.776 (DSYSB2) (Table 2.1). A maximum kurtosis value of $3.347 \approx 3$ and the maximum skewness value of $2.776 \approx 3$ were obtained. The normal range of absolute skewness and absolute kurtosis is $|\pm 3|$ according to Kline (2005) and Brown (2015). None of the kurtosis and skewness values of the study were above the $|\pm 3|$. In this study, based on the skewness and kurtosis values achieved, it is assumed that the data is normally distributed. Therefore, the structural models and the PLS-SEM analysis of the measurement model were estimated. The detailed analysis of normality is shown in Table 2.2.

The respondents' demographics analysis indicates a female representation was only 35.23% and a male majority of 64.77%. These results demonstrate male dominance in the drone delivery industry. Also, the majority (48.77%) of the study respondents were between 26 and 35 years. This is followed by those between 18 and 25, which constituted 25.84% of the study respondents. 15.10% were between 36 and 45 years, and 7.38% were between 46 and 60 years, while 2.91% were aged 61 years and above. Clearly, the data shows the predominance of young people within the drone delivery industry. This predominance is expected as young people have been perceived as technology savvy. In terms of educational qualifications, the majority (67.79%) of the respondents reported holding a bachelor's degree, followed by a master's (22.48%). The rest are PhD constituting 3.36% and other educational qualifications such as technical and vocational education and a diploma representing 6.37% of the total respondents.

Also, 44.97% of the respondents were pharmacists, representing the majority, 11.41% were medical laboratory scientists, and 7.38% were pharmacologists, with 5.03% being medical doctors and physician assistants. In terms of respondents' working experience within the drone delivery industry, about half (50.34%) reported up to 1-year experience. Others have 2–5 years, 6–10 years, and 11 years and above, representing 21.14%, 22.15%, and 6.37%, respectively. Most respondents' low level of experience indicates the relatively new adoption of drones for medical delivery within Africa's health sectors.

Regarding the country of residence, the majority (65.44%) of the study respondents were Ghanaians, whereas 34.56% are based in Rwanda. The study data also shows the majority (37.92%) received an annual salary between 10,001 and 15,000 US dollars. The respondents' demographics are summarized in Table 2.3.

2.5.2 Reliability and Validity Tests (Constructs Measurement)

In this study, Coltman et al. (2008) recommend analyzing the measurement model. The internal consistency, reliability, and discriminant and convergent validity of the item were analyzed. The constructs had item loadings of above the 0.7 thresholds and were modeled as reflective (Barclay et al., 1995) except for six items (INFOQUAL4, SYSQUAL5, SERVQUAL4, IU/SU5, ORGCON2, PFC3) (see Table 2.4). These six items recorded item loadings below the required 0.7 thresholds and were subsequently removed before the structural model analysis. Analysis of the internal consistency was done using Cronbach's alpha. Cronbach's alpha values greater than 0.7 were attained as recommended by Straub (1989), which suggests the validity of constructs. Composite reliability (CR) was also assessed since other researchers prefer that. To examine the reliability of constructs, CR was used. All the constructs attained CR values greater than 0.7, which is the recommended value of CR, for good reliability (Hair et al., 2010), as shown in Table 2.4.

Table 2.3 Demographic characteristics of the respondents

Demographic	Value	Frequency	Percentage	Cum.
Gender	Female	105	35.23	35.23
	Male	193	64.77	**100**
Age (years)	18–25	77	25.84	25.84
	26–35	145	48.77	74.61
	36–45	45	15.10	89.71
	46–60	22	7.38	97.09
	61 and above	9	2.91	**100**
Education	Bachelor's	202	67.79	67.79
	Master's	67	22.48	90.27
	PhD	10	3.36	93.63
	Others	19	6.37	**100**
Occupation	Pharmacologist	22	7.38	7.38
	Pharmacist	134	44.97	52.35
	Service/customer support	33	11.07	63.42
	Nutritionist	6	2.01	65.43
	Nurse	14	4.70	70.13
	Medical laboratory scientist	34	11.41	81.54
	Medical doctor/physician assistant	15	5.03	86.57
	Drone technician/operator	14	4.70	91.27
	Biochemist	14	4.70	95.97
	Executive/manager	12	4.03	**100**
Income (annual in US$)	Less than 3000	30	10.06	10.06
	3000–10,000	113	37.92	47.98
	10,001–15,000	105	35.23	83.21
	15,001–20,000	13	4.36	87.57
	20,001–25,000	25	8.39	95.96
	25,001 and above	12	4.04	**100**
Country of residence	Ghana	195	65.44	65.44
	Rwanda	103	34.56	**100**
Years of working experience	Up to 1 year	150	50.34	50.34
	2–5 years	63	21.14	71.48
	6–10 years	66	22.15	93.63
	11 years and above	19	6.37	**100**
Affiliation	The staff of the healthcare facilities	202	67.79	67.79
	The staff of the drone operation centers	96	31.21	**100**

The average variance extracted (AVE) was used to measure the convergent validity. The convergent validity further validates each construct's reflective nature through its indicators. The convergent validity ensures the unidimensionality of multiple-item factors (Gefen et al., 2000) and the elimination of unreliable indicators (Bollen, 1989). All AVE values were above 0.5 as obliged by Wixom and Watson (2001). A latent variable's square root of AVE against correlations with

Table 2.4 Item loadings and construct validity and reliability

Constructs	Indicators	Item loadings	Cronbach's alpha	Composite reliability	Average variance extracted (AVE)
Information quality	INFOQUAL1	0.880	0.867	0.909	0.716
	INFOQUAL2	0.887			
	INFOQUAL3	0.863			
	INFOQUAL4	0.546			
	INFOQUAL5	0.746			
System quality	SYSQUAL1	0.819	0.882	0.919	0.740
	SYSQUAL2	0.871			
	SYSQUAL3	0.932			
	SYSQUAL4	0.814			
	SYSQUAL5	0.433			
Service quality	SERVQUAL1	0.838	0.900	0.930	0.769
	SERVQUAL2	0.891			
	SERVQUAL3	0.913			
	SERVQUAL4	0.601			
	SERVQUAL5	0.863			
Intention to use/ system use	IU/SU1	0.733	0.817	0.879	0.647
	IU/SU2	0.861			
	IU/SU3	0.868			
	IU/SU4	0.747			
	IU/SU5	0.578			
Perceived financial control	PFC1	0.904	0.609	0.832	0.713
	PFC2	0.780			
	PFC3	0.543			
Organizational considerations	ORGCON1	0.968	0.787	0.890	0.804
	ORGCON2	0.577			
	ORGCON3	0.818			
User satisfaction	USERSAT1	0.713	0.825	0.896	0.745
	USERSAT2	0.922			
	USERSAT3	0.936			
Net drone system benefits	DSYSB1	0.919	0.873	0.923	0.800
	DSYSB2	0.829			
	DSYSB3	0.932			

other latent variables was compared to measure the discriminant validity (Fornell & Lacker, 1981). All correlation values were greater than the AVEs of constructs, preferred by Fornell and Lacker (1981) and shown in Table 2.4.

Furthermore, a multicollinearity test was analyzed by calculating the variance inflation factor (VIF). Meanwhile, VIF values of less than 3 are necessary to prevent the occurrence of multicollinearity (Hair et al., 2016). Multicollinearity was shown not to be present in the sample data with the highest VIF of 2.793. Table 2.5 shows the result of the discriminant validity test and multicollinearity test.

Table 2.5 Discriminant validity test (Fornell and Lacker criteria)

	AVE	VIF	DSYSB	INFOQUAL	IU/SU	ORGCON	PFC	SERVQUAL	SYSQUAL	USERSAT
DSYSB	0.800	2.547	**0.894**							
INFOQUAL	0.716	2.481	0.301	**0.846**						
IU/SU	0.647	1.406	0.576	0.559	**0.805**					
ORGCON	0.804	1.414	0.519	0.194	0.353	**0.896**				
PFC	0.713	1.836	0.491	0.386	0.754	0.385	**0.844**			
SERVQUAL	0.769	3.002	0.359	0.537	0.599	0.308	0.609	**0.877**		
SYSQUAL	0.740	2.937	0.146	0.733	0.524	0.033	0.364	0.775	**0.860**	
USERSAT	0.745	1.406	0.744	0.394	0.537	0.381	0.443	0.524	0.449	**0.863**

Factor correlation matrix with $\sqrt{\text{AVE}}$ on the diagonal; *AVE* average variance extracted, *VIF* variance inflation factor

2.5.3 Structural Model Results

The structural model was estimated with the bootstrap technique (100 samples). Kock (2011) stresses this method is appropriate when the sample size is greater than 100. The PLS analysis results are shown in Fig. 2.3. The path coefficients are shown on the arrows, whereas the R-squared values are indicated in percentages. With p-values less than 0.05, the path coefficients were considered significant. Figure 2.3 indicates that INFOQUAL, SYSQUAL, SERVQUAL, ORGCON, and PFC explained 66.8% of the variance in intention to use and system use (IU/SU). Moreover, INFOQUAL, SYSQUAL, and SERVQUAL combined with IU/SU accounted for 35.4% of user satisfaction variance (USERSAT).

In contrast, USERSAT and IU/SU explained 59.7% of the variance in net drone system benefits (DSYSB). Many of the suggested relationships were again supported. Specifically, INFOQUAL ($\beta = 0.181$, $p < 0.001$), SYSQUAL ($\beta = 0.221$, $p < 0.001$), and PFC ($\beta = 0.609$, $p < 0.001$) significantly affected IU/SU. Furthermore, SERVQUAL ($\beta = 0.281$, $p < 0.001$) and IU/SU ($\beta = 0.333$, $p < 0.001$) impacted significantly on USERSAT, whereas IU/SU ($\beta = -0.248$, $p < 0.001$) and USERSAT ($\beta = 0.611$, $p < 0.001$) significantly affected DSYSB. Meanwhile, **SERVQUAL** ($\beta = -0.070$, $p > 0.05$) and ORGCON ($\beta = 0.09$, $p > 0.05$) failed to affect IU/SU, whereas **SYSQUAL** ($\beta = 0.050.0310$, $p > 0.05$) and INFOQUAL ($\beta = 0.033$,

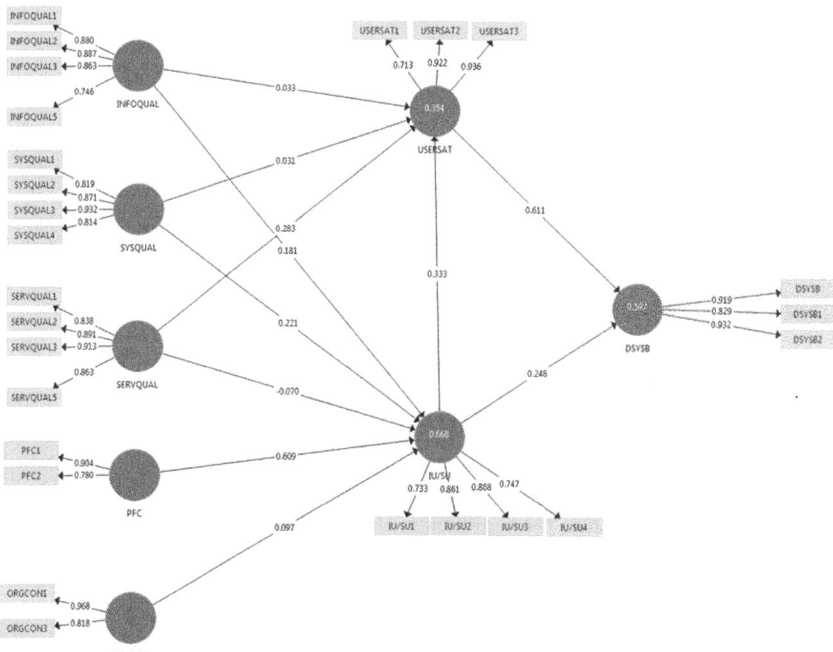

Fig. 2.3 PLS analysis of structural model

Table 2.6 Significance of path coefficients

Relationship	Hypothesis	Original sample (O)	Standard deviation (STDEV)	T statistics (|O/STDEV|)	Coefficient	P values	Supported
INFOQUAL -> IU/SU	H1a	0.181	0.058	3.141	0.181	0.001	Yes
INFOQUAL -> USERSAT	H1b	0.033	0.103	0.325	0.033	0.372	No
SYSQUAL -> IU/SU	H2a	0.221	0.070	3.182	0.221	0.001	Yes
SYSQUAL -> USERSAT	H2b	0.031	0.099	0.314	0.031	0.377	No
SERVQUAL -> IU/SU	H3a	−0.070	0.057	1.234	−0.070	0.109	No
SERVQUAL -> USERSAT	H3b	0.283	0.079	3.569	0.281	0.000	Yes
PFC -> IU/SU	H4	0.609	0.038	16.163	0.609	0.000	Yes
ORGCON -> IU/SU	H5	0.097	0.065	1.504	0.097	0.066	No
IU/SU -> USERSAT	H6a	0.333	0.077	4.309	0.333	0.000	Yes
IU/SU -> DSYSB	H6b	0.248	0.076	3.246	0.248	0.001	Yes
USERSAT -> DSYSB	H7	0.611	0.070	8.690	0.611	0.000	Yes

$p > 0.05$) also failed to affect USERSAT. The projected relationships, p-values, their path coefficients, and whether they were supported or not are summarized in Table 2.6.

2.5.4 *Conditions and Factors That Facilitate the Implementation of Drone Delivery System for Healthcare*

Relative importance index (RII) analysis was performed to determine how significant the various statements are as factors and conditions associated with implementing a drone delivery system for healthcare. The relative importance index (RII) was given as:

$$\text{RII} = \frac{\sum w}{AN} \tag{2.1}$$

Table 2.7 Relative importance of conditions and factors that facilitate the implementation of drone delivery system for healthcare

Conditions and factors	1	2	3	4	5	N	EW	x	RII	Remarks
Deplorable road networks	0	0	10	90	198	298	1380	4.6	0.93	H
Traffic congestions in cities	0	7	28	77	186	298	1336	4.5	0.89	H
Quick delivery time for drones	0	0	7	29	262	298	1447	4.9	0.97	H
Healthcare facilities located in remote areas	0	0	7	21	270	298	1455	4.9	0.98	H
Late arrival of some medical supplies	0	7	14	56	221	298	1385	4.7	0.93	H
High or strong wind affects safe delivery of medical supplies	0	14	112	132	40	298	1092	3.7	0.91	H
The weight a drone delivers can affect the quantity of medical supply to order	7	14	12	175	90	298	1207	4.1	1.00	H
Sometimes drugs and blood do not get the right temperature in transportation	56	42	112	28	60	298	888	3.0	0.61	M
Sometimes drone operators do not supply the right prescription of medical supplies	70	147	35	28	18	298	671	2.3	0.41	L
Availability of telecommunication infrastructures	0	7	36	189	66	298	1208	4.1	1.00	H

where w is the weighting given to each statement by respondents ranging from 1 (strongly disagree) to 5 (strongly agree), A is the highest weight, and N is the total number of respondents. The conditions and factors associated with drone delivery system implementation are presented in Table 2.7 with their relative importance index (RII). The conditions and factors were categorized into five (5) based on their relative importance to the respondents using the RII. The classification is based on the work of Akadiri (2011) given as $0.8 \leq \text{RII} \leq 1$ as high (H), $0.6 \leq \text{RII} \leq 0.8$ as high-medium (H–M), $0.4 \leq \text{RII} \leq 0.6$ as medium (M), $0.2 \leq \text{RII} \leq 0.4$ as medium-low (M-L), and $0 \leq \text{RII} \leq 0.2$ as low (L). Based on the results, it is noted that all conditions and factors were rated by the respondents as high conditions except temperature of blood and medicines in transportation and supply of right medicines and medication by drone operators, which were rated as medium and low, respectively. This result indicates that the conditions and factors indicated in Table 2.6 facilitate implementing a drone delivery system.

2.6 Discussions

In this chapter, the updated and modified DeLone and McLean Information Systems Success Model (DMISSM) was adopted as a theoretical lens to investigate the drivers, motivations, conditions, and factors facilitating the successful implementation of drones for healthcare delivery in Africa. The theory was extended with relevant constructs (perceived financial cost and organizational considerations) to expand the proposed conceptual framework's strength. The framework specifically investigated the influence of information quality, system quality, service quality, perceived financial cost, and organizational consideration on the intention to use/system use and the influence of information quality, system quality, service quality, and intention to use/system use on user satisfaction. It also investigated the effects of user satisfaction and intention to use or actual usage of drones on healthcare delivery.

The findings show that a reasonable amount of the variance in intention to use or the actual usage of drone delivery system (66.8%) is explained by the exogenous variables (information quality, system quality, and perceived financial cost). The drone delivery system's variance in user satisfaction (35.4%) is explained by the exogenous variables (service quality and intention to use/system use). Finally, the variance in the impact of drone system use on healthcare delivery (59.7%) is explained by exogenous variables of user satisfaction and intention to use or actual drone system use. Information quality, system quality, and perceived financial cost directly influenced usage intention. This influence confirms the studies of Eichleay et al. (2019) and Gangwal et al. (2019), who argued that system quality and information quality predict use intention, and Venkatesh et al. (2012) and Eichleay et al. (2019) who believe cost plays a critical role in information system adoption.

Contrary to previous studies (Jeyabalan et al., 2020; McCall, 2019), service quality and organization consideration did not affect use intention. This finding is surprising, as medical drones' quality of service was expected to have motivated the use of drones by medical staff and healthcare facilities. Perhaps this result could be due to the drone system technical staff's inability to promptly and accurately resolve challenges. As the desire to use drones for medical supply intensifies in some parts of Africa, drone operators such as Zipline may have measures to improve the quality of their services to healthcare facilities across Africa. User satisfaction was directly influenced by service quality and use intention. This finding is consistent with Jeyabalan et al. (2020) and McCall (2019). They argued that the availability of human resources, competent staff, and the ability to resolve technical challenges faced in drone implementation influence drones' adoption in healthcare. However, this study contradicts McCall (2019) on the influence of drones' information quality on user satisfaction derived from using medical drones.

Finally, the findings show that drone technology has contributed significantly to the work of medical professionals within the healthcare sector. The direct benefits of drones have derived the satisfaction of healthcare providers and stakeholders alike. The drone system's effects on healthcare delivery were directly influenced by user satisfaction and intention to use/system use. This finding is consistent with other studies that have asserted that the use of drones for medical supply has substantially impacted healthcare delivery positively (Braun et al., 2019; Hügler et al., 2018; Lin et al., 2018).

The study identified poor road networks, quick delivery time for drones, healthcare facilities in remote areas, and late arrival of medical supply through the traditional supply chain as conditions and factors that facilitate the successful implementation of a drone delivery system for healthcare. Others include traffic congestion in cities and the small quantity of drugs drone can deliver. These findings are consistent with previous studies. Scott and Scott (2017) argued that drones are faster transportation than the traditional transportation system, hence their effective use in emergency medical supplies delivery. Boukoberine et al. (2019) assert that drones facilitate smaller quantity items' delivery faster. The study results rejected the claim that drone operators do not supply the right prescription of medical supplies. This result, therefore, presupposes that medical professionals get the exact medical supplies requested.

2.7 Conclusion and Recommendations

2.7.1 Conclusion

The use of digital technologies to expand health access is getting impetus in Africa. Moreover, the health-related aspects of the Millennium Development Goals (MDGs), the Sustainable Development Goals (SDGs), and the Universal Health Coverage (UHC) policies all call for innovative and technological strategies to support the implementation of healthcare on the continent. Fortunately, drones have been confirmed as a potential technology to facilitate product delivery worldwide, and healthcare products could not be an exception. Drones can solve supply chain challenges, improve logistical efficiency, and eliminate barriers that hinder access to remote and underserved populations with lifesaving medicines. This chapter makes significant progress by investigating the drivers, conditions, and factors facilitating drones' use for medical delivery and its health, social, and economic impacts. Responses from 298 participants were rigorously analyzed using partial least squares structural equation modeling.

The study's outcome suggests that the quality of information (e.g., accuracy, timely usability) provided by the drone system, system quality (e.g., flexibility, response time), is confirmed as driving drone adoption and use in Africa. Moreover, the drone service quality (e.g., drone operators' reliability and technical competence) and perceived financial cost are confirmed drivers facilitating drone adoption in parts of Africa. Medical professionals have underscored how they have been satisfied with the information quality, system quality, and service quality of deployed drones for medical delivery. The confirmation of perceived financial cost indicates that drones' impacts and benefits far outweigh the cost incurred. The findings further show that drone use has substantially impacted healthcare delivery. It has contributed immensely in saving lives through the emergency supply of drugs and medical equipment to remote areas. Also, quick delivery time for drones, healthcare facilities in remote areas, and late arrival of medical supplies through the traditional supply chain were identified as the most important factors and conditions facilitating drones' implementation for healthcare delivery in Africa.

2.7.2 Main Contribution and Advancement of Research

This study's main contribution is toward the effective and efficient implementation of drone usage in Africa's remote communities for healthcare delivery and its health and social impacts to guide research, policy, and practice. This chapter contributed significantly to addressing a significant gap in extant medical drone delivery technology literature, particularly concerning drivers, motivations, conditions, and factors that facilitate the successful implementation and use of drone systems for healthcare delivery. It further contributed to assessing the medical drone delivery technology's impact on the healthcare system and the communities being served. The significant theoretical contribution of this chapter is the modification of DMISSM for medical drone technology delivery systems. The generalizability of DMISSM is extended from an information system success context to a more specific for medical drone delivery usage. In the specific case of using the drone for medical supply, other important drivers come to play. Factors such as perceived financial cost and organizational considerations are important in implementing digital innovation and technologies in the health sector. Empirical support has been offered for the pertinency of DMISSM in different industry and cultural settings to offer a better explanation for the adoption and use of information systems.

2.7.3 Managerial and Practical Implications

Drone technology has emerged as a critical digital transformation tool in the healthcare delivery of Africa. The study's findings have several practical and managerial implications. The findings also present practical, relevant information to stakeholders within the health sector of Africa, particularly governments, donor partners, healthcare professionals, and digital technology transformation enthusiasts. Further, the study results have shown that drones have substantially impacted healthcare delivery and saved many lives in rural Africa. It is recommended for governments in Africa to begin large-scale implementation of medical drone delivery services. Such delivery will contribute significantly to providing medical healthcare services to difficult to reach areas in Africa and provide quality healthcare to people as envisaged by the Sustainable Development Goals (Goal 3).

2.7.4 Limitations and Direction for Future Research

The respondents for the study were sampled using the non-probabilistic sampling technique (convenient sampling). This approach presents the issue of sampling bias and places limitations on the generalizability of the findings. A more representative sampling approach, such as clustering and simple random sampling, could be adopted in future studies to eliminate sampling biases and better understand the use of drone technology for healthcare delivery. Future studies could also extend the study's scope by examining barriers and challenges that confront the successful implementation of drone delivery systems in Africa context-specific. Further study could consider drones' assessment in healthcare success from specific perspectives like the staff of the delivering drone operating centers and the staff of receiving healthcare centers. Also, community members and policymakers such as government officials could be rolled in as study respondents in future studies to understand better the perceptions, motivations, concerns, and drivers associated with the adoption and use of drones for healthcare delivery.

References

Agatz, N., Bouman, P., & Schmidt, M. (2015). *Optimization approaches for the traveling salesman problem with drone, ERIM report series research in management*. Erasmus Research Institute of Management, Erasmus University Rotterdam.

Akadiri, P. (2011). Development of a multi-criteria approach for the selection of sustainable materials for building projects. (Doctoral dissertation, University of Wolverhampton). Retrieved from https://file:/C:/Users/Mansah/Downloads/DEVELOPMENT_OF_A_MULTI_CRITERIA_APPROACH.pdf.

Amukele, T., Ness, P. M., Tobian, A. A., Boyd, J., & Street, J. (2017). Drone transportation of blood products. *Transfusion, 57*(3), 582–588.

Bagozzi, R. P., Yi, Y., & Phillips, L. W. (1991). Assessing construct validity in organizational research. *Administrative Science Quarterly, 36*(3), 421–458.

Barclay, D., Higgins, C., & Thompson, R. (1995). The partial least squares (PLS) approach to casual modeling: Personal computer adoption and use as an illustration. *Information Management & Computer Security, 8*, 131–143.

Bollen, K. A. (1989). A new incremental fit index for general structural equation models. *Sociological Methods & Research, 17*(3), 303–316.

Boukoberine, M. N., Zhou, Z., & Benbouzid, M. (2019). A critical review on unmanned aerial vehicles power supply and energy management: Solutions, strategies, and prospects. *Applied Energy, 255*, 113823.

Braun, J., Gertz, S. D., Furer, A., Bader, T., Frenkel, H., Chen, J., Glassberg, E., & Nachman, D. (2019). The promising future of drones in prehospital medical care and its application to battlefield medicine. *Journal of Trauma and Acute Care Surgery, 87*(1S), S28–S34.

Brown, T. A. (2015). *Confirmatory factor analysis for applied research* (2nd ed.). New York: Guilford Publication.

Choi-Fitzpatrick, A., Chavarria, D., Cychosz, E., Dingens, J. P., Duffey, M., Koebel, K., Siriphanh, M., Tulen, Y., Watanabe, H., Juskauskas, T., & Holland, J. (2016). *Up in the air: A global estimate of non-violent drone use 2009–2015*. San Diego: University of San Diego.

Clarke, R. (2014). Understanding the drone epidemic. *Computer Law and Security Review, 30*(3), 230–246.

Coltman, T., Devinney, T. M., Midgley, D. F., & Venaik, S. (2008). Formative versus reflective e measurement models: Two applications of formative measurement. *Journal of Business Research, 61*(12), 1250–1262.

D'Andrea, R. (2014). Guest editorial, can drones deliver? *IEEE Transactions on Automation Science and Engineering, 11*(3), 647–648.

DeLone, W. H., & McLean, E. R. (1992). Information systems success: The quest for the dependent variable. *Information Systems Research, 3*(1), 60–95.

Delone, W. H., & McLean, E. R. (2003). The DeLone and McLean model of information systems success: A ten-year update. *Journal of Management Information Systems, 19*(4), 9–30.
DeLone, W. H., & McLean, E. R. (2016). Information systems success measurement. *Foundations and Trends® in Information Systems, 2*(1), 1–116.
Eichleay, M., Evens, E., Stankevitz, K., & Parker, C. (2019). Using the unmanned aerial vehicle delivery decision tool to consider transporting medical supplies via drone. *Global Health: Science and Practice, 7*(4), 500–506.
Fornell, C., & Larcker, D. F. (1981). Evaluating structural equation models with unobservable variables and measurement error. *Journal of Marketing Research, 18*(1), 39–50.
French, S. (2015). Drone delivery is already here – And it works. *Market Watch* [online] https://www.marketwatch.com/story/drone-delivery-is-already-here-and-it-works-2015-11-30?mod=article_inline. Accessed 28 Nov 2020.
Gangwal, A., Jain, A., & Mohanta, S. (2019). Blood delivery by drones: A case study on Zipline. *International Journal of Innovative Research in Science, Engineering and Technology, 8*(8), 8760–8766.
Gefen, D., Straub, D., & Boudreau, M. C. (2000). Structural equation modeling and regression: Guidelines for research practice. *Communications of the Association for Information Systems, 4*(1), 7.
Hair, J. F., Jr., Hult, G. T. M., Ringle, C., & Sarstedt, M. (2016). *A primer on partial least squares structural equation modeling (PLS-SEM)*. Thousand Oaks: Sage.
Hair, J. F., Black, W. C., & Babin, A. (2010). *Multivariate data analysis*. Pearson Education.
Hair, J. F., Risher, J. J., Sarstedt, M., & Ringle, C. M. (2019). When to use and how to report the results of PLS-SEM. *European Business Review, 31*(1), 2–24.
Hügler, P., Roos, F., Schartel, M., Geiger, M., & Waldschmidt, C. (2018). Radar taking off: New capabilities for UAVs. *IEEE Microwave Magazine, 19*(7), 43–53.
Ibeneme, S., Ukor, N., Ongom, M., Dasa, T., Muneene, D., & Okeibunor, J. (2020). Strengthening capacities among digital health leaders for the development and implementation of national digital health programs in Nigeria. In *BMC Proceedings* (Vol. 14, No. 10, pp. 1–12). BioMed Central.
Jeyabalan, V., Nouvet, E., Meier, P., & Donelle, L. (2020). Context-specific challenges, opportunities, and ethics of drones for healthcare delivery in the eyes of program managers and field staff: A multi-site qualitative study. *Drones, 4*(3), 44.
Kellermann, R., Biehle, T., & Fischer, L. (2020). Drones for parcel and passenger transportation: A literature review. *Transportation Research Interdisciplinary Perspectives, 4*, 100088.
Khazan, O. (2016). A drone to save the world. *The Atlantic*. https://www.theatlantic.com/technology/archive/2016/04/a-drone-to-save-the-world/476592/. Accessed 24 Nov 2020.
Kline, R. B. (2005). *Principles and practice of structural equation modeling* (2nd ed.). New York: The Guilford Press.
Kock, N. (2011). Using WarpPLS in e-collaboration studies: Mediating effects, control, and second-order variables, and algorithm choices. *International Journal of e-Collaboration (IJeC), 7*(3), 1–13.
Lin, C. A., Shah, K., Mauntel, L. C. C., & Shah, S. A. (2018). Drone delivery of medications: Review of the landscape and legal considerations. *The Bulletin of the American Society of Hospital Pharmacists, 75*(3), 153–158.
Lu, V. N., Wirtz, J., Kunz, W. H., Paluch, S., Gruber, T., Martins, A., & Patterson, P. G. (2020). Service robots, customers and service employees: What can we learn from the academic literature and where are the gaps? *Journal of Service Theory and Practice, 30*(3), 361–391.
McCall, B. (2019). *Sub-Saharan Africa leads the way in medical drones*. Available at Sub-Saharan Africa leads the way in medical drones (uswr.ac.ir). Accessed 01 Dec 2020.
Olu, O., Muneene, D., Bataringaya, J. E., Nahimana, M.-R., Ba, H., Turgeon, Y., Karamagi, H. C., & Dovlo, D. (2019). How can digital health technologies contribute to sustainable attainment of universal health coverage in Africa? A perspective. *Frontiers in Public Health, 7*, 341.

Pepitone, J. (2015). *First FAA-approved drone delivery drops medicine in Virginia*. https://www.nbcnews.com/tech/tech-news/first-faa-approved-drone-delivery-drops-medicine-virginia-n393986. Accessed 15 Nov 2020.

Preimesberger, C. (2016). Drones will soon be dropping medicines to save lives in Rwanda. *eWeek*. https://www.eweek.com/mobile/drones-will-soon-be-dropping-medicines-to-save-lives-in-rwanda. Accessed 23 Oct 2020.

Preko, M., Osei-Boateng, R., & Durosinmi, A. E. (2020). Digitalising healthcare in developing economies: Challenges and mitigating strategies. In R. Boateng (Ed.), *Handbook of research on managing information systems in developing economies* (pp. 332–353). Hershey: IGI Global.

Prigg, M. (2014). The ambulance drone that could save your life: Flying defibrillator can reach speeds of 60mph. *Daily Mail*. https://www.dailymail.co.uk/sciencetech/article-2811851/The-ambulance-drone-save-life-Flying-defibrillator-reach-speeds-60mph.html. Accessed 23 Oct 2020.

Raptopoulos, A. (2013). No roads? There's a drone for that. In *TED conference*. Available online at: https://www.ted.com/talks/andreas_raptopoulos_no_roads_there_is_a_drone_for_that. Accessed 23 Oct 2020.

Rosser, J. C., Jr., Vignesh, V., Terwilliger, B. A., & Parker, B. C. (2018). Surgical and medical applications of drones: A comprehensive review. *JSLS: Journal of the Society of Laparoendoscopic Surgeons, 22*(3), e2018.00018.

Sandbrook, C. (2015). The social implications of using drones for biodiversity conservation. *Ambio, 44*(4), 636–647.

Saunders, M., Lewis, P., Thornhill, A., & Wilson, J. (2009). Business research methods. *Financial Times*.

Scott, J., & Scott, C. (2017). Drone delivery models for healthcare. In *Proceedings of the 50th Hawaii international conference on system sciences*. Hawaii 2017.

Straub, D. W. (1989). Validating instruments in MIS research. *MIS Quarterly, 13*(2), 147–169.

Tilley, A. (2016). *UPS experiments with drone delivery in partnership with Zipline*. https://www.forbes.com/sites/aarontilley/2016/05/09/ups-experiments-with-drone-delivery-in-partnership-with-zipline/#1593b26545a4. Accessed 28 Nov 2020.

Varnholt, H. (2016). DHL's drone demonstration fails to deliver. *Wall Street Journal*. https://www.wsj.com/articles/dhls-drone-demonstration-fails-to-deliver-1453226792. Accessed 23 Nov 2010.

Venkatesh, V., Thong, J. Y., & Xu, X. (2012). Consumer acceptance and use of information technology: Extending the unified theory of acceptance and use of technology. *MIS Quarterly, 36*, 157–178.

Wagstaff, A., & Claeson, M. (2004). *The millennium development goals for health: Rising to the challenges*. Washington, DC: World Bank. https://openknowledge.worldbank.org/handle/10986/14954. Accessed 23 Oct 2020.

Welch, A. (2015). *A cost-benefit analysis of Amazon Prime Air.* https://scholar.utc.edu/honors-theses/47. Accessed 23 Oct 2020.

Wixom, B. H., & Watson, H. J. (2001). An empirical investigation of the factors affecting data warehousing success. *MIS Quarterly, 25*, 17–41.

Wynn, M., & Jones, P. (2019). *The sustainable development goals: Industry sector approaches*. Routledge.

Samuel Anim-Yeboah is a Doctoral Candidate in Information Systems (IS) at the University of Ghana Business School and a lecturer in pharmacy informatics at the Dept. of Pharmacy Practice of the Kwame Nkrumah University of Science and Technology. He holds a Bachelor of Pharmacy degree, a Master of Science in Pharmaceutical Analysis and Quality Control, and a Master of Business Administration in Management Information Systems. Samuel is a professional pharmacist and a consultant in management information systems. He is the CEO of Sims Technologies Ltd. (a management information systems and solutions company). He is interested in digital technology and enterprise research, focusing on health informatics, entrepreneurship, management, digitalization, and transformation of health systems. Samuel can be reached at ssanim-yeboah@st.ug.edu.gh and samaniyeb@yahoo.com.

Richard Apau is a cybersecurity and digital forensics specialist with over 7 years of experience in information technology research and consultancy. He has extensive university teaching experience, having lectured at the University of Education Winneba (UEW) and Kwame Nkrumah University of Science and Technology (KNUST). He is currently an adjunct lecturer at the Ghana Institute of Management and Public Administration (GIMPA). He is the founder and CEO of Africa Digital Innovations Centre (AfriDIC) Limited and cofounder and managing partner of CERIT Research and Consultancy Limited. Richard is a Doctoral Candidate in Computer Science specializing in data and information security at KNUST, Ghana. He holds a Master of Philosophy (M.Phil.) degree in Computer Science and Bachelor of Science (BSc.) degree in Computer Science from KNUST. He also possesses a Master of Science (MSc) in Cybersecurity and Management from the University of Warwick, UK. He has published extensively in international peer-reviewed journals. Richard can be reached at apaur@ceritgh.com.

Mansah Preko is a final-year Doctoral Candidate in Information Systems (IS) at the University of Ghana Business School and an adjunct lecturer at the Ghana Institute of Management and Public Administration (GIMPA). She holds a Bachelor of Science degree in Information and Communication Technology (ICT) and a Master of Science degree in Management Information Systems (MIS). Her research interest is in digital transformation, with emphasis on the healthcare industry of developing economies and Africa, in particular. Mansah's interest is also found in IS implementations in both social and organizational contexts. Mansah can be reached at mansah.preko@gmail.com.

Chapter 3
Validating Digital Value from Digital Technology Adoption for Entrepreneurial Behaviour in Africa

Kobina A. Benson, Muesser C. Nat, Divine Q. Agozie, Sam A. Edu, and Oseyenbhin S. Osemeahon

Abstract Much evidence exists on the benefits of digital technology for innovation and entrepreneurship. In that, digital technologies impact individual innovation, which intends generates value. However, this assertion is often evident at the unit level and requires a broader understanding of digital value and entrepreneurial behaviour on the larger society and its relevance for policy overall. A paucity of investigations largely exists on this consideration. This study examines and validates the theoretical and economic effects of digital technology adoption and value generation on macro entrepreneurial behaviour. It also examines the feedback effects between these interactions. This chapter employs a partial least squares (PLS) estimator to validate the empirical model developed for these interactions based on World Bank data on 54 African states. At scale, technology adoption facilitates entrepreneurial behaviour, thus increasing SME start-up, likewise value generation and digital value. Thus, digital value generated from technology adoption will facilitate entrepreneurial behaviour (SME start-up) at scale.

Keywords Digital technologies · Digital value · SME start-up · Value generation · Africa · PLS

K. A. Benson · M. C. Nat · D. Q. Agozie (✉) · S. A. Edu · O. S. Osemeahon
Faculty of Applied Sciences, Cyprus International University, Haspolat, Cyprus
e-mail: mnat@ciu.edu.tr; dagozie@ug.edu.gh; aedu@ug.edu.gh; ose.sunday@ciu.edu.tr

R. Boateng et al. (eds.), *Digital Innovations, Business and Society in Africa*,
Advances in Theory and Practice of Emerging Markets,
https://doi.org/10.1007/978-3-030-77987-0_3

3.1 Introduction

In sub-Saharan Africa, slow economic growth and poverty remain a cutting-across challenge. There are several states in the African subregion still struggling with severe poverty because of slow economic growth and lack of employment (World Bank, 2016). To exacerbate the issue, the recent recession faced by the world as a result of the global pandemic (COVID-19) has gravely impacted many economies adversely and continues to worsen the adverse impact of poverty in Africa. The effect of the global recession from the pandemic is mostly felt by the region's larger economies, particularly in the area of stalled economic growth and employment which are both likely to worsen the poverty situation and endanger livelihood (World Bank Economic Review, 2020). For instance, the economic and social impacts are estimated to cost up to $79 billion in estimated output losses, reduced productivity, and limited job prospects (World Bank Economic Review, 2020). With these consequences, economic growth is estimated to contract by −5.1% by 2021 from 2.4% in 2019 to −2.1% in 2020 (World Bank Economic Review, 2020).

The collapse of economic activity and growth will require the creation of value and expansion of existing operations by leveraging on existing technological innovations to facilitate access to international markets and productivity (World Bank Economic Review, 2020; Nam, 2020; McHenry & Welch, 2018). Therefore, discerning how to stimulate entrepreneurial behaviour by identifying new possibilities and increased capability to venture into new markets is of the essence if African economies wish to impact the vicious cycle of poverty and stalled economic growth (World Bank Economic Review, 2020). Scholarly works on entrepreneurial activity have largely focused on the evaluation of business and organizational behaviour (Ndubisi & Iftikhar, 2012; Bierwerth et al., 2015) and the conceptualization of entrepreneurship as a means of achieving economic policy goals (Braunerhjelm & Henrekson, 2013; Galindo & Méndez, 2014; Hurtado et al., 2017). In line with the latter, entrepreneurship drives growth and innovation (Galindo-Martin et al., 2019), and these elements impact different social entities, including consumers, employees and shareholders. It is worthy to note that entrepreneurship goes beyond business creation to include the ability to *recognize opportunities*, *take risks over security* and *implement innovation* (Galindo & Méndez, 2014; GEM, 2017). However, little examinations exist on how concepts like recognizing opportunities and implementing innovation interact among themselves to promote entrepreneurial behaviour (Galindo & Méndez, 2014).

For instance, while examining innovation and entrepreneurship, Ndung'u (2018) observes that it is necessary to note the essence of implementing innovation for value generation to stimulate business and economic growth. Similarly, recognizing new opportunities through the adoption and use of technology influences idea development and entrepreneurial collaboration (Galindo-Martin et al., 2019). Innovations for business value generation are driven by different events (OECD, 2017). In recent times, it has been the digital revolution and superior digital dividends that accrue to the adoption of digital technologies (OECD, 2017; World Bank

Economic Review, 2020). Thus far, the digital transformations provide much dividend and business benefits, such as sustaining entrepreneurial behaviour and value creation (Galindo-Martin et al., 2019). This presents an important feedback process for improving on the challenge of slow economic growth and value generation (Rebensdorf et al., 2015). Yet, there is limited understanding of the overall relevance of the concepts of value generation, digitization and entrepreneurial behaviour, particularly from an aggregated perspective (Galindo-Martin et al., 2019; Narayan & Thenmozhi, 2014; Rebensdorf et al., 2015). The notion of entrepreneurship is steadily increasing in Africa (African Economic Outlook, 2020); therefore, a strong understanding of the nexus between entrepreneurial behaviour and the current digital developments in the region's emerging market economies may positively influence an upward trend of the needed growth and development required.

Therefore, this chapter explores the interrelationships between entrepreneurial behaviour, technology adoption and digital value and the feedback that arises from these interactions to examine how these concepts will promote entrepreneurial behaviour. This examination considers data on 54 economies in Africa from the World Bank data repository. The rest of the chapter is structured as follows: Sect. 3.2 presents the literature review and Sect. 3.3 the methodology and the hypotheses development. Sections 3.4 and 3.5 present the result and discussion and the conclusions respectively.

3.2 Prior Studies

3.2.1 Business Start-Up, Technology Adoption and Digital Value

The literature identifies three key components of entrepreneurial behaviour: opportunity, self-autonomy and innovation (Galindo-Martin et al., 2019; Nambisan, 2017). Autonomy reflects the self-sufficient decisions and behaviour of an entrepreneur when pursuing established objectives and making use of available possibilities (Rindova et al., 2009; Autio et al., 2014). Innovation, considered as a general context, concerns the implementation of emerging ideas with accompanying technological apparatus (Autio et al., 2014). However, in the current context of this examination, innovation extends to cover the utilization and performance of diverse applications, while the opportunity is understood as the ensuing prospects which depend on individual choices, which are susceptible to variations (Autio et al., 2014).

By incorporating this view, entrepreneurial behaviour will generate associated value, thus pursuits that add value to service offerings of businesses (Adner & Kapoor, 2009). By inference, greater value generation stimulates entrepreneurial effectiveness. In fact, several extant studies have focused on this relationship – value generation and entrepreneurial effectiveness (see Ireland et al., 2001; Van Praag & Versloot, 2007; Adner & Kapoor, 2009; Hitt et al., 2011; Huarng & Yu, 2011;

Mishra, 2017). The relevance of this nexus does accrue, not only to business evolution but also the economy as a whole, making it necessary to analyse what elements could improve value generation. It is worth noting that innovation highly aligns with digitization. This presents opportunities for venturing into new markets to access a broader range of consumers (Nambisan, 2017).

This examination surmises that the implementation of these three mechanisms also favour entrepreneurial behaviour. This is because, in Galindo-Martin et al. (2019), the authors argue that digital technologies facilitate information asymmetry on the labour market, and allows firms to access best-trained labour for specialized tasks. Similarly, new jobs will emerge from these tasks, resulting in more opportunities in the labour market. Further, other reports observe that increased labour opportunities and capabilities via digital applications also increase productivity (Nambisan, 2017; OECD, 2017), thus resulting in reduced output cost and increased revenue. Also, economies of scale are created to support innovation, thus reinforcing and maximizing the advantages of a strong digital economy (Deichmann et al., 2016). These benefits notwithstanding have other positive effects that benefit the broader economy. For example, increased employment, on one side, strengthens the socioeconomic environment, favourably affecting households and the cycle of economic growth (Galindo & Méndez, 2014).

Similarly, higher labour productivity contributes to increased quality service offerings, reduced costs, growing market surplus and improved demand to impact economic growth (Cumming et al., 2014; Galindo & Méndez, 2014). By implication, enhanced adoption of digital technologies intricately underlies benefits accrued to these economic agents (McHenry & Welch, 2018). For instance, the Internet promotes business entry to global markets, via ensuring online visibility and partnerships, and it breeds foreign trade and competitiveness, which then encourages innovation (Castaño et al., 2016; McHenry & Welch, 2018). It lowers the cost of production, culminating in lower prices. It also supports the creation of new digital job openings for households (d'Agostino & Scarlato, 2015). Coupled with these, governments can also use these digital technologies to offer citizens public services more effectively and conveniently. These benefits to businesses and households in the opinion of the authors should promote entrepreneurial behaviour in the long term to foster high standards of living. In light of the aforementioned, the outcomes of adopting digital technologies for public and private service offerings mainly include increased economic growth from higher consumption, lowered production and operating costs and increased employment and labour productivity.

The adoption of digital technologies with innovations yields a digital value that may stimulate entrepreneurial behaviour in the form of business creation and startups. Further, the response effect ought to be considered. Benefits including new target markets, higher competition and increased demand stimulate entrepreneurial activity (Nam, 2020; OECD, 2017). Businesses would encounter stronger competitiveness, which should motivate them to pursue more innovation with allied digital technologies, leading to a higher digital value. This leads to a positive influence on poverty through increased employment avenues and greater economic growth.

3.2.2 Enabling Drivers for Sustainable Entrepreneurship Activities

Literature suggests that the drive for entrepreneurial activity is a result of individual behaviour (Han & Park, 2017). Other strands of literature have also argued that institutional and environmental ecosystems promote groups or individual into entrepreneurial activities (Hoffman, 1999). Factors such as personality traits, risk-taking, new methods, proactiveness and novelty of products and services also influence entrepreneurial activities (Janson & Wrycza, 1999). Besides all these prevailing enablers, significant studies in recent times have posited that emerging technologies play a vital role in the entrepreneurial start-up and improve existing ones (Umar et al., 2020; Neumeyer et al., 2020; Ejemeyovwi et al., 2019). For example, Ejemeyovwi et al. (2019) acknowledged that the survival of twenty-first century entrepreneurial start-ups is influenced by the level of technology innovation. Further evidence from the adoption of emerging technological applications and platforms significantly advance the translation of inputs into outputs by start-up entrepreneurs (Dy et al., 2017: LeBlanc, 2015).

The context of innovative technology deployment is therefore perceived as the functions and benefits created through the usage of such technology. As such, substantial growths among start-up entrepreneurs are through specific innovations from technology promoting digital value and value generation. A framework such as Technology, Organization and Environment (TOE) (Tornatzky & Fleischer, 1990) advocates that specific factor or factors can be explored to identify the direction of innovation to ultimately change the overall goal of firms' strategy. In view of that, this chapter focuses on innovative technologies to drive entrepreneurial attitude for promoting start-up businesses. Therefore, proper implementation of innovation in technology functions supports perceived digital value and significantly affects value generation. Accordingly, the technology acceptance model (TAM) also identifies the acceptance and adoption of technology hinges on perceived utilities and perceived ease of application (Davis, 1989).

This chapter, hence proposes that the level to which entrepreneurs believe (utilities) the adoption of technology and ease of usage enhances productivity for SME start-ups. Given the above, it advocates that perceived digital value (utilization) and value generation through the ease of use from technology adoption inspire new entrepreneurs to create new businesses. The proposed conceptual framework shown in Fig. 3.1 reflects the emphasis on how digital technology adoption promotes digital value and value generation for SME start-up.

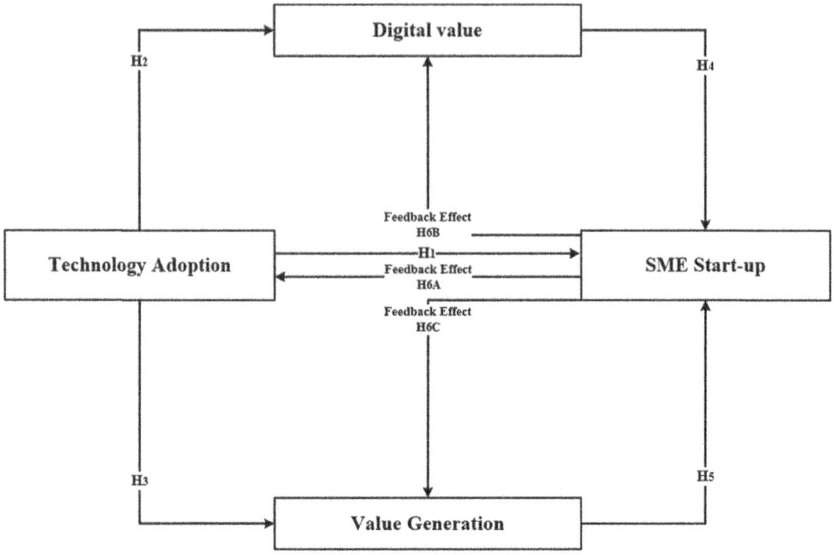

Fig. 3.1 Conceptual framework

3.3 Hypotheses Development

The study develops an empirical model, which is evaluated to verify the following hypotheses. There are six hypotheses in total; the initial three hypotheses seek to validate the relationships between the selected constructs, while the final three examine the feedback effects between entrepreneurial behaviour and the constructs.

H1: Technology adoption positively influences entrepreneurial behaviour.

In that, digital technologies make collaboration, idea generation and information access for creating a start-up easier, thus encouraging entrepreneurial behaviour (Umar et al., 2020; Neumeyer et al., 2020; Ejemeyovwi et al., 2019). The adoption of digital technologies will offer an avenue to penetrate new target markets and motivate African entrepreneurs to increase their entrepreneurial efforts to create new start-ups.

H2: Technology adoption positively influences digital value among the selected African states.

H3: Technology adoption positively influences business value generation among the selected African states.

Long and Ascent, (2020) posit that innovation remains a critical component of value generation, and digital technologies facilitate the ability to innovate. As a result, the digital transformation that accompanies innovation would promote value generation.

H4: High digital value increases entrepreneurial behaviour in the form of high start-ups.
H5: High value generation increases entrepreneurial behaviour in the form of high start-ups.

Technology adoption contributes to greater levels of production-consumption, job opportunities and reduced costs. In retrospect, these are gains from digital implementations, which will inspire entrepreneurial behaviour to widen the creation of new businesses or start-ups (McHenry & Welch, 2018).

H6a, b and c: Entrepreneurial behaviour, technology adoption, digital value and value generation establish positive feedbacks.

Implementation of digital technologies promotes innovation (Galindo-Martin et al., 2019), which contributes to increased competitiveness and emerging opportunities. In essence, enabling entrepreneurs to introduce innovative technologies is backed by digital values

The adoption of digital technologies produces potential digital value. This value is that which benefits society and the firm. Based on these positive returns, entrepreneurs are encouraged to expand or create more (Castaño et al., 2016).

3.4 Method

3.4.1 Data and Model Indicators

The study sources data on African countries based on the World Bank and IMF average GDP growth estimations for 2020. African countries are predicted to push up Africa's overall average economic growth rate to 3.8% compared to the global average of 3.4% (World Bank Economic Review, 2020).

The study collects world bank data from its open data repository (https://data.worldbank.org/) on all economies in Africa. The study averages data over the period of 2014–2018 to reflect the state of affairs over this period. This is to cater for the challenge of missing data points in some countries over the period. In line with Galindo-Martin et al. (2019), four broad indicators broadly determine entrepreneurial behaviour. These include value generation, technology adoption and digital value. In this chapter, entrepreneurial behaviour is considered the dependent variable, while value generation, technology adoption and digital value all enter as the independent variables. For each broad construct, sub-indicators identified with the World Bank's performance indicators were selected as proxies to measure the main constructs (see Table 3.1).

Relative to entrepreneurial behaviour, the percentage of SME ownership per population and the proportion of SME account with financial institutions per population of business accounts were the indicator items. The conception of entrepreneurial processes may occur arbitrarily at any stage, giving the expanded view of

Table 3.1 Constructs, indicators and their sources

Constructs	Indicators	Source
Entrepreneurial Behaviour	SME ownership as a percentage of the population	Global Financial Inclusion Database, World Bank http://www.doingbusiness.org/
	Proportion of SME accounts with financial institutions per number of business accounts	
Value generation	Operations performance index	Doing Business project, World Bank (https://www.worldbank.org/lpi)
	Service value created	
Technology adoption	Mobile Internet subscription per 100 SMEs	International Telecommunication Union, World Telecommunication / ICT
	Modern communication technologies	Development report and database
	Secured server	
Digital value	Financial consumption expenditure	World Bank national accounts data and OECD National Accounts and data files
	GPD at market prices, current prices, dollar per capita	

entrepreneurship considered in this chapter. To cater for this arbitrariness, the study draws on the description of entrepreneurship indicators determined by the Global Entrepreneurship Monitor (GEM, 2017) by using the period-by-period proportion of SME financial activity indicator and SME ownership as a percentage of the population. These variables describe the development of new entrepreneurial activity such as setting up new start-ups or expanding an existing one and involvement in the entrepreneurial venture (Bosma et al., 2013).

Secondly, concerning value generation, literature perceives value generation as behaviour intended to increase the value of service offerings. Giving the company data available, it is perceived that firm productivity affects performance. Thus far, the indicator operation performance and service value created per firm goods and services emerge useful determinants of productivity.

Thirdly, technology adoption mirrors business improvements necessary to innovate and use digital technology as well as incorporate a set of digital trade variables depicted in Table 3.1.

Lastly, the digital value exemplifies the positive effects derived from using digital technologies. These predominantly hinge on higher consumer surplus associated with increased demand for economic growth. The metrics are final consumer expense and gross domestic product at market price. In general, all indicators for the constructs particularly entrepreneurial behaviour and value generation are drawn from the World Bank data on the private sector, doing business survey. Similarly, the remaining variables of technology adoption data are drawn from science and technology survey.

3.4.2 Method Justification

The model depicted in this study is empirically evaluated in PLS (partial least squares) with Smart PLS 3.0. The PLS-SEM emphasizes prediction in estimating statistical models designed to provide causal explanations (Hair et al., 2019). PLS has seen extensive use in business research (see Chang & Rieple, 2018; Becker & Rosnita, 2016; Kock & Hadaya, 2018; Dinev & Hart, 2004). Ponsignon et al. (2014) assert that the PLS' ability to analyse the measurement of latent constructs, as well as the relationships between independent and dependent variables, accounts partly for its popularity. The covariance-based SEM and the PLS are the two main SEM methods used. This study employs PLS-SEM for the following reasons: First, the PLS-SEM is suited for models designed to test causal explanations, like the current model in this examination (Hair et al., 2019). It is also suitable for testing theory in exploratory studies, like the model underlying this chapter. The PLS-SEM approach relaxes the restrictions of the measurement scales, residual distributions and sample size; as such, this examination applies the rule of thumb in line with Kock and Hadaya (2018) in that the sample size should be more than ten times the number of constructs. Moreover, the lack of normality and the predictive nature of the proposed research model advocates estimating this type of relationships under the PLS method (Becker & Rosnita, 2016).

For an empirical evaluation of this kind, the PLS estimator is preferred over the ordinary least squares (OLS) estimator; in case of comparing the predictive accuracy of both estimators, the number of countries required to integrate the sample must be greater in the case of the OLS estimator.

3.4.3 Model Evaluation

The literature on the psychometric properties of the PLS-SEM suggests that to avoid misinterpreting the structural model, the measurement items should first be estimated before model and hypothesis testing is done (Malhotra et al., 2004). By evaluating the measurement model, the convergent and discriminant validity of the research instrument is assessed. In this analysis, four tests, composite reliability (CR), Cronbach's alpha reliability, Rho_A reliability and the average variance extracted (AVE), were used to assess convergent validity. Table 3.2 presents the results from the measurement model evaluation and shows the values for CR, AVE, Rho_A and Cronbach's alpha. Item reliability was examined using the loadings of each item on the respective constructs. The reliability of all items was above the 0.7 thresholds (Fig. 3.2). In addition, all-composite reliabilities were above the 0.7 level, and AVEs are greater than 0.5 for all constructs, an indication that more variance was adequately shared between an item and its construct than the error variance (Hair et al., 2016). As such, the model in this study establishes adequate convergent reliability.

Table 3.2 Item loadings and reliability tests

Construct	Items	Loadings	CR	Rho_A	Alpha	AVE	R^2
Digital value	CPc	0.88	0.87	0.701	0.701	0.77	0.308
	GDPpc	0.875					
Technology adoption	TA1	0.802	0.9	0.78	0.779	0.819	
	TA2	0.813					
	TA3	0.831					
Value generation	VG1	0.872	0.857	0.749	0.749	0.666	0.345
	VG2	0.887					
SME start-up	SEM_DEV1	0.908	0.904	0.83	0.791	0.825	0.530
	SEM_DEV2	0.901					

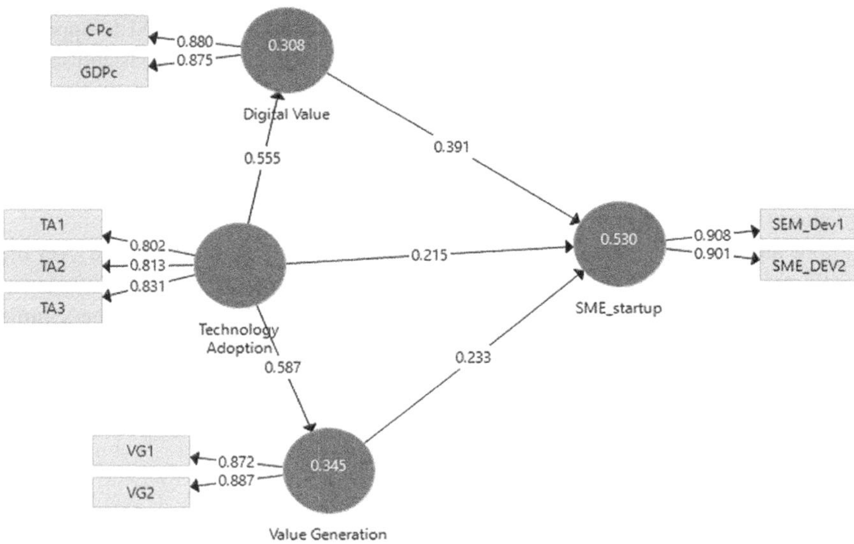

Fig. 3.2 Model evaluation

For discriminant validity, the study assesses the Fornell-Lacker criteria to ensure adequate discriminant validity. The Fornell and Larcker criterion compares the square root of the average variance extracted (AVE) with the inter-construct correlations. The latent constructs should explain better the variance of their indicator than the variance of other constructs (Hair et al., 2016; Hayes, 2015; Kline, 2011). Thus, the square root of the constructs' AVEs (on the diagonal) must be greater than the inter-item correlation coefficients (off the diagonal) relative to each row and column (Hair et al., 2016). Discriminant validity ratios are presented in Table 3.4, and all items in this study fulfilled the requirement of discriminant validity.

3.5 Results and Discussion

The hypothesized relationships are evaluated using a partial least squares SEM estimator. The estimations were done with Smart PLS 3. While evaluating the measurement model, the analysis assesses convergent validity using the item loadings, AVE, composite reliability, Rho_A and Cronbach's alpha estimates of these tests that are presented in Table 3.2. All items showed sufficient reliability, thus, above 0.7 and all AVEs above 0.5 (Hair et al., 2016). The average variance extracted (AVE) assesses the convergent validity with a minimal standard value of 0.50 (Fornell & Larcker, 1981; Chin, 1998). This suggests the variables have to describe no less than half the value of the variance of their individual indicators. A value less than 0.50 suggests the variance of an error is higher than the variance described. The least AVE value in this study was 0.66, suggesting high discriminant validity in this sense. Likewise, CR, Rho_A and the alpha coefficients were above the 0.7 level. Importantly, the indicators suit the latent variables, as the high item loading values show a match for the constructs in the model.

Further, the study analyses the mean degrees of fit for the structural model. Specifically, it reports the Nagelkerke R^2 coefficients consistent with latent variable regressions in the endogenous constructs. The R^2 value shows the variance of the structure explained by the model. A reasonable fit for the model is where endogenous latent variables show values > 10% (Falk & Miller, 1992). Thus, the model after being evaluated shows sufficient fit for the latent variable's digital value (30.8%), SME start-up (53.0%) and value generation (34.5%).

Further assessments of discriminant validity employed two main test criteria. First is the item factor loading, which shows the variance explained by an item on a particular construct. Kurfali et al. (2017) conclude that 0.7 or higher factor loadings represent a factor that extracts sufficient variance from a particular construct. Next is the Fornell-Lacker criterion. The cross-loading value evaluates the square roots of the AVEs whether they are greater than construct cross-correlations. All estimates generated for this analysis indicate sufficient discriminant validity (Table 3.3).

The measurement model assessments provided ample evidence of sufficient validity and reliability required to provide reliable model estimates. Although the

Table 3.3 Cross-loadings

Items	Digital value	SME start-up	Technology adoption	Value gen.
CPc	**0.88**	0.542	0.551	0.59
GDPc	**0.875**	0.632	0.421	0.605
SEM_Dev1	0.62	**0.908**	0.526	0.567
SME_DEV2	0.59	**0.901**	0.504	0.565
TA1	0.518	0.459	**0.802**	0.516
TA2	0.4	0.462	**0.813**	0.407
TA3	0.43	0.47	**0.831**	0.504
VG1	0.585	0.559	0.474	**0.872**
VG2	0.612	0.542	0.556	**0.887**

Table 3.4 Fornell-Lacker criterion

	Digital value	SME start-up	Technology adoption	Value gen.
Digital value	**0.88**			
SME start-up	0.67	**0.90**		
Technology adoption	0.55	0.57	**0.82**	
Value gen.	0.68	0.63	0.59	**0.88**

PLS-SEM does not provide the overall goodness of fit index, the R^2 estimates also showed a significant amount of variance explained in the exogenous variables.

Given the ability to compute the significance of path estimates with Smart PLS, the study uses the bootstrapping method to determine the significance of the hypothesized relationships. Table 3.4 reveals sufficiently significant relationships between the constructs. A 5% significance level in most situations is adequate, implying that the *p values* ought to be less than 0.05 to make the relationship significant (Hair et al., 2016). The results show all three initial hypotheses validated with the model explaining 0.53 variance in entrepreneurial behaviour (SME start-up).

The results herein the analysis rightly support the three initial hypotheses. In that, technology adoption encourages entrepreneurial behaviour, thus enabling SME start-up (0.215, $t = 4.87$, $p < 0.000$). As per the World Bank Economic Review (2020) projections, value generation (0.587, $t = 18.55$, $p<0.000$) and digital value (0.391, t=7.50, $p<0.000$) stimulate entrepreneurial behaviour in the form of SME start-up when both are perceived to increase. In essence, this confirms the (OECD, 2017) framework of economic expansion for member states (Nambisan, 2017). Specifying the specific indirect effects between the constructs under consideration, the results show a 0.217 effect size along with technology adoption to digital value to SME start-up. Similarly, between technologies' adoption to value generation and SME start-up, an effect size of 0.137 is shown. By implication, high technology adoption reveals positive indirect effects via digital value and value generation.

Considering the feedback effects in Hypotheses 4–6 suggests a feedback effect between entrepreneurial behaviour (SME start-up) and technology adoption, digital value and value generation. The results are shown in Fig. 3.3, and Table 3.5 presents the feedback effects between the constructs. A second PLS regression is conducted to examine the existence of feedback effects among entrepreneurial behaviour, technology adoption, digital value and value generation constructs. This is expressed in Fig. 3.3.

The analysis shows positive feedback effects between all three constructs examined. Entrepreneurial behaviour (SME start-up) and digital value established a strong positive association of 0.673 (Galindo-Martin et al., 2019), whereas technology adoption and value generation both revealed positive effects of 0.568 and 0.626, respectively.

As per the estimations shown in Table 3.6 for the new model, the standards of reliability and validity have been met by the model, as AVE values are >0.5 and composite reliability, Cronbach's alpha and Rho_A values were all > 0.7. Similarly, all the R^2 coefficients showed values greater than 0.1.

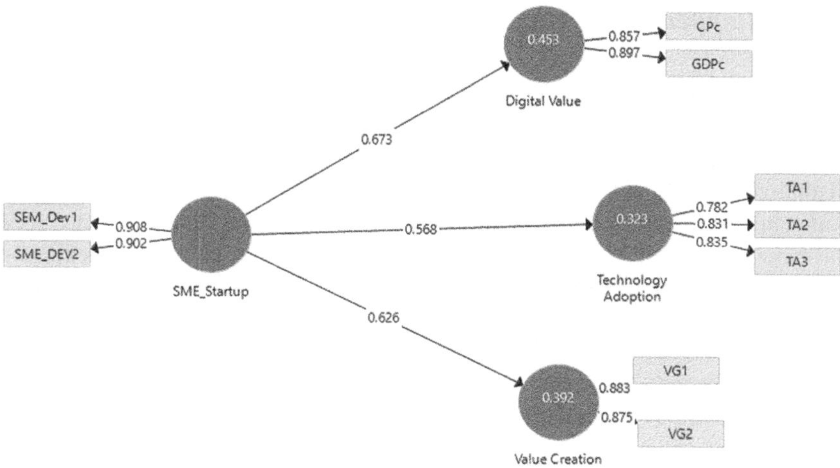

Fig. 3.3 Feedback effects model

Table 3.5 Summarized hypotheses results

Path	Coefficient	T Stats	P-value
Digital value -> SME start-up	0.391	7.50	0.000
Technology adoption -> digital value	0.555	15.03	0.000
Technology adoption -> SME start-up	0.215	4.87	0.000
Technology adoption -> value gen.	0.587	18.55	0.000
Value generation -> SME start-up	0.233	3.90	0.000
Feedback effects			
SME start-up-> digital value	0.673	26.29	0.000
SME start-up-> technology adoption	0.568	15.97	0.000
SME start-up-> value creation	0.626	17.72	0.000

Table 3.6 Reliability and validity of the feedback effect model

Construct	**Cronbach's alpha**	**Rho_A**	**CR**	**AVE**
Digital value	0.701	0.712	0.869	0.769
SME start-up	0.779	0.779	0.900	0.819
Technology adoption	0.749	0.749	0.857	0.666
Value creation	0.707	0.708	0.872	0.773
Discriminant validity: Fornell and Lacker				
	Digital value	**SME start-up**	**Tech_Adopt**	**Value creation**
Digital value	**0.877**			
SME start-up	0.673	**0.905**		
Tech_Adopt	0.543	0.568	**0.816**	
Value creation	0.680	0.626	0.581	**0.879**

3.5.1 *Implications of the Study*

The findings from this analysis provide support to the assertion that emerging digital technologies when deployed to create value will influence a paradigm shift for new entrepreneurs toward digital business. As revealed in the analysis, the adoption of digital technologies with the relevant productive and digital value associated, stimulates entrepreneurial behaviour. This is consistent with findings on drivers of business start-ups in Neumeyer et al. (2020). Allied with this are the benefits of increased demand, growth and competitiveness, which forces large businesses as well as start-ups to adopt more technology for faster innovation and greater digital dividends (Galindo-Martin et al., 2019; Bosma et al., 2013; Ejemeyovwi et al., 2019). Significantly, these findings provide insights for business and SME managers to pay attention to digital innovation in the digital ecosystem as a way to improve or create more value. For new start-up managers, particular attention should be paid to identifying emerging digital applications and platforms that help to create new businesses and support business processes (Dy et al., 2017: LeBlanc, 2015). More importantly, the COVID-19 pandemic has created a huge opportunity for entrepreneurs to harness emerging technology and innovative platforms and applications (mobile applications) to drive business strategy.

Additionally, another implication of this examination is that the assessed framework provides evidence to highlight the extent to which entrepreneurial behaviour is influenced by the concepts, digital technology, digital value and value generation. The fundamental question of what drives entrepreneurial spirit is still an area worth considering for future research. As such, the study suggests the need to provide a platform that integrates digital innovation to influence start-up businesses for value creation.

Lastly, although the review of literature positions three key components (opportunity, self-autonomy and innovation) of entrepreneurship behaviour, findings from this examination suggests that innovation aligns with digital technology to facilitate the formation of start-ups. Thus, this finding extends these three key components to include digital technology as crucial to the drivers of entrepreneurial behaviour.

3.6 Conclusion

This investigation employs data on African states, from the World Bank data survey, to validate the influence of value generation, technology adoption and digital value on entrepreneurial behaviour (SME start-up). The study carefully considers the conceptual and empirical implications of how technology adoption and digital value influence business start-up activities across Africa. Although many evaluations exist on the association between entrepreneurship and value generation, it is also relevant to evaluate other related effects which are likely to drive entrepreneurial activity, particularly business start-ups. In essence, the extent of technology adoption impacting business innovation to generate value is the main factor considered.

The analysis of the phenomenon among African states validates the existence of these relationships; thus, digital values obtained from technology adoption facilitates entrepreneurial behaviour (SME start-up). Besides, the respective feedback effects accruing to these relationships are of equal relevance, since the varied consequential effects such as increased competitiveness, new market entrance, increased demand and specialization, among others, are all potential facilitators of entrepreneurial behaviour. The above-discussed relationships were examined using a partial least squares structural equation model (PLS-SEM)

Just like any inquiry, the current examination has some limitations. Firstly, only a few variables were used to evaluate the phenomenon, as such, this may not provide a complete picture of how the relationship is formed. Future studies can consider increasing the scope of items and determinants of entrepreneurial behaviour to improve on the findings. Subsequently, future examinations could consider grouping the countries based on regions, size, GDP, etc. to examine if differences exist between the countries along with these demographic characteristics relative to the relationships between the variables and entrepreneurial behaviour.

References

Adner, R., & Kapoor, R. (2009). Value creation in innovation ecosystems: How the structure of technological interdependence affects firm performance in new technology generations. *Strategic Management Journal, 31*, 306–333. https://doi.org/10.1002/smj.824

African Economic Outlook (2020). *Developing Africa's workforce for the future*. African Development Bank Group: Abidjan, Cote d'Ivoire.

Autio, E., Kenney, M., Mustar, P., Siegel, D., & Wright, M. (2014). Entrepreneurial innovation: The importance of context. *Research Policy, 43*, 1097–1108.

Becker, J. M., & Rosnita, I. (2016). Accounting for sampling weights in PLS path modelling: Simulations and empirical examples. *European Management Journal, 34*, 606–617.

Bierwerth, M., Schwens, C., Isidor, R., & Kabst, R. (2015). Corporate entrepreneurship and performance: A meta-analysis. *Small Business Economics, 45*, 255–278. https://doi.org/10.1007/s11187-015-9629-1

Bosma, N., Wennekers, S., Guerrero, M., Amorós, J. E., Martiarena, A., & Singer, S. (2013). *Global entrepreneurship monitor*. Special report on entrepreneurial employee activity.

Braunerhjelm, P., & Henrekson, M. (2013). Entrepreneurship, institutions, and economic dynamism: Lessons from a comparison of the united states and Sweden. *Industrial and Corporate Change, 22*, 107–130. https://doi.org/10.1093/icc/dts048

Castaño, M. S., Méndez, M. T., & Galindo, M. A. (2016). Innovation, internationalization and business-growth expectations among entrepreneurs in the services sector. *Journal of Business Research, 69*, 1690–1695.

Chang, J., & Rieple, A. (2018). Entrepreneurial decision-making in a microcosm. *Management Learning, 49*(4), 471–497.

Chin, W. W. (1998). The partial least squares approach to structural equation modelling. In G. A. Macoulides (Ed.), *Modern methods for business research* (pp. 295–336). Psychology Press.

Cumming, D., Johan, S., & Zhang, M. (2014). The economic impact of entrepreneurship: Comparing international datasets. *Corporate Governance: An International Review, 22*, 162–178.

d'Agostino, G., & Scarlato, M. (2015). Innovation, socio-institutional conditions and economic growth in the Italian regions. *Regional Studies, 49*, 1514–1534. https://doi.org/10.1080/00343404.2013.838000
Davis, F. D. (1989). "Perceived Usefulness, Perceived Ease of Use and User Acceptance of Information Technology," *MIS Quarterly 13*(3), 319–339.
Deichmann, U., Goyal, A., & Mishra, D. (2016). Will digital technologies transform agriculture in developing countries? *Agricultural Economics, 47*, 21–33.
Dinev, T., & Hart, P. (2004). Internet privacy concerns and their antecedents – measurement validity and a regression model. *Behaviour & Information Technology, 23*(6), 413–423.
Dy, A. M., Marlow, S., & Martin, L. (2017). A web of opportunity or the same old story? Women digital entrpreneurs and intersectionality theory. *Human Relations, 3*, 286–311.
Ejemeyovwi, J. O., Osbuohien, E. S., Bowle, E. K., et al. (2019). Information and Communication Technolpgy adoption and innovation for sustainable entrpreneurship. *Journal de Physique, 1378*.
Falk, R. F., & Miller, N. B. (1992). *A primer for soft modeling*. University of Akron Press.
Fornell, C., & Larcker, D. F. (1981). Evaluating structural equation models with unobservable variables and measurement error. *Journal of Marketing Research, 18*, 39–50.
Galindo-Martín, M. Á., Castaño-Martínez, M. S., & Méndez-Picazo, M. T. (2019). Digital transformation, digital dividends and entrepreneurship: A quantitative analysis. *Journal of Business Research, 101*, 522–527.
Galindo, M. Á., & Méndez, M. T. (2014). Entrepreneurship, economic growth, and innovation: Are feedback effects at work? *Journal of Business Research, 67*, 825–829. https://doi.org/10.1016/j.jbusres.2013.11.052
Hair, J. F., Hult, G. T. M., Ringle, C., & Sarstedt, M. (2016). *A primer on partial least squares structural equation modelling (PLS-SEM)*. SAGE.
Hair, J. F., Risher, J. J., Sarstedt, M., & Ringle, C. M. (2019). *When to use and how to report the results of PLS-SEM*. European business review.
Han, J., & Park, C. (2017). Case study on adoption of new technology for innovation: Perspective of institutional and corporate entrepreneurship. *Asia Pacific Journal of Innovation and Entrepreneurship, 2*, 144–158.
Hayes, A. F. (2015). An index and test of linear moderated mediation. *Multivariate behavioral research, 50*(1), 1–22.
Hitt, M. A., Ireland, R. D., Sirmon, D. G., & Trahms, C. A. (2011). Strategic entrepreneurship: Creating value for individuals, organizations, and society. *Academy of Management Perspectives, 25*, 57–75.
Hoffman, A. J. (1999). Institutional evolution and change: Environmentalism and the US chemical industry. *Academy of Management Journal, 42*, 351–371.
Huarng, K. H., & Yu, T. H. K. (2011). Entrepreneurship, process innovation and value creation by a non-profit SME. *Management Decision, 49*, 284–296. https://doi.org/10.1108/00251741111109160
Hurtado, R. A., Velásquez, H., & Támara, A. (2017). La creación de empresas bajo un enfoque estructural: Un caso de aplicación. *Espacios, 38*, 289–300. https://doi.org/10.1007/s11187-010-9307-2
Ireland, R. D., Hitt, M. A., Camp, S. M., & Sexton, D. L. (2001). Integrating entrepreneurship and strategic management actions to create firm wealth. *The Academy of Management Executive, 15*, 49–63.
Janson, M. A., & Wrycza, S. (1999). Information technology and entrepreneurship: Three cases from Poland. *Intelligent Information Management, 19*, 351–367.
Kline, R. B. (2011). *Convergence of structural equation modeling and multilevel modeling*.
Kock, N., & Hadaya, P. (2018). Minimum sample size estimation in PLS-SEM: The inverse square root and gamma-exponential methods. *Information Systems Journal, 28*(1), 227–261.
Kurfalı, M., Arifoğlu, A., Tokdemir, G., & Paçin, Y. (2017). Adoption of e-government services in Turkey. *Computers in Human Behavior, 66*, 168–178.

LeBlanc, C. (2015). Why the rise of DIY business tools is good for women business owners. *Huffington Post, 29*.

Long, A., & Ascent, D. (2020). *World Economic Outlook*. International Monetary Fund.

Malhotra, N. K., Kim, S. S., & Agarwal, J. (2004). Internet users' information privacy concerns (IUIPC): The construct, the scale, and a causal model. *Information Systems Research, 15*(4), 336–355.

McHenry, J. E. H., & Welch, D. E. (2018). Entrepreneurs and internationalization: A study of Western immigrants in an emerging market. *International Business Review, 27*, 93–101. https://doi.org/10.1016/j.ibusrev.2017.05.008

Mishra, C. S. (2017). Entrepreneurial orientation. *Entrepreneurship Research Journal – De Gruyter, 7*, 1–20.

Monitor GGE GEM–Global Entrepreneurship. "GEM Global report." London

Nam, C. W. (2020). *World economic outlook for 2020 and 2021*. In CESifo Forum (Vol. 21, No. 02, pp. 58–59). München: ifo Institut-Leibniz-Institut für Wirtschaftsforschung an der Universität München.

Nambisan, S. (2017). Digital entrepreneurship: Toward a digital technology perspective of entrepreneurship. *Entrepreneurship: Theory and Practice, 41*, 1029–1055.

Narayan, P. C., & Thenmozhi, M. (2014). *Do cross-border acquisitions involving emerging market firms create value: Impact of deal characteristics*. Management Decision.

Neumeyer, X., Santos, S. C., & Morris, M. H. (2020). Overcoming barriers to technology adoption when fostering entreprenuership among the poor: The role of technology and digital literacy. *IEEE Transactions on Engineering Management, 1*, 14.

Ndubisi, N. O., & Iftikhar, K. (2012). Relationship between entrepreneurship, innovation and performance: Comparing small and medium-size enterprises. *Journal of Research in Marketing and Entrepreneurship, 14*, 214–236.

OECD. (2017). *Key issues for digital transformation in the G20* (p. 163). OECD Publication.

Ponsignon, F., Maull, R. S., & Smart, P. A. (2014). Four archetypes of process improvement: a Q-methodological study. *International Journal of Production Research, 52*(15), 4507–4525.

Rebensdorf, A., Gergert, A., Oosthuizen, G. A., & Böhm, S. (2015). Open community manufacturing–development challenge as a concept for value creation for sustainable manufacturing in South Africa. *Procedia CIRP, 26*, 167–172.

Rindova, V., Barry, D., & Ketchen, D. J. (2009). Entrepreneuring as emancipation. *The Academy of Management Review, 34*, 477–491.

Tornatzky, L., & Fleischer, M. (1990). *The processes of technological innovation*. D.C. Heath.

Umar, M. F., Nugroho, I., Darmadji, D., & Suwarta, S. (2020). The study of Entrepreneurship and innovation adoption by Farmer in improving lowland rice farming. *Journal of Socioeconomics and Development, 3*, 253–261.

Van Praag, C. M., & Versloot, P. H. (2007). What is the value of entrepreneurship? A review of recent research. *Small Business Economics, 29*, 351–382. https://doi.org/10.1007/s11187-007-9074-x

World Bank. (2016). *World development report 2016: Digital dividends*. International Monetary Fund.

World Bank Economic Review (2020). *Design Thinking for Social Innovation*. https://doi.org/10.1596/1020-797X_12_1_29

Kobina A. Benson is a PhD student in management information systems with the School of Applied Sciences at the Cyprus International University. His research interest is in data mining and predictive analysis. He is currently working on his thesis on a research on educational data mining to predict student performance in less deprived communities.

Muesser C. Nat is an Associate Professor and the Director of the School of Applied Sciences in Cyprus International University. She is also the head of department and a faculty at the Department of Management Information Systems at Cyprus International University. She has conducted research in the areas of social media technology for student engagement, social media engagement and message classification. She also has several publications in the field of educational technology and learning from different domains.

Divine Q. Agozie is an assistant lecturer in the Operations and Management Information Systems Department at the University of Ghana Business School and a final-year PhD student in information systems at the Cyprus International University. Agozie's research interest concentrates on natural language processing (text mining), online privacy and sustainable development. He has authored some scholarly articles on privacy fatigue and online engagement on social media. He also has some publications coming up on applications of text mining approaches to data from the advocacy domain for organizational communication.

Sam A. Edu is a final-year doctoral candidate in management information systems at Cyprus International University in Lefkosa, North Cyprus. He has a background in big data, cloud and IOT systems security. His research interest is consistent with his knowledge background. He is also an adjunct faculty with the Department of Management Information Systems at Cyprus International University.

Oseyenbhin S. Osemeahon holds a doctorate degree in management information systems which he attained in 2020. His research interest is in social media engagement and brand communication. Osemeahon has publications in this area and contributes mainly to fashion brand platform interactivity and organizational communication on social media.

Chapter 4
Impact of Mobile Payments on Micro-Business Activities: A Developing Country Experience

Impact of Mobile Payments

Eunice Yeboah Afeti and Acheampong Owusu

Abstract While mobile payment has received much attention, little research has focused on the suitability of mobile payment technology for payment for micro-businesses. This exploratory study seeks to provide a deeper understanding of how technology improves payment transactions in trading activities. The study draws on the task-technology fit (TTF) theory and the transaction cost theory as the theoretical lens. Based on qualitative data from 20 micro-businesses, the research findings indicate that micro-businesses' adoption of mobile payments generates strategic and operational benefits. Also, micro-businesses regard the use of mobile technology as suitable in their payment transactions. This study's contribution lies in the use of the TTF theory to determine the impact of mobile payment and its linkage with user performance on micro-businesses' livelihood. This study also provides guidelines for national policy discussions on payment systems and their legal framework development.

Keywords Mobile payments · Micro-traders · Developing country

4.1 Introduction

Mobile payments are arguably one of the most influential digital technologies with potential future business value. Its rapid evolution and increasing diffusion have given significant opportunities for innovative companies to create new payment solutions and offer value-added services to their customers (Hsiao, 2019). Arguably,

E. Y. Afeti · A. Owusu (✉)
University of Ghana Business School, Accra, Ghana
e-mail: eunice.yafeti@upsamail.edu.gh; aowusu@ug.edu.gh

R. Boateng et al. (eds.), *Digital Innovations, Business and Society in Africa*, Advances in Theory and Practice of Emerging Markets,
https://doi.org/10.1007/978-3-030-77987-0_4

the impact of mobile payment adoption has significantly been noticed in sub-Saharan Africa (SSA). This is due mainly to the lack of robust payment systems, weak institutional foundations, and the fact that mobile phones are becoming increasingly part of the everyday lives of the poor (Humbani & Wise, 2018). The global statistical report on mobiles demonstrates that global subscription has exceeded 7 billion, with an estimated 770 million to be in Africa alone (Giuntini, 2020). They are engendering hope that mobile payments have the strategic potential of meeting the financial service needs of the poor (Peruta, 2017). More importantly, mobile payments have enormous potential to introduce cashless payments and serve as a gap bridging mechanism for micro- and small businesses to circumvent the national constraints to leverage mobile payment benefits for greater financial inclusion (Afutu-Kotey et al., 2017).

Essentially, mobile payment is making many waves across industries, such as banking, agriculture, insurance, health, and commerce. In commerce, for example, businesses are trying to leverage mobile payment to support new business models, enhance business transactions, and transform market mechanisms to facilitate a new business climate (Oliveira et al., 2016). For instance, some micro-businesses like retailers, eateries, fashion shops, taxi drivers, churches, mechanic shops, and many small-scale service providers have strategically started to leverage mobile payment innovation for their businesses in Ghana. These micro- and small businesses depend on mobile payment capacity to support a much cheaper and faster financial transaction. Through mobile payment, they develop new market and business opportunities, improve consumer's experience, and create a different basis for competitive advantage (Gomber et al., 2018). The expanding significance of mobile payment services to micro-businesses has led to discussions about how mobile payments' potential can be entirely harnessed in socioeconomic development in Africa and other developing economies (Peruta, 2017; Oliveira et al., 2016).

In developing countries, the contribution of micro-businesses cannot be underestimated. For instance, in Ghana, micro-businesses play a significant role in employment generation (predominantly female employment), contribute to tax revenue, and facilitate the distribution of goods and services that contribute an estimated 70% of Ghana's GDP (Afutu-Kotey et al., 2017). Nevertheless, much of this money is unbanked, denying the government revenue that could be used for development purposes. Hence, mobile payments provide a way for small businesses to achieve efficiency and the government to track the financial system and do better projects that create value for the vulnerable in society. Micro-businesses leveraging mobile payments in this manner make it legitimate to understand the impact of its adoption on small-scale businesses and how mobile payments' potential can be entirely harnessed to develop micro-businesses in Africa and other developing economies (Peruta, 2017; Oliveira et al., 2016).

Despite the importance of mobile payment to the development of micro-business activities, previous studies have not investigated the fit of mobile payment to the task of payment in micro-business activities and to understand how mobile payments generate value and create benefit to the micro-business. The literature on mobile payments has explored and conceptualized mobile payment's benefits and challenges, technical dimensions that affect consumer intentions to adopt mobile payments (Madan & Yadav, 2016). Though helpful, these studies are often silent on how micro-businesses leverage mobile payments for business benefit as well as various ways in which mobile payment adoption and use impact the livelihood of small businesses. Also, these studies failed to provide comprehensive explanations of how indigenous technologies like mobile payment systems in resource-poor contexts are leveraged to create value (Duncombe & Boateng, 2009). Arguably, it is essential to respond to this question because there is a lack of resources in developing countries, and we need to find other means to leapfrog these challenges. If future research ignores this research question, we will not understand or learn the phenomenon nor be able to replicate the sound effects of locally generated technologies in other resource-poor contexts (de Albuquerque et al., 2016). The underpinning question is, how does mobile payments technology fit the task needs of micro-businesses, and how does it influence the adoption and use of mobile payments to impact their business activities for business development? This research will employ the task-technology fit (TTF) theory and the transaction cost theory as the theoretical lens.

In an attempt to address the research question outlined above, the study covers six sections. Section 4.1 introduces readers to the paper. Section 4.2 examines mobile payments and the market traders and develops research constructs on the value mobile payments bring to market traders and their stakeholders. Section 4.3 presents the research framework and methods for the research. Section 4.4 looks at the case study of the market traders and their stakeholders. The analysis of the case study is presented in Sect. 4.5. The conclusion and direction for future research are discussed in Sect. 4.6.

4.2 Literature Review

4.2.1 Conceptualizing Mobile Payments

Conceptually, mobile payment is a new form of value transfer, similar to other payments; however, the point of difference is mobile devices as a medium. The concept of mobile payments has been defined severally in the literature from a different perspective. Researchers including Liu et al. (2015) have defined mobile payments as utilizing mobile devices and technology to initiate and authorize payments for goods and services. The definition above examines mobile payment features from the technical angle, thus seeing mobile payments as taking advantage of technology to make payment via the mobile device. Zhong (2009) defined mobile payments as a type of payment transaction processing. The payer uses mobile communication techniques in association with mobile devices for initiation, authorization, or payment completion. This definition considers the distinguishing characteristics that point to mobile payment as having strategic, participatory, and operational functions, which allows for mobile payments to have typology. Upadhyay and

Chattopadhyay (2015) also looked at mobile payments (m-payment) as a subset of e-commerce. In this scenario, mobile payments provide a method for conducting practical and innovative micropayment to facilitate mobile commerce transactions. The mobile payment provides a nonbanking channel (mainly retail) to offer and extend the financial services to subscribers who are not profitable to be reached by formal and traditional financial service providers. Furthermore, m-payment is a way of using a mobile device to transfer money from payer to receiver through an intermediary or directly. This definition describes mobile payments broadly, categorizing the many ways mobile payments bring innovation to business and service delivery, such as e-commerce, and classifying mobile payments as a service and an infrastructure for e-commerce.

4.2.1.1 Adoption and Use of Mobile Payments

Mobile payment adoption has received a lot of attention in the literature, the reason that researchers have lamented on lower than predicted mobile payment usage and adoption (Williams et al., 2017). As a result, researchers are anxious about mobile payment user behavior and looking for responses to factors affecting consumer's adoption and use of mobile payments (Zhou, 2014). Li et al. (2014) argue that mobile payment systems like compatibility and perceived complementarity and user characteristics like mobile payment knowledge and risk-related factors in the form of perceived risk are drivers of mobile payment adoption. Perceived compatibility is how consistent an innovation is to existing values and past experiences. The perceived complementarity relates to network externalities, thus the number of people in a user's social networks. Mobile payment knowledge is how informed the customer is of an innovation and its advantages to using. Finally, perceived risk is the negative factor associated with mobile payment adoption (Li et al., 2014). Upadhyay and Chattopadhyay (2015), in their research on mobile payment adoption issues, argue that mobile payment adoption is influenced mainly by innovativeness, discomfort, system quality, perceived usefulness, and ease of use task-fit, connectivity, absorptive capacity, and structural assurance.

Also, Kim et al. (2009), in their paper "Factors Influencing the Intention to Use Mobile Payments," mentioned that for customers to adopt and use mobile payments depends on individual differences and system characteristics through perceived ease of use and perceived usefulness. They classified individual differences as innovativeness and mobile payment knowledge. The system's attributes consist of mobility, reachability, compatibility, and convenience. Also, Chandra et al. (2010) examined the role of trust in consumer adoption of mobile payment systems and suggest that service providers' characteristics and mobile technology characteristics affect the consumer's trust usefulness and perceived ease of use and user adoption. Furthermore, Schierz et al. (2010), in an empirical analysis of electronic commerce, noted that perceived security, perceived usefulness, perceived ease of use, and mobility are the characteristics that affect consumer attitude, which also affects usage intentions. The literature reviewed points to the fact that most of the studies focused on consumer adoption and neglect activities of end users, concerning whether or not using the technology enables productivity gains for large organizations, individuals, and micro-business (Li et al., 2014).

Benefits of Mobile Payments More importantly, several studies have shown that mobile payments generate operational and strategic benefits for users. Taylor (2016), in her work "Potential Benefits and Risks of Mobile Payments," reiterated that mobile payments are beneficial to consumers and retailers alike. The use of mobile payments leads to transformation and innovation in brick-and-mortar sales. According to her, mobile payments make payment transactions more straightforward and faster, saving time and effort.

Furthermore, research into mobile payment adoption by Zhao and Kurnia (2014) posits that mobile payments enable quick transactions in an environment with large volumes of payments, save operational turnaround time, and ensure productivity gains. Besides, Kim et al. (2010) have also indicated that mobile payments enable organizations to achieve competitive advantage through the efficient use of mobile payments for transactions. Arguably in developing countries, Duncombe and Boateng (2009) posit that with the high prevalence of mobile phone usage and limited access to financial systems, mobile payments hold the key to positively influencing financial inclusion. Specifically, in Africa, due to micro-business minimal access to regular banking service, mobile payments provide an avenue for micro-businesses excluded from the financial sector to be reached through mobile payments (Talom & Tengeh, 2020). In Ghana, for example, mobile payment technology enables micro-businesses to make payments, send money to family members, and safely store monetary value (Narteh et al., 2017).

Additionally, mobile payments make it possible for micro-businesses to access loans or insurance products. This makes mobile payments one of the most accessible means to promote financial inclusion in developing countries and to revolutionize the world of e-commerce. Existing research has shown that the adoption and use of mobile payments have a potential impact on the livelihood of adopters. Due to the less expensive nature of mobile payment charges, individuals can transfer a small amount of money and make payments at fewer fees to poor households. In addition to the cost-savings, mobile payments enable users to access financial services to include financial inclusion for the unbanked (Hayashi, 2012). Also, researchers like Boateng (2011) from developing country contexts have emphasized that mobile payment technologies allow users to strategically use their mobile phones to store value on an account linked to their handset. Again, users can transfer funds to their suppliers and receive payments for their sales irrespective of their location and time, allowing payment transactions to be made in real time.

Additionally, mobile payments make it possible for users to access loans or insurance products. Due to the less expensive nature of mobile payment charges, individuals can transfer a small amount of money and make payments at fewer fees to micro-businesses. In addition to the cost-savings, mobile payments enable users to access financial services to include financial inclusion for the unbanked (Hayashi, 2012).

Despite the positive attributes of mobile payments, there are some challenges faced by merchants and consumers, which could significantly impact mobile payment adoption negatively. Among them are the scarce knowledge regarding mobile payments, the user confidence doubts, the complexity of the systems, privacy concerns, and lack of security (Yu et al., 2018; Qin et al., 2017).

4.2.2 Theoretical Foundations

The TTF theory is adopted for this study because it offers significant explanatory power to utilize technology and its linkage with user performance. The TTF is deemed appropriate for this study because of the match between user task needs and the available functionality of the technology (Dishaw & Strong, 1999). The TTF theory argues that tasks constitute an individual's actions to generate outputs from inputs in order to satisfy information needs (Goodhue & Thompson, 1995). The use of information technology by an individual to perform a task is considered a task characteristic. The task can be classified as routine, interrelated, or time-critical. In this study, the task is constructed as payment transactions market traders engage in, using mobile payments as part of their payment transactions. Technology is the tool (hardware, software, data) used by market traders in carrying out their payment transaction tasks. The features of these technologies can affect customer utilization and their perception of the technology. The TTF theory's importance is how well the functionality and technological features fit the user's needs. Studies have shown that a better fit will improve perceived performance (McGill & Klobas, 2009).

Moreover, the technology must have different functionalities to provide support for various aspects of the task. For instance, a researcher like Davis (1989) asserted that it results in higher performance when technology is utilized. However, performance will not improve if there is a poor task-technology fit, irrespective of higher utilization (Davis, 1989). This study looks at a mobile device (mobile phone) and the payment software's applicability in the trader's day-to-day payment transactions.

More so, the adoption and use of IT depends mainly on the role of the individual. The TTF view is on IT use, and users look at the relationship between task requirements, individual abilities, and how well the IT system functions. There is an emphasis on the alignment between the three aspects of inducing positive IT-enabled performance (Nan, 2011). This study considers payments by market traders using a mobile device as an IT system. The specific attributes of mobile payment users may affect the mobile payments' perceived fit in meeting the user's task-related needs. Evaluating the fit of technology and perceptions of performance may vary depending upon individual experience in using computers and mobile devices and related software and expertise and training in information skills.

Nevertheless, according to the TTF theory, effective adoption and technology use are that the individual must be willing to accept and use that particular technology (Goodhue & Thompson, 1995). According to the TTF theory, a positive impact on technology adoption is created when there is a fit among the constructs: the task, the technology, and the user. This then leads to performance, which is the execution of specific tasks by an individual. If the task's performance is high, it signifies a high TTF level and satisfaction with the IT (Goodhue &Thompson, 1995). Whenever there is a high TTF, there is an increase in the performance impact of the system. Market traders do payment transactions to support their trading activities and send money to their friends and relatives. These payment transactions are means by which traders enhance their trading activities. Traders have been using traditional means of payments over the years without the contribution of IT. However, this context is changing with the emergence of mobile payments that offer the same service but deliver additional value not possible with traditional payments. This process has changed the interaction between traders and their customers. Nonetheless, the impact of this change on performance is yet to be determined.

According to Goodhue and Thompson (1995), the antecedents of utilization are about beliefs of using a system. They argue that the TTF should provide the basis of belief about the utility and importance of a system and the advantages gained from using a system. Also, if a user of a technology believes in the technology's capacity to support the task at hand, the user will adopt and use the technology. This means that the software and its applications help with the efficient performance of the task. Also, it helps to reduce the cost involved in task performance and the effortless execution of the task. In this study, utilization is the use of mobile phones and other mobile devices by market traders to make payment transactions. Usage must be considered since the use of mobile payments by market traders is discretionary. Utilization at any level greater than zero and technology with a maximum TTF will give a better performance. Hence, performance will be a function of both utilization and TTF (Goodhue & Thompson, 1995).

Based on the TTF discourse above, the model stipulates that market traders may adopt mobile payment technology for mini, micro, or macro payment transactions. The application of the technology by the market traders provides alternative means of payments which is likely to add value to enhance their task performance. Arguably, the literature points to the fact that the application of technology in a task's performance leads to the efficient delivery of that particular task.

In addition to appropriate technology in payment transactions, trading is driven by the efficient and valuable exchange of goods and services and profitable transactions at a minimal cost (Liu et al., 2015). Further, a scholar like Boateng (2011) has posited that the generation of value in any business depends on efficient transactions. This assertion relates very well to the transaction cost theory, which is any cost an individual incurs in the form of money, time, effort, or other disutility during a process of economic exchange (Lehdonvirta et al., 2009). The theory postulate that transaction efficiency increases when the cost per transaction decreases. The greater the transaction efficiency gains enabled by a particular business, the lower the cost, the more valuable it will be. Typically, transactional cost consists of the time, effort, and attention required to locate and pay for a good or service (Lehdonvirta et al., 2009). From this perspective, a trader always looks for innovative ways to create and capture value in their trading activities. With the application of technology to payment transactions using the mobile phone, market traders can

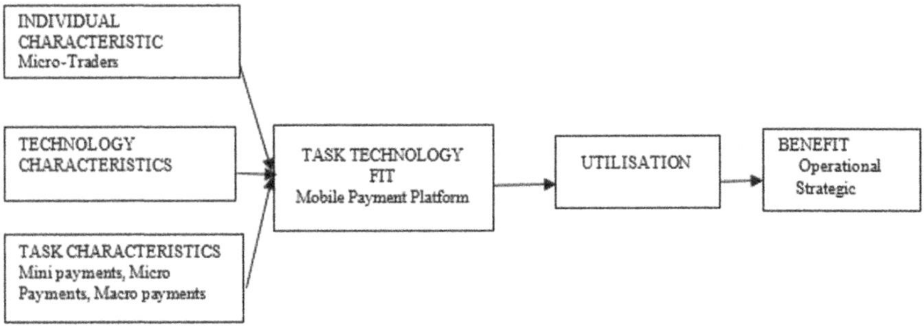

Fig. 4.1 Conceptual model on the impact of mobile payment adoption and use on micro-traders

generate value based on the features of a mobile device such as mobility, flexibility, convenience and ubiquity, localization immediacy, and instant connectivity (Yang et al., 2012).

Additionally, these characteristics, combined with the vastly reduced cost of information processing, allow efficient payment transactions, which affect the way these traders operate. Mobile payments enable traders to transact business and make payment any time, everywhere conveniently, and in real time, including payment upfront for goods and services. According to the literature, these characteristics generate strategic and operational benefits for the traders. These benefits can be attributed to innovation through IT, which can be associated with the mobile device (Wu et al., 2017; Oliveira et al., 2016). The above discussions are depicted in Fig. 4.1 as the conceptual framework for the study.

4.3 Research Methodology

This study, as stated earlier, aims to empirically explore how mobile payment technology fits the task needs of micro-businesses and how it impacts business activities for business development. The study conducted an in-depth interview with micro-business owners in order to address the research objectives. As recommended by Churchill (1999), the research adopted a qualitative method as an appropriate methodology to understand whether or not mobile devices' technology is suitable for the task of payment. This study's data collection was through a semi-structured set of questions designed to throw light on how mobile payment adoption and use impact these micro-businesses. We started our data collection by reviewing published and public online and offline documents relating to microenterprises, press articles, websites, and newspapers. The micro-businesses interviewed are classified in Ghana as operating in the informal sector. Most of the companies operate as sole proprietors employing less than five persons. Most of these businesses serve small semi-organized and mostly unregulated business sectors primarily concentrated in the cities and the rural areas. Such companies are managed and operated by the owners, who are also the managers. These businesses are found in market stalls, open yards, residential houses, and open grounds.

The profile sought was very difficult to come by; therefore, the researchers depended on the National Board for Small Scale Industries (NBSSI), the institution responsible for coordinating small-scale micro-businesses in Ghana, to identify the micro-businesses. Two regional managers (Greater Accra region and Eastern region) were contacted through telephone and emails; through their contacts, the managers gave us different contacts of their members who are micro-businesses. We selected our interviews randomly from the list and interviewed those who accepted to participate in the research. The interviews were conducted with micro-business owners in two regions in Ghana. The authors conducted interviews with micro-businesses such as fruit and vegetable retailers, wholesalers and retailers of provisions and household items, shoe sellers, importers of general goods, and restaurant operators. The recruitment of interviews stopped at the point of theoretical saturation, where there was no new knowledge coming out from the interview. This point was attained with 12 interviewees (Eisenhardt, 1989; Glaser & Strauss, 1967).

This number is believed to be adequate based on Guest et al.'s (2006) recommendations that "saturation occurred within the first 12 interviews. However, basic elements for meta-themes were present as early as six interviews". The initial interviews were all selected from a market setting. Therefore, there was a further supplementary data collection using small-scale businesses that included value addition and processing such as restaurants, fresh fish processing, fresh juice processing, dressmaking, and fashion designing. For the later interviews, we spoke to an incubation center in the city. We adopted a snowballing sampling approach to select the respondent: The first respondent interviewed was asked to recommend and introduce the researcher to a small-scale manufacturing company. We adopted this approach because it enables the research to reach the hard-to-reach individuals (Atkinson & Flint, 2001). Eight respondents were legible as the above respondents were selected.

In all, data was collected from a sample size of 20 respondents, 14 females and 6 males ranging from 28 to 50 years who have a diverse socioeconomic background, family status, and geographical location. Our in-depth interviews were adopted face-to-face and, in some cases, in telephone because we wanted to mitigate the effect of COVID-19. The length of the interview was between 45 minutes and 1 hour. The interviews were recorded and transcribed in their entirety for subsequent content analysis (Weber, 1990). The profiles of the respondents and their businesses are listed in Table 4.1. The content analysis was carried out using the conventional manual approach. At the initial stage, the researcher read the transcription repeatedly to identify some themes in the transcribed data. Further, each respondent's discussions were analyzed word by word to discover the diverse answers and to capture coding schemes, emergent categories, and subcategories that were derived directly from the data. In the following section, we develop our findings in detail.

Table 4.1 Summary profile of interviewees

Informant	Age	Gender	Business type	Educational background	Region	Payment platform type
Alice	43	Female	Retailing of fresh pineapple	School certificate	Eastern NBSSI	Service provider network mobile phone
Dora	38	Female	Importer of shoes and bags	Ordinary level	Greater Accra NBSSI	Service provider network smartphone
Esther	53	Female	Mini supermarket	Degree	Greater Accra NBSSI	Service provider network smartphone
Francis	36	Male	Pharmaceutical retailing	Degree	Greater Accra NBSSI	Service provider network smartphone
Pommayee	28	Female	Fresh fish distribution	Diploma	Incubation	Third-party providers' point-of-sale device
Steven	42	Male	Pizza shop	Secondary	Greater Accra NBSSI	Service provider network smartphone
Josephine	39	Female	Retailing of consumables	Diploma	Eastern NBSSI	Service provider network mobile phone
Olivia	34	Female	Lingerie retailing shop	Diploma	Eastern NBSSI	Service provider network mobile phone
Florence	41	Female	Retailing of consumables	JHS	Eastern NBSSI	Service provider network mobile phone
Grace	42	Female	Retailing of consumables	Degree	Greater Accra NBSSI	Service provider network smartphone
Percy	50	Male	Retailing of coconut oil	Masters	Incubation center	Service provider network smartphone
David	19	Male	Micro-banking (susu)	Diploma	Incubation center	Service provider network smartphone
Sara	35	Female	Mobile restaurant	Secondary	Incubation	Service provider network mobile phone
Agyeiwaa	32	Female	Shoe retailing (side job)	Diploma	Greater Accra NBSSI	Service provider network smartphone

(continued)

Table 4.1 (continued)

Informant	Age	Gender	Business type	Educational background	Region	Payment platform type
Gloria	40	Female	Mothercare Shop	Degree	Eastern NBSSI	Third-party provider's point-of-sale device
Bukala	28	Female	Cottage juice processing	Degree	Incubation	Service provider network Mobile phone
Alby	28	Female	Local processing of cosmetics	Degree	Incubation	Service provider network smartphone
Tina	53	Female	Mushroom processing	Diploma	Incubation	Service provider network smartphone
Nicholas	48	Male	Fashion designing	Diploma	Incubation	Service provider network smartphone
Joyce	44	Female	Retailing of building materials	Degree	Eastern NBSSI	Service provider network smartphone

4.4 Analysis of Research Findings

4.4.1 Mobile Payment Meeting the Task Needs

Our research emerged that micro-business owners expressed satisfaction with using the mobile device (mobile phone) in making payments. All informants believed that mobile device was suitable for various payment transactions, including paying suppliers for goods and services, paying bills, sending money to friends and relatives, withdrawing cash, and topping up airtime accounts.

From Dora, an importer and a retailer: With mobile money, I can send my clearing agent money right from my shop or the house, and he also uses mobile payment. So, he does the clearing without me going there physically. Again, I do not go round to collect my money from the retailers I supply, and they send me mobile money whenever they are unable to come, and their credit term is due.

Esther is an owner-manager of a supermarket: Mobile money helps me access my cash in times of emergency easily, and mostly I use my mobile money to buy airtime to top up my account.

From Agyeiwaa, a retailer of lady's shoes: Selling is my side job, so mobile payment is the most suitable payment option. I have registered my SIM with the service provider so are my trading partners. I mostly order the products I sell from my wholesaler and pay with mobile money, and then the products are delivered to me in the office or home because I do not have the time to go. In selling, I take both cash and mobile payment.

I have to be stationed at my shop as a resident pharmacist, so mobile payment has been helping me to pay my suppliers, so they supply the drugs without me going to town since I adopted mobile payment; I use it very often: as intimated by Francis, an owner-manager of a pharmaceutical retailing shop.

From the discussions above, our respondents were convinced that mobile payment through the mobile device positively influences payments by saving them physical effort and promoting their job performance. The positive effect of using a mobile device for payment transactions motivates the micro-traders to adopt mobile payment in their transactions. Again, because mobile payments are commonly done through mobile phones and are accessible to a large segment of the population, it makes it easy and convenient for traders to make payment transactions to their customers and their suppliers. Further, since the micro-traders understand the benefit they derive from using mobile payments, it has engendered a positive evaluation of the value of mobile payment use, which influences the willingness of the micro-trades to adopt the technology for their payment transactions.

Regarding the payment characteristics, our informants mentioned that they mostly use micropayments and macro payments and do not use the mini payments and the large ends of the macro payments because of transaction fees and perceived financial risk. The micro-business owners disclosed that they are confident to use mobile payments because their transaction amounts are not significant. The analysis points out that most micro-businesses do not consider large payment forms suitable for mobile payment transactions because of perceived financial risk and transaction costs.

Alice, a fresh vegetable retailer, stated that I usually receive any amount from 20 cedis to 800 cedis (GHC20–800) and send between 200 and 400 cedis (GHC200–400).

The biggest I have sent is 1000 Ghana cedis (GHC1000), and the lowest I have received is 10 cedis (GHC10), as mentioned by Bukala, owner-manager of a fruit juice processing factory.

However, it was identified that the value-adding micro-businesses use the macro payment in their transactions but mentioned that if the transactions exceed macro payments, they will prefer to use check or bank transfer because of perceived financial risk and transaction cost.

As intimated by an owner-manager of the juice processing company: I am not sure of sending big money through mobile payment when something goes wrong. I lose money. It will affect my operations.

As a remark by Alby, a local cosmetic producer: I usually will send 1000 cedis (GHC1000). Beyond that, I will do cash or bank transfers. But for my sales, I receive from 10 cedis (GHC10) to 100 cedis (GHC100). When I am receiving, I do not care because it is sending that face the risk.

I am a small business, so I do not receive so much in a day, but mobile payment is beneficial: as mentioned by Tina, a mushroom retailer.

The analysis demonstrates that micro-businesses are more inclined to use a mobile device for payment transactions. Nevertheless, it was observed from the data that micro-businesses perform these transactions when the payment characteristics do not exceed a particular value. Because they perceive mobile payments as suitable for small value payments, that notwithstanding, all our interviewees were convinced that there was an excellent relationship between their task of payment transactions and the technology, and they see mobile payment as a good fit, hence facilitating the use of the technology to make the payment, which is generating usage and impact on their business activities.

Concerning the individual characteristics, it was identified from the data that all the respondents are educated and have experience with computer usage and were willing to use technology. Hence there was a positive effect on the task-technology fit in performing payment transactions.

> Grace, a retailer of fast-moving consumables, commented that: The features of my phones are easy to operate, and I am conversant with the use of mobile payment. I do not have difficulty using the technology, so anytime there is an opportunity to make any payment transaction, I prefer to use mobile payment.
>
> According to Olivia, a lingerie retailer: Mobile payments are effortless and not challenging to learn. I have the skills as it does not require much to operate mobile payment and can also be done in the local language. For me, I prefer mobile payments to cash.
>
> I am abreast of the operations of mobile payment. I usually buy online using my mobile payment. It is straightforward to maneuver, as commented by David, a mobile phone retailer.
>
> Josephine informed us, a retailer of fast-moving consumer goods, that I understand using a mobile phone in performing different functions. Therefore, using it for payment is also very easy because I am familiar with the steps.

The researchers found that most mobile handsets are easy to operate on the technological characteristics and have the required functionalities needed for mobile payment technology. The finding shows that micro-business who use mobile phones consider technology (mobile phones) convenient and suitable and support the task of payments. More importantly, according to the business owners, the mobile phone and the mobile payment platforms are easy to navigate and fit into the daily routine of payment transactions associated with trading, which have many advantages for their trading activities.

> The mobile payment procedure is very simple, is about six simple steps, and you are through to make payments: as stated by Nicholas, the fashion designer.
>
> Sarah, a mobile restaurant operator, affirmed that: I do not struggle using my mobile phone for payment transactions. I understand the procedure. It is very simple.

4.4.2 Benefits of Using Mobile Payments

This section seeks to explain the benefits micro-businesses obtained from performing the payment task using mobile payments. Our respondents in the micro-business mentioned that their mobile payment deployment in their companies is enhancing their service delivery and generating organizational growth. The interviewees agreed that mobile phone features such as mobility, flexibility, convenience, ubiquity, localization, immediacy, and instant connectivity help their micro-businesses facilitate their daily business activities. Again, they can conveniently transact business and make payment any time, everywhere, and in real time, including payment upfront for goods and services.

> For example, Florence, a retailer of fast-moving consumer products, told us that: Mobile payments help a lot in preventing outstanding payment. According to her, mobile payment has helped reduce the outstanding debt because clients can fall on mobile payments or fall on relatives to transfer payments on their behalf.
>
> Alice intimated that: I do not have to travel to the pineapple farms any longer because the farmers send the pineapples via a truck, and I pay by mobile money. As soon as I receive the consignment, if not for mobile payment, I will have to go from village to village to make an advance payment at the various villages, which is time-wasting.
>
> I do not remember the last time I went to the market, since I started using mobile money. I can preorder my raw materials and pay with my mobile money. My customers also pay and order my products in advance, enabling me to plan my daily production, Percy, a coconut oil distributor, mentioned.

The micro-business owners interviewed point to using mobile payments as a relatively cheaper alternative, an easy way of delivering cash to their suppliers and business partners. They also consider it to be a personal means of making transactions anywhere and at any time. The use of mobile payments by micro-businesses improves service quality to their suppliers and business partners because cash delivery is easier through mobile payments. The use of mobile payments for transactions by the micro-business reduces traveling and its cost. Doing so helped reduce their transactional cost and improved efficiency in their trading activities, which generates strategic and operational benefits for their businesses. The record-keeping advantage of mobile payments keeps records on the phone concerning how much the supplier has sent or the trader has received transparency and enhances their trading activities.

> According to Agyeiwaa, a shoe retailer: mobile payment is convenient and transparent. If I send money, the amount is recorded, and the date is also registered as evidence of payment on the phone. Before then, sometimes somebody can send the money through people who may not deliver or not deliver the entire amount, but with mobile payment, nobody can cheat you. Once the money is transferred, it produces records that are there for all to see.

Besides, mobile payment allows users to store value on their phones for other transactional purposes. Also, mobile payment transactions are safe and reduce stealing and petty theft at the market.

> Pomayee, the fresh fish processing business owner, also stated that: I use mobile money because I know that whenever I lose my phone, once I get my SIM, my money is safe. It also helps me save money because when the money is small, I do not go for it and keep it on my phone until I have enough, which allows me to save.

The advantage of mobile payments is reducing the inherent risks in cash-based payment systems, improving transparency in fund flows, and enhancing the potential for risk associated with trading with cash at the market.

4.4.3 *The Impact of Mobile Payments on Market Traders*

This section aims to enrich mobile payment adoption by small businesses by defining opportunities and leverages that lead to operational and strategic benefits. Mobile payments significantly affect adopters, such as easy accessibility, low cost, security in transactions and business dealings, convenience, and availability.

Concerning the impact of mobile payments on micro-businesses, the findings show that mobile payments have become an innovative way of making payments and receiving payments. Mobile payments are gradually shaping market traders' trading activities; more so, it has become a demand-driven phenomenon and a compelling case for diversifying payments.

> Josephine told us that: These days, customers prefer to pay with mobile money, and they do so without much difficulty, which has increased sales and revenue for my business.

Also, all the respondents indicated that mobile payments help them save money on their mobile phones. Again, they can send money to friends and family, pay school fees, and conveniently make all their payment transactions right at their office without leaving their office. This has generated a transformational effect for the individuals as well as their businesses. The transformational impact of mobile payment is seen where micro-business uses mobile payments to control their bank accounts, store value right, and convert cash in and out of the stored value on their mobile device, no matter the amount, the place, and time. Mobile payments by micro-businesses in their transaction activities mean more sales and improvement in revenue.

Constraints of Mobile Payments Micro-businesses face a lot of constraints in using mobile payment in their trading activities. The data analysis demonstrates that using mobile payments by the market traders has some constraints such as double fee payment, complexities involved in doing mobile money, level of education of trader's fraud, and non-operability of the networks.

> Percy, the virgin coconut oil distributor: service providers are not fair in terms of the charges. Even though they give concessions to merchants, the costs are very high for the consumer. This serves as a barrier to usage by both the consumer and the merchant. The more the consumer patronizes the payment system, the more merchants are interested in using the system.
>
> Also, Yaa, who deals in men's outfits, told us that I get all kinds of calls supposedly coming from providers, but it turns out to be intruders who can generate codes that should be coming from service providers, which are a little bit suspicious if fraudsters can do that.

Micro-businesses are uncertain about the transaction's security because intruders can generate codes to wipe out the merchant's wallet; hence there is more room for safety. There is evidence that people can steal from the merchants without knowing the merchant's code, so the codes are not enough for protecting them.

Our data demonstrate that mobile payments' inherent financial risk serves as a constraint on small business intention to adopt them. This assertion by the business owners portrays mobile payments as potentially having significant financial risk. Micro-businesses are skeptical about using mobile payment for large transactions because mobile payment is a wireless network and is susceptible to intruders, affecting transactional security. The micro-businesses were particularly concerned about security, fraud, payment transaction errors, and potential cash loss.

4.5 Discussions of Research Findings

4.5.1 Mobile Payments and Micro-Businesses

From the 20 interviews conducted with micro-business owners who have decided to adopt mobile payments for their payment transactions, the study contributes new theoretical and empirical insight to an extensive phenomenon that is underestimated and understudied. While the literature to date has mainly focused on the consumer and large-size corporate organizations, this study addresses this gap with an in-depth examination of the mobile device being a fit for a payment transaction and the benefit micro-businesses derive from using mobile payments as well as its impact on their business activities.

The findings demonstrate that the use of a mobile device (mobile phone) in payment transactions is suitable for the task of various forms of payment transactions, including paying suppliers for goods and services, paying bills, sending money to friends and relatives, withdrawing cash, and topping up airtime accounts. The use of mobile payment transactions by the micro-businesses has a positive influence on the task of payments. This is because mobile payments are commonly done through mobile phones and are accessible to a large segment of the population. It makes it easy and convenient for traders to make payment transactions to their customers and their suppliers. Concerning characteristics of mobile payments, the findings show that market traders use mostly the micropayments and the macro payments and do not use the mini payments and the large ends of the macro payments because of transaction fees and the financial risk. The business owners do not consider those payment forms as suitable for their payment transactions. The data analysis points to the fact that both micro- and macro payments are used by both retailers and value-adding micro-businesses who are engaged in retailing and wholesaling and supports the findings of Sarika and Vasantha (2019) and Liu et al. (2015).

Further, the analysis shows that micro-businesses engaged in trading tend to use primarily micropayment because the cost involved is not that much, but they use macro payments when they need to be. The findings demonstrate that the micro-business owners interviewed saw a perfect relationship between their task of payment transactions and the technology as a good fit and, as a result, used the technology to make payment generating usage and impact on their trading activities. All the micro-businesses interviewed were educated and had experience with computer usage and were willing to use technology; hence, there was a positive effect on the task-technology fit in performing payment transactions.

On technological characteristics, most mobile handsets are easy to operate and have the required functionalities needed for mobile payment technology. The findings show that market traders who use mobile phones consider the technology (mobile phone) convenient and suitable and support the task of payments. More importantly, according to the businesses, the mobile phone and the mobile payment platform are easy to navigate and use and fit into the daily routine of payment transactions associated with trading, which have a lot of advantages for their trading activities (Boateng et al., 2014). Also, personal identification numbers (PINs) and secret codes for mobile payments are perceived as safe by businesses. Shon and Swatman (1998) posited that an electronic financial transaction requires that the transactions include confidentiality, authentication, data integrity, and non-repudiation.

4.5.2 Benefits of Using Mobile Payments

Secondly, one of the study's objectives is to ascertain how mobile payments can benefit market traders. The analysis of the data indicates micro-business owners agreed that based on the features of mobile phones such as mobility, flexibility, convenience and ubiquity, localisation immediacy, and instant connectivity, have helped the businesses to facilitate their daily business activities conveniently, transact business and make payment any time, everywhere and in real-time including payment upfront for goods and services. The traders' use of mobile payments improves service quality to their suppliers and business partners because cash delivery is easier through mobile payments. The use of mobile payments for transactions by the micro-businesses helped reduce traveling and the cost associated with it, which helped reduce their transactional cost and improved efficiency in their trading activities, generating strategic and operational benefits for their businesses. The empirical findings are in line with the literature; mobile payment transactions come with several benefits for individuals and organizations, including market traders. Many studies on mobile payments have elaborated on how it can impact business and improve the company's efficiency (Mbogo, 2010; Williams et al., 2017).

4.5.3 The Impact of Mobile Payments on Market Traders

Concerning the impact of mobile payments on micro-business trading activities, the findings show that mobile payments have become an innovative way of making payments and receiving payments. Mobile payments are gradually shaping micro-traders' trading activities; more so, it has become a demand-driven phenomenon and a compelling case for diversifying payments. Modern-day customers prefer to pay with mobile money, which increases sales and revenue. Also, the data analysis shows that mobile payment enables micro-traders to save their money on their mobile phones. They can send money to friends and family, pay school fees, and conveniently make all their payment transactions at the market (Talom & Tengeh, 2020). This has generated a transformational effect for the individuals as well as their businesses. Also, the transformational impact is seen where micro-businesses use mobile payments to control their bank accounts, store value right, and convert cash in and out of the stored value on their mobile device, no matter the amount, the place, and time. Accepting mobile payments by micro-traders in their trading activities means more sales and improvement in revenue. These findings are not different from earlier research (Mbogo, 2010). However, there was no evidence of mobile payment enabling the traders to engage in mobile banking, access money, and capital through microfinance institutions for loans, contrary to existing research on "The Impact of Mobile Payments on the Success and Growth of Micro-Business" (Mbogo, 2010).

4.6 Conclusion and Recommendations

4.6.1 Summary of Research Findings

The research findings have produced many insights that will be very useful for future research and practice. The research findings indicate that micro-businesses use mobile payment for payments transacting in their trading activities, including payment of goods and services to their suppliers. They also accept payments from their customers, all in their palms and through their mobile phones, regardless of time and place. Also, micro-businesses in Ghana store value on their mobile phones through mobile payments, enabling them to top up their mobile credit without using cash. Most of these micro-businesses innovatively use mobile payments to pay their children's school fees and send money to their relatives outside their reach.

Nevertheless, the use of mobile payments by micro-businesses is dependent mainly on their level of education and how familiar they are with the help of mobile phones and their features. The findings of the study based on the data show that the micro-businesses that are using mobile payment in their trading activities achieve strategic and operational efficiencies, which translate to the transformational effect that empowers the micro-businesses to manage and control their financial activities using mobile payments. However, for the micro-businesses to achieve the stated impact on mobile payment in their trading activities, their stakeholders in the value chain must be willing also to do the same. Hence, mobile payment is significant only when actors within the market traders' value chain are eager to use mobile payments for their trading activities.

4.6.2 Implications of the Study

The study contributes to research by identifying mobile payments' impact on micro-businesses using the TTF theory and the transactional cost theory. Arguably, not many studies have looked at the impact of mobile payments on the lives of adopters from the perspective of TTF and how the characteristics of mobile technology fit the needs or task of micro-business to impact their livelihoods in the Ghanaian context, hence a contribution to the body of knowledge. Concerning practice, the study provides guidelines to actors in the mobile payment ecosystem to exploit the payment system's benefits and address the constraints and risks. Concerning policy implication, this study provides guidelines for discussions on national policy on payment systems and their legal framework and interoperability among the telecom providers to ensure that the country has the necessary infrastructure for mobile payment success.

4.6.3 *Future Research Directions*

This research was on micro-business and the focus was on two regions. With the rapid expansions of mobile payments, future research can concentrate on mobile payments and their influence on shopping behaviors and how mobile payments impact rural Ghana economies and farmer's communities.

References

Afutu-Kotey, R. L., Gough, K. V., & Owusu, G. (2017). Young entrepreneurs in the mobile telephony sector in Ghana: From necessities to aspirations. *Journal of African Business, 18*(4), 476–491.

Albuquerque, J. P., Diniz, E. H., & Cernev, A. K. (2016). Mobile payments: A scoping study of the literature and issues for future research. *Information Development, 32*(3), 527–553. https://doi.org/10.1177/0266666914557338

Atkinson, R., & Flint, J. (2001). *Accessing hidden and hard-to-reach populations: Snowball research strategies*. Social Research Update, p. 33.

Boateng, R. (2011). Mobile phones and micro-trading activities–conceptualising the link. *Info, 13*(5), 48–62.

Boateng, R., Hinson, R., Galadima, R., & Olumide, L. (2014). Preliminary insights into the influence of mobile phones in micro-trading activities of market women in Nigeria. *Information Development, 30*(1), 32–50.

Chandra, S., Srivastava, S. C., & Theng, Y. L. (2010). Evaluating the role of trust in consumer adoption of mobile payment systems: An empirical analysis. *Communications of the Association for Information Systems, 27*(1), 29.

Churchill, G. (1999). *Marketing research: Mythological foundations* (7th ed.). Dryden.

Davis, F. D. (1989). Perceived usefulness, perceived ease of use, and user acceptance of information technology. *MIS Quarterly, 13*(3), 319–334.

Dishaw, M. T., & Strong, D. M. (1999). Extending the technology acceptance model with task–technology fit constructs. *Information & management, 36*(1), 9–21.

Duncombe, R., & Boateng, R. (2009). Mobile phones and financial services in developing countries: A review of concepts, methods, issues, evidence and future research directions. *Third World Quarterly, 30*(7), 1237–1258.

Eisenhardt, K. M. (1989). Building theories from case study research. *Academy of Management Review, 14*(4), 532–550.

Glaser, B., & Strauss, A. (1967). *The discovery of grounded theory: Strategies in qualitative research*. Weidenfeld and Nicholson.

Gomber, P., Kauffman, R. J., Parker, C., & Weber, B. W. (2018). On the fintech revolution: Interpreting the forces of innovation, disruption, and transformation in financial services. *Journal of Management Information Systems, 35*(1), 220–265.

Goodhue, D. L., & Thompson, R. L. (1995). Task-technology fit and individual performance. *MIS Quarterly*, 213–236.
Guest, G., Bunce, A., & Johnson, L. (2006). How many interviews are enough? An experiment with data saturation and variability. *Field Methods, 18*, 59–82.
Giuntini, A. (2020). 2 ITU, Submarine Cables and African Colonies, 1850s–1900s. In *History of the International Telecommunication Union (ITU)* (pp. 37-54). De Gruyter Oldenbourg.
Hayashi, F. (2012). *Mobile payments: What's in it for consumers?* Economic Review-Federal Reserve Bank of Kansas City, p. 35.
Hsiao, M. H. (2019). Mobile payment services as a facilitator of value co-creation: A conceptual framework. *The Journal of High Technology Management Research, 30*(2), 100353.
Humbani, M., & Wiese, M. (2018). A cashless society for all: Determining consumers' readiness to adopt mobile payment services. *Journal of African Business, 19*(3), 409–429.
Kim, G., Shin, B., & Lee, H. G. (2009). Understanding dynamics between initial trust and usage intentions of mobile banking. *Information Systems Journal, 19*(3), 283–311.
Kim, C., Mirusmonov, M., & Lee, I. (2010). An empirical examination of factors influencing the intention to use mobile payment. *Computers in Human Behavior, 26*(3), 310–322.
Lehdonvirta, V., Soma, H., Ito, H., Yamabe, T., Kimura, H., & Nakajima, T. (2009, September). *Ubipay: Minimising transaction costs with smart mobile payments.* In Proceedings of the 6th international conference on mobile technology, application & systems (p. 1). ACM literature. *The Information Society, 24*, 140–159.
Li, H., Liu, Y., & Heikkilä, J. (2014). Understanding the factors driving NFC-enabled mobile payment adoption: An empirical investigation. In *PACIS* (p. 231).
Liu, J., Kauffman, R. J., & Ma, D. (2015). Competition, cooperation, and regulation: Understanding the evolution of the mobile payments technology ecosystem. *Electronic Commerce Research and Applications, 14*(5), 372–391.
Madan, K., & Yadav, R. (2016). Behavioural intention to adopt mobile wallet: A developing country perspective. *Journal of Indian Business Research, 8*(3), 227–244. https://doi.org/10.1108/JIBR-10-2015-0112
Mbogo, M. (2010). The impact of mobile payments on the success and growth of micro-business: The case of M-Pesa in Kenya. *Journal of Language, Technology & Entrepreneurship in Africa, 2*(1), 182–203.
McGill, T. J., & Klobas, J. E. (2009). A task–technology fit view of learning management system impact. *Computers & Education, 52*(2), 496–508.
Nan, N. (2011). Capturing bottom-up information technology use processes: A complex adaptive systems model. *MIS Quarterly, 35*(2), 505–532.
Narteh, B., Mahmoud, M. A., & Amoh, S. (2017). Customer behavioural intentions towards mobile money services adoption in Ghana. *Service Industries Journal, 37*(7–8), 426–447. https://doi.org/10.1080/02642069.2017.1331435
Oliveira, T., Thomas, M., Baptista, G., & Campos, F. (2016). Mobile payment: Understanding the determinants of customer adoption and intention to recommend the technology. *Computers in Human Behavior, 61*(2016), 404–414.
Peruta, M. D. (2017). Adoption of mobile money and financial inclusion: A macroeconomic approach through cluster analysis. *Economics of Innovation and New Technology, 20*(1).
Qin, Z., Sun, J., Wahaballa, A., Zheng, W., Xiong, H., & Qin, Z. (2017). A secure and privacy-preserving mobile wallet with outsourced verification in cloud computing. *Computer Standards & Interfaces, 54*, 55–60.
Sarika, P., & Vasantha, S. (2019). Impact of mobile wallets on cashless transaction. *International Journal of Recent Technology and Engineering, 7*(6), 1164–1171.
Schierz, P. G., Schilke, O., & Wirtz, B. W. (2010). Understanding consumer acceptance of mobile payment services: An empirical analysis. *Electronic commerce research and applications, 9*(3), 209–216.
Shon, T. H., & Swatman, P. M. (1998). Identifying effectiveness criteria for Internet payment systems. *Internet Research, 8*(3), 202–218.

Talom, F. S. G., & Tengeh, R. K. (2020). The impact of mobile money on the financial performance of the SMEs in Douala, Cameroon. *Sustainability, 12*(1), 183.

Taylor, E. (2016). Mobile payment technologies in retail: A review of potential benefits and risks. *International Journal of Retail & Distribution Management, 44*(2), 159–177.

Upadhyay, P., & Chattopadhyay, M. (2015). Examining mobile based payment services adoption issues. *Journal of Enterprise Information Management, 28*(4), 490–507. https://doi.org/10.1108/JEIM-04-2014-0046

Weber, R. P. (1990). *Basic content analysis*. Sage.

Williams, M. D., Roderick, S., Davies, G. H., & Clement, M. (2017). *Risk, trust, and compatibility as antecedents of mobile payment adoption*. In Twenty-third Americas Conference on Information Systems, Boston, 2017

Wu, J., Liu, L., & Huang, L. (2017). Consumer acceptance of mobile payment across time. *Industrial Management & Data Systems, 117*(8), 1761–1776. https://doi.org/10.1108/IMDS-08-2016-0312

Yang, S., Lu, Y., Gupta, S., Cao, Y., & Zhang, R. (2012). Mobile payment services adoption across time: An empirical study of the effects of behavioral beliefs, social influences, and personal traits. *Computers in Human Behavior, 28*(1), 129–142.

Yu, X., Kywe, S. M., & Li, Y. (2018). Security issues of in-store mobile payment. In *Handbook of blockchain, digital finance, and inclusion* (Vol. 2) (pp. 115–144). Academic.

Zhao, Y., & Kurnia, S. (2014). Exploring Mobile Payment Adoption in China. In *PACIS* (p. 232).

Zhong, J. (2009). *A comparison of mobile payment procedures in Finnish and Chinese markets*. BLED 2009 Proceedings, p. 37.

Zhou, T. (2014). Understanding the determinants of mobile payment continuance usage. *Industrial Management & Data Systems, 114*(6), 936–948. https://doi.org/10.1108/IMDS-02-2014-0068

Eunice Yeboah Afeti is a PhD candidate at the Operations and Management Information Systems (OMIS) Department, University of Ghana Business School (UGBS), Accra, Ghana. She holds an MPhil and Executive MBA in Business Administration from the University of Ghana. Eunice has worked in the manufacturing sector for more than half a decade with vast international experience, working to bring social and economic change to out-grower farmers in the Akwapim South municipalities of the Eastern region of Ghana. Her research interest includes mobile commerce, electronic business, social media, innovative business models, mobile payment adoption, impact, and use. She can be reached at eunice.yafeti@upsamail.edu.gh.

Acheampong Owusu holds a PhD in Information Systems from the Limkokwing University of Creative Technology, Cyberjaya, Malaysia. He is a lecturer at the Operations and Management Information Systems (OMIS) Department at the University of Ghana Business School (UGBS). Acheampong is a multidisciplinary researcher with research interests including information systems, business intelligence systems and analytics, technology diffusion, cloud computing, and e-commerce. Acheampong has published several research articles in peer-reviewed journals. He can be reached at aowusu@ug.edu.gh.

Chapter 5
Creating Value in Organizational Communication: Analyzing Twitter Messages for Effective Message Characteristics

Divine Q. Agozie, Muesser C. Nat, Sam A. Edu, Kobina A. Benson, and Oseyenbhin S. Osemeahon

Abstract Effective messaging for organizational communication on social media like Twitter depends on certain message features and characteristics. These characteristics contribute to making organizational messages amenable to desirable engagement actions. Thus, an implementation of these features will create value for organizational communication on social media. Given the recent developments in text-mining and analysis capabilities, it is possible to extract and combine textual content to attain valuable insights and predictions. This chapter investigates the characteristics of textual content shared by interest group organizations. It does this by first classifying these messages into a dichotomous group of high and low effective messages. It then employs a computerized content analysis procedure to extract the characteristics underlying high effective messages. Five thousand, seven hundred and forty-one Twitter posts of 123 interest group organizations (IGOs) were analyzed. Largely, high effective messages reveal an average of 9 verbs and 3.5 nouns per message, average of 37 words per message and 13.5 words per sentence. They also possessed an informal tone and are written in a direct style. Practically, this examination offers useful guidelines for creating organizational messages that are likely to draw desirable engagement reactions in the form of increased dissemination and comments from Twitter audiences.

Keywords Organizational communication · Effective messaging · Interest group organizations (IGOs) · Text mining · Twitter

---

D. Q. Agozie (✉) · M. C. Nat · S. A. Edu · K. A. Benson · O. S. Osemeahon
Faculty of Applied Sciences, Cyprus International University, Haspolat, Cyprus
e-mail: dagozie@ug.edu.gh; mnat@ciu.edu.tr; aedu@ug.edu.gh; ose.sunday@ciu.edu.tr

R. Boateng et al. (eds.), *Digital Innovations, Business and Society in Africa*,
Advances in Theory and Practice of Emerging Markets,
https://doi.org/10.1007/978-3-030-77987-0_5

5.1 Introduction

For many organizations, social media present low-cost avenues to interact and build relationships with audiences. They also present forums for users to share their experiences and provide feedback relevant for service improvement (Schreiner et al., 2019). Given the opportunities for mass communication through social media, users are constantly exposed to a deluge of messages (Louisa, 2017; Pentina & Tarafdar, 2014). As such, influencing user intentions and attitudes through messaging on social media has grown in difficulty (Chung, 2017). While related examinations into user and brand relationships on social media exist (Labrecque, 2012), sustaining social media use, considering their fast evolution requires additional inquiry (Schreiner et al., 2019). This makes the need for renewed understanding of how to "write for social media" more relevant (Joo et al., 2020).

Different organizations communicate differently depending on the organization type, objective, and target audience (Joo & Cahil, 2019). For instance, among interest group organizations (IGOs) which struggle with the challenge of collective action, a focus on relationship building and member engagement is paramount as a communication goal (Guo & Saxton, 2014). Therefore, social media messages in this context must seek interactions or intimacy with audiences, thus user engagement (Kanol & Nat, 2017). Chung (2017) describes user engagement in the social media context to include different user responses to social media content. For example, sharing, commenting, liking, tagging, and retweeting among others. Others also perceive user engagement actions to be metrics for assessing effectiveness of social media use (Darren et al., 2017; Paul & Dredze, 2014).

However, from an IGO perspective, effective communication depends on several evolving factors (Ziegele et al., 2014), like group type, group location, platform type, and group cause, among others. As such, examinations exploring the user-organization communication nexus require similar basis to present a state-of-the-art engaging communication framework for communication on social media (Joo et al., 2020). Various approaches exist to pursue this objective. For instance, text-mining approaches exist to analyze textual social data to reveal relevant content, user, and network characteristics of messages for effective engagement (Nguyen et al., 2015, 2017; Darren et al., 2017; Andalibi et al., 2016; Liu, 2015; Paul & Dredze, 2014).

For example, Sewwandi et al. (2017) employed the Linguistic Inquiry and Word Count (LIWC) to identify linguistic features of personality identification. Nazneen and Raymond (2017) analyzed lexical structures of twitter messages, using auxiliary features to determine victims' chances of leaving or staying in abusive relationships. Darren et al. (2017) undertook a similar analysis to identify the drivers of political mobilization. These and other evidences of the feasibility of text-mining social data exist to show the usefulness of text characteristics for predicting various phenomena. Although these evidences also suggest much application of this concept, a few gaps still exist in this application area. First, there is limited evidence of what characteristics typify an effective organizational message (Suhaimin et al., 2017). Second, from a contextual perspective, examinations of social media content of IGO and their related communication activities online are scant. Thus far, this study extends the discourse of detection and classification to effective messaging, to examine message characteristics underlying desirable organizational messages on Twitter.

As such the study is organized as follows: the review of literature and then the method in Sect. 5.3 followed by the results and discussion. Finally, the conclusion, limitations, and suggestion for future studies on the gaps contributing in this are presented.

5.2 Review of Literature

5.2.1 Message Effectiveness on Social Media

Social media technologies have steadily evolved since their inception likewise the modes and mechanisms for communication (Zhang & Mao, 2016). As a result, there are discrepancies on what makes an effective use of social media for communication irrespective of the type of platform (Zhang & Mao, 2016). This review pursues the understanding of effective communication on social media through the lens of the hierarchy-of-effects framework popularly used in advertising communication (Lavidge & Steiner, 1961; Smith et al., 2008). The theory perceives that consumers go through multiple phases while determining or modifying their intentions and attitudes toward a brand. Specifically, it depicts a sequential progression from knowing and feeling to doing, to form an attitude (Solomon et al., 2016). Other applications of the hierarchy-of-effects theory also propose that attitude is unidirectional, that is, relative to being determined solely by affect, the extent of favorability with the attitude object also matters (Lutz, 1981). In practical sense, consumers shape their beliefs by collecting and analyzing relevant aspects of information they acquire (Solomon et al., 2016). By inference, user intentions and actions online are influenced by the information or content they receive (Szmigin & Piacentini, 2015), and this subsequently drives their engagement action toward the information or content (in this case, the social media message). For example, a message may facilitate sharing, comments, and like actions from users because the user believes it is relevant to them or their networks (Rossiter & Percy, 2017). The hierarchy sequence depicted in the theory suggests that users are mostly interested in gathering as much information as possible including alternative information in order to arrive at an optimal engagement decision (Rossiter & Percy, 2017).

Some scholars still share doubts about the sequence and even the existence of a hierarchy of effects in real-life cases (Goodrich, 2011, Smith et al., 2008). Similar to this assertion, insufficient evidence exists on its relevance to influencing the effectiveness of online user engagement actions. Therefore, there is the need to further understand its role relative to specific organizational contexts such as brand communication (Rossiter & Percy, 2017). Thus far, the study presented here draws on the standard learning hierarchy of the hierarchy-of-effects model to understand the effectiveness of social media messaging for organizational communication and user engagement decision. This study, thus, proposes that an effective message on social media like Twitter possesses inherent features that lead users into thinking, feeling, or undertaking certain engagement actions, prior to the user's intended decision to engage or disregard (Zhang & Mao, 2016; Rossiter & Percy, 2017).

5.2.2 IGOs and Social Media Use

The reason why and how interest group organizations (IGOs) use social media tools still remains partly illusive. To make matters worse, the well-known resource-based theoretical view offers some contrasting evidences (Kanol & Nat, 2017). For instance, a part of the literature sees social media as a tool for the "weak," thus largely for resource-poor groups like interest and pressure groups (Eyal, 2016; Kanol & Nat, 2017). However, in other viewpoints, it is a tool for the "powerful," like large corporations and business organizations (Van der Graaf et al., 2013). In addition, the resource-based view only shows the resource capability of an organization to use social media technologies and not necessarily how and why they use these technologies. Efforts to understand social media use by organizations in general have focused on factors that make social networking technologies appealing to organizations (Kanol & Nat, 2017; Chalmers & Shotton, 2016). These efforts have largely assessed how social media technologies facilitate organizational communication practices. For example, among IGOs, it is asserted that social media have mainly facilitated garnering support or advocacy (Kanol & Nat, 2017; Eyal, 2016). This view proves relevant because until recently, scholars were unsure whether social media technologies were useful for "inside" or "outside" lobbying strategies (Kanol & Nat, 2017). For instance, Binderkrantz (2012) opines that policy-relevant information cannot be disseminated on social media effectively how traditional media channels will, whereas the kind of protest strategies typified by outside strategies favor what social media offers.

These misconceptions, perhaps, exist because the analysis of social media's role among IGOs has not extensively examined their news making potential (Eyal, 2016; Joo & Cahil, 2019). Instead, most have conceptualized social media use as a part of the traditional media or a new paradigm operating parallel to it (Kanol & Nat, 2017). Based on the latter view, two arguments emerge to explain social media use among IGOs: first, the organization's position on shaping policy debates and, second, its place on controlling the organizational image in the public (Chalmers & Shotton, 2016).

The nature of policy issues and lobbying debates usually narrows these issues to which dimension of the debate is to be projected or relegated. Parties that successfully frame policy issues can start debates on their terms and possess more influence to shape the debate (Chalmers & Shotton, 2016). In essence, to gain control over a debate is crucial to shaping policy. Edwards and Hoefer (2010) believe that the ability to construe issues and raise awareness is distinct to traditional news media. Therefore, social media currently present new opportunities to frame debates, raise significant awareness, and shape policy with specific organizational information exchange.

Literature suggests that shaping of both the organizational image and policy debates depends on the information communicated (Kanol, 2016; Binderkrantz, 2012). This is termed as the "medialization" of communication, which has led to advocacy actors all seeking media presence (Chalmers & Shotton, 2016). As such, IGOs no longer subscribe to the traditional pressure-centered approach but rather dwell on in-house expertise to shape debates via evidence-based communication (Obar et al., 2012; Chalmers & Shotton, 2016). Traditional news media will mainly generate attention toward IGOs themselves (Obar et al., 2012; Schultz et al., 2011), whereas social media channels will sustain the organization's online presence and impression (Castello & Morsing, 2013). An effective online presence goes with a reputation or image (Conrad & Sollitto, 2017; Ziegele et al., 2014). Compared with corporate reputation and brand building context, little evidence exists on this issue in the advocacy and IGO perspective (Conrad & Sollitto, 2017). Therefore, this study contends that the new opportunities handed to IGOs by affordances of social media provide an important apparatus for effective brand communication and relationship strategies. This leads to the study's proposition that characteristics exist of effective messages for social media communication.

5.2.3 Text Analysis

Social media are crucial to the nature of interactions of organizations in recent (Kanol & Nat, 2017) as they offer channels to exchange messages with audiences aiming to attract positive appeals to drive diverse interactive actions. The result of these exchanges is a deluge of social data that become inputs for analysis like text-mining. Text-mining refers to a process of transforming unstructured text data into structured form to derive underlying insights and patterns (Nguyen et al. 2017). Numerous applications of the text-mining procedure have used social data to investigate real-life and online phenomena (Wang et al., 2017). For instance, in a healthcare study, mental disorders were predicted by analyzing textual medical documents (Nguyen et al., 2015, 2017). Balani and Choudhury (2015) also predicted depression conditions with language styles expressed in text (e.g., use of swear words or sadness-related words). Current text-mining models have the ability to analyze unstructured texts (Wang et al., 2017) (see other studies Andalibi et al., 2016; Lui, 2015; Paul & Dredze, 2014). To capture such language characteristics in unstructured text, the Linguistic Inquiry and Word Count (LIWC) technique emerges as a widely used tool by prior studies (Andalibi et al., 2016). The LIWC converts unstructured textual content into meaningful categorizations (Andalibi et al., 2016; Lui, 2015; Paul & Dredze, 2014).

For example, Sewwandi et al. (2017) employed the LIWC to investigate linguistic features of personality identification. Similarly, Pankajdeep (2015) employed the LIWC, to establish that linguistic features of text are domain specific, as characteristics such as hashtags, special characters, and mentions convey emphasis to make messages persuasive. Andalibi et al. (2016) showed that, in seeking support on advocacy platforms, characteristics as first-time disclosure and length of post can predict stigmatization using the LIWC. Nazneen and Raymond (2017) analyzed lexical structures of Twitter messages, using auxiliary features to predict victims' chances of leaving or staying in abusive relationships. Darren et al. (2017), in analyzing what drives political mobilization in the digital age, classified political messages into two groups: direct and indirect political messages to mobilize support. The direct types report the situation as if it were from the location where an event is occurring, while indirect message types reecho direct messages already posted from other platforms (Al-garadi et al., 2016). Despite the evidences that much application of the text-mining for prediction abounds, a number of gaps still exist unresolved. First, there is limited evidence of studies that focus on the constituents of an effective message (Subramani et al., 2017). Second, empirical evaluations of features of an effective advocacy-related message remain unresolved. Thus far, this study extends the discourse of detection and classification with text-mining to the organizational communication domain while focusing on interest group organizational messaging.

5.3 Method

This study focuses on organizational posts of IGOs. Literature describes IGOs as organized membership groups that seek to influence policy and social phenomena (Kanol & Nat, 2017). They are classified into "cause" and "sectional" groups. Cause groups are nonmembership-based and focus primarily on issues broadly benefiting the larger society, whereas sectional groups are membership-based and focus on issues benefiting members only, e.g., worker unions and professional bodies (Kanol & Nat, 2017). Groups identified for the study were randomly identified from a list of active IGOs published in the Worldwide NGO directory (https://www.wango.org/resources.aspx?=Africa) (see extract in Table 5.1). The directory lists a total of 2340 NGOs in total. Out of this total number, 250 NGOs were randomly drawn from the list. The online presence of each identified group was checked by visiting the websites and subsequently their official Twitter pages through the link provided on the websites. This is in line with Kanol and Nat (2017) in order to determine the social media activeness of each group and also determine if it shared sufficient posts during the period identified for the data collection. A final sample comprising of 123 groups was selected out of the 250 initially identified IGOs. Only groups that had active Twitter pages and also shared posts in English were selected, thus resulting in the sample size of 123 selected groups.

Table 5.1 An extract of IGOs used in the study

IGO	Web address	Twitter page address
Africa Advocacy Foundation	https://www.africadvocacy.org/	https://twitter.com/africadvocacy
Urgent Action Fund	https://www.uaf-africa.org/	https://twitter.com/UAFAfrica/
Green African Youth Organization	https://greenafricayouth.com/	https://twitter.com/gayoghana
Green Peace	https://www.greenpeace.org/africa/en/	https://twitter.com/Greenpeaceafrica/
High Atlas Foundation	http://www.highatlasfoundation.org/	https://twitter.com/AtlasHigh/status/
Nelson Mandela Foundation	https://www.nelsonmandela.org/	https://twitter.com/NelsonMandela
The Samburu Project	https://thesamburuproject.org/	https://twitter.com/samburuproject
Somali Women Development Centre	http://www.swdcsom.org/	https://twitter.com/swdc_org
Tostan: Dignity for All	https://www.tostan.org/	https://twitter.com/tostan
Ubuntu Pathways	https://ubuntupathways.org/	https://twitter.com/UbuntuPathways
West African Aids Foundation	https://waafweb.org/	https://twitter.com/WAAFoundation
Gift of Hope	https://www.sheldrickwildlifetrust.org/	https://twitter.com/SheldrickTrust
Naankuse: Wildlife Conservation	https://naankuse.com/	https://twitter.com/Naankuse/en

5.3.1 Data

Twitter exists as a popular social media platform used by organizations globally as 75% of B2B businesses market their products and services on Twitter. It generates over 500 million tweets a day and has over 192 million daily users and 353.1 million monthly users, respectively (Twitter, 2021). Reports estimate 77% of IGOs have active Twitter accounts and attract thousands of followers (Guha, 2015). In all, 5,741 tweets were drawn for the dataset over a 2-month duration between August 1 and October 2, 2019. Tweets extracted did not center on a specific subject. The broad and unrestricted scope of messages drawn is to offer an unrestricted scope of writing for Twitter, in the IGO domain. Table 5.2 provides a sample of the original input data. The study employs Rapid Miner analytics software, and the Linguistic Inquiry and Word Count (LIWC, 2015) software were sequentially used. Linguistic features of the messages were extracted using the LIWC. The LIWC uses an empirically validated dictionary of about 4500-word terms, condensed into 80 categories (Pennebaker et al., 2015).

In line with Tausczick and Pennebaker (2010), the study creates a linguistic profile using the LIWC software to classify each tweet in terms of its linguistic (syntactic, pragmatic, and prosodic) usage. The LIWC analysis takes each tweet and

Table 5.2 Sample input data collected from interest groups

Text	Retweets	Comments
COTTON CRIMES - government forces people go to pick cotton. This letter confirms, public employees are forced to pick cotton, anyone who refuses loses their job	587	312
Next week is #AlcoholAwarenessWeek: how does alcohol affect your asthma? And does asthma change how you drink?	47	84
URGENT! Please sign and share… and help put an end to this terrible slavery trade	1123	631
Please don't forget to look out for the little guys tonight and always #CheckBonfires before lighting!	9	23
AAH Annual Conference, Call for Papers deadline 7 March. If you want to propose a paper do it this week! http://aah.org.uk/	105	9

analyzes it a word at a time. Where a word occurs, matching with the LIWC dictionary, it is credited to the appropriate category. The study captures the number of retweets and the number of comments on a post as engagement actions to determine message effectiveness. In line with Kumar et al. (2017), a dichotomous category of message effectiveness was determined (high and low effective messages). In that, a "high" effective message has retweets and number of comments greater than the average number of counts of total retweets and number of comments, and "low" effective messages have retweets and number of comments less than the average total number of retweets and comments, respectively.

Message characteristics drawn for the analysis were categorized into linguistic, pragmatic, and prosodic characteristics of messages (Subramani et al., 2017). Therefore, linguistic characteristics assessed for this analysis included the proportion of nouns (mentions), verbs per message, sentence length, pronouns per message, and words per sentence (Labrecque et al., 2020; Subramani et al., 2017). The pragmatic characteristics included the counts of hashtags (#), special characters (' ' and " "), and links or URLs present in the messages (Suhaimin et al., 2017; Desmet & Hoste, 2018). Lastly, the prosodic features in the messages consisted the message tone and the writing style (Burgers, 2010; Kumar et al. 2017). Kumar et al. (2017) evaluate message tone by determining whether it is written in a formal (official) or informal communicative language. A similar approach is adopted in this analysis.

5.3.2 Modeling and Preprocessing

Data preprocessing and subsequent text classifications were conducted in Rapid Miner. To begin with, the data was divided into training and testing sets for each process run: 80% to train the model (4593 messages) and 20% (1148 messages) for testing the model. In line with Williams and Gong (2014), the data was transformed into usable forms that are indicative of message effectiveness. Each transformed message was vectorized to make them suitable for use by the predictive algorithms.

The text preprocessing followed the guidelines of existing approach of Denny and Spirling (2017) and Miner et al. (2012). The messages were reduced into word units (tokenized), and all words were converted into lower cases (case transformation). "Stop-words" in the form of prepositions or articles were removed. Common English words like "but," "and," "so," etc. were removed at this stage. A text unification technique, lemmatization, was used to reduce inflected word forms into a common base (Manning et al., 2009). Then relative pruning is applied after lemmatization to reduce the challenge of interpreting word stems. For example, the word "organized" when stemmed would be "organ" while its lemma is "organize." Manning and Schultz (2003) and Weiss et al. (2010) suggest that relative pruning reduces the instances of reoccurrence of words in a document vocabulary. The process also applied the "generate n-grams terms feature" which creates term n-Grams of the tokens in the document. It describes a series of consecutive tokens for a certain length n. This analysis generated bigrams for the word tokens.

5.3.3 Classification Models

An initial classification process employed three classifiers (decision trees, KNN, and naïve Bayes) to classify each message into a dichotomous (high or low effective) category. Then, an ensemble model combined the three models to boost the accuracy of the initial predictions. A fivefold validation procedure is used for testing and training the data combinations in this analysis. The same number streams of random seeds were used for each predictive model to make it easy to compare the outputs of each classification.

- Decision trees—the term-frequency document matrix selects n- terms based on the weights generated for them with the TF-IDF formulation. The three weighting algorithms used are gain ratio, log odds ratio, and chi-square. Similar to Chang and Lin (2011).
- K-nearest neighbor (KNN)—similarly, three factors are used to weight the word document matrix. These include the collection frequency, term frequency, and the normalization factor. The cosine normalization and term frequency were used mainly for the weighting process. Similar to the parameters used in the decision tree model; the top n terms identified were selected and their values used as the inputs for the KNN model, instead of the popular known absence or presence of a term. The cosine similarity model employed compares messages to each other with a k ranging between 1 and 10.
- Naïve Bayes—this classification model employs similar weighting process used under the KNN algorithm. However, a latent semantic analysis, with the singular value decomposition (SVD), is employed for dimension reduction in this case.

5.4 Results

A summary of the model predictions is provided in Table 5.3. The results on the model accuracies, class precisions, and class recalls are shown in detail. Precision values determine the extent to which a classifier finds all members of the positive class, and the recall rate indicates the proportions of false-negative predictions. A high recall value implies that the classifier is permissive in its criteria for classifying objects as positive. From this analysis (shown in Table 5.3), the naïve Bayes algorithm showed the highest accuracy. It predicts "low" effective messages with a high precision rate of 98.28%. Then the KNN algorithm showed second highest model accuracy of 93.75% and highly predicted high effective messages at 98.04% precision rate. Thirdly, the decision tree algorithm showed the least precision rate of 59.86% and best predicts high effective messages of 72.73% precision.

A recall rate indicates the proportion of messages correctly predicted by each model from the testing set. Overall, the KNN algorithm showed the best recall for both category of messages, and it best classifies low effective messages. Next, the naïve Bayes algorithm performed second best with a high recall (97.37%) rate for high effective messages. The decision tree algorithm best predicted low effective messages with a class recall value of 99.18% but poorly predicts low effective messages. Overall low effective messages showed the most reliable classifications.

In order to optimize the initial classifications, we employed an ensemble model, incorporating the initial three classifiers. The ensemble model showed an optimized accuracy and precision, particularly for low effective messages. It revealed an overall accuracy level of 98.74% and with precision rate for low effective messages at 99.17% and 97.40% for high effective messages. The ensemble model like the individual models performed best at predicting low effective messages. Thus, it showed the higher recall rate of 98.77% for low effective messages compared with a 98.68% for high effective messages and also a higher precision (99.17%) for low effective messages. To add to the information presented in Table 5.3, the best prediction run from the ensemble model shown in Tables 5.4 and 5.5 also provides an extract of the actual messages classified from the best model run of the ensemble model output shown in Table 5.5.

To extract the characteristics of the predicted effective messages, the cluster of high effective messages determined by the best ensemble model run is retrieved and fed into the LIWC text analysis software. At this stage, the analysis extracts the syntactic, pragmatic, and prosodic characteristics as proportions and counts for

Table 5.3 Model predictions

Model	Accuracy	Precision		Class recall	
		High	Low	High	Low
Decision tree (DT)	59.86%	72.73%	59.51%	5.24%	99.18%
K-NN	93.75%	98.04%	91.25%	98.68%	98.77%
Naïve Bayes (NB)	97.19%	90.80%	98.28%	97.37%	94.24%
Ensemble model (numeric)	98.74%	97.40%	99.17%	98.68%	98.77%

Table 5.4 Confusion matrix for best ensemble model run

	Actual low effective	Actual high effective	Class precision
High effective	401	57	87.29%
Low effective	2	688	99.71%
Class recall	98.77%	98.68%	

Table 5.5 Sample message classifications from the best ensemble model run

	Low effective		High effective
131	this amazing footage shows our proud west #african #black crowned #crane parents keeping a close watch over their new chick!!	1271	tune in live to our facebook page at 7.45pm tonight, to ask bowel cancer survivor nicola any questions about her experience with cancer.
546	change of venue for the #wbtiuk2016 report launch. https://t.co/xydorhvglh	116	take a look at our game season advice here: http://bit.ly/2cerja6
741	#@@born free foundation is attending, and participating in the first public hearing of the #wildlife #justice commission# (wjc) at the #hague.#tune in: https://wildlifejustice.org/1512-2/	526	share the call to support nestle-free week with your networks #nestlefreeweek https://t.co/meje14rzvd https://t.co/v02sz6dbit
803	#loving animals? #or loving keeping them? #wild animals belong in the wild and deserve our #respect.	638	what is ulab? according to a new report – www.worstpolluted.org #lppw2019 #leadfreekids #factfriday
1071	#pressure mounts against #new zealand's #scion to stop their #ge trees: http://stopgetrees.org/new-zealand-forestry-research-wing-pressure-propagation-ge-trees/	728	the ivory market must shut down! please sign & share this petition today. visit: https://petition.parliament.uk/petitions/165905

further content analysis. A sample of this output from the text analysis in the LIWC software is presented in Table 5.6.

Analysis of the syntactic features of the classified high effective messages revealed the messages possess an average message length of 37.44 words per message and 13.5 words per sentence. By inference, effective organizational messages in this context show substantial brevity and relative conciseness to engender significant engagement actions such as high retweets or comments.

Further, special characters were prominently represented in these messages. Special characters such exclamations (!) and quotations (“ “) were most apparent. About 72% of the messages had one or more special characters, resulting in an average of 4.68 special characters per message. It also identified that these special characters were employed to emphasize words or phrases. Similar to Chung (2017), special characters such as “@” in social media messages emphasized a personality, thing, or place. This finding supports the current finding that effective messages use mechanisms like special characters to show emphasis or draw reader attention. In addition, the use of verbs in the messages was substantial, a suggestion that these messages were generally composed in active terms. Average verb per sentence was 5.26.

Table 5.6 Sample output/extractions from the LIWC analysis

WC	Analytic	Clout	Authentic	Tone	WPS	Sixltr	Dic	Function	Verbs	Pronoun	Style	ppron	Noun
70	99.00	71.61	13.15	52.57	23.33	30.00	72.86	35.71	2.86	2.86	0.00	1.43	1.43
28	93.26	99.00	52.86	87.20	14.00	28.57	85.71	39.29	10.71	10.71	0.00	10.71	0.00
1	93.26	50.00	1.00	25.77	1.00	100.00	0.00	0.00	0.00	0.00	0.00	0.00	0.00
17	68.29	99.00	89.63	25.77	7.00	14.29	100.00	2.86	14.29	14.29	0.00	0.00	14.29
39	98.87	86.68	4.97	99.00	9.00	22.22	88.89	3.33	11.11	0.00	0.00	0.00	0.00
76	62.04	99.00	1.00	99.00	6.00	33.33	83.33	50.00	16.67	16.67	0.00	0.00	16.67
7	68.29	99.00	89.63	25.77	7.00	42.86	71.43	42.86	14.29	14.29	0.00	14.29	0.00
14	5.89	76.25	52.86	1.00	14.00	21.43	100.00	42.86	7.14	0.00	0.00	0.00	0.00
6	99.00	95.20	23.51	1.00	6.00	0.00	83.33	16.67	0.00	0.00	0.00	0.00	0.00
10	1.00	99.00	3.37	25.77	3.33	0.00	90.00	60.00	30.00	20.00	0.00	10.00	10.00
36	66.17	99.00	8.57	99.00	14.33	24.42	81.40	48.84	16.28	12.79	0.00	6.98	5.81
59	64.55	99.00	5.20	99.00	12.71	16.85	80.90	42.70	17.98	12.36	0.00	5.62	4.49
38	82.31	99.00	4.59	52.99	15.33	17.39	81.88	43.48	13.04	11.59	1.45	2.17	2.90
42	99.00	98.33	1.06	25.77	21.00	16.67	71.43	35.71	7.14	7.14	0.00	4.76	2.38
21	99.00	68.29	68.01	25.77	10.50	19.05	66.67	23.81	0.00	0.00	0.00	0.00	0.00
28	83.81	63.97	13.15	25.77	14.00	35.71	78.57	39.29	10.71	3.57	0.00	0.00	3.57
40	98.58	97.69	7.84	96.76	20.00	45.00	90.00	30.00	5.00	5.00	0.00	5.00	0.00
14	83.81	92.33	13.15	99.00	4.67	7.14	85.71	35.71	7.14	0.00	0.00	0.00	0.00
41	93.26	99.00	1.00	99.00	13.67	26.83	78.05	41.46	7.32	7.32	0.00	2.44	4.88
46	47.75	99.00	16.76	66.89	9.20	19.57	76.09	45.65	13.04	13.04	0.00	4.35	8.70
27	96.08	93.07	33.94	88.52	27.00	25.93	59.26	25.93	7.41	7.41	0.00	3.70	0.00
22	96.54	81.84	61.34	25.77	11.00	13.64	68.18	36.36	4.55	4.55	0.00	0.00	4.55

Analysis of the pragmatic features reveals 49.27% of the messages also had in them a link to an external source, while 43.33% possessed hashtags to highlight an action. The messages averaged 1.09 and 3.25 links and hashtags per message, respectively. The highest number of hashtags in a single message was 9. Despite the relevance hashtags, this particular message was classified as a low effective message. By inference, many hashtags in a message do not necessarily increase its pliability to desirable engagement actions.

It also worth to note that links attached to the messages were to redirect users to access additional information, thus serving as a means for attaining message brevity. Perhaps platform requirements on Twitter also contribute to this observation. Thus, the effective messages generally mimicked the concept of brevity. In Chung (2017), breast cancer messages shared on breast cancer awareness day largely shared URLs to external sources which users are to access additional information.

The prosodic features examined revealed the messages (67%) possessed unofficial tones while written (58%) in direct-style forms. In the opinion of this study, effective organizational messages may also be designed with some informal language or content. Particularly, organizations like IGOs who seek to build relationships with followers or members require some element of informality in their organizational communication to eliminate excessive formality or forms of corporate relationship on their social media platforms to encourage interactivity from followers.

5.5 Discussion

Organizations like IGOs use Twitter to share information and build relationships with members and the general public. In this light, this study extends the works of some prior investigations (de Vries et al., 2012; Swani et al., 2017) to examine characteristics of effective organizational messages. By extending the discourse to cover organizational messaging, this study evaluates tweets of 123 IGOs using text-mining to determine what linguistic characteristics underlie such messages on Twitter.

The messages were dichotomously classified into high and low effective groups using an ensemble model, and a computerized content analysis using LIWC software extracted three main characteristics (syntactic, pragmatic, and prosodic) underlying high effective messages. Results showed a high sense of brevity in high effective messages. For example, these messages showed an average of 37.44 words per message and 13.5 words per sentence. Aside from the fact that the objective of brevity is consistent with Twitter's policy of limiting messages to a number of characters (Chung, 2017), this finding also projects that brevity in messages facilitates specificity in organizational communication. Twitter users are exposed to large amounts of messages daily from multiple networks and risk being driven into experiencing information fatigue (Choi et al., 2018). Thus, fatigue is characterized by abandonment and disengagement behavior. Therefore, concise and brief messages reduce the risk of information overload, thus facilitating desirable engagement actions with organizational message content.

Findings on the pragmatic features show characteristics such as links (URL) and hashtag use vary across the categories of effectiveness. For example, the use of links may appear to facilitate sharing of large information yet achieving brevity, whereas hashtag use was largely consistent with low effective messages. Perhaps organizations use the links to redirect users to specific sites including their websites and other social media platforms. Thus, in our opinion, the use of links could be purposely used to drive desirable engagement actions such as likes and comments from users on their main websites. Prosodic features as informal tone were largely associated with high effective messages. Perhaps this could be how organizations can build stronger relationships and online communities for their brand. Scholars like Guo and Saxton (2014) and Kanol and Nat (2017) describe this type of messages as "community-type" messages. Thus, they facilitate the building of a community replicating the offline environment of social interactions online. Hence, the incorporation of this concept into organizational messages may increase the likelihood of desirable interactions with organizational messages.

Practically, the study offers useful guidelines for creating organizational messages for IGO members on Twitter. This is likely to increase desired engagement actions. For instance, if an IGO wishes to increase cognitive interactivity online, i.e., to generate more comments on organizational posts, message length should be less than 45 words, and informal language with direct writing style is likely to make a message appealing. Further, the inclusion of links in organizational post on Twitter should be encouraged. However, these links should redirect followers to organizational websites or other social media pages to facilitate engagement actions for the organization irrespective of the platform. Lastly, effective organizational messages on Twitter should possess a moderate number of hashtags and special characters to emphasize important words or phrases and not to emphasize the entire message.
Conclusion

The study analyzes shared posts of selected IGOs in Africa. It classifies the posts into high and low effective messages using an ensemble model of decision tree, KNN, and naïve Bayes classifiers and analyzes the syntactic, pragmatic, and prosodic features underlying high effective messages. Largely, IGOs focus on building strong relationships and constituency online to facilitate collective action. Because most IGOs face the challenge of collective action (Kanol & Nat, 2017), the need to design and create effective messages for social media for effective engagement is a means of creating value with digital technology for communication and brand development. Limitations and Future Research

Like all inquiries, this study has some limitations that should be addressed in future research. The first limitation of this study is the use of cause interest groups on Twitter for this analysis. Given the categorization of IGOs, other types of IGOs like "sectional groups" communicate and pursue different objectives. Further, interest organizations also engage audiences on other social media platforms like Facebook and Instagram, among others. Thus, the consideration of only cause interest groups on the Twitter platform alone may be quite limiting. This notwithstanding, prior researches also establish that interest groups, although employing different or specialized social media platforms, also find Twitter as a famous channel (Van der Graaf et al., 2016). In essence, analyzing IGO messages on Twitter alone may not be as problematic as initially considered.

Though studying effectiveness of organizational messages of IGOs alone can reveal valuable insights, it will not only be interesting but necessary if all features of effective message contents such images and videos can be included in future analysis. Finally, future studies can also expand the scope to include low effective messages as well as the volume of data used for this current study to provide an even deeper insight on the phenomenon of effective organizational communication on Twitter.

Conflict of Interest Statement The authors of this chapter collectively declare they have no conflict of interest whatsoever regarding this research work.

References

Al-garadi, M. A., Khan, M. S., Varathan, D. K., Mujtaba, G., & Al-Kabsi, A. M. (2016). Using online social networks to track a pandemic: A systematic review. *Journal of Biomedical Informatics, 62*(4), 1–11.

Andalibi, N., Haimson, O. L., De Choudhury, M., & Forte, A. (2016). *Understanding social media disclosures of sexual abuse through the lenses of support seeking and anonymity*. In Proceedings of the 2016 CHI Conference on Human Factors in Computing Systems. ACM, pp. 3906–3918.

Balani, S., & De Choudhury, M. (2015). *Detecting and characterizing mental health related self-disclosure in social media*. In Proceedings of the 33rd Annual ACM Conference Extended Abstracts on Human Factors in Computing Systems. ACM, pp. 1373–1378.

Binderkrantz, A. S. (2012). Interest groups in the media: Bias and diversity over time. *European Journal of Political Research, 51*(4), 117–139. https://doi.org/10.1111/ejpr.2012.51.issue-1

Burgers, C. F. (2010). Verbal irony: Use and effects in written discourse. [Sl: sn].

Chalmers, A. W., & Shotton, P. A. (2016). Changing the face of advocacy? Explaining interest organizations' use of social media strategies. *Political Communication, 33*(3), 374–391. https://doi.org/10.1080/10584609.2015.1043477

Choi, H., Park, J., & Jung, Y. (2018). The role of privacy fatigue in online privacy behavior. *Computers in Human Behavior, 81*, 42–51. https://doi.org/10.1016/j.chb.2017.12.001

Conrad, C., & Sollitto, M. (2017). History of Organizational Communication. The International Encyclopedia of Organizational Communication, (1–32).

Chung, J. E. (2017). Retweeting in health promotion: Analysis of tweets about Breast Cancer Awareness Month. 74, 112–119. Computers and Human Behaviour. http://dx.doi.org/10.1016/j.chb.2017.04.025

Darren G. L., & Koc-Michalska, K. (2017). What Drives Political Participation? Motivations and Mobilization in a Digital Age, *Political Communication, 34*(1), 21–43, https://doi.org/10.1080/10584609.2016.1225235

Desmet, B., & Hoste, V. (2018). Online suicide prevention through optimized text classification. *Information Sciences, 4*(3), 61–78.

De Vries, L., Gensler, S., & Leeflang, P. S. H. (2012). Popularity of brand posts on brand fan pages: An investigation of the effects of social media marketing. *Journal of Interactive Marketing, 26*, 83– 91.

Denny, M. J., & Spirling, A. (2017). Text Preprocessing For Unsupervised Learning: Why It Matters, When It Misleads, And What To Do About It. SSRN Electronic Journal.

Edwards, H. R., & Hoefer, R. (2010). Are social work advocacy groups using Web 2.0 effectively? *Journal of Policy Practice, 9*(4), 220–239. https://doi.org/10.1080/15588742.2010.489037

Eyal, H. (2016). Digital fit as a leg-up for nongovernmental organizations' media and political Success. *Political communication, 33*(1), 118–135. https://doi.org/10.1080/15588742.2010.489037

Goodrich, K. (2011). Anarchy of effects? Exploring attention to online advertising and multiple outcomes. *Psychology and Marketing, 28*, 417– 440.

Guha, I. (2015). *How do the world's top 100 brands use Facebook?* Retrieved from http://dazeinfo.com/2015/01/03/world-top-100brands-facebook-usage-q3-2014/

Guo, C., & Saxton, G. D. (2014). "Tweeting social change: How social media are changing Nonprofit advocacy", *Nonprofit and Voluntary Sector Quarterly, 43*(1), 57–79.

Joo, S., & Cahill, M. (2019). "The relationships between library resources and children's use of public libraries: an exploratory analysis of IMLS public library statistics data", *Journal of Librarianship and Information Science, 51*(2), 307–316.

Joo, S., Lu, K., & Lee, K. (2020). Analysis of content topics, user engagement and library factors in public library social media based on text mining, *Emerald publishing, 44*(1), 258–277.

Kanol, D., & Nat, M. (2017). Interest groups and social media: An examination of cause and sectional group's social media strategies in the EU. J of Public Affairs. 17: e1649. 9

Kumar, V., Choi, J. W. B., & Greene, M. (2017). Synergistic effects of social media and traditional marketing on brand sales: Capturing the time-varying effects. *Journal of the Academy of Marketing Science, 33*, 524– 541.

Labrecque, L. I., Zanjani, S. H. A., & Milne, G. R. (2012). Authenticity in online communications: Examining antecedents and consequences. In A. G. Close (Ed.), Online consumer behavior: Theory and research in social media, advertising, and e-tail (pp. 133–156). New York, NY: Routledge.

Labrecque, L. I., Swani, K., & Stephen, A. T. (2020). The impact of pronoun choices on consumer engagement actions: Exploring top global brands' social media communications. *Psychol Mark.*, 1–19. https://doi.org/10.1002/mar.21341

Lavidge, R. J., & Steiner, G. A. (1961). A model for predictive measurements of advertising effectiveness. *Journal of Marketing, 25*, 59– 62.

Liu, B. (2015). *Sentiment analysis: Mining opinions, sentiments, and emotions*. Cambridge University Press.

Lutz, R. (1981). A reconceptualization of the functional approach to attitudes. *Research in Marketing, 5*, 165– 210.

Maloney, W. (2009). Interest groups and their vitalization of democracy: Are we expecting too much? *Representation, 45*(3), 277–287. https://doi.org/10.1080/00344890903129541

Manning, C. D., & Schütze, H. (2003). Foundations of statistical natural language processing (6. print with corr.). Cambridge, MA: MIT Press.

Miner, G., Elder, J., Hill, T., & Delen, D. (2012). *Fast, practical text mining and statistical analysis for non-structured text data applications*. Academic.

Nazneen F. R., & Raymond J. M. (2017). Stacking With Auxiliary Features. In Proceedings of the 26th International Joint Conference on Artificial Intelligence (IJCAI-17), pp. 2634–2640, Melbourne, Australia.

Nguyen, T., Duong, T., Venkatesh, S., & Phung, D. (2015). Autism blogs: Expressed emotion, language styles and concerns in personal and community settings. *IEEE Transactions on Affective Computing, 6*(3), 312–323.

Nguyen, T. O., Dea, B., Larsen, M., Phung, D., Venkatesh, S., & Christensen, H. (2017). Using linguistic and topic analysis to classify sub-groups of online depression communities. *Multimedia Tools and Applications, 76*(8), 10653–10676.

Obar, J. A., Zube, P., & Lampe, C. (2012). Advocacy 2.0: An analysis of how advocacy groups in the United States perceive and use social media as tools for facilitating civic engagement and collective action. *Journal of Information Policy, 2*(2), 1–25. https://doi.org/10.5325/jinfopoli.2.2012.0001

Pankajdeep, K. N. V. (2015). An ontology based text analytics on social media. *International Journal of Database Theory and Application, 8*(5), 45–78.

Paul, M. J., & Dredze, M. (2014). Discovering health topics in social media using topic models. *PloSone, 9*(8), 10–34.

Pennebaker, J. W., Boyd, R. L., Jordan, K., & Blackburn, K. (2015). *The development and psychometric properties of LIWC2015*. University of Texas at Austin.

Pentina, I., & Tarafdar, M. (2014). From "information" to "knowing": Exploring the role of social media in contemporary news consumption. *Computers in Human Behavior, 35*, 211– 223.

Rossiter, J. R., & Percy, L. (2017). Methodological guidelines for advertising research. *Journal of Advertising, 46*, 71– 82.

Schreiner, M., Fischer, T., & Riedl, R. (2019). "Impact of content characteristics and emotion on behavioral engagement in social media: literature review and research agenda", Electronic Commerce Research, pp. 1–17.

Schultz, F., Utz, S., & Göritz, A. (2011). Is the medium the message? Perceptions of and reactions to crisis communication via Twitter, blogs and traditional media. *Public Relations Review, 37*(1), 20–27. https://doi.org/10.1016/j.pubrev.2010.12.001

Smith, R. E., Chen, J., & Yang, X. (2008). The impact of advertising creativity on the hierarchy-of-effects. *Journal of Advertising, 37*, 47– 61.

Smith, M. C. (2012). The interaction of social media and the law and how to survive the social media revolution. *New Hampshire Bar Journal, 52*, 24–39.

Solomon, M. R., Bamossy, G., Askegaard, S., & Hogg, M. K. (2016). Consumer Behavior: A European Perspective (6th ed.). Edinburgh: Pearson.

Subramani, S., Quan, H. V., & Wang, H. (2017). *Intent classification using feature sets for domestic violence discourse on social media*. 4th Asia-Pacific World Congress on Computer Science and Engineering.

Suhaimin, M. S. (2017). Natural Language Processing Based Features for Sarcasm Detection: An Investigation Using Bilingual Social Media Texts. Proceeding of the 8th International Conference on Information Technology, Amman, Jordan

Szmigin, I., & Piacentini, M. (2015). Consumer behavior. Oxford: Oxford University Press

Swani, K., Milne, G. R., Brown, B. P., Assaf, G. A., & Donthu, N. (2017). What messages to post? Evaluating the popularity of social media communications in business versus consumer markets. *Industrial Marketing Management, 62*, 77–87.

Tausczik, Y. R., & Pennebaker, J. W. (2010). The psychological meaning of words: LIWC and computerized text analysis methods. *Journal of Language and Social Psychology, 29*(1), 24–54.

Vu, H. Q., Li, G., Law, R., & Zhang, Y. (2017). Travel diaries analysis by sequential rule mining. *Journal of Travel Research, 4*(2), 39–51.

Wang, H., Zhang, Z., & Taleb, T. (2017). Special issue on security and privacy of IOT. *World Wide Web*, 1–6.

Weiss, S. M., Indurkhya, N., & Zhang, T. (2010). *Fundamentals of predictive text mining*. Springer Verlag.

Zhang, J., & Mao, E. (2016). From online motivations to Ad clicks and to behavioral intentions: An empirical study of consumer response to social media advertising. *Psychology and Marketing, 33*, 155–164.

Ziegele, M., Breiner, T. & Quiring, O. (2014). What Creates Interactivity in Online News Discussions? An Exploratory Analysis of Discussion Factors in User Comments on News Items. Journal of Communication. https://doi.org/10.1111/jcom.12123

Divine Q. Agozie is an Assistant Lecturer in the Operations and Management Information Systems Department at the University of Ghana Business School and a final-year PhD student in Information Systems at the Cyprus International University. Agozie's research interest concentrates on natural language processing (text-mining), online privacy, and sustainable development. He has authored some scholarly articles on privacy fatigue and online engagement on social media. He also has some publications coming up on applications of text-mining approaches to data from the advocacy domain for organizational communication.

Muesser C. Nat is an Associate Professor and the Director of the School of Applied Sciences in Cyprus International University. She is also the Head of Department and a Faculty at the Department of Management Information Systems at the Cyprus International University. She has conducted research in the areas of social media technology for student engagement, social media engagement, and message classification. She also has several publications in the field of educational technology and learning from different domains.

Sampson A. Edu is a final-year Doctoral Candidate in Management Information Systems at Cyprus International University in Lefkosa, North Cyprus. He has a background in big data, cloud, and IOT systems security. His research interest is consistent with his knowledge background. He is also an adjunct faculty with the Department of Management Information Systems at Cyprus International University.

Kobina A. Benson is a PhD student in management information systems with the School of Applied Sciences at the Cyprus International University. His research interest is in data mining and predictive analysis. He is currently working on his thesis on a research on educational data mining to predict student performance in deprived African communities.

Oseyenbhin S. Osemeahon holds a Doctorate Degree in Management Information Systems which he attained in 2020. His research interest is in social media engagement and brand communication. Osemeahon has publications in this area and contributes mainly to fashion brand platform interactivity and organizational communication on social media.

Chapter 6
Dealing with the Unexpected: Exploring the Unintended Negative Consequences of Digitalisation in Africa's Healthcare Industry

Mansah Preko, Patrick Shabaya, and Samuel Anim-Yeboah

Abstract Unintended consequences of digitalisation are usually outcomes that are not anticipated during the planning, development, implementation, and use of digital technologies within social contexts. These consequences are generally observed as either positive or negative, desirable or undesirable. In the healthcare industry, for example, such observations abound due to the increasing number of digitalisation initiatives that are continually being executed in most healthcare settings. While the information systems (IS) healthcare literature unanimously documents and advocates the desirable outcomes of digitalisation, very little theoretical and practical insights exist concerning the unintended and rather negative consequences of digitalisation in the healthcare industry. This chapter, therefore, employs the updated DeLone and McLean IS success model to explore such unintended negative consequences of healthcare digitalisation in the African context by answering the following research questions: (1) What are the distinguishing unintended negative consequences of healthcare digitalisation in the African context? (2) How do we deal with such unexpected and undesirable outcomes with negative impacts? The theoretical and practical insights introduced in this study regarding the unintended negative consequences of digitalisation and how they could be alleviated in Africa's healthcare industry spell out the contribution of this chapter.

Keywords Healthcare · Unintended consequences · Africa · eHealth · Ghana · Kenya

---

M. Preko (✉) · S. Anim-Yeboah
University of Ghana Business School, Accra, Ghana
e-mail: mpreko@st.ug.edu.gh; ssanim-yeboah@st.ug.edu.gh

P. Shabaya
School of Computing and Engineering Sciences, Strathmore University, Nairobi, Kenya
e-mail: pshabaya@strathmore.edu

R. Boateng et al. (eds.), *Digital Innovations, Business and Society in Africa*,
Advances in Theory and Practice of Emerging Markets,
https://doi.org/10.1007/978-3-030-77987-0_6

6.1 Introduction

Intended and unintended consequences of digitalisation are outcomes that are usually interpreted and understood in several subjective ways by heterogeneous users of information systems (IS) (Luciano et al., 2020). Both consequences generally trigger various natural reactions from these users, some of which are documented and further explored. In the context of IS research, for instance, several studies on healthcare (e.g. Kumar & Mostapha, 2020; Gann 2019; Pluye et al., 2019; Gabre-Mariam & Bygstad, 2019; etc.) have explored and discussed a plethora of intended consequences of digitalisation in the health sector through empirical studies. Some of these include the reduction of cumbersome documentation and paperwork in healthcare settings, increase in the efficiency and quality of data aggregation and data analysis routines to support decision-making (Gabre-Mariam & Bygstad, 2019), collection and use of data for achieving better health statuses both at the patient and public health levels (Kumar & Mostapha, 2020), and opportunities and consolidation of the patient empowerment concept which has proven positive health outcomes (Gann 2019; Pluye et al., 2019), among others.

Intended consequences, in principle, are those desirable outcomes that are carefully assessed to have high positive impacts on an organisation and its stakeholders before corresponding investments are made (Mosadeghrad, 2014). Currently, the concept of 'digitalisation', i.e. the development and implementation of information and communication technologies (ICTs) and its concomitant organisational changes (Gabre-Mariam & Bygstad, 2019), has been one of the hugely invested and growing initiatives for most organisations with proven ability to produce, mostly, intended positive outcomes. As earlier noted, the healthcare industry has not been an exception to this global phenomenon because the permeation of digitalisation in the medical field was largely driven by its potential, as well as the associated positive health outcomes. However, while extant literature has widely advocated and documented these benefits, very little theoretical and practical insights exist concerning the unintended negative consequences of these initiatives in the health sector. Unintended consequences, of digitalisation, are those outcomes that were not anticipated during the planning, development, implementation, and use of digital technologies and are generally observed to be either positive or negative – desirable or undesirable (Zheng et al., 2016).

In this study, we underscore the rather unintended negative consequences of digitalisation in the healthcare industry, with particular emphasis on the African context. This emphasis is justified on four fronts. First, the increasing unintended negative consequences are seen to have a direct relationship with technology adoption (Coiera et al., 2016). Therefore, exploring these negative consequences within the African context, taking cognisance of their peculiar circumstances, may present an understanding of the causalities and subsequently contribute to the technology adoption discourse in Africa's health sector. Second, the complex and dynamic nature of healthcare settings requires robust pre-emptive mechanisms that can forestall the adverse outcomes of digitalisation, especially in regions where medical resources are known to be limited (World Economic Forum, 2019). Third, studies have revealed that some unintended negative consequences of digitalisation have had error-producing effects on patients and, in worst cases, harmed them (Coiera et al., 2016). Since the health sector cannot be likened to the manufacturing or banking sectors, in terms of the critical nature of the human life, exploring such negative outcomes from an arguably vulnerable population, and subsequently suggesting ways to surmount them, contributes to both literature and practice in Africa's healthcare industry. Finally, while we do acknowledge that some earlier studies (e.g. Luciano et al., 2020; Gogia et al., 2016; Thomas & Bond, 2014; etc.) have explored the unintended negative consequences of digitalisation in the health sector of other developed countries, much of these studies have not been conducted from the African context. This study, therefore, attempts to fill this gap by adopting the updated Delone and McLean IS success model (2016) as its theoretical lens to answer the following research questions: (1) What are the distinguishing unintended negative consequences of healthcare digitalisation in the African context? (2) How do we deal with such unexpected and undesirable outcomes with negative impacts? The theoretical and practical insights introduced in this study spell out the contribution of this chapter.

The rest of the chapter is structured as follows: Section 6.2 presents brief perspectives of digitalisation in Africa's healthcare industry. Section 6.3 discusses the theoretical underpinning of the chapter. Section 6.4 presents the methodologies adopted in this study. Section 6.5 presents the case descriptions and discussions of the chapter. Section 6.6 presents the implications of the study, as well as the conclusion and recommendations for future studies.

6.2 Perspectives of Digitalisation in Africa's Healthcare Industry

The African continent is one that is better positioned to benefit from the emerging digital revolution in healthcare. This is because information technologies have proven to be a catalyst in tackling the rising burden of diseases and other major obstacles in its infrastructure and environments (World Economic Forum, 2019). According to the World Economic Forum (2019), digitalisation in Africa's healthcare industry holds the potential to bridge the gaps in healthcare provision by directing limited medical resources to these regions where they are needed the most. Similarly, the perspectives of the World Health Organisation (WHO) also suggest that the same principles underpin the Organisation's objective of leveraging the opportunities of digitalisation to deliver the Sustainable Development Goals (SDGs) and achieving the Universal Health Coverage (UHC) (WHO, 2019). These initiatives by the WHO, for instance, are intended to be universal and applicable to all continents, including Africa. Hence, a comprehensive understanding of the consequences of using these technologies in providing healthcare is a good starting point for realising the potential of digitalisation in Africa's healthcare industry. The argument comes at the back of studies (Luciano et al., 2020; Coiera et al., 2016) that have established that the adoption of IT-based solutions in both organisational and social contexts generally brings consequences (i.e. intended and unintended), and Africa's healthcare industry is no exception.

In view of the foregoing, a number of studies have explored several perspectives on digitalisation in various health sectors within Africa that invariably reveal the impact of digitalisation in these regions. Preko and Boateng (2020), for example, reported how digitalisation has helped to curb certain pressing issues in some healthcare facilities in the Ghanaian context. Notable among them included the standardisation and streamlining of work practices as mandatory replacements of the traditional paper-based systems while tackling the issues of financial malfeasance, missing folders, and storage systems, among others. Other studies, (Tambo et al., 2016; Olu et al., 2019) also outlined the implications of digital health in Africa's health systems and how digitalisation has been successfully applied to prevent some non-communicable diseases such as cancer and promote maternal and child health, immunisation, HIV/AIDS management, essential medicines, and other medical product supply chain management. From an economic perspective, Preko et al. (2019a) shared insights on how digitalisation of the health sector of developing countries, which included several cited African countries, could help in mitigating the menace of brain drain in the medical field.

Practically, there have been reports about some African countries that have implemented digital technologies as key elements of their clinics, as well as the creation of digital patients. Olu et al.'s study in 2019 gave an account of the practicality and applicability of these digital health technologies in certain African countries. It included, among others, the use of computer-aided detection of tuberculosis by chest X-ray in Gambia, South Africa, and Zambia. In Tanzania, digital ultrasound (using mHealth/telemedicine) solutions are being utilised for similar purposes. Countries including Kenya, Tanzania, and Ghana were also reported to have adopted rapid diagnostic tests (RDT) that are integrated into cloud-based mHealth smart reader systems, while Uganda and Malawi were reported to be utilising smartphone-powered, cloud-enabled portable electrocardiograph (ECG) in healthcare provision. More recently, the use of drones to deliver blood supplies has been successfully piloted in Ghana (Preko et al., 2020) and Rwanda (Olu et al., 2019). Interestingly, most of these countries mentioned herein were part of the early adopters of digital health in Africa. These include Malawi which developed and adopted eHealth strategy in 2003, Cabo Verde in 2007, Ghana in 2010, and Kenya in 2011; after which several other countries on the continent began to adopt the concept of digital health as a strategy to improve health service delivery (Olu et al., 2019).

Despite the above promising potential of digitalisation in Africa's healthcare industry, there have been several reports about the challenges that confront the implementation of these technologies in various African contexts. These challenges are deemed multifaceted from the aggregation of perspectives of several authors who have explored the phenomena from technological, behavioural, governmental, regulatory, legal, and social perspectives. For example, Preko et al. (2020)

catalogued a myriad of challenges that confront healthcare digitalisation in the Ghanaian and Nigerian contexts. These included infrastructural challenges such as network connectivity issues and electricity instability, the complexity of systems, funding, human resource constraints, and user acceptance of technology, among others. Similarly, Olu et al. (2019) noted how the implementation of digital health in Africa has mostly been slow due to the lack of requisite governance framework, institutional capacity, and funding. The authors further noted the lack of adequate legal framework and capacity for addressing ethical issues such as digital health data ownership, consent to use, and availability and security as bottlenecks for the successful implementation of digitalisation in Africa's healthcare industry. Other reported challenges worth mentioning include the complexity and interrelationship between context and action that usually underlie the digitalisation process, thereby creating huge infrastructural gaps and limited consideration for operational and cultural needs for scalability (Gabre-Mariam & Bygstad, 2019).

6.3 Theoretical Foundation: The IS Success Model

The success or failure of an information systems can be largely determined or assessed by a number of factors but, most importantly, by the type of outcomes it produces. While such assessments can be highly subjective, some IS studies (DeLone & McLean, 1992, 2003, 2016) have developed models to guide both researchers and practitioners in evaluating information systems. The original DeLone and McLean IS success model (1992) and the updated DeLone and McLean IS success model (2003), for instance, have been very useful over the years for measuring and understanding the categories of IS success. These categories were originally assessed through 'individual impact' and 'organisational impact' (DeLone & McLean, 1992) and, subsequently, through the 'net benefits' (DeLone & McLean, 2003). However, a careful review of this endpoint assessment of success naturally implied that outcomes were expected to be only positives since the word 'benefit' has an affirmative connotation. Thus, the term 'net impacts' was used in DeLone and McLean (2016) to recognise the possibility of having both positive and negative outcomes in an IS implementation.

Theoretically, the DeLone and McLean IS success model has been applied in several studies to examine the success of different information systems. Studies, including Yakubu and Dasuki (2018) and Jaafreh (2017), for instance, have applied the IS success model to assess the successes of eLearning and banking systems, respectively. In the context of healthcare, Ali et al. (2017) adopted this model to develop a knowledge management system success model for healthcare organisations. Al-Fadhli et al. (2017) similarly applied the IS success model to determine health professionals' intention to use telehealth. Additionally, authors, including Jeyaraj (2020), have through literature reviews catalogued a number of studies that have found the applicability of the IS success model useful in assessing the success of various systems. These include enterprise systems, expert systems, and online shopping and e-commerce systems, among others. Despite the theory's wide applicability in IS studies, no study has arguably applied it directly to explore the unintended negative outcomes of an IS implementation in the context of healthcare. This study, therefore, fills the theoretical gap by employing the modified version of the updated DeLone and McLean (2003) model (Fig. 6.1) to explore the negative outcomes of IS implementations in Africa's healthcare industry.

The variables used in the adopted model (Fig. 6.1) are described in DeLone and McLean (2016) as follows:

- System quality looks at the desirable characteristics of an IS. This includes the ease of use, system flexibility, system reliability, ease of learning, and also the features of intuitiveness, sophistication, flexibility, and response times.
- Information quality focuses on the desirable characteristics of the system outputs, i.e. management reports and web pages, for instance, relevance, accuracy, understandability, completeness, conciseness, timely, usability, and currency.
- Service quality is the quality of support that system users receive from the IS organisation, as well as IT support personnel. Service quality includes accuracy, responsiveness, reliability, technical competence, and empathy of the IT support staff.
- System use looks at the degree and manner in which employees and customers utilise the capabilities of an IS. This includes, for instance, the amount of use, frequency of use, nature of use, appropriateness of use, extent of use, and purpose of use.
- User satisfaction looks at users' level of satisfaction with reports, websites, and support services.
- Net impact focuses on the extent to which an IS contributes (or does not contribute) to the success of individuals, groups, organisation, industries, and nations. These are assessed by, for example, improved decision-making, improved profits, market efficiency, consumer welfare, and economic development, among

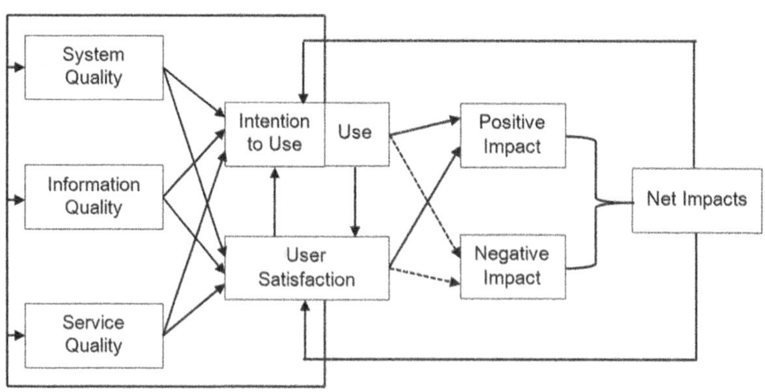

Fig. 6.1 Updated DeLone and McLean 2003 IS success model (modified). (Source DeLone & McLean (2016))

others. Hence, these net impacts can be either positive or negative, depending on the type of outcome, i.e. beneficial or detrimental.

In this conceptualisation, it is posited that after the net impact is realised, i.e. positively or negatively, there are feedback loops to 'user satisfaction' and to 'use', causing a new iteration of more (or less) 'use' and greater (or lesser) 'user satisfaction' depending on whether the impact is negative or positive (DeLone & McLean, 2016). However, our focus in this chapter is limited to the exploration of those negative outcomes that could consequently lead to lesser user satisfaction and use of digital technologies in healthcare settings. This is necessary because, as we earlier indicated, some authors (e.g. Coeira et al., 2016) have noted the relationship between such negative unintended outcomes and technology adoption in the health sector, of which the African context is no exception.

6.4 Methodology

6.4.1 Research Approach

This study adopted an exploratory research approach, using a qualitative research design. The approach was considered most appropriate in the current study because it has the natural propensity to provide richer, deeper, and more nuanced insights and understanding of a phenomenon being studied and usually leads to the answering of many overarching research questions in the phenomenon (Mapesa, 2016). Also, qualitative studies of this nature provide flexible and contextual interpretations of specific social phenomena that relate to the experiences and perspectives of a population regarding the phenomena under study (Warren, 2017). The study also makes a strong case for adopting a multiple case study approach in exploring the phenomenon under study. This choice was justified to the extent that case studies allow the researcher to observe participants, collect data in the participants' words or language through interviews, and analyse data from verbal responses, which also enhances the contextual meaning in the process of exploring the phenomenon (Yilmaz, 2013). Moreover, the multiple sources of data in multiple case study research generally enhance the trustworthiness of qualitative studies (Yin, 2014).

6.4.2 Research Context

The qualitative multiple case study was conducted from four selected healthcare facilities from the Ghanaian and Kenyan contexts. These included two facilities each from both contexts. The selection of these facilities was typically based on the extent of digitalisation (i.e. fully digitised facilities) and the length of time the facilities had been digitised. The subsections below present brief descriptions of the respective contexts of this study:

The Ghanaian Healthcare Industry Ghana is a developing country within the West African subregion, with a middle-income status and constitutional democracy (Alagidede & Ibrahim, 2017). The country has an estimated population of about 27.41 million people (Gyamfi et al., 2017). Through a national digitisation agenda of the Government of Ghana in recent years, the country has made tremendous leaps in digitising most of its sectors across the economy. The healthcare industry in Ghana has been one of the key beneficiaries of the ongoing national digitisation agenda. This is observed in how Ghana has consistently developed routine health information systems (HIS) in both government and district hospitals for collecting routine health information (Asare et al., 2017; Preko et al., 2020). Additionally, the country has progressively redesigned its healthcare systems to include ICTs and its applications to improve healthcare delivery and facilitate the quality of care for its citizens. Following these initiatives, studies, including Preko et al. (2019b) and Preko and Boateng (2020), identified some factors that are giving traction to the Ghanaian healthcare industry as far as digitalisation is concerned. These included, firstly, the introduction of electronic payment systems through visa platforms and the use of mobile money wallets and transfers at various healthcare facilities. Secondly, the collaborations between different state institutions such as the telecommunication, banking, and healthcare institutions that have enabled the seamless transfer of funds between these institutions were noted as providing a foundation for digitalisation in the health sector. Thirdly, the proliferation of smartphones and other mobile and digital devices that support data and information sharing across various healthcare platforms was seen to support digitalisation in Ghana's health sector. In more recent developments, Preko et al. (2020) identified the piloting of drones for delivering blood supplies in the Ghanaian healthcare industry. This innovation was championed by the Government of Ghana as part of its agenda to reduce mortality and morbidity rates of citizens across the entire country.

As with most African countries, however, the implementation of the aforementioned initiatives in the Ghanaian health sector has not been free from challenges. Preko et al., 2020, for example, revealed how the non-existence of policy guidelines for HIS implementations and data sharing between hospitals has affected some digitalisation initiatives in the Ghanaian health sector. Other studies (Asare et al., 2017) have also revealed the lack of regulatory bodies to monitor eHealth applications in Ghana, as well as the lack of skilled ICT personnel with the ability to deliver large-scale eHealth projects, as the major underlying factor that inhibits digitalisation in Ghana's health sector. From the legislative perspective, Gyamfi et al. (2017) noted how privacy laws have become bottlenecks for healthcare facilities that wish to exchange information beyond organisational boundaries in Ghana. In their empirical study, the authors revealed how a hospital expanded beyond its borders and required parliamentary approval before data sharing across its platforms could be approved and legalised for its operations. Unfortunately, these legislative issues became a major challenge for the facility because there were no clear guidelines for sharing electronic data in the health sector of Ghana.

The Kenyan Healthcare Industry Kenya is situated in the eastern part of Africa and covers approximately 580,360 KM2. In the year 2019, Kenya recorded a population of 47,560,000 people living in 47 administrative counties (KNBS Census, 2019), served by approximately 12,300 healthcare facilities. As part of Kenya's efforts to digitise its economy, successive governments have been committed to the automation and modernisation of its health sector. In 2009, for instance, the 'OpenClinica' (OC) community edition project, an open-source software system, was installed in conjunction with the Kenya Medical Research Institute (KEMRI-Wellcome Trust Research Programme – KWTRP) to support clinical trials and data management at KEMRI (Ngari et al., 2014). In 2010, the government launched a countrywide open-source web-based District Health Information Software (DHIS-2) project for capturing, analysing, sharing, and reporting healthcare information (Karuri et al., 2014). In 2011, a committee was commissioned by the government to review 17 electronic medical records (EMRs) systems against standards and selected those (i.e. OpenMRS, AMPATH, IQ Care, and C-PAD) that government hospitals could implement after further evaluation to support HIV patient care (Kenya's EMRs review towards standardisation, 2011). Again, the national eHealth strategy was also developed and launched in 2011 to accelerate the implementation of eHealth systems in Kenya (Njoroge et al., 2017). In 2014, the Afya Electronic Health Management System was launched to improve healthcare delivery at the county level (Muinga et al., 2018). Other successful projects, including the KenyaEMR (open medical record) system and the International Quality Care (IQCare) system, were further implemented by the Kenyan government across the various counties in Kenya. Currently, with more than 98% of mobile phone uptake and penetration in Kenya, the concept of mobile health (mHealth) is also gaining popularity in the health sector and presenting great potential for revolutionising the healthcare industry in Kenya (Salte, 2014). This has consequently impacted the proliferation of mobile money payments as an effective payment system for healthcare services in the country (Salte, 2014). Interestingly, the foregoing developments are not observed in the public sector alone, as several private facilities are also implementing various eHealth systems to improve the quality of healthcare while reducing costs to stay competitive in the industry.

Although Kenya's healthcare industry presents promising opportunities for digitalisation, the country is also confronted with some surmountable challenges, most of which have been reported by other African countries. For instance, Njoroge et al. (2017) reported that the implementation of eHealth systems in Kenya's public sector is hindered by multifaceted factors, including inadequate infrastructure and equipment, insufficient human resources and skilled ICT personnel in healthcare, inadequate legislation, insufficient or unreliable power supply, insecurity, trust, scarce funding, low government and other user buy-in, and weak evaluation mechanisms. Boore (2018) also reported how the Government of Kenya's ICT policy has been silent on mHealth initiatives, although the MOH recognizes its importance within its ICT policies. The disconnect between these units is of great concern to a country that seeks to achieve universal healthcare status. Other reports about the government's weak tracking mechanisms to track eHealth implementations have also led to an overlap in the interventions, resulting in high failure rates in mHealth projects (Njoroge et al., 2017). Nonetheless, such knowledge is needed to identify and understand the potential pitfalls in digitalising the healthcare industry in Africa, if positive outcomes are to be expected.

6.4.3 Data Collection

The empirical data presented in this study was collected in Ghana and Kenya over a period of 10 weeks. The study participants, which included healthcare practitioners (i.e. physicians, nurses, and pharmacists), hospital administrators, as well as patients, were selected through purposeful sampling, a sampling technique that has been emphasised in IS research (Creswell & Sheikh, 2013). The selection of these groups of participants was geared towards achieving the widest range of responses. Data was collected using semi-structured interviews with open-ended questions, which aimed at answering the main research questions of the study, i.e. to specifically identify and describe the unintended negative consequences of the various IS implementations in the respective contexts. The interview guide was designed with concepts of the theoretical underpinning of the study, as well as the guiding research questions. A total of 37 participants were interviewed from two healthcare facilities each, in Ghana and Kenya. Responses were mostly given in English and each interview lasted between 40 and 60 minutes. The interviews were recorded with the permission of participants, in each case. Other data collection techniques, such as observation, were also employed as part of the data collection process for this study.

6.4.4 Data Analysis

The qualitative data was transcribed and analysed. Qualitative data analysis, according to Preko et al. (2019a), is a process of noticing, collecting, and thinking about interesting 'things' in the material. 'Things' in this study were, therefore, related to the net benefits that were considered and assessed to be undesirable or negative from the various IS implementations in both contexts. The process was iterated a number of times to identify major meaningful themes, patterns, and descriptions of the post-digitalisation outcomes that were not originally planned during the acquisition and implementation of the IT-based solutions. The extraction of these themes was geared towards answering the research questions of this study (Yin, 2014).

6.5 Results and Discussion

In spite of the several expected positive outcomes regarding digitalisation in Africa's healthcare industry that warrants and justifies its investments, such initiatives are also accompanied by some unexpected negative consequences at both individual and organisational levels. In this section, we discuss findings of the study by drawing out themes from the adopted conceptual framework, with a focus on answering the underpinning research questions: (1) What are the distinguishing unintended negative consequences of healthcare digitalisation in the African context? (2) How do we deal with such unexpected and undesirable outcomes with negative impacts? In answering these questions, we first explored the negative unintended outcomes of the various digitalisation initiatives in the four healthcare facilities used for this study. Subsequently, we explored those surmountable solutions or options available for these facilities to deal with such unexpected and undesirable outcomes of digitalisation. In the subsections below, we provide details of these findings and its relationship with extant literature.

6.5.1 Findings Based on Study's Conceptual Framework

System Quality As explained by DeLone and McLean (2016), system quality relates to the desirable characteristics of an information system, such as the ease of use, system flexibility, system reliability, ease of learning, and also the features of intuitiveness, sophistication, flexibility, and response times. However, in exploring the undesirable outcomes of the various digital technologies that emanated from system quality, it was noted that some of its attributes were accountable for such unintended consequences. The sampled transcripts below are themed responses that are related to system reliability, flexibility, sophistication, ease of use and learning, as well as system response time (Table 6.1).

Information Quality Information quality, according to DeLone and McLean (1992, 2003, 2016), is the desirable characteristic of the system outputs, including its reports and web pages. Based on this definition and understanding, the following transcripts were themed as unintended consequences that emanated from information quality (Table 6.2).

Service Quality DeLone and McLean (1992, 2003, 2016) defined service quality as the quality of support that system users receive from the IS organisation, as well as IT support personnel. Service quality includes accuracy, responsiveness, reliability, technical competence, and empathy of the IT support staff. Based on the responses gathered, the following themed transcripts were captured under service quality as producing negative unintended consequences in the facilities under study (Table 6.3).

Table 6.1 Negative unintended consequences based on system quality

Unintended consequences	Transcript	Respondent
Increased patient waiting time	*The network issues cause unnecessary delays on the part of the patient*	Nurse (KN)
	The unexpected system malfunctions cause patients to wait unnecessarily. For example, the unexpected breakdown of machines usually stalls the delivery process	Hospital administrator (GH)
	Network issues cause a lot of stress to patients when they have to wait, and they don't know how long they have to wait for	Physician (KN)
	Because of how electronically and digitally connected we are, unstable power supplies render the facility helpless, and it goes back to the poor patient	Physician (GH)
	There have been times that I've had to be here for almost 5 hours, just waiting for the system to come up	Patient (KN)
	Honestly, the issue of 'network is down' is really frustrating to hear, especially in healthcare settings where human lives are on the line	Patient (GH)
	I made observations at two hospitals and noted long queues caused by technology failure or slow speed	Researcher (KN)
Increased costs on the part of patients	*There have been instances where patients' bills have been increased because they could not be discharged from the system, which resulted from the usual network challenges*	Nurse (GH)
	My wife delivered in this hospital, and we were supposed to be discharged on a particular day. However, we couldn't go home on the said day because they said the system was down, and we still needed to be discharged through the system. The extra stay in the hospital caused us extra money even though it wasn't our fault. For me, I think we still have a long way to go if we indeed want to catch up with the developed world	Patient (GH)
Loss of patient's medical history resulting from system complexity	*You know I was born before computer so I find myself struggling with using most of the systems because of their nature. It is too complex. Sometimes you think you have saved the data but later you will realise that it wasn't saved. How do you get the patient's records back? It is worrying*	Nurse (GH)
	Everything has to be typed, which is a bit difficult for me. I would naturally prefer to write but since everything has to be keyed in the system, I try to do so. Unlike writing, you can forget to save the record and lose it entirely	Physician (KN)
Technostress	*Our overreliance on the system (HIS) brings a lot of frustration when there are power interruptions or network issues*	Physician (GH)

Table 6.2 Negative unintended consequences based on information quality

Unintended consequences	Transcript	Respondent
Wrong entries and its associated risks	*The time format of the system can cause wrong entries, which usually leads to misinformation on patient scheduling, among others*	Physician (GH)
	Wrong entries cannot be changed after 1 hour. For example, if someone delivers a girl in this ward and I enter a boy instead of a girl, I cannot make any changes to the record after 1 hour, and it cannot be deleted too. So, unless a new record is created for the baby. You can image when the error is not even noted on time. It means that the person's gender and records associated with him or her will forever be wrong till it is realised; by which time they have some medical history attached to those records. It is really complicated	Nurse (GH)
	Some of the systems are too sensitive; before you realise, you have made a wrong input; and if this is not rectified on time, it may lead to other dire consequences	Physician (KN)
Wrong self-diagnosis and medication by the Internet-informed patient	*Because most people believe that everything is now on the Internet, a lot of patients leverage this platform to make several wrong diagnosis and self-medication without coming to the hospital for proper assessment. This has resulted in a lot of complications for some patients*	Physician (GH)

Table 6.3 Negative unintended consequences based on service quality

Unintended consequences	Transcript	Respondent
Security risks emanating from system and staff attitudes	*IT support for us has been very poor, and even within here, we like to depend on only but a few of the numerable IT staff. Hence, if he is away, then we know we have to wait until he comes back*	Lab physician (KN)
	Data can be easily comprised if conscious efforts are not made to secure it. I know our IT team does well in securing our patients' records	Physician (GH)
	The system is not fool-proof… what I'm saying is that the nurse can easily get away with some frivolous transactions on drugs for in-patient clients	Nurse (KN)
	Viral threats on the system. We have, therefore, installed antiviruses and other firewalls to protect the system and patient information	Hospital administrator (GH)
	If you forget to log out from your interface, someone can use your ID to perform malicious acts in your name. So, the system forces us to change our passwords every 4 weeks	Nurse (GH)

6.5.2 Other Unintended Consequences Identified

Apart from the thematic analysis (using the conceptual framework of the study) that revealed some negative unintended consequences of digitalisation in the facilities, further analysis of the data also revealed some other unexpected outcomes which were deemed undesirable by the users of the various systems. The table below summarises these other unintended consequences of digitalisation in the facilities under study (Table 6.4).

6.5.3 Analysis of Findings Between the West and East of Africa

An analysis between the two contexts (i.e. Ghana and Kenya), representing the West and the East of Africa, respectively, was conducted by comparing the outcomes of the study findings using the constant comparative method (Preko et al., 2020). The comparison revealed similar outcomes across both countries, especially with regard to some attributes of *system quality* (DeLone & McLean, 2016), e.g. network challenges, which resulted in delays and increased waiting times of patients at the four facilities under study. The same challenge also dovetailed into other observed unintended consequences across both countries. This included the technostress experienced by both providers and clients in healthcare settings, increased workload on the part of providers regarding data entries, and loss of 'essence' in the current medical practice, among others. However, the attendant effects of such network delays, i.e. the increased costs on the part of patients, were only experienced from the Ghanaian context, as none was mentioned from the Kenyan context.

With the unintended consequences that stemmed from some attributes of *information quality* (DeLone & McLean, 2016), it was noted that the outcomes of risks (e.g. health, psychological, emotional, etc.) associated with wrong entries in the systems were similar across both contexts. However, although the issue of wrong self-diagnosis and medication by the Internet-informed patient was mentioned from the Ghanaian context, it could still be generalised across the entire African continent as the use of the Internet has become a global phenomenon in recent times.

Further analysis of the unintended consequences that emanated from *service quality* (DeLone & McLean, 2016), however, revealed some interesting findings regarding the security risks that result from both systems and staff attitudes. While reports from the Ghanaian context suggested extreme support from its IT personnel in the facilities under study, the Kenyan context presented contrary views, which suggested the relatively small number of IT personnel and the lack of IT support in the Kenyan health sector. These findings reveal the gap in IT staffing from the Kenyan healthcare context and the threats it tends to pose in the digital era if policies are not specifically instituted to address this concern.

Table 6.4 Other findings from the study

Unintended consequences	Transcript	Respondent
Increased workload	*The workload has become even more stressful now because of the double entries that have to be made in both the system and in our books. It is virtually like doing the same thing twice*	Nurse (GH)
	The development of policies and guidelines to guard or regulate the operations of our system (HIS) has actually increased the workload because of the ever-increasing demand on us to get these records up to date. We also develop and update standard operating procedures (SOPs) to manage key aspects of the system and other hospital operations	Hospital administrator (GH)
	The downtime issue is a big problem for me because I have to key in data after the system comes back into operation	Physician (KN)
Loss of certain core practices in the medical field	*I think this whole idea of digitalisation is fading out some of the core practices in the medical field. You know, in medical school, we're taught to draw scenarios to aid in making judgements on cases. Now, we're forced to type whatever we're looking at or assessing, and this wastes a lot of time, trust me, especially for those of us who are not conversant with typing. At least, at first, we could scribble quickly and get things done in real time, but this is where we are now*	Physician (GH)
	IT and digitisation are taking away scribbling and replacing it with comfort, sensation, typing, etc. which can make natural mistakes when keying in	Physician (GH)
	I agree that a time will come where we will lose that touch of face-to-face interaction with our patients with the introduction of these technologies	Physician (KN)
Loss of 'essence' in the medical practice	*The fact that this is health, we don't have to take chances. In healthcare, we deal with emergencies and that means time. Also, the fact that healthcare issues have to do with emergencies, we shouldn't liken it to the financial sector in terms of system downtimes. The essence involved in the health sector should never be compromised because it is a very delicate area*	Physician (GH)
	The health sector should always be thought of as a critical environment so that it can guide our behaviours, because, when the Electoral Commission (EC) loses data, it can be replaced; however, when a medical record is lost, it can never be replaced	Physician (GH)

(continued)

Table 6.4 (continued)

Unintended consequences	Transcript	Respondent
Loss of trust on the part of patients	*Yes, true! A doctor was telling me about how his patients feel when he is talking to them and typing at the same time. Sometimes, the patients think he is Googling their condition and telling them about the results since they don't know exactly what he is doing. So, in the patient's mind, this is not the usual interaction they have with the doctor (typing while talking)*	Pharmacist (KN)
Privacy concerns	*I don't know how robust their system is but once we're talking about electronic data, it can easily be shared without a trace*	Patient (KN)
	Nowadays, people like to take screenshots of everything, and I wouldn't be surprised if it happens with our health records	Patient (KN)
	I know it is unethical to share people's personal health records but so far as we're dealing with people and systems, you can never be too sure	Patient (GH)

Other findings analysed from the data also revealed the loss of trust on the part of patients as an unintended consequence of digitalisation from the Kenyan context, while the loss of medical records, 'essence', and some core practices in the medical field was mentioned from the Ghanaian context. The privacy concerns on the part of patients regarding the digitisation of health records were, however, similar across both contexts.

6.5.4 *Comparison of Study Findings with Extant Literature*

Based on the findings of this study, we noted that some earlier studies have identified and corroborated similar unintended negative consequences of digitalisation in the health sector, which were in line with our study findings. This included studies (Adu et al., 2017) which discussed privacy concerns on the part of healthcare consumers (Zeckhauser & Sommers, 2013) which identified wrong self-diagnosis and medication as a result of the online health-seeking behaviours of the Internet-informed consumer and (e.g. Coiera et al., 2016; Zheng et al., 2016) which discussed new types of patient safety risks including wrong entries leading to wrong diagnosis, wrong medication, and wrong patient selection, among others. Other studies including Mihailescu and Mihailescu (2018) also discussed the increased delays resulting from poor network connectivity issues and system downtimes and Luciano et al. (2020) that discussed the security risks resulting from the negligence of providers. Again (e.g. Zheng et al., 2016; Strong et al., 2014), further identified wrong data entries result from inexperienced medical practitioners regarding the use of digital technologies, as well as the poorly designed user interfaces and complexities of such technologies in healthcare settings. Finally, the overdependence on digital technologies and the associated technostress that come along with delays on these systems, especially in DE contexts, was discussed by Gogia et al. (2016), while Zheng et al. (2016) identified the additional demands on documentation resulting from emergent regulatory requirements enabled and enforced by digitalisation in the healthcare industry.

Although most of the above unintended negative consequences identified in this study have been discussed in extant literature, the study revealed four new key findings as its contribution to literature. These included the following:

1. The loss of patients' medical history resulting from the unconscious acts of providers to save data and, in other instances, as a result of system complexities and poor user interface designs
2. The loss of certain core practices in the field of medicine resulting from practitioners' inability to scribble and illustrate patients' medical conditions and scenarios with diagrams that aid judgements and decisions in the medical practice
3. Loss of 'essence' in the medical field resulting from the delays that characterise network connectivity and stability issues associated with healthcare digitalisation in most African contexts
4. Loss of trust on the part of patients resulting from some emerging trends associated with digitalisation (e.g. 'talking while typing' on electronic devices in the consulting room)

6.5.5 Dealing with the Unexpected Outcomes

Pre-emptive Approaches Proposed from This Study Based on the identified unintended negative consequences of digitalisation identified in the earlier part of this study, some surmountable solutions have been proposed to minimise or preempt the occurrences of such outcomes. These pre-emptive approaches that were geared towards answering the second research question of this study are summarised in Table 6.5.

6.6 Conclusion

Digitalisation in the medical field has been paradoxical due to its tendencies to produce both desirable and undesirable consequences to users and implementing organisations alike. In this study, the rather negative unintended consequences of digitalisation in the Ghanaian and Kenyan healthcare industries are explored and underscored. The study reveals 12 distinct outcomes that were not originally planned during the purchase and implementation of various HIS and other digital health technologies in 4 healthcare facilities under study. Although several studies (e.g.

Table 6.5 Pre-emptive approaches proposed from this study

Unintended consequence	Pre-emptive approach
Increased patient waiting time and its concomitant effects	This can be pre-empted by the development and adoption of offline versions of solutions (systems) that could be synchronised with online versions. By doing so, the issue of customer delays, which sometimes lead to increased costs on the part of patients, could also be curbed. In addition, the automatic and systemic synchronisation of data could further curb the issue of increased workload on the part of providers, who need to key in data after every system reconnection. Finally, the issue of 'essence' that is associated with urgency in the medical field would be restored and maintained in healthcare settings of the African continent.
Wrong entries and its associated risks	This can be pre-empted by adopting the following approaches: 1. Employing healthcare professionals who have considerable knowledge and expertise in the field of IT to be able to manage health information systems and other digital technologies, as mentioned by Luciano et al. (2020) 2. Inclusion of IT modules in the medical schools and nursing colleges to raise new kinds of medical professionals for Africa's healthcare industry 3. Periodic training and refresher programmes for medical staff to enable them to acquaint themselves with emerging technological trends 4. Design of user-friendly interfaces by developers and programmers to enable novice IT users of such systems to use them with ease
Wrong self-diagnosis and medication by the Internet-informed patient	The unintended negative consequences that arise from wrong self-diagnosis and medication could be surmounted by frequent intensive public education on the responsible use of the Internet, especially with regard to medical and health issues. This is due to the rising online health-seeking behaviours among Internet-informed consumers of healthcare (Zeckhauser & Sommers, 2013). Also, the frequent public education and sensitisation on the concept of digitalisation in the healthcare industry would further encourage and maintain *trust* in such healthcare settings
Privacy risks and concerns	The privacy risks and concerns that arise from digitalisation in Africa's healthcare industry could be surmounted by strengthening and empowering its regulatory machineries to deliver their mandate adequately (i.e. by overseeing the collection and responsible use of electronic data in the healthcare industry). By so doing, public confidence in the use of digital technologies to deliver healthcare services would be developed and restored
Loss of certain core practices in the medical field	This unintended outcome could be pre-empted by the creation and inclusion of interfaces and modules that allow scribbling when designing health information systems. This would allow physicians to scribble and have diagrammatic representations of scenarios about patients' conditions, as was done in the traditional paper-/folder-based systems

Luciano et al., 2020; Mihailescu & Mihailescu, 2018; Adu et al., 2017; Coiera et al., 2016; Zheng et al., 2016; Gogia et al., 2016; Zeckhauser & Sommers, 2013; etc.) have identified and discussed a number of unintended negative consequences of digitalisation in the healthcare industry, this study revealed four new unique findings from the Ghanaian and Kenyan healthcare contexts. These included the loss of medical records due to the negligence of professionals and system complexities; loss of certain core practices in the medical field resulting from practitioners' inability to scribble and illustrate patients' medical conditions and scenarios with diagrams; loss of trust on the part of patients resulting from some of the emerging trends associated with digitalisation; as well as the loss of 'essence' in the medical field due to delays that characterise the poor network connectivity in most African countries. The comparative analysis conducted in this study also revealed some similarities and differences between the study findings from both contexts, which represent a cross section of the African continent, i.e. East and West.

The new knowledge documented in this study contributes to the IS healthcare literature, especially in the African context where such knowledge is needed to guide IS investments and technology adoption in the healthcare industry. Also, the study contributes to theory and enhances the rigour around the DeLone and McLean IS success model by applying it directly to explore the unintended negative outcomes of IS implementations in Africa's healthcare industry. In terms of practice and policy implications, the study could serve as a guide to showcase the challenges in Africa's attempt to digitalise its healthcare system. The documented knowledge could further improve the health system preparedness and proactively reduce the adverse effect of digitalisation in Africa's healthcare industry. Finally, the study could guide policymakers and practitioners to minimise the unintended negative consequences of technology, which will help create a shared strategic understanding of what works in Africa.

6.6.1 Limitations and Recommendations for Future Research

We do acknowledge that this study was limited to only two African countries, i.e. Ghana and Kenya, and four healthcare facilities. However, our results were generalised for the entire African continent. Due to this limitation of the study, we do admit that the outcomes of this study are not exhaustive. Hence, future research is recommended to focus on a similar phenomenon in other African healthcare contexts to unearth further such undesirable outcomes of digitalisation in the health sector. Future studies can also build on the foundations of this study by adopting different theoretical approaches to explore the phenomenon. This would, again, unveil an appreciable number of the overarching contributing factors of this phenomenon in Africa's healthcare industry to guide policy development and practice.

References

Adu, E. K., Mills, A. M., & Todorova, N. (2017). *The digitization of healthcare: Understanding personal health information disclosure by consumers in developing countries – An extended privacy calculus*. Australasian Conference on Information Systems, pp. 1–9. Hobart, Australia.

Alagidede, P., & Ibrahim, M. (2017). On the causes and effects of exchange rate volatility on economic growth: Evidence from Ghana. *Journal of African Business, 18*(2), 169–193.
Al-Fadhli, A. A., Othman, M., Ali, N., & Al-Jamrh, B. A. (2017). *Understanding health professionals' intention to use telehealth in Yemen: Using the DeLone and McLean IS success model* (pp. 627–638). Springer.
Ali, N., Tretiakov, A., Whiddett, D., & Hunter, I. (2017). Knowledge management systems success in healthcare: Leadership matters. *International Journal of Medical Informatics, 97*, 331–340.
Asare, S., Otoo-Arthur, D., & Frimpong, K. O. (2017). Assessing the readiness of the digitalization of health records: A case of a municipal hospital in Ghana. *International Journal of Computer Science and Information Technology Research, 5*(4), 76–90.
Boore, C. (2018). *A framework for eHealth implementation in the healthcare sector in Kenya: A grounded theory approach*. University of Nairobi.
Coiera, E., Ash, J., & Berg, M. (2016). The unintended consequences of health information technology revisited. *IMIA Yearbook*, 163–169.
Cresswell, K., & Sheikh, A. (2013). Organizational issues in the implementation and adoption of health information technology innovations: An interpretative review. *International Journal of Medical Informatics, 82*(5), 73–86.
DeLone, W., & McLean, E. (1992). Information systems successes: The quest for the dependent variable. *Information Systems Research, 3*(1), 60–95.
DeLone, W. H., & McLean, E. R. (2003). The DeLone and McLean model of information systems success: A ten-year update. *Journal of Management Information Systems, 4*, 9–30.
DeLone, W. H., & McLean, E. R. (2016). Information systems success measurement. *Foundations and Trends in Information Systems, 2*(1), 1–116.
Gabre-Mariam, M., & Bygstad, B. (2019). Digitalization mechanisms of health management information systems in developing countries. *Information and Organisation, 29*, 1–22.
Gann, B. (2019). Transforming lives: Combating digital health inequality. *International Federation of Library Associations and Institutions, 45*(3), 187–198.
Gogia, S. B., Maeder, A., Mars, M., Hartvigsen, G., Basu, A., & Abbott, P. (2016). Unintended consequences of tele-health and their possible solutions. *IMIA and Schattauer GmbH*.
Gyamfi, A., Mensah, K. A., Oduro, G., Donkor, P., & Mock, C. N. (2017). Barriers and facilitators to electronic medical records in the emergency centre at Komfo Anokye Teaching Hospital. *Kumasi-Ghana. African Journal of Emergency Medicine*, 177–182.
Jaafreh, A. B. (2017). Evaluation information system success: Applied DeLone and McLean information system success model in context banking system in KSA. *International Review of Management and Business Research, 6*(2), 828–854.
Jeyaraj, A. (2020). DeLone & McLean models of information system success: Critical meta-review and research directions. *International Journal of Information Management, 102139*, 1–15.
Karuri, J., Waiganjo, P., Daniel, O., & Manya, A. (2014). DHIS2: The tool to improve health data demand and use in Kenya. *Journal of Health Informatics in Developing Countries, 8*(1).
Kenya's EMR Review Towards Standardisation. https://www.ghdonline.org/uploads/Kenya_EMR_Review_Towards_Standardization_Report.pdf. Last accessed 21 Sept 2020.
KNBS Census. https://www.knbs.or.ke/?page_id=3142. Last accessed 17 Sept 2020.
Kumar, M., & Mostafa, J. (2020). Electronic health records for better health in the lower- and middle-income countries: A landscape study. *Library Hi Tech*, 1–17.
Luciano, E., Mahmood, M., & Rad, P. M. (2020). Telemedicine adoption issues in the United States and Brazil: Perception of healthcare professionals. *Health Informatics Journal*, 1–18.
Mapesa, N. M. (2016). *Health information technology implementation strategies in Zimbabwe*. Walden University.
Mihailescu, M., & Mihailescu, D. (2018). *The emergence of digitalisation in the context of health care*. 51st Hawaii International Conference on System Sciences, pp. 3066–3071. Hawaii.
Mosadeghrad, A. M. (2014). Factors influencing healthcare service quality. *International Journal of Health Policy and Management, 3*(2), 77–89.

Muinga, N., Magare, S., Monda, J., Kamawu, O., Houston, S., Fraser, H., ... Paton, C. (2018). Implementing an open souce electronic health record system in Kenyan healthcare facilities: Case study. *JMIR Medical Informatics, 6*(2).

Ngari, M. M., Waithira, N., Chilengi, R., Njuguna, P., Lang, T., & Fegan, G. (2014). Experience of using an open source clinical trials data management software system in Kenya. *BMC Research Notes, 7*(1), 845.

Njoroge, M., Zurovac, D., Ogara, E. A., Chuma, J., & Kirigia, D. (2017). Assessing the feasibility of eHealth and mHealth: A systematic review and analysis of initiatives implemented in Kenya. *BMC Research Notes, 10*(1), 90.

Olu, O., Muneene, D., Bataringaya, J. E., Nahimana, M.-R., Ba, H., Turgeon, Y., ... Dovlo, D. (2019). How can digital health technologies contribute to sustainable attainment of universal health coverage in Africa? A perspective. *Frontiers in Public Health, 7*(341).

Pluye, P., El Sherif, R., Granikov, V., et al. (2019). Health outcomes of online consumer health information: A systematic mixed studies review with framework synthesis. *Journal of the Association for Information Science and Technology, 70*(7), 643–659.

Preko, M., & Boateng, R. (2020). Assessing healthcare digitalisation in Ghana: A critical realist's approach. *Health Policy and Technology, 9*(2). https://doi.org/10.1016/j.hlpt.2020.03.006

Preko, M., Boateng, R., & Effah, J. (2019a). *Health informatics and brain drain mitigation in Ghana*. 25th America's Conference on Information Systems (pp. 1–10). Cancun, Mexico.

Preko, M., Boateng, R., & Effah, J. (2019b). *Healthcare digitalisation in Ghana: An assessment based on the realist social theory*. 25th Americas Conference on Information Systems (pp. 1–5). Cancun, Mexico.

Preko, M., Osei-Boateng, R., & Durosinmi, A. E. (2020). Digitalising healthcare in developing economies: challenges and mitigating strategies. In R. Boateng (Ed.), *Handbook of research on managing information systems in developing economies* (pp. 332–353). Hershey, PA.

Salte, T. (2014). *ICTs and access to health care in Kenya*. Master's Thesis.

Strong, D. M., Johnson, S. A., Tulu, B., Trudel, J., Volkoff, O., Pelletier, L. R., ... Garber, L. (2014). A theory of organization-EHR affordance actualization. *Journal of Association for Information Systems, 15*(2), 53–85.

Tambo, E., Madjou, G., Mbous, Y., Olalubi, O. A., Yah, C., Adedeji, A. A., & Ngogang, J. Y. (2016). Digital health implications in health systems in Africa. *European Journal of Pharmaceutical and Medical Research, 3*(1), 91–93.

Thomas, J. G., & Bond, S. D. (2014). Review of innovations in digital health technology to promote weight control. *Curr Diab Rep, 14*(485), 1–10.

Warren, R. A. (2017). *Exploring strategies for successful implementation of electronic health records*. Walden University.

WHO Public consultation on the draft global digital health strategy. https://extranet.who.int/dataform/upload/surveys/183439/files/Public-Consultation-on-the-Draft-Global-Strategy-on-Digital-Health.pdf. Last accessed 23 June 2020.

World Economic Forum. (2019). *How to start a digital healthcare revolution in Africa in 6 steps*. https://www.weforum.org/agenda/2019/08/6-ways-digital-technology-can-transform-healthcare-in-africa/. Last accessed 19 Sept 2020.

Yakubu, M. N., & Dasuki, S. (2018). Assessing eLearning systems success in Nigeria: An application of the DeLone and McLean Information Systems Success Model. *Journal of Information Technology Education Research, 17*, 183–203.

Yilmaz, K. (2013). Comparison of quantitative and qualitative research traditions: Epistemological, theoretical, and methodological differences. *European Journal of Education, 48*, 311–325.

Yin, R. K. (2014). *Case study research design and methods*. Sage.

Zeckhauser, R., & Sommers, B. (2013). Consumerism in health care: Challenges and opportunities. *American Medical Association Journal of Ethics, 15*(11), 988–992.

Zheng, K., Abraham, J., Novak, L. L., Reynolds, T. L., & Gettinger, A. (2016). A survey of the literature on unintended consequences associated with health information technology: 2014–2015. *IMIA Yearbook of Medical Informatics*, 13–29.

Mansah Preko is a final-year Doctoral Candidate in Information Systems (IS) at the University of Ghana Business School. She holds a Bachelor of Science degree in Information and Communication Technology (ICT) and a Master of Science degree in Management Information Systems (MIS). Her research interest is in the area of digital transformation, with emphasis on the healthcare industry of developing economies and Africa, in particular. Mansah's interest is also found in IS implementations in both social and organisational contexts. Mansah can be reached at mpreko@st.ug.edu.gh.

Patrick Shabaya is a Doctoral Student in Information Systems Management at the School of Computing and Engineering Sciences in the University of Strathmore, Kenya. He holds a Bachelor's degree in Software Engineering and a Master's degree in Information Systems. Patrick's research interest is in information systems implementation. He is currently working on healthcare systems implementation in low- and middle-income countries. Patrick can be reached on pshabaya@strathmore.edu.

Samuel Anim-Yeboah is a Doctoral Researcher at the University of Ghana Business School and the CEO of Sims Technology Ltd. He is also a lecturer and consultant in informatics, management information systems, entrepreneurship, and management. Samuel is interested in technology and enterprise research, focusing on digital entrepreneurship, digital transformation, and enterprise systems. Samuel can be reached at ssanim-yeboah@st.ug.edu.gh.

Part II
Digital Disruption and Transformation

Chapter 7
Influencer Marketing: A Bibliometric Analysis of 10 Years of Scopus-Indexed Research

Sheena Lovia Boateng

Abstract In recent years, influencer marketing has garnered considerable research interest from scholars. However, scholars have yet to examine the volume and impact of such research. Using data from Scopus, this study identifies 243 journal articles by 538 authors. Through a bibliometric approach, using VOSviewer and Bibliometrix software, the study quantitatively and visually analyzed these papers. The results reveal that papers on influencer marketing had been indexed in the Scopus database for over 10 years, beginning from 2011. Further, most papers did not use any underpinning theory or model, and quantitative methods dominated the research methodology used. The USA emerged as the most productive country in terms of the number of publications, followed by the UK and the Netherlands. South Africa was the only African country to have a researcher as the first author of a paper on this subject. Regarding keywords, scholars have mainly focused on influencer marketing via social media platforms such as Instagram, YouTube, and Twitter. The results of the analysis found a potential research opportunity for more persuasive forms of influencer marketing targeted at children and adolescents. This may change the direction of future research in influencer marketing especially for developing regions such as Africa where research on the area has been nascent.

Keywords Influencer marketing · Influencers · Social media · Bibliometric analysis · Africa

---

S. L. Boateng (✉)
University of Ghana Business School, Legon, Accra, Ghana
e-mail: slboateng@ug.edu.gh

R. Boateng et al. (eds.), *Digital Innovations, Business and Society in Africa*, Advances in Theory and Practice of Emerging Markets,
https://doi.org/10.1007/978-3-030-77987-0_7

7.1 Introduction

Influencer marketing has become an integral part of retailers' marketing strategies (De Veirman et al., 2016; Cuevas et al., 2020). Glucksman (2017) defined influencer marketing as the "process of identifying, engaging, and supporting individuals who create conversations with a brand's customers" (p. 77). Khamis et al. (2017) argued that influencer marketing has emerged alongside the growth of digital technology, particularly social media, thereby creating an opportunity for brand marketing by what are termed social media influencers. Freberg et al. (2011) defined social media influencers as a "new type of independent, third-party endorsers who shape an audience's attitudes through blogs, tweets, and the use of other social media channel[s]" (p. 1). Such endorsers are different from traditional endorsers who are usually famous TV show hosts, sports personalities, movie stars, and music celebrities (Khamis et al., 2017).

For many retailers, influencer marketing is a new way of marketing to increase sales and profits (Cuevas et al., 2020). Consumers on their part are increasingly using larger network opportunities available to them via social media to acquire better and more trustworthy information about goods and services (Alves et al., 2016; Stubb et al., 2019). Hence, many businesses, especially in retail, are devoting increased marketing resources to this domain as the prospects of reaching a vast audience are considerably higher (Campbell & Marks, 2015). Particularly, retailers sign partnership agreements with influencer marketers, otherwise known as social media influencers (Khamis et al., 2017), to draw consumer traffic to their online stores and increase interest in their goods and services (Ryu & Park, 2020).

The model of influencer marketing has been applied to various aspects of marketing, including fashion marketing (Wiedmann et al., 2010; Sudha & Sheena, 2017) and political marketing (Lewis, 2020; Laaksonen et al., 2020), and in some platform-specific contexts such as Instagram (Carah & Shaul, 2016; Argyris et al., 2020) and YouTube (Xiao et al., 2018; Nandagiri & Philip, 2018).

Despite this increasing research on influencer marketing and social media influencers, no bibliometric analysis has been undertaken to analyze the main topics, sources, methodologies, theories, and authors or the impact of studies published in this research domain. Such an analysis will provide researchers with useful information on publication trends, relevant authors, sources, methodologies, theories, countries, and institutions involved. Such an analysis will also provide valuable insights to researchers by providing a better understanding of the academic relevance of the topic, gaining useful information about current research trends, and identifying future research trends. This study uses a carefully selected sample of 243 journal articles that have been indexed in the Scopus database.

The remainder of this study is structured as follows: The next section reviews existing literature and identifies gaps. Then, the methodology is presented, following which the results and discussion are presented. The subsequent section presents some future research directions drawn out of the results and discussion of the present study that can be explored. Finally, the conclusions, limitations, and future research trends in this study are presented.

7.1.1 Filling the Bibliometric Research Gap

Bibliometrics is a scientific approach aimed at measuring the level of productivity and impact of research in a particular discipline (Costas et al., 2010; Merigó & Yang, 2017). Ye et al. (2012) defined bibliometrics as an assessment of statistical information regarding research in an area to identify the main topics and sources of that research. Systematic reviews are often restricted to literature that is familiar to the author and lacks the tendency to account for a considerable number of research papers, if not all the papers, that have been done in a particular research field (Mallett et al., 2012); bibliometric analysis, on the other hand, does not only show the development of a subject area such as authors and critical papers through visualization networks and figures but also provide trends regarding further research in this domain of research (Zupic & Čater, 2015), hence directing both experienced and budding researchers what to look out for in the journals when researching a particular area as well as authors, countries, and institutions to target for collaborations. Further, while systematic reviews tend to focus more on analysis of the content of papers to draw out theoretical models (Finfgeld-Connett, 2014), bibliometrics focuses on numerical counts to tease out the most influential characteristics of a particular research topic (Zhang et al., 2018).

Many disciplines have been subjected to bibliometric analysis (Zupic & Čater, 2015), for example, education (Fellnhofer, 2019; Kosmützky & Krücken, 2014; Diem & Wolter, 2013), tourism and leisure (Köseoglu et al., 2016; Okumus et al., 2018), engineering (Garousi & Mäntylä, 2016; Gerdsri et al., 2017), finance (Chang & Ho, 2010; Zhang et al., 2019), agriculture (Velasco-Muñoz et al., 2018; Giraldo et al. 2019), management (Podsakoff et al., 2008), and information technology (Madani, 2015; Mora et al., 2017).

Similarly, bibliometric studies also exist in the field of marketing. For example, Kim and McMillan (2008) studied Internet marketing, and Samiee and Chabowski (2012) examined international marketing. These bibliometric analyses pertain to marketing, but they do not focus on influencer marketing. Bibliometric analyses related to marketing—similar to the aim of this study (influencer marketing)—include those by Kim et al. (2019). However, they explored digital marketing communication rather than influencer marketing or how technologies aid business agents or endorsers in influencing consumers. Their focus was on digital marketing communication, which refers to the adoption of technologies to collaborate with customers and partners for communicating their business ideas on delivering and sustaining value (Lamberton & Stephen, 2016; Guercini et al., 2018). Alves et al. (2016) reviewed social media marketing research with a focus on the Web of Science database, but their search keyword term was limited to "social media marketing." This resulted in the discovery of a relatively low number of papers (44 papers).

Moreover, they focused on social media marketing rather than social media influencers. Additionally, they remain silent on other aspects of bibliometrics, such as authors, institutions, and countries spearheading research in a particular direction, as asserted by Kumar et al. (2020). Kim et al. (2019) have also stated that their bibliometric analysis on digital marketing embraces too broad an area, and hence there is a need to bibliometrically analyze papers on subfields of digital marketing communications.

Unlike studies by Kim and McMillan (2008), Samiee and Chabowski (2012), Kim et al. (2019), and Alves et al. (2016), this study aims to analyze research trends in influencer marketing—where third-party endorsers who shape audience attitudes through social media channels are particularly engaged to drive consumer interests in products and services (De Veirman et al., 2016; Cuevas et al., 2020; Glucksman, 2017; Khamis et al., 2017; Freberg et al., 2011). This study will shed light on the volume and nature of published research on influencer marketing (Pillania, 2011; Haustein & Larivière, 2015), thus examining the properties of scholarly research in the area.

7.2 Methodology

This section describes the methodology that was used when conducting the study. It specifically discusses the process of acquiring data and the analytics tools used in undertaking this study.

7.2.1 Source of Data

This study focuses on journal articles published in Elsevier's Scopus database. The Scopus database indexes a larger number of journals than other popular databases, such as Web of Science and Google Scholar (Falagas et al., 2008). The Scopus database includes approximately 36,377 published article titles from approximately 11,678 publishers. There are 34,346 leading peer-reviewed multidisciplinary journal articles in the fields of social science, business management, physical science, economics, finance, and life sciences, among others. Hence, choosing the Scopus database ensures that the data source used in this study is of the highest quality.

7.2.2 Data Extraction

Articles were extracted from the source database using specific search keywords. The search words were "influencer marketing," "social media influencers," or "social media personalities." In the search, 388 documents were obtained, which were later reduced to 243, since only journal articles published in English were considered for this analysis. Only journal articles were considered because they are generally regarded as reliable and top-quality communication for researchers (Martí-Parreño et al., 2016, p. 5) compared to other documents such as conference proceedings, books, book chapters, reviews, editorials, and doctoral theses (Martí-Parreño et al., 2016). Moreover, journal articles tend to contain the most rigorous research and are often subjected to peer review (Durieux & Gevenois, 2010). Further, the time range for the extraction of articles did not have a specified start point but had an endpoint of 2020; hence, papers published in 2021 were excluded by the timeframe restriction.

7.2.3 *Analysis of Data*

This study adopted R, the open-source statistical application, to construct the influencer marketing bibliometric analysis. Specifically, the Bibliometrix package in R was installed. Multiple studies have used Bibliometrix (Cirillo et al., 2020; Arfaoui et al., 2019). Such studies have measured the most cited articles and sources, leading authors, countries, and institutions contributing to the research and provided information on a publication pattern in that area of research.

7.3 Results and Discussion

This section presents the results and discussion of the bibliometric analysis conducted on characteristics such as methods and theories used, the most influential authors and sources, most cited documents, and institutions and countries that are contributing to research on influencer marketing. The commonly used keywords are also presented here through keyword co-occurrence and overlay visualization analysis.

7.3.1 *Overview of Data Extracted*

Table 7.1 provides an overview of the contents of the data. It shows that 583 authors have contributed to 243 journal articles from 150 sources on influencer marketing. Among them, 541 authors have collaboratively written more than 1 document (authors of multiauthored documents), and 42 authors have independently written a document (authors of single-authored documents). Another notable item from the timespan in Table 7.1 is that the indexing of papers on influencer marketing in Scopus began in 2011 and papers continue to be published.

Table 7.1 Overview of data extracted

Description	Results
Main information about data	
Timespan	2011:2020
Sources (journals only)	150
Documents	243
Average years from publication	1.76
Average citations per documents	8.909
Average citations per year per doc	2.542
References	12873
Document types	
Articles	243
Document contents	
Keywords Plus (ID)	394
Author's keywords (DE)	708
Authors	
Authors	583
Author appearances	665
Authors of single-authored documents	42
Authors of multiauthored documents	541
Author's collaboration	
Single-authored documents	45
Documents per author	0.417
Authors per document	2.4
Coauthors per documents	2.74

7.3.2 *Trends in Yearly Publications*

As shown in Fig. 7.1, the number of papers published on influencer marketing has increased over the last 5 years from 4 papers in 2016 to 139 papers in 2020. Before 2016 (between 2011 and 2015), the number of papers had been relatively low (one to two papers). There was no publication in 2013. This insignificant number of publications in the period from 2011 to 2015 may be attributed to less interest in the area of research or a low level of maturity in the development of the technologies and platforms that can support influencer marketing. Dabi et al. (2016) describe this period as the budding period for a research area, where many aspects of a research field still have to be explored.

As of January 2021, when the data was collected and analyzed, the number of papers published in Scopus for the year 2020 was 139 (74 more publications than the number recorded in 2019). Generally, the yearly trend indicates that publication on influencer marketing is increasing. This further shows that the topic is receiving a significant level of attention, and it will continue to be a primary topic of discussion for researchers studying contemporary ways of marketing to drive sales and profits.

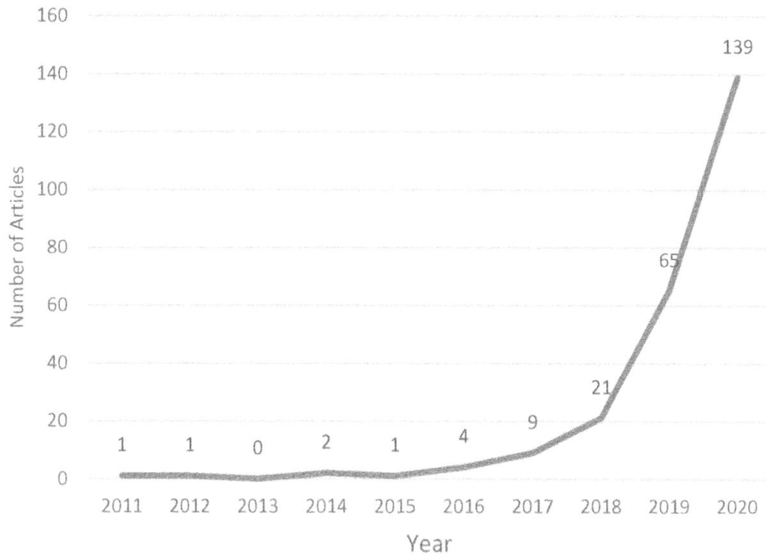

Fig. 7.1 Trend in yearly publication

7.3.3 Methodologies and Theoretical Adoption

Table 7.2 presents the classification of influencer marketing articles based on methodology and theoretical adoption. Empirical studies include articles that adopted qualitative, quantitative, and mixed-methods approaches; nonempirical studies only include literature reviews and conceptual studies.

The review and analysis pointed to the use of the three major empirical methodological approaches (Creswell & Creswell, 2017) used in research, which are the "qualitative" (e.g., Coco & Eckert, 2020), "quantitative" (e.g., Shan et al., 2020; Cuevas et al., 2020), and "mixed-methods" approach. Also, two nonempirical approaches, which are literature reviews/conceptual papers (e.g., Gupta et al., 2020) and papers that sought to do computational analysis or mathematical modeling (e.g., Britt et al., 2020; Huynh et al., 2020), were identified.

The preference for many authors was a quantitative approach, probably because influencer marketing predominantly happens on social media (Xu & Pratt, 2018). As such, it was easy to conduct online surveys to solicit the views of consumers, influencers, and businesses who are involved in this model of marketing. Regarding underpinning theoretical adoptions, the choice of use of theories by authors was relatively low as compared to authors who applied conceptual models and those who did not apply any theories or models. Examples of theories are Theory of Planned Behaviour (TPB) (Chetioui et al., 2020; Taillon et al., 2020), Technology Acceptance Model (TAM) (Al-Khalaf & Choe, 2020), Social Learning Theory (Soltani et al., 2020), Gratification Theory (Morton, 2020), and the Source Credibility Theory (Balaban & Mustățea, 2019). Balaban and Mustățea (2019), for

Table 7.2 Methodology and theoretical adoption

Methods		**2011**	**2012**	**2014**	**2015**	**2016**	**2017**	**2018**	**2019**	**2020**	**Total**
Empirical	Qualitative			1		1	2	4	11	34	53
	Quantitative			1			2	14	42	87	146
	Mixed-methods							1	2	4	7
Nonempirical	Review/conceptual	1	1			1	4	1	10	12	30
	Computational analysis				1	2	1	1		2	7
Total		**1**	**1**	**2**	**1**	**4**	**9**	**21**	**65**	**139**	**243**
Theoretical adoptions											
Conceptual model/framework				1			3	5	20	37	66
Theory/model/framework								5	4	7	16
Combination of theories/models/frameworks										1	1
No model/framework/theory		1	1	1	1	4	6	11	41	94	160
Total		**1**	**1**	**2**	**1**	**4**	**9**	**21**	**65**	**139**	**243**

example, apply the Source Credibility Theory to explore "users' perspectives on the credibility of social media influencers in Romania and Germany." Notably, among all the 243 studies, the Theory of Planned Behavior was identified to have been used in more than one study. Taillon et al. (2020) used it in "understanding the relationships between social media influencers and their followers," while Chetioui et al. (2020) applied it to understand "how fashion influencers contribute to consumers' purchase intention."

7.3.4 *Most Relevant Authors, Sources, and Influential Documents*

This section presents characteristics of the scholarly publications on influencer marketing from the bibliometric point of view per the objectives set out in the introduction of this study.

Most Relevant Authors

Table 7.3 presents a picture of the most relevant authors. From the total citations (TC) and the number of publications (NP), "Hudders L" leads in the number of citations with 226 citations and the most productive with 7 papers. Followed by "De Veirman M" with 256 citations and 5 publications and then by "Cauberghe V" with 228 citations and 2 publications. Further, comparing the year that the author started publications (PY_Start), though "Hudders L," "De Veirman M," and "Cauberghe V" started their publications in the same year (2017), "Hudders L" has been more productive and received more citations on productions than "De Veirman M" and "Cauberghe V." Therefore, "Hudders L" is considered to be the most relevant in the field, strongly contributing to the growth (publications) and knowledge (citations) of the academic literature in the field of influencer marketing.

One interesting fact is that though authors such as "Freberg K," "Freberg LA," "Graham K," and "McGaughey K" began publications earlier (2011) than authors

Table 7.3 Top 10 most relevant authors

Author	TC	NP	PY_Start
Hudders L	266	7	2017
De Veirman M	256	5	2017
Cauberghe V	228	2	2017
Freberg K	196	1	2011
Freberg La	196	1	2011
Graham K	196	1	2011
McGaughey K	196	1	2011
Ang L	193	1	2017
Khamis S	193	1	2017
Welling R	193	1	2017

TC total citations, *NP* number of publications, *PY_Start* publication start year

such as "Hudders L," "De Veirman M," and "Cauberghe V" who began publications 6 years later (2017), the former authors produced a lower number of papers and have received less citations. This suggests that the themes discussed by "Hudders L," "De Veirman M," and "Cauberghe V" are of more interest to researchers in the field as compared to the publications by "Freberg K," "Freberg LA," "Graham K," and "McGaughey K" who started publishing 6 years earlier. Notably, although other authors such as "Ang L," "Khamis S," and "Welling R" also started publication in 2017 like authors such as "Hudders L," "De Veirman M," and "Cauberghe V," the former made fewer contributions and had little influence on other researchers in the field as they have produced only 1 paper each and received 193 citations each over 3 years.

Generating a network of the coauthors or collaborations with VOSviewer resulted in six colored clustered nodes (red, green, blue, purple, yellow, and sky-blue) (see Fig. 7.2). Five hundred forty-one coauthors and 42 single authors constituted the 583 authors. The red cluster contains five items, the green cluster has five items, the blue cluster has four items, the yellow cluster has three items, the sky-blue cluster has three items, and the purple cluster has three items. Each node represents an author, and a clustering of nodes represents a collaboration between authors. The larger the size of the node, the higher the linkages and total link strength of the author. The total link strength indicates the cumulative number of publications in which the author occurs, and the linkages refer to the number of nodes that the author is connected to (Van Eck and Waltman, 2013). Hence, from Fig. 7.2, the

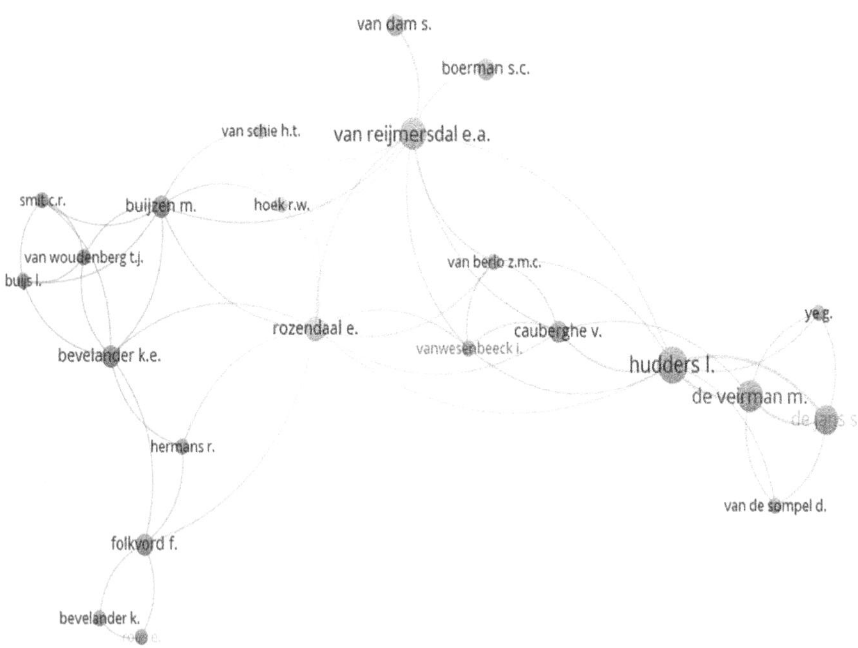

Fig. 7.2 Coauthorship analysis. (Coauthors)

topmost collaborating author is the largest green node representing "Hudders L" who has nine links and total link strength of 17. The authors who are mostly collaborating with "De Veirman M" are "De Jans S," "Van de Sompel D," and "Ye G," all belonging to the same green cluster. Notably, "Hudders L" is the most relevant author as seen in Table 7.3. "van Reijmersdal E A" who is the second most collaborating as seen in Fig. 7.2 has five links and total link strength of 11. Interestingly, however, this author is not listed among the ten most relevant authors (see Table 7.3) despite the author's significant level of collaborations with other authors in the research area. The authors who are mostly collaborating with "van Reijmersdal E A" are "Boerman S C" and "Van Dam S," all belonging to the sky-blue cluster. This further indicates that though "van Reijmersdal E A" is the second most collaborative author, the author is not making a lot of impact in terms of papers spearheading contributions and citations. These findings are indications that most collaborative authors are not necessarily the most relevant, as they may only be coauthors to papers and not the brains behind the publications. On the flip side, an author such as "Hudders L" who emerged as the most relevant author had the most collaborations with other authors. This suggests that in many of the papers (e.g., De Veirman et al., 2017; De Veirman & Hudders, 2020; van Reijmersdal et al., 2020; De Jans et al., 2020; De Jans & Hudders, 2020) that the author produced, there were contributions from other authors.

Most Relevant Sources

A total of 150 sources (journal outlets) were identified to have published the 243 articles on influencer marketing. Table 7.4 shows the ten most relevant journals in influencer marketing, detailing the number of articles (NP), total number of citations (TC), and the publication start year (PY_Start). The publication start year refers to the year in which a paper on influencer marketing was first published in that particular source. Generally, according to Table 7.4, almost all the journals that are publishing papers in the area of influencer marketing have strong marketing, advertising, social media, or celebrity orientation as their names denote. The journals that have the highest number of publications were *International Journal of*

Table 7.4 First ten most relevant sources

Source	TC	NP	PY_Start
International Journal of Advertising	316	7	2017
Public Relations Review	219	5	2011
Celebrity Studies	193	1	2017
Journal of Interactive Advertising	118	7	2018
Computers in Human Behavior	113	5	2017
Journal of Retailing and Consumer Services	109	4	2018
Social Media and Society	65	6	2016
Journal of Marketing	62	2	2018
Journal of Business Research	54	4	2020
Journal of Marketing Management	46	5	2018

TC total citations, *NP* number of publications, *PY_Start* publication start year

Advertising and *Journal of Interactive Advertising* (seven publications each), *Social Media and Society* (six publications), as well as *Public Relations Review*, *Computers in Human Behavior*, and *Journal of Marketing Management* (six publications each).

Moreover, *International Journal of Advertising* and *Journal of Interactive Advertising*, which had the highest number of publications, focus on research articles that have a scope on advertising and interactive advertising respectively. Notably, also, the presence of a journal such as *Social Media and Society* among the first ten most relevant journals is not surprising, as influencer marketing relies mostly on social media platforms to thrive (Jin et al., 2019; Coates et al., 2019).

Another aspect used to identify the influence of journals is the number of citations received by each journal. According to Table 7.4, the most cited journal, with 316 citations, is the *International Journal of Advertising* which also emerged as the journal with the highest number of publications. The next most cited journals are *Public Relations Review* with 219 citations and *Celebrity Studies* with 193 citations. *International Journal of Advertising* targets author publications that revolve around aspects of marketing communications, advertising and media, direct marketing, sales promotions, sponsorship, and public relations from practitioner and public policy perspectives. Aside from these 3 most cited journals, 3 other journals have over 100 citations: *Journal of Interactive Advertising*, *Computers in Human Behavior*, and *Journal of Retailing and Consumer Services*. Notably, most of these journals focus specifically on human and consumer engagements or interactions in advertising and marketing; therefore, the high frequency of citations could be the consequence of strong interest in this theme in the area of influencer marketing.

Most Cited Documents

The most cited author document shows the specific journal articles that the highest number of researchers have cited in authoring their papers. This points to the strong relevance of the arguments being made in the document to the studies that are being conducted by other authors in the field of influencer marketing. From Table 7.5 which shows the top 10 most cited author documents or articles, the article titled "Marketing Through Instagram Influencers: The Impact of Number of Followers and Product Divergence on Brand Attitude" (De Veirman et al., 2017) in *International Journal of Advertising* was the most cited paper with a total citation of 221. The paper sought to examine the impact of the number of followers and product divergence on brand attitude using Instagram influencers as a case study (De Veirman et al., 2017), followed by the paper titled "Who Are the Social Media Influencers? A Study of Public Perceptions of Personality" (Freberg et al., 2011) published in *Public Relations Review* with a total of 196 citations. It is worth noting that the difference in the citation count between the first and second most cited papers is 25 citations which suggests a fairly strong interest by researchers in the most cited paper to contribute to their arguments and discussions.

Regarding the journals in which these most cited papers are published, unsurprisingly, the journals in which the most cited publications are published appear in the order of the most cited journals, at least for the first three most cited journal articles (see Table 7.5) and the first three most cited journal sources (see Table 7.4).

Table 7.5 Ten most cited author documents

Authors	Title	Source title	Citations
De Veirman et al. (2017)	Marketing Through Instagram Influencers: The Impact of Number of Followers and Product Divergence on Brand Attitude	*International Journal of Advertising*	221
Freberg et al. (2011)	Who Are the Social Media Influencers? A Study of Public Perceptions of Personality	*Public Relations Review*	196
Khamis et al. (2017)	Self-Branding, "Micro-Celebrity," and the Rise of Social Media Influencers	*Celebrity Studies*	193
Lou and Yuan (2019)	Influencer Marketing: How Message Value and Credibility Affect Consumer Trust of Branded Content on Social Media	*Journal of Interactive Advertising*	93
Arora et al. (2019)	Measuring Social Media Influencer Index: Insights from Facebook, Twitter, and Instagram	*Journal of Retailing and Consumer Services*	63
Chae (2017)	Virtual Makeover: Selfie-Taking and Social Media Use Increase Selfie-Editing Frequency Through Social Comparison	*Computers in Human Behavior*	61
Schouten et al. (2020)	Celebrity vs. Influencer Endorsements in Advertising: The Role of Identification, Credibility, and Product-Endorser Fit	*International Journal of Advertising*	53
Audrezet et al. (2018)	Authenticity Under Threat: When Social Media Influencers Need to Go Beyond Self-Presentation	*Journal of Business Research*	43
Hughes et al. (2019)	Driving Brand Engagement Through Online Social Influencers: An Empirical Investigation of Sponsored Blogging Campaigns	*Journal of Marketing*	40
Jin et al. (2019)	Instafamous and Social Media Influencer Marketing	*Marketing Intelligence and Planning*	38

The *International Journal of Advertising*, *Public Relations Review*, and *Celebrity Studies* appear in first, second, and third place as the most cited journal sources and also in the first, second, and third place for the most cited articles.

7.3.5 Keywords Co-occurrence and Trend

This section presents terms that have dominated the studies done on influencer marketing, how terms occur in their use by researchers, and the implication of the dominance and occurrence of the use of these terms through a keyword trend analysis.

Commonly Used Terms

Table 7.6 presents the commonly used terms in the 243 journal articles published in influencer marketing. Examining such terms through author keywords helps to predict the research trend in a discipline over time (Madani and Weber, 2016). Hence, from Table 7.6, the most commonly used term is "influencer marketing" with 80 occurrences, followed by "social media" with 68 occurrences and "social media influencers" with 54 occurrences.

Keyword Co-occurrence

Figure 7.3 presents a deeper analysis of the relationships between the most common keywords. The occurrence of keywords is presented in three major clusters (yellow, green, and blue) and two minor clusters (red and purple). The primary node represents the most co-occurring keyword and is found at the center of the network. The thicker the lines that connect keywords, the more those keywords occur with each other. Hence, as seen in Fig 7.3, the central co-occurring keyword is "influencer marketing," which was also identified as the most frequently used keyword in Table 7.6.

"Influencer marketing" (yellow node) has the largest node in the network because it is connected to most other node clusters in the network and has words such as "Instagram," "social media marketing," and "social influence" as words that are often used alongside "influencer marketing" because they have the same color code. Similarly, the second most co-occurring keyword is "social media" (largest green node) and has words such as "influencers," "marketing," "public relations," and "Twitter," as words that are often used alongside it because they have the same color code. The third most co-occurring keyword is "social media influencers" (largest blue node) and has words such as "purchase intention," "celebrity endorsements," "source credibility," and "trust," as words that are often used alongside it because they have the same color code. Also, the red nodes reveal there has been discussion centered on "persuasion knowledge," which is done to keep people (e.g., adolescents) in the know on how influencer marketing is done, hence the presence of words such as "advertising," "adolescents," "children," "disclosure," "native advertising," and "YouTube" in the same red-colored cluster. The purple cluster reveals that research has been done which revolves around "digital marketing," "microcelebrity," and "authenticity."

Table 7.6 The most commonly used keywords

Words	Occurrences
Influencer marketing	80
Social media	68
Social media influencers	54
Influencers	36
Instagram	32
Social media marketing	13
Marketing	12
Purchase intention	10
Persuasion knowledge	9
Public relations	9

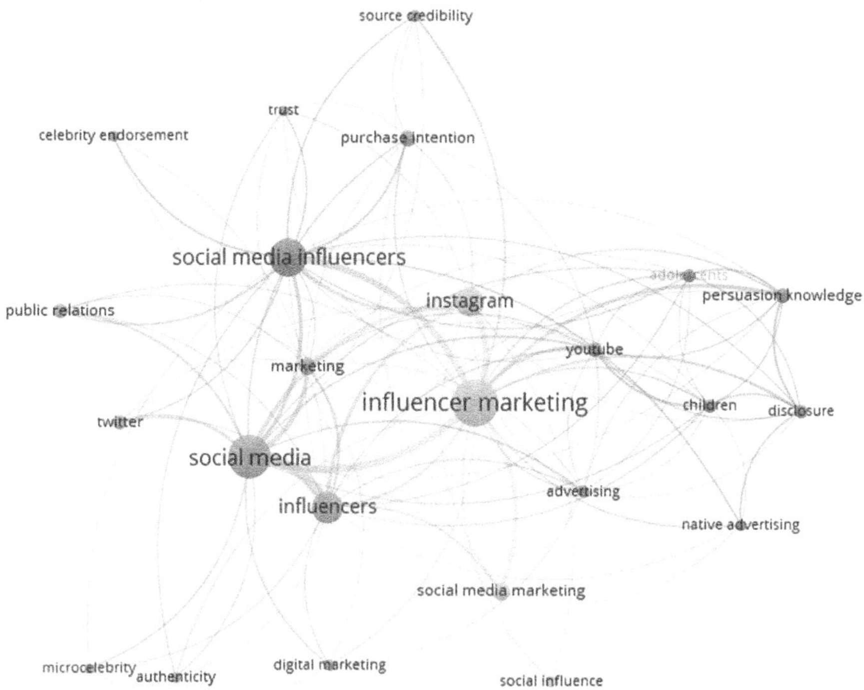

Fig. 7.3 Map of keyword co-occurrence

Emerging/Trending Keywords

Figure 7.4 presents the trends in the appearance of keywords in influencer marketing research using an overlay visualization of keywords between early 2018 and mid-2018, end of 2018 and mid-2019, and end of 2019 and 2020. Between early 2018 and mid-2018, researchers focused on "public relations," "Twitter," and "social influence." However, at the end of 2018 to mid-2019, attention shifted more to discussions that centered on marketing and advertising by influencing consumers using notable personalities, hence the appearance of words such as "social media marketing," "influencers," "influencer marketing," "advertising," and "marketing." This suggests that social media platforms and the measures and strategies to rank influencers according to their online social influence and interaction patterns attracted the attention of scholars in the research area. Notably, the emergence of words such as "trust," "source credibility," and "celebrity endorsement" during this period (2018 to mid-2019) is not surprising as authenticity and trust in a world that barrages users with exasperating, disturbing, and deceitful advertisements is necessary within the context of influencer marketing (Lou & Yuan, 2019; Schouten et al., 2020). Then, at the end of 2019 to 2020, studies largely focused on persuasion and purchase intentions of consumers, especially children through native advertising means using platforms such as YouTube and Instagram, hence the appearance of words such as "purchase intention," "persuasion knowledge," "children,"

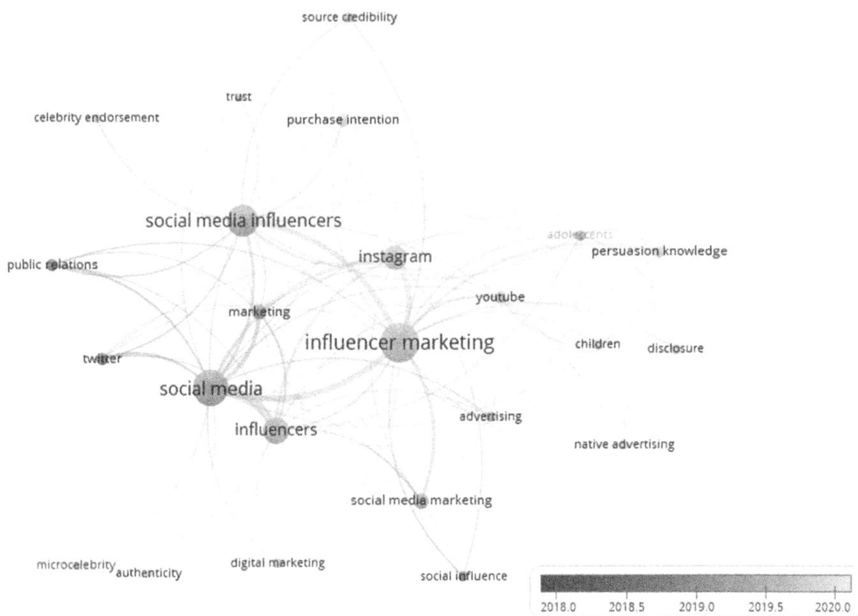

Fig. 7.4 Trend in the use of keywords

"disclosure," "native advertising," and "YouTube." For example, van Reijmersdal et al. (2020) aver that there is a growing trend in the development of influencer marketing content using children's digital media (online content), while Coates et al. (2019) assert that "children's liking of a character increases the probability of imitating the character's action" (p. 2). Hence, the apparent interest in and attention to research on influencer marketing regarding young people (e.g., adolescents and children) is not out of place.

7.3.6 Contributing Countries and Institutions

The top 10 most productive countries are listed in Table 7.7. These constitute the countries that have paid the most attention to research on influencer marketing. According to Cristino et al. (2018), country and institutional productions in bibliometric studies are determined by the first author's affiliation. The USA, UK, and Netherlands stand out as the leading three countries above all others, being the countries with the highest number of contributions. The USA has 40 articles, followed by the UK with 14 articles and the Netherlands with 13 articles. Specifically, authors from the USA are identified as the major facilitators for research in influencer marketing. The paper by Freberg, Graham, McGaughey, and Freberg (2011), which sought to understand public perceptions regarding the personality of social media influencers (SMIs) in optimizing an organization's SMI capital, and the paper by Xiao et al. (2018) who used a heuristic-systematic model to explore the factors affecting YouTube influencer marketing credibility using Amazon's Mechanical Turk (MTurk) platform as a case study were some of the research in the US category.

The table further indicates that, regionally, the majority of the leading countries (60%) were from Europe, suggesting a high interest by countries in these regions in research on influencer marketing.

Regarding country collaborations as seen in Table 7.8, the three leading pairs of countries that have collaborated are the USA and S. Korea (six collaborations) followed by the USA and the UK (five collaborations) and then by the USA and Canada, as well as the USA and Hong Kong (three collaborations each). This indicates there have been a lot more collaborations happening among countries located in North America (e.g., USA) and Europe (e.g., UK). Therefore, these countries have widespread cooperation with other countries when it comes to research on the topic. Highlighting further on the level of multiregional or multicountry collaborations, most of the country collaborations were seen to be coming from collaborations between North America and Europe and also among authors only affiliated to European countries. An example is a study by Hughes et al. (2019) where they explore the factors that drive the success of online brand engagement at different stages of the consumer purchase funnel. The collaboration was between authors from the USA and UK. Also, there was collaboration between authors from two European countries (Netherlands and Belgium) where van Reijmersdal et al. (2020) explored the effects of sponsorship disclosure on children's attitudes toward the sponsoring brand, the video, and the influencer.

The top 10 institutions leading the research on the topic are listed in Table 7.9. Among these 10 institutions, the leading 3 are the University of Liverpool (21 papers), followed by Ghent University (20 papers) and Radboud University (13 papers). Specifically, three of the top 10 institutions are located in the Netherlands. One of the papers from the University of Liverpool, located in the UK, which leads in terms of the number of authors' institutional affiliations is the study by Coates

Table 7.7 The ten most productive countries

Country	Region	Articles
USA	North America	40
UK	Europe	14
Netherlands	Europe	13
Germany	Europe	10
India	South Asia	9
Spain	Europe	7
Australia	Europe	6
Belgium	Europe	6
Hong Kong	Asia	5
S. Korea	Asia	5

Table 7.8 Top 10 country collaborations

From	Region	To	Region	Frequency
USA	North America	S. Korea	Asia	6
USA	North America	UK	Europe	5
USA	North America	Canada	North America	3
USA	North America	Hong Kong	Asia	3
Finland	Europe	Sweden	Europe	2
Netherlands	Europe	Spain	Europe	2
UK	Europe	Canada	North America	2
UK	Europe	France	Europe	2
UK	Europe	Germany	Europe	2
USA	North America	Australia	Oceania	2

Table 7.9 Most productive institutions

Affiliations	Country	Articles
University of Liverpool	UK	21
Ghent University	Belgium	20
Radboud University	Netherlands	13
Nanyang Technological University	Singapore	12
Universiti Malaysia Kelantan	Malaysia	12
University of Amsterdam	Netherlands	9
New York University	USA	8
The Hong Kong Polytechnic University	Hong Kong	8
Erasmus University Rotterdam	Netherlands	7
University of Tennessee	USA	7

et al. (2019) who investigate the impact of social media influencer marketing on children's intake of healthy and unhealthy foods.

Spotlight on Africa

Findings from this bibliometric review show a seeming lack of research from authors in African countries and African institutions. Out of the 243 journal publications on influencer marketing, South Africa was the only African country with a first author from Africa, though it is not listed among the list of the ten countries making the most contributions. The paper was authored by Iqani (2019), who explored social media influencers' cultural labor on marketing luxury brands using their Instagram profiles. Reiterating the assertion made by Cristino et al. (2018), country and institutional productions in bibliometric studies are determined by the first author's affiliation. Hence, author contributions are counted based on the first author affiliation.

However, in terms of author appearances, there are a total of 11 authors who were affiliated to Africa who appeared as coauthors in influencer marketing research. Leading the author appearances from Africa is South Africa, followed by Morocco.

7.3.7 Future Research Directions

Based on the results and discussions of this bibliometric study, the following suggestions in terms of research directions are proposed:

First, considering that the attention on influencer marketing research has predominantly been in the past 4 years (2016–2020), keeping an eye on the level of scholarly research attention it receives in the next 10 years will be important.

Second, the predominant methodological approach identified in this study is quantitative. Hence, researchers tend to rely on a generalization rather than gaining in-depth understanding of consumers, influencers, and businesses' perceptions of influencer marketing (Clark et al., 2008). Further, considering that theory adoption has been low, authors need to consider focusing more on theoretical adoption to understand a marketing model such as influencer marketing, in order to contribute to existing theories.

Third, having identified the leading authors and journals in research on influencer marketing, it will also be worth identifying the co-citations between authors and how journals are also co-cited and coupled with each other. It will also be valuable to explore journal-specific bibliometric reviews of the sources (journal outlets) that have spearheaded much of the influencer marketing literature (e.g., *International Journal of Advertising*, *Public Relations Review*, and *Celebrity Studies*).

Fourth, considering the growing interest in adopting influencer marketing from businesses (De Veirman et al., 2016; Cuevas et al., 2020), coupled with active collaborations among scholars from different geographical regions, future empirical studies should also compare research from developed countries in Europe, America, and Asia with research from developing countries to understand the dynamics within these contexts. Finally, influencer marketing analytics may be at the cusp of bringing a paradigm shift in the field of marketing. Hence, it is important to explore, through empirical studies, how data analytics technologies transform the marketing field in terms of interactivity and effectiveness in tracking return on investment (ROI) (Alampi, 2019).

Research Directions for Africa

The study identified that only a very limited number of countries from Africa were making a contribution to influencer marketing research as the topic had predominantly been explored in North America and Europe. South Africa was the only country to have contributed a paper; though authors from other African countries had collaborated with non-African authors, they were not the lead author of the contributions (see Table 7.10). It will therefore be worth exploring further studies that place a premium on developing regions to determine the level of research there and the extent of country collaborations within that context.

Further, following in the path of the ten most cited papers on influencer marketing (see Table 7.5), there are a number of research leaps that could be explored by researchers and their institutions in African countries, to make up for the research deficit that has characterized the research area of influencer marketing in the region

Table 7.10 Author appearance from African countries

Country	Region	Appearance
South Africa	Southern Africa	5
Morocco	North Africa	3
Kenya	East Africa	1
Nigeria	West Africa	1
Uganda	East Africa	1

of Africa. Table 7.11 provides a summary of possible future study directions that researchers in Africa could explore.

7.4 Conclusion

Based on 243 articles which were identified to have been published between 2011 and 2020, significant findings emerged from the bibliometric analyses of influencer marketing research. This study has identified the key methods, theories, authors, journals, countries, institutions, and keywords. Furthermore, the study predicts that social media will continue to dominate as a focus area for researchers, and persuasion targeted at influencing children and adolescents toward accepting brands will linger on in the agenda for researchers.

By using VOSviewer and Bibliometrix to quantitatively investigate a research discipline, this study has demonstrated how to investigate a discipline in a short duration. Compared to a systematic review, which reviews extant literature, the bibliometric method employed in this study not only traces the development of a subject, its important authors, and critical papers through visualization maps and figures but also reveals future research trends in this discipline.

7.4.1 Limitations of the Study

This study is not immune to limitations. First, the study has focused on only journal articles indexed in the Scopus database. Future studies can include other sources of data, such as the Web of Sciences (WoS). Second, this study focused exclusively on peer-reviewed journal articles. Future studies should analyze other types of papers (e.g., conference papers) as well as expand to journals related to influencer marketing, such as the *International Journal of Advertising*. The citation analysis and visualization of co-citation networks depict the invisible aspects within a discipline (Zupic & Čater, 2015). Hence, future studies should examine cumulative citation and co-citation networks to offer a broader view of the discipline. Further, an inherent weakness in this study is that bibliometric studies/software do not consider self-citation bias. We, therefore, consider this as one of the limitations of bibliometric

Table 7.11 Summary of possible future study directions for researchers in Africa

Theme	Possible questions	Further reading
Followership of the influencer	How does an influencer's number of followers affect perceptions of the uniqueness of a product and accordingly brand attitudes? What is the impact of factors such as familiarity, similarity, and likeability on an endorser's persuasiveness? What is the impact of influencers' personality traits (e.g., self-esteem, need for uniqueness) on consumers' decision to follow a brand?	De Veirman et al. (2017)
Content posted by influencers	How does the topic posted by influencers shape their followership and ability to influence consumers? What is the impact of the quality (photography, text, etc.) of the content posted by influencers on their followership and influence?	De Veirman et al. (2017) and Freberg et al. (2011)
Influencers and brands	Are influencers more likely than others to influence brand perceptions in a beneficial way? What factors impact a brand's decision to engage an influencer? What are the motivating factors for an influencer's decision to sign up as a brand influencer? What is the impact of factors such as daily hits on a blog, number of times a post is shared, or number of followers on a brand's decision to engage an influencer? Online influencer's quality or quantity, which matters to brands? What types of brands engage the services of influencers?	De Veirman et al. (2017) and Jin et al. (2019)
Technology and influencer marketing	What technologies/platforms are used by influencers to reach their target audience? What factors inform the influencer's decision to adopt a particular social media platform? What technologies are adopted by brands to track the influence and ROI of their brand influencers? What affordances do social media platforms create for influencer marketing? How do different social media platforms compare to each other in influencer marketing?	Khamis et al. (2017) and Jin et al. (2019)
Expenditure on influencer marketing	How does influencer marketing affect consumer expenditure? How does influencer marketing affect brand expenditure?	Lou and Yuan (2019)
Effects of the sources of influence	How does the channel of influence determine its effectiveness on influencer marketing? How does the medium through which persuasion is made impact on a consumer's decision to purchase or follow a brand?	Lou and Yuan (2019) and Hughes et al. (2019)

(continued)

Table 7.11 (continued)

Theme	Possible questions	Further reading
General directions	How does influencer marketing impact on specific social networking sites (SNSs).	Lou and Yuan (2019)
Sampling of respondents	What is the role of cultural factors in social media following? How does a consumer's generation and age impact their decision to be influenced by influencer marketers?	Lou and Yuan (2019) and Chae (2017)
Methodologies	Future research can use other methods, such as experimental designs, to study causal relationships for influencer marketing	Lou and Yuan (2019)
Celebrities and influencer marketing	What are the types of social media endorsements with different levels of product engagement? How do traditional celebrities become influencers on social media? Test the effects of two types of celebrities (Instagram celebrity vs. traditional celebrity) on source trustworthiness, brand attitude, envy, and social presence	Schouten et al. (2020) and Jin et al. (2019)

studies that our study inherits (in essence, self-citation bias is rarely discussed in bibliometric studies). Also, bibliometric software is unable to draw out theories/models, hence, a limitation of this study.

References

Alampi, A. (2019). The future is micro: How to build an effective micro-influencer program. *Journal of Digital and Social Media Marketing, 7*, 203–208.

Al-Khalaf, E., & Choe, P. (2020). Increasing customer trust towards mobile commerce in a multicultural society: A case of Qatar. *Journal of Internet Commerce, 19*(1), 32–61.

Alves, H., Fernandes, C. M., & Raposo. (2016). Social media marketing: A literature review and implications. *Psychology and Marketing, 33*, 1029–1038.

Arfaoui, A., Ibrahimi, K. F., & Trabelsi. (2019). Biochar application to soil under arid conditions: A bibliometric study of research status and trends. *Arabian Journal of Geosciences, 12*(2), 45.

Argyris, Y. A., Wang, Z., Kim, Y. Z., & Yin. (2020). The effects of visual congruence on increasing consumers' brand engagement: An empirical investigation of influencer marketing on Instagram using deep-learning algorithms for automatic image classification. *Computers in Human Behavior, 112*, 106443.

Arora, A., Bansal, S., Kandpal, C., Aswani, R., & Dwivedi, Y. (2019). Measuring social media influencer index-insights from Facebook, Twitter and Instagram. *Journal of Retailing and Consumer Services, 49*, 86–101.

Audrezet, A., de Kerviler, G., & Moulard, J. G. (2018). Authenticity under threat: When social media influencers need to go beyond self-presentation. *Journal of Business Research, 117*, 557–569.

Balaban, D., & Mustățea, M. (2019). Users' perspective on the credibility of social media influencers in Romania and Germany. *Romanian Journal of Communication and Public Relations, 21*(1), 31–46.

Britt, R. K., Hayes, J. L., Britt, B. C., & Park, H. (2020). Too big to sell? A computational analysis of network and content characteristics among mega and micro beauty and fashion social media influencers. *Journal of Interactive Advertising, 20*(2), 111–118.

Campbell, C., & Marks, L. J. (2015). Good native advertising isn't a secret. *Business Horizons, 58*(6), 599–606.

Carah, N., & Shaul, M. (2016). Brands and Instagram: Point, tap, swipe, glance. *Mobile Media & Communication, 4*(1), 69–84.

Chae, J. (2017). Virtual makeover: Selfie-taking and social media use increase selfie-editing frequency through social comparison. *Computers in Human Behavior, 66*, 370–376.

Chang, C. C., & Ho, Y. S. (2010). Bibliometric analysis of financial crisis research. *African Journal of Business Management, 4*, 3898–3910.

Chetioui, Y., Benlafqih, H., & Lebdaoui, H. (2020). How fashion influencers contribute to consumers' purchase intention. *Journal of Fashion Marketing and Management: An International Journal., 24*, 1–20.

Cirillo, B., Tzabbar, D., & Seo, D. (2020). A bibliometric and topic modeling analysis of the structural divide in the multidisciplinary research on employee mobility. In *Employee inter-and intra-firm mobility*. Emerald Publishing Limited. https://doi.org/10.1108/S0742-332220200000041001

Clark, V. L. P., Creswell, J. W., Green, D. O. N., & Shope, R. J. (2008). Mixing quantitative and qualitative approaches. In *Handbook of emergent methods* (p. 363).

Coates, A. E., Hardman, C. A., Halford, J. C., Christiansen, P., & Boyland, E. J. (2019). Food and beverage cues featured in YouTube videos of social media influencers popular with children: An exploratory study. *Frontiers in Psychology, 10*, 2142.

Coco, S. L., & Eckert, S. (2020). # sponsored: Consumer insights on social media influencer marketing. *Public Relations Inquiry, 2046147X20920816*. https://doi.org/10.1177/2046147X20920816

Costas, R., Van Leeuwen, T. N., & Bordons, M. (2010). A bibliometric classificatory approach for the study and assessment of research performance at the individual level: The effects of age on productivity and impact. *Journal of the American Society for Information Science and Technology, 61*, 1564–1581.

Creswell, J. W., & Creswell, J. D. (2017). *Research design: Qualitative, quantitative, and mixed methods approaches*. Sage.

Cristino, T. M., Neto, A. F., & Costa, A. F. B. (2018). Energy efficiency in buildings: Analysis of scientific literature and identification of data analysis techniques from a bibliometric study. *Scientometrics, 114*(3), 1275–1326.

Cuevas, L. M., Chong, S. M., & Lim, H. (2020). Influencer marketing: Social media influencers as human brands attaching to followers and yielding positive marketing results by fulfilling needs. *Journal of Retailing and Consumer Services, 55*, 102133.

Dabi, Y., Darrigues, L., Katsahian, S., Azoulay, D., De Antonio, M., & Lazzati, A. (2016). Publication trends in bariatric surgery: a bibliometric study. *Obesity Surgery, 26*(11), 2691–2699.

De Jans, S., & Hudders, L. (2020). Disclosure of vlog advertising targeted to children. *Journal of Interactive Marketing, 52*, 1–19.

De Jans, S., Van de Sompel, D., De Veirman, M., & Hudders, L. (2020). # Sponsored! How the recognition of sponsoring on Instagram posts affects adolescents' brand evaluations through source evaluations. *Computers in Human Behavior, 109*, 106342.

De Veirman, M., Cauberghe, V., & Hudders, L. (2016). *Why are people interacting with brands on Facebook: Unraveling consumers' motivations for lurking and posting on Facebook brand pages*. In EMAC 2016.

De Veirman, M., Cauberghe, V., & Hudders, L. (2017). Marketing through Instagram influencers: the impact of number of followers and product divergence on brand attitude. *International Journal of Advertising, 36*(5), 798–828.

De Veirman, M., & Hudders, L. (2020). Disclosing sponsored Instagram posts: the role of material connection with the brand and message-sidedness when disclosing covert advertising. *International Journal of Advertising, 39*(1), 94–130.

Diem, A., & Wolter, S. C. (2013). The use of bibliometrics to measure research performance in education sciences. *Research in Higher Education, 54*, 86–114.
Durieux, V., & Gevenois, P. A. (2010). Bibliometric indicators: Quality measurements of scientific publication. *Radiology, 255*, 342–351.
Falagas, M. E., Pitsouni, E. I., Malietzis, G. A., & Pappas, G. (2008). Comparison of PubMed, Scopus, Web of Science, and Google Scholar: Strengths and weaknesses. *The FASEB Journal, 22*, 338–342.
Fellnhofer, K. (2019). Toward a taxonomy of entrepreneurship education research literature: A bibliometric mapping and visualization. *Educational Research Review, 27*, 28–55.
Finfgeld-Connett, D. (2014). Use of content analysis to conduct knowledge-building and theory-generating qualitative systematic reviews. *Qualitative Research, 14*(3), 341–352.
Freberg, K., Graham, K., McGaughey, K., & Freberg, L. A. (2011). Who are the social media influencers? A study of public perceptions of personality. *Public Relations Review, 37*, 90–92.
Garousi, V., & Mäntylä, M. V. (2016). A systematic literature review of literature reviews in software testing. *Information and Software Technology, 80*, 195–216.
Gerdsri, N., Kongthon, A., & Puengrusme, S. (2017). Profiling the research landscape in emerging areas using bibliometrics and text mining: A case study of biomedical engineering (BME) in Thailand. *International Journal of Innovation and Technology Management, 14*, 1740011.
Giraldo, P., Benavente, E., Manzano-Agugliaro, F., & Gimenez, E. (2019). Worldwide research trends on wheat and barley: A bibliometric comparative analysis. *Agronomy, 9*, 352.
Glucksman, M. (2017). The rise of social media influencer marketing on lifestyle branding: A case study of Lucie Fink. *Elon Journal of Undergraduate Research in Communications, 8*, 77–87.
Guercini, S., Bernal, P. M., & Prentice, C. (2018). New marketing in fashion e-commerce. *Journal of global fashion marketing, 9*(1), 1–8.
Gupta, N., Dorfman, R., Saadat, S., & Roostaeian, J. (2020). The plastic surgery social media influencer: Ethical considerations and a literature review. *Aesthetic Surgery Journal, 40*, 691–699.
Haustein, S., & Larivière, V. (2015). The use of bibliometrics for assessing research: Possibilities, limitations and adverse effects. In *Incentives and performance*. Springer.
Hughes, C., Swaminathan, V., & Brooks, G. (2019). Driving brand engagement through online social influencers: An empirical investigation of sponsored blogging campaigns. *Journal of Marketing, 83*(5), 78–96.
Huynh, T., Nguyen, H., Zelinka, I., Dinh, D., & Pham, X. H. (2020). Detecting the influencer on social networks using passion point and measures of information propagation. *Sustainability, 12*, 3064.
Iqani, M. (2019). Picturing luxury, producing value: The cultural labour of social media brand influencers in South Africa. *International Journal of Cultural Studies, 22*(2), 229–247.
Jin, S. V., Muqaddam, A., & Ryu, E. (2019). Instafamous and social media influencer marketing. *Marketing Intelligence & Planning, 37*(5), 567–579.
Khamis, S., Ang, L., & Welling, R. (2017). Self-branding, 'micro-celebrity' and the rise of social media influencers. *Celebrity studies, 8*, 191–208.
Kim, J., & McMillan, S. J. (2008). Evaluation of internet advertising research: A bibliometric analysis of citations from key sources. *Journal of Advertising, 37*, 99–112.
Kim, J., Kang, S., & Lee, K. H. (2019). Evolution of digital marketing communication: Bibliometric analysis and network visualization from key articles. *Journal of Business Research*. https://doi.org/10.1016/j.jbusres.2019.09.043
Köseoglu, M. A., Sehitoglu, Y., Ross, G., & Parnell, J. A. (2016). The evolution of business ethics research in the realm of tourism and hospitality. *International Journal of Contemporary Hospitality Management, 28*, 1598–1621.
Kosmützky, A., & Krücken, G. (2014). Growth or steady state? A bibliometric focus on international comparative higher education research. *Higher Education, 67*, 457–472.
Kumar, S., Sureka, R., & Pandey, N. (2020). A retrospective overview of the Asian Review of Accounting during 1992–2019. *Asian Review of Accounting, 28*, 445–462.

Laaksonen, S. M., Pantti, M., & Titley, G. (2020). Broadcasting the movement and branding political microcelebrities: Finnish anti-immigration video practices on YouTube. *Journal of Communication, 70*, 171–194.

Lamberton, C., & Stephen, A. T. (2016). A thematic exploration of digital, social media, and mobile marketing: Research evolution from 2000 to 2015 and an agenda for future inquiry. *Journal of Marketing, 80*(6), 146–172.

Lewis, R. (2020). "This is what the news won't show you": YouTube creators and the reactionary politics of micro-celebrity. *Television and New Media, 21*, 201–217.

Lou, C., & Yuan, S. (2019). Influencer marketing: How message value and credibility affect consumer trust of branded content on social media. *Journal of Interactive Advertising, 19*(1), 58–73.

Madani, F. (2015). 'Technology Mining' bibliometrics analysis: Applying network analysis and cluster analysis. *Scientometrics, 105*, 323–335.

Madani, F., & Weber, C. (2016). The evolution of patent mining: Applying bibliometrics analysis and keyword network analysis. *World Patent Information, 46*, 32–48.

Mallett, R., Hagen-Zanker, J., Slater, R., & Duvendack, M. (2012). The benefits and challenges of using systematic reviews in international development research. *Journal of Development Effectiveness, 4*(3), 445–455.

Martí-Parreño, J., Méndez-Ibáñez, E., & Alonso-Arroyo, A. (2016). The use of gamification in education: A bibliometric and text mining analysis. *Journal of Computer Assisted Learning, 32*, 663–676.

Merigó, J. M., & Yang, J. B. (2017). A bibliometric analysis of operations research and management science. *Omega, 73*, 37–48.

Mora, L., Bolici, R., & Deakin, M. (2017). The first two decades of smart-city research: A bibliometric analysis. *Journal of Urban Technology, 24*, 3–27.

Morton, F. (2020). Influencer marketing: An exploratory study on the motivations of young adults to follow social media influencers. *Journal of Digital & Social Media Marketing, 8*(2), 156–165.

Nandagiri, V., & Philip, L. (2018). Impact of influencers from Instagram and YouTube on their followers. *International Journal of Multidisciplinary Research and Modern Education, 4*, 61–65.

Okumus, B., Koseoglu, M. A., & Ma, F. (2018). Food and gastronomy research in tourism and hospitality: A bibliometric analysis. *International Journal of Hospitality Management, 73*, 64–74.

Pillania, R. K. (2011). The state of research on technological uncertainties, social uncertainties and emerging markets: A multidisciplinary literature review. *Technological Forecasting and Social Change, 78*, 1158–1163.

Podsakoff, P. M., MacKenzie, S. B., Podsakoff, N. P., & Bachrach, D. G. (2008). Scholarly influence in the field of management: A bibliometric analysis of the determinants of university and author impact in the management literature in the past quarter century. *Journal of Management, 34*, 641–720.

Ryu, S., & Park, J. (2020). The effects of benefit-driven commitment on usage of social media for shopping and positive word-of-mouth. *Journal of Retailing and Consumer Services, 55*, 102094.

Samiee, S., & Chabowski, B. R. (2012). Knowledge structure in international marketing: A multimethod bibliometric analysis. *Journal of the Academy of Marketing Science, 40*, 364–386.

Schouten, A. P., Janssen, L., & Verspaget, M. (2020). Celebrity vs. Influencer endorsements in advertising: The role of identification, credibility, and Product-Endorser fit. *International Journal of Advertising, 39*(2), 258–281.

Shan, Y., Chen, K. J., & Lin, J. S. (2020). When social media influencers endorse brands: The effects of self-influencer congruence, parasocial identification, and perceived endorser motive. *International Journal of Advertising, 39*, 590–610.

Soltani, M., Nejad, N. S., Azad, F. T., Taheri, B., & Gannon, M. J. (2020). Food consumption experiences: A framework for understanding food tourists' behavioral intentions. *International Journal of Contemporary Hospitality Management, 33*(1), 75–100.

Stubb, C., Nyström, A. G., & Colliander, J. (2019). Influencer marketing. *Journal of Communication Management, 23*, 109–122.
Sudha, M., & Sheena, K. (2017). Impact of influencers in consumer decision process: The fashion industry. *SCMS Journal of Indian Management, 14*, 14–30.
Taillon, B. J., Mueller, S. M., Kowalczyk, C. M., & Jones, D. N. (2020). Understanding the relationships between social media influencers and their followers: The moderating role of closeness. *Journal of Product and Brand Management*. https://doi.org/10.1108/JPBM-03-2019-2292
Van Eck, N. J., & Waltman, L. (2013). VOSviewer manual. *Leiden: Univeristeit Leiden, 1*(1), 1–53.
van Reijmersdal, E. A., Rozendaal, E., Hudders, L., Vanwesenbeeck, I., Cauberghe, V., & van Berlo, Z. M. (2020). Effects of disclosing influencer marketing in videos: An eye tracking study among children in early adolescence. *Journal of Interactive Marketing, 49*, 94–106.
Velasco-Muñoz, J. F., Aznar-Sánchez, J. A., Belmonte-Ureña, L. J., & López-Serrano, M. J. (2018). Advances in water use efficiency in agriculture: A bibliometric analysis. *Water, 10*, 377.
Wiedmann, K. P., Hennigs, N., & Langner, S. (2010). Spreading the word of fashion: Identifying social influencers in fashion marketing. *Journal of Global Fashion Marketing, 1*, 142–153.
Xiao, M., Wang, R., & Chan-Olmsted, S. (2018). Factors affecting YouTube influencer marketing credibility: A heuristic-systematic model. *Journal of Media Business Studies, 15*, 188–213.
Xu, X., & Pratt, S. (2018). Social media influencers as endorsers to promote travel destinations: An application of self-congruence theory to the Chinese Generation Y. *Journal of Travel & Tourism Marketing, 35*, 958–972.
Ye, Q., Song, H., & Li, T. (2012). Cross-institutional collaboration networks in tourism and hospitality research. *Tourism Management Perspectives, 2*, 55–64.
Zhang, Y., Hua, W., & Yuan, S. (2018). Mapping the scientific research on open data: A bibliometric review. *Learned Publishing, 31*(2), 95–106.
Zhang, D., Zhang, Z., & Managi. (2019). A bibliometric analysis on green finance: Current status, development, and future directions. *Finance Research Letters, 29*, 425–430.
Zupic, I., & Čater, T. (2015). Bibliometric methods in management and organization. *Organizational Research Methods, 18*, 429–472.

Dr. Sheena Lovia Boateng is a lecturer at the Department of Marketing and Entrepreneurship at the University of Ghana Business School. She is a fellow of the Academy of Marketing Science. She also served as a member of the Editorial Advisory Board for the *Emerald Emerging Markets Case Study Journal*, Emerald Publishing Limited, UK, from 2018 to 2020. She has published seven journal publications, three books, four book chapters, five published conference papers, one working paper, and one industry report. Her academic work has been published in the *International Journal of Bank Marketing*, *Journal of Financial Services Marketing*, and *Journal of Educational Technology Systems*. Her research interests include online relationship marketing, fashion and beauty marketing, digital business strategy, electronic learning adoption, entrepreneurship, online branding and advertising, social media marketing, and structural equation modeling in marketing. She can be reached at slboateng@ug.edu.gh.

Chapter 8
Thirty-Four Years of Online Pharmaceutical Marketing Research: A Bibliometric Analysis

Sheena Lovia Boateng and Paul Owusu Donkor

Abstract This study seeks to uncover the state of scientific research and trends in online pharmaceutical marketing. A total of 541 journal documents were obtained from Scopus and classified based on country, institutions, most impactful authors, influential journals, and keywords in the research area using VOSviewer and the bibliometrix package in R Studio. The findings reveal that research on online pharmaceutical marketing has revolved around three themes: digital technologies that facilitate the marketing of pharmaceutical products, the dark side of marketing pharmaceutical products online, and the legislation and regulation of online pharmaceutical marketing. Contributions to research in the area were also found to mostly originate from North America (USA) and Europe, with developing regions such as Africa being barely represented. Findings show that the USA and the University of Hertfordshire are the most productive country and institution, respectively, in respect to online pharmaceutical marketing research. At the same time, the *International Journal of Drug Policy* emerged as the most productive and most cited journal, with "Mackey TK" and "Liang BA" being the most relevant authors and "Schifano F" involved in most of the author collaborations. These results provide insights into online pharmaceutical marketing, in addition to valuable information to enable researchers to identify hot topics, new perspectives and research frontiers in the area, as well as potential collaborators and partner institutions. Furthermore, the findings point to the need for an enhanced research focus on other themes in online pharmaceutical marketing, particularly by researchers in Africa.

S. L. Boateng (✉)
University of Ghana Business School, Legon, Accra, Ghana
e-mail: slboateng@ug.edu.gh

P. O. Donkor
University of Ghana School of Pharmacy, Accra, Ghana
e-mail: powusudonkor@ug.edu.gh

R. Boateng et al. (eds.), *Digital Innovations, Business and Society in Africa*,
Advances in Theory and Practice of Emerging Markets,
https://doi.org/10.1007/978-3-030-77987-0_8

Keywords Online pharmaceutical marketing · Online marketing · Internet-based direct-to-consumer advertising (eDTCA) · Pharmaceutical marketing · Bibliometric analysis

8.1 Introduction

Marketing refers to all the activities performed by a business to satisfy customers' needs in a profitable manner (Todor, 2016). In the recent past decade, the rapid evolution of the Internet has created myriad opportunities for satisfying these customer needs in what is termed as digital marketing (Parekh et al., 2016; Mullner & Gurău, 2005). Lad et al. (2017) define digital marketing as a means of marketing products using digital technology, often referred to as "online marketing," "Internet marketing," or "web marketing" (Todor, 2016).

For several businesses, online marketing provides a means of enhancing commercial opportunities by establishing "digital relationships" with customers (Phillips, 2015). These are enabled by technologies such as artificial intelligence, deep learning, and the Internet of things (IoT) (Kannan, 2017), the application of which can be observed in various sectors. These sectors include tourism (e.g., Howison et al., 2015), manufacturing (e.g., Wajid & Bhullar, 2019; Kimergård et al., 2014), fashion and beauty (e.g., Chan & Astari, 2017), and education (e.g., Constantinides & Stagno, 2012; Constantinides & Zinck Stagno, 2011; Adams & Eveland, 2007). Thus, many firms in the pharmaceutical sector have followed suit by investing heavily in acquiring these digital tools for the marketing of their products and services. These investments were made despite the observed operational and regulatory challenges in digital pharmaceutical marketing at both national and global levels (Jawaid & Ahmed, 2018; De Freitas et al., 2013; Mullner & Gurău, 2005), (Parekh et al., 2016).

As executed online via websites or through social media, online pharmaceutical marketing has gained significant interest globally (Liang & Mackey, 2011). In countries like the USA and New Zealand, pharmaceutical marketing is undergoing a substantial shift from more traditional forms of direct-to-consumer advertising (DTCA) to the use of more Internet-based DTCA approaches (eDTCA), given the growing popularity of electronic health (eHealth) (Mackey et al., 2015). This shift has led to the emergence of several new technologies that have been designed to facilitate eHealth practices. "DTCA 2.0" is an example of such technology, which makes use of interactive web programs and tools such as podcasts, blogs, Really Simple Syndication (RSS) feeds, social networking sites (Facebook, Twitter), and forums (Jawaid & Ahmed, 2018; Liang & Mackey, 2012). Despite the growing body of research in utilizing these digital technologies for marketing pharmaceutical products and services, a specific bibliometric analysis on scientific publications in the area is yet to be performed. Furthermore, there have been calls for the recognition of the decades of research in the area (Mackey & Liang, 2012). Thus, this study seeks to respond to these calls by conducting a bibliometric analysis to recognize scientific research in online pharmaceutical marketing.

8.1.1 Responding to the Call

Bibliometric analysis is a statistical analysis method for studying scientific publications in a particular research area (Hicks et al., 2015; Broadus, 1987). This method has been applied in many research fields to evaluate patterns in publications with regard to the countries, institutions, journals, authors, and keywords associated with specific research types. Studies of this nature have been performed in education (e.g., Fellnhofer, 2019; Kosmützky & Krücken, 2014), medicine and wellness (e.g., Kokol et al., 2020; Han & Ho, 2011), tourism and leisure (e.g., Okumus et al., 2018; Köseoglu et al., 2016), manufacturing (e.g., Marzi et al., 2017), finance (Zhang et al., 2019; Chang & Ho, 2010), agriculture (Giraldo et al., 2019; Velasco-Muñoz et al., 2018), and information technology (Mora et al., 2017; Madani, 2015), among others.

Nonetheless, previous bibliometric studies conducted within the context of this study have focused broadly on pharmaceutical marketing (e.g., López-Muñoz et al., 2015; Babar & Atif, 2014; Basak & Sathyanarayana, 2010; Rivera et al., 2010). For instance, Babar and Atif (2014) performed a bibliometric review of publications on the differential pricing of pharmaceutical products. Basak and Sathyanarayana (2010) also analyzed literature regarding community pharmacy practice in India from 1998 to 2008. However, there is arguably no identifiable study of this nature that focuses specifically on the concept of marketing pharmaceutical products and services online. As a result, a bibliometric analysis of online pharmaceutical marketing research is performed in this study, highlighting the nature and trends of research in the area while providing directions for future research.

The ensuing sections of the study are organized as follows: In Sect. 8.2, the research methodology is elaborated, including the data acquisition process and the analysis tools for processing the acquired data. The research results and discussion are then presented, including an analysis of the most relevant authors and journals, countries and institutions, a network of author collaborations, keyword co-occurrence, and possible future research directions, as presented in Sect. 8.3. The final section concludes the study and highlights some limitations that can be addressed in further research.

8.2 Methodology

This section describes the methodology that was used in conducting the study. It discusses the process for acquiring the data, as well as the analytics tools used in undertaking the study.

8.2.1 Data Acquisition

For purposes of this study, the Scopus database was used to obtain research data in online pharmaceutical marketing. Compared to other scientific databases, the Scopus database is a repository of multidisciplinary peer-reviewed literature (Mongeon & Paul-Hus, 2016). It contains indexed articles from approximately 38,046 journals and captures one of the widest ranges of scientific articles among all electronic databases, with publications dating as far back as 1788 (Elsevier, 2020). Previous researchers, including Kipper et al. (2020); Sweileh (2018); Veer and Khiste Gajanan (2017); and Palomo et al. (2017), have all conducted bibliometric studies using the Scopus database for data acquisition, thereby emphasizing the selection of this database for the current study.

A search strategy was designed to collect data for the study by capturing all the relevant published indexed articles referring to "online pharmaceutical marketing." Other keywords that are used in reference to engagements in "online pharmaceutical marketing" were also considered. These keywords were chosen based on previous literature reviews on similar topics, the authors' own research experience, and expert views from fellow academics as proposed by Xu et al. (2018). As such, the following string words were used: online **or** digital **or** Internet **and** pharmaceutical marketing **or** drug marketing **or** pharma marketing. The search was carried out on the titles, abstracts, and keywords of the articles (Zupic & Čater, 2015). The timeframe for the search was made open, with no time limits. The document type was also limited to journal articles written in English. Table 8.1 provides a breakdown of the bibliometric information derived after the acquisition process. Journal articles are considered because they are "generally regarded as the top-quality communication type for researchers" (Martí-Parreño et al., 2016, p. 5) among other communication types like conference proceedings, books, book chapters, reviews, editorials, and doctoral theses (Martí-Parreño et al., 2016). Also, journals are known to publish relatively rigorous research which is usually subjected to peer review in the given field of study (Durieux & Gevenois, 2010).

8.2.2 Analysis Tools

VOSviewer and the bibliometric package in R Studio were utilized as the analysis tools to generate the visualization maps and networks for this bibliometric study. Visualization maps consist of nodes of different colors and links. Different nodes in a given map represent specific elements such as a cited author or keywords. Herein, the links between nodes represent relationships of collaboration/co-occurrence or co-citations (Liang et al., 2017), with the largest nodes often regarded as turning points or pivotal points in the field under study (Xie, 2015).

Table 8.1 Overview of bibliometric information realized after curation

Description	Results
Main information about data	
Timespan	1985:2020
Sources (journals)	288
Documents	541
Average years from publication	8.46
Average citations per document	16.25
Average citations per year per document	2.028
References	15748
Document types	
Journal articles	541
Document contents	
Keywords Plus (ID)	4298
Author's keywords (DE)	1246
Authors	
Authors	1517
Author appearances	1723
Authors of single-authored documents	136
Authors of multiauthored documents	1381
Author collaborations	
Single-authored documents	159
Documents per author	0.357
Authors per document	2.8
Coauthors per documents	3.18
Collaboration index	3.62

8.3 Results

In this section, the results of three central elements are presented to measure research performance in online pharmaceutical marketing. Research countries and institutions are analyzed, along with the most impactful authors, most cited articles, most influential journals, keyword co-occurrence, and trends.

8.3.1 Analysis of the Yearly Publication Trend

Figure 8.1 shows the yearly trend in publications on online pharmaceutical marketing. The figure shows that the total number of publications in the area increased over the 34-year period of scholarly work on the topic, but with some fluctuations. This

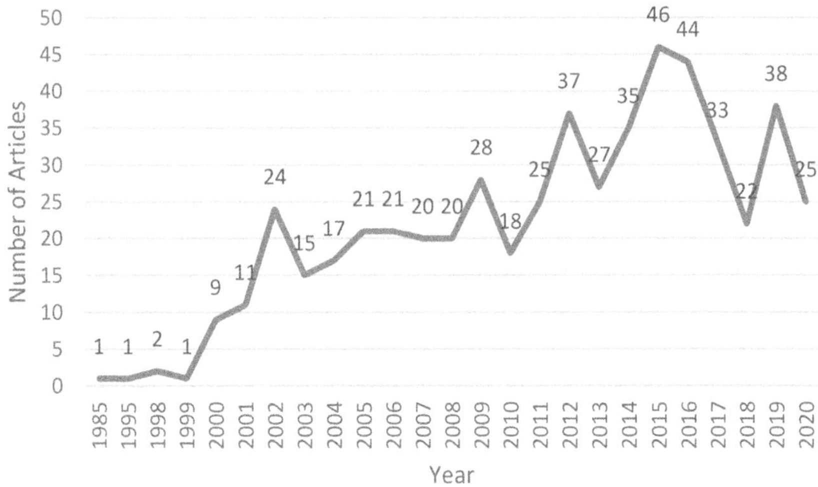

Fig. 8.1 Number of papers according to the years of publication

trend can be divided into three periods. The first period ran from 1985 to 1995; there was one paper in 1985 and another in 1995. However, within this early period, the years from 1986 to 1994 were fallow, with no articles published. This may be attributed to less interest in the area of research or a low level of maturity in the development of online platforms or digital technologies that could support the marketing of pharmaceutical products. Dabi et al. (2016) describe this period as the budding period for a research area, where many aspects of the field are yet to be explored.

The second period ran from 1998 to 2002, where there was a fluctuation in research, after which publications fell in 2003. Then came the third period, which ran from 2004 to 2020. However, within this third period, the publication trend in terms of numbers was relatively high, though there were fluctuations in the numbers compared to the first and second periods. Notably, the yearly publication trend, especially in the past decade, indicates that online pharmaceutical marketing is receiving increased attention and may continue to receive attention even though fluctuations in the number of publications in the years ahead can be expected.

8.3.2 Countries and Institutions

In Table 8.2, the top 20 countries producing most of the research in the area of online pharmaceutical marketing are presented. The country and institutional productions are determined by the first author's affiliation (Cristino et al., 2018). The top 3 countries from the list are the USA (148 papers), the UK (34 papers), and Australia (13 papers). Notably, from Table 8.2, most of these countries with the

Table 8.2 Top 20 countries leading in publications

Country	Region	Articles	SCP	MCP
USA	North America	148	142	6
UK	Europe	34	28	6
Australia	Europe	13	12	1
India	South Asia	12	10	2
Canada	Europe	11	10	1
Japan	East Asia	11	10	1
France	Europe	10	10	0
Germany	Europe	9	8	1
Switzerland	Europe	8	7	1
Italy	Europe	7	3	4
China	Asia	6	5	1
Denmark	Europe	5	4	1
Netherlands	Europe	5	2	3
Ireland	Europe	4	3	1
Korea	Asia	4	4	0
Spain	Europe	4	3	1
Finland	Europe	3	3	0
Poland	Europe	3	3	0
Romania	Europe	3	3	0
Austria	Europe	2	1	1

highest number of articles also have the highest single-country publications (SCP) and multiple-country publications (MCP) figures. SCP refers to publications that occur with authors from the same country, while MCP refers to publications with authors from more than one country. The USA (142 papers) tops the list of SCPs, followed by the UK (28 papers) and Australia (12 papers). The top 3 MCP countries are the USA and the UK (six papers each), followed by Italy (seven papers). The general picture painted by the country publication shows that a lot more first authors prefer to publish either as sole authors or with other authors who are affiliated to the same countries as the first author. Table 8.2 further points to a cumulative high number of European and Asian contributions, despite the significant number of American productions. Among the top 20 most productive countries, as shown in Table 8.2, one can count as many as 15 (75%) countries from Europe and 3 (15%) from Asia, with the remaining (10%) from North America.

More so, in Table 8.2, a seeming interest in online pharmaceutical marketing research can be observed in North America, Europe (e.g., Netherland), and even Asia (e.g., China). This can be attributed to the dominance of online pharmaceutical marketplaces, coupled with the concerns of counterfeit medicines, which "pose a public health risk" (World Health Organization, 2010; Aldridge & Décary-Hétu, 2016) within these geographical regions. It is also noteworthy that aside from China, other countries from Asia (i.e., India and Japan) make it among the top 10 countries that contribute to the papers. A country such as India is known to be one of the world leaders in drug manufacturing (Economic Times, 2017). In contrast, countries in Africa continue to adopt digital platforms for online marketing and trade (Boateng, 2020; Mohamed et al., 2019; Duffett et al., 2019), but at an insignificant pace when it comes to online pharmaceutical marketing. In this study, South Africa is identified as the only country in Africa that has contributed to research on online pharmaceutical marketing, though it is not listed among the 20 countries making the most contributions.

Additionally, the institutional affiliations of the authors in the publications are identified and discussed. As presented in Table 8.3, the University of Hertfordshire, located in the UK, produced authors with the most publications (35 papers), followed by an anonymous institution (not reported) and the University of California (with 24 papers each), King's College London, UK (20 papers), the University of New South Wales (19 papers), and Harvard Medical School (18 papers). The table corroborates the findings in Table 8.2, which suggests that the USA is the most productive country in the research area, as most of the institutions presented in the table are located in the USA. As many as 7 (35%) out of the top 20 most productive institutions are from the USA; the remaining (65%) can be found in the UK, China, Japan, Italy, Germany, Australia, the Netherlands, and two anonymous countries. Hence, institutionally, authors making publications on online pharmaceutical marketing are mostly from America and Europe, corroborating previous findings naming countries in America and Europe as the dominant contributors in the area.

Table 8.3 Top 20 contributing institutions

Affiliations	Country	Region	Articles
University of Hertfordshire	UK	Europe	35
Not reported	Anonymous	Anonymous	24
University of California	USA	North America	24
King's College London	UK	Europe	20
University of New South Wales	Australia	Europe	19
Harvard Medical School	USA	North America	18
Huazhong University of Science and Technology	China	Asia	17
Kanazawa University	Japan	East Asia	15
University of Pécs	Hungary	Europe	15
University of Brescia	Italy	Europe	14
Institute for Quality and Efficiency in Health Care	Germany	Europe	12
The University of Sydney	Australia	Europe	10
University of Ottawa	USA	North America	10
University of Pennsylvania	USA	North America	10
Texas Heart Institute	USA	North America	9
University of Michigan	USA	North America	9
University of Southern California	USA	North America	9
Utrecht University	Netherlands	Europe	9
Charité – University Medicine Berlin	Germany	Europe	8
Liverpool John Moores University	UK	Europe	8

8.3.3 Most Relevant Authors

The number of publications of an author in a given period is considered to indicate the author's scientific activity in a given research field. In total, 1517 distinct authors were identified to have contributed to the 541 journal articles on online pharmaceutical marketing, reflecting a dispersion of authorship. About 91% of these authors collaborated to contribute papers (authors of multiauthored papers), which is common in relatively new research fields that have not yet reached maturity (Casillas & Acedo, 2007), while the remaining 9% represents independently authored papers (authors of single-authored papers). It is also important to indicate that these authors may have contributed to the publication of other papers that were not included in the current study, as this study is only limited to datasets regarding online pharmaceutical marketing articles.

Table 8.4 presents a picture of the most productive authors. NP refers to the number of publications by an author, while TC refers to the total citations received by an author. PY_Start on the other hand refers to the year of first publication by the author as indexed in the Scopus database. "Mackey TK" and "Liang BA" lead in the productions with 11 papers each; thus, they may be considered influential in the field, strongly contributing to the growth of the academic literature on online pharmaceutical marketing. The third most productive author is "Schifano F" with seven articles, followed by "Deluca P" with six articles. Also, in Table 8.4, the most influential authors based on the number of citations are presented. The number of citations implies the influence of authors' research efforts in the field (Bengoa et al., 2020). Most of them have received more than 100 citations. As seen in Table 8.4, the most influential authors identified are "Mackey TK" with 11 publications and 353 citations, followed by "Liang BA" who also has 11 publications but 351 citations, 2 citations short of the number of citations received by "Mackey TK." This, therefore, puts "Mackey TK" ahead of "Liang BA" in terms of relevance to the research area as both authors began to publish in the research area in the same year (2011).

One interesting fact is that though authors such as "Schifano F" and "Deluca P" began publications earlier (in 2006) than the likes of "Mackey TK" and "Liang BA" who began publications 4 years later (in 2011), the former authors produced a smaller number of publications and have received a smaller number of citations. This is an indication that the topics discussed by "Mackey TK" and "Liang BA" are of more interest to researchers in the area than those discussed by "Schifano F" and "Deluca P."

Subsequently, a network of the coauthors and collaborations was generated with VOSviewer, resulting in seven-colored clustered nodes (red, green, blue, purple, orange, yellow, and sky blue) (see Fig. 8.2). Altogether, 1381 coauthors and 136 single authors were realized to have constituted the 1517 authors. The red cluster contained nine items, the green cluster had six items, the blue cluster had six items, the orange cluster had four items, the yellow cluster had five items, and the sky-blue cluster had four items, while the purple cluster had five items. Each node represents an author, and a clustering of nodes represents a collaboration between authors. The

Table 8.4 Top 10 most influential authors

Author	NP	TC	PY_Start
Mackey TK	11	353	2011
Liang BA	11	351	2011
Schifano F	7	339	2006
Deluca P	6	131	2006
Barratt MJ	5	140	2016
Dargan PI	5	105	2011
Van Hout MC	5	178	2011
Wood DM	5	105	2011
Bruno R	4	65	2011
Burns L	4	65	2014

TC total citations, *NP* number of publications, *PY_Start* publication start year

Fig. 8.2 Coauthorship analysis. (Coauthors)

larger the size of the node, the higher the linkages and total link strength of the author in question. The total link strength indicates the cumulative number of publications in which the author occurs, and the linkages refer to the number of nodes that the author is connected to (Van Eck and Waltman, 2013). Hence, from Fig. 8.2, the topmost collaborating author is the largest orange node representing "Schifano F," who has 19 links and a total link strength of 22. The authors who are mostly collaborating with "Schifano F" are "Feinmann C" and "Sharma A," all belonging to the same orange cluster. Notably, "Schifano F" is the third most influential author as seen in Table 8.4. "Deluca P" who is the fourth most influential author is seen in Fig. 8.2 as the second most collaborating author with nine links and a total link strength of 15. The authors who are mostly collaborating with "Deluca P" are "Kimergard A," "Drummond C," "Wadsworth E," "Davey Z," "Brobbine E," "Jennings S," and "Forley M," all belonging to the red cluster. This further indicates that though "Mackey TK" and "Liang BA" are the most relevant authors they are not the most collaborative. Thus, the most influential authors are not the most collaborative, even though a considerable number of them collaborated with other authors in contributing to the research area. An author such as "Schifano F" who emerged the third most influential author had the most collaborations with other authors. This suggests that in many of the papers that the author produced (e.g.,

Orsolini et al., 2017; Orsolini et al., 2015; Corazza et al., 2012; Schmidt et al., 2011; Schifano et al., 2006), there were contributions from other authors.

8.3.4 Most Cited Publications

The most cited author publications show the specific journal articles that most researchers have referred to in authoring their papers. This points to the strong relevance of the arguments made in these publications to the studies that other authors are conducting on online pharmaceutical marketing. A look at Table 8.5 shows the top 20 most cited author documents or articles. The publication titled "Heavy Metal Content of Ayurvedic Herbal Medicine Products" (Saper et al., 2004) published in *JAMA – the Journal of the American Medical Association* was the most cited paper with a total citation of 445. The paper sought to identify the prevalence and concentration of heavy metals in Ayurvedic HMPs manufactured in South Asia and sold in Boston area stores by comparing estimated daily metal ingestion with standards set up by regulatory bodies (Saper et al., 2004).

The influence of Saper, Phillips, Sehgal, Khouri, Davis, Paqui, and Kales in the online pharmaceutical marketing literature should also be stressed. This is because their article titled "Lead, Mercury, and Arsenic in US- and Indian-Manufactured Ayurvedic Medicines Sold via the Internet" (Saper et al., 2008), published in *JAMA – the Journal of the American Medical Association*, was the second most cited paper with a total citation of 309. Similar to the paper by Saper et al. (2004), where they explored the presence of heavy metals in Ayurvedic medicines, the purpose of the latter paper was to determine the prevalence of Ayurvedic medicines available through online platforms that contain detectable lead, mercury, or arsenic and to compare the prevalence of toxic metals among US and Indian manufactured medicines (Saper et al., 2008). This is followed by the paper titled "Mechanisms of Prescription Drug Diversion Among Drug-Involved Club- and Street-Based Populations" (Inciardi et al., 2007), published in *Pain Medicine*, with a total citation of 225. It is worthy to note that the difference in the citation count between the first and second most cited papers is 136 citations, which suggests an extreme interest by researchers in the most cited paper to contribute to their arguments and discussions. Again, a notable trend regarding the first and second most cited papers indicates an interest in studies on heavy metals in drug manufacturing since they both discuss heavy metal content (e.g., mercury and lead) in Ayurveda. Regarding the journals in which these most cited papers are published, surprisingly, *JAMA – the Journal of the American Medical Association* is not listed among the 20 most publishing and cited journals, though it is the source of the top-cited publication in the research area. The journal is also the source for the second most cited publication. This suggests that many authors in preparing their manuscripts have not been keen on which journal is the most influential to cite from but tend to focus more on the publication's subject matter. This is evident in the titles of the two most cited papers, as they focus on issues relating to heavy metal content (e.g., mercury and lead) in a

Table 8.5 Top 20 most cited author documents

Authors	Title	Source title	Citations
Saper et al. (2004)	Heavy Metal Content of Ayurvedic Herbal Medicine Products	*JAMA – the Journal of the American Medical Association*	445
Saper et al. (2008)	Lead, Mercury, and Arsenic in US- and Indian-Manufactured Ayurvedic Medicines Sold via the Internet	*JAMA – the Journal of the American Medical Association*	309
Inciardi et al. (2007)	Mechanisms of Prescription Drug Diversion Among Drug-Involved Club- and Street-Based Populations	*Pain Medicine*	225
Griggs et al. (2009)	Clinical Research for Rare Disease: Opportunities, Challenges, and Solutions	*Molecular Genetics and Metabolism*	195
Morris and Avorn (2003)	Internet Marketing of Herbal Products	*Journal of the American Medical Association*	192
Inada and Inagaki (2015)	Psychotropic Dose Equivalence in Japan	*Psychiatry and Clinical Neurosciences*	162
McCabe et al. (2004)	The Use, Misuse and Diversion of Prescription Stimulants Among Middle and High School Students	*Substance Use and Misuse*	160
Schmidt et al. (2011)	"Legal Highs" on the Net-Evaluation of UK-Based Websites, Products and Product Information	*Forensic Science International*	151
Bonn-Miller et al. (2017)	Labeling Accuracy of Cannabidiol Extracts Sold Online	*JAMA – the Journal of the American Medical Association*	145
Anbarasi and Kumar (2019)	Various Online Marketing and Promotions Strategies to Improve the Validation Towards the Organic Products in the Pharmaceutical Sectors	*Indian Journal of Public Health Research and Development*	137
Lo and Friedman (2002)	Teratogenicity of Recently Introduced Medications in Human Pregnancy	*Obstetrics and Gynecology*	135
Bell et al. (2000)	The Educational Value of Consumer-Targeted Prescription Drug Print Advertising	*Journal of Family Practice*	132
Mackey and Liang (2011)	The Global Counterfeit Drug Trade: Patient Safety and Public Health Risks	*Journal of Pharmaceutical Sciences*	119
Richard and Chandra (2005)	A Model of Consumer Web Navigational Behavior: Conceptual Development and Application	*Journal of Business Research*	119
Ventola (2011)	Direct-to-Consumer Pharmaceutical Advertising: Therapeutic or Toxic?	*P and T*	115
Cross et al. (2002)	Post-marketing Drug Dosage Changes of 499 FDA-Approved New Molecular Entities, 1980–1999	*Pharmacoepidemiology and Drug Safety*	106

(continued)

Table 8.5 (continued)

Authors	Title	Source title	Citations
Corazza et al. (2012)	Phenomenon of New Drugs on the Internet: The Case of Ketamine Derivative Methoxetamine	*Human Psychopharmacology*	103
Van Hout and Bingham (2014)	Responsible Vendors, Intelligent Consumers: Silk Road, the Online Revolution in Drug Trading	*International Journal of Drug Policy*	99
Cohen et al. (2001)	Medications as Social Phenomena	*Health*	96
Jung et al. (2006)	Anorectic Sibutramine Detected in a Chinese Herbal Drug for Weight Loss	*Forensic Science International*	86

traditional herbal drug called "Ayurveda." Ayurveda is a traditional Indian medication with potency in preserving health and wellness by keeping the mind, body, and soul in check through preventive care rather than curative care (Sudha et al., 2011).

8.3.5 *Most Relevant Journals*

A total of 288 sources (journal outlets) published the 541 publications that were realized in this study. The relevance of journals, or how influential they are in the development of the online pharmaceutical marketing field, was measured as a function of their productivity (the number of articles published in that journal) and the number of citations received by the journal. Table 8.6 shows the 20 most relevant journals in online pharmaceutical marketing research, detailing the number of articles, number of citations, and average citations per article. Generally, per Table 8.6, almost all the journals published in the area of online pharmaceutical marketing have a strong pharmaceutical, medical/clinical, and drug orientation, as their names denote. The journals that have the highest number of publications were *International Journal of Drug Policy* (30 publications), *Drug Information Journal* (13 publications), and *Pharmaceutical Journal* and *Plos One* (11 publications each).

Moreover, the *International Journal of Drug Policy*, which had the highest number of publications, publishes research articles that have a scope on the social, political, legal, and health contexts of psychoactive substance use, both licit and illicit with a particular interest in articles that explore the effects of drug policy and practice on drug-using behavior and its health and social consequences. Notably also, the presence of a journal such as *Forensic Science International* among the first 20 most relevant journals is not surprising, given that the field of online pharmaceutical marketing is characterized by legal and regulatory issues (Mackey & Liang, 2013; Schmidt et al., 2011; Liang & Mackey, 2011; Spain et al., 2001).

Another aspect used to determine the influence of journals is the number of citations received by each journal. As observed in Table 8.6, the most cited journal, with 719 citations, is the *International Journal of Drug Policy* which also emerged as the

Table 8.6 Most influential journals

Source	NP	TC
International Journal of Drug Policy	30	719
Drug Information Journal	13	76
Pharmaceutical Journal	11	5
Plos One	11	192
European Pharmaceutical Contractor	10	1
Pharmaceutical Technology Europe	10	4
Forensic Science International	9	413
International Journal of Pharmaceutical Sciences Review and Research	9	2
Drug and Alcohol Dependence	8	154
Human Psychopharmacology	8	201
Drug Testing and Analysis	7	144
EPC – European Pharmaceutical Contractor	7	0
Pharmaceutical Manufacturing and Packing Sourcer	6	0
Journal of Psychoactive Drugs	5	134
Pharmazeutische Industrie	5	2
Social Science and Medicine	5	73
Annals of Pharmacotherapy	4	54
BMJ (online)	4	62
BMJ Open	4	55
Clinical Pharmacology and Therapeutics	4	84

TC total citations, *NP* number of publications, *PY_Start* publication start year

journal with the highest number of publications. The next most cited journal is *Forensic Science International*, which targets author publications that revolve around research "where science and medicine interact with the law" with 413 citations, and *Human Psychopharmacology* with 201 citations. Aside from these 3 most cited journals, 4 other journals have over 100 citations: *Plos One*, *Drug and Alcohol Dependence*, *Drug Testing and Analysis*, and the *Journal of Psychoactive Drugs*. Markedly, most of these journals focus specifically on drug testing and addictive behaviors of drug use which changes a person's mental state; therefore, the high frequency of citations could be the consequence of strong interest in this theme as it relates to online pharmaceutical marketing.

8.3.6 Keyword Co-occurrence and Trend

Table 8.7 projects the commonly used terms in the 541 journal articles that have been published in the field of online pharmaceutical marketing. The most widely used keywords were generated from the authors' keywords and are useful in predicting the research trend in a particular discipline or field of research over a period of time (Madani & Weber, 2016). A total of 1246 author keywords were realized

Table 8.7 Top 20 commonly used keywords

Words	Occurrences
Internet	39
Pharmaceutical marketing	20
Cryptomarkets	18
Social media	14
Marketing	11
Advertising	10
Cannabis	10
Direct-to-consumer advertising	10
New psychoactive substances	10
Prescription drugs	9
Drug markets	8
Legal highs	8
Online pharmacies	8
Pharmacovigilance	8
Internet pharmacy	7
Pharmaceutical industry	7
Pharmaceuticals	7
Public health	7
Survey	7
Darknet	6

from 541 publications. As shown in Table 8.7, the most used keyword is *Internet* followed by *pharmaceutical marketing*, *cryptomarkets*, *social media*, and *marketing*.

In Fig. 8.3, a deeper analysis of the relationships between the commonly used keywords is presented. Five clusters of keywords can be observed. These are the yellow, red, blue, green, and purple clusters. The primary and largest node represents the most co-occurring keyword and is found at the center of the network. Nodes of the same color strongly co-occur and indicate that the concepts behind those words are closely discussed in papers that have been published in the research area (Zupic & Čater, 2015). In other words, authors use such words alongside each other in their studies on online pharmaceutical marketing. As can be observed from Fig. 8.3, "Internet" (the largest yellow node) was identified as the most frequently used keyword. The word Internet co-occurs with words such as *online pharmacies* and *public health*. The second most co-occurring keyword is "pharmaceutical marketing" (largest red node) and has words such as *pharmaceutical industry*, *direct-to-consumer advertising*, *health policy*, *social media*, and *survey* often being used alongside it, given that they have the same color code in the network. The third most co-occurring keyword is "cryptomarkets" (largest purple node) and has words such as *darknet* and *drug markets* often used alongside it, as they have the same color

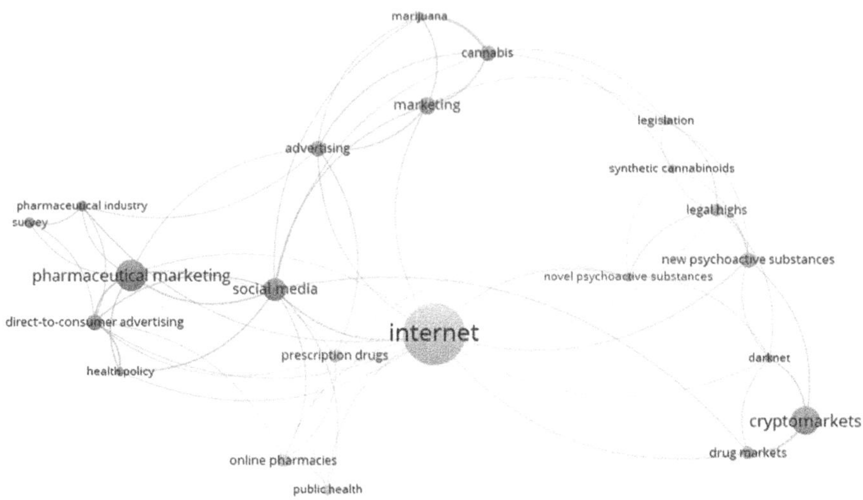

Fig. 8.3 Most commonly used keywords

code in the network. Also, the blue nodes indicate that there have been some discussions centered on "new psychoactive substances" done around "legal highs," "synthetic cannabinoids," and "legalization." These blue nodes indicate discussions centered on the *marketing* and *advertising* of *cannabis* and *marijuana*.

Figure 8.4 presents the trend in the appearance of keywords in online pharmaceutical marketing research. Between 2009 and 2012, researchers focused their attention on the "pharmaceutical industry," "online pharmacies," "Internet pharmacies," "direct-to-consumer advertising," and "pharmaceutical marketing." It is essential to point out that *pharmaceutical marketing*, which formed the red cluster's pivot, was the most used and discussed topic during the period, as seen in Fig. 8.4. Notably, between the year 2013 and 2014, studies largely focused on the marketing of drugs generally purported to be "illegal" or "highly regulated," coupled with regulatory and legal issues concerning online pharmaceutical marketing. Consequently, words like *synthetic cannabinoids*, *legalization*, *legal highs*, *online pharmacy*, and *Internet* were the most used and discussed topics during the period. The third phase in the trend on keyword usage was between 2015 and 2020, where the research agenda focused on issues relating to social media and the dark side of online pharmaceutical marketing of purported "illegal," "highly regulated" drugs or "medicinal cannabis," hence the emergence of words such as *cryptomarkets*, *social media*, *darknet*, *cannabis*, and *marijuana*.

These results indicate that the majority of keywords used in online pharmaceutical marketing revolve around three themes. The first theme covers discussions on the digital aspects of marketing pharmaceutical products, hence the use of words such as "Internet," "social media," and "online pharmacy marketing." The second theme encompasses discussions on the dark side of marketing pharmaceutical products online. With the emergence of the dark side of marketing pharmaceutical products online, a third theme bordering on legalization and regulation also emerged,

Fig. 8.4 Trend in the use of keywords

hence the presence of words such as "legalization" and "legal highs." Impliedly, the emergence of keywords such as "marijuana" and "cannabis" suggests attention to research regarding purportedly "illegal" or "highly regulated" drugs, thereby emphasizing the pertinent role of legislation and regulation in online pharmaceutical marketing as discussed earlier. Legislation and regulation are a necessity in the space of online pharmaceutical marketing as some of the products (e.g., medicinal cannabis and marijuana) that are marketed online are considered to be potentially dangerous to the health of consumers. Thus, their sale needs to be regulated by laws to ensure proper sale and use among consumers (Gorlach & Pham-Kanter, 2013; Mackey & Liang, 2012; Liang & Mackey, 2011).

8.3.7 Future Research Directions

In respect of the findings presented in the previous sections, the following research directions are proferred for future studies on online pharmaceutical marketing:

First, it emerged that the growth pattern in the number of publications on online pharmaceutical marketing has been inconsistent over the past 35 years, especially in the last two decades (2000–2020). Therefore, it will be beneficial to expand the bibliometric analysis to include scholarly research across multiple databases over the next decade (i.e., an analysis of the growth pattern will be necessary to know if the growth pattern remains the same or changes).

Second, the study identified the most impactful authors and influential journals in the field of online pharmaceutical marketing. A significant additional contribution would be to explore another aspect of bibliometrics on how authors, journals, and their associated references are bibliometrically coupled with each other. The area can also benefit from exploring journal-specific bibliometric reviews of the journal outlets that have spearheaded much of the research in the area, including the *International Journal of Drug Policy*, *Drug Information Journal*, *Forensic Science International*, *Pharmaceutical Journal*, and *Plos One*.

Third, the study identified research from countries in developing regions (e.g., India and South Africa), though premium was placed on dominant countries and institutions, which showed that the research area has predominantly originated from developed countries such as America and Europe. Therefore, future studies can explore online pharmaceutical marketing in developing regions/countries to determine the level of attention given by researchers in that context to the area and the ongoing country collaborations. Studies on online pharmaceutical marketing in Africa are critical. This is because African leaders, in the "Cotonou Declaration," signed in Benin, Africa, agreed to work to eliminate counterfeit ("falsified") drugs to ensure adequate and affordable access to quality medication and healthcare for persons living in Africa (Fernandez et al., 2011).

Fourth, there is a growing interest in online pharmaceutical marketing research (Chaffey & Smith, 2017; Kladou & Mavragani, 2015; Teo, 2005) coupled with the active collaborations among scholars from different geographical locations, as identified in this study. Therefore, future studies may be conducted to empirically compare research from developed countries in Europe, America, and Asia with the research from developing countries to understand the dynamics of online pharmaceutical marketing research within these contexts.

Finally, as identified in this study, research on the drug markets and the marketing of purportedly "illegal or highly regulated" drugs such as marijuana and cannabis may be at the edge of bringing a different paradigm shift in the field of online pharmaceutical marketing. Hence, it will be worthy to explore how such drugs are marketed online across geographical contexts through empirical studies.

8.3.8 Possible Research Themes from the 20 Most Cited Papers

To provide further directions for future research, we perform a content review of the top 20 most cited publications to identify other possible directions for future research. Based on the themes developed, research questions (see Table 8.8) are proposed for exploration in future studies.

Table 8.8 Excerpts of future research from the most cited papers

Theme	Rationale	Possible questions	Further reading
Technologies for ensuring safer purchase of medicines online	One of the primary reasons for consumers not purchasing from Internet sources is the belief that the drugs that are purchased online are not safe, and the presence of toxic substances such as mercury and lead in medicinal products remains one of the concerns on the pharmaceutical industry. Schmidt et al. (2011), for example, aver that most medicines that are sold online have poor-quality product information provided to consumers, with a large minority of products not listing ingredients at all	What technologies can be implemented on online pharmaceutical marketing platforms to provide consumer-side checks during online purchases to avert the purchase of intoxicated medicines? What technologies can be implemented on online pharmaceutical marketing platforms to provide supplier-side checks during their demand for medicine from suppliers regarding the presence of toxic substances in the medication they provide to clients?	Saper et al. (2004, 2008), Inciardi et al. (2007), Griggs et al. (2009), Schmidt et al. (2011), and Bell et al. (2000)
Different contextual-level studies	A national probability sample of adults polled by the Pew Internet and American Live Project in 2004 found about only 4% of Americans use the Internet to purchase drugs and that most sites required a physician's prescription. Given this, it is likely that opportunities and mechanisms for obtaining prescription drugs in other jurisdictions and context other than America will be useful	What probability sample of adults uses the Internet to purchase drugs in developing countries? What are the major online pharmaceutical platforms used by consumers of purchasing medicines online? What are the clinical protocols required by the sites before purchases can be made online by consumers in developing country markets?	Inciardi et al. (2007)
Regulation of online pharmaceutical markets	With regard to the online marketing of medicines, especially herbal medicines, consumers are easily misled by vendors into thinking that such products can treat or cure some specific diseases through acts such as product branding and descriptions	What effective regulations are required to avert vendors' deceptions in misleading consumers regarding online marketing of medicines, especially herbal products?	Morris and Avorn (2003)

(continued)

Table 8.8 (continued)

Theme	Rationale	Possible questions	Further reading
Regulation of online pharmaceutical markets	Discrepancies between regulatory laws, especially for medicinal cannabis, have resulted in inadequate regulation and oversight, leading to inaccurate labeling of some products. This suggests the need for manufacturing and testing standards and regulatory oversight in the marketing of medicinal cannabis products	How do regulatory frameworks guide online pharmacies toward the sale of regulated medicinal products (e.g., medicinal cannabis)?	Bonn-Miller et al. (2017)
Regulation of online pharmaceutical markets	The responsible generation and sharing of information regarding illicit online pharmacies and suspected counterfeit products across multiple stakeholders globally have become critical, especially in the fight against illegal drugs. To accomplish needed information collation and timely reporting of surveillance data, the formation of a centralized and standardized reporting system accessible to these actors for collective reporting should be engaged. Though recent global enforcement efforts have led to arrests of online counterfeit sellers, such actions have not curtailed supplies from illegal online sellers or kept up with their creativity in illegally selling their products	What global policy frameworks utilizing public-private partnership models with centralized surveillance reporting can be developed to enable cooperation and coordination to combat the supply and sale of illegal drugs online?	Mackey and Liang (2011)
Regulation of online pharmaceutical markets	Currently, available evidence, although limited, indicates that the effect of direct-to-consumer pharmaceutical advertising (DTCPA) on consumers is both positive and negative. An increased understanding of the effects of DTCPA will have important implications for public health in countries such as America and Europe, as well as other countries and regions where the ban on such advertising medicine online is being challenged due to activities of illegal drug dealers	What are the benefits and risks of direct-to-consumer pharmaceutical advertising (DTCPA) as a medium of improving public health?	Ventola (2011) and Corazza et al. (2012).

8.4 Conclusion

Based on a bibliometric analysis of 541 articles published on online pharmaceutical marketing between 1985 and 2020, several significant findings have emerged from this study. Key authors, journals, countries, institutions, and keywords in online relationship marketing research have been identified, as shown in the tables and figures presented in this paper. Furthermore, the study predicts that the focus on the Internet, pharmaceutical marketing, cryptomarkets, and social media will continue to dominate the area. A focus of research on the online marketing of purported "illegal or highly regulated" drugs such as cannabis and marijuana may also continue to feature strongly in future research.

This study has demonstrated a research method supported by VOSviewer and bibliometrix for quantitatively investigating the area of online pharmaceutical marketing research, which has hitherto not been performed. In comparison with systematic reviews, which simply review extant literature, the bibliometric method employed in this study does not only show the development of a subject area such as online pharmaceutical marketing by analyzing important authors and critical papers through visualization networks and figures, but it also provides trends regarding further research in this domain of research. Furthermore, the study provides sufficient information about the critical papers in the field of online pharmaceutical marketing, hence directing both experienced and budding researchers to the journals to consider when researching in the area and the authors, countries, and institutions to target for collaborations.

Online pharmaceutical marketing continues to receive research attention and constitutes a significant phenomenon in this digital marketing era. To avoid misunderstanding and to guide future investigations, the following are noted as limitations of this study: First, the current study focused only on journal articles indexed in the Scopus database. Future studies can explore other sources, such as the Web of Sciences (WoS) and a possible comparative study of papers in these two databases (Scopus and WoS). Also, this study focused exclusively on peer-reviewed journal articles. Future studies may analyze other document types (e.g., conference papers). Also, bibliographic coupling networks present a depiction of invisible aspects within a particular field of research (Zupic & Čater, 2015). Hence, future studies on the coupling of authors, publications, and references should be pursued in online pharmaceutical marketing research to offer a bigger picture in the domain of bibliographic analysis. Despite these limitations, this study has contributed significantly to scholarly work in the field of digital and pharmaceutical marketing by highlighting the number of publications, keyword occurrence and citations, and number of publications in studies on online pharmaceutical marketing which hitherto had not been done, thereby contributing significantly to scholarly work in the field of digital and pharmaceutical marketing.

References

Adams, J., & Eveland, V. (2007). Marketing online degree programs: How do traditional residential programs compete? *Journal of Marketing for Higher Education, 17*(1), 67–90.

Aldridge, J., & Décary-Hétu, D. (2016). Hidden wholesale: The drug diffusing capacity of online drug cryptomarkets. *International Journal of Drug Policy, 35*, 7–15.

Anbarasi, M., & Kumar, S. P. (2019). Various online marketing and promotions strategies to improve the validation towards the organic products in the pharmaceutical sectors. *Indian Journal of Public Health Research and Development, 10*(1), 263–269.

Babar, Z. U. D., & Atif, M. (2014). Differential pricing of pharmaceuticals: A bibliometric review of the literature. *Journal of Pharmaceutical Health Services Research, 5*(3), 149–156.

Basak, S. C., & Sathyanarayana, D. (2010). Community pharmacy based research activity in India: A bibliometric study of the past ten years. *Southern Med Review, 3*(1), 7–10.

Bell, R. A., Wilkes, M. S., & Kravitz, R. L. (2000). The educational value of consumer-targeted prescription drug print advertising. *Journal of Family Practice, 49*(12), 1092–1092.

Bengoa, A., Maseda, A., Iturralde, T., & Aparicio, G. (2020). A bibliometric review of the technology transfer literature. *The Journal of Technology Transfer*, 1–37.

Boateng, S. L. (2020). Enhancing calculative commitment and customer loyalty through online relationship marketing: The mediating role of online trust. In G. Ekren, A. Erkollar, & B. Oberer (Eds.), *Advanced MIS and digital transformation for increased creativity and innovation in business* (pp. 50–76). IGI Global.

Bonn-Miller, M. O., Loflin, M. J., Thomas, B. F., Marcu, J. P., Hyke, T., & Vandrey, R. (2017). Labeling accuracy of cannabidiol extracts sold online. *JAMA, 318*(17), 1708–1709.

Broadus, R. N. (1987). Toward a definition of "bibliometrics". *Scientometrics, 12*(5-6), 373–379.

Casillas, J., & Acedo, F. (2007). Evolution of the intellectual structure of family business literature: A bibliometric study of FBR. *Family Business Review, 20*(2), 141–162.

Chaffey, D., & Smith, P. (2017). *Digital marketing excellence: Planning, optimizing and integrating online marketing* (5th ed.). Routledge.

Chan, A., & Astari, D. (2017). The analysis of content marketing in online fashion shops in Indonesia. *Review of Integrative Business and Economics Research, 6*(2), 225–233.

Chang, C. C., & Ho, Y. S. (2010). Bibliometric analysis of financial crisis research. *African Journal of Business Management, 4*(18), 3898–3910.

Cohen, D., McCubbin, M., Collin, J., & Pérodeau, G. (2001). Medications as social phenomena. *Health, 5*(4), 441–469.

Constantinides, E., & Stagno, M. C. Z. (2012). Higher education marketing: A study on the impact of social media on study selection and university choice. *International Journal of Technology and Educational Marketing (IJTEM), 2*(1), 41–58.

Constantinides, & Zinck Stagno, M. C. (2011). Potential of the social media as instruments of higher education marketing: A segmentation study. *Journal of Marketing for Higher Education, 21*(1), 7–24.

Corazza, O., Schifano, F., Simonato, P., Fergus, S., Assi, S., Stair, J., & Blaszko, U. (2012). Phenomenon of new drugs on the Internet: The case of ketamine derivative methoxetamine. *Human Psychopharmacology: Clinical and Experimental, 27*(2), 145–149.

Cristino, T. M., Neto, A. F., & Costa, A. F. B. (2018). Energy efficiency in buildings: Analysis of scientific literature and identification of data analysis techniques from a bibliometric study. *Scientometrics, 114*(3), 1275–1326.

Cross, J., Lee, H., Westelinck, A., Nelso, J., Grudzinskas, C., & Peck, C. (2002). Postmarketing drug dosage changes of 499 FDA-approved new molecular entities, 1980–1999. *Pharmacoepidemiology and Drug Safety, 11*(6), 439–446.

Dabi, Y., Darrigues, L., Katsahian, S., Azoulay, D., De Antonio, M., & Lazzati, A. (2016). Publication trends in bariatric surgery: a bibliometric study. *Obesity Surgery, 26*(11), 2691–2699.

De Freitas, J., Falls, B. A., Haque, O. S., & Bursztajn, H. J. (2013). Vulnerabilities to misinformation in online pharmaceutical marketing. *Journal of the Royal Society of Medicine, 106*(5), 184–189.

Duffett, R., Petroşanu, D. M., Negricea, I. C., & Edu, T. (2019). Effect of YouTube marketing communication on converting brand liking into preference among millennials regarding brands in general and sustainable offers in particular. Evidence from South Africa and Romania. *Sustainability, 11*(3), 1–24.

Durieux, V., & Gevenois, P. A. (2010). Bibliometric indicators: Quality measurements of scientific publication. *Radiology, 255*(2), 342–351.

Economic Times. (2017). *Here's how India can be the world leader in drug manufacturing*. https://economictimes.indiatimes.com/blogs/et-commentary/heres-how-india-can-be-the-world-leader-in-drug-manufacturing/. Accessed 24 Dec 2020.

Elsevier. (2020). *How Scopus works*. Elsevier. https://www.elsevier.com/solutions/scopus/how-scopus-works/. Accessed 1 Dec 2020.

Fellnhofer, K. (2019). Toward a taxonomy of entrepreneurship education research literature: A bibliometric mapping and visualization. *Educational Research Review, 27*, 28–55.

Fernandez, F. M., Hostetler, D., Powell, K., Kaur, H., Green, M. D., Mildenhall, D. C., & Newton, P. N. (2011). Poor quality drugs: Grand challenges in high throughput detection, countrywide sampling, and forensics in developing countries. *Analyst, 136*(15), 3073–3082.

Giraldo, P., Benavente, E., Manzano-Agugliaro, F., & Gimenez, E. (2019). Worldwide research trends on wheat and barley: A bibliometric comparative analysis. *Agronomy, 9*(7), 352.

Gorlach, I., & Pham-Kanter, G. (2013). Brightening up: the effect of the Physician Payment Sunshine Act on existing regulation of pharmaceutical marketing. *The Journal of Law, Medicine & Ethics, 41*(1), 315–322.

Griggs, R. C., Batshaw, M., Dunkle, M., Gopal-Srivastava, R., Kaye, E., Krischer, J., & Merkel, P. A. (2009). Clinical research for rare disease: Opportunities, challenges, and solutions. *Molecular Genetics and Metabolism, 96*(1), 20–26.

Han, J. S., & Ho, Y. S. (2011). Global trends and performances of acupuncture research. *Neuroscience and Biobehavioral Reviews, 35*(3), 680–687.

Hicks, D., Wouters, P., Waltman, L., De Rijcke, S., & Rafols. (2015). Bibliometsrics: The Leiden Manifesto for research metrics. *Nature, 520*(7548), 429–431.

Howison, S., Finger, G., & Hauschka, C. (2015). Insights into the Web presence, online marketing, and the use of social media by tourism operators in Dunedin, New Zealand. *Anatolia, 26*(2), 269–283.

Inada, T., & Inagaki, A. (2015). Psychotropic dose equivalence in Japan. *Psychiatry and Clinical Neurosciences, 69*(8), 440–447.

Inciardi, J. A., Surratt, H. L., Kurtz, S. P., & Cicero, T. J. (2007). Mechanisms of prescription drug diversion among drug-involved club-and street-based populations. *Pain Medicine, 8*(2), 171–183.

Jawaid, M., & Ahmed, S. J. (2018). Pharmaceutical digital marketing and its impact on healthcare physicians of Pakistan: A national survey. *Cureus, 10*(6), e2789. https://doi.org/10.7759/cureus.2789

Jung, J., Hermanns-Clausen, M., & Weinmann, W. (2006). Anorectic sibutramine detected in a Chinese herbal drug for weight loss. *Forensic Science International, 161*(2–3), 221–222.

Kannan, P. K. (2017). Digital marketing: A framework, review and research agenda. *International Journal of Research in Marketing, 34*(1), 22–45.

Kimergård, A., McVeigh, J., Knutsson, S., Breindahl, T., & Stensballe, A. (2014). Online marketing of synthetic peptide hormones: Poor manufacturing, user ssafety, and challenges to public health. *Drug Testing and Analysis, 6*(4), 396–398.

Kipper, L. M., Furstenau, L. B., Hoppe, D., Frozza, R., & Iepsen, S. (2020). Scopus scientific mapping production in industry 4.0 (2011–2018): A bibliometric analysis. *International Journal of Production Research, 58*(6), 1605–1627.

Kladou, S., & Mavragani, E. (2015). Assessing destination image: An online marketing approach and the case of TripAdvisor. *Journal of Destination Marketing and Management, 4*(3), 187–193.

Kokol, P., Blažun Vošner, H., & Završnik, J. (2020). Application of bibliometrics in medicine: A historical bibliometrics analysis. *Health Information and Libraries Journal*. https://doi.org/10.1111/hir.12295

Köseoglu, M. A., Sehitoglu, Y., Ross, G., & Parnell, J. A. (2016). The evolution of business ethics research in the realm of tourism and hospitality. *International Journal of Contemporary Hospitality Management, 28*(8), 1598–1621.

Kosmützky, A., & Krücken, G. (2014). Growth or steady state? A bibliometric focus on international comparative higher education research. *Higher Education, 67*(4), 457–472.

Lad, P., Muragundi, P., & Ligade, V. S. (2017). Digitalize pharmaceutical marketing: Medical representative perspective. *Research Journal of Pharmacy and Technology, 10*(7), 2179–2182.

Liang, B. A., & Mackey, T. (2011). Direct-to-consumer advertising with interactive internet media: Global regulation and public health issues. *JAMA, 305*(8), 824–825.

Liang, B. A., & Mackey, T. K. (2012). Vaccine shortages and suspect online pharmacy sellers. *Vaccine, 30*(2), 105–108.

Liang, Y. D., Li, Y., Zhao, J., Wang, X. Y., Zhu, H. Z., & Chen, X. H. (2017). Study of acupuncture for low back pain in recent 20 years: A bibliometric analysis via CiteSpace. *Journal of Pain Research, 10*, 951–964. https://doi.org/10.2147/JPR.S132808

Lo, W. Y., & Friedman, J. M. (2002). Teratogenicity of recently introduced medications in human pregnancy. *Obstetrics and Gynecology, 100*(3), 465–473.

López-Muñoz, F., Srinivasan, V., Gutiérrez-Soriano, A., Shen, W. W., García-García, P., Rubio, G., & Álamo, C. (2015). A bibliometric analysis of scientific research on atypical antipsychotic drugs in India during 1998–2013. *Molecules and Medicinal Chemistry, 1*. https://doi.org/10.14800/mmc.1113

Mackey, T. K., & Liang, B. A. (2011). The global counterfeit drug trade: Patient safety and public health risks. *Journal of Pharmaceutical Sciences, 100*(11), 4571–4579.

Mackey, T. K., & Liang, B. A. (2012). Combating healthcare corruption and fraud with improved global health governance. *BMC International Health and Human Rights, 12*(1), 1–7.

Mackey, T. K., & Liang, B. A. (2013). Pharmaceutical digital marketing and governance: Illicit actors and challenges to global patient safety and public health. *Globalization and Health, 9*(1), 45. https://doi.org/10.1186/1744-8603-9-45

Mackey, T. K., Cuomo, R. E., & Liang, B. A. (2015). The rise of digital direct-to-consumer advertising? Comparison of direct-to-consumer advertising expenditure trends from publicly available data sources and global policy implications. *BMC Health Services Research, 15*(1), 1–9.

Madani, F. (2015). Technology mining' bibliometrics analysis: Applying network analysis and cluster analysis. *Scientometrics, 105*(1), 323–335.

Madani, F., & Weber, C. (2016). The evolution of patent mining: Applying bibliometrics analysis and keyword network analysis. *World Patent Information, 46*, 32–48.

Martí-Parreño, J., Méndez-Ibáñez, E., & Alonso-Arroyo, A. (2016). The use of gamification in education: A bibliometric and text minings analysis. *Journal of Computer Assisted Learning, 32*(6), 663–676.

Marzi, G., Dabić, M., Daim, T., & Garces, E. (2017). Product and process innovation in manufacturing firms: A 30-year bibliometric analysis. *Scientometrics, 113*(2), 673–704.

McCabe, S. E., Teter, C. J., & Boyd, C. J. (2004). The use, misuse and diversion of prescription stimulants among middle and high school students. *Substance Use and Misuse, 39*(7), 1095–1116.

Mohamed, M. E., Hewedi, M., Lehto, X., & Maayouf, M. (2019). Marketing local food and cuisine culture online: A case study of DMO's websites in Egypt. *International Journal of Tourism Cities, 6*(4), 1045–1068.

Mongeon, P., & Paul-Hus, A. (2016). The journal coverage of Web of Science and Scopus: A comparative analysis. *Scientometrics, 106*(1), 213–228.

Mora, L., Bolici, R., & Deakin, M. (2017). The first two decades of smart-city research: A bibliometric analysis. *Journal of Urban Technology, s24*(1), 3–27.
Morris, C. A., & Avorn, J. (2003). Internet marketing of herbal products. *JAMA, 290*(11), 1505–1509.
Mullner, R., & Gurau, C. (2005). Pharmaceutical marketing on the Internet: Marketing techniques and customer profile. *Journal of Consumer Marketing, 22*(7), 421–428.
Okumus, B., Koseoglu, M. A., & Ma, F. (2018). Food and gastronomy research in tourism and hospitality: A bibliometric analysis. *International Journal of Hospitality Management, 73*, 64–74.
Orsolini, L., Papanti, G. D., Francesconi, G., & Schifano, F. (2015). Mind navigators of chemicals' experimenters? A web-based description of e-psychonauts. *Cyberpsychology, Behavior, and Social Networking, 18*(5), 296–300.
Orsolini, L., Papanti, D., Corkery, J., & Schifano, F. (2017). An insight into the deep web; why it matters for addiction psychiatry?. *Human Psychopharmacology: Clinical and Experimental, 32*(3), e2573.
Palomo, J., Figueroa-Domecq, C., & Laguna, P. (2017). Women, peace and security state-of-art: A bibliometric analysis in social sciences based on SCOPUS database. *Scientometrics, 113*(1), 123–148.
Parekh, D., Kapupara, P., & Shah, K. (2016). Digital pharmaceutical marketing: A review. *Research Journal of Pharmacy and Technology, 9*(1), 108–112.
Phillips, E. (2015). Retailers scale up online sales distribution networks. *The Wall Street Journal.* Available at: http://www.wsj.com/articles/retailers-scale-up-onlinesales-distribution-networks-1447792869. Accessed 23 Sept 2020.
Richard, M. O., & Chandra, R. (2005). A model of consumer web navigational behavior: Conceptual development and application. *Journal of Business Research, 58*(8), 1019–1029.
Rivera, G., Puras, G., Palos, I., Ordaz-Pichardo, C., & Bocanegra-Garcia, V. (2010). Bibliometric analysis of scientific publications in the field of medicinal chemistry in Latin America, the People's Republic of China, and India. *Medicinal Chemistry Research, 19*(6), 603–616.
Saper, R. B., Kales, S. N., Paquin, J., Burns, M. J., Eisenberg, D. M., Davis, R. B., & Phillips, R. S. (2004). Heavy metal content of ayurvedic herbal medicine products. *JAMA, 292*(23), 2868–2873.
Saper, R. B., Phillips, R. S., Sehgal, A., Khouri, N., Davis, R. B., Paquin, J., & Kales, S. N. (2008). Lead, mercury, and arsenic in US-and Indian-manufactured Ayurvedic medicines sold via the Internet. *JAMA, 300*(8), 915–923.
Schifano, F., Deluca, P., Baldacchino, A., Peltoniemi, T., Scherbaum, N., Torrens, M., ... & Psychonaut 2002 Research Group. (2006). Drugs on the web; the Psychonaut 2002 EU project. *Progress in Neuro-Psychopharmacology and Biological Psychiatry, 30*(4), 640–646.
Schmidt, M. M., Sharma, A., Schifano, F., & Feinmann, C. (2011). Legal highs on the net – Evaluation of UK-based Websites, products and product information. *Forensic Science International, 206*(1-3), 92–97.
Spain, J. W., Siegel, C. F., & Ramsey, R. P. (2001). Selling drugs online: Distribution-related legal/regulatory issues. *International Marketing Review, 8*(4), 432–449.
Sudha, P., Zinjarde, S. S., Bhargava, S. Y., & Kumar, A. R. (2011). Potent α-amylase inhibitory activity of Indian Ayurvedic medicinal plants. *BMC Complementary and Alternative Medicine, 11*(1), 5. https://doi.org/10.1186/1472-6882-11-5
Sweileh, W. M. (2018). Bibliometric analysis of peer-reviewed literature in transgender health (1900–2017). *BMC International Health and Human Rights, 18*(1), 16. https://doi.org/10.1186/s12914-018-0155-5
Teo, T. S. (2005). Usage and effectiveness of online marketing tools among Business-to-Consumer (B2C) firms in Singapore. *International Journal of Information Management, 25*(3), 203–213.
Todor, R. D. (2016). Blending traditional and digital marketing. Bulletin of the Transilvania University of Brasov. *Economic Sciences. Series V, 9*(1), 51–56.
Van Eck, N. J., & Waltman, L. (2013). VOSviewer manual. *Leiden: Univeristeit Leiden, 1*(1), 1–53.

Van Hout, M. C., & Bingham, T. (2014). Responsible vendors, intelligent consumers: Silk Road, the online revolution in drug trading. *International Journal of Drug Policy, 25*(2), 183–189.

Veer, D. K., & Khiste Gajanan, P. (2017). Digital Library Output in Scopus during 1995–2016: A Bibliometric Analysis. *International Journal of Scientific Research in Computer Science, Engineering and Information Technology, 2*(5), 779–784.

Velasco-Muñoz, J. F., Aznar-Sánchez, J. A., Belmonte-Ureña, L. J., & López-Serrano, M. J. (2018). Advances in water use efficiency in agriculture: A bibliometric analysis. *Water, 10*(4), 377. https://doi.org/10.3390/w10040377

Ventola, C. L. (2011). Direct-to-consumer pharmaceutical advertising: Therapeutic or toxic? *Pharmacy and Therapeutics, 36*(10), 669–984.

Wajid, U., & Bhullar, G. (2019). Towards interoperability across digital manufacturing platforms. In *Enterprise interoperability VIII* (pp. 81–91). Springer.

World Health Organization (WHO). (2010). *Medicines: Counterfeit medicines*. Fact sheet no 275. Available at : http://www.who.int/mediacentre/factsheets/fs275/en/. Accessed 24 Dec 2020.

Xie, P. (2015). Study of international anticancer research trends via co-word and document co-citation visualization analysis. *Scientometrics, 105*(1), 611–622.

Xu, X., Chen, X., Jia, F., Brown, S., Gong, Y., & Xu, Y. (2018). Supply chain finance: A systematic literature review and bibliometric analysis. *International Journal of Production Economics, 204*, 160–173. https://doi.org/10.1016/j.ijpe.2018.08.003

Zhang, D., Zhang, Z., & Managi, S. (2019). A bibliometric analysis on green finance: Current status, development, and future directions. *Finance Research Letters, 29*, 425–430. https://doi.org/10.1016/j.frl.2019.02.003

Zupic, I., & Čater, T. (2015). Bibliometric methods in management and organization. *Organizational Research Methods, 18*(3), 429–472.

Dr. Sheena Lovia Boateng is a lecturer at the Department of Marketing and Entrepreneurship at the University of Ghana Business School. She is a fellow of the Academy of Marketing Science. She also served as a member of the Editorial Advisory Board for the Emerald Emerging Markets Case Study Journal, Emerald Publishing Limited, UK, from 2018 to 2020. She has published seven journal publications, three books, four book chapters, five published conference papers, one working paper, and one industry report. Her academic work has been published in the *International Journal of Bank Marketing*, *Journal of Financial Services Marketing*, and the *Journal of Educational Technology Systems*. Her research interests include online relationship marketing, fashion and beauty marketing, digital business strategy, electronic learning adoption, entrepreneurship, online branding and advertising, social media marketing, and structural equation modeling in marketing. She can be reached at slboateng@ug.edu.gh.

Paul Owusu Donkor has extensive experience in the field of pharmacy. He has worked as a Senior Research Scientist with LaGray Chemical Company, involved in the R&D of active pharmaceutical ingredients (APIs), and served in the Business Development Department of the same company as a Zonal Manager for 2 years. He has lectured at the University of Health and Allied Sciences and the Kwame Nkrumah University of Science and Technology. Dr. Owusu Donkor currently advises the Pharmacy Council of Ghana on the rollout of the Council's e-Pharmacy policy. He also lectures at the University of Ghana School of Pharmacy.

Chapter 9
Platform Business Models: E-logistics Platforms in Sub-Saharan Africa

Olayinka David-West

Abstract Transaction digital platforms in sub-Saharan Africa exist across diverse verticals, addressing a plethora of market, resource and institutional constraints. With the growth of digital start-ups attracting venture capital and private equity funds, e-logistics platforms have yet to advance beyond seed and series A funding rounds to scale. Notwithstanding these developments, little is known about the dynamics and performance of platform businesses and their operational considerations on the continent. Using the platform business model (PBM) analysis and map, this chapter examines the platform design and ecosystem development of funded e-logistics platforms. The chapter sources data from public sources, identifying and profiling platform customers, the value units exchanged (physical, information and financial) and the ability to customer types attract (pull) other customer types (build network effects). By highlighting the similarities and differences of logistics platforms, the findings also show that even though the core interaction, a platform design and architecture component is homogeneous across industry platforms, ecosystem building strategies that differentiate platforms are unique to platform businesses. Though the chapter presents findings from an external perspective, the findings are insightful to current and prospective platform business owners. Apart from building the platform technologies for the core interaction, platform business owners should also focus on design strategies that will build and enhance the platform ecosystem (interactions and value to secondary platform participants).

Keywords Digital platforms · E-logistics · Platform business model

O. David-West (✉)
Lagos Business School, Pan-Atlantic University, Lagos, Nigeria
e-mail: ydavid-west@lbs.edu.ng

R. Boateng et al. (eds.), *Digital Innovations, Business and Society in Africa*, Advances in Theory and Practice of Emerging Markets,
https://doi.org/10.1007/978-3-030-77987-0_9

9.1 Introduction

Africa's logistics sector, though critical, lacks modern development. With parts of the 1970s trans-African highway proposed by the United Nations Economic Commission for Africa either yet to be built or in poor condition, poor transportation infrastructure and inadequate rail and road links plague logistics in Africa (Knight Frank, 2016). Because of these infrastructure gaps, industry experts estimate the cost of moving goods in Africa to be 2–3 times higher than in developed markets, increasing the retail cost of goods and services (Teravaninthorn & Raballand, 2009). The increasing growth in e-commerce is also increasing the demand for logistics services. However, these services are often hindered by traffic congestion in cities like Lagos and Nairobi, which has warranted the use of smaller vehicles or motorcycles (which carry less) or the use of collection centres for customers to pick up orders.

New technologies are being applied in the logistics industry to ease value chain tensions, enhance trade and commerce and reduce the high associated costs, for example, drones delivering healthcare products to remote locations.

Africa's platform evolution dates back to the late 1990s, resulting from the ubiquity of Internet and mobile technologies (David-West & Evans, 2016). Transaction platforms in diverse industry sectors dominate the platform landscape with emerging ecosystem hubs developing in the western, eastern and southern African regions. Investment platform groups also operate in the region. The ubiquity of global systems for mobile technology has advanced mobile telephony adoption in a "mobile first" market. Hence, Web or mobile apps dominate platform channels (David-West & Evans, 2016). In addition, the market, resource and institutional voids (Bhatti, 2012) that constrain markets in sub-Saharan Africa (SSA) compel platform operators to innovate (David-West & Evans, 2016).

- Market constraints: SSA markets boast large, poor populations. Despite the economic thrusts and the rise of the middle class, poverty abounds, affecting broad participation in the digital and platform economies. For example, dominant feature (non-smart) phones among the wider population have platform owners operating a hybrid of online and offline models. The offline locations serve as order taking and delivery/pickup locations (David-West, 2017).
- Resource constraints: Infrastructure to operate digital business such as grid power, financial services and payment systems, digital and Internet penetration, logistics/distribution, uniform addressing systems and talent and venture financing, to name a few, are scarce in the region. For example, platforms operate a payment-on-delivery scheme (cash included) to pull users and transactions (David-West, 2017; David-West & Evans, 2016).
- Institutional voids: Weak legal and business policies create institutional voids that distort the ability to provision an enabling environment. For example, poor contract enforcement and consumer protection practices have reduced trust levels. In the platform economy, this is further exaggerated by cybercrime. Despite

these obstacles, backward integration into complementary business areas like warehousing and logistics is necessary.

9.1.1 Logistics Platforms

In African markets, moving physical goods and services is a critical success factor and trade facilitator of e-commerce, business-to-business interactions and regional initiatives such as the African Continental Free Trade Agreement. Be it first mile, middle mile or last mile, trade-delimiting logistics constraints vary across the continent. The digitisation of logistics services through platforms that match supply and demand is one such emerging area seeking to address this gap. Aside from transportation (ridesharing) platforms, embedding logistics services into the value offerings of e-commerce marketplaces is commonplace (David-West, 2017; David-West & Evans, 2016). Because of market failures in African markets, businesses incur higher logistics costs, reducing competitiveness. The emerging innovation ecosystem is seeking to address the sectoral inefficiencies in logistics like the underutilisation of assets, warehouse management platforms and delivery apps (Giuliani & With, 2019). Briter Bridges' Innovating Logistics in Africa (Giuliani & With, 2019) highlights advancing independent e-logistics platforms and over 120 start-ups offering shipping and freighting, freight forwarding and management, courier services and last-mile delivery, storage and warehousing, cold chain and addressing systems (Hashi, 2019). Combining physical assets like trucks with digital solutions will transform domestic and intra-African trade. Venture capital and private equity funding inflows offer another lens to track platform performance. While the sector is witnessing international funding attention and the top 5 funded companies have cumulatively raised over $60 million, funding rounds have yet to exceed series A (Giuliani & With, 2019). The asset-light models of tech-enabled operators – matching partner assets with existing demand – warrant sustainability funding. According to Giuliani and With (2019), seed- and growth-stage funding top start-up challenges, and exploring the scale potential of digital technologies requires insights to explore platform growth opportunities through ecosystem development. This chapter addresses the knowledge gaps, highlighting recommendations for e-logistics platform ecosystem development.

Using the platform business model (Rogers, 2016), the chapter analyses the business models of the most funded transport and logistics digital platforms (Digest Africa, 2019) to identify ecosystem development opportunities for platform growth. By analysing platform design and architecture and ecosystem development strategies, we find that while the core interactions of industry-based platforms are homogeneous, platform growth and development strategies hinge on the unexplored ecosystem development opportunities. In addition, we highlight the similarities and differences of the business models of the logistics platform businesses. The chapter focuses on e-logistics platforms facilitating the movement of goods as opposed to persons, akin to mobility platforms. Following this introduction, we introduce digital platforms, distinguishing them from regular linear businesses called pipelines and introducing digital platforms in the goods logistics sector. Section 9.3 presents the approach undertaken in evaluating logistics platform business models. The presentation of the core interaction of logistics platforms follows this as well as their maps generated from the platform business model analyses. The chapter concludes with a discussion on platform design and strategy considerations in the logistics ecosystem.

9.2 Digital Platforms

Traditional businesses as we know them have created value by controlling a series of linear activities, beginning with the supply of raw materials and ending with the delivery of products or services to consumers. Such businesses, also known as pipes or pipelines, differ from platforms. Unlike pipes, platforms create value by facilitating interactions between two or more parties (see Table 9.1 for differentiating factors).

Hence, platforms are multi-sided networks that facilitate interactions between two or more parties (Eisenmann et al., 2006). Though platforms like the credit card have existed for decades, digital technologies like the Internet enhance their dominance and prevalence. Figure 9.1 and Table 9.2 illustrate the multiple actors in a platform ecosystem and their roles (with examples).

Table 9.1 Summary of pipes vs. platforms

Attribute	Pipeline	Platform
Objective	Maximise customer lifetime value	Maximise ecosystem value
Business emphasis	Dictating processes	Persuading participants
Focus	Internal optimisation	External orientation
Resource orientation	Resource control	Orchestration
Basis for competition	Assets, resources and capabilities (scarce, imitable and valuable)	Network of producers and consumers
Supply chain/ inventory	Fixed	Dynamic
Value creation and internal organisation	Linear processes that produce products and services consumed by customers (sales)	Interactions and information usually co-created by producers and consumers (interactions)
Process flow	Linear	Circular, iterative, feedback driven
Scale	Efficient, repetition	Quantity, quality
Product design/ development	Closed – controlled by "experts"	Open – controlled by consumer needs/market signals

Van Alstyne et al. (2016)

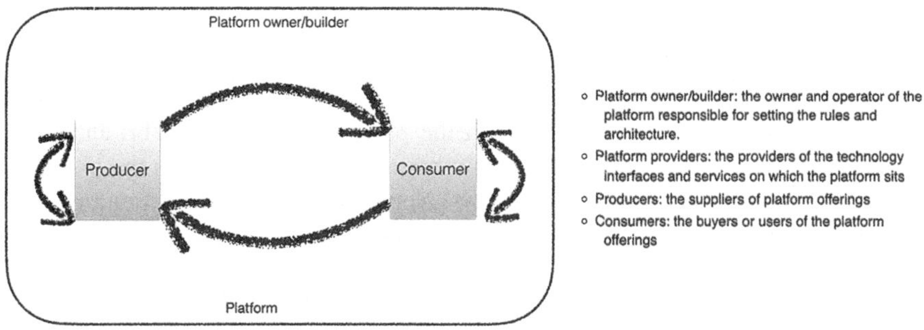

Fig. 9.1 Author's adaptation of digital platforms. (Van Alstyne et al., 2016)

Table 9.2 Platform examples

Name	Owner	Providers	Producer(s)	Consumer(s)
Windows	Microsoft	Intel computers	Software developers	PC owners/users
App Store	Apple	Apple Mac/iPhone/iPad	Software developers	Apple device owners/users
Google Play	Google	Android device producers (Samsung)	Software developers	Android device owners/users
Amazon Marketplace	Amazon	Internet, browser, iOS, Android, etc.	Sellers	Buyers
Uber	Uber Technologies	iOS, Android, etc. Google Maps	Drivers	Riders
Sony PlayStation	Sony	Console and accessory manufacturers	Video game developers	Video game players

Source: compiled by author

9.2.1 *Platform Types*

Depending on the interaction, Evans and Gawer (2016) introduce four platform archetypes – transaction, innovation, integrated and investment. Transaction platforms like Uber and Amazon Marketplace facilitate transactional exchanges, while innovation platforms provide the foundations upon which other actors can develop complementary products or services (e.g., GitHub). Integrated platforms such as Apple's App Store facilitate both transactional and innovation interactions, and investment platforms are companies like Rocket Internet with a portfolio of platforms in a holding company structure.

The primary functions (or use cases) vary by platform type. Transaction platforms excel at providing efficient interactions and matching services, while innovation platforms stimulate innovation through complementors.

9.2.2 *Platform Dynamics*

Network effects are a platform dynamic where the value of the platform increases as more users interact and engage with the platform (Gatautis, 2017; Jacobides et al., 2019; Kenny & Zysman, 2016). As more people interact with the platform, the platform attracts new users and grows. Network effects are direct and indirect (Hagiu, 2009; Zhu & Iansiti, 2012). We encounter direct network effects when users attract more users on the same side of the platform. For example, Facebook users attract their friends to interact and engage on the platform. We observe indirect network effects when users of one side of the platform attract more users from the other side. For example, more rideshare users attract more drivers to the platform, and more video game developers attract more users to a gaming platform.

Because network effects are susceptible and subject to change, poor platform management and negative feedback loops may affect the platform if rule-based platform governance mechanisms are not enforced (Parker et al., 2016).

9.2.3 *Platform Functions*

The distinguishing differences between traditional pipeline businesses and platforms warrant alternative business strategies and activities (Van Alstyne et al., 2016; Parker & Alstyne, 2014). Notable among these are access decisions, design and architecture (design principles), launch strategies (ecosystem building) and platform governance (controls and rules).

Design and Architecture The design and architectural considerations of a platform are another critical responsibility of platform owners. Platform design and architecture considerations entail designing the core interaction, resourcing to conduct key platform activities and designing new interactions to scale the platform.

The core interaction is an integral component that attracts users to the platform – it is the primary purpose of the platform that brings producers and consumers to engage with it (Van Alstyne et al., 2016; Parker et al., 2016). Platform core interactions are not unique to a specific platform business and are common across the industry. For example, the core interactions of ridesharing platforms or marketplaces are similar. The core interaction comprises three components – the participants (customers), the value unit created by the producer and consumed by the consumer and the filter or curation method that enables the efficient exchange of value among the participants.

Complementary to the core interaction are key platform activities – pull, facilitate and match. First, the platform must attract (pull) producers and consumers to engage on the platform. Then the platform must facilitate the efficient exchange of value units between the platform participants through effective matching algorithms to ensure the exchange of the value unit between the producers and consumers.

To scale the platform and drive user engagement, platform owners need to design and accommodate new ecosystem participants and interactions that will drive economies of scale and scope.

Launch Strategies Critical to platform performance are the tactics applied to launch and the build-out of the ecosystem that will drive network effects and growth (Parker & Alstyne, 2014). Platform businesses need to be deliberate about attracting (pulling) the different participants that will engage (and not register/sign up) on the platform, the market development plans and the structure of incentives for both sides of the platform. Having developed the strategies for attracting the producer and consumer of the core interaction, platform owners also need to enhance the value of the ecosystem and drive user engagement through complementary ecosystem participants and additional interactions that enhance platform growth.

Governance Aside from the design and strategic considerations, platform owners should avert platform (market) failure by using governance rules and tools that direct and control the behaviours of all platform participants, promoting a healthy ecosystem for all (Kenny & Zysman, 2016; Parker et al., 2016).

9.2.4 Digital Platforms in Sub-Saharan Africa

Even though digital platforms on the continent date back to 1999, the surge began much later because of high-speed cable and mobile telephony networks. The earliest survey paper exploring the existence of platforms in Africa identifies key distinguishing characteristics (David-West & Evans, 2016).

- Innovation clusters: The concentration of platforms in regional innovation clusters spanning southern, western and eastern Africa.
- Transaction focused: Marketplace platforms facilitating transactions across diverse industries dominate the platform landscape.
- Ownership: The majority of the platforms are privately owned entities, merely focusing on delivering the core interactions between two sides of the market (buyers and sellers, travellers and accommodations, etc.) with few platforms exploring ecosystem development.

Subsequent work exploring the nexus between digital platforms and financial services identifies mobile and Web (browsers) as dominant accessibility interfaces (Smit et al., 2019).

E-logistics Platforms According to Meyer et al. (2018), the benefits of digital technologies in the transportation sector and the potential impact of new business models are apparent. Using the business morphological box to categorise and compare rail sector business models, Meyer et al. identify a preference for digital business models focusing on information management, simple business optimisations and advanced analytics. Regarding platform business models, they recognise the difficulty of building network effects by mobilising users as a challenge that can be addressed by integrating cyber-physical systems. In sub-Saharan Africa, David-West and Evans (2016) highlight the dearth of delivery logistics infrastructure for the movement of physical goods to support marketplace platforms and backward integration of some platform operators. Still, logistics platforms were not identified as a dominant business category until the work of Smit et al. (2019), with Giuliani and With's (2019) survey classifying the sector by products and services – shipping/freighting, courier services and last-mile delivery, cold chain, freight forwarding or management, storage and warehousing and addressing systems.

9.3 Approach

In this chapter, we analyse e-logistics platforms using the platform business model (PBM) analysis and map (Rogers, 2016) to explain two aspects – the core interaction (Parker et al., 2016) and their ecosystem development or economic (Kenny & Zysman, 2016) capabilities.

Define the core interaction: Identify the components that make up the core interaction – the participants (producer and consumer), value unit and curation filters.

Map the platform ecosystem development capabilities: Notwithstanding similarities in core interactions, platform businesses distinguish themselves through their business models. Rogers' (2016) platform business model map provides a visual representation of the platform business, highlighting the customer types (participants), the roles they play in the ecosystem and the value units exchanged among customers and between customers and the platform. The value units exchanged may be physical goods and services, information or financial (currency).

Profile the Participants Rogers (2016) defines four platform archetypes depending on the role each customer type plays in the platform ecosystem. The customer type that attracts more customer types is the linchpin. Customers are considered either primary payers or payers, depending on the monetary value the platform receives. Other customer types that do not provide monetary value but provide value units to other customers are sweeteners.

9.3.1 Platform Sampling

We select our sample from Digest Africa's (2019) report of the ten most funded platforms listing. Of the top 10 funded platforms, six provide ridesharing or transportation, three are e-logistics services, and one is a data and journey planning service. The three e-logistics platforms (see Table 9.3) are the scope of this chapter.

Table 9.3 Most funded e-logistics platforms

Platform	Description	Founding	Amount raised (USD)	Headquarters	Countries of operations
Kobo360	Connects truckers to companies with freight needs	2017	27.3M	Nigeria	Nigeria, Kenya, Ghana, Togo
Lori Systems	Connects cargo owners to transport in frontier markets	2016	14.9M	Kenya	Kenya, Nigeria, Uganda
Sendy	On-demand door-to-door package delivery	2014	8M	Kenya	Kenya, Uganda

9.3.2 Data Collection

Using publicly available information, this chapter explores platform business models highlighting the design components (customers and value units using Rogers's platform business model map). We collected Internet data in two stages. First, a website review was conducted to identify the customer segments, value units exchanged and network effects. The second data collection phase sourced Internet data using a keyword search for "Logistics Platform AND (Kobo360 OR Sendy OR Lori Systems)". We archived the 688 search references for review. Further keyword searches of the company names alone resulted in 47, 192 and 71 articles referencing Sendy, Kobo360 and Lori Systems, respectively.

Detailed review of the websites of each of the platforms was conducted to identify the elements of the platform business model, customer segments served, value unit exchanged (physical and/or financial) and network effects, assigning profiles based on their roles.

9.4 Logistics Platform Business Model Analysis

E-logistics platforms facilitate logistics and freight services between transporters and freight companies and cargo owners. By providing access to their assets and resources, transporters and freight companies offer freight/cargo delivery services to cargo owners, facilitating trade and commerce across the middle and last miles. Fig. 9.2 illustrates the core interaction.

	Producer (creation)	Consumer (consumption)	Curation/Filter
Participants	Transporters/haulage	Cargo owners	Order specifications, truck details, cargo/freight specifications (volume/weight), trip details, driver preferences, goods handling specifications
Value Unit	Asset/resource accessibility	Freight/cargo delivery	

Fig. 9.2 E-logistics platforms: the core interaction

9.4.1 Core Interaction

9.4.2 Kobo360

Kobo360 is Nigeria's e-logistics platform focusing on "getting the continent moving". The Kobo360 platform serves both its primary stakeholders (cargo owners and haulage companies) and provides value-added services to both drivers and haulage companies through additional ecosystem actors (see Table 9.4 and Fig. 9.3). Besides facilitating cargo movements, Kobo360's ecosystem development encompasses access to financial services – digital wallets for drivers, working capital (fuel and parts), goods and health insurance and asset financing and job creation with driver onboarding resources for haulage companies with trucks needing drivers. Through the asset financing scheme, the Kobo360 ecosystem seeks to empower drivers and scale the supply of logistics assets available.

9.4.3 Lori Systems

Lori Systems operates from Nairobi, Kenya, and removes the burden of cargo and freight delivery from cargo owners by facilitating shipment with transporters. Their ability to optimise shipments also reduces the overall costs. The financial services support on the Lori Systems platform is limited to working capital (fuel) and goods in transit insurance. While the Lori ecosystem is open to independent drivers, limited benefits are available. The platform business analysis and map are illustrated in Table 9.5 and Fig. 9.4.

Table 9.4 Kobo360 platform business model analysis

Customer type	Value received from the other customers	Value received from the platform	Value provided to the other customers	Value provided to the platform	Attracts	Profile
Haulage companies/ truckers	Truck/asset utilisation (cargo owners/recipients) **Delivery service fees (cargo owners)**	**Asset/resource accessibility**	**Truck/asset (drivers)**	Data	Haulage companies/ truckers	Payer
	Truck asset financing, trip financing (financial institutions, individuals)	Work performance records	Cargo movement (cargo owners/ recipients)	**Intermediation fee (commission)**	Drivers	Linchpin
		Truck marketplace			Truck parts/fuel suppliers	
					Cargo owners	
Drivers	Truck/asset utilisation (haulage companies/ truckers)	**Work opportunity**	Ratings (cargo owners/recipients)	Data	Haulage companies/ truck owners	Payer
	Driver support (service stations)	Driver empowerment (healthcare, discounted diesel, education, working capital)	Cargo movement (cargo owners/ recipients)	**Intermediation fee (commission)**	Drivers	
	Health insurance (insurance providers)				Citizen investors	

(continued)

Table 9.4 (continued)

Customer type	Value received from the other customers	Value received from the platform	Value provided to the other customers	Value provided to the platform	Attracts	Profile
Cargo owners/producers and distributors (individuals/SMEs[a]/corporates/government)	**Accounts receivable (cargo recipients)**	Trucking/haulage and delivery services (scheduled and on demand)	Goods and services (cargo recipients)	Data	Drivers	Primary payer
	Goods-in-transit insurance (insurance providers)	Price estimation tools/two-way quote system		**Delivery fee (weight/volume based)**	Clearing agents	
		Supply chain management tools			Haulage companies/truck owners	
		Collection services			Cargo recipients	
		Access to markets				
Cargo recipients (individuals/SMEs/corporates/government)	Goods and services (cargo owners)	Trucking/haulage tracking services	**Accounts payable (cargo owners)**	Data	N/A	Sweetener
Clearing agents	**Patronage (cargo owners/recipients)**	**Access to markets**	Goods and services (cargo recipients)	Data	Cargo owners/recipients	Payer
				Delivery fee (weight/volume based)	Haulage companies/truck owners	
Financial institutions	**Patronage (drivers, truck owners)**	**Access to markets**	**Truck (asset) financing (haulage companies/truck owners)**	Data	Haulage companies/truck owners	Sweetener
		Performance records		User engagement		
		Credit references				
Truck parts/fuel suppliers	**Patronage (truck owners)**	**Access to markets**	Car parts/fuel credits (drivers, cargo owners)	Data	Haulage companies/truck owners	Sweetener
				User engagement		

Customer type	Value received from the other customers	Value received from the platform	Value provided to the other customers	Value provided to the platform	Attracts	Profile
Insurance providers (general and health)	**Patronage (drivers, truck owners)**	**Access to markets**	Insurance coverage (drivers, cargo owners)	Data	Haulage companies/ truck owners	Sweetener
				User engagement	Drivers	
Citizen investors (individuals)	Principal + interest income (truck owners)	**Investment opportunity**	**Truck (asset) financing (drivers)**	Data	Haulage companies/ truck owners	Sweetener
				User engagement	Drivers	
					Citizen investors (individuals)	

Monetary value exchanges in bold
[a]Small and medium enterprises (SMEs)

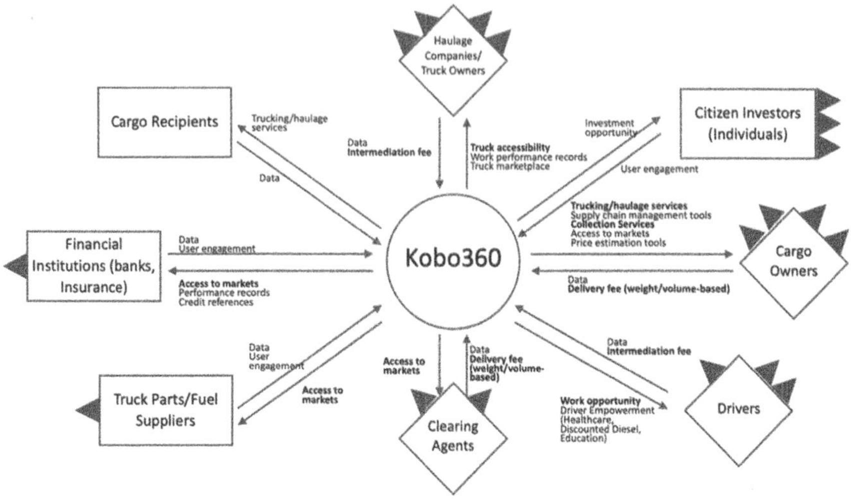

Fig. 9.3 Kobo360 platform business model map

9.4.4 Sendy

Sendy facilitates on-demand, door-to-door (last-mile) package deliveries. With a simpler ecosystem (see Table 9.6 and Fig. 9.5), Sendy's ability to provide both middle-mile (freight) and last-mile (door-to-door) services makes the ecosystem attractive to enterprises and e-commerce providers.

9.5 Platform Design Considerations

9.5.1 Value Units

The middle mile of cargo and freight shipments requires assets and resources like trucks and working capital, providing opportunities for creating new value units for platform participants.

Financial Services Distribution As evidenced in the analyses of the platforms providing e-logistics services, digital platforms are alternative distribution channels for financial services. Combining financial products and services in the platform offerings is common. The bundled financial services provide assurance of the goods and services transit and enhance asset utilisation by keeping the trucks moving. Kobo360 offers innovative crowdsourced financing of trucks that expands the funding sources for drivers and haulage companies. As an investment opportunity, this enables individuals to take part in the logistics ecosystem without managing drivers and opens drivers to self-employment and entrepreneurship. Cash resources

Table 9.5 Lori Systems platform business model analysis

Customer type	Value received from the other customers	Value received from the platform	Value provided to the other customers	Value provided to the platform	Attracts	Profile
Transporters	Fuel (service stations)	**Asset/resource accessibility**	Work opportunity (drivers)	Data	Transporters	Payer/ linchpin
	Truck/asset utilisation, **Delivery service fee (cargo owners, freight forwarders)**	Invoicing	**Patronage (service stations, insurance providers)**	**Intermediation fee**	Service providers (service stations, insurance providers)	
		Working capital (fuel financing and insurance)			Drivers	
					Cargo owners	
Cargo owners (individuals/SMEs/ corporates/ government)	**Accounts receivable (cargo recipients)**	Reliable trucking/ haulage services	Truck/asset utilisation (transporters)	Data	Freight forwarders/ clearing agents	Primary payer
	Goods-in-transit insurance (insurance providers)	Supply chain management solutions	Goods and services (cargo recipients)	**Delivery fee (weight/volume based)**	Transporters	
		Transporter verification			Cargo recipients	
		Goods tracking/ transit notifications			Insurance providers	
					Cargo owners	
Cargo recipients (individuals/ SMEs/ corporates/ government)	Goods and services (cargo owners)	Reliable trucking/ haulage services	**Accounts payable (cargo owners)**	Data	N/A	Sweetener

(continued)

Table 9.5 (continued)

Customer type	Value received from the other customers	Value received from the platform	Value provided to the other customers	Value provided to the platform	Attracts	Profile
Freight forwarders, clearing agents	**Patronage (cargo owners/ recipients)**	**Access to markets**	Cargo movement (cargo owners and recipients)	Data	Cargo owners/ recipients	Payer
		Goods tracking/ transit notifications		**Delivery fee (weight/volume based)**	Transporters	
Service stations	**Patronage (transporters)**	**Access to markets**	Fuel (transporters)	Data	Transporters	Sweetener
				User engagement		
Insurance providers	**Patronage (transporters)**	**Access to markets**	Insurance coverage (cargo owners)	Data	Cargo owners	Sweetener
				User engagement		
Drivers	**Work opportunity (transporters)**	Driver verification	Truck/asset utilisation (transporters)	Data	Transporters	Payer
				Intermediation fee	Drivers	

Monetary values in bold
[a]Small and medium enterprises (SMEs)

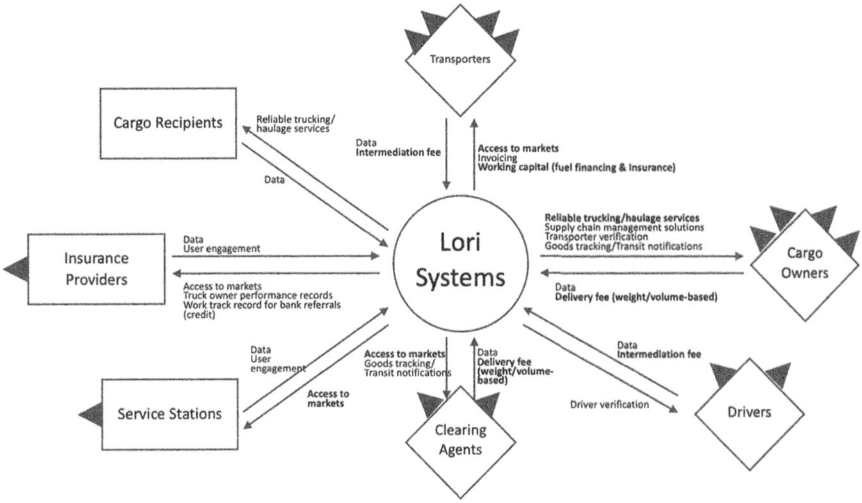

Fig. 9.4 Lori Systems platform business model map

(liquidity) to keep the trucks fuelled and operational are an additional value offering on logistics platforms. In a market like Nigeria, access to parts suppliers and service garages are beneficial additions to the platform ecosystem. These arrangements ensure asset optimisation through fuelling, servicing and maintaining cargo trucks. To enhance platform transparency, the Kobo360 platform supports digital wallets, maintaining a running total of all driver monetary benefits.

Supply Chain Management Supply chain management tools are another feature offered to enterprises, with Kobo360 also exploring further integration with enterprise systems like SAP. Lori is also extending back-office support to the transporters with invoicing solutions. Integrating these capabilities aligns with the recommendations of Meyer et al. (2018) of combining platforms and cyber-physical systems.

Co-creation While Sendy's simplified ecosystem does not cater to asset financing or working capital schemes, their partner engagement tactics that capitalise on customer knowledge result in product/service co-creation opportunities. Including diverse ecosystem actors enables the platform to provide diverse offerings and economies of scope.

9.5.2 Ecosystem Development

By extending the core interaction and creating additional value units, the platform ecosystem multiplies. Aside from creating the value units for the main platform participants, extending the platform should also foster the creation of additional value units among platform actors that will enhance the direct and indirect network effects.

Table 9.6 Sendy platform business model analysis

Customer type	Value received from the other customers	Value received from the platform	Value provided to the other customers	Value provided to the platform	Attracts	Profile
Partners (drivers/riders)	Asset utilisation	**Asset/resource accessibility**	Delivery (goods and documents) service (senders/e-commerce merchants)	**Intermediation fee**	Customers/senders	Payer
	Delivery payments (senders)	Training		Data	Partners (drivers/riders)	
		Micro-financing (loans)				
		Supplementary insurance		Product suggestions (co-creation)	E-commerce merchants	
Freight transporters	Truck/asset utilisation, **Delivery service fee (senders)**	**Asset/resource accessibility**	**Patronage (insurance providers)**	Data	Freight transporters	Payer
				Intermediation fee	Insurance providers	
					Senders	
Customers/senders (individuals/businesses)	**Accounts receivable (recipients)**	Delivery order tracking tools (scheduled and on demand)	Goods/services (recipients)	Data	Recipients (individuals and businesses)	Primary payer
	Goods-in-transit insurance (insurance providers)	Multi-location deliveries		**Delivery fee (distance based)**	Customers/senders	
		Cost management tools			Insurance providers	
E-commerce merchants	**Accounts receivable (recipients)**	**Access to markets**	Goods/services (buyers)	Data	Recipients (individuals and businesses)	Payer
	Goods-in-transit insurance (insurance providers)	Delivery order tracking tools (scheduled and on demand)		**Delivery fee (distance based)**	E-commerce merchants	
					Insurance providers	

Customer type	Value received from the other customers	Value received from the platform	Value provided to the other customers	Value provided to the platform	Attracts	Profile
Recipients/buyers (individuals/ businesses)	Goods/services (customers/senders)	Delivery service notifications	**Accounts payable (customers/senders)**	Data	N/A	Sweetener
Insurance providers	**Patronage (customers/senders)**	**Access to markets**	Insurance coverage (customers)	Data	Customers/ senders	Sweetener
				User engagement	E-commerce merchants	

Monetary values in bold

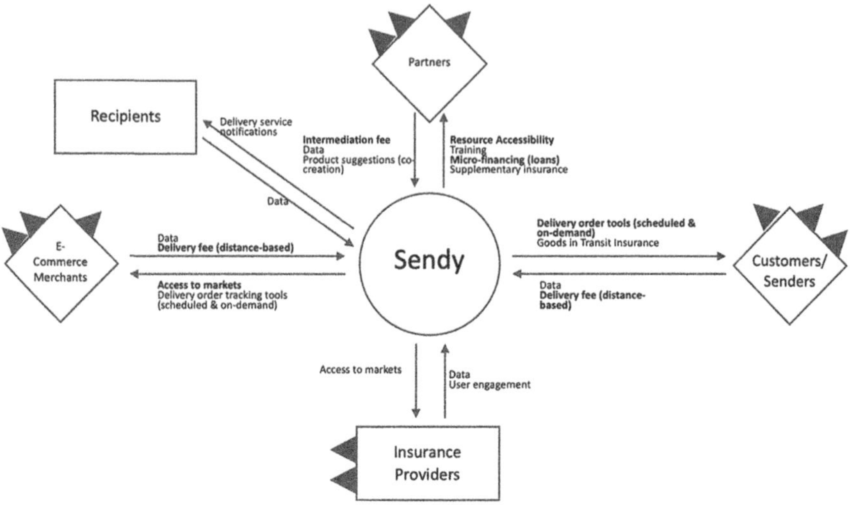

Fig. 9.5 Sendy platform business model map

The assigned profiles of each ecosystem actor suggest the platforms' ability to scale and produce additional value units and hence network effects (Parker et al., 2016; Rogers, 2016). The core participants of logistics platforms – transporters and cargo owners – are linchpins that pull other participants into the platform ecosystem, producing strong direct and indirect network effects. The summary of similarities and differences is highlighted in Fig. 9.6.

Figure 9.6 highlights that the value of e-logistics platforms extends beyond the movement of physical goods and services. Other than addressing market failures common in SSA, such platforms are potential mechanisms propagating access to finance and distributing financial services (Smit et al., 2019). This concept is especially important in markets where retail payment systems like mobile money have yet to become mainstream and embedding financial services within industry value chains is a viable adoption strategy (David-West et al., 2016). Another critical feature of e-logistics platforms is the ability to formalise and digitise informal businesses dominant in SSA by, for example, aggregating and optimising the use of physical assets typically held by micro and small enterprises (Cenamor et al., 2019; OECD, 2021).

Access to quality data for decision- and policymaking is another structural gap logistics platforms can address. As evidenced in the platform business models, data generated by the various platform interactions provide a complementary value unit – advanced analytics (Meyer et al., 2018). For policymakers, the chapter emphasises the micro and macro benefits of e-logistics platforms and the growing need for enabling environments prompting platform businesses and attendant issues like anti-competitive practices (Giuliani & With, 2019; OECD, 2021), labour as it

Similarities	Differences
Impact: Logistics platforms have high impact in not only addressing market and trade gaps but also in providing employment and entrepreneurial opportunities to drivers.	**Context:** Based on their operating context, platform businesses are addressing institutional, market and resource constraints.
Financial services distribution: Addressing financial inclusion limitations on the continent by distributing financial services like access to credit, insurance and crowdfunding expands the use of financial services and value chain efficiency.	**Digital solutions provider:** Where the cargo owners lack solutions, the platform businesses provide solutions for supply chain activities.
Enterprise integration: Serving large and midsized enterprises that have automated internal processes, integrating into their supply chain management systems.	**Pricing:** Atypical to freight and cargo shipments is the use of volume/weight pricing. Last mile shipments are adopting distance-based (fixed) pricing models.
Data harvesting: Logistics platforms are a critical source of data on road and transportation systems and networks. The management of such data can not only enhance the algorithms of platform businesses but also enhance journey planning and management to a larger audience, a potential new interaction.	

Fig. 9.6 E-logistics platform similarities and differences

pertains to employer-employee relationships and livelihoods (Berg et al., 2018) and financial services integrations facilitating payments and fundraising activities.

The study contributes to practice by highlighting platform design strategies as a key focus area for platform business owners, a requisite to building and enhancing the platform ecosystem (i.e. interactions and value to secondary platform participants). By exploiting these platform management strategies, platform owners can leverage additional growth-stage funding opportunities. For policymakers, the chapter recognises emergent policy areas for a thriving platform economy.

9.6 Conclusion

Business models illustrate how organisations create and deliver value (Osterwalder & Pigneur, 2004; Alexander Osterwalder & Pigneur, 2010). Platform business models highlight the value units (physical, information and monetary) exchanged among customers and the platform (Rogers, 2016) and focal areas for platform strategy and management (Alstyne et al., 2016). Unlike pipeline businesses, platforms require different strategies to build substantial network effects that will drive scale.

Leveraging data is one such strategy. Aside from facilitating core interactions, platforms are aggregating vast amounts of data that can optimise their curation or matching capabilities. Further, by applying analytics, platform owners can improve and optimise service delivery by analysing behaviours and patterns (e.g. allocating time-sensitive trips to reliable drivers or predicting spare part replacements based on trip history and truck service records). Because platform subscription by the core participants/asset owners (transporters and cargo owners) is non-exclusive, platforms need strategies that prevent switching. Limiting multi-homing is a strategic imperative for platforms (Eisenmann et al., 2006; G. Parker & Alstyne, 2014), guaranteeing their ability to facilitate the core interaction. In the logistics sector, facilitating the core interaction is securing access to different classes of assets (trucks) for different cargo types when required. For example, multi-homing strategies for last-mile platforms for package delivery will differ from those of middle-mile platforms requiring cold chains. Though platforms need to innovate to produce additional value units that extend the ecosystem, the models highlight the gaps. By employing only secondary data, the study does not incorporate future platform business strategies. While this external-only perspective is limiting, the findings are nonetheless insightful to current and prospective platform business owners, highlighting design and ecosystem development dynamics in the e-logistics sector. Further research opportunities include deep dive case studies of the platforms, including platform ecosystem sizing.

References

Alstyne, M. W. V., Parker, G. G., & Choudary, S. P. (2016, April). *Pipelines, platforms, and the new rules of strategy*. Harvard Business Review.

Berg, J., Furrer, M., Harmon, E., Rani, U., & Silberman, M. S. (2018). *Digital labour platforms and the future of work Towards decent work in the online world*. International Labour Organisation.

Bhatti, Y. A. (2012). What is frugal, what is innovation? Towards a theory of frugal innovation. *SSRN Electronic Journal*. https://doi.org/10.2139/ssrn.2005910

Cenamor, J., Parida, V., & Wincent, J. (2019). How entrepreneurial SMEs compete through digital platforms: The roles of digital platform capability, network capability and ambidexterity. *Journal of Business Research, 100*, 196–206. https://doi.org/10.1016/j.jbusres.2019.03.035

David-West, O. (2017). *E-Commerce management in emerging markets. In undefined* (pp. 200–222). IGI Global. https://doi.org/10.4018/978-1-4666-9787-4.ch016

David-West, O., & Evans, P. C. (2016). *The rise of African platforms: A regional survey*. http://thecge.net/wp-content/uploads/2016/04/AfricanPlatformSurveyFinal.pdf

David-West, O., Ajai, O., Umokoro, I., Salami, D., Isheyemi, O., Ihenachor, N., Adetunji, O., & Kelikume, I. (2016). *Digital financial services in Nigeria: State of the market report 2016* (pp. 1–112). Undefined. https://doi.org/10.13140/rg.2.2.24491.23849

Digest Africa. (2019, August 15). These are Africa's 10 most funded transport and logistics startups. *DigestAfrica*. https://digestafrica.com/africa-funded-transport-logistics-startups

Eisenmann, T., Parker, G., & Alstyne, M. W. V. (2006, October 1). Strategies for two-sided markets. *Harvard Business Review*, 12.

Evans, P. C., & Gawer, A. (2016). *The rise of the platform enterprise: A global survey (Thecge. Net)*. The Centre for Global Enterprise. http://www.thecge.net/wp-content/uploads/2016/01/PDF-WEB-Platform-Survey_01_12.pdf

Frank, K. (2016). *Logistics Africa*. Knight Frank. https://www.knightfrank.com/research/report-library/logistics-africa-2016-4022.aspx

Gatautis, R. (2017). The rise of the platforms: Business model innovation perspectives. *Engineering Economics, 28*(5), 585–591. https://doi.org/10.5755/j01.ee.28.5.19579

Giuliani, D., & With, L. H. (2019). *Digitising logistics in Africa: The role of technology and innovation*. Briter Bridges. https://static1.squarespace.com/static/5ab2a4d655b02c29746fc58c/t/5d84f29c0a997e4f96ae2dae/1568993955203/20092019_Digitising_Logistics_in_Africa_Report.pdf

Hagiu, A. (2009). Two-sided platforms: Product variety and pricing structures. *Journal of Economics & Management Strategy, 18*(4), 1011–1043. https://doi.org/10.1111/j.1530-9134.2009.00236.x

Hashi, S. (2019, October 9). The 3 trends shaping the future of logistics in African markets. *The Africa Report*. https://www.theafricareport.com/18341/the-3-trends-shaping-the-future-of-logistics-in-african-markets/

Jacobides, M. G., Sundararajan, A., & Alstyne, M. W. V. (2019). *Platforms and ecosystems: Enabling the digital economy*. Undefined. http://www3.weforum.org/docs/WEF_Digital_Platforms_and_Ecosystems_2019.pdf

Kenny, M., & Zysman, J. (2016). The rise of the platform economy. *Issues in Science and Technology, 3*(32).

Meyer, N., Horvat, D., Hitzler, M., & Doll, C. (2018). *Business models for freight and logistics services*. Working Paper Sustainability and Innovation, No. S08/2018.

OECD. (2021). *SMEs in the online platform economy*. Undefined. https://doi.org/10.1787/1386638a-en

Osterwalder, A., & Pigneur, Y. (2004). In W. Currie (Ed.), *An ontology for e-business models. Value creation from E-business models*. Butterworth-Heinemann.

Osterwalder, A., & Pigneur, Y. (2010). *Business model generation*. Wiley.

Parker, G., & Alstyne, M. W. V. (2014). Platform strategy. *SSRN Electronic Journal*. https://doi.org/10.2139/ssrn.2439323

Parker, G. G., Alstyne, M. W. V., & Choudary, S. P. (2016). *Platform revolution: How networked markets are transforming the economy and how to make them work for you*. WW Norton & Company.

Rogers, D. L. (2016). *The digital transformation playbook: Rethink your business for the digital age*. Columbia University Press. https://doi.org/10.7312/roge17544-toc

Smit, H., Johnson, C., Hunter, R., Dunn, M., & van Vuuren, P. F. J. (2019). *Africa's digital platforms and financial services: An eight-country overview* (pp. 1–42).

Teravaninthorn, S., & Raballand, G. (2009). *Transport prices and costs in Africa: A review of the international corridors*. The World Bank.

Zhu, F., & Iansiti, M. (2012). Entry into platform-based markets. *Strategic Management Journal, 33*(1), 88–106. https://doi.org/10.1002/smj.941

Olayinka David-West is a Professor of Information Systems with over three decades' experience in the IT and financial services industry and a passionate advocate for digital transformation and inclusive finance. Her research and practice engagements involve policy and strategic management interventions towards using digital technologies for transforming businesses and society. Olayinka is a renowned thought leader in digital transformation and applications in financial services. She has expert certifications in financial inclusion policy and digital money and is a governing council member of the Fintech Association of Nigeria and a member of the African Women in Finance and Payments. She mentors young women in STEM and has featured on the Tech Women of Lagos exhibition, listed among the Leading Women in Nigeria's Financial Technology Industry and profiled on Fintech Times as a regional thought leader in financial inclusion and digital transformation.

Chapter 10
COVID-19 Pandemic and the Small- and Medium-Sized Enterprise: Digital Strategies for Surviving in a Developing Economy

Eric Ansong and Charles Turkson

Abstract **Situation faced:** Various restrictions were imposed to curb the spread of COVID-19. The owners of a small- and medium-sized enterprise (SME) in the food sector faced challenges that span from keeping their employees and customers safe, shoring-up cash and liquidity, reorienting operations to navigating complicated government support programs.

Action taken: The case SME in Ghana adopted several digital strategies that revolutionized their business model and ensured that revenue came in, keeping the business alive and strong. Some measures included enhanced social media engagements and introducing a mobile application (app) for online ordering of meals and making payments.

Results achieved: Adopting and implementing strategies utilizing digital technology brought considerable benefits to the SME even though the initial stages were marred with some challenges. One related organizational challenge was an organizational culture accustomed to manual service delivery procedures, hence hampering the smooth implementation of the digital strategies in the initial stages. But the digital strategies enabled the SME to remain profitable in the face of the challenges the COVID-19 pandemic created.

Lessons learned: Adoption of affordable and or low-cost digital tools – rather than buying expensive proprietary software – was one of the most important critical success factors in implementing digital strategies. The willingness of the staff – their desire for change and the cordial relationship among them – was very crucial in innovation implementation. Electronic payment channels such as mobile money

---

E. Ansong (✉)
Wisconsin International University College, Accra, Ghana
e-mail: eric.ansong@wiuc-ghana.edu.gh

C. Turkson
University of Kent, Kent, UK
e-mail: C.Turkson@kent.ac.uk

R. Boateng et al. (eds.), *Digital Innovations, Business and Society in Africa*, Advances in Theory and Practice of Emerging Markets,
https://doi.org/10.1007/978-3-030-77987-0_10

services supported the SME's digital strategies. Also, their collaboration with strategic partners in the downstream supply chain enhanced their operational efficiency.

Keywords COVID-19 pandemic · Digital strategies · SMEs · Food sector

10.1 Introduction

Small- and medium-sized enterprises (SMEs) in Ghana contribute significantly to developing the economy. It is asserted in extant research (Quartey et al., 2017; Abor & Quartey, 2010) that SMEs account for 92% of all formal businesses and offer 80% employment besides contributing to 70% of gross domestic products. SMEs in Ghana are owned and mostly managed by a single person. This entrepreneur is in charge of all major decisions and often has limited or no formal education and may lack adequate information in using new technologies. This phenomenon attests to why most SMEs are characterized by weak management skills and a lack of technical know-how (Mensah, 2004). SMEs in Ghana serve mainly the local market. Only a handful of these SMEs have the capability and resources to suit international needs. This is partly due to the enormous capital requirements for engaging in export trade and perhaps the owner's inadequate knowledge and awareness of opportunities. Most of these SMEs are labor-intensive and operate with low technological know-how and innovation (Donkor et al., 2018).

In 2011, a Ghanaian couple set up a restaurant and named it Melabites Enterprise (a pseudonym). The initial intention was to set up a small restaurant showcasing some of the favorite dishes from places this couple had traveled to around the world. The purpose was to provide patrons with contemporary flavors from the Americas to Asia fused with Ghanaian dishes to compliment all tastes. The first branch was therefore opened in East Legon, a suburb of Accra, Ghana. The intention to set up their first branch in East Legon was due to the cosmopolitan nature of the suburb, which provided a conducive venue for attracting potential clients interested in such contemporary dishes.

Melabites uses produce grown and made locally for freshly prepared food throughout the day. Melabites' affordable price policy, combined with the quality and tasty dishes for all, has grown at a fast pace within the years of operation. The SME has therefore opened eight other outlets in Ghana within Accra and Kumasi, which are the two biggest cities in Ghana. Melabites has 25 full-time employees and over 30 temporary staff.

10.2 Situation Faced

Governments, in an effort to contain and reduce the rate of spread of COVID-19, instituted lockdowns in most parts of their jurisdictions. Some countries instituted total lockdowns, which included the whole country, while others instituted partial lockdowns, which affected hotspots and areas with rising numbers of confirmed COVID-19 cases. These restrictions on movements made nonessential workers stay at home, limiting activities and leading to the temporary closure of some businesses. For instance, in a survey conducted on over 5,800 SMEs, 41.3% reported that they were temporarily closed because of COVID-19 (Bartik et al., 2020).

On 30 March 2020, a partial lockdown of Accra and Kumasi in Ghana took effect because of the COVID-19 global pandemic. To this effect, the government of Ghana banned all public gatherings, including restaurants and bars, from operating while members of the executive, legislature, and judiciary were allowed to operate. Some services, such as those that were involved in the production, distribution, and marketing of food, beverages, pharmaceuticals, and medicine, were also exempted from the restrictions (Nyavor, 2020).

Later in a televised address, the president extended the ban on social gatherings till the last day of May 2020 to reduce the spread of the virus. However, on 11 May 2020, the government of Ghana again, through the office of the Ghana Tourism Authority, gave hotels, bars, and restaurants permission to reopen but to operate under enhanced social distancing procedures. Among the directives was for operators of pubs and bars to remain closed. Restaurants and eateries were to stay open. These restaurants were only to operate through pick-up and delivery services (Cromwell, 2020).

While the lockdown was a good measure by the government to curb the spread of the virus from infecting people, its effect on businesses and enterprises was a nightmare. The COVID-19 pandemic caused many food businesses to close their doors. However, others quickly adapted to support their employees by generating income and still delivering quality products and services to customers through digital technology.

Because of the increased spread of COVID-19, many businesses worldwide have been inconvenienced a great deal. Food businesses are one of the most hit enterprises. The survival of Melabites was challenged. Melabites had to temporarily close five of its branches because of the lockdown and restrictions. 80% of the employees were also temporarily laid off. Melabites had to re-evaluate their operations to survive and meet the needs of their customers while ensuring safety for both themselves and consumers in the face of the COVID-19 pandemic.

10.2.1 Challenges Melabites Faced Because of COVID-19

The challenges COVID-19 has caused are enormous. To businesses, it has led to closures. Most companies have shut down as a measure to stop the spread of the virus and many enterprises have to devise innovative ways of restructuring and operating.

Like many other food businesses worldwide, the coronavirus adversely impacted food companies operating in Ghana. Government policies and safety measures have caused many consumers to forgo commutes to public gatherings and rather focus on expending resources mostly for necessities instead of certain luxuries like meals from restaurants. The need for social distancing and hygiene has increased consumers' self-reliance on preparing meals at home to reduce the possibility of viral spread. What this essentially means is people will instead cook their food themselves than have others outside their safety nucleus do so for them.

The virus has also affected the country economically. Many businesses are struggling to generate revenue resulting in layoffs, delayed payments, and salary cuts. There is a reduction in the purchasing power of consumers too. Many consumers will be more interested in spending less money on a sufficient meal that will satisfy them. In this period, the standard prices of dishes from restaurants may seem relatively expensive to the consumer than other cheaper priced substitute products that could be purchased or cooked at home.

Melabites struggled to generate enough revenue to continuously operate with fewer customers patronizing services. This led to the enterprise reducing the number of days it operated in a week. Some of its branches do not open on Tuesdays and Sundays to reduce the number of resources being utilized. This has graduated into a full-blown layoff of nonessential staff. The microentrepreneurs indicated that they have laid-off their waiting staff because fewer people come into the restaurant to stay and eat. Most customers now prefer to either pick up or have their orders delivered to them. This has interrupted the original flow of work of the enterprise, which involved dine-in services within their premises.

In these times, where the focus is mainly on safety and survival, consumers' attention is more directed toward information about the coronavirus. Ads related to protecting oneself from the virus have been given more priority and have dominated the traditional media spaces. Consumers who now spend more time at home are barely exposed to the outdoor ads of restaurants or external food businesses like Melabites. Overall, this has affected the ability of the SME to continue operating, generate enough funds, and pay employees.

10.3 Action Taken

The main problems so far identified include maintaining brand loyalty and patronage and facilitating deliveries to customers. This has forced the enterprise to boost its digital and online efforts to ensure the business survived and remained profitable. With the many digital tools relatively accessible in the ever-growing digital age, it has become almost easy to conduct business virtually. The following are the digital technology-enabled strategies Melabites implemented.

Social Media Tools Melabites mainly utilized social media to get their message across to consumers. With more time available to most people staying at home, the Internet and social media, by extension, became one of the most visited places. Melabites took advantage of this to advertise through popular social media platforms such as Instagram and Facebook, among others.

The managers of Melabites engaged the services of social media influencers who further engaged consumer interests. The majority of their online impressions, leads, and conversions originated from paid ads over the various social media platforms. This meant that for a relatively low price than in traditional media, Melabites pushed their ads further online over a certain geographic space, for varying periods to social media accounts using GPS tags and keywords among other unique categories over the platform.

Enhanced Enterprise Website Other digital communication strategies involved enhancing the Melabites website. The SME engaged a professional website manager to redesign and rebrand their website. The enterprise's website is up and running and shows every meal and service on offer in high-quality graphics. Making good use of digital marketing tools available with Google Ads, the enterprise has been able to effectively advertise using search engine ads, banner display ads, and video ads to draw a large pool of customers to the site. This has aided Melabites in remaining relevant in the eyes of a large customer base and increased their reach and patronage.

Strategic Partnerships In terms of delivering service to consumers in this period of the pandemic, Melabites also resorted to using digital technologies to facilitate a smooth customer experience. Formerly, customers could only walk into the premises or make phone calls to order food. Melabites has now partnered with Jumia Foods, a subsidiary of the parent company Jumia, to facilitate online delivery of services to customers. Jumia Foods is one of the most convenient online food ordering service providers in Ghana. Jumia Foods has both a website and a mobile app which simply connects customers to restaurants within Accra, Ghana (Jumia Foods, 2020). Through this partnership, Melabites was listed on Jumia Foods' digital platforms and customers ordered for food.

Melabites strategically partnered with some mobile money service providers in Ghana. These mobile money service providers created accounts with special codes for Melabites, which allowed customers to electronically transfer money as payment for services. These accounts waived the transaction charges which customers would have paid.

Introduction of a Mobile App In response to meeting consumer needs on their own, Melabites fast-tracked the development of their mobile app. The Melabites app allows consumers to make orders by merely choosing what they want from the menu in the app. After filling out the details, the customer is prompted when the order will be fulfilled and the time the dispatch rider will arrive at the customer's premises with the food. The app also has an artificial intelligence (AI) bot that autonomously interacts with customers in case of complaints or any other problem. This helps to reduce the man-hours of employees and save resources while enabling continued service provision.

The mobile app also serves the purpose of communication and advertising to consumers. Like most mobile applications, the Melabites app can send notifications. Most notifications sent from the app are to alert consumers that their order is ready and dispatch riders are within range to make deliveries. Still, it has also been used to send ad notifications about the brand and its offerings. This is beneficial as it helps to ensure continued patronage by consumers with the application.

Cashless Transactions Digital technology has not only improved service delivery and communication with consumers of Melabites but also enabled cashless transactions. Many consumers can pay for goods and services from the comfort of their homes through mobile wallet services provided by most of Ghana's telecommunication service providers. While mobile wallet technology has been around for a long time (Talom & Tengeh, 2020), Melabites has, in the wake of the COVID-19 pandemic, encouraged consumers to pay for their orders with mobile money to ensure a better transaction of business at low risks of infection between consumers and staff. Melabites uses MTN MoMo, Vodafone Cash, and AirtelTigo Money and also accepts credit/debit card payments.

10.4 Results Achieved

The founders of Melabites attested to the positive impact of implementing the various strategies utilizing digital tools, even though there were initial challenges encountered. First, some difficulties the SME faced during the initial stages of implementing the digital strategies are outlined below;

These challenges encountered in the implementation have been discussed in three folds: organizational-related challenges, technological-related challenges, and lastly, environmental-related challenges. One organizational-related challenge was an organizational culture accustomed to manual service delivery procedures, hence hampering the smooth implementation of the digital strategies. Digital technologies are disruptive (Christensen, 2013). Most organizations, therefore, find it challenging in the initial stages of adoption, especially in adjusting to the new business procedures introduced by digital technologies.

In the technologically related challenges, the employees initially had to be trained in utilizing the digital tools introduced within the SME. Interactions with some employees for this case study showed that they initially had difficulties carrying out some activities such as social media campaigns, processing orders electronically, and managing inquiries electronically, among others. The microentrepreneurs justified the investment in the training of the employees by indicating that the employees are now using the skills acquired to manage the digital technologies introduced in their operations.

In the environmentally related challenges, the current and potential customers found it difficult to come to terms with the new procedures involved in placing orders and making payments. Interactions with one employee indicated that most customers had to be guided on how to use the mobile app and other electronic platforms to place orders. This resulted in an initial dip in the number of orders. The number of orders rose after the customers became accustomed to the new digital technologies implemented by the SME.

10.4.1 Benefits Derived from Implementing Digital Strategies

There is no gainsaying the positive impact of digital strategies on the survival of SMEs. Generally, digital technologies present enormous benefits for SMEs, which include reduced cost of transactions and an increase in operational efficiency (Lätti, 2016). Implementing digital strategies yielded significant positive results for the SME and its business operations. Besides the SME surviving during the COVID-19 pandemic, the following are benefits it derived from implementing the digitally enabled strategies.

Creation of an Online Brand Identity The brand identity is the physical or tangible part of the brand that enables consumers to identify a particular product, service, or even a company (Wäckerlin et al., 2020). A new brand identity was created for Melabites after it implemented its digital strategies. This included a name, logo, color scheme, brand guideline, and other relevant digital media on its social media platforms, website, mobile app, and partner platforms. Then social media handles were created for the business using the logos as profile pictures and brand elements as well. This helped customers or audience to quickly identify the business or page whenever they chanced upon it in their feed.

Improved Customer Experience Implementation of the digital strategies have helped the SME to maintain the majority of its old customers besides new ones. This can be attributed to the convenience the digital tools offer to the customers. The customers can now place orders in the comfort of their homes via the mobile app and other electronic platforms. The very high efficiency rate of digital tools provides an excellent experience for the customers. Customers can thus place their orders by vividly specifying their requirements. An employee of Melabites asserted that the digital platforms document the customers, which has helped to drastically reduce errors in executing orders. Unlike the paper receipts, which can get lost – mostly indicating no proof of purchase – the digital platforms present good storage space for good documentation. Again, digital tools such as the mobile app can track purchase history, and hence, more focused marketing messages are delivered to customers.

Reduction in Overhead Costs and Increased Revenue Businesses were challenged to reduce their overhead costs to survive in the COVID-19 pandemic. The reduction of overhead expenses is very critical in the operations of every business. One tool asserted to contribute to the reduction of overhead cost is digital technologies (Talom & Tengeh, 2020). Digital technologies allow SMEs to manage their operations more efficiently. Implementing digital technologies has replaced time-consuming business procedures. The digital platforms presented high-quality data for planning. Through digital platforms, the SME can forecast sales trends and patterns. The co-founder of the SME indicated that, based on data from the online platforms, they now know their most active days, less active days, and most demanded dishes, among others.

Electronic Financial Management An indirect benefit of implementing digital strategies was electronic financial management. Electronic financial management refers to the efficient management of a firm's finances using digital tools. Mararo and Ngahu (2017) assert that mobile money wallets present readily available accounts for SMEs. Thus, the electronic financial transactions platforms introduced allow for sales invoicing and up-to-date and automated accounting. The electronic payment platforms enable financial management and follow-up of the SMEs position regardless of time and place. On the whole, the electronic financial management tools significantly enhanced the SME's operational efficiency, thereby speeding up its financial processes resulting in cost savings.

10.5 Lessons Learned

COVID-19 has affected the world. This virus has forced most organizations and businesses to adapt by allowing the majority of their employees to work from home. In contrast, some institutions have been forced to shut down altogether. But in these moments, online transactions have become a viable option for people asked to stay at home for long periods. Digital technologies are critical for the survival of businesses. Bartik et al. (2020) assert that SMEs able to develop strategies around digital technologies survived the challenges posed by the COVID-19 pandemic. Such firms, including Melabites, moved most of their operations online, utilizing social media and online payment channels.

SMEs must embrace electronic payment systems. In a cash-dependent economy as one which prevails in Africa (Talom & Tengeh, 2020), the COVID-19 pandemic has severely affected transactions that involve the physical exchange of cash. To reduce the contamination and spread of the virus, people have been advised to resort to cashless means of transactions. This was a challenge because the majority of the populace did not have the digital means to receive and make payments and some also preferred to use physical cash for a variety of reasons.

All information gathered about Melabites proved that the firm understood its weaknesses during the COVID-19 pandemic and hence had to strategize to survive quickly. The enterprise soon realized the two major sectors that could improve the situation of their business, which were brand patronage and ensuring high-quality service delivery. They tailored specific plans suited to handle the two fields simultaneously. If not for their speed in discerning the situation and finding solutions, they would have suffered more significant losses at the initial stage, which had the potential to halt their operations. The SME's ability to work on two projects simultaneously – the mobile app and partnering with Jumia Foods – gave them the right impetus to offer continued services to clients. In implementing all the strategies, the owners did not only realize the importance of technology as an essential tool embedded in almost every facet of human life but had the technical know-how necessary to use it. Although the SME outsourced some of the heavy technical aspects, including mobile app development, most of the other technical configurations were done in-house. Information gathered from the case indicated that an in-house communication team implemented all social media campaigns using social media influencers and paid ads. Designing of graphical and message content, management of online orders through the apps and website were also done in-house. By taking advantage of the technical knowledge on social media management and application utilization at their disposal, Melabites was, therefore, able to essentially operate over the Internet with little effort.

10.5.1 Critical Success Factors in Digital Strategy Implementation

Based on interactions with the founders and employees of Melabites Enterprise, some critical success factors that contributed to the utilization of digital technologies are presented in Table 10.1.

The critical success factors are organized into the three major contexts that influence technology adoption within organizations (Tornatzky & Fleischer, 1990). These are technological factors, organizational factors, and environmental factors.

The technological factors consist of both the internal and external technologies that assisted the firm in its utilization of digital technologies during the COVID-19 pandemic. Table 10.1 shows that the critical success factors related to the technology context include the availability of relatively free to use social media platforms.

Table 10.1 Critical success factors

Context	Critical success factors
Technological success factors	1. The availability of free to use social media platforms made it easy to adopt and integrate into services (Facebook, Instagram, etc.) 2. Availability of affordable handheld devices for the staff 3. Availability of electronic payment platforms
Organizational success factors	1. The skills and technological literacy of the staff supported the utilization of digital tools 2. Staff knowledge of using social media, coordinating online transactions, and managing content on the website supported utilization 3. The IT-friendly microentrepreneurs facilitated the implementation of digitally enabled strategies
Environmental success factors	1. Government directive on social distancing and delivery of only pick-up and delivery services influenced the introduction of strategies enabled by digital technologies 2. Pressure from competing SMEs influenced the implementation of digital strategies 3. The availability of third-party support services contributed to implementing digital strategies

This confirms the assertion of Yan and Musika (2018) that most SMEs resort to social media due to its affordability and ease of use. Also, the availability of affordable handheld devices for staff contributed to the successful implementation of the digitally enabled strategies. The availability of electronic payment platforms also facilitated the implementation of digitally enabled strategies.

The organizational factors also refer to the various features within the organization, including its size, management, employees, and culture, among others, which contributed to implementing the digitally enabled strategies leading to the survival of the SME. The willingness of the microentrepreneurs – the founders and the managers of the SME – to accept and invest in the digital tools was very critical in creating a conducive atmosphere for implementing the digitally enabled strategies (Awiagah et al., 2016). The innovations within the SME were primarily championed by the microentrepreneurs. Other organizational factors that contributed to the survival of the SME include the staff with IT skills and hence that were digitally literate. These staff had the skill in using social media and other digital tools to coordinate online transactions and manage content on the website. It is asserted that the success of every intervention depends mostly on the people within the organization (Kovačič et al., 2018). The willingness of the staff – their desire for change and the cordial relationship among them – are very crucial in innovation implementation. Interaction with some employees in this case study indicated that the digitally enabled strategies received the full cooperation and support of all employees. The employees, thus, must be appropriately educated and well-motivated to understand and accept all the digital innovations introduced within the firm. At Melabites, the two founders were in constant communication with all the employees, including educating them on how to utilize the digital tools.

Environmental factors refer to the firm's interactions with external agents such as competitors, service providers, and government agencies whose activities contributed to the successful implementation of the SME's digital strategies. A significant driver in implementing the digitally enabled strategies was the support of the government of Ghana. Awiagah et al. (2016) assert that the level of digital innovation implementation by SMEs in developing economies has been dramatically enhanced by the government's participatory role in providing the empowering infrastructure. The influence of government policies and regulations has a direct or indirect impact on technology adoption. Government policies and initiatives could stimulate the progression of IT/IS infrastructure and information flow to hasten technology adoption (Ocloo et al. 2020). With Melabites, the government of Ghana has introduced policies such as mobile money interoperability services. Mobile money interoperability is a service that allows direct and seamless transfer of funds from one mobile money wallet to another mobile money wallet across networks (Ghana Interbank Payment and Settlement Systems Limited (GhIPSS) (2020)). This service was instrumental in the peak of the COVID-19 lockdown when social distancing regulations were imposed warranting electronic fund transfers. Other environmental factors that contributed to implementing digitally enabled strategies for survival include pressure from competing SMEs and the availability of third-party support services. Competing SMEs within the country in their quest to survive also implemented digital strategies, which made it mandatory for Melabites to also implement similar strategies. Ocloo et al. (2020) assert that a typical survival factor for competing firms is mostly digital innovations. Implementation of digital strategies in one firm influences competition for firms to also adopt. The availability of third-party firms also offered support to the SME, which also contributed to its survival. With Melabites, Jumia Foods served as a supportive platform during the COVID-19 pandemic.

10.6 Teaching with This Case

Applicable Topics This case may be applied in teaching topics such as electronic business, e-entrepreneurship, digital business strategy, total quality management, and business process digitalization.

Sample Questions for Discussion:

1. What factors were critical for the successful implementation of the digital strategies in Melabites?
2. What are the characteristics of an entrepreneur that could lead to the success of innovations in a business?
    - How do you see these characteristics manifesting in the case firm's microentrepreneurs?

3. Assuming you are the head of IT at Melabites, what would you have done differently to help the firm overcome the COVID-19 challenges?

Theories/Conceptual Frameworks That Could Be Used for Analyzing the Case

The technology-organization-environment (TOE) framework developed by Tornatzky and Fleischer (1990) may be applied in analyzing the case. The TOE framework is an organizational-level theory that explains the three elements from a firm's context that influence adoption decisions (Baker, 2012). These three elements are the technological context, the organizational context, and the environmental context. All three are advanced to influence technological innovation. The technological context deals with both the internal and external technologies relevant to the firm. The organizational context addresses descriptive measures regarding the organization, such as firms' scope and size, internal resources, and managerial structure. In contrast, the environmental context refers to the area in which a firm conducts its business.

The TOE framework, originally adapted in IT adoption studies, provides a useful analytical framework that can be used for studying the adoption and assimilation of different types of IT innovation. The TOE framework has a compact theoretical basis, steady empirical support, and the potential of application to IS innovation domains, though specific factors identified within the three contexts may vary across different studies and cases (Oliveira & Martins, 2010).

Teaching Cohort (Graduate/Undergraduate) This case may be applied in teaching both at the undergraduate and graduate levels.

References

Abor, J. Y., & Quartey, P. (2010). Issues in SME development in Ghana and South Africa. *International Research Journal of Finance and Economics, 39*(6), 215–228.

Awiagah, R., Kang, J., & Lim, J. I. (2016). Factors affecting e-commerce adoption among SMEs in Ghana. *Information Development, 32*(4), 815–836.

Baker, J. (2012). The technology–organization–environment framework. In *Information systems theory* (pp. 231–245). Springer.

Bartik, A. W., Bertrand, M., Cullen, Z., Glaeser, E. L., Luca, M., & Stanton, C. (2020). The impact of COVID-19 on small business outcomes and expectations. *Proceedings of the National Academy of Sciences, 117*(30), 17656–17666.

Christensen, C. (2013). *The innovator's dilemma: When new technologies cause great firms to fail.* Harvard Business Review Press.

Cromwell, A. (2020). *Food chains, restaurants to operate through pick-up and deliveries only.* https://www.myjoyonline.com/news/national/food-chains-restaurants-to-operate-through-pick-up-and-deliveries-only/. Accessed 23 Aug 2020.

Donkor, J., Donkor, G., & Kwarteng, C. (2018). Strategic planning and performance of SMEs in Ghana: The moderating effect of market dynamism. *Asia Pacific Journal of Innovation and Entrepreneurship, 12*(1), 62–76.

Ghana Interbank Payment and Settlement Systems Limited (GhIPSS). (2020). *Mobile money interoperability FAQs*. https://ghipss.net/products-services/gh-link/mobile-money-interoperability-faqs. Accessed 25 Aug 2020.

Jumia Foods. (2020). *About us*. https://food.jumia.com.gh/contents/about.htm. Accessed 23 Aug 2020.

Kovačič, A., Hauc, G., Buh, B., & Štemberger, M. I. (2018). BPM adoption and business transformation at Snaga, a public company: Critical success factors for five stages of BPM. In J. vom Brocke & J. Mendling (Eds.), *Business process management cases* (pp. 77–89). Springer.

Lätti, R. (2016). *Value creation and strategy in the hyperconnected world: The current wave of digitalization explained through the study of Finnish forerunner companies*. Aalto University.

Mararo, M. W., & Ngahu, S. (2017). Influence of mobile money services on the growth of SME in Nakuru town, Kenya. *IOSR Journal of Humanities and Social Science, 22*, 64–72.

Mensah, S. (2004). *A review of SME financing schemes in Ghana*. http://semcapitalgh.com/downloads/research/SME_Financing_Schemes_in_Ghana.pdf. Accessed 26 Aug 2020.

Nyavor, G. (2020). *Coronavirus: Lockdown in Accra and Kumasi comes into force*. https://www.myjoyonline.com/news/national/coronavirus-lockdown-in-accra-and-kumasi-comes-into-force/. Accessed 23 Aug 2020.

Ocloo, C. E., Xuhua, H., Akaba, S., Shi, J., & Worwui-Brown, D. K. (2020). The Determinant Factors of Business to Business (B2B) E-Commerce Adoption in Small-and Medium-Sized Manufacturing Enterprises. *Journal of global information technology management, 23*(3), 191–216.

Oliveira, T., & Martins, M. F. (2010). Information technology adoption models at firm level: Review of literature. 4th European conference on information management and evaluation. *ECIME, 2010*(May 2014), 312–322.

Quartey, P., Turkson, E., Abor, J. Y., & Iddrisu, A. M. (2017). Financing the growth of SMEs in Africa: What are the constraints to SME financing within ECOWAS? *Review of Development Finance, 7*(1), 18–28.

Talom, F. S. G., & Tengeh, R. K. (2020). The impact of mobile money on the financial performance of the SMEs in Douala, Cameroon. *Sustainability, 12*(1), 183–190.

Tornatzky, L., & Fleischer, M. (1990). *The processes of technological innovation*. Lexington Books.

Wäckerlin, N., Hoppe, T., Warnier, M., & de Jong, W. M. (2020). Comparing city image and brand identity in polycentric regions using network analysis. *Place Branding and Public Diplomacy, 16*(1), 80–96.

Yan, L., & Musika, C. (2018). *The social media and SMEs business growth: How can SMEs incorporate social media*. Linnaeus University.

Eric Ansong is a lecturer in Information Systems at Wisconsin International University College, Ghana. He holds a PhD in Information Systems. His research interests cover the digital economy, digital business strategy, technology-mediated teaching and learning, and design science. He has published a number of research articles in peer-reviewed academic journals and books and has presented papers in international conferences which include the Hawaii International Conference on System Sciences (HICSS). He can be reached via eric.ansong@wiuc-ghana.edu.gh. His ORCID ID is http://orcid.org/0000-0002-0262-3485.

Charles Turkson is a lecturer in Business Analytics at the University of Kent, United Kingdom. He has a background in operations management and performance measurement and a PhD in Management Science. His research interest is in the use of operations research and management science techniques in industry. His current research focuses on efficiency modeling of systems with complex internal structures. He has published in high impact journals with both academic and practitioner focus. His ORCID ID is https://orcid.org/0000-0002-1173-2819.

Chapter 11
Exploring the Problematic Consumption of Digital Platforms During the COVID-19 Pandemic Among University Students in Africa

Makafui Nyamadi and Pitso Tsibolane

Abstract This research explores the process leading to digital platforms' problematic consumption among university students during the COVID-19 pandemic in Africa. Literature generally focuses on the positive and tremendous impact of digital platforms on economies. Although this is essential, there is a developing trend of students' problematic use of these platforms, especially during the COVID-19 pandemic lockdown. Therefore, there is the need to examine the nature, causes, and consequences of these platforms from developing countries' contexts by interrogating students from Ghana and South Africa; (RQ1) What are the nature and causes of digital platforms' problematic consumption during COVID-19 lockdown? (RQ2) What are the consequences of problematic consumption of digital platforms on students' academic performance? Fifty (50) students were sampled for this study, four (4) experienced severe forms of problematic use of these platforms. This study revealed that digital platforms are used for hedonic and utilitarian benefits. During the lockdown, the platforms were used mainly for *communication and social interactions*, *education and virtual learning*, and *perform religious activities, business, and politics*. These activities led users to use these platforms frequently, which resulted in problematic use with the following consequences: *mental health complications (depression and frustration)*, *health complications and impaired social life functions*, and *emotional instability (despair and mood swings)*. These can be regulated through *self-regulation*, which serves as an IS use reduction mechanism. A model for the problematic consumption of digital platforms was developed. This

M. Nyamadi (✉)
University of Ghana, Accra, Ghana
e-mail: mnyamadi@st.ug.edu.gh

P. Tsibolane
University of Cape Town, Cape Town, South Africa
e-mail: pitso.tsibolane@uct.ac.za

R. Boateng et al. (eds.), *Digital Innovations, Business and Society in Africa*,
Advances in Theory and Practice of Emerging Markets,
https://doi.org/10.1007/978-3-030-77987-0_11

study's contribution to research, practice, policy, and future research directions are expounded in the main work.

Keywords Problematic consumption · Digital platforms · COVID-19 pandemic

11.1 Introduction

The global outbreak of severe acute respiratory syndrome coronavirus (SARS-CoV-2), also known as novel coronavirus or COVID-19, was first identified in December 2019 and declared by the World Health Organization (WHO) as a pandemic on March 11, 2020 (Király et al., 2020). This pandemic has brought the need for social or physical distancing and technological or digital togetherness (Király et al., 2020; Dessalegn & Frissa, 2020). While humans observe social distancing, staying at home, and self-isolating, there is an emerging and intense increase in the use of digital platforms. The term digital platforms is an integral part of Information Systems (IS) literature and comprise interfaces and components that form a standard structure using software, hardware, Internet, and communication networks (Parmentier & Gandia, 2017). IS research tries to understand digital platforms' omnipresent characteristics (Tiwana, 2014; Hein et al., 2020). The predominant and ubiquitous digital platforms on mobile and smartphones are social applications (apps). They are applications offered through dominant technology marketplaces such as the Apple iOS App Store, Microsoft Windows Store, and Android Play Store for easy accessibility and download (Sedrati et al., 2016; Ding et al., 2016; Eric et al., 2016).

During the COVID-19 lockdown, there was an upsurge of problematic usage of these digital platforms (Király et al., 2020; Barnes, 2020; King et al., 2020). Families and friends who could not meet and socialize adopted these platforms to stay connected, which came with consequences, e.g., the problematic use of the Internet during the COVID-19 pandemic lockdown (Király et al., 2020; Islam et al., 2020); the COVID-19 pandemic lockdown resulted in the problematic playing of online games (King et al., 2020), social media (Drouin et al., 2020), etc. The COVID-19 pandemic has necessitated the need to engage on these platforms for utilitarian and hedonic benefits (Wu & Lu, 2013; Chitturi et al., 2008; Lin & Lu, 2015). Therefore, this study explores these platforms' benefits due to the COVID-19 pandemic lockdown and its negative consequences. Self-regulatory IS use behavior is theorized and validated to plummet the negative consequences (Osatuyi & Turel, 2020).

Information systems research on digital platforms is generally centered on the disruptive and tremendous positive impact of digital platforms on economies. For example, PayPal, Square, Apple Pay, and the like are disrupting the financial sector, and Uber, Taxify, and Airbnb are creating a "sharing economy." Artificial intelligence, the Internet of Things (IoT), 3D/4D printing technologies, robotics and blockchain technologies, big data, and cloud computing disrupt every facet of life.

Although this is essential, there is a developing trend of parents and their children problematic engagement on these platforms, especially during the COVID-19 pandemic lockdown (Drouin et al., 2020). Therefore, there is the need to examine the nature, causes, and consequences of this problematic usage from developing countries' contexts by interrogating students from the University of Ghana and University of Cape Town, South Africa. This study's main contribution is exploring the nature, causes, and consequences of digital platforms' problematic consumption during the COVID-19 pandemic among university students in Africa.

While these technologies and services continue to disrupt various facets of life, there is an emerging need to critically look at mobile social apps and their tendencies to disrupt almost every facet of life, including family and friend relationships and general well-being. Research about emerging digital business models and disruptive technologies is centered on digital business platforms, sharing economies, social media interactions, smart devices, and services that generally revolve around enablers and inhibitors of value creations. There is an increasing need to explore the problematic, dependence, and addictive use of these platforms and their consequences. This research focuses on mobile social apps such as Facebook, Instagram, YouTube, LinkedIn, Twitter, WeChat, etc. (Zhitomirsky-Geffet & Blau, 2016; Wei et al., 2018; Ozkan & Solmaz, 2015). These devices' usage was seen as esoteric in the past, but things have changed; it is currently the most pervasive and ubiquitous smart device in the universe (Cohen & Lemish, 2003). Mobile devices are seen to be integral and significant components of everyday life. Addiction to phones is expected on a record high and has been compared with substances, i.e., opium and cocaine searches of addiction to mobile devices reported worldwide (Brown et al., 2017; Liu et al., 1999; Feng et al., 2017). There was limited research from Africa on technology addictions. However, Nyamadi and Boateng recorded a paper from Ghana that identified various game design features and their inherent elements that result in problematic playing, leading to flow that eventually results in addiction (Nyamadi & Boateng, 2018). Few papers recorded from Africa's continent on other technology-related addictions were mainly focused on Internet use (Thatcher et al., 2008; Orsal et al., 2013). There are also several forms of addictions and problematic related use of technologies in literature and have engaged the attention of researchers such as excessive microblogging (Li et al., 2012), mobile email (Turel & Serenko, 2010), instant messaging (Huang & Leung, 2009), and social network site (SNS) excessive usage (Andreassen, 2015), to mention a few.

11.2 Literature Review

This review section conceptualizes mobile social applications as prevalent digital platforms, the problematic use of digital applications beyond platforms, different kinds of problematic behaviors, the hedonic and utilitarian value created on these platforms, and self-regulation construct as a reduction mechanism.

11.2.1 Mobile Social Applications (Apps) as Prevalent Digital Platforms

Digital technologies, by their nature, have the characteristics of homogenization of data, editability, programmability, distributedness, and self-referentiality (Kallinikos et al., 2013; Yoo et al., 2010). Digital platforms encompass APIs, machine learning techniques, AI engines, and analytical engines, which must be integrated to give extreme user experiences (Di Mitri et al., 2017; Mohammadi et al., 2018; Lee & Ha, 2018; Perriam et al., 2020). Digital platforms, in a broad term, are any electronic tool for communication, including desktop, mobile, social, and email software. This covers websites and social media platforms (Wei et al., 2018; Perriam et al., 2020). Mobile social application platforms are typical examples of digital platforms available for users during the COVID-19 lockdown. Mobile social apps is an integration of several other platforms such as online or Internet gaming addiction (Bargeron & Hormes, 2017; Cho et al., 2014; Ng & Wiemer-Hastings, 2005), smartphone addiction (Capon et al., 2016; Bae, 2017; Elhai et al., 2017), social network site (SNS) addiction (Andreassen, 2015; Kuss, 2012), and online gambling and betting (LaPlante et al., 2008; Chrétien et al., 2017; He et al., 2017). All of the above led to some common realities among young people who are mostly university students (Zhitomirsky-Geffet & Blau, 2016). These common realities are that these various activities have now been repackaged and developed on mobile applications. Thus, social applications which were conceptualized and centered games and social services originally on PCs have been transferred to mobile phones to enable users to interact and share in real-time, irrespective of location and time (Lin & Lu, 2015). These mobile applications on smartphones assume new forms or characteristics that are ubiquitous and always available to users (Choi et al., 2015; Wang et al., 2016). Literature suggests that users usually rely on their mobile social apps when on their smartphones (Najjar & Ngoc Bui, 2012). The various forms of technology addictions are now being put together into an easily accessible, ubiquitous, and readily available form for users. This research will focus on the problematic use of these apps among university students in Ghana and South Africa.

11.2.2 Toward an Understanding of Problematic Behaviors

In IS literature, various terms describe problematic use of digital platforms. These are addictive, excessive, compulsive, voluntary, mandatory, dependency, and habitual. Some of these behaviors are discussed in this section. *Mandatory behavior* is also defined as a behavior that one needs to execute, follow, or comply with, usually because of being officially required (Aoki & Downes, 2003) or being parentally mandated. *Voluntary action* is a reasoned behavior that is supposed to be driven by specific motivations, but voluntary behavior is toward positive effects (Kang et al., 2007). *Compulsive behavior* is an impulse disorder that is the inability to restrain or control an impulse (Faber et al., 1992; Hanley & Wilhelm, 1992; O'Guinn & Faber, 1989). While addictive behavior tends to be a continuing or unending pattern, compulsive behavior is frequently associated with relieving stress (Rook & Rook, 1987). Compulsive behavior is often attached to attaining interpersonal and self-esteem goals; when the first attempt is successful, it reinforces compulsive behavior (Hanley & Wilhelm, 1992; O'Guinn & Faber, 1989). Often, a habit regularly performed is termed as a *habitual behavior* (Biel et al., 2005). Abraham Maslow's theory of needs stated clearly that human behavior is a performance or evidence of intentions (Maslow, 1943). These various types of digital behaviors are referred to in this book chapter as problematic behavior.

11.2.3 Hedonic and Utilitarian Values of Digital Platforms

11.2.3.1 Hedonic Value

Information systems research has focused on hedonic benefits (Venkatesh et al., 2012; Van Der Heijden, 2004a). It is the "degree to which performing an activity is perceived as providing pleasure and joy in its own right, aside from performance consequences" (Davis, 1989; Venkatesh & Davis, 2000) and is defined as the consumer's overall evaluation of experiential, aesthetic, and enjoyment-related benefits derived from technologists (mobile social apps) (Chitturi et al., 2008). The hedonic benefits of digital platform consumption are based on affective consumer behavior from emotive and multi-sensory elements (Cyr & Head, 2008). The hedonic value of digital platforms is conceptualized in terms of intrinsic benefits or non-functional benefits derived from these platforms, such as enjoyment, pleasure, relationships, interactivity, and so on (Venkatesh & Davis, 2000). The users will persist and be more willing to continue using technologies and systems if they experience enjoyment and interest (Dec et al., 1999). Perceived enjoyment is emphasized to be "important in hedonic or semi-hedonic technology settings, in which the mere intrinsic joy of using the technology is an important determinant of user perceptions and behaviors, over and above its utilitarian usefulness" (Van Der Heijden, 2004a; Turel et al., 2011). This research will explore the hedonic benefits of these platforms during the COVID-19 lockdown.

11.2.3.2 Utilitarian Value

Utilitarian value in this research is the use of mobile social apps by users for specific tasks. It is defined as the consumer's overall evaluation of users' functional benefits and costs achieving their purpose or benefits from these technologies (Hoffman & Novak, 1996). It is also the functional, instrumental, and practical benefits derived from the technologies (Najjar & Ngoc Bui, 2012). Utilitarian value is often task-related and rational-based (Wu, 2009). Thus, users are concerned about using the platforms to perform their respective tasks and achieve their goals. Every platform is built or developed to perform specific functions, and users normally engage the digital platforms for those specific benefits (Ampong et al., 2018; Han et al., 2016). The utilitarian consumption of digital platforms has focused on predestined benefits in cognitive consumer behavior (Lyons et al., 2012). The hedonic and utilitarian values as the value of digital platforms are stimuli that users derive. The greater these values, the greater the behavioral intentions to revisit these platforms, resulting in problematic behaviors (Chang et al., 2014).

11.2.3.3 Self-Regulation as Reduction Mechanism

Self-regulation has been treated in problematic use of digital platform literature as an inherent strength that prevents or reduces the loss of control (Bandura, 1991). It is "the process of self-control through psychological sub-functionalism such as self-monitoring, judgment, and self-reactive" (Khang et al., 2013). This research posits that users who restrain and regulate their digital consumption behavior are likely not to increase digital platform consumption behavior to problematic levels (LaRose et al., 2003). Individuals with low-self-control would have difficulty controlling themselves on technologies (i.e., the Internet) and therefore are prone to be more addicted (Song, 2004). The literature on self has reported that users' attitudes about self, which is constructed through self-esteem, self-efficacy, and self-control, are significant indicators of users' over-reliance on technologies (Khang et al., 2013). Therefore, researchers posit that users who restrain and regulate their digital consumption behavior are likely not to increase digital platform consumption behavior to problematic levels.

This literature review has led to the model below, Fig. 11.1. It depicts the process leading to problematic digital platform consumption behaviors during the COVID-19 lockdown. This process and the various constructs or components of the diagram will be interrogated in this research to ascertain the activities undertaken by users during COVID-19 lockdown, the hedonic and utilitarian benefits, and the resultant problematic consumption behaviors.

11.2.4 Research Methodology

11.2.4.1 Research Design

This research was designed and conducted in two stages. The first stage is screening to get problematic digital platform users, i.e., mobile social apps users. Fifty students were engaged from two universities; twenty-five (25) from the University of Ghana and twenty-five (25) from the University of Cape Town, South Africa. The participants were reached with Google Forms to complete the 20 items questions from the Internet Addiction Test (IAT) by Dr. Kimberly Young, a valid measure of addiction to the Internet. It consists of 20 questionnaire items and measures mild,

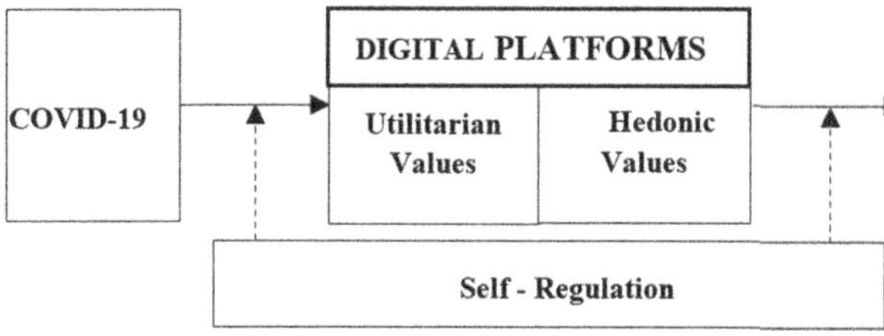

Fig. 11.1 The model for the problematic consumption of digital platforms

moderate, and severe Internet addiction (Young, 2009). The participants who scored 20 to 49 points were average digital platform users, followed by participants having occasional problems with the platforms who were graded between 50 to 79, and finally, participants with severe forms of addiction were those having significant problems with the digital platforms, they scored between 80 and 100. Since the focus of this work is the addiction to digital platforms, the two(2) participants who had severe forms of digital platform addiction voluntarily availed themselves and were sampled for this work. In the second level of interviews, the four (4) participants who were heavily addicted to digital platforms were further interviewed using the semi-structured interview guides within a 1-year and 9-month period from March 2019 to December 2020. The interviews were recorded and later transcribed verbatim. The duration was between 30 mins and 1 h. The transcribed words ranged from 1,584 to 2,018. The problematic users spent between 7 h and 15 h a day on the digital platforms, while average users spent 1 h and 30 mins to 3 h a day on the digital platforms during the COVID-19 lockdown.

This research adopts qualitative content analysis to "provide knowledge and understanding of the phenomenon under study" p.314 (Downe-Wamboldt, 1992). Qualitative research (QR) "tends to explore the meanings, attitudes, values, and beliefs people associate with a phenomenon to establish a better understanding, rather than to test to either support or disprove a relationship" (Schwandt et al., 1994). QR is about a broad range of empirical processes designed to elucidate and construe research participants' experiences in a context-specific setting (Ponterotto, 2005). The semi-structured questionnaire was based on the components model of addiction by Griffiths (2005). The interviewees were interrogated based on their experiences with the digital platforms during the COVID-19 lockdown.

11.2.4.2 Data Collection

This research's collection process enabled researchers to gather opinions, views, and useful information from targeted respondents about a research topic or topic (Churchill, 1987). Several data collection methods were identified in the literature, such as meeting face-to-face with participants, telephone calls, postal services, sending electronic mails, and combining all these methods (Cooper & Schindler, 2001; Zikmund, 2000). However, this study adopted a face-to-face interview with participants. The qualitative data collection was purposeful sampling and focused on individuals who use digital platforms (VanderStoep & Johnston, 2009) (Tables 11.1 and 11.2).

11.2.5 Findings, Results, and Analysis

The Internet Addiction Test (IAT) by Dr. Kimberly Young is a valid measure of addiction to the Internet. It consists of 20 questionnaire items and measures mild, moderate, and severe Internet addiction (Young, 2009). This scale helped us find two (2) users who had severe forms of addictions from the University of Ghana and two (2) severe users from University of Cape Town out of the mobile social apps' sample users during the COVID-19 pandemic period. These four (4) problematic users found in this category were further examined to find the nature and causes of their engagement with the device.

Two (2) relations each of the addicts were also interviewed to authenticate or otherwise some of the interviewees' responses. Three (3) experts or professionals made up of two (2) males and one (1) female were also interviewed to verify the findings of this study. The female is a Cyber Psychologist/Counselor who lectures

Table 11.1 Table of participants, relations, and experts interviewed

Participants (addicts and experts)	Codes	Profiles
Participant 1	P1	Female Law student at the University of Ghana (online relationship)
Relation 1	P1a	The younger sister of P1
Relation 2	P1b	The mother of P1
Participant 2	P3	Male undergraduate dropout at Korle Bu Addiction Centre, Ghana (online gambling and betting)
Relation 1	P2a	A friend of the P3
Relation 2	P2b	The father of P3
Participant 3	P3	Male Computer Science student (University of Cape Town); betting and online relationship
Relation 1	P3a	A cousin of P4
Relation 2	P3b	The father of P4
Participant 4	4	Female Business Administration student (University of Cape Town)
Relation 1	P4a	A brother of P5
Relation 2	P4b	The father of P5
Expert 1	Exp1	A Clinical Psychologist (Addiction Center Manager) with 25 years of experience
Expert 2	Exp2	A Professional Cyber Psychologist and a Senior Lecturer at the University of Ghana
Expert 3	Exp3	A Lecturer and a Mobile Social Apps Developer in South Africa

Table 11.2 Depicting the total number of interviewees

Participants data				
	Dependent users	Relations	Experts	Total number
Male	2	4	2	8
Female	2	4	1	7
Total	4	8	3	15

in the Psychologist Department of the University of Ghana. The males are; a Clinical Psychologist in charge of Korle Bu Addiction Center with 25 years of experience working with both substance and behavioral addicts and Psychiatric Doctor lecturing at the University of Health and Allied Services and a Lecturer of one of the addicts and a Mobile Social Applications Developer. These experts were interviewed to validate the findings of this research from the addicts and their relations. The following issues were covered: (a) The technology users were interviewed and observed on the nature of the characteristics of the mobile social media apps that are addictive, (b) the nature in terms of motivations and circumstances during COVID-19 that likely get users into problematic usage, and (c) the impact of problematic usage of digital platforms on the general well-being of users. They were interviewed on their profiles, nature, and causes of their addictions, the process of addiction, the constructs used in the model, and the impact of addiction on their academic performance and their general well-being. In the process, the researcher also found out if they lose control, crave, or felt compulsive to use mobile social apps and their adverse negative effect on them.

The experts were made to authenticate the findings based on their specialty. They provided the technical and professional view in authenticating the findings in their various disciplines. This study's data analysis technique abstracts problematic technology consumption in its constitutive structures and causal powers. Descriptive data analysis will be used to analyze the qualitative data. After coding, the themes and subthemes that emerged from the themes guided the findings and discussions. First, the four (4) problematic users were observed at different times within 1-year and 9-month periods. Within that period, two (2) of their relations and colleagues were interviewed to corroborate the addicts' responses. The responses were subjected to the views of experts such as a Clinical Psychologist, a Psychiatric Doctor, an Educationist, and a Technologist to authenticate and clarify the findings before the analysis and conclusions. The audio recordings were transcribed verbatim by clearly and legibly writing down the written documents and giving them back to the interviewees to cross-check for accuracy. After their approval, the write-ups were subdivided into umbrella codes and subcodes using a code tree.

The research purpose, objectives, and questions directed this research and helped generate the codes for analysis. The theories were used to revise the codes' context by providing labels and defining the data to reflect or be a true representation of the actual raw data. The subsequent coding recommendations were done using the data-driven method; this enabled codes to be written down paragraph by paragraph and sentence by sentence levels (DeCuir-Gunby et al., 2011). The individual respondents were investigated independently using the framework provided to enhance the data's validity and reliability using analytical triangulation (Padgett, 1998). The patterns identified from the interviews were categorized to show convergence and saturation. The data were analyzed using qualitative methodology.

This research adopted multiple perspectives to enhance the data's reliability and validity (Yin, 1984; Uhan et al., 2013; Miles & Huberman, 1984). The participants who were problematic users of the digital platforms, their relations, and experts were interviewed to authenticate the data and ensure its reliability and validity. The data analysis techniques deployed for this research assisted in analyzing problematic technology consumption. The initial steps used were open coding, which involved breaking, renaming, and labeling the data into discrete acts or events (Miles & Huberman, 1984; Miles & Huberman, 1994). The codes generated were very close to participants' vocabulary to ensure the emerging coded dataset's faithfulness. The next step was axial coding (Strauss et al., 1990). This was an inductive recursive process to combine similar codes into second-order codes, as shown in Table 11.3 below. The second-order code led to generating a selective coding scheme.

11.3 Discussions

This section discusses the findings from the data representation and their coding in the table above. The COVID-19 lockdown mainly led to users of mobile social apps stay at home and practice social distancing but reached their family, friends, clients, employers, and business partners to perform or carry out the following activities: *communication and social interactions, for education and virtual learning, to perform religious activities, business, and politics*. This research revealed that the main activities that users, in general, perform on these devices during the lockdown were centered around the findings, which are the main functions of mobile social apps. The digital platforms provided utilitarian and hedonic benefits to users during the COVID-19 lockdown. The hedonic benefits identified by researchers were as follows: *seeking online pleasures, excitement, social interactions to be happy, joyous, self-fulfillment and satisfaction*; *for relaxation, relief, and releasing of tension release emotional stress and keep users busy*; and *for self-esteem (belongingness and accomplishment) through virtual presence*. It stretches across several platforms and apps. The utilitarian values or benefits derived from these platforms are as follows: *ubiquitous and information availability*, *quick means of making money*, *convenience for buying and selling*, *developing and maintaining relationships*, and *fast user interface fit to create and share images, videos, and audios*. The utilitarian benefits are actual practical benefits and functions derived from these apps, and they also cut across several platforms and technologies due to their usefulness. These activities, therefore, are the real forces that enable users to connect to social media platforms (Han et al., 2016; Chang et al., 2014; Etemad-Sajadi & Ghachem, 2015). However, it was found in the literature that "perceived usefulness loses its dominant predictive value in favor of ease of use and enjoyment" (van der Heijden, 2004b).

Table 11.3 Qualitative data evidence of theoretical dimensions, 1st and 2nd codes

Qualitative data evidence: theoretical dimensions, 2nd-order constructs, 1st-order codes (data rep)	
Theoretical dimensions (First- and second-order codes)	Data representation
COVID – 19	
Communication and social interactions	
A. For communication	A1. I use the apps to receive and share images and text messages (P4)
	A2. The mobile social apps are used for voice and video calls (Exp3)
B. For social interaction	B1. My boyfriend sometimes travels outside Ghana; therefore, mobile social platforms allow us to always in contact and enable easy interactions (P1)
	B2. The mobile social apps assist in social interactions (Exp2)
Education and virtual learning	
C. Virtual learning	C1. I read novels and storybooks online during COVID -19 (P1)
	C2. Mobile social apps assist me in learning virtually during the COVID-19 lockdown (P4)
D. For studies	D1. I use mobile social media apps for studies during the lockdown (P3)
	D2. Yes, she reads her novels and all that, but I think she's just found of always being on mobile social apps (P1a)
Religious activities	
E. For religious activities	E1. I read my Quran and other religious books during the lockdown (P3)
	E2. I read my Bible and evangelize on mobile social apps (P1)
Business	
F. For marketing	F1. I use mobile social apps to promote my business (P3)
	F2. Mobile social apps are used to market goods and services (Exp1)
G. To develop and maintain customers	G1. I develop and maintain the customer base of my business on these apps (P2)
	G2. My son has been into cyber fraud, online betting, and gambling (P2b)
Politics	
H. For political activities	H1. Some people mainly use mobile social apps for politics (Exp1)
	H2. My sister uses the apps to sometimes comment on political issues (P4a)
I. To get current news updates	I1. I check news headlines and news update often during COVID-19 (P4)
	I2. News portals alert assist me regularly with current news (P4)

(continued)

Table 11.3 (continued)

Qualitative data evidence: theoretical dimensions, 2nd-order constructs, 1st-order codes (data rep)	
Utilitarian value	
Ubiquitous and information availability	
	J1. These mobile apps are ubiquitous because they are with me everywhere (P2)
J. Ubiquitous in nature	J2. The mobile social apps are universal and ubiquitous (Exp3)
K. Information availability	K1. These apps enable users to access information anytime and anywhere (Exp2)
	K2. These apps help make information available 24/7 (Exp1)
Quick means of making money, convenience for buying and selling	
L. Quick means of making a profit	L1. These platforms aid my cyber business and assist in making quick money (P2)
	L2. He uses these apps to make quick money (P2a)
M. Convenience for buying and selling	M1. I use the apps for shopping and ordering goods and services online (P4)
	M2. There are a lot of apps now that are convenient for assisting buying and selling (Exp3)
Developing and maintaining relationships	
	N1. I use mobile apps to develop relationships with new friends (P3)
N. Develop new relationships	N2. During the COVID -19 lockdown, I used online dating sites to connect to new friends (P3)
O. Maintain relationships	O1. These apps help to maintain a relationship with family and friends (Exp2)
	O2. I use these apps to have constant touch with family and friends (P4)
	O3. I easily use these apps to connect to my boyfriend (P1)
Fast user interface fit for creating and sharing images, videos, and audios	
P. Fast user interface	P1. The user interfaces of apps are faster than normal text messages (P3)
	P2. The user interface of these apps responds to my actions faster than other platforms (P4)
Q. Easy ways for creating and sharing images, audio, and video recording	Q1. Mobile social apps provide interfaces for easy and quick audio, videos, and image creations (Exp3)
	Q2. During the COVID-19, I generated a lot of videos, audios, and images and shared them with family and friends (P3)
Hedonic value	
Seeking online pleasures, excitement, social interactions to be happy, joyous, self-fulfillment and satisfaction	
R. Online pleasures and excitement	R1. I seek online pleasures on these apps during the lockdown (P1)

(continued)

Table 11.3 (continued)

Qualitative data evidence: theoretical dimensions, 2nd-order constructs, 1st-order codes (data rep)	
	R2. I seek online excitement during the lockdown (P4)
S. Happy and joyous	S1. My son is happy on these platforms during the lockdown (P2b)
	S2. My son is joyous on this platform (P2b)
T. Online satisfaction, social interaction, and happiness for self-fulfillment	T1. These apps keep me satisfied during COVID-19 lockdown (P3)
	T2. I have social interactions that keep me fulfilled (P4)
For relaxation, relief, and releasing of tension release emotional stress and keep users busy	
U. Generate interest and keeps users busy	U1. During the lockdown, when I'm bored, I get myself busy with these apps (P1)
	U2. These mobile platforms generate interest and keep users busy (Exp2)
V. Relaxation and releasing tension	V1. I use mobile social apps to relax during the lockdown (P4)
	V2. I use mobile social apps to release tension during COVID-19 (P3)
For self-esteem (belongingness and accomplishment) through virtual presence	
W. Looking for belongingness and accomplishment	W1. Mobile social apps help me to belong (P1)
	W2. I look for accomplishment on these platforms (P3)
	W3. I thought I could make money and accomplish myself, but it never came (P2)
X. Have a virtual presence	X1. I forget about my immediate environment while on these apps (P2)
	X2. I enjoy a virtual presence on these apps during the lockdown (P3)
Self-regulation	
Set time and regulate the amount of time on mobile apps	
Y. Regulate the amount of time on the mobile social apps	Y1. Problematic users must regulate their amount of time on these apps (Expt 1)
	Y2. I always try to regulate the amount of time on these apps (P4)
Z. Set time for the mobile social apps	Z1. During the lockdown, I tried to regulate myself but failed (P3)
	Z2. I tried to set time for myself and only use mobile social apps when I'm less busy, which helped my recovery (P2)
Switch off your data and alerts when necessary	
AA. Switch off data when not in use	AA1. I switch off my data anytime I'm busy to avoid disruptions (P2)
	AA2. To limit my problematic usage, I tried to keep my data offline (P3)
AB. Switch off mobile social apps alerts	AB1. Users must only leave very important alerts on their apps (Exp3)

(continued)

Table 11.3 (continued)

Qualitative data evidence: theoretical dimensions, 2nd-order constructs, 1st-order codes (data rep)	
	AB2. The best thing to do is to switch off the alerts on these apps (Exp2)
Avoid unnecessary social interactions and checking regular updates	
AC. Avoid unnecessary interactions and frequent checking up of others statuses	CC1. I normally advise my students to limit the number of interactions with others on mobile social apps to regulate their problematic usage (Exp2)
	CC3. I have advised myself to avoid regular and frequent checking up of other users' status on all social media platforms (P2)
AD. Perform only important tasks on these apps	CD1. Going through only important messages on mobile social platforms (P4)
	CD2. Avoid unnecessary comments and reactions (Exp1)
Avoid forms of adverts to make quick money on mobile social apps	
AE. Avoid online gambling and betting adverts	AE1. I try not to respond to online ads on making quick money on these apps (P2)
	AE2. Most of these online quick money-making adverts are to lure users to online gambling or betting or online cyber fraud, so they must be avoided (Exp1)
AF. Avoid all forms of quick online money-making adverts	AF1. I try to avoid all forms of alerts that may prompt me to make quick money on these apps (P3)
	AF2. Users should be taught to avoid these easy ways of making money adverts on social media apps (Exp2)
Uninstall all unnecessary alert tools and apps	
AG. Uninstall all tools and apps that are not necessary	AG1. I uninstall all alert tools that cause me to frequently and regularly engage with mobile social apps (P2)
	AG2. I advised my client to uninstall apps that lure him to bet and gamble online (Exp1)
Problematic usage	
Mental health disorders (depressions and frustration)	
AH. Mental disorder	AH1. My thought became skewed, and I couldn't think about anything else than mobile social apps during the COVID-19 (P2)
	AH2. Problematic consumption of these platforms can lead to mental disorder (Exp2)
AI. Depression and frustrations	AI1. Problematic usage can lead to depression and frustrations (Exp2)
	AI2. He was hallucinating, got frustrated, and lost control of his life, so he was sent to the hospital and then to the addiction center (P2a)
Health complications	
AJ. Health complications	AJ1. I use any money I find to play games online, and it became difficult even to eat well and maintain a healthy life, so I was fallen sick frequently (P2)

(continued)

Table 11.3 (continued)

Qualitative data evidence: theoretical dimensions, 2nd-order constructs, 1st-order codes (data rep)	
	AJ2. I am unable to make friends in my physical world because I already have millions of friends when playing mobile social games (P3)
Impaired social life, functions, and emotional instability	
AK. Impaired social life and functions	AK1. My son became unstable and unable to interact with family and friends (P2b)
	AK2. Problematic consumption leads to an impaired social function. Addicts are unable to complete their works at home, school, or work (Exp1)
AL. Emotional instability	AL1. My daughter became emotionally unstable (P4b)
	AL2. I became emotionally unstable during the COVID-19 period; I got frustrated with staying home alone (P4)

The benefits of these platforms made users relegate their general well-being to the back and were more focused on using the digital platforms, which resulted in the following: *mental health complications (depression and frustration)*, *health complications*, and *impaired social life, functions, and emotional instability (despair and mood swings.* These problems are generic and may influence any individual user who has either excessively, habitually, compulsively, or addictively consume digital platforms without any restrictions or regulations. The final model of the study, Fig. 11.2, has the self-regulation construct, which serves as a reducing mechanism to control users' addictive or problematic behavior. Therefore, for users to manage their consumption of these platforms, the following were the activities that should be done to restrain or regulate their problematic behaviors on digital platforms. The activities are as follows: *set time and regulate the amount of time on mobile apps*, *switch off your data and alerts when necessary*, a*void unnecessary social interactions and checking regular update*, a*void forms of adverts to make quick money on mobile social apps*, and *uninstall all unnecessary alert tools and apps.* The above activities identified in the literature tend to reduce users' frequent engagement on mobile social apps and prevent problematic behaviors platforms.

11.3.1 Conclusions, Implications, and Future Research Directions

The COVID-19 lockdown resulted in users practicing social distancing and using the technology to reach family, friends, clients, employers, and business partners for the following based on our findings, such as *communication and social interactions*, *education and virtual learning*, and *perform religious activities*, *business*, and *politics*. The digital platforms provided the following hedonic benefits to clients: *seeking online pleasures, excitement, social interactions to be happy, self-fulfillment and*

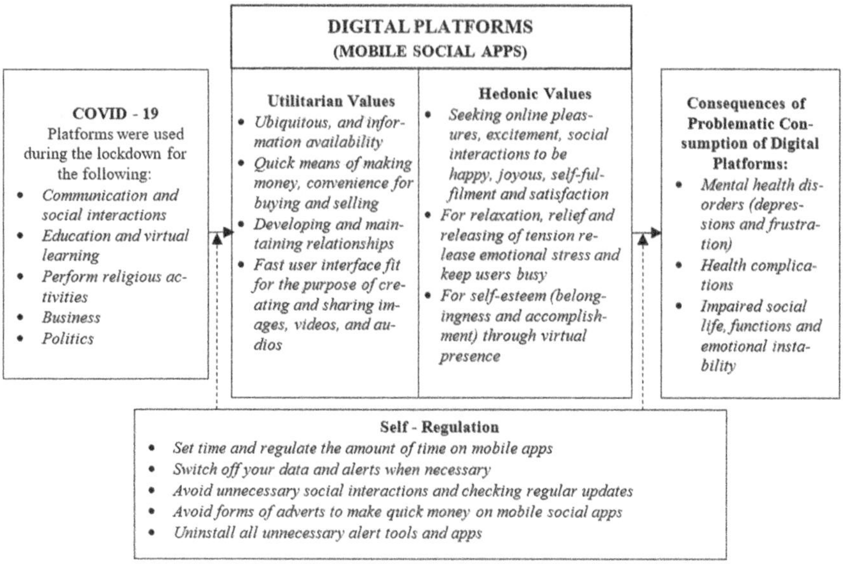

Fig. 11.2 The final model for the problematic consumption of digital platforms

satisfaction; *for relaxation, relief, and releasing of tension*; *release emotional stress and keep users busy*; as well as *self-esteem (belongingness and accomplishment) through virtual presence*. The utilitarian values or benefits derived from these platforms are as follows: *ubiquitous and information availability*, *quick means of making money*, *convenience for buying and selling*, *developing and maintaining relationships*, and *fast user interface fit to create and share images, videos, and audios*. The benefits enable or lead users to use these mobile social platforms frequently, and those four (4) highly problematic users interviewed experienced the following: *mental health complications (depression and frustration)*, *health complications*, and *impaired social life, functions, and emotional instability (despair and mood swings)*. The problematic use of digital platforms can be regulated by *setting time and regulating the amount of time on mobile apps*, *switch off your data and alerts when necessary*, *avoid unnecessary social interactions and checking regular updates*, *avoid forms of adverts to make quick money on mobile social apps*, and *uninstall all unnecessary alert tools and apps*.

The study contributes to practice by explaining the causes and nature of problematic use of digital platforms during the COVID-19 pandemic lockdown. It further elaborated the self-regulatory IS use practices on digital platforms, which may be applied to regulate all users, including kids. This chapter will assist the government, policymakers, and regulators in developing and implementing policies to regulate digital platform use. The model developed also provides the basis for researchers and tech developers to collaborate and develop software applications to assist users who cannot self-regulate.

For future research, the relationship among the constructs could be hypothesized and analyzed quantitatively. There is also the need for future research to explore the problematic use of new and emerging digital platforms, such as social media platforms, the Internet of Things (IoT), artificial intelligence (AI), and fake news, etc.

References

Ampong, G. O. A., Mensah, A., Boakye, K. G., Simpson, G., Ofori, K. S., & Addae, J. A. (2018). Exploring mobile social networking sites continuance intention from the perspective of network externalities and mobile value. *Proceedings International Conference Electronic Bus, 2018*, 295–303.

Andreassen, C. S. (2015). Online social network site addiction: A comprehensive review. *Current Addiction Reports, 2*(2), 175–184.

Aoki, K., & Downes, E. J. (2003). An analysis of young people's use of and attitudes toward cell phones. *Telematics and Informatics, 20*(4), 349–364.

Bae, S.-M. (2017). The relationship between the type of smartphone use and smartphone dependence of Korean adolescents: National survey study. *Children and Youth Services Review, 81*(May), 207–211.

Bandura, A. (1991). Social cognitive theory of self-regulation. *Organizational Behavior and Human Decision Processes.*

Bargeron, A. H., & Hormes, J. M. (2017). Psychosocial correlates of internet gaming disorder: Psychopathology, life satisfaction, and impulsivity. *Computers in Human Behavior, 68*, 388–394.

Barnes, S. J. (2020). Information management research and practice in the post-COVID-19 world. *The International Journal of Information Management, 55*(June), 102175.

Biel, A., Dahlstrand, U., & Grankvist, G. (2005). Habitual and value-guided purchase behavior. *Ambio, 34*(4–5), 360–365.

Brown, P. N., Lund, J. A., & Murch, S. J. (2017). A botanical, phytochemical and ethnomedicinal review of the genus Mitragyna Korth: Implications for products sold as kratom. *Journal of Ethnopharmacology, 202*(March), 302–325.

Capon, H., Hall, W., Fry, C., & Carter, A. (2016). Realising the technological promise of smartphones in addiction research and treatment: An ethical review. *The International Journal on Drug Policy, 36*, 47–57.

Chang, C. H., Shu, S., & King, B. (2014). Novelty in theme park physical surroundings: An application of the stimulus-organism-response paradigm. *Asia Pacific Journal of Tourism Research, 19*(6), 680–699.

Chitturi, R., Raghunathan, R., & Mahajan, V. (2008). Delight by design: The role of hedonic versus utilitarian benefits. *Journal of Marketing, 72*(3), 48–63.

Cho, H., et al. (2014). Development of the internet addiction scale based on the internet gaming disorder criteria suggested in DSM-5. *Addictive Behaviors, 39*(9), 1361–1366.

Choi, S., Kim, J., & Qu, M. (2015). The flipside of ubiquitous connectivity by smartphone-based social networking service(SNS): Social presence and privacy concern. *Pacific Asia Conference on Information Systems*, 1–13.

Chrétien, M., Giroux, I., Goulet, A., Jacques, C., & Bouchard, S. (2017). Cognitive restructuring of gambling-related thoughts: A systematic review. *Addictive Behaviors, 75*(July), 108–121.

Churchill, G. A. (1987). *Marketing research: Methodological foundations*. Rinehart and Winston, Holt.

Cohen, A. A., & Lemish, D. (2003). Real time and recall measures of mobile phone use: Some methodological concerns and empirical applications. *New Media & Society, 5*(2), 167–183.

Cooper, D. R., & Schindler, P. S. (2001). *Business research methods*. McGraw-Hill.

Cyr, D., & Head, M. (2008). Hedonic and utilitarian contexts in website viewing: The impacts of framing and time constraints. *Proceedings Seventh Pre-ICIS HCI Research MIS Workgroup*, 35–39.
Davis, F. D. (1989). Perceived usefulness, perceived ease of use, and user acceptance of information technology. *MIS Quarterly, 13*(3), 319–339.
Dec, E. L., Ryan, R. M., & Koestner, R. (1999). A meta-analytic review of experiments examining the effects of extrinsic rewards on intrinsic motivation. *The American Psychological Association, 125*(6).
DeCuir-Gunby, J. T., Marshall, P. L., & McCulloch, A. W. (2011). Developing and using a codebook for the analysis of interview data: An example from a professional development research project. *Field Methods, 23*(2), 136–155.
Dessalegn, B. S., & Frissa, S. M. (2020). The mental health impact of the COVID-19 pandemic: Implications for sub-Saharan Africa. *OSF Prepr.*
Di Mitri, D., Börner, D., Scheffel, M., Ternier, S., Drachsler, H., & Specht, M. (2017). Learning pulse: A machine learning approach for predicting performance in self-regulated learning using multimodal data. *ACM International Conference Proceedings Series*, 188–197.
Ding, X., Xu, J., Chen, G., & Xu, C. (2016). Beyond smartphone overuse: Identifying addictive mobile apps. *CHI Extension Abstracts Human Factors Computer System*, 2821–2828.
Downe-Wamboldt, B. (1992). Content analysis: Method, applications, and issues. *Health Care for Women International, 13*(3), 313–321.
Drouin, M., McDaniel, B. T., Pater, J., & Toscos, T. (2020). How parents and their children used social media and technology at the beginning of the COVID-19 pandemic and associations with anxiety. *Cyberpsychology, Behavior, and Social Networking, 23*(11), 727–736.
Elhai, J. D., Dvorak, R. D., Levine, J. C., & Hall, B. J. (2017). Problematic smartphone use: A conceptual overview and systematic review of relations with anxiety and depression psychopathology. *Journal of Affective Disorders, 207*(February 2016), 251–259.
Eric, H., Hyunji, K., Sang, S., Han, P., & Oh, W. (2016). Excessive dependence on mobile social apps: A rational excessive dependence on mobile social apps: A rational addiction perspective, no. November.
Etemad-Sajadi, R., & Ghachem, L. (2015). The impact of hedonic and utilitarian value of online avatars on e-service quality. *Computers in Human Behavior, 52*, 81–86.
Faber, R. J., Guinn, T. C. O., Faber, R. J., & Guinn, T. C. O. (1992). Linked references are available on JSTOR for this article: A Clinical Screener for Compulsive Buying. *Journal of Consumer Research, 19*(3), 459–469.
Feng, L.-Y., Battulga, A., Han, E., Chung, H., & Li, J.-H. (2017). New psychoactive substances of natural origin: A brief review. *Journal of Food and Drug Analysis, 25*(3), 461–471.
Griffiths, (2005). A components model of addiction within a biopsychosocial framework. *Journal of Substance Use, 10*(4), 191–197.
Han, S., Min, J., & Lee, H. (2016). Building relationships within corporate SNS accounts through social presence formation. *International Journal of Information Management, 36*(6), 945–962.
Hanley, A., & Wilhelm, M. S. (1992). Compulsive buying: An exploration into self-esteem and money attitudes. *Journal of Economic Psychology, 13*(1), 5–18.
He, W., et al. (2017). Abnormal reward and punishment sensitivity associated with internet addicts. *Computers in Human Behavior, 75*, 678–683.
Hein, A., et al. (2020). Digital platform ecosystems. *Electronic Markets, 30*(1), 87–98.
Hoffman, D. L., & Novak, T. P. (1996). Marketing in hypermedia computer-mediated environments: Conceptual foundations. *Journal of Marketing, 60*(3), 50–68.
Huang, H., & Leung, L. (2009). Instant messaging addiction among teenagers in China: Shyness, alienation, and academic performance decrement. *CyberPsychology Behavior, 12*(6), 675–679.
Islam, M. S., et al. (2020). Problematic Internet use among young and adult population in Bangladesh: Correlates with lifestyle and online activities during the COVID-19 pandemic. *Addictive Behaviors Reports, 12*(November), 100311.

Kallinikos, A., Jannis, A., & Aleksi, M. (2013). The ambivalent ontology of digital artifacts. *MIS Quarterly, 37*(2), 357–370.
Kang, I., Lee, K. C., Lee, S., & Choi, J. (2007). Investigation of online community voluntary behavior using cognitive map. *Computers in Human Behavior, 23*(1), 111–126.
Khang, H., Kim, J. K., & Kim, Y. (2013). Self-traits and motivations as antecedents of digital media flow and addiction: The internet, mobile phones, and video games. *Computers in Human Behavior, 29*(6), 2416–2424.
King, D. L., Delfabbro, P. H., Billieux, J., & Potenza, M. N. (2020). Problematic online gaming and the COVID-19 pandemic. *Journal of Behavioral Addictions, 9*(2), 184–186.
Király, O., et al. (2020). Preventing problematic internet use during the COVID-19 pandemic: Consensus guidance. *Comprehensive Psychiatry, 100*, 1–4.
Kuss, D. J. (2012). AS32-01 - Internet addiction or else? A way out of conceptual crisis and a call for nosological precision. *European Psychiatry, 27*(i), 1.
LaPlante, D. A., Schumann, A., LaBrie, R. A., & Shaffer, H. J. (2008). Population trends in internet sports gambling. *Computers in Human Behavior, 24*(5), 2399–2414.
LaRose, R., Lin, C. A., & Eastin, M. S. (2003). Unregulated internet usage: Addiction, habit, or deficient self-regulation? *Media Psychology, 5*(3), 225–253.
Lee, K., & Ha, N. (2018). AI platform to accelerate API economy and ecosystem. *International Conference on Information and Network, 2018*, 848–852.
Li, Q., Guo, X., & Sun, C. (2012). The shadow of microblogging use: Relationship between usage types and addiction. *ICIS, 9*(2), 579–612.
Lin, K. Y., & Lu, H. P. (2015). Predicting mobile social network acceptance based on mobile value and social influence. *Internet Research, 25*(1), 107–130.
Liu, J.-L., Liu, J.-T., Hammitt, J. K., & Chou, S.-Y. (1999). The price elasticity of opium in Taiwan, 1914–1942. *Journal of Health Economics, 18*(6), 795–810.
Lyons, E. J., Tate, D. F., Komoski, S. E., Carr, P. M., & Ward, D. S. (2012). Novel approaches to obesity prevention: Effects of game enjoyment and game type on energy expenditure in active video games. *Journal of Diabetes Science and Technology, 6*(4), 839–848.
Maslow, A. H. (1943). A theory of human motivation. *Psychological Review, 50*(4), 370–396.
Miles, M. B., & Huberman, A. M. (1984). *Qualitative data analysis*. Sage.
Miles, M. B., & Huberman, A. M. (1994). *Qualitative data analysis: An expanded sourcebook*. Sage.
Mohammadi, M., Al-Fuqaha, A., Sorour, S., & Guizani, M. (2018). Deep learning for IoT big data and streaming analytics: A survey. *IEEE Communication Surveys and Tutorials, 20*(4), 2923–2960.
Najjar, M. S., & Ngoc Bui, S. (2012). The influence of technology characteristics on privacy calculus: A theoretical framework. *18th America Conference on Information Systems 2012, AMCIS 2012, 1*, 218–225.
Ng, B. D., & Wiemer-Hastings, P. (2005). Addiction to the internet and online gaming. *Cyberpsychology & Behavior, 8*(2), 110–113.
Nyamadi, M., & Boateng, R. (2018). The influence of IT artifacts on players leading to internet gaming addiction among university students in Africa. In *Americas conference on information systems* (pp. 1–10).
O'Guinn, T. C., & Faber, R. J. (1989). Compulsive buying: A phenomenological exploration. *Journal of Consumer Research, 16*(2), 147.
Orsal, O., Orsal, O., Unsal, A., & Ozalp, S. S. (2013). Evaluation of internet addiction and depression among university students. *The Procedia – Social and Behavioral Science, 82*, 445–454.
Osatuyi, B., & Turel, O. (2020). Conceptualisation and validation of system use reduction as a self-regulatory IS use behaviour. *European Journal of Information Systems, 29*(1), 44–64.
Ozkan, M., & Solmaz, B. (2015). Mobile addiction of generation Z and its effects on their social lifes. *The Procedia – Social and Behavioral Sciences, 205*(May), 92–98.
Padgett, D. K. (1998). Does the glove really fit? Qualitative research and clinical social work practice. *Social Work, 43*(4), 373–381.

Parmentier, G., & Gandia, R. (2017). Redesigning the business model: From one-sided to multi-sided. *The Journal of Business Strategy, 38*(2), 52–61.

Perriam, J., Birkbak, A., & Freeman, A. (2020). Digital methods in a post-API environment. *International Journal of Social Research Methodology, 23*(3), 277–290.

Ponterotto, J. G. (2005). Qualitative research in counseling psychology: A primer on research paradigms and philosophy of science. *Journal of Counseling Psychology, 52*(2), 126–136.

Rook, D. W., & Rook, D. W. (1987). Linked references are available on JSTOR for this article: The Buying Impulse. *The Journal of Consumer Research, 14*(2), 189–199.

Schwandt, T. A., Denzin, N. K., & Lincoln, Y. S. (1994). *Handbook of qualitative research.* Ed Denzin Lincoln.

Sedrati, H., Nejjari, C., Chaqsare, S., & Ghazal, H. (2016). Mental and physical mobile health apps: Review. *Procedia Computer Science, 100*, 900–906.

Song, N. O. (2004). *University student's stress, self-control, self-esteem, and Internet usage.* Unpublished masters thesis, Yonsei University Seoul, Korea.

Strauss, A., Corbin, J., Strauss, A., & Corbin, J. (1990). *Basics of qualitative research: Grounded theory procedures and techniques.* Sage.

Thatcher, A., Wretschko, G., & Fridjhon, P. (2008). Online flow experiences, problematic internet use and internet procrastination. *Computers in Human Behavior, 24*(5), 2236–2254.

Tiwana, A. (2014). *Platform ecosystems: Aligning architecture, governance, and strategy.* Morgan Kaufmann. https://doi.org/10.1016/C2012-0-06625-2

Turel, O., & Serenko, A. (2010). Is mobile email addiction overlooked? *Communications of the ACM.*

Turel, O., Serenko, A., & Giles, P. (2011). Integrating technology addiction and use: An empirical investigation of online auction users. *MIS Quarterly, 35*(4), 1043–1061.

Uhan, S., Malnar, B., & Kurdija, S. (2013). Grounded theory and inductive ethnography: A sensible merging or a failed encounter? *Teor. Praksa, 50*, 642–657.

Van Der Heijden, H. (2004a). User acceptance of hedonic information systems. *Source MIS Quarterly, 28*(4), 695–704.

van der Heijden, H. (2004b). User acceptance of hedonic information systems. *MIS Quarterly, 28*(4), 695–704.

VanderStoep, S. W., & Johnston, D. D. (2009). Planning your qualitative study: Design, sampling, and data analysis. *Research Method Everyday Life Blending Qual Quantitative Approaches*, 181–199.

Venkatesh, V., & Davis, F. D. (2000). A theoretical extension of the technology acceptance model: Four longitudinal field studies. *Management Science, 46*(2), 186–204.

Venkatesh, V., Thong, J. Y. L., & Xu, X. (2012). Consumer acceptance and use of information technology: Extending the unified theory of acceptance and use of technology. *MIS Quarterly, 36*(1), 157–178.

Wang, C., Lee, M. K. O., Yang, C., & Li, X. (2016). Understanding problematic smartphone use and its characteristics: A perspective on behavioral addiction. *Lecture Notes Information System Organs, 17*, 215–225.

Wei, R., Huang, J., & Zheng, P. (2018). Use of mobile social apps for public communication in China: Gratifications as antecedents of reposting articles from WeChat public accounts. *Mobile Media & Communication, 6*(1), 108–126.

Wu, H.-L. (2009). Utilitarian and hedonic values of social network services. *15th Americs Conference on Information Systems 2009, AMCIS 2009, 4*, 2132–2140.

Wu, J., & Lu, X. (2013). Effects of extrinsic and intrinsic motivators on using utilitarian, hedonic, and dual-purposed information systems: A meta-analysis. *Journal of the Association for Information Systems, 14*(3), 153–191.

Yin, R. K. (1984). *Applied social research methods series case study research: Design and methods.*

Yoo, Y., Henfridsson, O., & Lyytinen, K. (2010). The new organizing logic of digital innovation: An agenda for information systems research. *Information Systems Research, 21*(4), 724–735.

Young, K. (2009). Internet addiction: The emergence of a new clinical disorder. *Cyberpsychology & Behavior, 1*(3), 237–244.
Zhitomirsky-Geffet, M., & Blau, M. (2016). Cross-generational analysis of predictive factors of addictive behavior in smartphone usage. *Computers in Human Behavior, 64*, 682–693.
Zikmund, W. G. (2000). *Business research methods*. Dryden.

Makafui Nyamadi is a Lecturer at Ho Technical University, Ghana. He is also a Doctoral Researcher in Information Systems at the University of Ghana Business School. He was an Americas Conference on Information Systems (AMCIS) Doctoral Fellow in 2018, International Federation for Information Processing (IFIP WG 8.6) Doctoral Fellow, and Hawaii International Conference on Systems Sciences (HICSS) Doctoral Fellow in 2019. He published in ICIS, HICSS, and AMCIS. His research interests include technology addictions, digital platforms, cybersecurity, and theory development. Makafui can be reached at mnyamadi@htu.edu.gh

Pitso Tsibolane is currently a Senior Lecturer at the University of Cape Town, South Africa, Centre for Information Technology and National Development in Africa (CITANDA). He is the Director (At-Large) at Southern African Chapter of the Association for Information Systems (AISSAC), City of Cape Town, Western Cape, South Africa. He obtained a Masters in IT from the University of Pretoria, an MA in Creative Writing from Rhodes University, and a BSc (Hons) in Computer Science from the University of Cape Town. His broad research interests lie at the intersection of technology, development, and culture. He has several publications to his credit and can be reached at pitso.tsibolane@uct.ac.za

Part III
Digital Innovation and Development

Chapter 12
Fairness in the Platform Economy: A Bibliometric Analysis of Journal Research Articles

Richard Boateng, Obed Kwame Adzaku Penu, Thomas Anning-Dorson, and Joseph Budu

Abstract An increasing number of journal articles have been published on fairness in the platform economy from diverse perspectives. However, no study has yet attempted to assess the quantities and impact of such publications. In this study, 473 Scopus-indexed journal articles were analyzed using a bibliometric method to identify the leading authors and journal outputs as well as the evolutionary trends in knowledge on fairness in the platform economy. The results revealed that contributions to research in the area mostly originated from North America (the USA), Europe, and Asia, with no substantive research emerging from Africa. However, some researchers who are not from Africa partnered researchers from Africa to produce papers. This suggests the need for substantive research attention on fairness in the platform economy by researchers in Africa. The knowledge domains of research focused mainly on the topic categories of crowdsourcing, crowdfunding, sharing economy, and the gig economy. Evolutionary trends in fairness in the platform economy tend to move from discussions revolving around digital platforms and resources that facilitate platform work to issues related to discrimination, bias, inequality, and equity in engaging in the platform economy. This study provides insights into fairness-related issues to address in the platform economy so that positive outcomes can be generated for the economy. A spotlight on Africa and future directions for its researchers have also been highlighted.

R. Boateng (✉) · O. K. A. Penu
University of Ghana Business School, Legon, Accra, Ghana
e-mail: richboateng@ug.edu.gh; okapenu@st.ug.edu.gh

T. Anning-Dorson
University of the Witwatersrand, Johannesburg, South Africa
e-mail: thomas.dorson.anning@wits.ac.za

J. Budu
Ghana Institute of Management and Public Administration, Accra, Ghana
e-mail: josbudu@gimpa.edu.gh

R. Boateng et al. (eds.), *Digital Innovations, Business and Society in Africa*,
Advances in Theory and Practice of Emerging Markets,
https://doi.org/10.1007/978-3-030-77987-0_12

Keywords Platform economy fairness · Platform economy · Bias · Inequality · Africa · Bibliometric analysis

12.1 Introduction

Digital platforms are evolving and shaping livelihood due to the rapid development of information and communication technology (ICT) (Chatterjee et al., 2018; Chauhan et al., 2018). Such digital platforms and ICTs have facilitated the temporary sharing of underutilized resources or assets in what is known as the sharing economy, also called the platform economy (Parente et al., 2018; Sovani & Jayawardena, 2017). Mobile technology, in particular, has contributed to the use of sharing options (Zamani et al., 2019) and created digital business models that "have found far-reaching economic and social application during the past decade at a pace unparalleled in history" (Mueller et al., 2017, p. 367).

The platform economy has become a part of social life. Its prevalence has created employment opportunities in the form of informal and vulnerable employment, which can be underpaid and unpaid, especialy in low-income countries (ILO, 2018). Globally, the platform economy has created collaborative marketplaces that have facilitated the sharing of resources such as cars, accommodation, and tools among individuals who need to use such resources and those who need to use underutilized resources (Ter Huurne et al., 2017). An example is in the housing sector, where consumers pay for short-term accommodation online (Sovani & Jayawardena, 2017), and in the transportation sector, online platforms are used to request a sharing ride in private vehicles at a fee (Kuswanto et al., 2019; Lee et al., 2018).

The platform economy is also known to have many issues regarding fairness, legislation, and regulation (Gonzalez-Padron, 2017). For example, it is characterized by algorithms that are seen to be gender-biased, are discriminatory to marginalized groups, and offer poor wage and welfare system for workers (Wood et al., 2019). Its novelty has created labor policy challenges where there are no laws to protect both the workers and employers (Bates & Kirman, 2019).

The aforementioned vulnerabilities have arguably generated considerable research interest regarding fairness in the platform economy. Presently, academic literature that assesses the number of studies and the impact of the sources and authors of the studies has not received attention to guide future research in this burgeoning field of study. In particular, there has been no bibliometric study on prior research to identify patterns and trends in the platform economy (Io & Lee, 2017; Zupic & Čater, 2015). A few studies that used a bibliometrics approach on the platform economy have not focused on fairness (e.g., Andreu et al., 2020; Ertz & Leblanc-Proulx, 2018; Kraus et al., 2020). This paper considers that performing specific bibliometric reviews on a particular topic is helpful in critically determining the extent scholars have dealt with a focal research field and the characteristics of the literature of such field (Gundes & Aydogan, 2016; Rocha & Rodrigues, 2017).

Considering the aforementioned drawbacks in existing studies, a threefold bibliometric objective is set to analyze literature on fairness in the platform economy. Bibliometric analysis is considered an appropriate method for establishing the amount of work regarding published research works and the properties of the research (Haustein & Larivière, 2015). A study of this nature provides meaningful lead to future researchers in this area. The first objective is to perform a descriptive analysis of the literature, showing the growth of the field over time and providing useful information for measuring different aspects such as journals, authors, institutions, and countries. The results include a general perspective of research pertaining to fairness in the platform economy to identify the yearly publications, articles, journals, and scholars as well as their collaborations that have made relevant contributions to the development of the research area and the most productive institutions and countries. The second objective is to identify areas of interest and potential directions for future research by categorizing the research topics of papers according to the similarities of their themes (Braun and Clarke, 2006).

The remainder of this study is organized as follows. Section 12.2 presents the methodology, whereas Sect. 12.3 presents the results and discussion of the study including an analysis of relevant author and journal, leading countries and institutions, most popular keyword, and their network co-occurrence. Following this section is a section on proposed future research directions in general and a spotlight on Africa for researchers in Africa to consider. Then the final section concludes this study and provides recommendations for future research.

12.2 Methodology

Bibliometric analysis is a fundamental and powerful method of exploring the patterns and future trends of a research topic (Zupic & Čater, 2015). Many researchers have used this method to explore the research trends in different areas, such as healthcare (e.g., Adunlin et al., 2015; Sweileh et al., 2018), education (e.g., Heradio et al., 2016; Shen & Ho, 2020), marketing (e.g., Kim et al., 2019; Martínez-López et al., 2018), supply chain (e.g., Feng et al., 2017; Mishra et al., 2018; Xu et al., 2018), finance (e.g., Baker et al., 2019; Costa et al., 2019), manufacturing (e.g., Caviggioli & Ughetto, 2019; Laengle et al., 2018), and agriculture (e.g., Luo et al., 2020; Raparelli & Bajocco, 2019).

Unlike other methods such as systematic review, which is deficient in providing a better understanding of how a research area has evolved over time, bibliometric reviews through an analysis of the authors, institutions, countries and journals make impactful contributions regarding a research area. In the view of Mallett et al., (2012), systematic studies are often restricted to literature that is familiar to the author; hence, the same studies are frequently cited, and this introduces biases to the literate that are reviewed. Therefore, systematic literature review approaches lack the tendency to account for all, if not a considerable number of, research done in a particular field.

12.2.1 Information Retrieval

There are two major sources of information retrieval for bibliometric studies: (1) the Institute for Scientific Information (ISI) Web of Science (WoS) and (2) Scopus (Kumar, Pandey, & Tomar, 2020). However, the Scopus database was chosen because it has the largest databases of multidisciplinary peer-reviewed literature (Mongeon & Paul-Hus, 2016) and contains indexed articles from approximately 38,046 journals. It further captures one of the widest ranges of scientific articles among all electronic databases, with articles dating back to 1788 in some cases (Elsevier, 2020). Moreover, the preliminary search in the two databases using keywords shows that Scopus contains more articles on the theme under discussion than the WoS database.

The search strategy was designed to capture all relevant published indexed articles referring to "fairness" and the "platform economy." In this study, we consider other keywords that are used in reference to engagements in the "platform economy" and "fairness" in the platform economy. These keywords were chosen based on previous literature reviews on similar topics, the authors' own research experience, and expert views from fellow platform economy academics as proposed by Xu et al. (2018). As such, the following string words were used (TITLE-ABS-KEY (("platform economy" OR "online labor" OR "gig economy" OR "sharing economy" OR "access economy" OR "platform work" OR "digital labor" OR "digital labor platforms" OR "digital work" OR "online labor markets" OR "collaborative economy")) OR TITLE-ABS-KEY (("collaboration economy" OR "collaborative consumption" OR "on-the-demand economy" OR "on-demand economy" OR "crowd work" OR crowdwork OR crowdsourcing OR "gig work" OR "online outsourcing")) AND TITLE-ABS-KEY (("fairness" OR "unfairness" OR "decency" OR "equity" OR "equality" OR "inequality" OR "inequalities" OR "discrimination" OR "justice" OR "injustice" OR "bias" OR "fairwork" OR "decent work")). The search was done on the titles, abstracts, and keywords of the articles (Zupic & Čater, 2015). The search had no time limits. Initial results of searching the keywords generated 825 papers (comprising journal articles, editorials, book chapters, reviews, conference proceedings, and surveys and unidentified papers). However, further refinement of the search was done through inclusion and exclusion criteria as presented in the next subsection.

12.2.2 Inclusion and Exclusion Criteria

For papers to be included, they must discuss an issue regarding "fairness" and the "platform economy" or any of the string of keywords used. To ensure that this was achieved, five research assistants, with the authors of this study, screened the abstract of the papers at a deliberated sitting. Papers were excluded if they do not present any issue related to "fairness" of the "platform economy" or any of the string of keywords used. Only journal articles were considered as they are regarded as top quality and peer-reviewed research documents (Durieux & Gevenois, 2010; Martí-Parreño et al., 2016). Moreover, many researchers (e.g., Avila-Robinson & Wakabayashi, 2018; Hew, 2017; Martí-Parreño et al., 2016; Xu et al., 2018) have restricted their bibliometric studies to journal articles as they are the preferred source of information by researchers and practitioners and they communicate highly scrutinized research findings (Ngai & Gunasekaran, 2007). Table 12.1 provides a breakdown of the bibliometric information that were realized after the inclusion and exclusion criteria. As shown in Table 12.1, 1377 authors contributed to 473 journal articles on the theme of fairness of the platform economy. Among them, 1277

Table 12.1 Breakdown of bibliometric information

Description	Results
Main information about data	
Timespan	2006:2020
Sources (journals articles only)	346
Documents	473
Average years from publication	2.88
Average citations per documents	16.84
Average citations per year per document	2.904
References	24,689
Document types	
Articles	473
Document contents	
Keywords plus (ID)	2314
Author's keywords (DE)	1599
Authors	
Authors	1377
Author appearances	1533
Authors of single-authored documents	100
Authors of multi-authored documents	1277
Authors collaboration	
Documents per author	0.344
Authors per document	2.91
Co-authors per documents	3.24
Collaboration index	3.43

authors collectively collaborated to produce more than one document (authors of multi-authored documents) and 100 independent authors produced a document each (authors of single-authored documents).

12.2.3 Data Analysis Tools

This study adopted the VOSviewer, a widely used software for bibliometric analysis (e.g., Martínez-López et al., 2018; Valenzuela et al., 2017) as the visualization tool. The software can visualize the co-citation networks and cluster the related articles for a specific research area so that researchers can understand the development of the research area more efficiently (Van Eck & Waltman, 2010). In this study, the data to be analyzed were exported from Scopus as a comma-separated values (CSV) file into VOSviewer because the research objective is to investigate the trend of scholarly research that has been done on "fairness" in the "platform economy." The "bibliometrix-biblioshiny" package from RStudio is, however, used to generate keyword occurrence and trend analysis (Aria & Cuccurullo, 2017; Nasir et al., 2020).

12.3 Results and Discussion

This section presents the results and discussion of the scholarly publications on fairness in the platform from the bibliometric point of view per the objectives set out in the introduction of this study.

12.3.1 Trend in Yearly Publications

The time frame for research in fairness in the platform economy is between 2006 and 2020 (see Fig. 12.1). As shown, the number of papers published on the topic has significantly increased over the last 5 years from 21 papers in 2015 to 136 papers in 2020. Before 2014 (between 2006 and 2012), the number of papers has been relatively low (1 to 2 papers) and increased to 12 papers in 2013 but declined to 11 papers in 2014. It is also important to note that within the period 2006 and 2013 when publications were at relatively lower levels, there were no publications for 2007 and 2008. This relatively lowers levels in publications within this period (2008–2012) coupled with the absence of publications for the years 2007 and 2008 that may be attributed to less interest in the area of research or a low level of maturity of the platform economy. A globally known platform such as Uber, for example, is known to have emerged in 2009 in the USA, before expanding to overseas countries in 2011 (Pelzer et al., 2019; Thelen, 2018). This is a period that is described by Dabi et al., (2016) as the budding period for a research area, a period where many

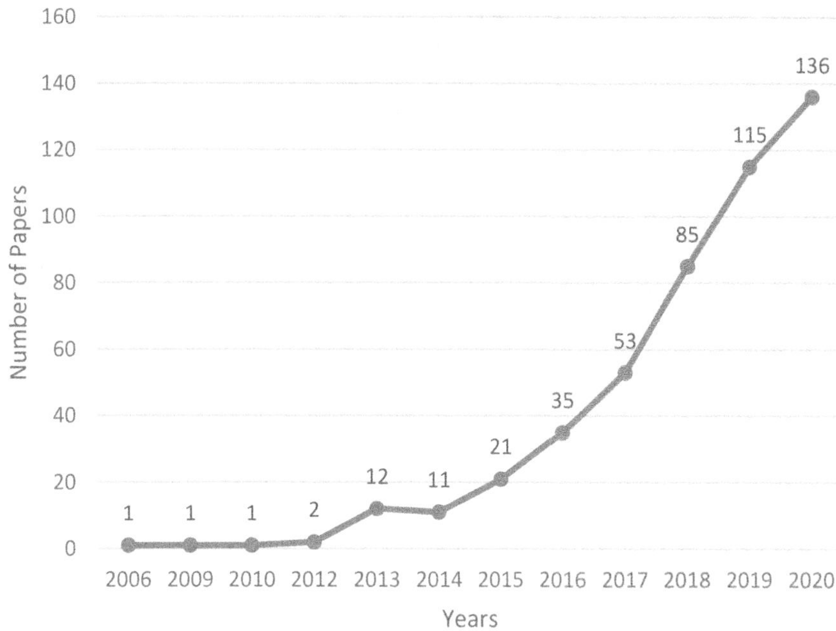

Fig. 12.1 Trend in yearly publication

aspects of a research field still have to be explored. As of December 31, 2020, when the data was extracted, the number of papers published was 136 (about 21 papers more the number of publications done in 2019). As per Fig. 12.1, one can allude that most of the research outputs are in the period 2013–2020, suggesting that research on fairness only gained interest and matured in recent past 7 years as opposed to the period 2006–2012 where publications were relatively low. The significant increase in the research output from 2015 can also be attributed to the emergence and adoption of online labor platforms or technologies. Moreover, as averred by Srnicek (2017), the emergence of Internet-based digital connectivity and matching technologies led to the emergence of the platform economy.

12.3.2 Bibliometric Analysis

In this section, we present the results of three central elements to measure research on fairness in the platform economy; we analyze the most relevant journals, authors and documents, the popular keywords and their trend, and the leading countries and institutions and provide future research direction based on the discussions of the findings.

12.3.2.1 Most Relevant Journals

There was a total of 346 sources for the 437 journal articles that were realized in this study. *Proceedings of the ACM on Human-Computer Interaction* was the most impactful with publications comprising 8 number of publications (NP) and total citation (TC) of 48, followed by *New Media and Society* with publications comprising 6 number of publications and total citation of 172 and *Journal of Business Ethics* with 5 publications and total citations. Though *New Media and Society* is by far the source with the most number of citations (172), it was not the most relevant as other factors such as the PY_Start (publication start year) come to play in the determination of the relevance of a journal. According to Hirsch (2005), the relevance or impact of a journal combines both quantity (number of papers), the period of publication, and an approximation of quality (citations to these papers) and not just having just a high number of publications or just a high number of citations. Comparing the publications start years for the most relevant source (*New Media and Society*) and second-most relevant journal (*Proceedings of the ACM on Human-Computer Interaction*), for example, shows that though the later has received a significant number of citations as compared to all the other sources in the top 20 most relevant sources, it has published a lesser number of papers within a longer time-space (2006–2020) as compared to the former which has published more papers within a shorter time-space (2017–2020), though its citations were 3 times less the citations received by the former. Table 12.2 summarizes the most impactful sources. Notably, the scope of the most cited journals suggests a preference for citations by authors in journals that focus on social contexts and consequences of new information and communication technologies for business models such as the platform economy. The top-cited journal is the *New Media and Society*.

12.3.2.2 Most Relevant Authors

An author's scientific activity in a research field in a given period can be considerably assessed by the author's number of publications (Bengoa et al., 2020, p.9). In Table 12.3, "Zhang J" tops the list as the most relevant author with 6 publications (NP), 64 total citations (TC), and a publication start year (PY_Start) of 2015. The publication start year is the year in which the author's first publications were recorded. Hence the relevance or impact of the author takes into consideration both quantity (number of papers), the period of publication, and an approximation of quality (citations to these papers) and not just having just a high number of publications or just a high number of citations (Hirsch, 2005). Hence, even though an author such as "Strickland JC" also has the same number of publications and PY_Start as "Zhang J," the latter has total citations that are higher than the former.

Notably, the authors publishing the most papers are not the most cited. For example, despite the relatively higher number of publications being made by "Zhang J," one can observe that taking into consideration and number of citations alone, "Schor JB," is the most cited author, having been cited as many as 285 times by other

Table 12.2 Top 20 most relevant sources

Source	NP	TC	TC/NP	PY_Start
Proceedings of The ACM on Human-Computer Interaction	8	48	6.00	2017
New Media and Society	6	172	28.66	2006
Journal of Business Ethics	5	50	10.00	2019
Proceedings of The National Academy of Sciences of The United States of America	4	154	38.50	2013
PLOS One	9	47	5.22	2014
Sustainability (Switzerland)	6	28	4.66	2017
Journal of Global Health	5	32	6.40	2015
IEEE Transactions on Knowledge and Data Engineering	4	49	12.25	2015
Information Communication and Society	4	25	12.25	2014
Management Science	4	29	7.25	2018
International Journal of Communication	3	55	18.33	2016
GeoJournal	4	8	2.00	2018
IEEE Access	4	20	5.00	2017
International Journal of Computer Assisted Radiology and Surgery	4	18	4.50	2016
Drug and Alcohol Dependence	3	38	12.66	2015
EPJ Data Science	3	4	1.33	2019
IEEE Transactions on Services Computing	3	12	4.00	2018
Journal of Medical Internet Research	3	18	6.00	2014
Scientific Reports	3	10	3.33	2017
Tourism Geographies	3	40	13.33	2019

Table 12.3 Top 10 most relevant authors

Author	NP	TC	PY_Start
Zhang J	6	64	2015
Strickland JC	6	47	2015
Rudan I	5	32	2015
Lutz C	4	14	2018
Schor JB	4	285	2016
Snyder J	4	79	2016
Stoops WW	4	45	2015
Wang Y	4	14	2018
Demartini G	3	25	2015
Gadiraju U	3	15	2019

authors. This number of citations is significant, considering that the number of citations is about 4 times the citations received by "Zhang J." Also there appears to be a lot of interest in publications that emerged in 2015 and 2016 as authors whose publications emerged in 2015 and 2016 emerged as the top most-cited authors. The instance can be given from Table 12.3 of "Schor JB" who has a PY_Start of 2016 with a total citation of 285 and "Snyder J" who also has a PY_Start of 2016 with a total citation of 79. In fact, "Schor JB" and "Snyder J" are the first and second most-cited authors, respectively.

Juxtaposing these findings to Fig. 12.1, one can see that the year 2015 and 2016 marked the beginning of a steady exponential rise in the number of publications in the research area. Hence, publications that were done in 2015 and 2016 were pivotal to the authoring of papers that were published in subsequent years as authors relied on these publications to publish their papers.

Author contribution to the research was done through independent research as well as collaborative research. Out of a total of 1377 authors who contributed to the research area, 100 were independent authors (single-authored documents), while the remaining 1277 collaborated (multi-authored documents) in producing research articles. In Fig. 12.2, a network map of the co-authors or collaborations between authors who have collaborated in a minimum of two documents is presented. The map is generated using the VOSviewer (Van Eck & Waltman, 2010).

Four clusters were realized from the network map. These are cluster 1 (red) with five items, cluster 2 (green) with four items, cluster 3 (blue) with three items, and cluster 4 (yellow) with two items. Each node represents an author, and a clustering of nodes represents a collaboration between authors. The larger the size of the node, the higher the linkages and total link strength of the author. The total link strength of the authors indicates the cumulative number of publications the two researchers have co-authored, and the linkages refer to the number of nodes that the author is connected to (Van Eck & Waltman, 2013). Thus, from Fig. 12.2, the topmost collaborating author is "Zhang J" who appears in cluster 3, has 5 links, and has a total link strength of 9. The authors who are mostly collaborating with "Zhang J" are "Wu X" and 'Sheng V.S.," all belonging to cluster 3. Notably, "Zhang J" is also the most impactful author as seen in Table 12.3. "Wang Y" is the second most collaborating author with 4 links and total link strength of 7. The authors who are mostly

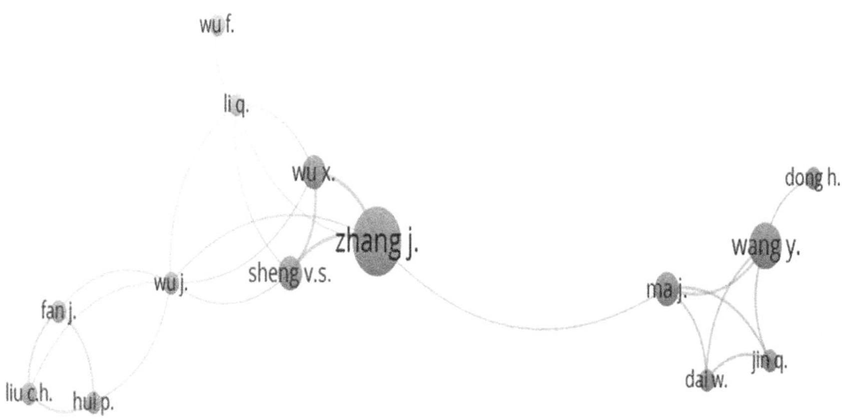

Fig. 12.2 Co-authorship analysis (co-authors)

collaborating with are "Ma J," "Dai W," "Jin Q," and " Dong H," all belonging to the red cluster.

12.3.2.3 Most Relevant Documents

Table 12.4 shows the top 20 most cited documents. It can be noted from the table that the paper titled "Data Collection in a Flat World: The Strengths and Weaknesses of Mechanical Turk Samples" (Goodman et al., 2013) published in the *Journal of Behavioral Decision Making* was the most cited paper with 1042 citations. The purpose of the paper was to compare personality, financial, and consumption dimensions, as well as decision-making biases among students and Mechanical Turk participants (Goodman et al., 2013). Following this paper in citation count is the paper titled "Citizen science as an ecological research tool: Challenges and benefits" (Dickinson et al., 2010) published in *Annual Review of Ecology, Evolution, and Systematics* which had 851 citations. The third leading paper titled "Reputation as a sufficient condition for data quality on Amazon Mechanical Turk" (Peer, Vosgerau, Acquisti, 2014) published in *Behavior Research Methods* had 583 citations. Interestingly, the publication outlet of the top-cited papers, especially the top three sources, do not emerge as the most relevant sources as seen in Table 12.2. The top three cited documents are published in *Journal of Behavioral Decision Making*; *Annual Review of Ecology, Evolution, and Systematics*; and *Behavior Research Methods*, respectively. However, the most relevant are published in *Proceedings of The ACM on Human-Computer Interaction*, *New Media and Society*, and *Journal of Business Ethics*, respectively.

Further, an analysis of the years in which the top 20 papers were published further corroborates the findings of this research that suggest that attention to research on fairness in the platform economy began to heighten 5–7 years ago (between 2012 and 2015) as many of the cited papers, especially the top five cited ones, were published within this period. Specifically, publications that were done in 2015 and 2016 appeared more (4 times) on the top 20 cited documents than any other years. Goodman et al. (2013), in particular, appear to have been seminal at the point where the interest in the research area heightened, having discussed biases among students and Mechanical Turk participants.

12.3.2.4 Countries and Institutions

Table 12.5 shows the countries that are contributing to research on fairness in the platform economy. Country and institutional contributions are determined by the affiliation of the first authors country and institutional affiliation, respectively (Cristino et al., 2018). The USA appears as the country contributing the most papers with 51 papers, followed by the UK with 17 papers and Canada with 10 papers. Notably, also from Table 12.5, most of these countries with the highest number of articles also have the highest single country publication (SCP) and multiple country

Table 12.4 20 most cited documents

Authors	Title	Source title	Citations
Goodman et al. (2013)	Data Collection in a Flat World: The Strengths and Weaknesses of Mechanical Turk Samples	*Journal of Behavioral Decision Making*	1042
Dickinson et al. (2010)	Citizen science as an ecological research tool: Challenges and benefits	*Annual Review of Ecology, Evolution, and Systematics*	851
Peer, Vosgerau, Acquisti (2014)	Reputation as a sufficient condition for data quality on Amazon Mechanical Turk	*Behavior Research Methods*	583
Edelman et al. (2017)	Racial discrimination in the sharing economy: Evidence from a field experiment	*American Economic Journal: Applied Economics*	221
Richardson (2015)	Performing the sharing economy	*Geoforum*	177
Raykar, Yu (2012)	Eliminating spammers and ranking annotators for crowdsourced labeling tasks	*Journal of Machine Learning Research*	162
John (2013)	The Social Logics of Sharing	*Communication Review*	133
Gant (2016)	Holiday rentals: The new gentrification battlefront	*Sociological Research Online*	118
Schor et al., (2016)	Paradoxes of openness and distinction in the sharing economy	*Poetics*	108
Deng et al., (2016)	The duality of empowerment and marginalization in microtask crowdsourcing: Giving voice to the less powerful through value sensitive design	*MIS Quarterly: Management Information Systems*	101
Vesdapunt et al., (2014)	Crowdsourcing algorithms for entity resolution	*Proceedings of the VLDB Endowment*	98
Franke et al., (2013)	Does this sound like a fair deal?: Antecedents and consequences of fairness expectations in the individual's decision to participate in firm innovation	*Organization Science*	98
Irani (2015)	The cultural work of microwork	*New Media and Society*	94
Schor (2017)	Does the sharing economy increase inequality within the eighty percent?: Findings from a qualitative study of platform providers	*Cambridge Journal of Regions, Economy and Society*	90
Schor, Attwood-Charles (2017)	The "sharing" economy: labor, inequality, and social connection on for-profit platforms	*Sociology Compass*	85
Jin et al., (2018)	Ridesourcing, the sharing economy, and the future of cities	*Cities*	81
Calo and Rosenblat (2017)	The taking economy: Uber, information, and power	*Columbia Law Review*	76

(continued)

Table 12.4 (continued)

Authors	Title	Source title	Citations
Budak et al., (2016)	Fair and balanced? Quantifying media bias through crowdsourced content analysis	*Public Opinion Quarterly*	69
Beaulieu et al., (2015)	A conceptual framework for understanding crowdfunding	*Communications of the Association for Information Systems*	69
Dushnitsky et al., (2016)	Crowd funding in Europe: Determinants of platform creation across countries	*California Management Review*	58

Table 12.5 Top 20 countries leading in publications

Country	Region/continent	Articles	SCP	MCP
USA	North America	51	46	5
UK	Europe	17	11	6
Canada	Europe	10	5	5
China	Asia	8	6	2
Korea	Asia	7	5	2
Australia	Europe	6	5	1
Germany	Europe	6	5	1
Netherlands	Europe	6	4	2
Austria	Europe	4	2	2
Belgium	Europe	4	4	0
Switzerland	Europe	4	3	1
Israel	Asia	3	3	0
Spain	Europe	3	2	1
France	Europe	2	1	1
Hong Kong	Asia	2	1	1
Italy	Europe	2	1	1
Norway	Europe	2	1	1
Poland	Europe	2	2	0
Sweden	Europe	2	0	2
Denmark	Europe	1	0	1

publication. SCP refers to publications that occur among authors in the same countries, while MCP refers to publications that are occurring among authors in more than one country. The USA (46 papers) tops the list of SCP, followed by the UK (11 papers) and China (5 papers). The top three MCP countries are the UK (6 papers) followed by Italy and Canada (5 papers each). The general picture painted by the country publication shows that a lot more authors prefer to publish with other authors within the geographical borders of their countries, either as sole authors or with authors within one country. Table 12.5 further points to a cumulative high number of contributions from European and Asian countries, despite the significant number of productions from the USA which is located in North America. This is so because, among the top 20 most productive countries as shown in Table 12.5, one can count as many as 15 (75%) countries from Europe, 3 (15%) from Asia, and the remaining (10%) from North America.

Table 12.6 shows the top contribution institutions around the world. Institutions of author affiliation that conduct fairness of the platform economy research are mostly the "Simon Fraser University" in Canada, the "University College London" in the UK, and the University of Oxford also in the UK. Each of these three institutions has 19 papers each. They are followed by the "University of Arizona" in the USA with 16 papers and the "University of Edinburgh," in the UK with 14 papers. However, in mapping the institutions to their country of origin, Table 12.6 corroborates the findings in Table 12.5 which suggests the USA is the most productive country in the research area as most of the institutions presented in the table are located in the USA. As many as 8 (40%) out of the top 20 most productive institutions are from the USA, while the remaining (60%) are between the UK, Austria, Canada, Australia, China, Norway, and the Netherlands. The impact made by the USA and its institutions is not far-fetched because the USA is one of the leading

Table 12.6 Top 20 contributing institutions

Affiliations	Country	Region	Articles
Simon Fraser University	Canada	Europe	19
University College London	UK	Europe	19
University of Oxford	UK	Europe	19
University of Arizona	USA	North America	16
University of Edinburgh	UK	Europe	14
International Institute for Applied Systems Analysis (IIASA)	Austria	Europe	10
University of Minnesota	USA	North America	10
University of Southern California	USA	North America	9
University of British Columbia	Canada	Europe	8
University of Melbourne	Australia	Europe	8
University of Washington	USA	North America	8
Xidian University	China	Asia	8
Arizona State University	USA	North America	7
BI Norwegian Business School	Norway	Europe	7
Delft University of Technology	Netherlands	Europe	7
Massachusetts Institute of Technology	USA	North America	7
Texas A&M University	USA	North America	7
University of Canterbury	UK	Europe	7
Wageningen University and Research	Netherlands	Europe	7
Yale University	USA	Europe	7

countries that is known to be spearheading academic publications in most fields of research (Wamba & Queiroz, 2020). Hence, identifying it to be a leader in a research field is not surprising. Also, identifying the USA to be the leader in terms of research contributions can be attributed to the origination and widespread use of platforms such as Uber, Airbnb, CrowdFlower, TaskRabbit, Amazon, and Lyft, among others (Thelen, 2018), in the country. The Uber ride-hailing platform, for example, emerged in the USA in 2009 and before moving to other overseas countries in 2011. Over the next 6 years, in particular, the Uber platform had expanded its reach to over 700 cities in 84 countries over the globe (Pelzer et al., 2019; Thelen, 2018). Again, issues regarding fairness in the platform economy had been very evident in the USA (Cohen, 2017), with prominent lawsuits regarding worker rights being brought by workers of Uber and Lyft against their respective companies in March 2015 (Rogers, 2016).

Spotlight on Africa Conspicuously missing from the country contributions are countries located in Africa. Specifically, no paper was identified to have originated from Africa, even though there were authors from South Africa, Kenya, Ghana, and Tunisia who had collaborated with other authors to produce some of the papers. It is important to note that the country and institutional productions in bibliometric studies are determined by the first author's affiliation (Cristino et al., 2018). Thus, per this specific research, no authors from Africa or affiliated to institutions in Africa were identified to be the first authors.

However, out of the 1377 authors, there were co-authors (authors other than first authors) who collaborated with other first authors not affiliated to Africa or institutions in Africa. Out of these, five authors were co-authors affiliated to South Africa, three were co-authors affiliated to Kenya, two were co-authors affiliated to Ghana, and two were co-authors affiliated to Tunisia. This suggests that authors from Africa had shown interest in research regarding fairness in the platform economy but were not doing so as the first authors who are considered owners of a particular research article because first authors are technically known to contribute a larger proportion toward the research output.

12.3.2.5 Commonly Used Terms and Co-occurrence

The commonly used terms were examined through authors' keywords (Comerio & Strozzi, 2019). A total of 1599 author keywords (DE) were identified from the 473 journal articles differently co-occurred in this analysis. To some extent, these keywords project the knowledge and trend in research in a particular paper and can be used to predict the trend in research over a period of time (Madani & Weber, 2016). Hence, in Table 12.7, the most commonly used keywords when researching fairness in the platform economy are presented. The table shows that the most used term is "crowdsourcing," which has 106 occurrences; followed by "sharing economy," which has 60 occurrences; and then followed by "crowdfunding" with 22 occurrences.

Table 12.7 Top 20 commonly used keywords

Words	Occurrences
Crowdsourcing	106
Sharing economy	60
Crowdfunding	22
Gig economy	20
Airbnb	15
Platform economy	14
Bias	11
Fairness	11
Citizen science	10
Discrimination	10
Inequality	10
Social media	9
Big data	7
Equity	7
Gender	7
Platforms	7
Collaborative consumption	6
Collaborative economy	6
Digital divide	6
Digital labour	6

A deeper analysis of the relationships between the most occurring keywords is presented in Fig. 12.3. In the view of Zupic and Čater (2015), keyword co-occurrence indicates that the concepts behind those words are closely related. The co-occurrence analysis revealed four major color clusters (yellow, red, green, sky-blue, and purple), with each cluster having a central node represented by the largest colored node of its kind.

The largest node represents the most co-occurring node. The primary and central co-occurring word is "crowdsourcing," which is the largest node in the network because it is connected to most of the other clusters in the network. The second most co-occurring node is "sharing economy," and it co-occurs mostly with "collaborative economy." The third most co-occurring node is "crowdfunding," which co-occurs mostly with "ethics," "bias," "platforms," and "discrimination." "Gig economy" co-occurs mostly with "gender," "Uber," and the "platform economy." "Tourism" is mostly used alongside (co-occurs) with "Airbnb," whereas "Internet" is most used alongside with "Amazon mechanical tuck." The results and co-occurrence of words are an indication of the terms around which research on the platform economy revolves and define the services offered by the platform economy. The term "crowdsourcing," for example, is used in reference to a business practice of outsourcing a task to deliver goods or services to a specialized group of people in the form of an open call via an online platform (Howe, 2008), rather than traditionally designating it to an agent (usually an employee) (Estellés-Arolas &

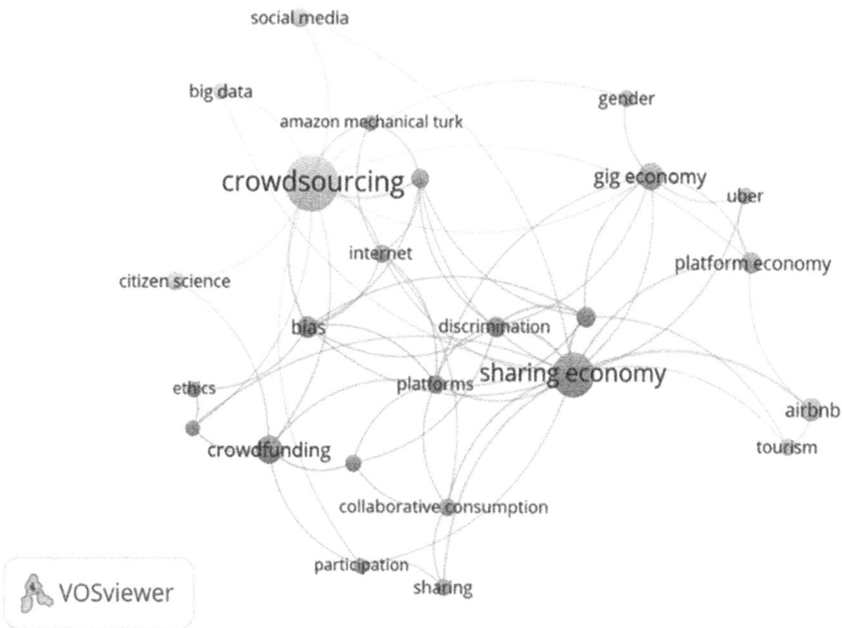

Fig. 12.3 Most commonly used keywords

González-Ladrón-De-Guevara, 2012). More importantly, the keywords regarding fairness revolving around these central keywords were identified as "bias," "discrimination," and "inequality." These words can particularly be observed in the red cluster where crowdfunding is the major concept of discussion. This suggests that many of the studies (e.g., Cumming et al., 2019; Kumar, Langberg, & Zvilichovsky, 2020; Martínez-Gómez et al., 2020; Troise et al., 2020; van Duynhoven et al., 2019) on fairness in the platform economy have been done on the subject of "crowdfunding." van Duynhoven et al. (2019), for example, aver that though medical crowdfunding provides individuals leverage to raise funds for health-related needs through social networks in order to avoid medical debt, there are ethical concerns of inequities in access to healthcare if persons from relatively wealthy backgrounds, media connections, tech-savvy, and educational attainments are best positioned to use and succeed with crowdfunding.

12.3.2.6 Emerging/Trending Keywords

Figure 12.4 presents the trend in the appearance of keywords in the past 4 years. The trend points to a four-phase shift: from 2016 to 2017 as phase one, from 2018 to mid-2019 as phase two, from mid-2019 to end of 2019 as phase three, and from the beginning of 2020 to the present as phase four. Between 2016 and 2017, researchers focused more resources and digital platforms to empower and allow people to

Fig. 12.4 Trend in the emergence of keywords

engage in digital labor, thereby bridging the digital divide, hence the presence of words such as "Internet," "resource allocation," "digital divide," and "digital labor." Then, between the year 2018 and mid-2019, research topics changed to mostly "crowdsourcing" and "crowdfunding" as well as tourism, accommodation rental, and sharing topics with discussions on gender-related issues, hence the presence of words such as "crowdsourcing," "crowdfunding," "Airbnb," "tourism," "Uber," "gender," and "sharing." Moving on from late-2018 to mid-2019, researchers had begun to emphasize fairness issues surrounding the "sharing economy" and "gig economy," hence the appearance of fairness-related keywords such as "bias," discrimination," and "inequality." In 2020, attention on fairness in the platform economy has so far revolved around "equity crowdfunding," which is almost similar to what has been seen from late-2018 to mid-2019. With the emergence of keywords such as equity crowdfunding in 2020 (post-2019), it is envisaged that there will be more platform-specific research on fairness.

12.4 Future Research Directions

Based on the results of this bibliometric study and discussions, the following suggestions in terms of research directions are proposed:

1. Considering that the attention on fairness in the platform economy research has predominantly been in the recent 7 years (2012–2020), it will be worth exploring the level of scholarly research attention given to it in the next 7–10 years.
2. Having identified the leading authors and journals in research on fairness in the platform economy, it will be worth identifying the co-citations between authors, and how journals are also co-cited and coupled with each other. It will also be worth exploring journal-specific bibliometric reviews of the source (journal outlets) that have spearheaded much of the fairness in the platform economy literature (e.g., *Journal of Behavioral Decision Making*; *Proceedings of The ACM on Human-Computer Interaction*, *New Media and Society*, and *Journal of Business Ethics*).
3. Considering the growing and evolving nature of the platform economy (Estellés-Arolas & González-Ladrón-De-Guevara, 2012), future studies may also be conducted empirically to compare research from developed countries in Europe, America, and Asia with the research from developing countries to understand and measure the differences and similarities in decent work standards in the platform economy. This can also be considered within the context of the developed countries, considering that issues such as pricing differentials (Chark, 2019) and racism (Vallas & Schor, 2020) may exist within different geographical spaces.
4. Platform fairness concerns within industry contexts remain a major concern (Thebault-Spieker et al., 2017). This study identified these concerns in the sectors of tourism and accommodation (Airbnb) (Ert et al., 2018) and ride-sharing (Uber) (Calo & Rosenblat, 2017). Discussion on gender discrimination and equity is yet another concern to be considered (Barzilay, 2018; Galperin, 2019). Future studies can explore variation in fair work in the platform economy across different platform sectors, genders, worker groups, and axes of difference.
5. Another issue that is worth investigating is the worker's experience and voice. To what extent are workers' voice heard and their inputs valued in the determination of workers' condition of service? How are can their experiences be improved by these platforms? These are many questions regarding experience and voice that will continue to be critical in the sharing economy.
6. An important research area that needs attention is the driver of digital value in networks. This research area has not received adequate attention as more and more worker agitations are being recorded around the world. Understanding the drivers of value in digital platform networks will help the further development of platforms with better shared value.
7. Lastly, empirical investigation is needed into informalization in the global south and how that is affecting the effectiveness of digital platforms. How are informal institutions within the global south affecting or facilitating the activities within the gig economy? Are there specific platform types that work better within the global south and why?

12.4.1 Future Research Spotlight on Africa

As per the results of the study, research that originated from African countries and their institutions seem very nascent. In other words, out of the 473 Scopus-indexed journal articles that were analyzed, no papers was identified to have been spearheaded by researchers from Africa or lead researchers affiliated to institutions in Africa. As averred by Cristino et al. (2018), in bibliometric studies the contributions to scientific knowledge rests largely on the efforts and inputs of the first author; hence country and institutional productions are determined by the first author's affiliation.

To begin with, given that premium was placed on dominant countries and institutions, which showed that research area has predominantly originated from developed countries such as America and Europe, future research can explore bibliometric studies that place a premium on developing regions such as Africa to determine the level of research given by researchers in the area of research and the ongoing country collaborations within that context.

Additionally, following in the path of the 20 most cited papers identified in this study, we present some research leaps that could be explored by researchers in Africa and their institutions in meeting up with the research deficit that has characterized the research area of fairness of the "platform economy" in Africa (see Table 12.8).

12.5 Conclusions

A total of 473 articles published between 2006 and 2020 on fairness in the platform economy were collected from 325 sources in the Scopus database for this study; they were then analyzed using a bibliometric method. The results on the keywords revealed that more scholars have focused on words such as "crowdsourcing," "sharing economy," and "crowdfunding" with issues of fairness being "ethics," "bias," and "discrimination" in the area of ride-hailing ("Uber"), "tourism", accommodation ("Airbnb"), and matters relating to gender. However, the concerns on fairness have predominantly been on the subject of crowdfunding.

The publication sources revealed the participation of multidisciplinary journals (i.e., social sciences, business and management, economics, computer sciences, psychology, and health) categories, which are productive and interested in publishing studies on fairness in the platform economy. Further, the diversity of journals from psychology to social sciences indicates that not only the development and design of innovation that is being published but also studies on social implications of technology.

Researchers from the USA were found to be the major contributors to fairness in the platform economy literature, followed by the UK and Canada. The results agree with the increasing presence of gig and online labor platforms (e.g., Uber, Salesforce,

Table 12.8 Summary of possible future study directions for researchers in Africa

Theme	Possible questions	Further reading
Attention to platform tasks	What level of attention do crowdsourcing platform participants (e.g., freelancers) in Africa give to task materials? What are the experiences of "crowdsourcers" regarding attention to detail to task materials and instructions by crowdsourcing participants in Africa?	Goodman et al. (2013)
Discrimination/inequalities/injustice/selection bias in the platform economy	Do platform workers in Africa feel marginalized in the selection of participants for online tasks? What are the experiences of low-reputation (entry-level) workers regarding sampling high-reputation workers in the platform economy in Africa? Which factors may be more critical for influencing the marginalized group's use of the platform economy? How should platform economy aggregators respond to the challenges faced by the marginalized groups in accessing the platform economy in Africa? How do current design choices of platform aggregators facilitate discrimination on platforms in Africa? What are the inequalities in sharing economy sites or platforms within the type of economic arrangement in Africa? Sharing platforms have become a part of urban governance. How does the digital divide affect social inclusion of citizens on the lower belt of the digital divide?	Peer et al., (2014), Edelman et al. (2017), Deng et al., (2016), Schor et al., (2016), Schor (2017), Schor and Attwood-Charles (2017) and Jin et al., (2018)
Methodologies for studying the platform economy	What methodologies have been adopted to platform economy research in Africa?	Richardson (2015)

(continued)

Table 12.8 (continued)

Theme	Possible questions	Further reading
Disruptiveness of the platform economy?	How is the sharing economy in Africa affecting traditional housing and transport providers? How does the emergence of the accommodation sharing economy displace middle- to low-income earners by the pressure of tourist investors?	Gant (2016)
Fairness impact and expectations	What is the rate of occurrence of platform injustice on different people in Africa? What is the impact of platform injustice on different people in Africa? How can the development of digital labor platforms be influenced positively in terms of fair and socially acceptable working conditions for workers in Africa? What are the fairness expectations of platform workers in the platform economy in Africa? (a) What are the antecedents of fairness expectations? (b) What factors make potential platform subscribers think that they will be treated fairly? (c) How do consequences of fairness expectations affect platform subscribers?.	Franke et al., (2013)
Unionization and bargaining	What factors inhibit labor unions in collectively bargaining on behalf of non-standard workers in the platform economy in Africa? How do regulatory frameworks guide platform economy aggregators to apply the regulations guiding the platform economy?	Jin et al., (2018)
Empirical studies on flexibility and job insecurity	What is the empirical nature of compensation levels of "on-demand workers" in the platform economy in Africa? What is the empirical nature of platform flexibility and insecurity in "on-demand work" in Africa?	Jin et al., (2018)
Theoretical application/ framework development	How do theoretical frameworks shape our understanding of the issue of social exclusion in the sharing economy?	Jin et al., (2018) and Beaulieu et al., (2015)

Upwork, Lyft, Amazon Flex, Airbnb, Fiverr, TaskRabbit, Share Now, Kickstarter, and Indiegogo) in these countries. The USA ranks high in the authoring of papers. Moreover, the number of countries participating in studying fairness in the platform economy means there is a growing interest among scholars from around the world. However, lagging far behind are scholars in developing regions such as Africa. As ride-hailing and online labor platforms are becoming prominent in these regions (Acheampong et al., 2020; Mäntymäki et al., 2019; Wood et al., 2019), there is an opportunity for fairness research.

This study has some limitations. First, only Scopus-indexed journal articles were considered. Future studies can explore other sources, such as the Web of Science (WoS). A systematic review of the extant research can also yield deeper insights into the conceptual and theoretical frameworks and thereby define new paths for theoretical contribution in this research space. Further, this study focused exclusively on peer-reviewed journal articles. Future studies may analyze other types of papers (e.g., conference papers, book chapters, and reviews).

Future studies could also analyze articles by focusing on co-citations and bibliometric coupling to understand how authors and journals are interlinked with each other. Nonetheless, this study has contributed by highlighting the increase in studies on fairness in the platform economy. Drawing upon these findings, fairness in the platform economy is a maturing theme, which is attracting research attention.

References

Acheampong, R. A., Siiba, A., Okyere, D. K., & Tuffour, J. P. (2020). Mobility-on-demand: An empirical study of Internet-based ride-hailing adoption factors, travel characteristics and mode substitution effects. *Transportation Research Part C: Emerging Technologies, 115*, 102638.

Adunlin, G., Diaby, V., & Xiao, H. (2015). Application of multicriteria decision analysis in health care: a systematic review and bibliometric analysis. *Health Expectations, 18*, 1894–1905.

Andreu, L., Bigne, E., Amaro, S., & Palomo, J. (2020). Airbnb research: an analysis in tourism and hospitality journals. *International Journal of Culture, Tourism and Hospitality Research., 14*, 2–20.

Aria, M., & Cuccurullo, C. (2017). bibliometrix: An R-tool for comprehensive science mapping analysis. *Journal of Informetrics, 11*(4), 959–975.

Avila-Robinson, A., & Wakabayashi, N. (2018). Changes in the structures and directions of destination management and marketing research: A bibliometric mapping study, 2005–2016. *Journal of Destination Marketing and Management, 10*, 101–111.

Baker, H. K., Kumar, S., & Pandey, N. (2019). Thirty years of the Global Finance Journal: A bibliometric analysis. *Global Finance Journal.*, Inpress, *100492*.

Barzilay, A. R. (2018). Discrimination without discriminating: Learned gender inequality in the labor market and gig economy. *Cornell Journal of Law and Public Policy, 28*, 545.

Bates, O., & Kirman, B. (2019). Sustainable platform cooperativism: Towards social and environmental justice in the future of the gig-economy. Limits 2019, available at https://eprints.lancs.ac.uk/id/eprint/134925/1/limits19_bates.pdf Accessed 21 Dec 2020.

Beaulieu, T., Sarker, S., & Sarker, S. (2015). A conceptual framework for understanding crowdfunding. *Communications of the Association for Information Systems, 37*(1), 1–31.

Bengoa, A., Maseda, A., Iturralde, T., & Aparicio, G. (2020). A bibliometric review of the technology transfer literature. *The Journal of Technology Transfer*, 1–37.

Braun, V., & Clarke, V. (2006). Using thematic analysis in psychology. *Qualitative research in psychology, 3*(2), 77–101.
Budak, C., Goel, S., & Rao, J. M. (2016). Fair and balanced? Quantifying media bias through crowdsourced content analysis. *Public Opinion Quarterly, 80*(S1), 250–271.
Calo, R., & Rosenblat, A. (2017). The taking economy: Uber, information, and power. *Columbia Law Review, 117*, 1623.
Caviggioli, F., & Ughetto, E. (2019). A bibliometric analysis of the research dealing with the impact of additive manufacturing on industry, business and society. *International Journal of Production Economics, 208*, 254–268.
Chark, R. (2019). Price fairness in the era of the sharing economy. *Cornell Hospitality Quarterly, 60*(3), 200–211.
Chatterjee, S., Kar, A. K., & Gupta, M. P. (2018). Success of IoT in smart cities of India: An empirical analysis. *Government Information Quarterly, 35*(3), 349–361.
Chauhan, S., Gupta, P., & Jaiswal, M. (2018). Factors inhibiting the Internet adoption by base of the pyramid in India. *Digital Policy, Regulation and Governance., 20*(4), 323–336.
Cohen, J. E. (2017). Law for the platform economy. *UCDL Review, 51*, 133.
Comerio, N., & Strozzi, F. (2019). Tourism and its economic impact: A literature review using bibliometric tools. *Tourism Economics, 25*(1), 109–131.
Costa, D. F., Carvalho, F. D. M., & Moreira, B. C. D. M. (2019). Behavioral economics and behavioral finance: A bibliometric analysis of the scientific fields. *Journal of Economic Surveys, 33*(1), 3–24.
Cristino, T. M., Neto, A. F., & Costa, A. F. B. (2018). Energy efficiency in buildings: analysis of scientific literature and identification of data analysis techniques from a bibliometric study. *Scientometrics, 114*(3), 1275–1326.
Cumming, D., Meoli, M., & Vismara, S. (2019). Investors' choices between cash and voting rights: Evidence from dual-class equity crowdfunding. *Research Policy, 48*(8), 103740.
Dabi, Y., Darrigues, L., Katsahian, S., Azoulay, D., De Antonio, M., & Lazzati, A. (2016). Publication trends in bariatric surgery: a bibliometric study. *Obesity surgery, 26*(11), 2691–2699.
Deng, X., Joshi, K. D., & Galliers, R. D. (2016). The duality of empowerment and marginalization in microtask crowdsourcing: Giving voice to the less powerful through value sensitive design. *Mis Quarterly, 40*(2), 279–302.
Dickinson, J. L., Zuckerberg, B., & Bonter, D. N. (2010). Citizen science as an ecological research tool: challenges and benefits. *Annual Review of Ecology, Evolution, and Systematics, 41*, 149–172.
Durieux, V., & Gevenois, P. A. (2010). Bibliometric indicators: quality measurements of scientific publication. *Radiology, 255*(2), 342–351.
Dushnitsky, G., Guerini, M., Piva, E., & Rossi-Lamastra, C. (2016). Crowdfunding in Europe: Determinants of platform creation across countries. *California management review, 58*(2), 44–71.
Edelman, B., Luca, M., & Svirsky, D. (2017). Racial discrimination in the sharing economy: Evidence from a field experiment. *American Economic Journal: Applied Economics, 9*(2), 1–22.
Elsevier. (2020). How scopus works. Elsevier, available at: https://www.elsevier.com/solutions/scopus/how-scopus-works/ Accessed 6 Dec 2020.
Ertz, M., & Leblanc-Proulx, S. (2018). Sustainability in the collaborative economy: A bibliometric analysis reveals emerging interest. *Journal of Cleaner Production, 196*, 1073–1085.
Ertz, M., Durif, F., Lecompte, A., & Boivin, C. (2018). Does "sharing" mean "socially responsible consuming"? Exploration of the relationship between collaborative consumption and socially responsible consumption. *Journal of Consumer Marketing. 35*(4), 392–402.
Estellés-Arolas, E., & González-Ladrón-De-Guevara, F. (2012). Towards an integrated crowdsourcing definition. *Journal of Information Science, 38*(2), 189–200.
Feng, Y., Zhu, Q., & Lai, K. H. (2017). Corporate social responsibility for supply chain management: A literature review and bibliometric analysis. *Journal of Cleaner Production, 158*, 296–307.

Franke, N., Keinz, P., & Klausberger, K. (2013). "Does this sound like a fair deal?": Antecedents and consequences of fairness expectations in the individual's decision to participate in firm innovation. *Organization science, 24*(5), 1495–1516.
Galperin, H. (2019). "This gig is not for women": Gender stereotyping in online hiring. *Social Science Computer Review*, 1–19.
Gant, A. C. (2016). Holiday rentals: The new gentrification battlefront. *Sociological Research Online, 21*(3), 112–120.
Gonzalez-Padron, T. L. (2017). Ethics in the sharing economy: Creating a legitimate marketing channel. *Journal of Marketing Channels, 24*(1–2), 84–96.
Goodman, J. K., Cryder, C. E., & Cheema, A. (2013). Data collection in a flat world: The strengths and weaknesses of Mechanical Turk samples. *Journal of Behavioral Decision Making, 26*(3), 213–224.
Gundes, S., & Aydogan, G. (2016). Bibliometric analysis of research in international construction. *Canadian Journal of Civil Engineering, 43*(4), 304–311.
Haustein, S., & Larivière, V. (2015). The use of bibliometrics for assessing research: Possibilities, limitations and adverse effects. In *Incentives and performance* (pp. 121–139). Cham: Springer.
Heradio, R., De, L. T. L., Galan, D., Cabrerizo, F. J., Herrera-Viedma, E., & Dormido, S. (2016). Virtual and remote labs in education: A bibliometric analysis. *Computers and Education, 98*, 14–38.
Hew, J. J. (2017). Hall of fame for mobile commerce and its applications: A bibliometric evaluation of a decade and a half (2000–2015). *Telematics and Informatics, 34*(1), 43–66.
Hirsch, J. E. (2005). An index to quantify an individual's scientific research output. *Proceedings of the National Academy of Sciences, 102*(46), 16569–16572.
Howe, J. (2008). *Crowdsourcing: how the power of the crowd is driving the future of business*. New York: Business Books.
ILO. (2018). *World employment and social outlook: Trends 2018*. Geneva: ILO.
Io, H. N., & Lee, C. B. (2017, December). Chatbots and conversational agents: A bibliometric analysis. In *2017 IEEE International Conference on Industrial Engineering and Engineering Management (IEEM)* (pp. 215–219). IEEE.
Irani, L. (2015). The cultural work of microwork. *New Media & Society, 17*(5), 720–739.
Jin, S. T., Kong, H., Wu, R., & Sui, D. Z. (2018). Ridesourcing, the sharing economy, and the future of cities. *Cities, 76*, 96–104.
John, N. A. (2013). The social logics of sharing. *The Communication Review, 16*(3), 113–131.
Kim, J., Kang, S., & Lee, K. H. (2019). Evolution of digital marketing communication: Bibliometric analysis and network visualization from key articles. *Journal of Business Research*. In Press. https://doi.org/10.1016/j.jbusres.2019.09.043.
Kraus, S., Li, H., Kang, Q., Westhead, P., & Tiberius, V. (2020). The sharing economy: a bibliometric analysis of the state-of-the-art. *International Journal of Entrepreneurial Behavior and Research., 26*(8), 1769–1786.
Kumar, P., Langberg, N., & Zvilichovsky, D. (2020). Crowdfunding, financing constraints, and real effects. *Management Science, 66*(8), 3561–3580.
Kumar, S., Pandey, N., & Tomar, S. (2020). Twenty years of Latin American Business review: A bibliometric overview. *Latin American Business Review, 21*(2), 197–222.
Kuswanto, A., Sundari, S., Harmadi, A., & Hariyanti, D. A. (2019). The determinants of customer loyalty in the Indonesian ride-sharing services: Offline vs online. *Innovation and Management Review, 17*(1), 75–85.
Laengle, S., Modak, N. M., Merigó, J. M., & De La Sotta, C. (2018). Thirty years of the International Journal of Computer Integrated Manufacturing: A bibliometric analysis. *International Journal of Computer Integrated Manufacturing, 31*(12), 1247–1268.
Lee, Z. W. Y., Chan, T. K. H., Balaji, M. S., & Chong, A. Y. L. (2018). Why people participate in the sharing economy: An empirical investigation of Uber. *Internet Research, 28*(3), 829–850.
Luo, J., Han, H., Jia, F., & Don, H. (2020). Agricultural co-operatives in the Western World: A bibliometric analysis. *Journal of Cleaner Production, 273*, 122945.

Madani, F., & Weber, C. (2016). The evolution of patent mining: Applying bibliometrics analysis and keyword network analysis. *World Patent Information, 46*, 32–48.

Mäntymäki, M., Baiyere, A., & Islam, A. N. (2019). Digital platforms and the changing nature of physical work: Insights from ride-hailing. *International Journal of Information Management, 49*, 452–460.

Mallett, R., Hagen-Zanker, J., Slater, R., & Duvendack, M. (2012). The benefits and challenges of using systematic reviews in international development research. *Journal of development effectiveness, 4*(3), 445–455.

Martínez-Gómez, C., Jiménez-Jiménez, F., & Alba-Fernández, M. V. (2020). Determinants of Overfunding in Equity Crowdfunding: An Empirical Study in the UK and Spain. *Sustainability, 12*(23), 2–29.

Martínez-López, F. J., Merigó, J. M., Valenzuela-Fernández, L., & Nicolás, C. (2018). Fifty years of the European Journal of Marketing: A bibliometric analysis. *European Journal of Marketing, 52*(1/2), 439–468.

Martí-Parreño, J., Méndez-Ibáñez, E., & Alonso-Arroyo, A. (2016). The use of gamification in education: a bibliometric and text mining analysis. *Journal of Computer Assisted Learning, 32*(6), 663–676.

Mishra, D., Gunasekaran, A., Papadopoulos, T., & Childe, S. J. (2018). Big Data and supply chain management: A review and bibliometric analysis. *Annals of Operations Research, 270*(1–2), 313–336.

Mongeon, P., & Paul-Hus, A. (2016). The journal coverage of Web of Science and Scopus: A comparative analysis. *Scientometrics, 106*(1), 213–228.

Mueller, S. C., Bakhirev, A., Böhm, M., Schröer, M., Krcmar, H., & Welpe, I. M. (2017). Measuring and mapping the emergence of the digital economy: a comparison of the market capitalization in selected countries. *Digital Policy, Regulation and Governance, 19*(5), 367–382.

Nasir, A., Shaukat, K., Hameed, I. A., Luo, S., Alam, T. M., & Iqbal, F. (2020). A bibliometric analysis of corona pandemic in social sciences: A review of influential aspects and conceptual structure. *IEEE Access, 8*, 133377–133402.

Ngai, E. W., & Gunasekaran, A. (2007). A review for mobile commerce research and applications. *Decision Support Systems, 43*(1), 3–15.

Parente, R. C., Geleilate, J. M. G., & Rong, K. (2018). The sharing economy globalization phenomenon: A research agenda. *Journal of International Management, 24*(1), 52–64.

Peer, E., Vosgerau, J., & Acquisti, A. (2014). Reputation as a sufficient condition for data quality on Amazon Mechanical Turk. *Behavior research methods, 46*(4), 1023–1031.

Pelzer, P., Frenken, K., & Boon, W. (2019). Institutional entrepreneurship in the platform economy: How Uber tried (and failed) to change the Dutch taxi law. *Environmental Innovation and Societal Transitions, 33*, 1–12.

Raparelli, E., & Bajocco, S. (2019). A bibliometric analysis on the use of unmanned aerial vehicles in agricultural and forestry studies. *International Journal of Remote Sensing, 40*(24), 9070–9083.

Raykar, V. C., & Yu, S. (2012). Eliminating spammers and ranking annotators for crowdsourced labeling tasks. *The Journal of Machine Learning Research, 13*(1), 491–518.

Richardson, L. (2015). Performing the sharing economy. *Geoforum, 67*, 121–129.

Rocha, P., & Rodrigues, R. C. (2017). Bibliometric review of improvements in building maintenance. *Journal of Quality in Maintenance Engineering, 23*(4), 437–456.

Rogers, B. (2016). Employment rights in the platform economy: Getting back to basics. *Harvard Law and Policy Review, 10*, 479.

Schor, J. B., Fitzmaurice, C., Carfagna, L. B., Attwood-Charles, W., & Poteat, E. D. (2016). Paradoxes of openness and distinction in the sharing economy. *Poetics, 54*, 66–81.

Schor, J. B. (2017). Does the sharing economy increase inequality within the eighty percent?: findings from a qualitative study of platform providers. *Cambridge Journal of Regions, Economy and Society, 10*(2), 263–279.

Schor, J. B., & Attwood-Charles, W. (2017). The "sharing" economy: labor inequality, and social connection on for-profit platforms. *Sociology Compass, 11*(8), e12493.
Shen, C. W., & Ho, J. T. (2020). Technology-enhanced learning in higher education: A bibliometric analysis with latent semantic approach. *Computers in Human Behavior, 104*, 106177.
Sovani, A., & Jayawardena, C. C. (2017). How should Canadian tourism embrace the disruption caused by the sharing economy? *Worldwide Hospitality and Tourism Themes, 9*(4), 464–470.
Srnicek, N. (2017). *Platform capitalism*. John Wiley and Sons.
Sweileh, W. M., Wickramage, K., Pottie, K., Hui, C., Roberts, B., Sawalha, A. F., & Zyoud, S. (2018). Bibliometric analysis of global migration health research in peer-reviewed literature (2000–2016). *BMC Public Health, 18*(1), 1–18.
Ter Huurne, M., Ronteltap, A., Corten, R., & Buskens, V. (2017). Antecedents of trust in the sharing economy: A systematic review. *Journal of Consumer Behaviour, 16*(6), 485–498.
Thebault-Spieker, J., Terveen, L., & Hecht, B. (2017). Toward a geographic understanding of the sharing economy: Systemic biases in UberX and TaskRabbit. *ACM Transactions on Computer-Human Interaction (TOCHI), 24*(3), 1–40.
Thelen, K. (2018). Regulating Uber: The politics of the platform economy in Europe and the United States. *Perspectives on Politics, 16*(4), 938–953.
Troise, C., Tani, M., & Jones, P. (2020). Investigating the impact of multidimensional social capital on equity crowdfunding performance. *International Journal of Information Management, 55*, 102230.
Valenzuela, L. M., Merigó, J. M., Johnston, W. J., Nicolas, C., & Jaramillo, J. F. (2017). Thirty years of the Journal of Business and Industrial Marketing: A bibliometric analysis. *Journal of Business and Industrial Marketing, 32*(1), 1–18.
Vallas, S., & Schor, J. B. (2020). What do platforms do? Understanding the gig economy. *Annual Review of Sociology, 46*, 273–294.
van Duynhoven, A., Lee, A., Michel, R., Snyder, J., Crooks, V., Chow-White, P., & Schuurman, N. (2019). Spatially exploring the intersection of socioeconomic status and Canadian cancer-related medical crowdfunding campaigns. *BMJ Open, 9*(6), e026365.
Van Eck, N. J., & Waltman, L. (2010). Software survey: VOSviewer, a computer program for bibliometric mapping. *Scientometrics, 84*(2), 523–538.
Van Eck, N. J., & Waltman, L. (2013). *VOSviewer manual. Leiden: Univeristeit Leiden, 1*(1), 1–53.
Vesdapunt, N., Bellare, K., & Dalvi, N. (2014). Crowdsourcing algorithms for entity resolution. *Proceedings of the VLDB Endowment, 7*(12), 1071–1082.
Wamba, S. F., & Queiroz, M. M. (2020). Blockchain in the operations and supply chain management: Benefits, challenges and future research opportunities. *International Journal of Information Management, 52*, 102064.
Wood, A. J., Graham, M., Lehdonvirta, V., & Hjorth, I. (2019). Good gig, bad gig: autonomy and algorithmic control in the global gig economy. *Work, Employment and Society, 33*(1), 56–75.
Xu, X., Chen, X., Jia, F., Brown, S., Gong, Y., & Xu, Y. (2018). Supply chain finance: A systematic literature review and bibliometric analysis. *International Journal of Production Economics, 204*, 160–173.
Zamani, E. D., Choudrie, J., Katechos, G., & Yin, Y. (2019). Trust in the sharing economy: the AirBnB case. *Industrial Management and Data Systems, 119*, 1947–1968.
Zupic, I., & Čater, T. (2015). Bibliometric methods in management and organization. *Organizational Research Methods, 18*(3), 429–472.

Richard Boateng is a Professor of Information Systems at the University of Ghana Business School (UGBS). Richard's experience covers the digital economy, cloud computing, e-learning, information and communication technologies (ICT) for development, electronic governance, social media, electronic business, gender and technology, mobile commerce, and mobile health at the national, industrial, organizational, and community levels. His papers have been published in or are forthcoming in the *International Journal of Information Management*, *Internet Research*, *Qualitative Market Research: An International Journal*, and many others. Richard can be reached at richboateng@ug.edu.gh

Obed Kwame Adzaku Penu is a PhD student in Information Systems at the University of Ghana. He holds an MPhil in Management Information Systems from the same University. Obed is also a Teaching and Research Assistant at the Operations and Management Information Systems (OMIS) Department, University of Ghana Business School (UGBS). He also has work experience as a software tester and documentation writer. His research interests is in the sharing/platform economy, digitalization (enterprise IS/IT implementation and usage), e-learning, artificial intelligence, business analytics, and information systems security. He can be reached at okapenu@st.ug.edu.gh.

Thomas Anning-Dorson (PhD) is an Associate Professor of Marketing at the University of the Witwatersrand, South Africa. He also serves as a Researcher with The Fairwork Foundation, Oxford Internet Institute, University of Oxford, and a QES Fellow at McGill University, Canada. His research interest spans the digital economy, innovation, marketing, strategy, and emerging markets. He can be reached at thomas.dorson.anning@wits.ac.za

Joseph Budu (PhD) is an Information Systems scholar with a keen interest in multi-sided digital platforms, information, communication and technology for development (ICT4D), and information systems education. He has several journal publications, book chapters, and conference papers. He is a lecturer at the School of Technology, Ghana Institute of Management and Public Administration (GIMPA), and blogs about research at www.researchcoa.ch. He can be reached via email at josbudu@gimpa.edu.gh

Chapter 13
A Review of Dominant Issues, Multi-dimensions, and Future Research Directions for Smart Cities

Patrick Annan-Noonoo, Bryan Acheampong, Joseph Budu, and Edward Entee

Abstract This study presents a systematic review of dimensions and dominant issues in smart city research. A total of 70 papers obtained from the top eight senior baskets of IS journals and five academic literature databases from 2016 to May 2020 were reviewed. Following the review, various issues were analyzed under five main elements that shape smart city projects, i.e., smart mobility, smart energy, smart living, smart urbanism, and the Internet of Things. Findings from the review showed that smart cities are multi-dimensional, comprising governmental, socio-economic, and environmental factors, each with unique dynamics and degree of context sensitivity. Information communication and technology serves as the backbone for smart city initiatives. The findings also suggest six main areas for future smart city research; stakeholder collaboration, IS policies governing smart cities, big data, citizen involvement, built environment, and smart healthcare. These future research areas are also necessary for the African research context. Cities that want to embark on sustainable smart city initiatives should involve public authorities, private businesses, and citizens. Future research should also examine the context-based factors that influence smart cities.

Keywords Smart cities · ICT · Big data · Internet of Things · Literature review

P. Annan-Noonoo (✉) · B. Acheampong · E. Entee
University of Ghana Business School, Accra, Ghana
e-mail: pannan-noonoo@st.ug.edu.gh; bacheampong016@st.ug.edu.gh; eentee001@st.ug.edu.gh

J. Budu
Ghana Institute of Management and Public Administration, Accra, Ghana
e-mail: josbudu@gimpa.edu.gh

R. Boateng et al. (eds.), *Digital Innovations, Business and Society in Africa*, Advances in Theory and Practice of Emerging Markets,
https://doi.org/10.1007/978-3-030-77987-0_13

13.1 Introduction

The emergence of "smart cities" or the "smart city" has attracted strong interest from researchers and practitioners (Guo et al., 2018; King & Kraemer, 2019; Kulkarni & Robles-Flores, 2019). Smart cities have been predicted to be the future of urban development as it is improving the quality of life through better use of space, cleaner air, less traffic, and more efficient civic services (Bosch, 2020; Forbes, 2020; PwC, 2020). Smart city solutions are even expected to manage post-COVID life because they have already proved handy for curbing the infection through real-time heatmaps of crowding in public spaces, remote temperature monitoring systems, robots acting as "safe-distance" ambassadors, and drones spraying disinfectants (Hasija, 2020).

Despite the growing trend in smart cities, there has not been a clear definition of a "smart city." The concept has enjoyed a plurality of definitions depending on the researcher's theme or perspective. For instance, based on smart growth and sustainability of urban environments, Hu and Zheng (2020) defined a smart city as the effort to make a metropolis more livable, workable, and sustainable. Others have emphasized the wide use of ICT to integrate critical infrastructure and improve city services (Dameri et al., 2019; Wataya & Shaw, 2019; Anthopoulos, 2017; Joss et al., 2019). A growing number of scholars have also taken a more comprehensive approach, asserting that the smart city concept involves multiple dimensions including governance, environment, people, technology, and the community (Hu & Zheng, 2020; Joss et al., 2019; Timeus et al., 2020; Monstadt & Coutard, 2019; Yigitcanlar et al., 2018; Komninos et al., 2019).

Studies on the smart city concept have been recently carried out in different fields (Jazzar, 2019; Yu & Peng, 2020). Although these studies provide useful insights into smart cities, some knowledge gaps remain, warranting additional research and review of relevant studies. For example, there is a need to carry out studies on trending issues related to smart cities similar to how it has been done for platform interoperability (Boateng et al., 2019) and gamification (Kasurinen & Knutas, 2018; Rapp et al., 2019).

Additionally, smart cities as an emerging concept are of interest to both public sector institutions and private businesses (Hu & Zheng, 2020). For the government, smart cities improve city administration, help manage resources efficiently, and create value for citizens (Ruhlandt, 2018; Lam & Yang, 2020). Despite these benefits associated with smart cities, there are still some challenges and limitations to planning, development, and sustainability (Wataya & Shaw, 2019; Marsal-Llacuna, 2018; Wilson & Chakraborty, 2019; Manitiu & Pedrini, 2016). These challenges could also be due to the complex phenomenon of smart cities with constraints in several dimensions like socioeconomic, environmental, technology, and government (Komninos et al., 2019). The complexity is further exacerbated by the fact these constraints differ by context – for example, from one city to another city, depending on the prevailing economic, sociotechnical, or political conditions

(Dameri et al., 2019; De Falco et al., 2019; Butler et al., 2020). Arguably, review articles on smart cities focusing on business and society seem insufficient. Since the smart city concept is a growing area, we need to take stock of existing data to shape future research. To this end, conducting extant research through a review may provide insights that can inform future research exploring smart cities and how to address the challenges (Senyo et al., 2018).

This study seeks to review relevant literature to establish dominant research issues, multi-dimensions, and future direction for smart city research. This paper is structured into six sections. Section 13.1 presents the introduction. The methodology used to conduct the study is presented in Sect. 13.2. Section 13.3 discusses the multi-dimensions identified in the papers, while Sect. 13.4 discusses the dominant issues. Section 13.5 discusses the directions for future research. Sections 13.6 and 13.7 discusses smart cities in the African context and the conclusion for the study, respectively.

13.2 Methodology for Review

A literature review is central to academic research. An effective review enables a researcher to create a firm foundation for advancing knowledge, facilitates theory development, identifies areas where a plethora of research exists, and uncovers new areas where research is needed (Webster & Watson, 2002). Reviewing literature entails gathering, assimilating, and analyzing extant literature from largely diverse academic-oriented sources (Boateng et al., 2008). A complete review is not confined to one set of journals, one research methodology, or one geographic region but rather covers relevant literature on the topic in a concept-centric approach (Webster & Watson, 2002).

In this review, EBSCOhost, Scopus, JSTOR, and the top 8 IS journals were searched to support the systematic review of the literature on smart cities. The book chapter focuses on digital innovations, business, and society. Coming from an IS perspective, we focused more on the business and managerial aspect of smart cities, than the technical aspect, which mainly focuses on developing new technologies for smart city development. Hence, a database like the Institute of Electrical and Electronics Engineers (IEEE) was omitted. Researchers mostly collect literature from electronic sources to gather literature that justifies arguments or assertions they make in their study on a particular subject (Petter & McLean, 2009).

In the search, only concepts directly related to smart cities, digital cities, or e-cities were used to understand how the literature presents these terms and what approaches and tools are used in the construction of smart cities. Searches were conducted with the phrases ["smart city" or "smart cities"], or ["digital cities"], or ["e-cities"] present in all fields across the databases. The search from the databases was also limited to peer-reviewed scholarly journals published between 2016 and May 2020 and written in the English language. According to a systematic review by

Cocchia (Cocchia, 2014), there has been a growing literature review on smart cities since 2005 and a spike since 2010. Existing systematic literature reviews have been conducted on papers published between 1993 and 2012 (Cocchia, 2014), 1997 to 2017 (Moustaka et al., 2018), and 2005 to 2017 (Lim et al., 2019). This study extends systematic literature review from 2016 to 2020 to provide insights on the most recent smart city issues, dimensions, and directions for future research. A total of 866 papers were returned, as highlighted in Table 13.1.

After generating the 866 papers, we moved to the second phase of the literature review process. This phase involved screening the papers gathered to identify the relevant literature to be included in the review. A title, keyword, and abstract search were first done to screen relevant articles. Duplicates were corrected in the databases to reduce the papers to 260. If the title and abstract were not informative enough to determine acceptance of the paper, further evaluation of the introduction and full paper were used as elimination criteria. Since the paper was limited to smart cities, digital cities, or e-cities, papers that focused on smart contracts, smart objects like smartphones, smart wristbands, and other non-related areas were eliminated. A total of 70 articles, therefore, qualified for evaluation. Figure 13.1 illustrates the methodological process described.

Table 13.1 Papers for repository

Paper Repository	Papers	Search string
JSTOR	109	("smart cities" OR "Digital cities" OR "E-cities")
EBSCOhost	170	(("Smart cit*") OR ("Digital cit*") OR ("E-cit*"))
Scopus	121	(("Smart cit*") OR ("Digital cit*") OR ("E-cit*"))
Google Scholar	96	(("Smart cit*") OR ("Digital cit*") OR ("E-cit*"))
Taylor and Francis	197	(("Smart cit*") OR ("Digital cit*") OR ("E-cit*"))
Top 8 senior basket of IS journals		
JIT	3	[All "smart cities"] OR [All "digital cities"] OR [All "e-cities"]
JAIS	120	[All "smart cities"] OR [All "digital cities"] OR [All "e-cities"]
ISR	8	[All "smart cities"] OR [All "digital cities"] OR [All "e-cities"]
EJIS	20	[All: "smart city"] OR [All: "smart cities"] OR [All: "digital city"] OR [All: "digital cities"] OR [All: "e-city"] OR [All: "e-cities"] AND [Publication Date: (01/01/2016 TO 12/31/2020)]
ISJ	18	[All "smart cities"] OR [All "digital cities"] OR [All "e-cities"]
JMIS	1	[All "smart cities"] OR [All "digital cities"] OR [All "e-cities"]
JSIS	2	[All "smart cities"] OR [All "digital cities"] OR [All "e-cities"]
MISQ	1	[All "smart cities"] OR [All "digital cities"] OR [All "e-cities"]
Total	**866**	

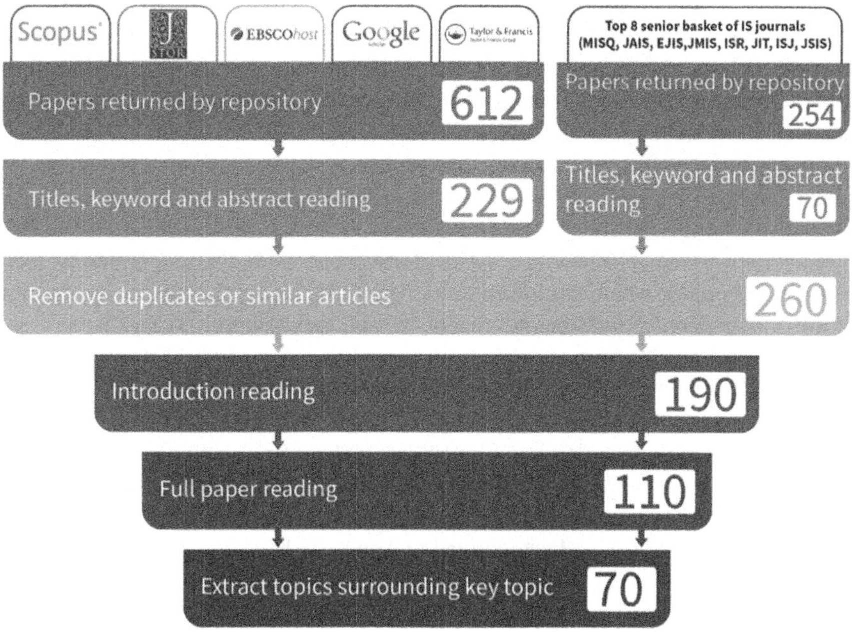

Fig. 13.1 The methodological process of papers included in the study

13.3 Multi-dimensional Concepts of Smart Cities

The reviewed papers recognized that the core concept of a smart city has been defined in myriad ways. Some researchers have highlighted smart growth and the sustainability of the urban environment, defining smart cities as the effort to improve the livability, workability, and sustainability of a city (Hu & Zheng, 2020; Macke et al., 2018). Others have emphasized the wide use of ICT to integrate critical infrastructure and improve city services (Dameri et al., 2019; Wataya & Shaw, 2019; Anthopoulos, 2017; Joss et al., 2019). However, a growing number of scholars have taken a more comprehensive approach asserting that the smart city concept involves multiple dimensions including governance, environment, people, technology, and the community (Hu & Zheng, 2020; Joss et al., 2019; Timeus et al., 2020; Monstadt & Coutard, 2019; Yigitcanlar et al., 2018; Komninos et al., 2019). In Komninos et al. (2019)'s evolutionary perspective on smart city planning, the authors defined smart city sustainability as "a set of dimensions, including socioeconomic, environmental, and governmental dimensions, which can be enhanced through the use of smart city applications, networks, and integration of digital, social, and institutional elements." Camboim et al. (2019)'s review and an empirical study showed that a smart city is an urban innovation ecosystem where knowledge easily flows from a deliberated interaction and collaboration among different stakeholders to create wealth, supported by a flexible institutional structure, an integrated-participative governance model, a digital-green infrastructure, and a functional urban design with diversified amenities and facilities. The authors concluded that cities that aim to become smarter should upgrade the elements related to their different dimensions, which are the techno-economic activity, the environ-urban configuration, and the socio-institutional structures in an integrated manner, guided by an integrated and comprehensive governance model. Yigitcanlar et al. (2018) further developed an understanding of a new city model by identifying and linking the key drivers to desired outcomes and then intertwining them in a multi-dimensional framework. The author's review revealed three types of drivers of smart cities, community, technology, and policy, which are linked to five desired outcomes, productivity, sustainability, accessibility, well-being, livability, and governance. These drivers and outcomes integrate to form a smart city framework, where each of them represents a distinctive dimension of the smart cities notion (Yigitcanlar et al., 2018). Hu and Zheng (2020) built on previous research and proposed a smart city initiative framework composed of the following dimensions: technology enablers, socioeconomic context, policy context, application domain, governance, and certain country-specific factors. A summary of key dimensions and elements falling within each of them is discussed below and categorized in Appendix II.

13.3.1 Governmental Dimensions

Existing research claims that smart city governance plays an important role in the success of smart city initiatives (Camboim et al., 2019; Castelnovo et al., 2016). Governance improves city administration to engage and deliver value for citizens (Camboim et al., 2019), mobilizes and allocates resources efficiently (Monstadt & Coutard, 2019), influences smart city implementation (Dameri et al., 2019), sets priorities for smart city projects, and engages multiple stakeholders in joint efforts to build smart cities (Ruhlandt, 2018; Lam & Yang, 2020). Cities vary in terms of political and administrative systems, power structure, and governance (Hu & Zheng, 2020). Larger cities in countries like Italy are organized with a multi-level governance structure, where power and competency descend from the central government to the local administrative agencies (Dameri et al., 2019). Hu and Zheng (2020) are of the view that without a well-designed and efficient governance system, it will be difficult for a city to build a smart city. Public-private partnership (PPP), as well as other stakeholder engagements with public authorities, private businesses, citizens, and academia, can enhance a city's effort in building smart cities and implementing smart city policies (Lam & Yang, 2020; Annan-Noonoo, 2020; Kempin Reuter, 2019; Caragliu & Del Bo, 2016).

13.3.2 Socioeconomic Dimensions

Socioeconomic factors such as population size and density, city size, income, and economic conditions can influence how cities adapt, plan, design, and develop their smart city initiatives (Hu & Zheng, 2020; Komninos et al., 2019; Camboim et al., 2019; Meijer et al., 2016). Cities with good socioeconomic factors can create significant value for citizens (Timeus et al., 2020). Komninos et al. (2019) argued that most urban socioeconomic indicators with population size are connected with agglomeration nonlinearities, making larger cities centers of innovation, wealth, and crime. Generally, large cities with higher population densities tend to demand more and better public services, compared with small towns (Hu & Zheng, 2020). Existing researchers point to the notion that cities with strong economies have access to essential resources like human and financial capital which enables them to adapt and innovate on smart city initiatives (Camboim et al., 2019; Meijer et al., 2016; De Falco, 2019). Cities with faster economic development and greater average household income also tend to attract more business or foreign direct investment and human capital (Kempin Reuter, 2019; De Falco, 2019). Human capital is important for smart city initiatives because people plan, contribute ideas, and provide feedback for smart city planning or development (Hu & Zheng, 2020). They also play the role of end users for smart city products and services. However, Corsini et al. (2016) argue that there is no correlation between economic wealth, city size, and smart city attributes when different European cities are considered at the same time. Nonetheless, making cities "smart" is becoming an emerging strategy to address challenges associated with increasing urban population growth.

13.3.3 Environmental Dimensions

Integrating environmental factors with other smart city dimensions play a crucial role in the success of smart living and quality of life. For instance, Macke et al. (2018) evaluated the perception of citizens' quality of life in a smart city and analyzed them against four main domains; environmental well-being, socio-structural relationship, material well-being, and community integration. The respondents' overall low satisfaction with the domains led to the calls for a better understanding of the planning and management of smart cities in conjunction with the QOL elements and their effects on citizens (Macke et al., 2018). Providing a green and sustainable environment is a critical success factor to improve quality of life and create a stronger community within a city. Globally, there are concerns for sustainability and how smart cities can support a more diverse, inclusive, and sustainable urban environment, including green cities, with lower carbon emissions, and less energy consumption (Komninos et al., 2019). Monstadt and Coutard (2019) assessed a collection of case studies to appraise how concepts of nexus and infrastructure integration have become guiding visions for the development of green, resilient, or smart cities. Such integration could help address environmental issues like pollution, traffic, and waste management (Jazzar, 2019; Hayat, 2016). Smart cities can deliver value to citizens in an economically, environmentally, and socially sustainable way (Timeus et al., 2020).

13.3.4 Technological Infrastructure (ICT)

The driving factor in the rapid development of smart cities has been attributed to the recent advances in technology, particularly ICT (Hu & Zheng, 2020; Butler et al., 2020; Lim et al., 2018; Shen et al., 2020; Hornillo-Mellado et al., 2020; Yang, 2019). Among the myriad of innovations in the field of ICT, many technological advances have helped shape smart city initiatives (Lea, 2017). IoT, for instance, helps predict the satellite coverage in urban areas (Hornillo-Mellado et al., 2020), enables cities to collect real-time data, delivers customized services (Lea, 2017), and optimizes sustainable energy and a greener environment (Monstadt & Coutard, 2019; Samih, 2019). AI, blockchain, cloud computing, and other related technologies play significant roles in collecting, storing, analyzing, sharing, and utilizing the huge volumes of data collected by IoT devices (Marsal-Llacuna, 2018; Allam & Dhunny, 2019; Kankanhalli et al., 2019). Although not a technology, big and open data is equally important. They leverage IoT, cloud computing, and other technological innovations to enhance smart city initiatives (Hu & Zheng, 2020; Lea, 2017). Government agencies can develop open data portals to share data with citizens and other agencies (Lea, 2017). Private businesses and other stakeholders can use data innovatively to create value and increase profitability (Hu & Zheng, 2020).

13.4 Dominant Issues in Smart Cities

Existing research about smart cities has centered on key thematic areas including smart mobility (Yu & Peng, 2020; Yang, 2019; Wang et al., 2016; Wang et al., 2017; Tironi & Valderrama, 2018; Ferreri & Sanyal, 2018; van der Graaf & Ballon, 2019; Iqbal & Khan, 2018; Vlahogianni et al., 2016; Freudendal-Pedersen et al., 2019; Yuan et al., 2020), smart energy (Jazzar, 2019; Cicea et al., 2019; Salvador et al., 2019), smart living (Macke et al., 2018; Baradaran et al., 2018; Mueller et al., 2018), smart urbanism (Lam & Yang, 2020; Nesti, 2020; Veselitskaya et al., 2019), artificial intelligence, big data, and the Internet of Things (Samih, 2019; Allam & Dhunny, 2019; Clim et al., 2020) (see Appendix I).

13.4.1 Smart Mobility

Research around smart cities has focused on automation and sustainability. Freudendal-Pedersen, Kesselring, and Servou (Freudendal-Pedersen et al., 2019) argued that discourses on automated mobility in urban spaces are in the process of creation and different stakeholders contribute to shaping the urban spaces and their infrastructures for automated driving in the future. Iqbal and Khan (Iqbal & Khan, 2018) also used smart roads in association with roadside units for data collection and data processing to develop an effective and robust approach for automatic incident detection for smart cities. The study found that the integration of multiple parameters like a lane change, speed, orientation, acceleration, and deviation factors increases the incident belief factor (the belief that an incident will occur) leading to the accuracy of incident detection.

The application of smart cities is also evidenced in the sharing or platform economy. The sharing economy has a profound impact on urban governance, mobility, policy planning, and urban environment as they disrupt traditional forms of transport, service industry, hospitality, and housing (Ferreri & Sanyal, 2018). Using Airbnb as an example, Ferreri and Sanyal (2018) looked at how sharing economy companies are involved in encouraging governments to change existing regulations, such as deregulating short-term subletting. In a related study, Yu and Peng (2020) used RideAustin to investigate the impact of the built environment on ride-sourcing demand. Findings from their study revealed a strong impact of the built environment on ride-sourcing or on-demand ride sharing and significant temporal heterogeneity.

Research under smart mobility has also looked at the smart city in the context of intelligent transportation systems and mobility in a citizen's everyday life. For instance, Wang et al. (2016) proposed a dynamic road lane management system to share appropriately the space devoted to traffic. By connecting a simulator and several 2D and 3D visualization tools, the authors were able to access the dynamic behavior of drivers, particularly their reaction related to vertical and horizontal road signs depending on the behavior of other vehicles around the driver. van der Graaf and Ballon (2019) also examined the traffic and navigation application, Waze, to explore manifestations of dynamics in mobility practices occurring between commerce and community in the public space of the city.

13.4.2 Smart Energy

Reviewed papers on smart energy focused on renewable energy as one of the key resources in ensuring sustainable smart city development (Cicea et al., 2019; Salvador et al., 2019; Mosannenzadeh et al., 2017a; Mosannenzadeh et al., 2017b). Mosannenzadeh et al. (2017b) adapted the 5W1H (why, what, who, where, when, how) model integrated with literature reviews and expert knowledge elicitation to define smart energy city development in both theoretical and practical concepts. Other studies around this issue include ways to integrate bioenergy (a form of renewable energy) into the functioning of such urban areas in Europe and a map of smart European cities making use of bioenergy to benefit the population's consumption (Cicea et al., 2019). Despite the potential of renewable energy to ensure the development of sustainable smart cities, the implementation of smart and sustainable energy projects in urban areas encounters different barriers (Mosannenzadeh et al., 2017a). Mosannenzadeh et al. (2017a) applied a case-based learning methodology to predict barriers to a given smart and sustainable energy project in Europe. The authors' results show that certain barriers with negative social or environmental impacts are more likely to occur. These include limited access to capital and cost disincentives, fragmented ownership of properties, and perception of interventions as being too expensive and complicated. Bulkeley et al. (2016) also examined how the smart city is being put to work for different ends and through different means. The authors argued that the constitution of urban areas as a site for carbon governance and a place where smart energy systems are developed is leading to novel forms of governmental intervention operating at the conjunction of the grid and the city.

Another issue closely related to smart energy is waste management. To address the issue of illegal waste dumping by waste generators, Jazzar (2019) developed an expert system to integrate scheduled waste management in Kuwait smart cities associated with the Internet of Things (IoT) technology.

13.4.3 Smart Living

Existing research about smart living has focused on the quality of life (QOL) (Macke et al., 2018; Grimaldi & Fernandez, 2017) and citizen participation in planning and developing smart cities (Baradaran et al., 2018; Mueller et al., 2018; Engelbert et al., 2019; Granier & Kudo, 2016). "Based on technology innovations, smart cities are complex ecosystems with the potential to improve urban livability, workability, and sustainability through a network of people, processes, and data"(Macke et al., 2018). In this regard, Macke et al. (2018) evaluated the perception of the quality of life in a smart city (Curitiba, Brazil, claimed to be a livable, green, and inclusive city) and analyzed the main elements of citizen's satisfaction with the city. Four main QOL domains were identified in the study: environmental well-being, material well-being, socio-structural relationships, and community integration. The authors concluded that meeting these four factors would enable a city to achieve success within the domain of smart living, thus improving citizens' QOL and creating a stronger community within the city. With a similar objective of improving citizens' QOL, Grimaldi and Fernandez (2017) analyzed the matching between a university curriculum and the innovative services of a smart city. A case study of four universities in Barcelona revealed that six emerging technology trends support the innovative services that the city is working on for the benefit of its citizens: IoT, mobile, big data, 3D printing, robotics, and renewable energy (Grimaldi & Fernandez, 2017).

Existing researchers have argued that sustainable energy supply and good infrastructure are not the only constituents of livable cities but also citizen input and feedback (Mueller et al., 2018; Engelbert et al., 2019). Engelbert et al. (2019) explored why, how, and with what effect for citizen participation smart city projects are shaped by specific visions for European cities in general and European smart cities in particular. Mueller et al. (2018) adapted a citizen design science approach for cities to integrate citizens' ideas and wishes in the urban planning process. Baradaran et al. (2018) proposed a model for evaluating and developing citizens' electronic readiness for deployment of a smart city. Granier and Kudo (2016) also analyzed citizen participation in Japanese smart communities. The results of the study indicated that very little input is expected from Japanese citizens. Instead, ICTs are used by municipalities and electric utilities to steer project participants and to change their behavior.

13.4.4 Smart Urbanism

"Smart urbanism is a loosely connected set of confluences between data, digital technologies, and urban sites and processes" (McFarlane & Söderström, 2017). It is an urban response to the explosive growth in the production (and potential) of data brought about by the permeation of digital technologies throughout the world (Kong & Woods, 2018). Smart cities are a new approach to urban development based on the extensive use of ICT and the promotion of environmental sustainability, economic development, and innovation (Nesti, 2020). Studies around this issue include reviews, interviews with experts, and insights from smart cities projects in Amsterdam, Turin, Barcelona, Lisbon, and Vienna on the drivers and barriers of smart city development and the transformational nature of smart city governance (Camboim et al., 2019; Nesti, 2020; Veselitskaya et al., 2019). Results from these studies show that a smart city is an urban innovation ecosystem where knowledge easily flows from a deliberated interaction and collaboration among different stakeholders to create wealth, supported by a flexible institutional structure, wide use of ICT, an integrated-participative governance model, a digital-green infrastructure, and functional urban design with diversified amenities and facilities. On the contrary, problems of information security and conflict of interest among stakeholders hinder smart city development.

Marsal-Llacuna (2018) showed how blockchain networks will disrupt the urban context, similar to what is happening in the financial technology (fintech) and insurance technology (insurtech) space. Using the UN's New Urban Agenda (NUA) as a case, Marsal-Llacuna (2018) showed the benefits of using blockchains in the urban field by breaking down the NUA in policies, planning, regulations, and standards. The case results confirm that blockchain will disrupt urban networks.

While public-private partnership (PPP) is considered by some researchers as viable for smart city projects, Lam and Yang (2020) call on the government to evaluate the available options using an objective approach such as multi-attribute utility analysis (MAUA). Results of their study show that not all projects are best suited to PPP and that there may be divergent views between the public and private sectors, with possibilities for a compromised decision which both sectors would accept. A smart city is a result of three interconnected processes: city development, city planning theories, and city rules and policy (Russo et al., 2016). The result of the case study indicated that a smart city seems to be the convergent point for all processes evolving in European urban areas.

13.4.5 Internet of Things (IoT) and Big Data

Existing research has shown that the use of urban big data from stakeholders and physical objects in cities is a key factor in transforming cities into smart cities (Lim et al., 2018; Abella et al., 2017; Bibri, 2018). Findings from Lim et al. (2018) study, for instance, classified the urban data use cases into four reference models (local government, companies, citizens, visitors) and identified six challenges (managing data quality; integrating different data; addressing privacy issues; understanding the needs of citizens, visitors, and employees; enhancing geographic information delivery methods; designing smart city services) in transforming data into information for smart cities.

Adapting an IoT-based futuristic scenario for optimizing the waste management processes in smart cities, Samih (2019) established a connection between IoT and the functions of smart cities. To provide information that could be useful in the IoT network planning process, Hornillo-Mellado et al. (2020) proposed an accurate and fast graphical method for predicting the satellite coverage in urban areas. Results from the study showed that the shadowed areas predicted by the method are corresponding almost perfectly with experimental data measured from a Eutelsat satellite in the urban area of Barcelona. Allam and Dhunny (2019) also centered on enhancing the integration of artificial intelligence and big data in smart cities to increase the livability of the urban fabric while boosting economic growth and opportunities. The authors reviewed the urban potential of AI and proposed a new framework binding AI technology and cities while ensuring the integration of key dimensions of culture, metabolism, and governance.

Big data has paved its way into the healthcare sector, as well. Clim et al. (2020) provided a theoretical framework for a clinical decision support system with the help of software as a medical device regime (CDS-SaMD). The software is implemented in smartphones and is helpful in cities for the diagnosis and treatment of chronic disease in an accurate and fast manner as compared to conventional diagnostic procedures. Using lung and skin cancers as case studies, Wray et al. (2018) presented smart prevention as a novel approach that uses smart city-enabled built environment monitoring to trigger local cancer prevention policies.

13.5 Future Research Direction for Smart Cities

From Table 13.2, our systemic review categorized future research direction under six main areas: stakeholder collaboration (Hu & Zheng, 2020; Timeus et al., 2020; Lam & Yang, 2020; Freudendal-Pedersen et al., 2019; Mosannenzadeh et al., 2017a; Mosannenzadeh et al., 2017b; Chatterjee et al., 2018; Angelidou, 2017), information systems (IS) policies (Manitiu & Pedrini, 2016; Lim et al., 2018), citizen engagement (Engelbert et al., 2019; Abella et al., 2017; Grossi & Pianezzi, 2017; Hatuka et al., 2018), smart healthcare (Clim et al., 2020; Wray et al., 2018), built environment (Yu & Peng, 2020; Hornillo-Mellado et al., 2020; van der Graaf & Ballon, 2019), and big data (Wilson & Chakraborty, 2019; Clim et al., 2020; Abella et al., 2017).

13.5.1 The Need for Stakeholder Collaboration

A systemic review of the literature showed several calls for stakeholder collaboration between government or public authorities, private businesses, academia, and citizens in planning and building sustainable smart cities. Hu and Zheng (2020) suggested that cities must carefully design governance mechanisms and related processes to engage key stakeholders in building and implementing smart city initiatives. Angelidou (2017) further suggested that innovative schemes of collaboration and funding with the participation of the public, private, and civic sectors are crucial to the development of smart cities. Stakeholder engagement is required in specific government and business sectors, as well. For instance, Lam and Yang (2020) mentioned that an appropriate representation of stakeholders is essential to find the optimal procurement mode. A review of big data research revealed that previous research has mainly focused on examining big data from the perspectives of the focal organization. Future research should endeavor to incorporate other stakeholders' perspectives (Wiener et al., 2020).

Mosannenzadeh et al. (2017b) suggested three future research gaps, which include an analysis of the interrelationship between stakeholders, investigating how the stakeholders shift from the institutional level to the policy level and determining how, by moving toward temporal and spatial dimensions, the objectives, solutions, and stakeholders change. The call for cities looking forward to implementing smart city initiatives to engage stakeholders has been encouraged by private businesses, as well. "The evolution of smart cities needs more than technology; it requires good relationships between key stakeholders. Government and the private sector must partner to turn their vision of connected, efficient, 24×7 citizen services into reality" (PwC, 2020).

Table 13.2 Summary of future research direction for smart cities

No.	Thematic area	Future direction	Authors
1	**Stakeholder collaboration**	Innovative schemes of collaboration and funding with the participation of the public, private, and civic sectors	Angelidou (2017)
2	**Stakeholder collaboration**	DSS can be integrated into existing well-known platforms such as the covenant of mayors, smart cities, and community stakeholder platforms or smart cities, and community information systems	Mosannenzadeh et al. (2017a)
3	**Stakeholder collaboration**	i. Analysis of interrelationship between stakeholders. ii. How do the stakeholders shift from the institutional level to the policy level? iii. How, by moving toward temporal and spatial dimensions, do the objectives, solutions, and stakeholders change?	Mosannenzadeh et al. (2017b)
4	**Stakeholder collaboration**	An appropriate representation of stakeholders is essential to find the optimal procurement mode	Lam and Yang (2020)
5	**Stakeholder collaboration**	Cities must carefully design governance mechanisms and related processes to engage key stakeholders in building and implementing smart city initiatives	Hu and Zheng (2020)
6	**Stakeholder collaboration**	Future research should explore the city model canvas (CMC) in higher-level decision-making processes that involve politicians and politically appointed executives as well as other stakeholders, such as citizen groups and private companies involved in smart city development	Timeus et al. (2020)
7	**Stakeholder collaboration**	Select respondents that make up a true representation of the whole population	Chatterjee et al. (2018)
8	**Stakeholder collaboration**	Future workshops with policymakers, citizens, and artists, which can serve as safe "imaginary spaces," where participants will be able to develop ontological expansion through reflecting on and talking about how the relations of future mobilities and the city can be repositioned, move into new directions, and be utilized to generate new and seriously smarter policies	Freudendal-Pedersen et al. (2019)
9	**IS policies**	Policy implications of smart cities in urban development	Manitiu and Pedrini (2016)
10	**IS policies**	More studies are required for policy development and ICT application toward developing smart cities with big data	Lim et al. (2018)
11	**Citizen involvement**	Role of cities in understanding counter-discourses of citizens in the development of smart city utopia	Grossi and Pianezzi (2017)
12	**Citizen involvement**	Engage with those citizen-led initiatives in the (smart) city that are not likely to fit the criteria for European funding	Engelbert et al. (2019)
13	**Citizen involvement**	Further analysis of the citizens' experiences in smart cities could be developed to provide a dashboard based on the identified indicators	Abella et al. (2017)

(continued)

Table 13.2 (continued)

No.	Thematic area	Future direction	Authors
14	**Citizen involvement**	i. How would the adoption of an urban concept influence people's lives? ii. What is the cost of urban concept adoption, and who in the city benefits from it?	Hatuka et al. (2018)
15	**Built environment**	i. Extend the understanding of smart cities at the disaggregated level to understand how the built environment affects ride-sourcing use ii. Investigate the relationships between public transit and ride-sourcing. Is ride-sourcing complementary to or a substitute for public transit?	Yu and Peng (2020)
16	**Built environment**	Systematically investigate an inclusive dynamic of the built environment and human conditioning – particularly motivated by citizen engagement, accountability, and well-being rather than understanding ownership as an exclusive proprietorship	van der Graaf and Ballon (2019)
17	**Built environment**	Future research can use the proposed approach to evaluate the performance of communication protocols for satellite-based IoT by simulations in real environments, especially in SatCom On-The-Move scenarios	Hornillo-Mellado et al. (2020)
18	**Big data**	Ethical and privacy concerns	Allam and Dhunny (2019)
19	**Big data**	Further research is needed to better understand the impact of civic technology in shaping and sustaining open data ecosystems, as well as the role it plays in planning and governing the smart city	Wilson and Chakraborty (2019)
20	**Big data**	New studies contrasting information with the real use of data can allow for improving the dimensions of MELODIA	Abella et al. (2017)
21	**Smart healthcare**	i. Focus on the potential of smart governance approaches to health problems ii. Expansion of SCC theories into a formalized theory of smart health and prevention would be beneficial in the grounding of future work in this field	Wray et al. (2018)
22	**Smart healthcare**	Future research on other robust and reliable decision-making with big data for doctors for fast diagnosis and treatment of patients	Clim et al. (2020)

13.5.2 IS Policies Governing Smart Cities

Future research can deal with issues relevant to IS policy. Researchers are encouraged to explore the policy implications of smart cities in urban development (Manitiu & Pedrini, 2016). Further studies are required for policy development and ICT application toward developing smart cities with big data (Lim et al., 2018). IS people can inform policy by considering the environment, the likely effects of the policy, and stakeholders' reactions to emerging concepts like the smart city (King & Kraemer, 2019).

13.5.3 Big Data

Through the emergence of big data from various smart city service providers, researchers have showcased numerous applications of AI. The emergence of big data has also raised several ethical and privacy concerns that require further research (Allam & Dhunny, 2019; Wiener et al., 2020). Further research is needed to better understand the impact of civic technology in shaping and sustaining open data ecosystems, as well as the role it plays in planning and governing the smart city (Wilson & Chakraborty, 2019). Big data is applicable in other sectors like healthcare. Researchers can look into other robust and reliable decision-making with big data for doctors for fast diagnosis and treatment of patients (Clim et al., 2020).

13.5.4 Citizen Involvement

Future research can examine the role of cities in understanding counter-discourses of citizens in the development of smart city utopia (Grossi & Pianezzi, 2017). Researchers can also engage with those citizen-led initiatives in the smart city that are not likely to fit the criteria for European funding (Engelbert et al., 2019). Further analysis of citizens' experiences in smart cities could be developed to provide a dashboard based on the identified indicators (Abella et al., 2017). Further studies are needed on how the adoption of an urban concept influences people's lives, the cost of urban concept adoption, and who in the city benefits from it (Hatuka et al., 2018).

13.5.5 Built Environment

Future research can systematically investigate an inclusive dynamic of the built environment and human conditioning – particularly motivated by citizen engagement, accountability, and well-being rather than understanding ownership as an exclusive proprietorship (van der Graaf & Ballon, 2019). Researchers can further extend the understanding of smart cities at the disaggregated level to understand how the built environment affects contexts like ride-sourcing use. This would explore the impacts of the built environment on the choice of ride-sourcing and the correlation and causality of ride-sourcing use associated with the built environment (which would provide the information needed for future planning) and investigate the relationships between public transit and ride-sourcing (Yu & Peng, 2020).

13.5.6 Smart Healthcare

Further research can focus on the potential of smart governance approaches to healthcare problems (Wray et al., 2018). Wray et al. (2018) further call for the expansion of smart and connected communities (SCC) theories into a formalized theory of smart health and prevention. This would be beneficial in the grounding of future work in this field. Future research on other robust and reliable decision-making for doctors for fast diagnosis and treatment of patients is also encouraged (Clim et al., 2020).

13.6 Spotlight on Africa

Findings from the literature review show a lack of research on smart cities in Africa. Only one out of the seventy papers reviewed focused on smart cities in Africa. Following African Union (2020)'s Agenda 2063 which aims to achieve "an integrated, prosperous and peaceful Africa, driven by its citizens, representing a dynamic force in the international arena," Slavova and Okwechime (2016) explored the strategies for making African cities smarter within 50 years. The authors' findings suggest infrastructure decoupling (using fewer resources effectively for the same or higher economic growth and impact (International Resource Planning, 2018)), strong leadership, and citizen participation as the key strategies for transforming African cities into smart cities. These strategies have worked in some European and Japanese cities (Engelbert et al., 2019; Granier & Kudo, 2016). Hence, African cities could explore the effectiveness of these strategies, considering all contextual circumstances to transform their cities into smart ones.

The continent is also not adequately represented on the global map when it comes to the database of smart city initiatives or implementations. For example, only Cape Town in South Africa was included in a comparative analysis of 60 municipal smart city plans drawn from countries globally (Tang et al., 2019). Such disparity needs to be restored.

Despite the lack of research on smart cities in Africa, the continent has made significant attempts at initiating smart city projects, albeit with delays and project failure. For example; Kenya's Konza Techno City, an urban initiative set to be completed in 2030, will incorporate advanced technology in telecommunications, education, and life sciences, among other innovations (Estate Cloud, 2020; Watson, 2015). Additionally, interconnectedness and embedded sensors will form the framework for the smart city once completed (Estate Cloud, 2020). Nigeria's Eko Atlantic City is set to have cutting-edge fiber-optic telecommunications, independent electricity supply, and advanced urban designs upon completion (ArcGIS, S. M, 2020).

Ghana's Hope City was planned to have Africa's tallest buildings, an ultra-modern technology park, and green space, but implementation has been stagnant since 2013 (Estate Cloud, 2020; Watson, 2015). Other smart city initiatives include Rwanda's Vision City and South Africa's Waterfall City encompassing innovation to drive digital transformation and integrated urban lifestyle (Estate Cloud, 2020; Murray, 2015; Gachuhi, 2020). While these long-term projects are yet to come to fruition, the continent has some success stories in terms of leveraging technological innovations to address some of the societal challenges facing Africa today such as inadequate waste management, poor healthcare, climate change, low-quality agriculture produce, fintech, and unreliable energy infrastructure. 3D printers have been made out of toxic electronic waste in the city of Lomé, Togo (Hostettler et al., 2018). Johannesburg has followed suit and initiated waste to energy technologies to promote a healthy and clean environment (Dlamini et al., 2019). Drones are used for emergency medicine and blood delivery in some inaccessible parts of Ghana. Satellite images are being used in Sudan to gather information about the performance of crops, and the information is shared to farmers in real-time via mobile phones (The World Bank, 2020). In the fintech space, mobile money interoperability powered by platforms such as Kenya's M-PESA, Ghana Interbank Payment and Settlement Systems (GhIPSS), and other similar platforms across Africa has promoted financial inclusion and transformed the nature of digital financial transactions (Kingiri & Fu, 2020; Agyapong, 2020; Mattern & McKay, 2018). Individuals and businesses are now able to make payments, transfer, and withdraw funds seamlessly across mobile networks and banks without physical cash. These initiatives have contributed to waste management, energy conversation, sustainable environment, and rapid urbanization through technology. These initiatives also show that Africa can and should build more sustainable smart cities to transform the continent.

13.7 Conclusion

This study is one of the first to review dominant issues and multi-dimensional concepts of smart city research. Two primary contributions are made from this study. First, it highlights the dominant issues in smart city studies and identifies the key elements or themes used in these studies. This includes categorizing smart city issues under five key elements (smart mobility, smart energy, smart living, smart urbanism, and IoT and big data) that shape sustainable smart city initiatives. Second, this review highlights the major concerns for future research. Researchers, public authorities, and private businesses looking to build smart city projects should pay attention to stakeholder collaboration, citizen involvement, the opportunities of big data, and the built environment. Policymakers should start thinking about IS policies that can govern smart city initiatives. A systemic review of the literature showed several calls for stakeholder collaboration in planning and developing sustainable smart cities. Future research can identify the various stakeholders and how they can collaborate on a given smart city project. Contextually, other future studies can also explore how developing countries can leverage the lessons from smart cities development in developed economies.

Appendices

Appendix 1: Dominant Issues in Smart City Research

Issue/elements/themes	Domains	Sub-themes	Authors
Smart mobility	Transportation and mobility	Road lane management system/traffic	Wang et al. (2016)
		Electric taxi	Wang et al. (2017)
		Self-tracking device	Tironi and Valderrama (2018)
		Sharing economy	Ferreri and Sanyal (2018)
		Ride-sourcing demand	Yu and Peng (2020)
		Navigating platform urbanism	van der Graaf and Ballon (2019)
		Automatic incident detection	Iqbal and Khan (2018)
		Real-time packing prediction	Vlahogianni et al. (2016)
		Location-based social media (LBSM) and its impact on smart city applications	Yuan et al. (2020)
		Automation and mobility	Freudendal-Pedersen et al. (2019)
		Developing a mobile mapping system for 3D geographic information systems (GIS) and smart city planning	Yang (2019)

Issue/ elements/ themes	Domains	Sub-themes	Authors
Smart energy	Sustainable energy and natural resources	Renewable energy	Mosannenzadeh et al. (2017a)
		Smart grid	Bulkeley et al. (2016)
		Natural resources and energy	Mosannenzadeh et al. (2017b)
		Technology parks (food-energy-water nexus)	Salvador et al. (2019)
		Integration of modern bioenergy	Cicea et al. (2019)
		Smart clean cities through a scheduled waste management system	Jazzar (2019)
Smart living	Quality of life (QOL) Citizen involvement	Smart utopia or neoliberal ideology/ smart reality	Anthopoulos (2017) and Grossi and Pianezzi (2017)
		Quality of life	Macke et al. (2018)
		Quality of life	Grimaldi and Fernandez (2017)
		Welfare and social inclusion	Tjønndal and Nilssen (2019)
		Citizen participation	Engelbert et al. (2019) and Granier and Kudo (2016)
		Citizen design science (citizen participation/crowdsourcing)	Mueller et al. (2018)
		Role of smart city project manager	Michelucci et al. (2016)
		Citizen readiness for the development of the smart city	Baradaran et al. (2018)
		Building inclusive, fair, and accessible cities	Kempin Reuter (2019)

Issue/ elements/ themes	Domains	Sub-themes	Authors
Smart urbanism	• City development, planning theories, and city rules • Public-private partnership (PPP) • Urban innovation ecosystem	Urban intelligence	Russo et al. (2016)
		Smart city planning	Marsal-Llacuna (2018) and De Falco (2019)
		An evolutionary perspective	Komninos et al. (2019)
		Blockchain	Marsal-Llacuna (2018)
		Drivers of smarter cities	Camboim et al. (2019)
		Smart city archetypes	Tang et al. (2019)
		Civic technologies	Wilson and Chakraborty (2019)
		Technology parks	Salvador et al. (2019)
		Wi-Fi facilities for smart city planning	Tang et al. (2019)
		Digital maps and spatial data infrastructure	Loo and Tang (2019)
		Transformational nature of smart city governance	Nesti (2020)
		Data-driven innovation and value generation for citizens and society	Lam and Yang (2020) and Abella et al. (2017)
		Status and progress of smart city development in China and the USA	Hu and Zheng (2020)
		Characteristics of smart cities	Angelidou (2017)
		Nexus and infrastructure integration as a guiding vision for smart cities	Monstadt and Coutard (2019)
		Urban experimentation and institutional arrangement	Joss et al. (2019)
		Upscaling of pilot projects	van Winden and van den Buuse (2017)
		Smart city framework	Yigitcanlar et al. (2018)
		Correlation between economic wealth, city size, and smart city attributes	Corsini et al. (2016)
		A global perspective of smart city	Hayat (2016)
		Drivers and barriers of smart city development	Veselitskaya et al. (2019)
		Smart city concept and urbanization challenges	Slavova and Okwechime (2016)
		Remote user authentication for e-governance application	Sharma and Kalra (2019)
		Comparing and contrasting resilient city, smart city, global city, creative city, sustainable city	Hatuka et al. (2018)
Sustainability	Toward sustainable smart cities	Urban smartness and sustainability	Manitiu and Pedrini (2016) and Cowley and Caprotti (2019)
		Development pattern optimization	Li et al. (2019)

Issue/ elements/ themes	Domains	Sub-themes	Authors
Gamification	Cities and the politics of gamification	Cities and the politics of gamification	Vanolo (2018)
Internet of Things (IoT), big data	• ICT adoption • Integration of big data and AI in smart cities	Development of knowledge and frameworks for data used for smart cities	Lim et al. (2018)
		IoT and its relationship with smart cities	Samih (2019)
		Satellite for IoT-different techniques for predicting the coverage of the satellite radio link in urban areas	Hornillo-Mellado et al. (2020)
		The urban potential of AI	Allam and Dhunny (2019)
		Effects of successful adoption of IT-enabled services from a user perspective	Chatterjee et al. (2018)
		Internet and space-time flexibility	Shen et al. (2020)
Health	Smart prevention	Health services in smart cities	Wray et al. (2018)
		Big data in the health sector to improve public health and fitness	Clim et al. (2020)
Global discourse network	Glocalization	Understanding smart cities as a global-local strategy	Dameri et al. (2019)
		Understanding smart cities as global discourse network	Joss et al. (2019)
Value creation/ cocreation		Role of soft assets in smart city development	Wataya and Shaw (2019)
		Delivering value to citizens in an economically, environmentally, and socially sustainable way	Timeus et al. (2020)

Appendix 2: Summary of Multi-dimensions of Smart City Research

	Multi-dimensions			
Author	Governmental	Socioeconomic	Environmental	Technological infrastructure
Wang et al. (2016)			x	
Mosannenzadeh et al. (2017a)			x	
Kempin Reuter (2019)		x		x

Author	Multi-dimensions			
	Governmental	Socioeconomic	Environmental	Technological infrastructure
Grossi and Pianezzi (2017)	x			
Macke et al. (2018)			x	
Manitiu and Pedrini (2016)		x	X	
Mosannenzadeh et al. (2017b)	x	x	x	
Lim et al. (2018)				x
Marsal-Llacuna (2018)				x
Ferreri and Sanyal (2018)		x		
Wray et al. (2018)			x	
Camboim et al. (2019)	x	x	x	x
Engelbert et al. (2019)		x		
De Falco (2019)			x	
Tang et al. (2019)		x	x	
Yu and Peng (2020)		x	x	
van der Graaf and Ballon (2019)		x		
Wilson and Chakraborty (2019)				x
Salvador et al. (2019)		x		
Dameri et al. (2019)	x	x	x	x
Wataya and Shaw (2019)	x	x		x
Tang et al. (2019)	x			x
Nesti (2020)	x			
Lam and Yang (2020)	x	x		
Shen et al. (2020)				x
Monstadt and Coutard (2019)	x		x	x
Anthopoulos (2017)		x		x
Abella et al. (2017)		x		
Joss et al. (2019)	x			
van Winden and van den Buuse (2017)	x	x	x	
Mueller et al. (2018)		x		

Author	Multi-dimensions			
	Governmental	Socioeconomic	Environmental	Technological infrastructure
Iqbal and Khan (2018)		x		
Komninos et al. (2019)	x	x	x	
Yigitcanlar et al. (2018)	x	x		x
Granier and Kudo (2016)	x	x		
Li et al. (2019)	x	x	x	x
Corsini et al. (2016)		x		
Michelucci et al. (2016)		x		
Hayat (2016)				x
Veselitskaya et al. (2019)	x	x		x
Cicea et al. (2019)		x	x	
Allam and Dhunny (2019)	x	x		x
Chatterjee et al. (2018)	x			x
Baradaran et al. (2018)		x	x	x
Jazzar (2019)			x	
Vlahogianni et al. (2016)		x		
Salvador et al. (2019)	x	X		
Loo and Tang (2019)	x	x	x	x
Hu and Zheng (2020)	x	x	x	x
Joss et al. (2019)	x			x
Timeus et al. (2020)		x	x	
De Falco (2019)		x	x	
Angelidou (2017)	x			x
Sharma and Kalra (2019)	x	x		
Hatuka et al. (2018)	x	x	x	x
Freudendal-Pedersen et al. (2019)		x	x	x
Hornillo-Mellado et al. (2020)				x
Yang (2019)				x
Cowley and Caprotti (2019)	x			

References

Abella, A., Ortiz-de-Urbina-Criado, M., & De-Pablos-Heredero, C. (2017). A model for the analysis of data-driven innovation and value generation in smart cities' ecosystems. *Cities, 64*, 47–53.

African Union. https://au.int/en/agenda2063/overview. Last accessed 2020/08/10.

Agyapong, D. (2020). Implications of digital economy for financial institutions in Ghana: An exploratory inquiry. *Transnational Corporations Review*, 1–11.

Allam, Z., & Dhunny, Z. A. (2019). On big data, artificial intelligence and smart cities. *Cities, 89*, 80–91.

Angelidou, M. (2017). The role of smart city characteristics in the plans of fifteen cities. *Journal of Urban Technology, 24*(4), 3–28.

Annan-Noonoo, P. (2020). Trends in smart cities: Implications for research and practice in developing economies. *AMCIS*.

Anthopoulos, L. (2017). Smart utopia VS smart reality: Learning by experience from 10 smart city cases. *Cities, 63*(3), 128–148.

ArcGIS, S. M. https://storymaps.arcgis.com/stories/0badb30335dd40268241729c4006571a. Last accessed 2020/14/09.

Baradaran, V., Farokhi, S., & Ahamdi, Z. (2018). A model for evaluation and development of citizens' electronic readiness for deployment of an E-city using structural equation modeling. *Journal of Global Information Management (JGIM), 26*(4), 135–157.

Bibri, S. E. (2018). The IoT for smart sustainable cities of the future: An analytical framework for sensor-based big data applications for environmental sustainability. *Sustainable Cities and Society, 38*, 230–253.

Boateng, R., Hinson, R., Heeks, R., & Molla, A. (2008). E-commerce in least developing countries: Summary evidence and implications. *Journal of African Business, 9*(2), 257–285.

Boateng, R., Acheampong, B., & Bedi, I. (2019). *Preliminary insights into dominant issues, theories and methodologies in platform interoperability research.*

Bosch. https://www.bosch.com/stories/smart-cities-of-the-future/. Last accessed 2020/05/04.

Bulkeley, H., McGuirk, P. M., & Dowling, R. (2016). Making a smart city for the smart grid? The urban material politics of actualising smart electricity networks. *Environment and Planning A: Economy and Space, 48*(9), 1709–1726.

Butler, J. S., Garg, R., & Stephens, B. (2020). Social networks, funding, and regional advantages in technology entrepreneurship: An empirical analysis. *Information Systems Research, 31*(1), 198–216.

Camboim, G. F., Zawislak, P. A., & Pufal, N. A. (2019). Driving elements to make cities smarter: Evidences from European projects. *Technological Forecasting and Social Change, 142*, 154–167.

Caragliu, A., & Del Bo, C. F. (2016). Do smart cities invest in smarter policies? Learning from the past, planning for the future. *Social Science Computer Review, 34*(6), 657–672.

Castelnovo, W., Misuraca, G., & Savoldelli, A. (2016). Smart cities governance: The need for a holistic approach to assessing urban participatory policy making. *Social Science Computer Review, 34*(6), 724–739.

Chatterjee, S., Kar, A. K., & Gupta, M. (2018). Success of IoT in smart cities of India: An empirical analysis. *Government Information Quarterly, 35*(3), 349–361.

Cicea, C., Marinescu, C., & Pintilie, N. (2019). Smart cities using smart choices for energy: Integrating modern bioenergy in consumption. *Theoretical and Empirical Researches in Urban Management, 14*(4), 22–34.

Clim, A., Zota, R., Constantinescu, R., & Ilie-Nemedi, I. (2020). Health services in smart cities: Choosing the big data mining based decision support. *International Journal of Healthcare Management, 13*(1), 79–87.

Cocchia, A. (2014). Smart and digital city: A systematic literature review. *Smart City*, 13–43.

Corsini, F., Rizzi, F., & Frey, M. (2016). Analysing smartness in European cities: A factor analysis based on resource efficiency, transportation and ICT. *International Journal of Global Environmental Issues, 15*(3), 235–254.

Cowley, R., & Caprotti, F. (2019). Smart city as anti-planning in the UK. *Environment and Planning D: Society and Space, 37*(3), 428–448.

Dameri, R. P., Benevolo, C., Veglianti, E., & Li, Y. (2019). Understanding smart cities as a glocal strategy: A comparison between Italy and China. *Technological Forecasting and Social Change, 142*, 26–41.

De Falco, S. (2019). Are smart cities global cities? *A European perspective. European Planning Studies, 27*(4), 759–783.

De Falco, S., Angelidou, M., & Addie, J.-P. D. (2019). From the "smart city" to the "smart metropolis"? Building resilience in the urban periphery. *European Urban and Regional Studies, 26*(2), 205–223.

Dlamini, S., Simatele, M. D., & Serge Kubanza, N. (2019). Municipal solid waste management in South Africa: From waste to energy recovery through waste-to-energy technologies in Johannesburg. *Local Environment, 24*(3), 249–257.

Engelbert, J., van Zoonen, L., & Hirzalla, F. (2019). Excluding citizens from the European smart city: The discourse practices of pursuing and granting smartness. *Technological Forecasting and Social Change, 142*, 347–353.

Estate Cloud. https://estatecloud.co.ke/top-5-smart-city-initiatives-in-africa/. Last accessed 2020/14/09.

Ferreri, M., & Sanyal, R. (2018). Platform economies and urban planning: Airbnb and regulated deregulation in London. *Urban Studies, 55*(15), 3353–3368.

Forbes. https://www.forbes.com/sites/jamesellsmoor/2019/05/19/smart-cities-the-future-of-urban-development/#5e283ab82f90. Last accessed 2020/04/18.

Freudendal-Pedersen, M., Kesselring, S., & Servou, E. (2019). What is smart for the future city? Mobilities and automation. *Sustainability, 11*(1), 221.

Gachuhi, L. (2020). *SME's Agribusiness Challenges & Solutions in Africa*. Exceller Books.

Granier, B., & Kudo, H. (2016). How are citizens involved in smart cities? Analysing citizen participation in Japanese "Smart Communities". *Information Polity, 21*(1), 61–76.

Grimaldi, D., & Fernandez, V. (2017). The alignment of University curricula with the building of a Smart City: A case study from Barcelona. *Technological Forecasting and Social Change, 123*, 298–306.

Grossi, G., & Pianezzi, D. (2017). Smart cities: Utopia or neoliberal ideology? *Cities, 69*, 79–85.

Guo, H., Gao, S., Li, J., & Xue, H. (2018). A conceptual framework for Smart City international standards. In *18th international conference on electronic business 2018* (pp. 1–8). International Consortium for Electronic Business.

Hasija, S. https://theconversation.com/smart-cities-can-help-us-manage-post-covid-life-but-theyll-need-trust-as-well-as-tech-138725. Last accessed 2020/06/05.

Hatuka, T., Rosen-Zvi, I., Birnhack, M., Toch, E., & Zur, H. (2018). The political premises of contemporary urban concepts: The global city, the sustainable city, the resilient city, the creative city, and the smart city. *Planning Theory & Practice, 19*(2), 160–179.

Hayat, P. (2016). Smart cities: A global perspective. *India Quarterly, 72*(2), 177–191.

Hornillo-Mellado, S., Martín-Clemente, R., & Baena-Lecuyer, V. (2020). Prediction of satellite shadowing in smart cities with application to IoT. *Sensors, 20*(2), 475.

Hostettler, S., Najih Besson, S., & Bolay, J.-C. (2018). *Technologies for Development: From innovation to social Impact*. Springer.

Hu, Q., & Zheng, Y. (2020). Smart city initiatives: A comparative study of American and Chinese cities. *Journal of Urban Affairs*, 1–22.

International Resource Planning: Introduction to Decoupling. (2018).

Iqbal, Z., & Khan, M. I. (2018). Automatic incident detection in smart city using multiple traffic flow parameters via V2X communication. *International Journal of Distributed Sensor Networks, 14*(11), 1550147718815845.

Jazzar, M. M. (2019). *Smart Clean City–Kuwait.*

Joss, S., Sengers, F., Schraven, D., Caprotti, F., & Dayot, Y. (2019). The smart city as global discourse: Storylines and critical junctures across 27 cities. *Journal of Urban Technology, 26*(1), 3–34.

Kankanhalli, A., Charalabidis, Y., & Mellouli, S. (2019). *IoT and AI for smart government: A research agenda.* Elsevier.

Kasurinen, J., & Knutas, A. (2018). Publication trends in gamification: A systematic mapping study. *Computer Science Review, 27*, 33–44.

Kempin Reuter, T. (2019). Human rights and the city: Including marginalized communities in urban development and smart cities. *Journal of Human Rights, 18*(4), 382–402.

King, J. L., & Kraemer, K. L. (2019). Policy: An information systems frontier. *Journal of the Association for Information Systems, 20*(6), 2.

Kingiri, A. N., & Fu, X. (2020). Understanding the diffusion and adoption of digital finance innovation in emerging economies: M-Pesa money mobile transfer service in Kenya. *Innovation and Development, 10*(1), 67–87.

Komninos, N., Kakderi, C., Panori, A., & Tsarchopoulos, P. (2019). Smart city planning from an evolutionary perspective. *Journal of Urban Technology, 26*(2), 3–20.

Kong, L., & Woods, O. (2018). The ideological alignment of smart urbanism in Singapore: Critical reflections on a political paradox. *Urban Studies, 55*(4), 679–701.

Kulkarni, U., & Robles-Flores, J. A. (2019). *Data analytics to improve citizen-centric Smart City services.*

Lam, P. T., & Yang, W. (2020). Factors influencing the consideration of Public-Private Partnerships (PPP) for smart city projects: Evidence from Hong Kong. *Cities, 99*, 102606.

Lea, R. J. (2017). *Smart cities: An overview of the technology trends driving smart cities.*

Li, X., Fong, P. S., Dai, S., & Li, Y. (2019). Towards sustainable smart cities: An empirical comparative assessment and development pattern optimization in China. *Journal of Cleaner Production, 215*, 730–743.

Lim, C., Kim, K.-J., & Maglio, P. P. (2018). Smart cities with big data: Reference models, challenges, and considerations. *Cities, 82*, 86–99.

Lim, Y., Edelenbos, J., & Gianoli, A. (2019). Identifying the results of smart city development: Findings from systematic literature review. *Cities, 95*, 102397.

Loo, B. P., & Tang, W. S. (2019). "Mapping" Smart Cities. *Journal of Urban Technology, 26*(2), 129–146.

Macke, J., Casagrande, R. M., Sarate, J. A. R., & Silva, K. A. (2018). Smart city and quality of life: Citizens' perception in a Brazilian case study. *Journal of Cleaner Production, 182*, 717–726.

Manitiu, D. N., & Pedrini, G. (2016). Urban smartness and sustainability in Europe. An ex ante assessment of environmental, social and cultural domains. *European Planning Studies, 24*(10), 1766–1787.

Marsal-Llacuna, M.-L. (2018). Future living framework: Is blockchain the next enabling network? *Technological Forecasting and Social Change, 128*, 226–234.

Mattern, M., & McKay, C. (2018). *Building inclusive payment ecosystems in Tanzania and Ghana.*

McFarlane, C., & Söderström, O. (2017). On alternative smart cities: From a technology-intensive to a knowledge-intensive smart urbanism. *City, 21*(3–4), 312–328.

Meijer, A. J., Gil-Garcia, J. R., & Bolívar, M. P. R. (2016). Smart city research: Contextual conditions, governance models, and public value assessment. *Social Science Computer Review, 34*(6), 647–656.

Michelucci, F. V., De Marco, A., & Tanda, A. (2016). Defining the role of the Smart-City manager: An analysis of responsibilities and skills. *Journal of Urban Technology, 23*(3), 23–42.

Monstadt, J., & Coutard, O. (2019). Cities in an era of interfacing infrastructures: Politics and spatialities of the urban nexus. *Urban Studies, 56*(11), 2191–2206.

Mosannenzadeh, F., Bisello, A., Diamantini, C., Stellin, G., & Vettorato, D. (2017a). A case-based learning methodology to predict barriers to implementation of smart and sustainable urban energy projects. *Cities, 60*, 28–36.

Mosannenzadeh, F., Bisello, A., Vaccaro, R., D'Alonzo, V., Hunter, G. W., & Vettorato, D. (2017b). Smart energy city development: A story told by urban planners. *Cities, 64*, 54–65.

Moustaka, V., Vakali, A., & Anthopoulos, L. G. (2018). A systematic review for smart city data analytics. *ACM Computing Surveys (CSUR), 51*(5), 1–41.

Mueller, J., Lu, H., Chirkin, A., Klein, B., & Schmitt, G. (2018). Citizen Design Science: A strategy for crowd-creative urban design. *Cities, 72*, 181–188.

Murray, M. J. (2015). Waterfall City (Johannesburg): Privatized urbanism in extremis. *Environment and Planning A, 47*(3), 503–520.

Nesti, G. (2020). Defining and assessing the transformational nature of smart city governance: Insights from four European cases. *International Review of Administrative Sciences, 86*(1), 20–37.

Petter, S., & McLean, E. R. (2009). A meta-analytic assessment of the DeLone and McLean IS success model: An examination of IS success at the individual level. *Information & Management, 46*(3), 159–166.

PwC. https://www.pwc.com/us/en/industries/capital-projects-infrastructure/library/future-smart-cities.html. Last accessed 2020/04/20.

Rapp, A., Hopfgartner, F., Hamari, J., Linehan, C., & Cena, F. (2019). *Strengthening gamification studies: Current trends and future opportunities of gamification research*. Elsevier.

Ruhlandt, R. W. S. (2018). The governance of smart cities: A systematic literature review. *Cities, 81*, 1–23.

Russo, F., Rindone, C., & Panuccio, P. (2016). European plans for the smart city: From theories and rules to logistics test case. *European Planning Studies, 24*(9), 1709–1726.

Salvador, D. S., Toboso-Chavero, S., Nadal, A., Gabarrell, X., Rieradevall, J., & da Silva, R. S. (2019). Potential of technology parks to implement Roof Mosaic in Brazil. *Journal of Cleaner Production, 235*, 166–177.

Samih, H. (2019). Smart cities and internet of things. *Journal of Information Technology Case and Application Research, 21*(1), 3–12.

Senyo, P. K., Addae, E., & Boateng, R. (2018). Cloud computing research: A review of research themes, frameworks, methods and future research directions. *International Journal of Information Management, 38*(1), 128–139.

Sharma, G., & Kalra, S. (2019). Advanced multi-factor user authentication scheme for E-governance applications in smart cities. *International Journal of Computers and Applications, 41*(4), 312–327.

Shen, Y., Ta, N., & Chai, Y. (2020). The Internet and the space–time flexibility of daily activities: A case study of Beijing, China. *Cities, 97*, 102493.

Slavova, M., & Okwechime, E. (2016). African smart cities strategies for agenda 2063. *Africa Journal of Management, 2*(2), 210–229.

Tang, Z., Jayakar, K., Feng, X., Zhang, H., & Peng, R. X. (2019). Identifying smart city archetypes from the bottom up: A content analysis of municipal plans. *Telecommunications Policy, 43*(10), 101834.

The World Bank. https://www.worldbank.org/en/news/speech/2017/11/30/innovation-in-africa. Last accessed 2020/11/08.

Timeus, K., Vinaixa, J., & Pardo-Bosch, F. (2020). Creating business models for smart cities: A practical framework. *Public Management Review, 22*(5), 726–745.

Tironi, M., & Valderrama, M. (2018). Unpacking a citizen self-tracking device: Smartness and idiocy in the accumulation of cycling mobility data. *Environment and Planning D: Society and Space, 36*(2), 294–312.

Tjønndal, A., & Nilssen, M. (2019). Innovative sport and leisure approaches to quality of life in the smart city. *World Leisure Journal, 61*(3), 228–240.

van der Graaf, S., & Ballon, P. (2019). Navigating platform urbanism. *Technological Forecasting and Social Change, 142*, 364–372.

van Winden, W., & van den Buuse, D. (2017). Smart city pilot projects: Exploring the dimensions and conditions of scaling up. *Journal of Urban Technology, 24*(4), 51–72.

Vanolo, A. (2018). Cities and the politics of gamification. *Cities, 74*, 320–326.
Veselitskaya, N., Karasev, O., & Beloshitskiy, A. (2019). Drivers and barriers for smart cities development. *Theoretical and Empirical Researches in Urban Management, 14*(1), 85–110.
Vlahogianni, E. I., Kepaptsoglou, K., Tsetsos, V., & Karlaftis, M. G. (2016). A real-time parking prediction system for smart cities. *Journal of Intelligent Transportation Systems, 20*(2), 192–204.
Wang, C., David, B., Chalon, R., & Yin, C. (2016). Dynamic road lane management study: A Smart City application. *Transportation Research Part E: Logistics and Transportation Review, 89*, 272–287.
Wang, Y., Ding, W., Huang, L., Wei, Z., Liu, H., & Stankovic, J. A. (2017). Toward urban electric taxi systems in smart cities: The battery swapping challenge. *IEEE Transactions on Vehicular Technology, 67*(3), 1946–1960.
Wataya, E., & Shaw, R. (2019). Measuring the value and the role of soft assets in smart city development. *Cities, 94*, 106–115.
Watson, V. (2015). The allure of 'smart city'rhetoric: India and Africa. *Dialogues in Human Geography, 5*(1), 36–39.
Webster, J., & Watson, R. T. (2002). Analyzing the past to prepare for the future: Writing a literature review. *MIS Quarterly*, xiii–xxiii.
Wiener, M., Saunders, C., & Marabelli, M. (2020). Big-data business models: A critical literature review and multiperspective research framework. *Journal of Information Technology, 35*(1), 66–91.
Wilson, B., & Chakraborty, A. (2019). Planning smart (er) cities: The promise of civic technology. *Journal of Urban Technology, 26*(4), 29–51.
Wray, A., Olstad, D. L., & Minaker, L. M. (2018). Smart prevention: A new approach to primary and secondary cancer prevention in smart and connected communities. *Cities, 79*, 53–69.
Yang, B. (2019). Developing a mobile mapping system for 3D GIS and smart city planning. *Sustainability, 11*(13), 3713.
Yigitcanlar, T., Kamruzzaman, M., Buys, L., Ioppolo, G., Sabatini-Marques, J., da Costa, E. M., & Yun, J. J. (2018). Understanding 'smart cities': Intertwining development drivers with desired outcomes in a multidimensional framework. *Cities, 81*, 145–160.
Yu, H., & Peng, Z.-R. (2020). The impacts of built environment on ridesourcing demand: A neighbourhood level analysis in Austin, Texas. *Urban Studies, 57*(1), 152–175.
Yuan, Y., Lu, Y., Chow, T. E., Ye, C., Alyaqout, A., & Liu, Y. (2020). The missing parts from social media–enabled smart cities: Who, where, when, and what? *Annals of the American Association of Geographers, 110*(2), 462–475.

Patrick Annan-Noonoo is a healthcare management expert and founder of ExpressMed Healthcare, a digital healthcare provider for the underprivileged. Patrick is constantly embarking on preventive health campaigns across Africa: notably COVID-19 prevention, HIV/AIDS sensitization in Cote D'Ivoire, malaria/cholera prevention in Nigeria, and teenage pregnancy prevention in Ghana. Patrick is a doctoral student in Information Systems with a keen interest in smart cities and innovations in healthcare. He has a publication on trends in smart cities: Implications for research and practice in developing economies. He also uses digital platforms (www.expressmedgh.com) to connect patients with healthcare providers. Over the past 5 years, he has specialized in facilitating foreign companies such as HexGn to establish and build partnerships in Ghana and Africa.

Bryan Acheampong is a Member of Parliament and the Chair of the Parliamentary Committee for Foreign Affairs, Ghana. He has served in leadership positions in business and politics over the last 20 years. His experience spans security analysis, project and team management, strategic planning, and budget management. He is also an avid entrepreneur who is currently building a hotel that is set to be one of the largest in Africa. Bryan is a doctoral researcher whose research examines mutual understanding in technology projects.

Joseph Budu is an Information Systems scholar with a keen interest in multi-sided digital platforms; information, communication, and technology for development (ICT4D); and information systems education. He has several journal publications, book chapters, and conference papers. He is a lecturer at the School of Technology, Ghana Institute of Management and Public Administration (GIMPA), and blogs about research at www.researchcoa.ch

Edward Entee is an information systems doctoral researcher. He has a Masters' Degree in Marketing and is currently pursuing a PhD Candidate in Information Systems at the University of Ghana Business School. Edward works as a consultant for leading TV and Radio stations in Ghana, in areas of sales management and programming. Edward has published four book chapters and two conference papers on the digital economy, social commerce and technology adoption. He is currently researching social commerce and value co-creation in his doctoral endeavour.

Chapter 14
Forecasting Internally Displaced People's Movements with Artificial Intelligence

Ayaka Oishi, Takeshi Teshima, Kunikazu Akao, Tsuyoshi Kano, Megumi Kiriha, Naoki Kojima, Takuya Sasaki, Kentaro Takahira, Jumpei Takami, Tomonari Takeuchi, Kenji Tajima, Chihiro Noda, Hikaru Hirose, and Shigeki Yamanaka

Abstract The rise of big data and artificial intelligence (AI) has paved the way for data-driven interventions in the field of international development. In this paper, a group of researchers (i) summarizes policies and implications of the use of advanced technology in the field and (ii) presents the result of the study they conducted which applies machine learning to forecast internally displaced people's (IDPs) movements in the Democratic Republic of the Congo. Despite methodological limitations, the results confer an exposition on how machine learning models and open-source data could enhance the predictive insights of forced displacement. Our approach could be used to predict not only IDP flows but also refugee flows, expanding the use of machine learning for social good. To counter future crises triggered by climate change and the COVID-19 pandemic, we believe our approach has a great possibility to support the effective distribution of limited funds and supplies. This study underscores the benefit of AI and highlights issues in implementations. Future research will need to widen target regions and periods as well as to include the pragmatic aspects of the implementations.

A. Oishi (✉)
Peloria Insights, Washington, D.C., USA
e-mail: ayaka.oishi@peloriainsights.com

T. Teshima
The University of Tokyo, Tokyo, Japan
e-mail: teshima@ms.k.u-tokyo.ac.jp

K. Akao
International Organization for Migration, Freetown, Sierra Leone

T. Kano
University of Michigan, Ann Arbor, MI, USA

M. Kiriha
NTT Data, Tokyo, Japan

R. Boateng et al. (eds.), *Digital Innovations, Business and Society in Africa*, Advances in Theory and Practice of Emerging Markets,
https://doi.org/10.1007/978-3-030-77987-0_14

Keywords Conflict · IDPs · Machine learning · Artificial intelligence · Democratic Republic of the Congo

14.1 Introduction

Forced displacement is a significant challenge to humanity affecting the lives of 79.5 million people worldwide (UNHCR, 2020c). The displaced are vulnerable, especially under the COVID-19 pandemic: they have limited medical access, limited income source under lockdowns, and exposure to the illicit economy. Meanwhile, the recent progress of artificial intelligence (AI) gave rise to new forms of solutions to this humanitarian challenge.

Given the recent development of technology as well as a related policy discussion, the primary objective of this study is twofold: (i) to sketch out the landscape of this novel field and to identify pitfalls based on the desktop research, especially highlighting how international organizations and governmental entities have addressed the issue of forced displacement leveraging the latest technology, and (ii) to experiment the utility of data-driven analysis on the forced displacement to better respond the pitfall we identify through the desktop research.

First, we find that international organizations such as the United Nations High Commissioner for Refugees (UNHCR), International Organization for Migration (IOM), and the World Bank have strongly promoted leveraging the novel technology for their operations. We confer the recent implications of these organizations in both strategic level and programmatic level. At the same time, it becomes clear that such implementations tend to be limited in locations, mainly in the Middle East and

N. Kojima
Link and Motivation, Tokyo, Japan

T. Sasaki · K. Tajima
Koei Research & Consulting, Tokyo, Japan

K. Takahira
Kyoto University, Kyoto, Japan

J. Takami
PASCO, Tokyo, Japan

T. Takeuchi · C. Noda
ICT for Development, Tokyo, Japan

H. Hirose
Peace Tech Foundation, Tokyo, Japan

S. Yamanaka
Actit, Tokyo, Japan

North Africa (MENA), and to involve private data due to the sensitive nature of displacement information, which we assume makes it difficult for researchers to collectively and freely produce insights for other regions than MENA.

Given this imperative, second, we examine the utility of machine learning methods with public data to predict the movement of internally displaced people (IDPs) in the less studied but critical country, the Democratic Republic of the Congo (DRC), where conflicts have continued since the 1990s. This study targets the most war-tone provinces in the eastern region, namely, Ituri, North Kivu, and South Kivu, and predicts the destination of the IDPs associated with conflict events. The dependent variable, the destination goal of IDPs, is obtained from a dataset provided by the Internal Displacement Monitoring Center (IDMC), while the main independent variable, namely, conflict events, is obtained from the Armed Conflict Location and Event Data Project (ACLED).[1]

Methodologically, we employ supervised machine learning to make predictions of IDP flows. We observe that, by incorporating more training data, the model's performance shows an acute improvement in two measures, namely, precision and recall. Although our result itself does not confer an actionable intelligence to decision-makers, it underscores the possibility to predict IDP flows associated with political violence and the importance of making more data available.

Based on these findings, we argue that the implications of data-driven approach in the international development which we find to currently be biased can be better adjusted by combining machine learning and open-source data. This study also sheds lights on the potential use case where IDP predictions rationalize the resource allocation under the current environment of pressing demand for humanitarian aid caused by the disaster, pandemic, or climate change.

Following the introduction, this paper provides the landscape of the use of advanced technology in the field of international development in Sect. 14.2 and highlights the key issues that are overlooked by previous studies in Sect. 14.3. After providing an overview of the conflict in our target country, the DRC, in Sect. 14.4, we provide detailed descriptions of methodologies and variables in Sect. 14.5. Following the empirical results presented in Sect. 14.6, this paper provides discussions and possible implications in Sects. 14.7 and 14.8 and concludes in Sect. 14.9.

[1] We also explored the potential of satellite imagery in tracking human movements due to our assumption that it may lead to additional dataset for human displacement. The current findings are still limited so that we report our attempt in the appendix.

14.2 The Landscape of the Use of Advanced Technology in International Development

The recent technological advancement of AI and big data has transformed many aspects of our lives. The field of international development is not an exception: as of 2019, 36 UN agencies have investigated and experimented how to improve their response to global challenges leveraging the new technologies (International Telecommunication Union, 2019). The trend is observed both in the high-level strategies of international actors and in the number of implications produced by academics and practitioners.

This section outlines the recent development of AI-related policies in the field of international development and confers some examples which specifically address forced displacement issues by using technology. We find that international organizations tend to have high-level strategies where they envision new intervention and evaluation mechanisms, while bilateral aid organizations tend to have limited or no such master plans.

14.2.1 Strategies

International organizations and bilateral aid organizations have made strategies on (1) supporting refugees/IDPs and (2) using data for better intervention. As a result of persecution, conflict, violence, human rights violations, or other events disturbing public order, the number of forcibly displaced people worldwide is estimated to be up to 79.5 million (UNHCR, 2020c).

In September 2016, the United Nations General Assembly decided to develop a global compact for safe, orderly, and regular migration. One year after GCM, the United Nations General Assembly affirmed the Global Compact on Refugees (IOM, 2016). These are the framework for more predictable and equitable responsibility-sharing, recognizing for governments, and international organizations. Even though these Global Compacts do not have compelling force, they still have certain impact on the international agencies as they incorporate the migration/refugee issue in their main strategies. For instance, the IDF committed 2.2 billion US dollars to refugees and host communities (World Bank, 2020).

Each multilateral organization is keen to use advanced technology as a solution. The World Bank has a new strategy for systematizing digital solutions in fragile and conflict-affected situations (World Bank, 2020). The UNHCR also plans to actively pursue innovative ways to amplify refugees' voices and take advantage of new technologies to enhance our ongoing dialogue with them and their connectivity with the global community. The IOM recently launched the Migration Data Portal as a unique access point to timely comprehensive migration statistics and reliable information about migration data globally (Message from Iraqi friends, Kodansha (2003), Tokyo Japan).

Concerning the refugee policies in bilateral aid organizations, whether they employ new technology depends on the situation that each country faces regarding asylum seekers and refugees (Czaika & Mayer, 2011). For example, Western countries tend to allocate their funds for prevention measures to the sending countries of asylum seekers rather than for IDPs to control the refugee migration to their countries, while Japan focuses on emergency funds due to less influence by asylum seekers (Czaika & Mayer, 2011).

As for the approach for data-driven interventions in bilateral aid organizations, some organizations have published digital strategies that focus not only on the benefits but also on the risks of data-driven development. While digital technology such as AI and machine learning is expected to strengthen accountability, transparency, and public engagement in humanitarian assistance (USAID, 2020; DFID, 2018), the USAID (2020) claims that international stakeholders need to discuss (1) how to protect the privacy of vulnerable populations, including IDPs and refugees, and (2) how to prevent amplifying biases that might be present in historical data when they are used for detecting patterns and making predictions.

14.2.2 Implications

Corresponding to such high-level strategies, the number of implementations of the advanced technology for international development has skyrocketed. In the refugee/IDP area, precedents of varying purposes and methodologies underscore the significance of the potential contribution enabled by technology. Table 14.1 categorizes such previous projects into five groups based on their objectives and methodologies.

Category 1: Object Detection Using Satellite Imagery

This category's objective is to visualize physical objects associated with, for instance, refugee/IDP tents and shelters or damaged sites due to natural disasters. The majority of projects in this category leverage remote sensing data and AI. Machine learning such as autoencoders is used for object detection in images, while satellite imagery is used to count various kinds of structures, for instance, tents and shelters of different materials, in refugee and IDP sites. Without automation, these tasks can be labor-intensive and time-consuming, and they may require experienced experts for adequate decision-making to respond to people's needs in crisis. Conversely, by leveraging the advanced technology, the United Nations Global Pulse and United Nations Institute for Training and Research built a deep learning model to automatically count the numbers of structures in multiple refugee camps in Africa and the Middle East (Quinn et al., 2018). A similar research was conducted by using deep learning for effective refugee tent extraction near Syria-Jordan border (Lu et al., 2020). In Bangladesh, satellite imagery and random forest algorithms are used to quantify deforestation caused by the establishment of Rohingya refugee camps (Hassan et al., 2018). There is also an activity among the

Table 14.1 Precedents using AI technologies for the refugee/IDP

#	Objective	Overview	Project example
1	Object detection using satellite imagery	Analysis of objects (tents, facilities, forests, geographic structures, etc.) in the satellite images. The main focus is on the accuracy of classification	Geographic Analysis of Refugee Camps in Africa and the Middle East by the United Nations Global Pulse and United Nations Institute for Training and Research (Quinn et al., 2018)
			Landslide Risk Analysis of Refugee Camps in Bangladesh by North South University (Ahmed et al., 2020)
			Deforestation through the establishment of refugee camps in Bangladesh by University of Florida and Virginia Tech (Hassan et al., 2018)
2	Visualization of migration routes chosen by refugees/IDPs	Visualization of the routes people use for traveling from one place to another, etc. Use Twitter, mobile usage data, and a variety of other data	Stop Corona Virus in the DRC by the government, GSMA, and other partners (GSMA, 2020)
			Distribution of city residents and travelers of Twitter data in the world by Mapbox (Migration Data Portal, 2020)
			Immigration in Facebook Data in the world by Facebook (Facebook, 2013)
			Trace Together in Singapore by the Government (Government of Singapore, 2020)
3	Prediction of the destinations and forecasts of trends in displacement of refugees/IDPs	Find patterns in the movement of people and their lives at the destination, and based on this, predict what kind of life can be lived under what conditions and where to move to for an ideal life, etc.	GeoMatch by Immigration Policy Lab (Immigration Policy Lab, 2020), Annie MOORE (Matching Outcome Optimization for Refugee Empowerment) used by HIAS in the USA and other agencies in the UK and Sweden (Teytelboym, 2020)
			Jetson in Somalia by the UNHCR Innovation Service (UNHCR Innovation Service, 2019; Parater, 2020)

(continued)

Table 14.1 (continued)

#	Objective	Overview	Project example
4	Sentiment analysis of both refugees/ IDPs and host communities	Analysis of the psychological conditions of host communities, refugees and migrants, refugee children, etc. and the correlation between behavior and psychological factors	Analysis of Psychological Factors in the Decision to Return Refugees in Syria by the World Bank (The World Bank, 2019)
			Correlation analysis of children's pictures and psychological trauma of Syrian refugees in Iraq, Jordan, and Lebanon (Baird et al., 2020)
			Sentiment analysis of host communities (in Europe) toward refugees and refugee reception in Greece by the UN Global Pulse and UNHCR (UN Global Pulse, 2017)
5	Improvement of work efficiency	Use of AI to improve business efficiency, e.g., to assist prioritization of tasks	Improving operational efficiency with AI for asylum procedures in refugee support groups in the USA by Microsoft, ASAP, and KIND (Spelhaug, 2019)

global data science community named "The Crowd AI mapping challenge" that aimed at detecting and mapping buildings using satellite imagery for humanitarian response (Crowd AI, 2018).

Category 2: Visualization of Migration Routes Chosen by Refugees/IDPs
The objective is to visualize human movement. Projects in this category often employ mobile data and SNS usage as well as AI. In fact, there are growing applications of mobile usage data for international development because tracking human movements is critical in the recent COVID-19 crisis. In the DRC where the national census has not been conducted since 1984, the government, GSMA, several mobile companies, and other partners implemented a project to analyze mobile usage data and visualize the population mobility trends, which also can be used for projects to prevent an epidemic (GSMA, 2020). Similarly, SNS data is also seen to be highly promising in the field of international development. Facebook conducted a project to map internal and international migrations using aggregated and anonymized Facebook profiles on departure and destination locations (Facebook, 2013). Mapbox, a company providing mapping platform services, supported a project to visualize human mobility within several major cities by using Twitter data and by updating the maps automatically using AI (Migration Data Portal, 2020).

Category 3: Prediction of the Destinations and Forecasts of Trends in Displacement of Refugees/IDPs
The main objective of this category is to predict forced displacement and to forecast future trends in human mobility. Some projects in this category also aim to identify host communities that best fit the refugees. Data used in this type of analysis varies from population data, local market data, climate indicators, to conflict dataset. For

example, in an attempt to predict displacements in Somalia, the UNHCR Innovation Service built a tool called Jetson, which is described as "a machine-learning based application [that] measures multiple variables to see how changes over time that affect movement of UNHCR's persons of concern, particularly refugees and internally displaced people" (UNHCR Innovation Service, 2019; Parater, 2020). Also, HIAS, a refugee resettlement agency of the USA, created a software called Annie™ MOORE. It uses "advanced machine learning and state-of-the-art integer optimization methods" to support the agencies that work on the appropriate placement of refugees to raise the chances for their employment and to ensure their access to services to meet their needs (Teytelboym, 2020).

Category 4: Sentiment Analysis of Both Refugees/IDPs and Host Communities
This category includes projects that analyze the human sentiment of both refugees/IDPs and people in the host communities and those that serve to improve the quality of lives of the displaced population after settlement. They obtain data from multiple sources, such as online media and children's paintings. For example, one research reviewed refugee children's drawings and metadata to understand the correlation between their psychological well-being and the exposure to violence experienced during displacement. Also, another study analyzed Twitter data to see the interactions among refugees as well as to understand the xenophobia sentiment in host communities toward displaced populations. There is also a study that uses survey data collected by humanitarian agencies such as the UNHCR and analyzes them by developing models with machine learning techniques.

Category 5: Improvement of Work Efficiency
This category is quite different from the others in terms of the objective and the use of AI. While others track movements and lives of refugees/IDPs to help them, this category focuses on helping an operation process in the organizations that support asylum seekers. In a collaboration between Microsoft and two NPOs called Asylum Seeker Advocacy Program (ASAP) and KIND, they took advantage of Microsoft's AI tools, such as speech-to-text artificial intelligence and an Azure-based database, to improve their work efficiency. It helped the staff members of ASAP to "efficiently track changing court dates and prioritize cases most in need of emergency legal services" in delivering legal assistance service to asylum seekers (Spelhaug, 2019). This is a unique and great example of multi-sector collaboration, where various parties bring their knowledge and technologies together to achieve a common goal.

14.3 Issues of Past Studies

Despite the enormous preceding contributions to the realm of international development, the past studies remain to have key issues. First, most of the implementations are limited to specific areas such as MENA or some host countries such as the

USA. The projects mentioned in Sect. 14.2 were largely conducted in Yemen, Somalia, Iraq, or Syria, whereas only a few examples target other countries such as Bangladesh or Nigeria. This bias makes sense as countries in MENA suffer refugee and IDP issues due to their unstable political dynamics. However, it does not explain why these cases overlook other critical regions such as sub-Saharan Africa or Latin America that also produce high numbers of forced displacements. For example, the number of forcibly displaced people in the DRC is the second highest in the world (UNHCR, 2020a). This selection bias may be partly because their ongoing conflicts make it hard to get quality data of displacement flow. Moreover, the forested geographical condition of these regions might limit the usability of satellite imagery. However, we argue that those less-focused countries are the ones that need to be better served by advanced technologies. Their long-lasting humanitarian crises not only cost millions of lives, but it also destabilizes the whole region.

Second, these precedents often rely on closed data that is not publicly available. For instance, Project Jetson led by the UNHCR made a strategic partnership with other institutes such as the World Meteorological Organization, the Met Office in the UK, academia, and other UN institutions to access proprietary data (UNHCR Innovation Service, 2019). In another case, a group of data scientists at Omdena leveraged satellite imagery and granular displacement data provided by the UNHCR to measure and predict displacement mobility in Somalia. Again, this data was not publicly available. The dependence on closed data serves its purpose to secure privacy and to ensure ethical aspects of the project deliverables. Yet, it ironically inhibits researchers to conduct similar studies and build collective knowledge in the field.

14.4 Part II

Acknowledging the issues raised by the precedents in part I, this part of the study conducts an empirical analysis by targeting a less-studied country and only using open-source data and investigates the utility of machine learning methods on the topic of forced displacement. This study choses the DRC as the main target country given the high number of forced displacement and humanitarian crisis of IDPs.

14.4.1 IDP Crisis in the DRC

The number of forcibly displaced persons in the DRC is the second highest in the world (UNHCR, 2020a). Most of these displacements are due to the long-lasting conflicts in the eastern region, notably North Kivu, South Kivu, and Ituri provinces. This section confers the overview of conflicts in the country and the key drivers of forced displacement.

14.4.2 Human Rights Violation in Three Provinces

The conflicts in the eastern region, North Kivu, South Kivu, and Ituri, date back to 1993, when the DRC was the Republic of Zaire. Various human rights violations have occurred in the eastern region since 1993, caused by three major factors, the failure of the democratization process in the Republic of Zaire, the influence of Rwanda genocide, and the Second Congo War (OCHA, 2010), and the conflict is still continued. In fact, the OCHA/UNJHRO (2020) reported that the cases of human rights violations from January to June 2020 in these three provinces were 1864 cases in North Kivu, 680 in Ituri, and 475 in South Kivu, marking the highest in the country. In addition, more than 1300 people (655 victims in Ituri, 617 victims in North Kivu, and 79 victims in South Kivu) were killed by armed perpetrators during the same period. The UN Security Council (2019) also condemns other types of human rights violations other than killing such as the recruitment and the use of child soldiers in armed groups, conflict-related sexual violence, and attacks against civilians.

14.4.3 Armed Groups and Mines in Three Provinces

A recent study estimated that approximately 120 armed groups operate in North and South Kivu provinces and that most of them are small-sized and primarily ethnocentric (Stearns & Voge, 2017). It has been reported that 57% of the human rights violations are committed by such non-state armed groups, e.g., Djugu-based armed assailants, FDLR, Nyatura, or Mayi-Mayi, while the other 43% are by state authorities including the Armed Forces of the Congo (FARDC) and Police Nationale Congolaise (PNC) (OCHA & UNJHRO, 2020). This dual nature of perpetrators, namely, the government and the non-government agents, is one of the unique features of conflicts in the DRC. This paper analyzes the political violences by both types. In addition, since the armed groups are mostly formed by ethnic or tribal identity, we take ethnic distribution into consideration. Another feature of this conflict is the deep relations to conflict minerals: tin, tantalum, tungsten, and gold (3TG). Surprisingly, 35.7% of total gold mines in the eastern region, 15.3% of tin, 11.3% of tantalum, and 9.5% of tungsten are estimated to be associated with either the DRC army or non-state armed groups (Hanai, 2019). Their illegal mining activities are a large part of their financial resources, while such activities themselves accelerate conflicts. Therefore, our analysis includes the locations of the mining sites, assuming that they influence refugee and IDP movements.

14.4.4 Overview of Displaced Persons: Refugees and IDPs

The displacement situation in the DRC, with more than 630,500 Congolese refugees and 4.49 million IDPs, is one of the most complex, challenging, prolonged, and forgotten crises in the world (UNHCR, 2018a). The number of IDPs has doubled since 2015, and approximately 428,000 persons have been displaced in the 3 months between October and December 2017 alone. In 2017, 120,000 Congolese fled to neighboring countries as refugees, namely, Uganda, Angola, Zambia, the United Republic of Tanzania, Burundi, the Republic of Congo, and Rwanda, joining the 510,000 already in exile. In addition, several thousand have also fled to southern Africa and to other countries such as the Central African Republic, Chad, Kenya, and South Sudan and even to the outside of Africa (UNHCR, 2018a).

14.4.5 IDP Situation in Three Provinces

Numerous armed groups continue to fight the FARDC and the United Nations Stabilization Mission (MONUSCO), causing significant harm to civilians. Intense fights in the Beni, Masisi, Rutshuru, and Lubero areas of North Kivu led to a large-scale displacement of people who escaped to neighboring provinces to become IDPs. In South Kivu, fighting in the Fizi and the Uvira areas led to the displacement of 50,000 people in 3 months in 2019. In addition, conflicts between the Lendu and Hema communities in Ituri province caused a mass displacement in early 2018 and June 2019, and Lendu militias attacked the national army and the civilians (UNHCR, 2019). As a result of these fightings, overall, 4.6 million IDPs have evacuated within the three provinces: 1.95 million IDPs in North Kivu, 0.98 million IDPs in South Kivu, and 1.67 million IDPs in Ituri (UNHCR, 2020b). In spite of a large population of IDPs, 93% of them are accommodated by host families and communities. Only 5% of the IDPs in North Kivu live in IDP sites and 7% in Ituri. There are no official IDP sites in South Kivu but spontaneous sites where 4% of IDPs live exist (UNHCR, 2019). This divergence of IDP locations renders most IDPs invisible to aid providers and makes it hard to deliver the support. The living condition of IDPs is severe: 34% of Ituri's population depends on some kind of humanitarian aid (Norwegian Refugee Council, 2020). Schools and hospitals are often attacked by armed groups, causing instability in the host communities.

14.5 Methodology

To explore further possibilities of data analysis for conflict resolution, we consider predicting the destinations of IDP movements associated with conflict events and human rights violations.

14.5.1 Data Sources

Here, we describe the data sources we employed for generating the predicted/predictor variables of our experiment. See Sect. 14.6.2 for the list of generated variables and how they were obtained.

Internal Displacement Updates (IDU): this dataset was provided by the IDMC via private communication. The IDU data is a collection of IDP movement information curated by the IDMC as a secondary data source collected from multiple primary sources, namely, the Office for the Coordination of Humanitarian Affairs (OCHA), United Nations High Commissioner for Refugees (UNHCR), IOM Displacement Tracking Matrix (IOM DTM), Intersos, European Civil Protection and Humanitarian Aid Operations (ECHO), and Radio Okapi. The IDU data contains the start date, the end date, and the destination of each reported IDP movement, along with other information. We first filtered out the records whose destination information was missing, and then we aligned the granularity of the destination to the same administrative level, namely, territory, for all the records. We treated the destination as the predicted variable. Since some records had few but multiple destinations, the predicted variable is essentially a list of destinations instead of a single destination. The number of destination territories that appeared in IDU data was 16. The preprocessed data contained records from Nov. 15, 2018, to Sept. 07, 2020.

Armed Conflict Location & Event Data (ACLED): this dataset was collected from the ACLED project website (Raleigh et al., 2010). It is a collection of the dates, actors, locations, fatalities, and types of political violence reported since 1997. ACLED is one of the most commonly used datasets in the peace and conflict study. While it has been pointed out to have a methodological limitation causing possible reporting bias and uneven quality in the dataset (Eck, 2012), this study relies on ACLED as it provides political events recorded at an ideal granularity. Each event has a pair of longitude and latitude, which was later used for calculating auxiliary input features for the predictors such as the routing distance from the conflict location to the destination candidates.

OpenStreetMap (OSM) is a collaborative project to create a free editable map of the world (OpenStreetMap Contributors, 2017). We use the data from OSM for reverse geocoding (i.e., looking up addresses by their global coordinates) via Nominatim (2012/2020), an open-source search engine for OSM data.

Open Source Routing Machine (OSRM) is an open-source router designed for use with the OSM data (Open Source Routing Machine, 2011/2020). It allows us to compute the walking distance and the walking duration from one location to another, specified by their longitudes and latitudes.

Territory Ethnic Composition (TEC) data: this dataset shows the different ethnic groups of the DRC by territory, published by the American Red Cross based on the work of Abbe Leon de Saint Moulin (American Red Cross, 2019/2020). The ethnic composition of each territory is referred to as the destination characteristics.

Subnational Population Statistics (SPS): this dataset shows subnational population in the DRC by subnational level, country, province, and territory in 2019 and 2020, contributed by the UNOCHA (OCHA DR Congo, 2019).

Mining Site Information (MSI): this dataset shows the mining site locations and the number of workers at the time recorded from Jan. 02, 2009, to July 19, 2019 (International Peace Information Service, 2019). We only use the latest information when multiple records exist for the same mining site.

14.5.2 List of Variables and Feature Engineering

We considered each IDU record as a data point, and we attached some additional data to each record as the predictor variables.

Predicted Variable We regarded the destination column of the IDU data to be the predicted variable. The variable is essentially a list of the territory names which are the reported destinations of the IDPs. Technically, the list of the territory names was converted to a fixed-length array of 0 or 1, indicating whether each candidate territory was a destination (1 if selected as a destination, 0 otherwise). The list of all candidate territories was determined by taking the unique list of territories that appeared in the IDU dataset as the destination.

Destination-Conflict Cross Features To create the input variables reflecting the information of the conflicts that occurred prior to each IDU record, we first associated the recent conflict records of ACLED, namely, those which reportedly occurred within 2 weeks before the reported starting date of the IDP movement. The number of conflict records associated with each IDU record ranged from 33 to 113, excluding those IDU records which were not assigned any conflict records. From the list of recent conflicts associated with each IDU record, we created the following predictor variables.

Routing distance: obtained using IDU, ACLED, and OSRM. For each recent conflict record associated with the IDU record, we obtained the representative coordinate of the conflict from ACLED, and we calculated the walking distance and duration from the coordinate to the representative coordinates of the destination candidate territories. We use the minimum walking distance and the minimum walking duration as predictive features out of those for the associated conflicts.

Ethnic composition dissimilarity: obtained by combining TEC and OSM. We first mapped the conflict coordinates to the corresponding territories by reverse geocoding using OSM. Then, the territories were converted to a list of its major ethnic groups by looking up in the TEC. In the end, to each pair of conflict record and destination candidate, we assigned 0 or 1 indicating the dissimilarity in the ethnic composition of the two territories (0 if the two territories share at least one ethnic group is common in their ethnic compositions and 1 if none is common. If

TEC has a missing record for the territory, we define this dissimilarity to be 1). We take the sum of the binary variable over all the associated conflict events to form the predictive feature.

Destination-Specific Features

Territorial population: obtained from SPS. We use the population at territorial level in 2019 as the destination feature, assuming that the population partly explains the cultural or economical importance of that area.

Wikipedia page importance: obtained from OSM via Nominatim. To each destination candidate territory, we assigned an importance score (in the range [0, 1]) calculated by Nominatim. The score is based on the page-link information on Wikipedia (Wikipedia-Wikidata, 2020/2020).

Mining site information: obtained by MSI via simple aggregation. As described in Sect. 14.4, the mining industry has been a key conflict driver in the eastern DRC. It is a general understanding in the field of civil war that mining concessions foster political violence in the region, hence resulting in the increase of IDPs (Sekeris et al., 2013). Based on this assumption, we count the mining sites and sum up the workers by each territory and assign these aggregation values to the corresponding territory as their features.

14.5.3 Integrated Dataset

We constructed our dataset by collecting the variables explained in Sect. 14.4.2. Among all IDU records, we disregarded the ones whose associated set of recent conflicts was empty. The resulting dataset consisted of 52 records of 8 variables (7 predictive features and 1 predicted variable):

1. *Walking distance* from recent conflict locations (aggregated over the recent conflict events by taking the minimum)
2. *Walking duration* from recent conflict locations (aggregated in the same way as the walking distance)
3. *Ethnic composition dissimilarity* (aggregated over the recent conflict events by taking the summation)
4. *Territorial population*
5. *Wikipedia page importance*
6. *Total number of mining sites*
7. *Total number of workers in the mining sites*
8. (Predicted variable) binary vector indicating whether each of the 16 candidates, namely, Aru, Beni, Bunia, Djugu, Irumu, Kabalo, Kalehe, Kisangani, Lubero, Mahagi, Masisi, Moba, Mwenga, Nyunzu, Rutshuru, and Walikale, was a destination. Each variable except the predicted variable and the ethnic composition dissimilarity was normalized by subtracting the average and dividing the standard deviation. The ethnic composition dissimilarity was normalized by dividing the value of one of the randomly selected destinations, namely, Nyunzu.

14.5.4 *Problem Setup and Evaluation Metric*

Here, we describe how we formulated the destination prediction as a machine learning problem setup.

The Multi-label Classification Problem Technically, we formulated the problem as multi-label classification (Tsoumakas et al., 2010). It is a variant of the classification problem where multiple labels are assigned to each instance. More concretely, we formulated the problem as predicting a binary vector indicating whether each of the destination candidates was selected as destination ("0" indicating "not selected" and "1" indicating "selected") for each record of IDU.

Evaluation Metric To evaluate the performance of the algorithm, we combine two evaluation metrics called precision and recall, devised for evaluating a rare phenomenon in the fields such as weather forecasting and information retrieval. We use these metrics since our multi-label classification is imbalanced, i.e., for each record of IDU, only a few of the destination candidates have the truth value "1." In such a case, it is easy to achieve more than 80% accuracy by predicting "0" for all destination candidates, which is unreasonable because this trivial predictor is not informative. On the other hand, the precision and the recall of this trivial predictor would be both 0, appropriately evaluating the uninformative predictions.

Precision and recall are both evaluation metrics of prediction results in binary classification. Precision is defined as the ratio of the correctly predicted instances among those for which the prediction was "1" (or positive), and recall is defined as the ratio of the positively predicted instances (i.e., those for which the prediction was "1") among those whose true label is "1." Together, these two metrics evaluate the characteristics of our algorithm: how it is accurate while maintaining sensitivity. We provide additional figures showing the results in terms of a few other performance metrics in Appendix E.

14.5.5 *Model and Training*

Model selection and corresponding parameter estimations are crucial for predicting the movement flow. Descent parameters can be obtained by optimizing the parameters to fit the model to explain the obtained data. We refer to this optimizing process as training.

Model We adopted a machine learning-based approach because of its appropriate characteristics to the refugee movement forecast. Compared to agent-based models like the ones proposed by Suleimenova et al. (2017), ML-based approaches are resilient with the sudden changes in a data structure (e.g., some features which were available in the modeling process cannot be observed when the model is in operation). This characteristic is essential in that the organizations generally need rapid predictions of refugee movements when conflicts occur. Besides, these characteristics make the prediction model more flexible to incorporate an alternative dataset which can be a good indicator for the refugee movement but whose relationship with the people movement is not always clear (e.g., Twitter logs at the time of conflicts).

To produce a prediction as precise as possible while maintaining the above characteristics, we employ eXtreme Gradient Boosting, or XGB (Chen & Guestrin, 2016), which is a commonly used machine learning algorithm based on gradient boosted trees. XGB is an optimized distributed gradient boosting library designed to be highly efficient, flexible, and portable. We chose this supervised learning model based on the following two reasons. First, it is empirically shown that XGB tends to produce high performance with structured tabular data like our dataset (Chen & Guestrin, 2016). Second, it is relatively easier to interpret the result compared to other nonlinear techniques like deep neural networks. The easiness of interpolation is often essential in the context where the model results lead to political decisions. To predict the whole destination choice of IDPs (expressed by a binary vector), we construct an XGB model for each territory to learn the probability of which each territory is chosen as a destination and combine their predictions into a binary vector expressing the whole destination selection.

Training and Experiment Procedure To train or find decent parameters, we split our dataset into test dataset and training dataset and feed only the training dataset into our model. We first randomly selected 30% of the 52 records and held it out as the test data. Out of the remaining 70%, in order to see the performance for different training data sizes, we randomly selected a varied number of data to use for training on the way how the training data size increased incrementally. The loss function of the model is logistic loss which is composed from the summation from all training data samples. Our model learns the parameters which minimize this objective function. We use the default hyperparameters specified in the XGBoost GitHub repository (XGBoost, 2014/2020), namely, the max depth of the tree is 6, the learning rate is 0.3, and the minimum child weight is 1. We repeated the initial procedure of test split 10 times to incorporate different train-test splits. After each test split, we varied the training data size in {5, …, 36} and randomly selected the specified number of data to train on.

14.6 Empirical Results

14.6.1 Performance Improvement for a Varied Number of Training Data

Figure 14.1 shows the performance improvement of the trained predictor trained on varied train data sizes. In both precision and recall, we can see that the performance improves in both metrics as we use more training data. The highest scores achieved at the training data size 30 are 0.175 for the precision and 0.186 for the recall.

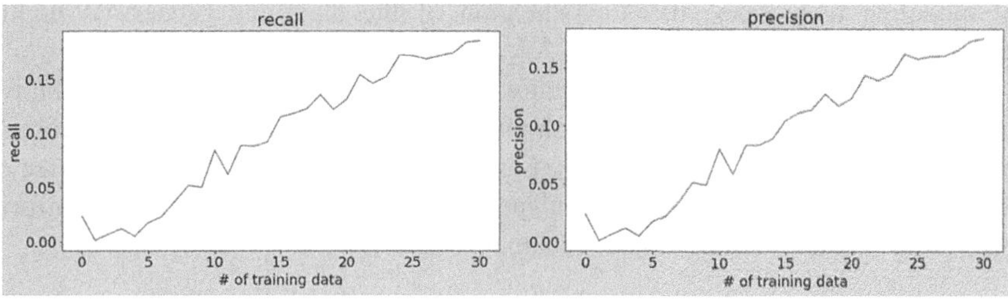

Fig. 14.1 Improvement of performance metrics (precision and recall; the higher the better) for varied sizes of training data

14.6.2 Implications

The values of the highest scores indicate that, with the current availability of data, we can build an alert system that can be trusted approximately only once in six alerts and misses 80% of the cases that should be alerted. Even though this result is superior to a random classifier's theoretical results (F1 scores of our model and a random classifier are 0.18 and 0.12 each), these performances are certainly unsatisfactory for actual deployment of the system to the real world. Nevertheless, the parallel upward trend in the evaluation metrics is clear, meaning that we can anticipate building a predictor that achieves high sensitivity (recall) and precision together by collecting more data.

14.7 Limitation and Caveat

While the results confer a robust exposition on how machine learning models and open-source data could enhance the predictive insights of forced displacement, it should be underscored that there are methodological challenges in our approach. First, it is worth noting that the data quality of displacement data should be improved in many ways. This study relies on the IDMC dataset to measure the flow of IDP in the DRC, as it was the most holistic and granular data source the research needed. Yet, the data the IDMC provides is secondary information, which is the collection of primary information provided by other organizations. This implies that the quality and methods to datafy IDP flow depend on the various primary providers and the numbers could be inconsistent based on who and how to count them. Although the IDMC does provide robust quality assurance, the possible misrepresentation of IDP data cannot be deniable. Furthermore, even with first-hand sources, measuring the number of moving persons in the midst of conflicts is fundamentally challenging, and there is no single way to be a hundred percent accurate on counting. This reminds researchers that the findings of this type of study, which heavily rely on data, are insights reflecting a counted data, and not necessarily the representation of the real phenomena on the ground. Together with the methodological advancement of modeling techniques, the sophistication of the datafying process is highly demanded.

Secondly, although the study indicates the significant improvement in predictive performance, it does not confer a high predictive accuracy to the extent where our models can be applied to real decision-making situations. With the greater size of data, future studies shall validate our methodological approach and could inform practitioners and decision-makers in actual circumstances.

14.8 Policy Implications

This paper presents great extensibility for implications that can serve practitioners at international organizations or governments to better respond and manage humanitarian challenges that IDPs face. Moreover, our approach could be used to predict not only IDP flows but also refugee flows, expanding the use of machine learning for social good. In fact, the UNHCR points out that its ineffective protection monitoring mechanism currently causes delay or a failure of service delivery to forcibly displaced persons and that it could be mitigated by building and leveraging an early warning system (UNHCR, 2018b). This shows the high demand of predictive insights. The long-term predictions may also rationalize the resource allocation that host countries require. Although it was not in the scope of our research, predicting the numbers of IDPs or refugees may provide a rationale for donors and host communities to determine how much resources, e.g., financial, material, and human resources, are required. To counter future crises triggered by climate change and the COVID-19 pandemic, we believe our approach has a great possibility to support the effective distribution of limited funds and supplies.

14.9 Conclusion

In the first part, we identified the previous applications of advanced technologies to the topic of forced displacement and pointed out the biased case selection issue as well as the potential of open-source data. Given this limitation of current implications, in the second part, we chose one of the less studied area, the DRC, and demonstrated that predictive performances improve as the number of training data increases using only open-source data and XGB model. The result shows the large potential of advanced technologies and open data in this field. Similar to most of the precedents, this research was conducted as an experimental project without an intention to integrate the results into real operations. Building off of our findings, the future research will need to widen target regions and periods as well as to include the pragmatic aspects of the implementations.

Acknowledgement The authors wish to extend their special thanks to Arata Otake, who provided enormous support for this study. Map data copyrighted OpenStreetMap contributors and available from https://www.openstreetmap.org.

Appendix

Introduction

The correlation between refugee migration and the environment change has gotten attention. This is because deforestation and land development are frequently seen in countries where refugees or IDPs arrive from neighboring countries due to conflicts (Van der Geest et al., 2010). The environmental causes of migration have been studied separately from its environmental impacts. This appendix shows the dynamics of migration and vegetation in the DRC and evaluates the relationship between three population-classified migrations and the environment change. We examine the utility of satellite imagery in measuring human movements from provinces into the destination of IDPs associated with political violence. As for the environmental impacts of migration, we look at three destination regions: Kisangani, Kitchanga, and Bukombo. Datasets of movements are utilized to calculate in-migration flows in this appendix and correlate with vegetation dynamics obtained from a remote sensing dataset. Please note that the first paragraph of a section or subsection is not indented. The first paragraphs that follows a table, figure, equation, etc. does not have an indent, either.

Materials and Methods

To assess the relationship between human migration and vegetation dynamics, we extract figures from datasets by the Internal Displacement Monitoring Center (IDMC) data and remote sensing data from Google Earth Engine. Migration data are utilized to determine in-migration at Kisangani, Bukombo, and Kitchanga. Remote sensing data are applied to calculate the trends in green and water content of vegetation change in time-series. The datasets and methods of extraction are described in more detail below.

Migration Data

The dependent variable, the destination of IDPs, is identified by leveraging the dataset provided by the IDMC. In Tshopo Province, including Kisangani, inter-community tensions produced the displacement of more than 34,000 people in April 2020. In addition, more than 6000 people have fled toward Bukombo town, in

Table 14.2 Summary of target migration data

Destination	Start date	End date	Qualifier	Figure
Kisangani	2020-04-01	2020-04-30	More than	34,000
Bukombo	2020-08-24	2020-09-07	More than	6000
Kitchanga	2019-01-07	2019-01-24	Approximately	1000

Adapted from the IDMC (2020)

Rutshuru territory, North Kivu, fleeing clashes between armed groups. Furthermore, about 1000 people fled clashes between government forces and armed groups occurring near villages west of Kitchanga, in Masisi territory, North Kivu, moving temporarily to stay in Kitchanga town. Table 14.2 shows migration data from the IDMC for each destination.

Remote Sensing Data and Indices

In this analysis we use two indices: normalized difference vegetation index (NDVI) and normalized difference water index (NDWI). NDVI is designed to understand the status of vegetation using remotely sensed data applied to an easy formula. It represents the quantity and activity level of vegetation. Vegetation is usually seen in green. This is because of the characteristics of light, as shown on the right figure, that vegetation especially reflects green light well and does not reflect red light so much among the lights from the sun. Therefore, a lot of green light can be reached to the eyes of humankind, which consequently makes us see the vegetation green. Besides the green light, vegetation has a characteristic to show a high reflectance on part of the near infrared of the band (NIR). Vegetation index is calculated making the best use of these characteristics (Geospatial Information Authority of Japan, 2020). NDWI is an indicator of the water area on the ground surface and the amount of water contained in vegetation. It is known that the reflection of light by water or snow is the largest in the visible light band and the smallest in short-wavelength infrared radiation (SWIR). This is caused by the absorption of SWIR by water, and NDWI takes advantage of these properties.

Calculation of vegetation and water index of each data observed is as follows.

1. **Calculation of NDVI**

$$NDVI = \frac{NIR - Red}{NIR + Red}$$

2. **Calculation of NDWI**

$$NDWI = \frac{Red - SWIR}{Red + SWIR}$$

Red: Visible red channel
NIR: Near infrared channel
SWIR: Shortwave infrared channel

To extract vegetation and water content indices, we use Google Earth Engine to compute a time-series of both values over three regions between Jan. 2019 and Sept.

2020. Google Earth Engine includes various kinds of satellite dataset and we use Landsat-8, Sentinel-2, and MODIS Aqua data for this analysis to create time-series graphs. Detailed information about satellite's products and quality assurance bands can also be obtained here:

Landsat8: USGS Landsat 8 Surface Reflectance Tier 1: https://developers.google.com/earth-engine/datasets/catalog/LANDSAT_LC08_C01_T1_SR

Sentinel-2: Sentinel-2 MSI: MultiSpectral Instrument, Level-2A: https://developers.google.com/earth-engine/datasets/catalog/COPERNICUS_S2_SR

MODIS Aqua Daily NDVI: https://developers.google.com/earth-engine/datasets/catalog/MODIS_MYD09GA_006_NDVI?hl=en

MODIS Aqua Daily NDWI: https://developers.google.com/earth-engine/datasets/catalog/MODIS_MYD09GA_006_NDWI?hl=en

To analyze the relation between migration and vegetation or water content in vegetation, we create polygon data of destinations, Kisangani, Bukombo, and Kitchanga, and calculate the NDVI and NDWI, respectively. We calculate the average NDVI and NDWI per day, 15 days, and month to identify densely and sparsely vegetated areas. We argue that averaged NDVI and NDWI are reasonably accurate proxy for the availability of natural resources depending on their livelihoods, because the greenness of the environment is largely determined by rainfall and soil conditions (Fig. 14.2).

Results

The results show a significant but weak correlation between migration and vegetation cover at each level. Due to use of three satellites and a narrow range of target destinations, daily NDVI and NDWI time-series graphs are fluctuated. We select images having cloud less than 10%, but there are still effects on both indices, especially on daily NDVI and NDWI time-series graphs. For this, 15-daily and monthly

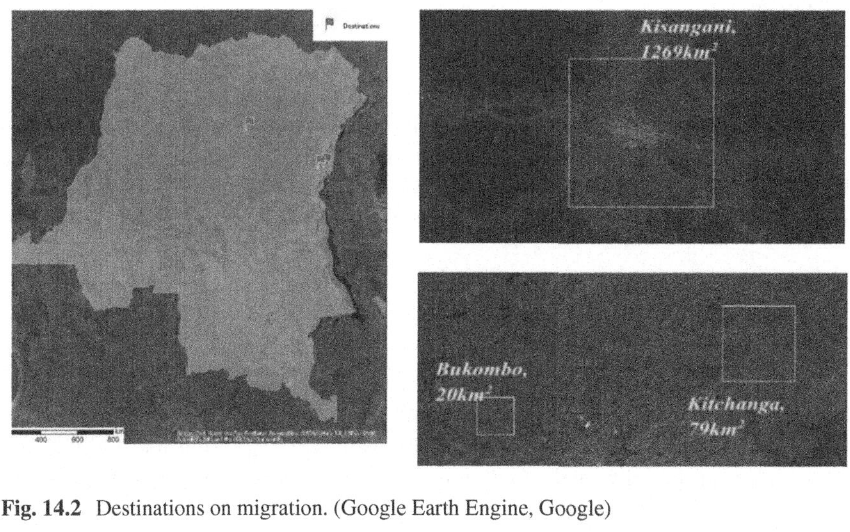

Fig. 14.2 Destinations on migration. (Google Earth Engine, Google)

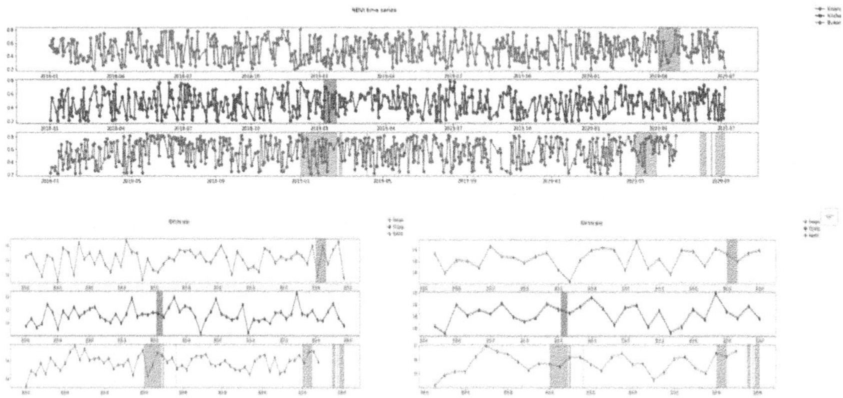

Fig. 14.3 Daily, 15-daily, and monthly NDVI time-series graphs (red Kisangani, blue Kitchanga, green Bukombo)

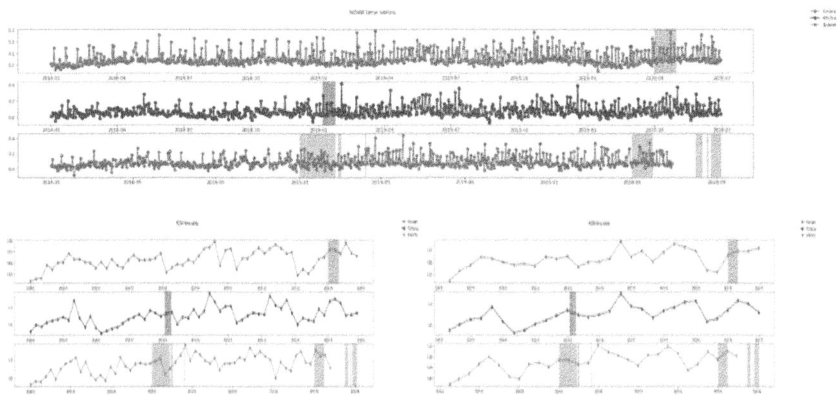

Fig. 14.4 Daily, 15-daily, and monthly NDWI time-series graphs

time-series graphs are suited for our analysis. Area with less populated migration, i.e., Kitchanga has low fluctuation in both indices compared to other overpopulated migration flows, i.e., Kisangani and Bukombo, and those trends toward NDVI and NDWI are more positive. The color bands in Fig. 14.3 determine the periods of migrations from the IDMC dataset (Fig. 14.4).

Conclusion

This substudy was conducted with the aim of expanding the emerging body of knowledge on migration-environment relationships by exploring the multiple ties between human mobility and vegetation and water content in vegetation dynamics in the DRC. We evaluate the role of environment changes in the DRC's three migration flows and explore the impact of migration on vegetation cover and water content in vegetation. Despite limitations in our analysis, this research provides an insightful exploration of migration and vegetation dynamics in migrations. Our findings suggest that although valid fluctuations are not indicated, the environmental factors play an important role in causing migration within the DRC depending on the area of target. A possible explanation could be that our target areas are too narrow to extract both indices and also the DRC does not have annual seasonal variation with constant temperature which may cause visible fluctuation of NDVI and NDWI. Indeed, other studies (Müller et al., 2016; Hassan et al., 2018) show the significance of utilizing NDVI and NDWI for the migrant's flow relation to vegetation change, but they set larger areas than our analysis. To assess the effective environmental impact of migration, larger areas are required to extract for both indices.

Detailed Experiment Results

Here, we show additional figures and tables to supplement the results shown in Sect. 14.5. Figure 14.5 shows the elements of the confusion matrix, the F1 score, and the average precision (AP), in relation to the training data size. Among these, the

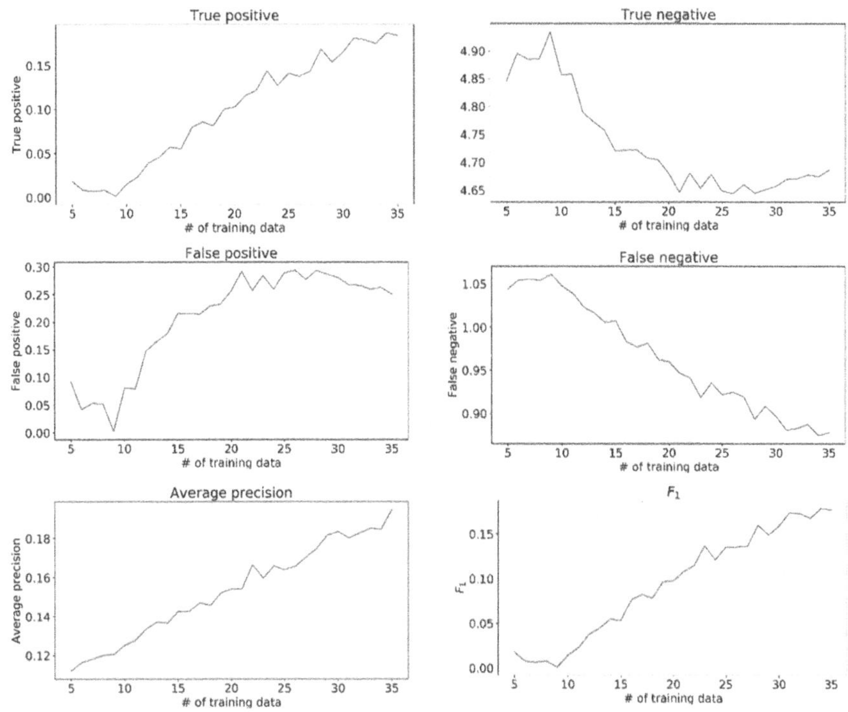

Fig. 14.5 Additional evaluation metrics: elements of the confusion matrix (# of true positives, true negatives, false positives, and false negatives), F1 score, and average precision

Table 14.3 F1 scores for each destination candidate

[a]Sample	Aru	Beni	Bunia	Djugu	Irumu	Kabalo	Kalehe	Kisangani	Lubero
5	0.02	0.02	0.01	0.02	0.02	0	0.03	0.03	0.01
10	0.02	0.04	0	0.01	0.01	0.03	0	0.01	0.01
15	0.01	0.09	0.03	0.06	0.07	0.07	0.08	0.04	0.04
20	0.03	0.12	0	0.12	0.1	0.09	0.15	0.04	0.08
25	0.04	0.17	0.03	0.19	0.15	0.1	0.24	0.07	0.11
30	0.1	0.16	0.01	0.2	0.17	0.17	0.25	0.04	0.12
35	0.05	0.21	0.01	0.29	0.2	0.18	0.3	0.02	0.1

[a]Sample	Mahagi	Masisi	Moba	Mwenga	Nyunzu	Rutshuru	Walikale	Average
5	0.02	0	0.01	0	0.03	0.04	0.03	0.02
10	0.01	0.01	0.01	0.02	0	0.03	0.03	0.01
15	0.01	0	0.05	0.06	0.06	0.17	0.03	0.05
20	0.03	0.04	0.08	0.17	0.11	0.3	0.1	0.1
25	0.03	0.05	0.12	0.17	0.19	0.39	0.13	0.14
30	0.07	0.05	0.1	0.21	0.19	0.5	0.22	0.16
35	0.05	0.09	0.1	0.2	0.2	0.55	0.3	0.18

[a]*Sample* shows the sample size, and *Average* shows the average of the figures over all destination candidates

average precision indicates the area under the precision-recall curve. In both the F1 and the AP, we observe similar trends as those of precision and recall, i.e., the scores improve as the training data size increases (Table 14.3).

References

Ahmed, N., Firoze, A., & Rahman, R. M. (2020). Machine learning for predicting landslide risk of Rohingya refugee camp infrastructure. *Journal of Information and Telecommunication, 4*(2), 175–198.

American Red Cross. (2020). *DRC tribes and ethnic cultural dataset* [Data set]. https://data.humdata.org/dataset/drc_cultural_social-data. (Original work published 2019).

Baird, et al. (2020). *Identifying psychological trauma among Syrian refugee children for early intervention: Analyzing digitized drawings using machine learning*. https://escholarship.org/uc/item/0fc7m5zm

Chen, T., & Guestrin, C. (2016). Xgboost: A scalable tree boosting system. In *Proceedings of the 22nd ACM SIGKDD international conference on knowledge discovery and data mining* (pp. 785–794).

Crowd AI. (2018). *Mapping challenge building missing maps with machine learning*. https://www.crowdai.org/challenges/mapping-challenge

Czaika, M., & Mayer, A. (2011). Refugee movements and aid responsiveness of bilateral donors. *Journal of Development Studies, 47*(3), 455–474. https://doi.org/10.1080/00220388.2010.492855

DFID. (2018). *Digital strategy 2018–2020*. https://assets.publishing.service.gov.uk/government/uploads/system/uploads/attachment_data/file/701443/DFID-Digital-Strategy-23-01-18a.pdf

Eck, K. (2012). In data we trust? A comparison of UCDP GED and ACLED conflict events datasets. *Cooperation and Conflict, 47*(1), 124–141. Retrieved November 7, 2020, from http://www.jstor.org/stable/45084688

Facebook. (2013). *Coordinated migration*. Posted on 18 December, 2013. https://www.facebook.com/notes/facebook-data-science/coordinated-migration/10151930946453859/

Geospatial Information Authority of Japan. (2020). *NDVI data*. Retrieved from https://www.gsi.go.jp/kankyochiri/ndvi_e.html

Government of Singapore. (2020). *Trace together*. https://www.tracetogether.gov.sg/

GSMA. (2020). *Using mobile big data to help inform the fight against COVID-19 in the Democratic Republic of Congo*. Posted on 29 July, 2020. https://www.gsma.com/mobilefordevelopment/blog/using-mobile-big-data-to-help-inform-the-fight-against-covid-19-in-the-democratic-republic-of-congo/

Hanai, K. (2019). Current situation and issues of conflict related minerals in the Democratic Republic of the Congo (in Japanese, コンゴ民主共和国における紛争資源問題の現状と課題). *International Affairs, 682*. http://www2.jiia.or.jp/kokusaimondai_archive/2010/2019-06_003.pdf?noprint. Accessed 5 Sept 2020.

Hassan, M., Smith, A., Walker, K., Rahman, M., & Southworth, J. (2018). Rohingya refugee crisis and forest cover change in Teknaf, Bangladesh. *Remote Sensing, 10*(5), 689. https://doi.org/10.3390/rs10050689

Immigration Policy Lab. (2020). *GeoMatch connecting people to places*. https://immigrationlab.org/geomatch/

International Organization for Migration (IOM). (2016). *Global compact for migration*. https://www.iom.int/global-compact-migration

International Peace Information Service. (2019). *Artisanal mining sites in Eastern DRC 2009–2019*. https://data.humdata.org/dataset/cod_mines_curated_all_opendata_p_ipis

International Telecommunication Union. (2019). *United Nations Activities on Artificial Intelligence (AI)*. https://www.itu.int/dms_pub/itu-s/opb/gen/S-GEN-UNACT-2019-1-PDF-E.pdf

Lu, Y., Koperski, K., Kwan, C., & Li, J. (2020). Deep learning for effective refugee tent extraction near Syria-Jordan border. *IEEE Geoscience and Remote Sensing Letters, 2020*, 1.

Migration Data Portal. (2020). *Mapping population distributions on city level, using Twitter data*. Posted on 28 September 2020. https://migrationdataportal.org/data-innovation/mapping-population-distributions-city-level-using-twitter-data

Müller, M. F., Yoon, J., Gorelick, S. M., Avisse, N., & Tilmant, A. (2016). Impact of the Syrian refugee crisis on land use and transboundary freshwater resources. *Proceedings of the National Academy of Sciences of the United States of America, 113*(52), 14932–14937. https://doi.org/10.1073/pnas.1614342113

Nominatim (3.5.2). (2020). [Computer software]. osm-search. https://github.com/osm-search/Nominatim. (Original work published 2012).

Norwegian Refugee Council. (2020). *Fear for safety for people in Ituri affected by armed groups attacks and intercommunal violence*. Norwegian Refugee Council. https://www.nrc.no/news/2020/february/dr-congo-new-displacement-in-ituri/. Accessed 8 Sept 2020.

OCHA. (2010). *Democratic Republic of the Congo, 1993–2003*. United Nations High Commissioner for Human Rights. https://www.ohchr.org/Documents/Countries/CD/DRC_MAPPING_REPORT_FINAL_EN.pdf. Accessed 8 Sept 2020.

OCHA DR Congo. (2019). *Democratic Republic of the Congo—Subnational Population Statistics* [Data set]. https://data.humdata.org/dataset/democratic-republic-of-the-congo-administrative-level-0-2-population-statistics

OCHA/UNJHRO. (2020). *Overview of the human rights situation during the first semester 2020*. United Nations High Commissioner for Human Rights (OCHA) and United Nations Joint Human Rights Office in the DRC (UNJHRO) MONUSCO – OHCHR. https://monusco.unmissions.org/sites/default/files/unjhro_-_analysis_of_the_human_rights_situation_in_drc_2020_6_month_eng_copy.pdf. Accessed 8 Sept 2020.

Omdena. (2019). *Predicting climate change and forced displacement*. https://omdena.com/projects/ai-climate-change/. Accessed 5 Sept 2020.

Open Source Routing Machine. (2020). *Project OSRM*. https://github.com/Project-OSRM/osrm-backend. (Original work published 2011).

OpenStreetMap Contributors. (2017). *Planet dump*. Retrieved from https://planet.osm.org. https://www.openstreetmap.org

Parater, L. (2020). *Jetson: Insights into building a predictive analytics platform for displacement*. Retrieved October 10, 2020, from https://www.unhcr.org/innovation/jetson-insights-into-building-a-predictive-analytics-platform-for-displacement/

Quinn, J. A., Nyhan, M. M., Navarro, C., Coluccia, D., Bromley, L., & Luengo-Oroz, M. (2018). Humanitarian applications of machine learning with remote-sensing data: Review and case study in refugee settlement mapping. *Philosophical Transactions of the Royal Society A: Mathematical, Physical and Engineering Sciences, 376*(2128), 20170363.

Raleigh, C., Linke, A., Hegre, H., & Karlsen, J. (2010). Introducing ACLED-armed conflict location and event data. *Journal of Peace Research, 47*(5), 651–660.

Sekeris, P., De Luca, G., Maystadt, J.-F., & Ulimwengu, J. (2013). Mineral resources and conflicts in DRC: A case of ecological fallacy. *Oxford Economic Papers, 66*. https://doi.org/10.1093/oep/gpt037

Spelhaug, J. (2019). Helping refugees and displaced persons by shifting the approach to how we help nonprofits. *Microsoft on the Issues*. https://blogs.microsoft.com/on-the-issues/2019/06/19/helping-refugees-and-displaced-persons-by-shifting-the-approach-to-how-we-help-nonprofits/

Stearns, J., & Voge, C. (2017). The landscape of Armed Groups in Eastern Congo Fragmented, politicized networks, KIVU SECURITY TRACKER. https://kivusecurity.nyc3.digitaloceanspaces.com/reports/5/Landscape%20of%20Armed%20Groups%20Essay%20KST.pdf. Accessed 5 Sept 2020.

Suleimenova, D., Bell, D., & Groen, D. (2017). A generalized simulation development approach for predicting refugee destinations. *Scientific Reports, 7*(1), 1–13.

Teytelboym, A (2020). *Annie™ Moore: Increasing employment of resettled refugees using matching, Machine learning and integer optimization*. University of Oxford. https://www.economics.ox.ac.uk/impact/annie-moore-increasing-employment-of-resettled-refugees-using-matching-machine-learning-and-integer-optimisation

The World Bank. (2019). *The mobility of displaced Syrians an economic and social analysis*. https://www.worldbank.org/en/country/syria/publication/the-mobility-of-displaced-syrians-an-economic-and-social-analysis

Tsoumakas, G., Katakis, I., & Vlahavas, I. (2010). Mining multi-label data. In O. Maimon & L. Rokach (Eds.), *Data mining and knowledge discovery handbook* (pp. 667–685). Springer. https://doi.org/10.1007/978-0-387-09823-4_34

UN Global Pulse. (2017). *Understanding movement and perceptions of migrants and refugees with social media* (Project Series, No. 28, 2017. https://reliefweb.int/sites/reliefweb.int/files/resources/Social%20Media%20Forced%20Displacement%20Europe%20Refugee%20Crises%20_0.pdf

UN Security Council. (2019). *Final report of the Group of Experts on the Democratic Republic of the Congo*. United Nations Security Council. https://reliefweb.int/sites/reliefweb.int/files/resources/S_2019_469_E.pdf. Accessed 5 Sept 2020.

UNHCR. (2018a). *Congolese situation – Responding to the needs of displaced Congolese and refugees – Supplementary Appeal, January–December 2018*. UN High Commissioner for Refugees, https://reporting.unhcr.org/node/20239. Accessed 10 Sept 2020.

UNHCR. (2018b). *Independent evaluation of UNHCR's response to the L3 emergency in the Democratic Republic of Congo, Evaluation Report, December 2018*. UN High Commissioner for Refugees, https://www.unhcr.org/en-us/5c5419fe4.pdf. Accessed 3 Nov 2020.

UNHCR. (2019). *Position on returns to North Kivu, South Kivu, Ituri and adjacent areas in the Democratic Republic of the Congo Affected by Ongoing Conflict and Violence – Update II*. UN High Commissioner for Refugees, https://www.refworld.org/docid/5d6d794a4.html. Accessed 10 Sept 2020.

UNHCR. (2020a). *Global trends forced DIsplaced in 2019*. UN High Commissioner for Refugees. https://www.unhcr.org/5ee200e37.pdf. Accessed 5 Sept 2020.

UNHCR. (2020b). *Weekly emergency update – Ituri, South Kivu and North Kivu Provinces, Democratic Republic of the Congo (8–22 June 2020)*. UN High Commissioner for Refugees. https://reliefweb.int/report/democratic-republic-congo/unhcr-weekly-emergency-update-ituri-south-kivu-and-north-kivu-7. Accessed 22 Oct 2020.

UNHCR. (2020c). *Refugee data finder*. https://www.unhcr.org/refugee-statistics/download/?url=R1xq

UNHCR Innovation Service. (2019). *Is it possible to predict forced displacement?* Medium.com. https://medium.com/unhcr-innovation-service/is-it-possible-to-predict-forced-displacement-58960afe0ba1

USAID. (2020). *Digital strategy 2020–2024*. https://www.usaid.gov/sites/default/files/documents/15396/USAID_Digital_Strategy.pdf

Van der Geest, K., Vrieling, A., & Dietz, T. (2010). Migration and environment in Ghana: a cross-district analysis of human mobility and vegetation dynamics. *Environment and Urbanization, 22*(1), 107–123. https://doi.org/10.1177/0956247809362842

Wikipedia-wikidata (commit 403060d). (2020). [Computer software]. osm-search. https://github.com/osm-search/wikipedia-wikidata. (Original work published 2020).

XGBoost (1.2.1). (2020). [Computer software]. Distributed (Deep) Machine Learning Community. https://github.com/dmlc/xgboost. (Original work published 2014).

Ayaka Oishi serves as a political analyst and project manager at Peloria Insights, a US-based company that leverages artificial intelligence to inform practitioners in the peace and security arena. As a former Fulbright fellow as well as a strategy consultant at International Business Machines (IBM), her interest resides in a multidisciplinary approach that combines insights both in data science and peacebuilding to better address one of the most challenging issues in the world, conflicts.

Takeshi Teshima is a Ph.D. student in machine learning at the University of Tokyo. After receiving the B.Econ. and the M.Sc. from the University of Tokyo, he has researched the topics of learning from imperfect information and causality-informed machine learning and published at multiple top-tier conferences such as the International Conference on Machine Learning, the Conference on Neural Information Processing Systems, and the AAAI Conference on Artificial Intelligence. His research interest lies in developing general machine learning methodologies that leverage the causal mechanism behind the data as well as in AI for Good. He is supported by Masason Foundation. (Personal website: https://takeshi-teshima.github.io/)

Kunikazu Akao is working in the International Organization for Migration (IOM) in Sierra Leone and managing several projects, including the Youth Vocational Training, the Youth Entrepreneurship, Ebola Crisis/COVID-19 response, Disaster Management, Diaspora coordination, the research project to evaluate the government's migration coordination, and enhancing activity for Global Compact for Migration (GCM). Before joining the IOM, he has worked in the Japan International Cooperation Agency (JICA), Ministry of Foreign Affairs of Japan (MOFA), and International Business Machines (IBM). He has a Master of Public Policy (MPP) in Tokyo University and a Bachelor of Liberal Arts in International Christian University. He published a book called "Messages from Iraqi friends" (Kodansha, 2003).

Tsuyoshi Kano is a Ph.D. candidate at the University of Michigan School of Information. His research interest is ICT industry development, digital human resource development, and innovation eco-system in developing countries. His research interests are built by his extensive practical experiences as (Ahmed et al., 2020) an economic development program officer at an international aid organization and (American Red Cross, 2020) an IT engineer (programmer, IT architect, and project manager) at a private company. Based on his diverse experiences, he is interested in approaching social issues from various perspectives such as psychology, information science, management, and development economics. (Personal website: https://tsuyoshi-kano.com)

Megumi Kiriha is a member of ICT for Development.JP (https://ict4d.jp).

Naoki Kojima is a member of ICT for Development.JP (https://ict4d.jp).

Takuya Sasaki received his Master's degree in International Peace Studies from the UN-mandated University for Peace. He is currently working in Peacebuilding and Reconstruction Group, Koei Research & Consulting Inc., and has engaged in several development projects of the Japan International Cooperation Agency (JICA) in Rwanda, Afghanistan, Palestine, Sudan, and Zambia. He specializes in peacebuilding, vocational training, and employment promotion targeting for vulnerable people such as youth, women, IDP, and refugees in conflict-affected areas.

Kentaro Takahira received his Master's degree in Informatics from Kyoto University. He is currently working as a data science practitioner at a private company. His research interests include the application of artificial intelligence to the socio-economic system. His work about the agent-based regulation method for transportation was published in the AAAI Conference on Artificial Intelligence.

Jumpei Takami is a satellite data analyst specifically for Optical and Synthetic Aperture Radar (SAR) data at Pasco Corporation. He received his Master's degree in Civil and Environmental Engineering from the University of Washington. He has worked on estimating vegetation and water body area from satellite data based on indices. His current research interests include the Interferometric SAR analysis for land subsidence or infrastructure monitoring, detection of water and wastewater leakage, machine learning analysis using geospatial and satellite information, and data analysis for flooding range and volume in disasters.

Tomonari Takeuchi is an ICT for Development (ICT4D) consultant, a visiting professor of Kobe Institute of Computing, and a co-founder of the general incorporated association ICT for Development in Japan. He has an MSc in ICT4D from the University of Manchester and a BA in Political Science from Keio University. He has been working for various kinds of development projects, especially in the ICT4D field, all over the world, including the experience working as a representative of the Japan International Cooperation Agency (JICA) Ghana office, a consultant for the Embassy of Japan in Ethiopia, and a manager of Deloitte Touche Tohmatsu LLC.

Kenji Tajima is working in Peacebuilding and Reconstruction Group, Koei Research & Consulting Inc., and is engaged in peacebuilding projects of the Japan International Cooperation Agency (JICA) in Afghanistan, Sudan, and Zambia. He specializes in peacebuilding and inclusive education and is studying self-esteem in conflict-affected areas. He received two Master's degrees in International Peace Studies from the University for Peace, created by UN General Assembly, and in Education from Tokyo Gakugei University. He has published seven research papers on the self-esteem/self-affirmation of children with disabilities studying in special schools. Before joining Koei Research & Consulting Inc., He spent 9 years as a teacher of special schools in Japan, Mongolia, Zambia, and Taiwan.

Chihiro Noda works for a US-based startup that provides AI model developers with training data in various areas from natural language processing (NLP) to speech technologies and computer vision (CV). She has contributed to the completion of data collection and validation projects that support the development of technologies used by smart assistant models, chatbots, image recognition, and so forth. Before joining the AI industry, she has worked on IT system development as a programmer and supported international development projects designed by the Japan International

Cooperation Agency (JICA) and the Ministry of Foreign Affairs of Japan (MoFA). Her interests are in the successful utilization of technologies for social good, as seen in her activities at ICT4D Lab.

Hikaru Hirose is working in a general incorporated association, Peace Tech Foundation (PTF), in Japan, and managing several Ed-tech projects, providing the skills such as programming and digital marketing to east African countries. Before joining PTF, he has worked as a representative of a local legal entity in Mozambique, Agro-Negocio para o Desenvolvimento de Mocambique, Lda (ADM). His research interests are built by his experiences in the projects with the Food and Agriculture Organization (FAO) and World Food Programme (WFP) in Mozambique.

Shigeki Yamanaka is the President of Actit Inc., an IT technology company. He is also a board member of the non-profit organization, the Forum for the Program of Revitalizing Japan. He has more than 20 years of experience as an IT engineer. He has a Master of Engineering degree in Natural Language Processing with Machine Learning from Yokohama National University. His interest is to contribute to the evolution of humanity and the realization of a sustainable world by combining the wisdom of humanity.

Chapter 15
COVID-19: Extracting the Pattern of Morbidity and Mortality Among Countries in the African Region

Donald Douglas Atsa'am, Emmanuel Awuni Kolog, Temidayo Oluwatosin Omotehinwa, Samuel Nii Odoi Devine, Oluwaseun Alexander Dada, Toluwalase Janet Akingbade, Richard O. Agjei, and Oluwafemi Samson Balogun

Abstract As the coronavirus disease 2019 (COVID-19) spreads worldwide, there were fears that the African continent would be torn apart by the pandemic. For instance, the World Health Organization reportedly warned that African countries

---

D. D. Atsa'am (✉)
University of the Free State, Qwaqwa Campus, South Africa
e-mail: donatsaam@alumni.emu.edu.tr

E. A. Kolog (✉)
University of Ghana, Accra, Ghana

Centre for Multidisciplinary Research and Innovation Abuja, Abuja, Nigeria
e-mail: eakolog@ug.edu.gh

T. O. Omotehinwa
Achievers University, Owo, Nigeria
e-mail: oluomotehinwa@achievers.edu.ng

S. N. O. Devine
Presbyterian University College Ghana, Abetifi-Kwahu, Ghana
e-mail: samuel.nodevine@presbyuniversity.edu.gh

O. A. Dada
University of Helsinki, Helsinki, Finland
e-mail: alexander.dada@helsinki.fi

T. J. Akingbade
Kogi State University, Anyigba, Kogi State, Nigeria

R. O. Agjei
Imperial College, London, United Kingdom

O. S. Balogun
University of Eastern Finland, Kuopio, Finland
e-mail: samson.balogun@uef.fi

R. Boateng et al. (eds.), *Digital Innovations, Business and Society in Africa*, Advances in Theory and Practice of Emerging Markets,
https://doi.org/10.1007/978-3-030-77987-0_15

should "prepare for the worst." In this study, non-parametric data analytics and data mining techniques were deployed on five COVID-19 datasets from the African region to extract knowledge on how the pandemic has affected the continent. Results from non-parametric tests, including the Friedman, Kendall's W, and Wilcoxon rank sum tests, showed that the distribution of morbidity and mortality figures across African countries and territories are statistically different. The agglomerative hierarchical clustering was deployed to extract four clusters of countries based on the similarity in the number of confirmed cases and deaths from the coronavirus infection. The clusters include the least-hit, moderately hit, badly hit, and worst-hit countries. These findings have established that though most African countries are underdeveloped, the effect of the pandemic is not uniform across the continent. It is therefore suggested that the better positioned countries should extend a hand of fellowship to the countries in need so that together, the African continent would be rid of the pandemic. This would pave the way for a uniform, post-pandemic, socioeconomic development across the continent.

Keywords COVID-19 · Morbidity and mortality · African region · Non-parametric test · Hierarchical clustering

15.1 Introduction

The coronavirus disease 2019 (COVID-19) is caused by the severe acute respiratory syndrome coronavirus 2 (SARS-CoV-2) (Rothan & Byrareddy, 2020; Shereen et al., 2020); and its main symptoms include difficulty in breathing, high body temperature, and coughing. The disease was initially detected in Wuhan, China, in December 2019 (Cortegiani et al., 2020; Khan & Atangana, 2020; Shereen et al., 2020) and has since spread to all continents of the world. As of August 12, 2020, the novel COVID-19 had spread to all African countries and territories with 1,055,964 confirmed cases, 23,582 deaths, 744,438 recoveries, and a fatality rate of 3.1% (Massinga Loembé et al., 2020). According to the World Health Organization (WHO) COVID-19 situation report of August 5, 2020, the five most-affected African countries in terms of morbidity and mortality include South Africa (confirmed cases 521,318 and confirmed deaths 8884), Nigeria (confirmed cases 44,433 and confirmed deaths 910), Ghana (confirmed cases 37,812 and confirmed deaths 191), Algeria (confirmed cases 32,504 and confirmed deaths 1248), and Kenya (confirmed cases 23,202 and confirmed deaths 388) (WHO, 2020a). With the available data, the African continent is the least affected by the COVID-19 pandemic to date.

African countries are so diverse in many ways, ranging from weak health systems, the high burden of infectious diseases (HIV, tuberculosis, hepatitis B or C), double burden of non-communicable diseases (cancers, diabetes, cardiovascular diseases, chronic respiratory diseases) (Mudie et al., 2019; WHO, 2010), and poverty. Among the 25 countries labeled as the most vulnerable or susceptible to infectious diseases, only three are outside the African region. Reports from the WHO suggest that within the African population, approximately 26 million are HIV positive, 213 million are infected with malaria, 2.5 million people are battling with tuberculosis, and 71 million are infected with hepatitis B or C (WHO, 2020b; WHO Regional Office for Africa, 2020a, b, c). A comparison among the top five most affected African countries reveals several distinctive factors associated with each country. Such disparity is evidenced in the presence of the winter "flu" season in the southern part of Africa. The winter season in Southern Africa is a disadvantage because the spread of all respiratory viruses is more effective and rapid in the winter. This informs the prediction of a worst-case scenario of COVID-19 between May and September 2020 (Mendelson, 2020; Hopman et al., 2020; Nachega et al., 2020a, b).

A modeling research by Gilbert et al. (2020) hinged on the State Party Self-Assessment Annual Reporting (SPAR), and the findings indicated that South Africa, Algeria, and Egypt had the highest COVID-19 importation risk from China; with the SPAR scores of 62, 76, and 87, respectively. Furthermore, the study showed that these countries had moderate to high capacity to respond to outbreaks, with Infectious Disease Vulnerability Index (IDVI) 2016 scores of 69, 49, and 53, respectively (Gilbert et al., 2020). Although Nigeria had moderate importation risk, with SPAR scores of 51, it had a high vulnerability with IDVI score of 27. More importantly, in Africa, a country's healthcare capacity is a major factor in the management and control of COVID-19. Unlike the developed countries such as the United Kingdom, Canada, or the United States with advanced healthcare systems and professionals, most African countries and territories have relatively poor and weaker healthcare systems and insufficient skilled personnel (OECD Development Matters, 2020; Boston Consulting Group, 2020). The African countries under consideration in this study have different but also limited testing capacities, limited number of healthcare professionals required for diagnostics test, and limited ventilators (Wood, 2020; Dahab et al., 2020). In the same way, majority of African countries have limited number of personal protective equipment (PPE) and intensive care units (ICU), lack of or scarcity of funds to combat COVID-19, and other healthcare challenges (OECD Development Matters, 2020; Boston Consulting Group, 2020; McKenzie, 2020). The general assertion has been that the African continent will be significantly impacted by the ongoing COVID-19 outbreak (African Development Bank Group, 2020; Center for Global Development, 2020; DW Africa, 2020a). However, the magnitude of the impact will depend on the management and control of COVID-19 within the respective countries.

This study is aimed at deploying data analytics and data mining techniques on several COVID-19 datasets from the African region to extract knowledge on how the pandemic has affected the continent. Is the morbidity and mortality of the pandemic uniform across countries and territories in the region or there are disparities? Which countries within the region have suffered a similar magnitude of confirmed cases and deaths from the disease? Several non-parametric statistical tests including the Friedman, Kendall's W, and Wilcoxon rank sum tests are deployed to resolve these questions. Furthermore, the hierarchical clustering technique of data mining is used to extract clusters of African countries exhibiting similarity in morbidity and mortality of COVID-19. It is expected that the findings of this study should reveal which countries need to strengthen or review their healthcare policies. Similarly, the study should reveal which countries should serve as reference points on how to manage the pandemic on the continent. Overall, the objective is to ensure a collaborative fight against the pandemic across Africa and thus, ensure a uniform post-pandemic socioeconomic development across the continent while other continents are dealing with the scourge of the pandemic.

15.2 Literature Review

15.2.1 The Morbidity and Mortality of COVID-19 in Africa

As COVID-19 spreads worldwide, there are fears that the African continent will be torn apart by the pandemic. For instance, the World Health Organization reportedly warned that African countries should "prepare for the worst" (France24, 2020). Among others, Melinda Gates was also quoted as saying, "I am worried.... I see dead bodies in the streets of Africa" (Africa Check, 2020). Months after the first COVID-19 incidences were recorded in different parts of Africa, the confirmed cases of infections (morbidity) and deaths (mortality) seem to be upsetting predictions made earlier by health experts and statistical models (Njenga, et al., 2020). As it turns out, the streets of Africa are not littered with dead bodies, and the fatality rate is below the global average despite fragile health systems (Mwai & Giles, 2020; Njenga, et al., 2020).

As of August 13, 2020, there were 20,405,695 confirmed cases and 743,487 deaths worldwide (WHO, 2020a). Africa accounts for about 5% of the global morbidity and approximately 3% of the mortality (BBC News, 2020). The low case numbers relative to other regions have generated a lot of debate. Some experts attribute it to the youthful population found on the continent (Dowd, et al., 2020). Others believe that the hot weather in most of Africa decreases the transmissibility of the virus. They also claim that Africa exhibits some preexisting immunity due to prior exposure to other types of coronavirus (Njenga, et al., 2020). There is another school of thought that claims the low morbidity and mortality of COVID-19 reported in Africa is due to cases of lack or insufficient testing (Soy, 2020). To understand how the pandemic may have affected Africa, one needs to consider the fact that Africa is not a single trajectory. Rather, it is made up of several countries, and each country has its own peculiarities and risk profiles. To make sense of the reported morbidity and mortality in different countries and territories of Africa, one may explore the following perspectives: healthcare, press freedom, poverty, and population age (Africacenter, 2020).

Research has shown that countries with high levels of poverty, relatively weaker healthcare systems, and crowded urban areas often have limited capacity for conducting COVID-19 testing and tend to report less confirmed cases (Africacenter, 2020; Soy, 2020). Nigeria is a typical example. However, some authors are of the opinion that the low morbidity and mortality reported in Nigeria is a confirmation of the idea that coronavirus is less active in hot weather and youthful population (Njenga, et al., 2020). In the same analogy, it can also be said that countries with more advanced healthcare systems tend to undertake more COVID-19 testing and report more cases when found. South Africa and Algeria are good examples (Africacenter, 2020). As of August 13, 2020, South Africa had the worst morbidity and mortality on the continent with 568,919 cases and 11,010 deaths (Johns Hopkins University, 2020). Despite the advanced healthcare system in Algeria (36,699 cases and 1333 deaths), the constant harassment of journalists (France-Presse, 2020) is an important factor to consider as press freedom has been shown to have a strong correlation with the morbidity and mortality (Shagam, 2020). Looking from the perspective of population age, Ghana (41,725 cases and 223 deaths) and Kenya (28,104 cases and 456 deaths) have relatively aged populations than the average African age. This indicates the possibilities that mortality rates may be higher (Africacenter, 2020).

15.2.2 Control Measures to Curtail COVID-19 Pandemic in Africa

As reports emerged across the globe amid calls for preparation and controls (Nkengasong & Mankoula, 2020), several African countries made efforts to manage and curtail the spread of the COVID-19 pandemic (Ogunleye et al., 2020). Notably, various countries including South Africa, Nigeria, Algeria, Ghana, and Kenya were in the lead. Several interventions were instituted as control measures. To ensure adequate responsiveness and preparedness, an Africa Task Force for Novel Coronavirus (AFCOR) was established by the Africa CDC (Nkengasong & Mankoula, 2020). Ghana, Nigeria, Algeria, Kenya, and others closed their boarders, suspended local flights, and restricted international air flights especially from COVID-19 ravaged countries (Quaresima et al., 2020). Many countries enforced a 14-day mandatory quarantine and self-isolation for persons arriving from countries where COVID-19 was detected or suspected to have COVID-19 (Nachega et al., 2020a, b).

As the case count increased, South Africa instituted a 30-day total lockdown; others such as Ghana and Kenya enforced partial lockdown and restriction of movement of people, while Algeria implemented a mixed lockdown approach (Ogunleye et al., 2020), with the aid of the police and military. In Ghana and Kenya, low income earning groups were provided free food, among others (Ogunleye et al., 2020), to mitigate the impact of these measures. These restrictions were gradually lifted due to the anticipated adverse socioeconomic impact (Lone & Ahmad, 2020). Aside training health personnel, community screening, mass testing, and contact tracing exercises were also conducted in suspected areas (Mehtar et al., 2020; Nachega et al., 2020a, b). Ghana and Egypt launched apps for tracing persons who may have had contact with COVID-19 patients (Ogunleye et al., 2020). Across the continent, schools were initially shutdown (Ogunleye et al., 2020). Similarly, many workers were directed to work from home. Public awareness campaigns were launched using both traditional and social media (Durotoye et al., 2020), advocating for all to "stay at home."

The WHO COVID-19 protocols including frequent handwashing, use of alcohol-based hand rubs/sanitizers, wearing face masks, social/physical distancing, and regular checking of body temperature were widely practiced (Durotoye et al., 2020; Taboe et al., 2020). Many countries including Ghana innovatively took to sewing non-medical face masks, often using local fabrics, and local manufacturing of hand sanitizers (Mehtar et al., 2020; Ogunleye et al., 2020). Mass gatherings, which often characterize religious events, marriage ceremonies, burials, and political rallies, were suspended (Ogunleye et al., 2020) and subsequently directed to be privately conducted. In some instances, stringent legislation was enacted to prevent such gatherings and persons who tested positive from physically interacting under similar circumstances (Mehtar et al., 2020; Nachega et al., 2020a, b). Others advocated for the use of electronic payment (Ogunleye et al., 2020) to avoid spread via physical cash. Further, various health facilities were provided personal protective equipment (PPE) for health workers, in addition to other incentives (Ogunleye et al., 2020). Many countries established quarantine centers to accommodate persons suspected to have COVID-19 (Ogunleye et al., 2020). Health facilities were converted, and others expanded to provide specialized retreatment for COVID-19 patients (Durotoye et al., 2020; Hopman et al., 2020). With effective compliance, Taboe et al. (2020) estimated a reduction in daily infection rates by 67% and more where public health control measures are activated in the West African region, thus Africa.

15.3 Materials and Methods

The materials deployed for this study are described in this section. These include the Friedman non-parametric test, the Kendall's W test for effect size, the Wilcoxon rank sum test, and the hierarchical clustering. Furthermore, the main experiments conducted for knowledge extraction are equally reported in this section.

15.3.1 Materials

15.3.1.1 Dataset

Five different COVID-19 datasets were deployed for experiments in this study. These include the COVID-19 situation reports across 49 African countries and territories as of August 1, 2, 3, 4, and 5, 2020, as reported by the WHO (2020a). Two dataset variables defined by the WHO are relevant to this study, namely, ConfCases

Table 15.1 Summary of COVID-19 morbidity and mortality across Africa

Dataset	Dataset description	Total confCases	Total deaths
COVID-19_ Aug1	COVID-19 data across Africa as of August 1 2020	788,448	13,545
COVID-19_ Aug2	COVID-19 data across Africa as of August 2, 2020	802,792	13,779
COVID-19_ Aug3	COVID-19 data across Africa as of August 3, 2020	815,996	14,062
COVID-19_ Aug4	COVID-19 data across Africa as of August 4, 2020	825,272	14,139
COVID-19_ Aug5	COVID-19 data across Africa as of August 5, 2020	834,147	14,750

and Deaths. The ConfCases records the cumulative number of confirmed COVID-19 cases within a country or territory from inception of the pandemic up to the specified date. On the other hand, Deaths records the cumulative number of confirmed deaths because of the coronavirus disease within a country or territory from inception up to the specified date. Each of the 49 countries and territories within Africa has values entered for these variables, which are updated daily by the WHO. This study used these two metrics to represent the morbidity and mortality of COVID-19 in Africa. The summary of the experimental datasets is given in Table 15.1.

It is important to point out that the WHO data on *ConfCases* and *Deaths* for any country are cumulative values from inception of the pandemic to the reporting date. This makes it appropriate to use data for any random dates for evaluating the morbidity and mortality of the pandemic. Furthermore, non-parametric testing requires at least two separate data groups on the same problem domain. To guarantee a robust and authentic finding, the present study selected up to five data groups both for *ConfCases* and *Deaths*. Two separate experimental datasets were formed by combining all the five datasets into singleton data, each for morbidity and mortality. That is, all confirmed cases per country/territory reported on the five days (August 1 to August 5) formed the *ConfCases* data. Furthermore, all deaths reported per country/territory on the five days formed the *Deaths* data. This was done to prepare the datasets for non-parametric analysis.

15.3.1.2 Friedman Test

According to Riffenburgh (2012), the Friedman test is a non-parametric statistic used for evaluating if there are discrepancies between the two-way data groups organized in an un-replicated complete block design. In this method, one variable serves as a treatment or group variable and the other variable as the blocking variable. The test checks to see whether the differences among paired groups are statistically significant. The Friedman test can be deployed only when the dataset does not follow a normal distribution (non-parametric) (Riffenburgh, 2012). In situations where the experimental dataset follows a particular distribution such as the normal distribution, the analysis of variance (ANOVA) is the appropriate metric to use.

15.3.1.3 Kendall's W Test for Effect Size

Kendall's W is used to measure the effect size of the Friedman test (Lakens, 2013; Tomczak & Tomczak, 2014). Whether the outcome of the Friedman test indicates that differences among groups are significant or not, effect size is evaluated to determine if the differences between the groups' averages are meaningfully large. The coefficient of Kendall's W assumes a value from 0 to 1 (Lakens, 2013; Tomczak and Tomczak, 2014). According to Tomczak and Tomczak (2014), Kendall's W uses the Cohen criteria for classification as follows: 0.1 to <0.3 (small effect), 0.3 to <0.5 (moderate effect), 0.5, and above (large effect).

15.3.1.4 Wilcoxon Rank Sum Test

This is a non-parametric test used to determine whether the distribution of values between two different groups on the same variable is statistically different from one another (Tomczak & Tomczak, 2014). The Wilcoxon rank sum test does not assume normality in the dataset, and as a result, it is an appropriate statistic when the data is not parameterized. While the Friedman test evaluates the differences between the groups generally, the Wilcoxon rank sum test evaluates the exact differences among paired groups. The distribution between two classes is said to be significantly different if the test between the classes returns a p-value <0.05 (Tomczak & Tomczak, 2014).

15.3.1.5 Hierarchical Clustering

Hierarchical clustering is an unsupervised learning technique that uses dendrograms to group data objects by means of nested partitions in a tree-like structure (Atsa'am et al., 2020; Nielsen, 2016). To perform clustering, similarity between pairs of observations is determined using distance measures such as Euclidean, Manhattan, and Minkowski distances (Nielsen, 2016; Yim & Ramdeen, 2015). The ultimate objective of clustering is to subgroup objects such that objects within the same cluster are very similar to each other and dissimilar to objects in another cluster.

15.3.2 Methods

This section reports the experiments conducted on the five COVID-19 datasets to extract the pattern of morbidity and mortality of the coronavirus among countries and territories in Africa.

15.3.2.1 Normality/Skewness Tests on the COVID-19 Experimental Datasets

Two techniques were employed to test whether the COVID-19 morbidity or mortality data follow a particular distribution such as normal, skewed, or is non-parametric. Density plots were visualized separately for the ConfCases and Deaths variables as shown in Figs. 15.1 and 15.2.

As noted in Figs. 15.1 and 15.2, the COVID-19 morbidity and mortality data, respectively, do not follow any distribution. For instance, a normally distributed data will generate a bell-shaped curve in a density plot (Kassambara, 2020). To further confirm that the data is non-parametric, Shapiro-Wilk's normality test (Ghasemi & Zahediasl, 2012; Kassambara, 2020) was also conducted on the *ConfCases* and *Deaths* data. The null hypothesis of Shapiro-Wilk's test assumes that the data is normally distributed (Ghasemi & Zahediasl, 2012). If the test turns out to be significant, it is concluded that the sample data is non-normal. In each case, the test yielded a p-value $0.00 < 0.05$ for both *ConfCases* and *Deaths*, effectively confirming the COVID-19 data across Africa as non-parametric.

Fig. 15.1 Density plot of *ConfCases* across Africa

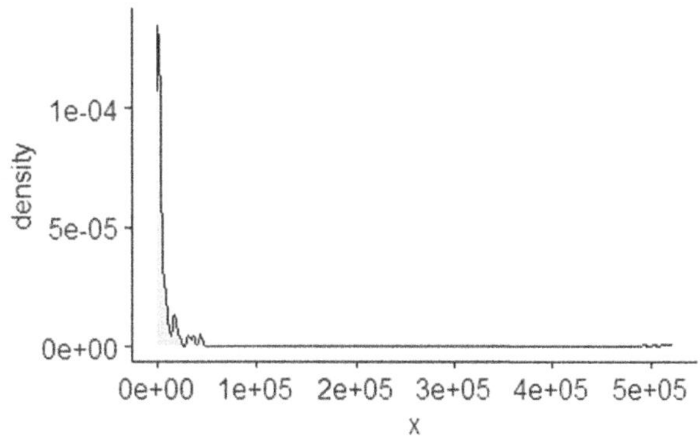

Fig. 15.2 Density plot of *Deaths* across Africa

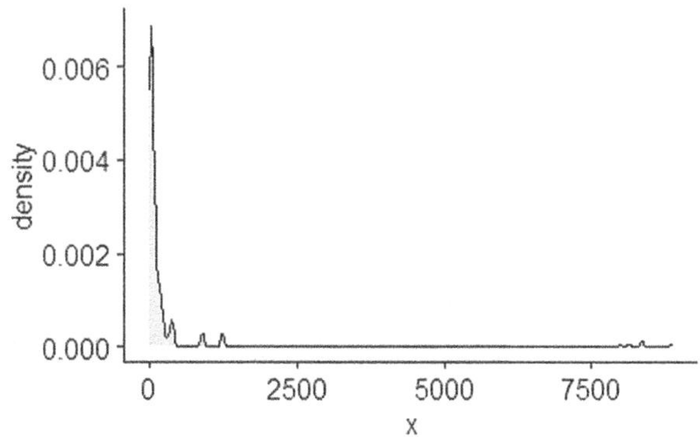

15.3.2.2 Experiment

It is instructive to note that the COVID-19 datasets have been confirmed to be non-parametric. Consequently, non-parametric tests (Friedman, Kendall's W, and Wilcoxon rank sum tests) were conducted to extract the patterns of confirmed cases and deaths across Africa. Prior to conducting the experiments, the names of each country/territory were abbreviated to enhance readability and reduce computing overheads. Detailed country/territory names and the abbreviations used in this study are presented in the Appendix.

The Friedman test was evaluated on the COVID-19 *ConfCases* data, and the following result was obtained: *Friedman test statistic = 240, df = 48, p-value = 0.00.* Furthermore, the same test was conducted on the COVID-19 *Deaths* data and the following results emerged: *Friedman test statistic = 222, df = 48, p-value = 0.00.* Furthermore, Kendall's W effect size test was conducted separately on the *ConfCases* and *Deaths* data. The test yielded the values, 1.0 and 0.9, for *ConfCases* and *Deaths*, respectively.

The Friedman test checks for significant differences in the distributions on the entire dataset. However, the Wilcoxon rank sum test checks the exact groups whose distributions are different, through pairwise comparisons. The results of the Wilcoxon test on *ConfCases* and *Deaths* are shown in Tables 15.2 and 15.3, respectively.

15.3.2.3 Extraction of Hierarchical Clusters from the COVID-19 Dataset

The agglomerative hierarchical clustering was deployed on the COVID-19 data as of August 5, 2020, and four clusters were extracted. Prior to executing clustering, the raw dataset was normalized to a uniform scale, using the min-max algorithm (Bodur & Atsa'am, 2019; Atsa'am, 2020). This effectively scaled all data points to the range [0, 1]. The criterion for cluster extraction was the extent of morbidity and

Table 15.2 Sample of pairwise comparisons of *ConfCases* using Wilcoxon rank sum exact test

	AL	AN	BE	BF	BR	BT	CA	CG
AN	0.0079							
BE	0.0112	0.0112						
BF	0.0079	**0.0749**	0.0112					
BR	0.0109	0.0109	0.0099	0.0109				
BT	0.0075	0.0075	0.0067	0.0075	0.0065			
CA	0.0112	0.0112	0.0102	0.0112	0.0099	0.0067		
CG	0.0079	0.0079	0.0112	0.0079	0.0109	0.0075	0.0112	–
NG	0.0079	0.0079	0.0112	0.0079	0.0109	0.0075	0.0112	0.0079
NI	0.0079	**0.3457**	0.0112	**0.3095**	0.0109	0.0075	0.0112	0.0079
UG	0.0079	0.0079	0.0112	**0.3095**	0.0109	0.0075	0.0112	0.0079
ZW	0.0112	0.0112	0.0102	0.0112	0.0099	0.0067	0.0102	**0.0907**

Table 15.3 Sample of pairwise comparisons of *Deaths* using Wilcoxon rank sum exact test

	AL	AN	BE	BF	BR	BT	CA	CG
AN	0.0097							
BE	0.0109	0.0285						
BF	0.0119	**0.0517**	**0.5232**					
BR	0.0075	0.0056	0.0065	0.0073				
BT	0.0075	0.0056	0.0065	0.0073	0.0040			
CA	0.0075	**0.1060**	**0.6501**	0.0073	0.0040	0.0040		
CG	0.0079	**0.1812**	0.0339	0.0119	0.0075	0.0075	**0.1188**	
CV	0.0112	**0.6623**	**0.6674**	**0.2031**	0.0067	0.0067	**0.6513**	**0.6723**
GB	0.0117	0.016	**0.6694**	**0.6733**	0.0071	0.0071	0.0071	**0.0117**
GU	0.0097	0.0075	**0.6613**	**0.6654**	0.0056	0.0056	0.0056	0.0097

Table 15.4 Distribution of countries/territories among clusters

Cluster	1	2	3	4
No. of countries/territories	1	2	4	42

mortality of the coronavirus disease within a country/territory. All countries/territories within a cluster can be said to exhibit some level of similarity in the number of confirmed cases and deaths caused by the pandemic. The country/territory distributions per cluster are shown in Table 15.4.

15.4 Results and Discussion

15.4.1 Results

The result of the Friedman's test showed that the significant value obtained (0.00) is less than 0.05, i.e., p-value <0.05. This implies that the null hypothesis must be rejected. Therefore, the alternate hypothesis, there is a significant difference in the distribution of morbidity and mortality among countries and territories in Africa, is accepted. In other words, the pattern of morbidity and mortality because of COVID-19 among countries and territories in Africa is significantly different. Having established the difference in the pattern of mortality and morbidity, we explored further with Kendall's W to establish the extent of the difference in the morbidity and mortality among countries/territories in Africa. As noted, Kendall's W adopts the Cohen's interpretation of effect size as follows: 0.1 to <0.3 (small effect), 0.3 to <0.5 (moderate effect), 0.5, and above (large effect). The result of Kendall's W effect size based on Cohen's interpretation of effect size implies that there is a large difference in the number of COVID-19 morbidity (1.0) and mortality (0.9) among countries/territories in Africa.

Table 15.2 shows some of the results of the pairwise comparisons of confirmed cases by each pair of country/territory. If a paired comparison yields a p-value <0.05, it means the number of COVID-19 confirmed cases among those countries is significantly different. The insignificant comparisons are marked in bold. It can be observed that the pattern of morbidity for these pairs of countries/territories (BF, Uganda; AN, Niger), (NI, Burkina Faso; AN, Niger), (NI, Burkina Faso; BF, Uganda), (UG, Liberia; BF, Uganda), (ZW, Congo; CG, Zimbabwe), and (ZM, Mauritania; MU, Zambia) are not significantly different.

These pairs of countries/territories (BF, Uganda; AN, Niger), (BF, Uganda; BE, Sierra Leone), (CA, Central African Republic; AN, Niger), (CA, Central African Republic; BE, Sierra Leone), (CG, Zimbabwe; AN, Niger), (CG, Zimbabwe; CA, Central African Republic), (CV, Mali; AN, Niger), (CV, Mali; BE, Sierra Leone), (CV, Mali; BF, Uganda), (CV, Mali; CA, Central African Republic), (CV, Mali; CG, Zimbabwe), (GB, Gabon; BE, Sierra Leone), (GB, Gabon; BF, Uganda), (GB, Gabon; CG, Zimbabwe), (GU, Guinea; BE, Sierra Leone), and (GU, Guinea; BF, Uganda) marked in bold in Table 15.3 are some of the countries/territories with insignificant differences in pattern of COVID-19 mortality in Africa. In other words, the pattern of COVID-19 mortality between each pair is similar.

It is instructive to note that the main non-parametric test for this study is the Friedman test which proved that the morbidity and mortality patterns of COVID-19 across Africa are significantly different, generally. The Wilcoxon rank sum test, which results are given in Tables 15.2 and 15.3, is a post hoc test that points out the few granular cases where insignificant differences might exist. However, this does not override the general result of the Friedman test.

The hierarchical clustering results group countries/territories in the hierarchy of the morbidity and mortality effect of COVID-19 across Africa. It can be observed from Table 15.4 that only one country, South Africa, is in cluster 1. South Africa has the highest morbidity (>500, 000) and mortality (>8000). Nigeria and Algeria are

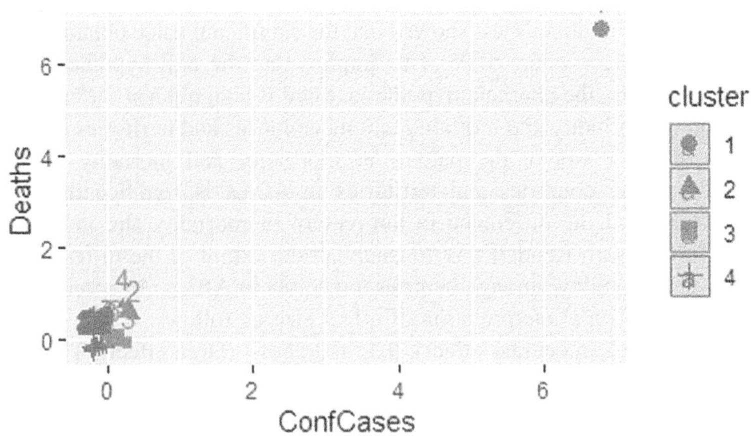

Fig. 15.3 Cluster plot

Table 15.5 Cluster characteristics

	ConfCases		Deaths	
	Min	Max	Min	Max
Cluster 1	521,318	Above	8884	Above
Cluster 2	32,504	44,433	910	1248
Cluster 3	17,718	37,812	191	391
Cluster 4	114	16,293	0	214

the two countries in cluster 2, while Ghana, Kenya, Ethiopia, and Cameroon belong to cluster 3. The remaining 42 countries/territories considered in this study belong to cluster 4.

The characteristics of each cluster in terms of the ranges of number of morbidity (*ConfCases*) and mortality (*Deaths*) as of August 5, 2020, are given in Table 15.5. In cluster 2, Algeria has the lowest number for morbidity (32,504) and the highest number for mortality (1248), while Nigeria has the highest number for morbidity and the lowest number for mortality. In cluster 3, Cameroon has the lowest number for morbidity and the highest number for mortality, while Ghana has the highest number for morbidity and the lowest number for mortality. Of the 42 countries/territories in cluster 4, Côte d'Ivoire has the highest number for morbidity (16,293), while the Republic of Seychelles has the lowest number for morbidity. Eritrea and Seychelles are yet to record any deaths, while Senegal and the Democratic Republic of the Congo have the highest numbers for mortality.

The cluster plot is given in Fig. 15.3. From the plot, it can be observed that the four clusters are well separated, and each cluster is well packed. These are indications that intra-cluster similarity and inter-cluster similarity are well maximized and minimized, respectively.

15.4.2 Discussion

The COVID-19 pandemic seems to have seeped into the societal fiber, disrupting among others the normal business and educational processes. Protocols issued against these exacerbated the use of virtual worlds among other technological infrastructure to facilitate especially business processes and teaching and learning experiences. The pandemic has not only exposed our unpreparedness but also shaped our thinking for future pandemic-like situations. The number of COVID-19 cases and deaths keep rising and has not shown any signs for retrogressing. The COVID-19 is touted to be part of human life which is now called the "new normal." This study has explored the levels of the effect of the pandemic on 49 African countries based on the available data gathered from WHO database on the reportages of various morbidity and mortality rates. By subjecting the data to normality tests by means of density plots shown in Figs. 15.1 and 15.2, it was found not to follow the bell-shaped or skewed. This prompted the need to explore the data with a non-parametric approach. Hence, we explored the variations in the confirmed cases and deaths in the various African countries using the Friedman non-parametric test. By checking with Friedman test, the study revealed that coronavirus morbidity and mortality among African countries are significantly different from country-to-country on a general note. Although the Friedman test established a significant variance in the morbidity and mortality rate in various African countries, Kendall's W test further yielded a large effect size for both the confirmed cases ($k = 1.0$) and the death cases ($k = 0.9$). This means that the average differences between the COVID-19 morbidity and mortality among African countries are meaningfully large.

This finding implies uniqueness in the way in which the novel coronavirus spread in the various countries of Africa. The variations may be because of the differing approaches/strategies in the management of the virus in terms of the treatment, protocol observations, and economic conditions of member countries. The WHO, at some point, observed that many countries in Africa lifted their lockdowns by downplaying the effect of the virus (World Health Organization Regional Office for Africa, 2020d). Downplaying the effect of the virus, at the early stages of the spread, could be attributed to various reasons known to Africans. Notable of these reasons was the public myth/theory about the inability of the virus to survive in the tropical region in Africa (DW Africa, 2020b). It was on this note that the World Health Organization and other leading health institutions warned that African countries should "prepare for the worst" (France24, 2020). Such assertions may, perhaps, been borne out of the weak economies of African countries with many predicting African countries' inability to execute lockdown for a longer time. Additionally, the high levels of poverty, relatively weaker healthcare systems, and crowded urban areas in Africa threatened the spread of the virus (Africacenter, 2020; Soy, 2020). Although the current situation is not as it was envisaged, some countries in Africa have been badly hit by the virus. At the granular level, we applied the Wilcoxon rank sum test to examine the exact pairwise country variations in the rate at which the confirmed cases and deaths are reported. As indicated in Table 15.2, the majority of the pairwise comparison among countries yielded significance, implying vast variations between countries. Few months after the virus was first detected in China, scientists sequenced the genomes of the virus and reported that it had mutated into different forms which were found to be respectively different from country to country (Kupferschmidt, 2020). The deadly nature of the mutated viruses was also found to vary from country to country (Kupferschmidt, 2020). This may have also accounted for the variations in the cases, especially the death toll. Nevertheless, studies have used machine learning and artificial intelligence techniques to predict the pattern of spread of the disease based on available data. Notably, Chaurasia and Pal (2020) in June 2020, predicted a slow increase of 600,000 death cases by January 2021.

Having found variations in the rate of confirmed cases and deaths in Africa, we further explored the magnitude of the effect of cases according to the way (time) they are reported. With unsupervised machine learning, we applied agglomerate hierarchical clustering technique to cluster the data according to countries with least-hit, moderately hit, badly hit, and worst-hit cases of the novel coronavirus.

This current study found South Africa to be the worst-hit country in Africa, while Nigeria and Algeria are found to be badly hit by the novel coronavirus. The technique for the clustering was based on the reported data and the rate of reporting cases, including death and confirmed cases. Ghana, Kenya, Ethiopia, and Cameroon are clustered together as the moderately hit countries. The remaining African countries, including Madagascar, Chad, and Senegal, are the least-hit countries. The percentages of the distribution of the countries among clusters are shown in a pie chart in Fig. 15.4.

While several studies have established the reasons for the spread of the virus, what seems to be the most notable is the mobility of people in public gatherings and apathy in following recommended protocols. In some study, it has been established that the virus spread faster in the temperate regions than the tropical regions (DW Africa, 2020b). While we agree that other factors contribute to the rise of cases in the spread of the virus, the findings of this study also sought to confirm the theory that the virus hardly survives in the tropical regions hence the low cases. For instance, South Africa is a cold region as compared to most of the African countries. The various countries clustered together have similarities in terms of the spread and rate at which cases are being reported. It is worth noting that countries that were clustered together also have similarities on the way this coronavirus is managed. It is prudent and for that matter our recommendation, in this study, for countries that are worst hit to review their policies and strategies in line with the least-hit countries toward taming the effect of the virus. It is also prudent, as a continental agenda, for the least-hit and moderately hit countries to collaborate and share ideas, resources, and strategies with countries in the worst-hit and badly hit clusters. This would certainly go a long way to salvage their situation.

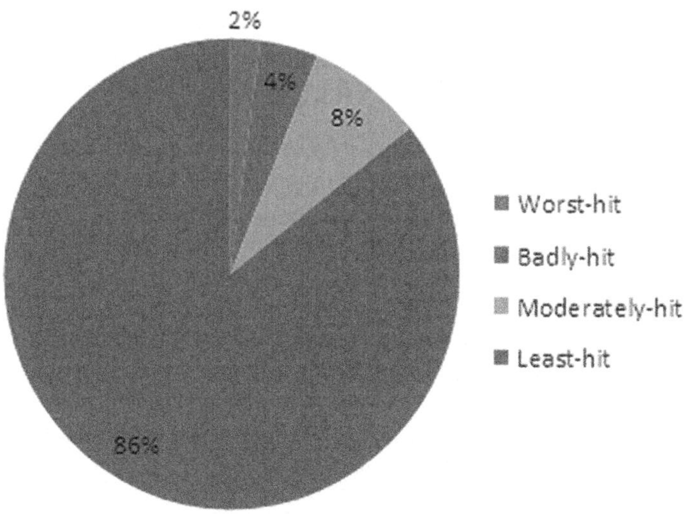

Fig. 15.4 Percentage distributions among clusters

15.5 Conclusion and Contribution

This study extracted the pattern of morbidity and mortality distribution of COVID-19 among countries and territories in Africa, using non-parametric tests (distribution-free tests). The datasets, sourced from the WHO COVID-19 daily situation reports, were first subjected to normality test using density plot and Shapiro-Wilk's normality test. The outcome indicated that the datasets are non-normal, thus suitable for non-parametric analysis. The Friedman test indicated that coronavirus confirmed and deaths cases among African countries are significantly different across countries. Kendall's W effect size test was performed on the morbidity and mortality cases with an output of 1.0 and 0.9, respectively. This implies that there is a large effect size in the morbidity and the mortality of COVID-19 cases in countries and territories in Africa. Furthermore, the Wilcoxon rank sum test was utilized to check the exact groups whose distributions are different, through pairwise comparisons, and the results show that there are significant discrepancies in most of the countries and territories on Africa.

Four clusters were extracted from the COVID-19 data using agglomerate hierarchical clustering which is an unsupervised machine learning technique. The results indicated that South Africa is the worst-hit country in Africa, while Nigeria and Algeria were found to be badly hit by the novel coronavirus. Ghana, Kenya, Ethiopia, and Cameroon were clustered together as the moderately hit countries. The other African countries, including Madagascar, Chad, and Senegal, were the least-hit countries by the pandemic. This study has effectively established that the morbidity and mortality of the pandemic is not uniform across Africa. At the beginning of the pandemic, several statements were credited to some institutions and personalities to indicate that the African continent was going to be uniformly hit by the pandemic, with dead bodies littering the streets of Africa.

This present study has interesting implications for both policy and practice. In terms of the policy, this study has reported the differences in patterns of spread of COVID-19 in Africa and therefore could guide policymakers on developing new policies for the pandemic. We have also shown which among the African countries are least hit and worst hit by clustering according to similarities in the spread and management of the virus. The findings from this present study will open up opportunities for countries within a particular cluster to reconsider their policies on managing the pandemic by benchmarking with countries in other clusters that are least hit.

The COVID-19 is still spreading which requires Africans to observe the recommended protocols specified by their respective countries and the WHO to reduce the rate of the spread. Based on the findings, we conclude that the badly hit and worst-hit countries have had challenges in dealing with the spread of the virus. This may be because of the differences in their management strategies, leadership style, and funds invested, among others. We envision that countries in the badly or worst-hit clusters confer with their counterparts in the least-hit cluster in managing the spread of the virus. Through non-parametric data analytics and data mining, this study has established that though majority of African countries are underdeveloped, the effect of the pandemic is not uniform across the continent. It is therefore suggested that the better positioned countries on the continent should extend a hand of fellowship to the countries in need so that, together, the African continent would be rid of the COVID-19 pandemic. This would pave the way for a uniform, post-pandemic, socioeconomic development across the continent.

Appendix: African Countries/Territories and Abbreviations

Country/territory	Abbreviation	Country/territory	Abbreviation
Algeria	AL	Madagascar	MD
Niger	AN	Cabo Verde	ML
Sierra Leone	BE	Zambia	MU
Uganda	BF	Malawi	MW
Burundi	BR	Guinea-Bissau	MZ
Botswana	BT	Nigeria	NG
Central African Republic	CA	Burkina Faso	NI
Zimbabwe	CG	South Sudan	NM
Côte d'Ivoire	CI	Réunion	RE
Cameroon	CR	Rwanda	RW
Mali	CV	South Africa	SA
Democratic Republic of the Congo	DRC	Benin	SL
Eritrea	ER	Senegal	SN
Ethiopia	ET	Namibia	SS
United Republic of Tanzania	GA	Sao Tome and Principe	ST
Gabon	GB	Seychelles	SY
Ghana	GH	Eswatini	SZ
Equatorial Guinea	GQ	Lesotho	TA
Guinea	GU	Togo	TD
Mozambique	GW	Chad	TO
Comoros	KM	Liberia	UG
Kenya	KY	Mayotte	YT
Gambia	LE	Mauritania	ZM
Angola	LI	Congo	ZW
Mauritius	MA		

References

Africacenter. (2020). *Mapping risk factors for the spread of COVID-19 in Africa*. https://africacenter.org/spotlight/mapping-risk-factors-spread-covid-19-africa/. Acessed 13 Aug 2020.

Africa Check. (2020). *Melinda Gates said she feared coronavirus in Africa would lead to dead being put out in street, as in Ecuador*. https://africacheck.org/fbcheck/melinda-gates-said-she-feared-coronavirus-in-africa-would-lead-to-dead-being-put-out-in-street-as-in-ecuador/. Accessed 13 Aug 2020.

African Development Bank Group. (2020). *African economic outlook 2020: Africa's economy forecast to grow despite external shocks*. https://www.afdb.org/en/news-and-events/press-releases/african-economic-outlook-2020-africas-economy-forecast-grow-despite-external-shocks-33839. Accessed 20 Aug 2020.

Atsa'am, D. D. (2020). Feature selection algorithm using relative odds for data mining classification. In A. Haldorai & A. Ramu (Eds.), *Big data analytics for sustainable computing* (pp. 81–106). IGI Global. https://doi.org/10.4018/978-1-5225-9750-6.ch005

Atsa'am, D. D., Wario, R., & Okpo, F. E. (2020). A new terrorism categorization based on casualties and consequences using hierarchical clustering. *Journal of Applied Security Research*. https://doi.org/10.1080/19361610.2020.1769461

Bodur, E. K., & Atsa'am, D. D. (2019). Filter variable selection algorithm using risk ratios for dimensionality reduction of healthcare data for classification. *PRO, 7*, 222. https://doi.org/10.3390/pr7040222

BBC News. (2020). *Coronavirus in Africa tracker*. https://www.bbc.co.uk/news/resources/idt-4a11d568-2716-41cf-a15e-7d15079548bc. Accessed 13 Aug 2020.

Boston Consulting Group. (2020). *Fighting COVID-19 in Africa will be different*. https://www.bcg.com/en-za/publications/2020/fighting-covid-in-africa.aspx. Accessed 13 Aug 2020.

Center for Global Development. (2020). *The economic impact of COVID-19 in Africa: A round-up of this week's analysis*. https://www.cgdev.org/blog/economic-impact-covid-19-africa-weeks-latest-analysis. Accessed 20 Aug 2020.

Chaurasia, V., & Pal, S. (2020). Covid-19 pandemic: Application of machine learning time series analysis for prediction of human future. *Research Square*, *12*, 1–16. 10.21203/rs.3.rs-39149/v1

Cortegiani, A., Ingoglia, G., Ippolito, M., Giarratano, A., & Einav, S. (2020). A systematic review on the efficacy and safety of chloroquine for the treatment of COVID-19. *Journal of Critical Care*. https://doi.org/10.1016/j.jcrc.2020.03.005

Dahab, M., van Zandvoort, K., Flasche, S., Warsame, A., Spiegel, P. B., Waldman, R. J., & Checchi, F. (2020). *COVID-19 control in low-income settings and displaced populations: What can realistically be done?* London School of Hygiene and Tropical Medicine. https://www.lshtm.ac.uk/newsevents/news/2020/covid-19-control-low-income-settings-and-displaced-populations-what-can. Accessed 13 Aug 2020.

Dowd, J. B., Andriano, L., Brazel, D. M., Rotondi, V., Block, P., Ding, X., Liu, Y., & Mills, M.C. (2020). Demographic science aids in understanding the spread and fatality rates of COVID-19. In: D. S. Masses (Ed.), *Proceedings of the National Academy of Sciences 117*(18), 202004911, 9696–9698. https://doi.org/10.1073/pnas.2004911117.

Durotoye, I., Odunola, R., Adeyemi, O., Akanmu, A., Bolarinwa, O., Adeboye, M., Abdullahi, A., Bolajoko, A., Durosinmi, W., Adebisi, G., & Aduloju, V. (2020). Pertinent roles of African higher institutions in the COVID-19 pandemic response: The University of Ilorin, Ilorin, Nigeria; an African model. *The International Journal of Health Planning and Management*. https://doi.org/10.1002/hpm.2984

DW Africa. (2020a). *World Bank: No African country can face this crisis alone*. https://www.dw.com/en/world-bank-no-african-country-can-face-this-crisis-alone/a-53142901. Accessed 24 Aug 2020.

DW Africa. (2020b). Africa has been spared so far from coronavirus. Why? https://www.dw.com/en/africa-has-been-spared-so-far-from-coronavirus-why/a-52382666. Accessed 24 Aug 2020

France-Presse. (2020). *Media watchdog: Algeria arrests independent journalist.* https://www.voanews.com/press-freedom/media-watchdog-algeria-arrests-independent-journalist. Accessed 23 Aug 2020.

France24. (2020). Burkina Faso reports sub-Saharan Africa's first coronavirus death as WHO warns 'prepare for worst'. https://www.france24.com/en/20200319-burkina-faso-sub-saharan-africa-coronavirus-covid19-death-who-tedros-adhanom-ghebreyesus. Accessed 13 Aug 2020

Ghasemi, A., & Zahediasl, S. (2012). Normality tests for statistical analysis: A guide for non-statisticians. *International Journal of Endocrinology and Metabolism, 10*, 486–489. https://doi.org/10.5812/ijem.3505

Gilbert, M., Pullano, G., Pinotti, F., Valdano, E., Poletto, C., Boëlle, P., et al. (2020). Preparedness and vulnerability of African countries against importations of COVID-19: A modelling study. *Lancet, 395*(10227), 871–877. https://doi.org/10.1016/S0140-6736(20)30411-6

Hopman, J., Allegranzi, B., & Mehtar, S. (2020). Managing COVID-19 in low-and middle-income countries. *JAMA, 323*, 1549–1550. https://doi.org/10.1001/jama.2020.4169.

Johns Hopkins University. (2020). COVID-19 dashboard by the Center for SystemScience and Engineering (CSSE) at Johns Hopkins University. https://coronavirus.jhu.edu/map.html. Accessed 13 Aug 2020.

Kassambara A (2020) Statistical tests and assumptions. https://www.datanovia.com/en/lessons/normality-test-in-r/. Accessed 11 Aug 2020.

Khan, M. A., & Atangana, A. (2020). Modeling the dynamics of novel coronavirus (2019-nCov) with fractional derivative. *Alexandria Engineering Journal.* https://doi.org/10.1016/j.aej.2020.033

Kupferschmidt, K. (2020). The pandemic virus is slowly mutating. But is it getting more dangerous? *Science Magazine*. https://doi.org/10.1126/science.abd8226.

Lakens, D. (2013). Calculating and reporting effect sizes to facilitate cumulative science: A practical primer for t-tests and ANOVAs. *Frontiers in Psychology, 4*, 863. https://doi.org/10.3389/fpsyg.2013.00863

Lone, S. A., & Ahmad, A. (2020). COVID-19 pandemic – An African perspective. *Emerging Microbes & Infections*, 1–28.

Massinga Loembé, M., Tshangela, A., Salyer, S. J., et al. (2020). COVID-19 in Africa: The spread and response. *Nature Medicine, 26*, 999–1003. https://doi.org/10.1038/s41591-020-0961-x

McKenzie, B. (2020). *The impact of COVID-19 on key African sectors.* https://www.bakermckenzie.com/en/insight/publications/2020/03/the-impact-of-covid19-on-key-african-sectors. Accessed 13 Aug 2020.

Mehtar, S., Preiser, W., Lakhe, N. A., Bousso, A., TamFum, J. JM., Kallay, O., & Nachega, J. B. (2020). Limiting the spread of COVID-19 in Africa: One size mitigation strategies do not fit all countries. *The Lancet Global Health.*

Mendelson, M. (2020). Could enhanced influenza and pneumococcal vaccination programs help limit the potential damage from SARS-CoV-2 to fragile health systems of southern hemisphere countries this winter? *International Journal of Infectious Diseases, 94*, 32–33. https://doi.org/10.1016/j.ijid.2020.03.030

Mudie, K., Tan, M. M. J., Kendall, L., Addo, J., dos-Santos-Silva, I., Quint, J., Smeeth, L., Cook, S., Nitsch, D., Natamba, B., Gomex-Olive, F. X., Ako, A., & Perel, P. (2019). Non-communicable diseases in sub-Saharan Africa: A scoping review of large cohort studies. *Journal of Global Health, 9*, 020409. https://doi.org/10.7189/jogh.09.020409

Mwai, P., & Giles, C. (2020). *Coronavirus: How fast is it spreading in Africa?* https://www.bbc.com/news/world-africa-53181555. Accessed 10 Aug 2020.

Nachega, J. B., Grimwood, A., Mahomed, H., Fatti, G., Preiser, W., Kallay, O., & Ngamije, D. (2020a). From easing lockdowns to scaling-up community-based COVID-19 screening, testing, and contact tracing in Africa: Shared approaches, innovations, and challenges to minimize morbidity and mortality. *Clinical Infectious Diseases, 31*, ciaa695. https://doi.org/10.1093/cid/ciaa695

Nachega, J. B., Seydi, M., & Zumla, A. (2020b). The late arrival of COVID-19 in Africa – Mitigating pan-continental spread. *Clinical Infectious Diseases*, ciaa353. https://doi.org/10.1093/cid/ciaa353

Nielsen, F. (2016). *Introduction to HPC with MPI for data science*. Springer.

Njenga, K. M., Dawa, J., Nanyingi, M., Gachohi, J., Ngere, I., Letko, M., Otieno, C. F., Gunn, B. M., & Osoro, E. (2020). Why is there low morbidity and mortality of COVID-19 in Africa? *The American Society of Tropical Medicine and Hygiene, 103*(2), 564–569. https://doi.org/10.4269/ajtmh.20-0474

Nkengasong, J. N., & Mankoula, W. (2020). Looming threat of COVID-19 infection in Africa: Act collectively, and fast. *The Lancet, 395*(10227), 841–842.

OECD Development Matters. (2020). *COVID-19 and beyond: How can Africa's health systems cope?* https://oecd-development-matters.org/2020/04/07/covid-19-and-beyond-how-can-africas-health-systems-cope/. Accessed 10 Aug 2020.

Ogunleye, O. O., Basu, D., Mueller, D., Sneddon, J., Seaton, R. A., Yinka-Ogunleye, A. F., … Massele, A. (2020). Response to the novel corona virus (COVID-19) pandemic across Africa: Successes, challenges and implications for the future. *Frontiers in Pharmacology*. https://doi.org/10.3389/phar.2020.01205

Quaresima, V., Naldini. M. M., & Cirillo, D. M. (2020). The prospects for the SARS-CoV-2 pandemic in Africa. *EMBO Molecular Medicine*, e12488. 10.15252/emmm.202012488.

Riffenburgh, R. H. (2012). Tests on ranked data. In: R. H. Riffenburgh (Ed.), *Statistics in medicine* (3rd edn. pp. 221–248). Elsevier. https://doi.org/10.1016/C2010-0-64822-X

Rothan, H. A., & Byrareddy, S. N. (2020). The epidemiology and pathogenesis of coronavirus disease (COVID-19) outbreak. *Journal of Autoimmunity, 109*, 102433. https://doi.org/10.1016/j.jaut.2020.102433

Shagam, L. (2020). Untangling factors associated with country-specific COVID-19 incidence, mortality and case fatality rates during the first quarter of 2020. medRxiv preprint. https://doi.org/10.1101/2020.04.22.20075580.

Shereen, M. A., Khan, S., Kazmi, A., Bashir, N., & Siddique, R. (2020). COVID-19 infection: Origin, transmission, and characteristics of human coronaviruses. *Journal of Advanced Research, 24*, 91–98. https://doi.org/10.1016/j.jare.2020.03.005

Soy, A. (2020). *Lack of Covid-19 testing undermines Africa's 'success'*. https://www.bbc.com/news/world-africa-52801190. Accessed 12 Aug 2020.

Taboe, H. B., Salako, K. V., Tison, J. M., Ngonghala, C. N., & Kakaï, R. G. (2020). Predicting COVID-19 spread in the face of control measures in West-Africa. *Mathematical Biosciences*. https://doi.org/10.1016/j.mbs.2020.108431

Tomczak, M., & Tomczak, E. (2014). The need to report effect size estimates revisited. An overview of some recommended measures of effect size. *TRENDS in Sports Sciences, 1*, 19–25.

World Health Organization. (2010). *Global status report on noncommunicable diseases 2010*. https://www.who.int/nmh/publications/ncd_report_full_en.pdf. Accessed 10 Aug 2020.

World Health Organization. (2020a). *Coronavirus disease (COVID-19) situation reports*. https://www.who.int/emergencies/diseases/novel-coronavirus2019/situation-reports. Accessed 23 Aug 2020.

World Health Organization. (2020b). *The World malaria report 2019 at a glance*. https://www.who.int/news-room/feature-stories/detail/world-malaria-report-2019, Accessed 6 Aug 2020.

World Health Organization Regional Office for Africa. (2020a). *World AIDS Day 2019 – Message of WHO Regional Director for Africa, Dr Matshidiso Moeti*. https://www.afro.who.int/regional-director/speeches-messages/world-aids-day-2019-message-who-regional-director-africa-dr. Accessed 10 Aug 2020.

World Health Organization Regional Office for Africa. (2020b). *World tuberculosis day 2019*. https://www.afro.who.int/media-centre/events/world-tuberculosis-day-2019. Accessed 13 Aug 2020.

World Health Organization Regional Office for Africa. (2020c). *World Hepatitis Day 2019 – Message of WHO Regional Director for Africa, Dr Matshidiso Moeti*. https://www.afro.who.

int/regional-director/speeches-messages/world-hepatitis-day-2019-message-who-regional-director-africa. Accessed 13 Aug 2020.

World Health Organization Regional Office for Africa. (2020d). *WHO urges caution as countries in Africa ease lockdowns*. https://www.afro.who.int/news/who-urges-caution-countries-africa-ease-lockdowns. Accessed 24 Aug 2020.

Yim, O., & Ramdeen, K. T. (2015). Hierarchical cluster analysis: Comparison of three linkage measures and application to psychological data. *The Quantitative Methods for Psychology, 11*, 8–21.

Dr. Donald Douglas Atsa'am is currently a postdoctoral research fellow at the Department of Computer Science and Informatics, University of the Free State, South Africa. He has been a lecturer of Computer Science in the University of Agriculture, Makurdi, Nigeria, since 2012. He holds a PhD in Applied Mathematics and Computer Science from the Eastern Mediterranean University, North Cyprus. Donald's research interests are in data mining, machine learning, and knowledge discovery. He has published over 20 articles and book chapters within these areas.

Dr. Emmanuel Awuni Kolog is a faculty member at the Department of Operations and Management Information Systems (OMIS) of the University of Ghana. He holds a PhD in Computer Science and MSc in Software Engineering from the University of Eastern Finland. He additionally holds an MBA degree in International Business Management from the Business School of Lapland University of Applied Sciences in Finland. Dr. Awuni's research interest is multidisciplinary which spans the fields of text mining, affect detection, learning analytics, machine learning applications, and digital platforms. He is the recipient of Queen Elizabeth II Scholarship to McGill University in Canada. In 2018, he won the best research paper award in a conference held in Hong Kong, and, in 2019, his paper was nominated with two others for the best paper award in knowledge management and information systems conference held in Vienna.

Dr. Temidayo Oluwatosin Omotehinwa is a senior lecturer in the Department of Mathematical Sciences, College of Natural and Applied Sciences, Achievers University, Owo, Nigeria. He holds a PhD degree in Computer Science from the University of Ilorin, Ilorin, Nigeria. His research interest includes machine learning, natural language processing, Web programming, embedded systems, the Internet of Things, algorithm design, and cloud computing. He is a RankSheet-Certified Programmer. He has authored and/or co-authored articles in refereed journals and conferences. Dr. Omotehinwa is a member of the Nigeria Computer Society (NCS) and an associate member of the Institute of Strategic Management (ISMN).

Samuel Nii Odoi Devine is a faculty member at the Information and Communication Technology department of the Presbyterian University College, Ghana. He holds an MSc in Information Technology from Sikkim Manipal University and a bachelor's degree in Information and Communication Technology, graduating with First Class (Honors). At both levels, he graduated top of his class and was the valedictorian at the bachelor's level. In the year 2019, his paper was nominated with two others for the best paper award at the knowledge management and information systems conference held in Vienna, Austria. As a researcher and technologist, Devine has a strong affinity for computing and its use to impact both academia and industry. He has several years of teaching experience and has been involved in several IS projects. His research interest is multidisciplinary, spanning the areas of knowledge management, machine learning applications, big data, and information security awareness.

Oluwaseun Alexander Dada is an Information Systems Specialist (cloud computing) at the Finland Institute for Molecular Medicine (FIMM) in the University of Helsinki. His academic background and work experience span the fields of computer science, educational technology, and business strategy. He is most interested in research related to education, educational technology, data science, business strategy, blockchain, and any aspect of computing (software development, architecture, cloud).

Dr. Toluwalase Janet Akingbade is a lecturer at Kogi State University, Anyigba, Kogi State, Nigeria. She has over 7 years of academic working experience as a lecturer and researcher. She holds a PhD degree in Statistics from the University of Nigeria, Nsukka, Nigeria. She has published academic research papers in different journals of repute. Her research interests are in the areas of sample survey, demography, quality control, data science, biostatistics, and modeling. She is an active member of the Nigerian Statistical Association (NSA-CISON).

Dr. Richard O. Agjei is currently a student at the Department of Medicine, School of Public Health of Imperial College London. He holds a PhD in Public Health and MSc in Research Chemist from the University of Eastern Finland. He additionally holds PGCE from Haaga-Helia University of Applied Sciences in Finland. His research interest is multidisciplinary which spans the fields of exposure assessment, affect detection, suicidal behaviors, health policy and analysis, machine learning, and data science applications in public health. He is a reviewer in Cogent Medicine and has published several articles in scientific journals.

Dr. Oluwafemi Samson Balogun is a Lecturer at the Department of Statistics and Operations Research, Modibbo Adama University of Technology, Yola, Adamawa State, Nigeria. He is currently a postdoctoral researcher at the School of Computing, University of Eastern Finland. He holds a PhD in Statistics from the Department of Statistics, University of Ilorin, Kwara State, Nigeria. He is a senior research fellow at Centre for Multidisciplinary Research and Innovation (CEMRI), and he is a member of the International Biometric Society (IBS), International Statistical Institute (ISI), Nigerian Statistical Association (NSA-CISON), and Nigerian Mathematical Society (NMS). He has several conference and journal papers in reputable international bodies, and he has also served as guest reviewer for several journals. His research interest is data science, machine learning, data mining, biostatistics, categorical data analysis, modeling, and probability distribution models.

Chapter 16
Assessing the Impact of Information and Communication Technologies on Human Development: A Regional Analysis for Africa

İpek Akad

Abstract This study examines the socio-economic effects of information and communication technologies (ICT) in Africa by region. Analysis-based data from countries in five regions of Africa show that the contribution of ICTs to socio-economic indicators varies according to the type of ICT and the region where these technologies are used. For example, Internet usage is prominent in the Middle, East, and North Africa, while telecommunication technologies are at the forefront in South, East, North, and West Africa. The study, therefore, contributes to the formation of policies according to the regional dynamics of the continent. Besides, this study argues that, contrary to the study performed by Njoh (2018) for the African continent, IC technologies can be effective on HDI with different types of ICT according to the regional dynamics of the continent. The result of this study is that using ICT alone does not adequately support development. Therefore, IC technologies should also be used in sectors such as agriculture, health, and education. Digital transformation in the agriculture sector can be a significant factor in solving the food problem facing the continent. Mobile phones and Internet use in the agricultural field can enable farmers to learn about new agricultural techniques and to use agricultural areas more efficiently. In healthcare, mobile phones and the Internet can enable these services to reach even remote regions of the continent. In education, the integration of IC technologies – especially the Internet and computers – can support human capital by ensuring that education reaches all levels of society equally and quickly. The use of IC technologies in these three sectors is the most effective way for Africa to achieve its sustainable development goals.

Keywords Information and communication technologies · Human development · Regional analysis

İ. Akad (✉)
Bitlis Eren University, Bitlis, Turkey
e-mail: iakad@beu.edu.tr

R. Boateng et al. (eds.), *Digital Innovations, Business and Society in Africa*, Advances in Theory and Practice of Emerging Markets,
https://doi.org/10.1007/978-3-030-77987-0_16

16.1 Introduction

The use of IC technologies such as mobile phones and the Internet, which have become an integral part of daily life, is increasing in Africa as well as in the rest of the world. With the discovery of certain features of IC technologies such as recording the acquired information and storing it for later use, IC technologies have started to be widely used in business life and public services. But the increase in the use of IC technologies is not at the same pace in all parts of Africa. In Figs. 16.1 and 16.2, regional data from Africa of Internet and mobile phone usage from IC technologies are visualized. As can be seen in both figures, North Africa ranked first in Internet and mobile phone usage, while Central and East Africa ranked last. The socio-economic consequences of this regional difference in the use of IC technologies in the African continent constituted the starting point of the study. IC technologies have become a part of human development with their role in the dissemination and

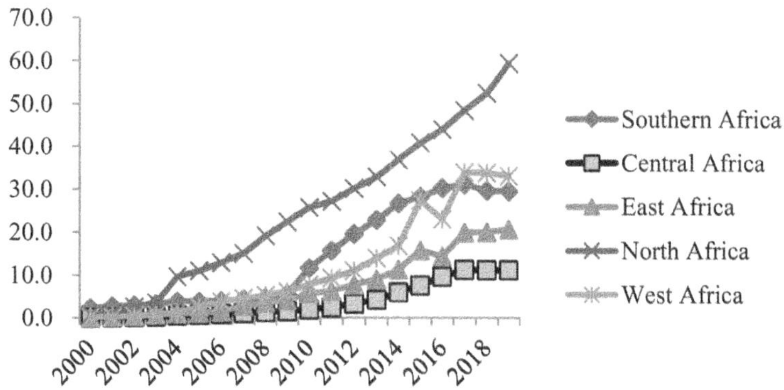

Fig. 16.1 Percentage of the population using the Internet. (Source: OECD Africa's Development Dynamics- Statistical Annex)

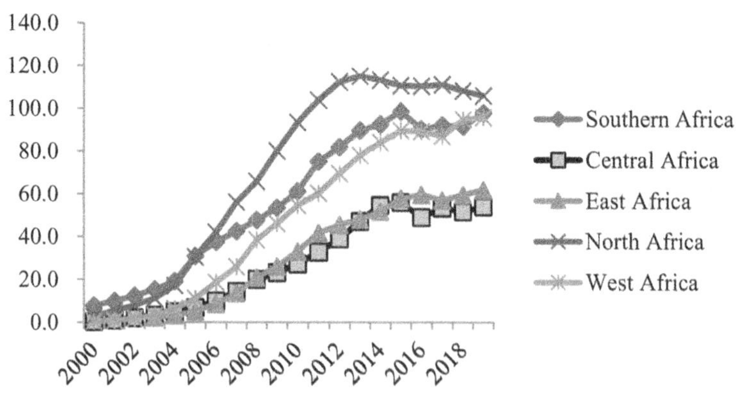

Fig. 16.2 Mobile-cellular telephone subscriptions per 100 inhabitants. (Source: OECD Africa's Development Dynamics- Statistical Annex)

sharing of knowledge (Polikanov & Abramova, 2003). Therefore, important conclusions have been made in this study, which includes findings on the effects of IC technologies on human development and how these technologies will play a role in achieving Africa's development goals. This study, which is carried out by taking into account the regional dynamics of Africa, is important in that it sheds light on the emergence of development policies of the continent by region.

Although IC technologies such as the Internet and mobile phones, which are used more in North and Southern Africa, have not reached the desired level in other regions, the positive trend in the numbers of the five regions shows that the continent is trying to keep up with the world. Kenya, located in the east of the continent, in contrast to the regional ICT indicators in Figs. 16.1 and 16.2, is an example of successful digitization in Africa (Schelenz & Schopp, 2018). Further examples of successful digitization are Nigeria in West Africa and South Africa in the South (Schelenz & Schopp, 2018). The success of these countries in digitization is directly related to the integration of ICTs into their public and private sector initiatives and services. Municipal services, agricultural services, and mobile banking are some examples where ICTs have been integrated and are found increasingly desirable by the public. The provision of digital services saves time and removes the need to travel, therefore, shortening distances. Thus, ICTs shorten the distances. Thus it is important to disseminate these services to the social base and facilitate the use of such technologies. To this end, African countries came together in 2013 to set up Smart Africa. The purpose of Smart Africa is to improve Africa through ICTs in terms of socio-economic development. Smart Africa declared, by publishing a manifesto, how ICTs are incorporated into social life with five main principles. According to the Smart Africa Manifesto, the ICTs aim to:

- Ensure prosperity and decrease poverty in Africa by considering the development strategies at a central point and promoting innovation production
- Ensure the development of productivity, prosperity, and poverty reduction in Africa by putting these at the center of development strategies and promoting the production of innovation
- Make infrastructure investments that will make broadband access more accessible and affordable
- Deliver public services to the public through applications such as e-government and pursue a more transparent and efficient government policy
- Help the shift toward a technology and innovation generating role of the private sector in the African continent as a whole by encouraging the private sector to use ICT
- Benefit from ICTs for sustainable development, empowering women, youth, and disabled people in socio-economic development and environmental sustainability

ICTs will play a part in achieving five fundamental principles (Summit, 2013). With this manifest, ICTs have been granted the role of creating both microeconomic and socio-economic value.

As stated in Smart Africa Manifesto, the development of technological innovations in the private sector and providing ICT production enables the commercialization of these technologies via ICTs through e-commerce channels. Thus, ICTs contribute to social development by providing economic gains in Africa. The next section will analyze the findings of research conducted in African countries on the microeconomic, macroeconomic, and socio-economic impacts of ICTs.

16.2 Literature Review

The economic values developed by IC technologies should be addressed to analyze the impact of the ICTs on social development. The development potential of these technologies is flexible from micro to macro scale. The emergence of this potential requires a transformation in public services and private sector production processes. Besides, for consumers to access these technologies, infrastructure services must be provided without any difficulties and these technologies must be offered to consumers at reasonable prices.

This reform on both sides for producers and consumers will be possible by increasing the investments made in these technologies. The social development expected to occur through these technologies is based on an economic foundation. This interrelated process is examined under two subheadings, particularly in the literature addressing the situation in African countries.

16.2.1 Microeconomic Effects of ICTs

Many entrepreneurs in Africa have also integrated incorporate ICTs into manufacturing or post-production processes. The ICTs used during and after production has created an expansion in the demand for goods with systems such as e-commerce in addition to increased labor productivity.

Kenya in particular is one of the prominent countries in the e-commerce sector in Africa. A review of 400 companies operating in Kenya indicated that 53% of such companies are operating in e-commerce (Wanyoike et al., 2012). A review of 400 companies operating in Kenya indicated that 53% of such companies were operating in e-commerce (Wanyoike et al., 2012). An additional study concluded that the corporate performance of companies in Kenya had been positively influenced by the use of ICTs (Wamuyu & Maharaj, 2011). Another study discovered that increasing ICT investments above a certain amount would have a positive effect on total factor productivity (TFP) in small and medium enterprises (SMEs) in Kenya and Tanzania (Wolf, 2001). Studies often concentrate on labor efficiency by specifying TFP. For example, in a study performed for the South African manufacturing sector, it was ascertained that telecommunications technologies have positive effects on labor productivity (Fedderke & Bogetic, 2006). In a similar study conducted at the level of a company in the Tunisian manufacturing sector, it has been found that the ICTs have a significant positive effect on productivity combined with human capital (Mouelhi, 2009).

ICTs used in other sectors, in addition to the manufacturing industry, present various benefits to the producers. In Zambia, for example, the functions of ICTs in agricultural sector growth have been investigated, and it has been reported that ICTs should be used more frequently and practically for agricultural sector development (Eden & Kalusopa, 2005). In a study for Mali and Burkina Faso, it was observed that the use of video on mobile telephones could boost agricultural services and farming activities by the communication between farmers (Sousa et al., 2016). In Nigeria, it has been concluded that the use of ICT in the construction sector improves the quality of service (Musa et al., 2010). In a study conducted in South Africa for the same sector, it was found that performance would increase as a result of saving time and cost if awareness was raised to a sufficient level among the stakeholders in terms of the transition of construction 4.0 (Osunsanmi et al., 2018). On the other hand, in another study examining ICTs from a macro perspective, it has been concluded that the highest contribution was obtained from ICTs regarding value-adding for SMEs in South Africa (Ismail et al., 2011). Findings regarding the negative aspects in addition to positive aspects of ICTs are available in the literature. For instance, a company-level study in Cameroon concluded that ICT investments do not affect productivity (Nkama, 2014).

The area of use for ICTs is rapidly expanding in Africa. For example, it was reported in the Ghana digital economy report of the World Bank that the telecommunications industry seems to be the principal sector in the Ghana economy and that the ICT and service sector provide 3.6% of Ghana's income (World Bank Group, 2019). Moreover, ICTs are successfully employed for health in Ghana, agriculture in Benin and Zimbabwe, and information access to remote rural areas in South Africa and Mozambique (Ponelis & Holmner, 2015).

Some countries in Africa continue to fight poverty and drought. Thus, investment in costly ICTs is not a priority for them. Instead, these countries have to focus on the provision of basic infrastructure, education, healthcare, food, and clean water (Ngwenyama et al., 2006). ICTs will not be able to improve before primary problems are solved. Because electricity, the Internet, mobile telephone, or fixed-line networks which will use these technologies are not common enough. A study mentioning the obstacles to the expansion of ICTs in Mozambique, Gillwald et al. (2019), highlighted the lack of infrastructure in Mozambique; nearly 66% of the population do not have access to electricity, and in this case, the development of the ICTs is hindered. Considering Nigeria, less than half of the country's citizens have Internet access. Also, the production cost of ICTs and insufficient investments in this sector make it difficult to integrate ICT systems (Ifinedo, 2006).

The problems faced by the private sector for the integration of ICTs in production models are due to general infrastructural shortcomings and inadequate investment in these technologies. In this case, it is necessary to concentrate on infrastructure services, as stated in the Smart Africa Manifesto, to expand these technologies widely. While these infrastructural services are provided by public authorities, citizens should have access to these technologies at a reasonable price and the infrastructure for IC technologies should be improved. The following section presents the findings of several studies into these technologies' macroeconomic and socio-economic impacts.

16.2.2 Macroeconomic and Socio-economic Effects of ICTs

16.2.2.1 Labor Productivity

Personal rights and freedoms are benefits from easy and rapid access to information. The willingness of people to compare and judge the diverse knowledge that they have access to from multiple sources through ICTs is an essential addition to the expansion of a developed society. People who use these tools in their social and professional life develop human capital and become more efficient in production. Hence, the impact of these technologies on labor productivity has been studied in many countries including developed or developing countries. Most of the studies conducted have found that ICT has a positive effect on labor productivity (Nurmilaakso, 2009; Ossadzifo, 2018; Piatkowski, 2003; Relich, 2017; Wamboye et al., 2016). Besides, a study in South Africa examined the macroeconomic impact of mobile technology and reported that widespread usage of mobile phone networks in rural South Africa would make a positive contribution to employment (Klonner & Nolen, 2008).

In addition to increasing labor productivity, the transformation of production processes with new technology to create job areas would also affect economic growth in the long term.

16.2.2.2 Economic Growth

Economic growth can be defined as the increase in the production of goods and services. The use of technology in the production of goods and services allows the production of products in a shorter period, and the transition of services to digital environments makes them more effective. Moreover, while digital technologies increase the quality of goods and services, they also make it possible to bring these products and services to consumers in a digital environment. This provides economic growth by generating higher income (Batuo, 2015; Nasab & Aghaei, 2009; Niebel, 2018; Wang, 1999).

The expectation that economies that use these technologies in production and post-production will grow faster than economies that use these technologies relatively less is popular in literature. The developed economies investing more in these technologies grow more compared to developing economies (Gruber & Koutroumpis, 2011; Stanley et al., 2018). Increased ICT investment by developing countries, such as African countries, can therefore save these countries from being developed countries' markets, as stated in the Smart Africa Manifesto.

The effect of this flexible growth potential of micro- to macro-scale ICTs on social development has been studied for a long time. The literature for answering this question is evaluated in the next section.

16.2.2.3 Socio-economic Development

The increased use of information and communication technology has made life simpler and quicker for people to access information by eliminating borders. While these innovations reduce the use of time and space, the socio-economic impact of these technologies remains a current question.

In addition to indicators such as income level, education, and health status, which are among the concepts of socio-economic development, the removal of barriers to people's rights and freedoms can be defined as individual social development (Roztocki & Weistroffer, 2016). Based on this definition, the flexible use of ICTs can lead to development in many ways. ICT integration, especially in the field of education, can contribute to socio-economic development both individually and socially. For example, university researchers may use these technologies to interact with and develop their work with researchers from different parts of the world and develop their studies (Adam, 1996). A doctor, anywhere in the world, can treat a patient anywhere in the world by using the Internet with telemedicine or a sportsman can be successful by communicating with a trainer via e-mail (Polikanov & Abramova, 2003).

The contribution of ICTs to indicators such as socio-economic growth and human development is a frequently examined subject in the literature. Information and communication technologies, in particular mobile phones, have played a significant role in socio-economic growth. The facilitation of communication and telephone links to the most remote areas has provided a great deal of comfort to human life. In particular, the development effects of such technologies have been frequently studied in the African continent, which is largely made up of developing countries. Most of the studies conducted in different countries in Africa have concluded that these developments have a positive effect on socio-economic development (Aker & Mbiti, 2010; Asongu & Le Roux, 2017; Moodley, 2005; Ngwenyama et al., 2006).

Studies on the micro, macro, and socio-economic impacts of ICT have typically highlighted the positive effects of these technologies and are concentrated on the need for further investment in these technologies. This study is different compared to the relevant studies in the literature since the effects of ICT on the human development index were examined by acknowledging the regional dynamics of the African continent.

16.3 Research Framework

The purpose of this study is to examine the impact of ICTs on the human development index, considering regional differences in the African continent. For this reason, Africa is divided into five separate regions, and the countries with available data are classified as regional. In this way, the aim is to determine if there is a regional difference on the African continent. The independent variables defining the ICTs in the study are Internet use and the use of mobile and fixed phones. Moreover, per capita income, which is directly related to human development, was also included as an independent variable in the study.

The fact that the income levels of the countries used in the study are different indicates that the production dynamics of those countries should also be considered. As mentioned in the literature section of the study and the Smart Africa Manifesto, an enhanced supply chain is also needed for growth. As a consequence, per capita, carbon emissions were included in the study as an independent variable due to its possible effect on the human development index.

ICT imports and exports are also used as independent variables in the study. The effect of ICT imports and exports on the human development index in a continent such as Africa, where ICT use is not yet common, would also provide information on the need for these technologies.

16.3.1 Carbon Emissions and Human Development

The United Nations (UN) Millennium Development Goals report indicated that carbon emissions should be minimized because they affect the quality of inhaled air and cause situations such as global warming and climate change (UN Millennium Project, 2005). Therefore, renewable resources should also be used by countries in their production processes. This transformation of production processes also requires more investment in technology. Nevertheless, this transformation of manufacturing processes is very expensive for countries that have not yet completed their industrialization. Hence, carbon emission thresholds should be re-evaluated based on developed and developing countries (Rybski et al., 2011). Based on this information, the effects of carbon emission rates on the human development index for five regions of Africa would also provide insights into the production processes in Africa.

16.3.2 ICT Trade and Human Development

Technology imports in developing countries increase innovation performance (Coe et al., 1997; Coe & Helpman, 1995; Kokko, 1996; Liu & Wang, 2003; Salomon & Shaver, 2005; Sinani & Meyer, 2004; Zhang, 2017). In an open economy with rising innovation performance, per capita income increases, which positively affects social welfare (Davies & Quinlivan, 2006; Flanders et al., 2001; Hoskins & Eiras, 2003). Trade is also a factor that has a positive impact on social development. ICT commerce (particularly ICT imports) is important for human development in terms of access to these technologies and the adoption of new technologies. While the import is an item of expenditure, it is a way to get access to these technologies. ICT imports and exports are indeed essential variables to assess the continent's need for information and communication technologies.

16.4 Methodology

16.4.1 Dataset

In this study, the African continent is divided into five regions. The distribution by region of 32 countries, the data of which are available, can be seen in Table 16.1.

Data for a total of seven variables for the countries as shown in Table 16.1 were taken from the OECD African Growth Dynamics and the World Bank World Development Indicator database. The data cover the years between 2000 and 2017. Among the data; human development index (HDI), percentage of individuals using the Internet (INT), mobile-cellular telephone subscriptions per 100 inhabitants (MTEL), and fixed-telephone subscriptions per 100 inhabitants (FTEL) are collected from OECD Africa's Development Dynamics database, while ICT goods exports (% of total goods exports) (ICT_{EXP}), ICT goods imports (% of total goods imports) (ICT_{IMP}), and CO_2 emissions (metric tons per capita) are collected from World Bank World Development Indicator database.

Table 16.1 Distribution of the countries included in the analysis by regions

Southern Africa	North Africa	Central Africa	East Africa	West Africa
Botswana	Algeria	Cameroon	Burundi	Benin
Lesotho	Egypt	São Tomé and Principe	Ethiopia	Ivory Coast
Namibia	Morocco		Kenya	Cape Verde
Eswatini	Tunisia		Madagascar	Ghana
South Africa			Mauritius	Gambia
			Rwanda	Mali
			Seychelles	Niger
			Tanzania	Senegal
			Mozambique	Togo
			Malawi	
			Zambia	
			Zimbabwe	

There are only two countries with data available for Central Africa. This might weaken the results for this area. However, the number of countries is adequate to represent other regions.

16.4.2 Model

The regression equation that is the basis of the study is shown in Eq. 16.1. According to this equation, a quadratic equation was constructed by including the squares of INT and CO_2 variables whose effects on the human development index were investigated. The increase in these two variables is represented by the squares of these variables. If the increase in these variables takes the shape of a U with a parabolic curve, these variables have a negative and then a positive effect on HDI. If this parabolic curve is in the shape of an inverted U, it is the opposite.

$$\begin{aligned} HDI_t &= \beta_0 + \beta_1 INT_t + \beta_2 INT_t^2 + \beta_3 MTEL_t + \beta_4 FTEL_t \\ &+ \beta_5 CO_{2,t} + \beta_6 CO_{2,t}^2 + \beta_7 GDP_t + \beta_8 ICT_{IMP_t} + \beta_9 ICT_{EXP_t} + \varepsilon_t \end{aligned} \tag{16.1}$$

The justification for preferring the use of the Internet and carbon emissions is that the Internet spreads faster on both computers and cell phones and is more of a knowledge-based technology. Assessing the degree to which the use of the Internet should be expanded can also act as an essential input for ICT policies. CO_2 emissions are an indication of the industrialization status of countries or regions. Consequently, the amount at which the metric ton of CO_2 per capita would have a negative impact on the human development index could be significant for transforming the production systems. Therefore, the level after which the metric ton of CO_2 per capita will have a positive or negative effect on the human development index can be an important indicator for transforming production systems and increasing the country's income. Country income levels are directly related to HDI. Therefore, GDP per capita figures are also included in the regression.

The fixed phone is linked to Internet usage because wired and wireless Internet uses the fixed telephone line infrastructure. Therefore, this variable is included in the regression as it constitutes the infrastructure of IC technologies (Njoh, 2018).

The connection of ICT import and export figures with HDI is also important. Related literature is given in subsection 3.2.

Equation 16.1 is separately estimated for the five regions in Table 16.1. Summary statistics of the variables are shown in Table 16.2.

Before selecting the estimation method for the regression equation in Eq. 16.1, the correlation between variables was tested. The results are shown in Table 16.3

Table 16.2 Summary statistics of the variables

	Obs	Mean	Std. Dev.	Min	Max
HDI	576	.519533	.1206295	.252	.797
INT_p	569	11.85735	14.72441	.006	64.191
MTEL	576	50.18893	44.19088	0	173.497
FTEL	576	4.949363	6.842161	.021	32.669
CO_2	544	1.241257	1.938852	.0193058	9.979458
GDP	576	4924.863	5027.711	441.818	28810.45
ICT_{exp}	529	.8627843	1.991531	.000058	20.94448
ICT_{imp}	544	4.247176	2.014472	.4483667	12.77396

	HDI	INT	TEL	FTEL
HDI	1.0000			
INT	0.6935*	1.0000		
MTEL	0.6489*	0.8261*	1.0000	
FTEL	0.7627*	0.5098*	0.3871*	1.0000
CO_2	0.6673*	0.4767*	0.4282*	0.6433*
GDP	0.8671*	0.6798*	0.6371*	0.8133*
ICT_{exp}	0.2952*	0.2830*	0.1746*	0.3040*
ICT_{imp}	0.1821*	0.0775	−0.0263	0.1919*

Table 16.3 Correlation matrix of the variables

	CO_2	GDP	ICT_{exp}	ICT_{imp}
HDI				
INT				
MTEL				
FTEL				
CO_2	1.0000			
GDP	0.7590*	1.0000		
ICT_{exp}	0.1690*	0.2120*	1.0000	
ICT_{imp}	0.3536*	0.1348*	0.3242*	1.0000

16.4.3 Method of Data Analysis

The variance and autocorrelation tests were then used to select the estimation approach to be used. These tests are the modified Wald variance test and the Box-Pierce autocorrelation test.

Heteroscedasticity is the condition where the variances of the terms of error vary from each other. In such a case, the panel ordinary least squares (OLS) would not yield reliable prediction results. Consequently, the identification of this condition is crucial to maintain reliable estimation results. Modified Wald test was used to ascertain the presence of varying variance in this study.

16.4.3.1 Modified Wald Test

Since the period (T) is 18 years and the number of panels (N) is less than 18, the use of the modified Wald test is appropriate in cases of $N < T$ (Baum, 2001).

Wald tests the following hypothesis: H_0, $\sigma_i^2 = \sigma^2$ for all. i represents the number of cross sections. Mathematical representation of the Wald test:

$$W = \sum_{i=1}^{N_g} \frac{\left(\hat{\sigma}_i^2 - \hat{\sigma}^2\right)}{V_i} \tag{16.2}$$

N_g is the cross-sectional number and V is the cross-sectional estimator. The Wald test fits the χ^2 distribution and can also be applied when the normality assumption is violated (Baum, 2001).

16.4.3.2 Box-Pierce Panel Autocorrelation Test

The Box-Pierce test has been used to detect autocorrelation on the panel. The Box-Pierce Q statistic is expressed as the product of the number of delayed observations h and the sum of the autocorrelation ρ, and its mathematical representation is described as in Eq. 16.3 (Box & Pierce, 1970).

$$Q_{BP} = n\sum_{k=1}^{h} \hat{\rho}_k^2 \tag{16.3}$$

The hypotheses of the test are the following: H_0, There is no autocorrelation in the data; H_1, there is autocorrelation in the data. In the presence of autocorrelation, the OLS estimator will not yield reliable results. A different estimator should be used to resolve the issue.

16.4.3.3 Generalized Least Square (GLS)

The GLS estimator is used in the absence of homoscedasticity and series correlation, one of the main assumptions of the Gauss-Markov theorem of the OLS estimator (Taboga, 2017). Besides, to use the GLS estimator, the time dimension T must exceed the number of panels N ($T > N$), which is a mathematical requirement for the use of GLS (Beck & Katz, 1995).

In this analysis, five separate forecasts have been made for five regions of Africa with 18 years of data. As each region includes more than one country, panel regression has been applied. The results of the models are included in Tables 16.4, 16.5, 16.6, 16.7, and 16.8. In the tables, autocorrelation and heteroscedasticity test results for each model are provided. These tests show the estimated GLS coefficients in only heteroscedasticity, autocorrelation, and both heteroscedasticity and autocorrelation conditions. Also, the presence of fixed or random effects in the regression was specified by using the Hausman test.

16.5 Findings

In this study, 32 African countries are classified regionally, and separate panel regressions are estimated for Eq. 16.1 for 5 regions of Africa. Heteroscedasticity and autocorrelation conditions were tested in regression estimates and OLS and GLS results were given together for comparison.

16.5.1 Southern Africa

Regression results for Southern Africa are shown in Table 16.4.

In the Botswana, Eswatini, Lesotho, Namibia, and South Africa region, while the effects of mobile and fixed phone usage among ICTs on the human development

Table 16.4 Regression results for Southern Africa

Southern Africa		
Dep. var:	OLS	FGLS
HDI	regression	regression
INT	−.0000883	−.0002628
	(.000696)	(.0006436)
INT^2	6.25e-06	.0000118
	(.0000127)	(.0000121)
MTEL	.0006145***	.0003642***
	(.0000926)	(.0000851)
FTEL	.0068464***	.0057188**
	(.0020205)	(.0016826)
CO_2	.0037672	.000343
	(.006651)	(.0055963)
CO_2^2	−.0009489	−.0001834
	(.0005745)	(.0004965)
GDP	8.54e-06***	.0000101***
	(1.33e-06)	(1.26e-06)
ICT_{imp}	.0087356***	.0032547***
	(.0020053)	(.0012188)
ICT_{exp}	.0020658***	.0002218
	(.0007517)	(.0004221)
CONS.	.3844795***	.4241064***
	(.0083076)	(.0076189)
Modified Wald test	Prob > χ^2 = 0.0000	
	Heteroscedastic	
Box-Pierce test	*P*-value > χ^2(1) 0.0000	
	AR(1) Panel autocorrelation	
Hausman test	Prob > χ^2 = 0.000 (fixed effects)	

Note: *** (**, *) indicate a significant level of 1%, (5, 10%)
Standard errors in parentheses

index have been positive and significant, no statistically significant effect of Internet use has been identified. In this situation, as emphasized by Olwal et al. (2013) in their study, the bandwidth and the price of this service in these countries decrease the demand of the household for this service. In the same study, it was established that the use of mobile phones in these countries increased even faster than the Internet subscription. As a consequence, it can be said that more work is needed on the infrastructure for Internet access in this area.

Although per capita income, which is directly linked to human development, has a positive and substantial impact on human development, no statistically and significant impact of CO_2 emissions has been found. On the other hand, ICT imports have a positive and significant impact on HDI, although ICT exports have no statistically significant effect. This shows that the need for IC technologies is provided by imports. With ICT imports, these technologies reach the public, creating a social welfare effect.

16.5.2 Central Africa

Regression results for Central Africa are shown in Table 16.5

Table 16.5 Regression results for Central Africa

Central Africa		
Dep. var:	OLS	FGLS
HDI	regression	regression
INT	.004528*	.004528**
	(.0024211)	(.0020396)
INT^2	−.0001434*	−.0001434**
	(.0000709)	(.0000598)
MTEL	−.000023	−.000023
	(.000165)	(.000139)
FTEL	.0005988	−.0005988
	(.0044762)	(.0037709)
CO_2	.1396318	.1396318
	(.1266335)	(.106679)
CO_2^2	.0111156	.0111156
	(.1727519)	(.1455302)
GDP	.0000461***	.0000461***
	(0000101)	(8.51e-06)
ICT_{imp}	−.0014388	−.0014388
	(.0015341)	(.0012924)
ICT_{exp}	.0041444***	.0041444***
	(.0014397)	(.0012128)
CONS.	.318722***	.318722***
	(.0103116)	(.0086867)

(continued)

Table 16.5 (continued)

Central Africa		
Dep. var:	OLS	FGLS
HDI	regression	regression
Modified Wald test	Prob > χ^2 = 0.4741	
	Homoscedastic	
Box-Pierce test	*P*-value > $\chi^2(1)$ 0.2949	
	No AR(1) panel autocorrelation	
Hausman test	Prob > χ^2 = 0.000 (fixed effects)	

Note: *** (**, *) indicate a significant level of 1% (5, 10%)
Standard errors in parentheses

The low number of countries representing Central Africa did not cause problems with heteroscedasticity and autocorrelation. Consequently, in Table 16.4, OLS and GLS coefficients are similar except for standard errors. The Central Africa sample is the smallest in the study. This region is represented by just two nations. According to the findings obtained from the data of these two countries, the influence of Internet subscriptions on the human development index is parabolically inverted U shape. The inflection point of this equation can be determined using the following formula: $-\frac{\beta 1}{2\beta 2}$. Internet use in Cameroon and Sao Tome has a positive impact on the human development index of up to 22.5%. However, the increase in the number of users accessing the Internet does not have a statistically significant effect on the HDI.

Mobile phones and carbon emission rates do not have a statistically significant effect. As expected, per capita income has a significant and positive impact on the HDI. In ICT trade, only ICT exports have a positive and significant effect. This implies that Cameroon and Sao Tome, which represent this region, prioritize higher incomes for human development.

16.5.3 *East Africa*

Regression results for East Africa are shown in Table 16.6.

Similar to Central Africa, if the number of citizens using the Internet in East Africa reaches 21%, it will be a positive and significant addition to the human development index. On the other hand, while ICT trade and carbon emissions have no statistically significant impact on HDI, mobile phone subscription and income per capita have a statistically positive and significant impact.

The positive impact of mobile phone users and individuals using the Internet on the human development index indicates that the area has a strong technology potential. Mobile phone use in the region is rising rapidly and the mobile market is growing in East Africa as well as in the rest of the world (Zanello & Maassen, 2011). Nevertheless, challenges remain that limit the use and access of ICT in Central and Eastern Africa (Haikin & Flatters, 2017).

Table 16.6 Regression results for East Africa

East Africa		
Dep. var:	OLS	FGLS
HDI	regression	regression
INT	.0049829***	.0042165***
	(.0015107)	(.0007122)
INT^2	−.0002384***	−.0001329***
	(.0000274)	(.0000187)
MTEL	.0007964***	.0005015***
	(.0002482)	(.0001146)
FTEL	−.0026046*	−.0005133
	(.0014706)	(.0010151)
CO_2	−.0269246	−.0001062
	(.016481)	(.0083658)
CO_2^2	.0012901	.0002822
	(.0015512)	(.0007259)
GDP	.0000343***	.0000207***
	(3.92e-06)	(2.72e-06)
ICT_{imp}	−.0014685	−.0002308
	(.0015642)	(.0005509)
ICT_{exp}	.0051062**	.0004055
	(.0019717)	(.0006528)
CONS.	.3730628***	.3936744***
	(.0092808)	(.0061643)
Modified Wald test	Prob > χ^2 = 0.0000	
	Heteroscedastic	
Box-Pierce test	*P*-value > $\chi^2(1)$ 0.0000	
	AR(1) panel autocorrelation	
Hausman test	Prob > χ^2 = 0.000 (fixed effects)	

Note: *** (**, *) indicate a significant level of 1% (5, 10%)
Standard errors in parentheses

16.5.4 North Africa

Regression results for North Africa are shown in Table 16.7.

In North Africa, if the percentage of individuals using the Internet in the population rises to 35%, it provides a positive and significant effect on the human development index. Besides, while mobile phone subscription did not have a statistically significant effect, fixed telephone subscription was found to have a positive and significant impact.

Although per capita income has a positive impact on the human development index in North Africa as in all regions, the rise in per capita carbon emissions above 3.5 metric tons per year negatively affects the human development index. For the per capita carbon emission amount to reach this level, the average CO_2 emission

Table 16.7 Regression results for North Africa

North Africa		
Dep. var:	OLS	FGLS
HDI	regression	regression
INT	−.0020732***	−.0007984
	(.000704)	(.0005612)
INT^2	.0000338***	.0000139*
	(9.80e-06)	(7.94e-06)
MTEL	.0003029**	.0001292
	(.0001393)	(.0001089)
FTEL	.0036583***	.0022244***
	(.0009442)	(.0008395)
CO_2	.1523713***	.0844208***
	(.0304178)	(.0257007)
CO_2^2	−.0164666***	−.012124***
	(.005071)	(.0045736)
GDP	2.56e-06	.0000117***
	(2.98e-06)	(2.16e-06)
ICT_{imp}	−.0036735*	−.0022423*
	(.0020395)	(.0012604)
ICT_{exp}	.0067963***	.0031393**
	(.0015141)	(.0012601)
CONS.	.3479182***	.4133343***
	(.031005)	(.0294828)
Modified Wald test	Prob > χ^2 = 0.7865	
	Homoscedastic	
Box-Pierce test	*P*-value > $\chi^2(1)$ 0.0000	
	AR(1) Panel autocorrelation	
Hausman test	Prob > χ^2 = 0.000 (fixed effects)	

Note: *** (**, *) indicate a significant level of 1% (5, 10%)
Standard errors in parentheses

amount in the region should be doubled. This demonstrates that there is a lack of industrialization in the region. Although ICT imports in the region have a negative impact on the human development index, ICT exports have a positive effect. This situation provides valuable clues as to the ICT potential of the area. The progress of Egypt, Tunisia, and Morocco in terms of ICT indicators (mobile phone and computer) is promising for the region (Bruno et al., 2004).

16.5.5 West Africa

Regression results for West Africa are shown in Table 16.8.

Table 16.8 Regression results for West Africa

West Africa		
Dep. var:	OLS	FGLS
HDI	regression	regression
INT	.0005656	.0001183
	(.0017075)	(.0008467)
INT^2	−.0000318	−.0000194
	(.0000383)	(.0000195)
MTEL	.0003626**	.0003206***
	(.0001564)	(.0000803)
FTEL	.0097103***	.0047335***
	(.0019326)	(.001324)
CO_2	.3536006***	.2326088***
	(.039591)	(.0305355)
CO_2^2	−.2826396***	−.177051***
	(.0434223)	(.0291991)
GDP	.0000272***	.0000422***
	(4.91e-06)	(4.85e-06)
ICT_{imp}	.0043251*	.0004568
	(.0025673)	(.0008975)
ICT_{exp}	−.0344331***	−.0018319
	(.0099729)	(.0022492)
CONS.	.2575703***	.2612487***
	(.0105447)	(.0083251)
Modified Wald test	Prob > χ^2 = 0.0000	
	Heteroscedastic	
Box-Pierce test	*P*-value > $\chi^2(1)$ 0.0000	
	AR(1) Panel autocorrelation	
Hausman test	Prob > χ^2 = 0.000 (fixed effects)	

Note: *** (**, *) indicate a significant level of 1% (5, 10%)
Standard errors in parentheses

No statistically significant effects of Internet usage and ICT trade on the human development index have been reported in West Africa. On the other hand, mobile phones, fixed phone use, and per capita income have a positive and significant impact. When the cell phone and fixed phone use coefficients are analyzed in Table 16.7, the lowest coefficients are those of West Africa relative to Southern Africa in Table 16.3 and East Africa in Table 16.5. Although the Ivory Coast is more successful in ICT expansion than other countries in the region, ICT investment in Senegal, Benin, and Burkina Faso is not being used effectively (Bollou, 2006).

16.6 Discussion

The amount of per capita carbon emissions selected as an indicator for the industrial growth of Africa suggests that industrialization on the continent has not yet achieved the desired level. According to the results of the regression, the CO_2 emission amounts in North and West Africa should be increased by 2 and 1.5 times, respectively, to have a positive effect on the HDI. Some African countries including Egypt, Tunisia, and Morocco in North Africa and the Ivory Coast in West Africa have made sound investments in ICT. These successful initiatives have taken place even though industrialization is yet to be completed. Moreover, the results of the FGLS regression in Table 16.6 indicate that increasing Internet use in North Africa would have a positive impact on the HDI. North Africa (see Fig. 16.1) also ranks first in mobile phone usage, with the continent's highest Internet usage rates. The intensive use of such IC technologies also positively affects the socio-economic indicators.

East Africa is the region where mobile phones contribute the most to human development. Fixed phone use is an IC technology that makes the greatest contribution to the HDI in Southern Africa. The fact that fixed phones are also Internet infrastructure indicates that this region needs more Internet infrastructure investment compared to North Africa.

In Central and East Africa, which rank lower in mobile phone and Internet usage rates, the need to increase the rate of Internet usage shows that both regions need more ICT investments. These two regions (East and Central Africa) need to be supported especially by agricultural ICTs. For example, by increasing the communication opportunities of farmers, farmers can reach the opinions of experts in the field of agriculture through a digital platform and can contribute to the solution of these agricultural problems (McCampbell et al., 2018). Because agriculture is the most important sector for creating economic value in the region, its development is essential.

16.7 Conclusions and Recommendations

This study contributes to regional policy-making in the continent, taking into account the regional dynamics of Africa. In the studies conducted so far, there are disagreements about the effects of ICTs on HDI in the African continent. The differences of opinion center around the infrastructure problems faced by the continent. While basic infrastructure deficiencies may prevent the development of ICTs, there are also opinions that expensive ICT investments will lead to neglect of infrastructure investments (Gillwald et al., 2019; Ifinedo, 2006; Ngwenyama et al., 2006). This situation makes it difficult to establish a balance between education, health, infrastructure, and ICT investments in the continent (Bollou, 2006).

As the main result of the study, it can be said that IC technologies have a positive effect on the HDI in all five regions of Africa. When this result is evaluated regionally, Internet usage should be increased in East, North, and Central Africa. Mobile and fixed phone use in South, North, and West Africa have a positive and significant impact on HDI. Despite the finding of Njoh (2018) for the African continent that ICTs (broadband and mobile phone) do not affect HDI, this study is supported by empirical findings that different ICTs have a positive effect on HDI in the continent. Considering these regional differences, in addition to individual users, the integration of IC technologies into production systems is important for both the economic and socio-economic development of Africa.

Africa has different dynamics than other continents. African countries have fallen behind the world in keeping up with these technologies due to fundamental problems they need to solve, such as education, health, and food. However, if the steps taken to solve basic infrastructure problems are supported by ICTs, they can create a development dynamic that is both fast and encompassing the whole society. For example, if the fertile agricultural structure of the continent is supported by the integration of ICTs into the agricultural sector, the food problem of the continent can be resolved. It can be ensured that farmers have information about agricultural markets by using mobile phones, and by consulting agricultural organizations on digital platforms, they can plant seeds suitable for their agricultural lands and find solutions for herbal diseases (Muriithi et al., 2009). Besides, the use of ICTs – especially the Internet, computer, and mobile phone – in the fields of education and health can provide uninterrupted and unlimited access to education and health services to all segments of society. For this, first of all, the infrastructure of IC technologies should be completed, and access to technologies such as faster and cheaper Internet, computers, and mobile phones should be provided to the public.

As a result, this study supports the view of Morawczynski and Ngwenyama (2007) that ICTs alone are not sufficient for development in the African continent. Also, development policies need to be reviewed by integrating IC technologies into agriculture, education, and health services.

References

Adam, L. (1996). Electronic communications technology and development of the Internet in Africa. *Information Technology for Development, 7*(3), 133–144.

Aker, J. C., & Mbiti, I. M. (2010). Mobile phones and economic development in Africa. *Journal of Economic Perspectives, 24*(3), 207–232.

Asongu, S. A., & Le Roux, S. (2017). Enhancing ICT for inclusive human development in Sub-Saharan Africa. *Technological Forecasting and Social Change, 118*, 44–54.

Batuo, M. E. (2015). The role of telecommunications infrastructure in the regional economic growth of Africa. *The Journal of Developing Areas*, 313–330.

Baum, C. F. (2001). Residual diagnostics for cross-section time series regression models. *The Stata Journal, 1*(1), 101–104.

Beck, N., & Katz, J. N. (1995). What to do (and not to do) with time-series cross-section data. *American Political Science Review*, 634–647.

Bollou, F. (2006). ICT infrastructure expansion in Sub-Saharan Africa: An analysis of six West African countries from 1995 to 2002. *The Electronic Journal of Information Systems in Developing Countries, 26*(1), 1–16.

Box, G. E., & Pierce, D. A. (1970). Distribution of residual autocorrelations in autoregressive-integrated moving average time series models. *Journal of the American Statistical Association, 65*(332), 1509–1526.

Bruno, G., Esposito, G., Iandoli, L., & Raffa, M. (2004). The ICT service industry in North Africa and the role of partnerships in Morocco. *Journal of Global Information Technology Management, 7*(3), 5–26.

Coe, D. T., & Helpman, E. (1995). International R&D spillovers. *European Economic Review, 39*(5), 859–887.

Coe, D. T., Helpman, E., & Hoffmaister, A. W. (1997). North-south R & D spillovers. *The Economic Journal, 107*(440), 134–149.

Davies, A., & Quinlivan, G. (2006). A panel data analysis of the impact of trade on human development. *The Journal of Socio-Economics, 35*(5), 868–876.

Eden, B. L., & Kalusopa, T. (2005). The challenges of utilizing information communication technologies (ICTs) for the small-scale farmers in Zambia. *Library Hi Tech, 23*(3), 414–424.

Fedderke, J. W., & Bogetic, Z. (2006). *Infrastructure and growth in South Africa: Direct and indirect productivity impacts of 19 infrastructure measures*. The World Bank.

Flanders, T., Quinlivan, G., & Therrien, M. (2001). *International debt relief: A moral and economic challenge* (Christian Thought Series, No. 2). Center for Economic Personalism at the Acton Institute for the Study of Religion and Liberty.

Gillwald, A., Mothobi, O., & Rademan, B. (2019). *The State of ICT in Mozambique 2018.*

Gruber, H., & Koutroumpis, P. (2011). Mobile telecommunications and the impact on economic development. *Economic Policy, 26*(67), 387–426.

Haikin, M., & Flatters, G. (2017). *Digital development: What is the role of international NGOs?* ICT for development programs and opportunities in the Horn, East, and Central Africa.

Hoskins, L., & Eiras, A. I. (2003). *Property rights: The key to economic growth. 2003 Index of economic freedom*. The Heritage Foundation and The Wall Street Journal.

Ifinedo, P. (2006). Towards e-government in a Sub-Saharan African country: Impediments and initiatives in Nigeria. *Journal of E-Government, 3*(1), 3–28.

Ismail, R., Jeffery, R., & Van Belle, J. P. (2011). Using ICT as a value-adding tool in South African SMEs. *Journal of African Research in Business & Technology, 2011*, 1–12.

Klonner, S., & Nolen, P. (2008). *Does ICT benefit the poor? Evidence from South Africa*. Unpublished mimeo. Accessed 10.12.2020.

Kokko, A. (1996). Productivity spillovers from competition between local firms and foreign affiliates. *Journal of International Development: The Journal of the Development Studies Association, 8*(4), 517–530.

Liu, X., & Wang, C. (2003). Does foreign direct investment facilitate technological progress?: Evidence from Chinese industries. *Research Policy, 32*(6), 945–953.

McCampbell, M., Schut, M., Van den Bergh, I., van Schagen, B., Vanlauwe, B., Blomme, G., ... Leeuwis, C. (2018). Xanthomonas Wilt of Banana (BXW) in Central Africa: Opportunities, challenges, and pathways for citizen science and ICT-based control and prevention strategies. *NJAS-Wageningen Journal of Life Sciences, 86*, 89–100.

Moodley, S. (2005). The promise of e-development? A critical assessment of the state ICT for poverty reduction discourse in South Africa. *Perspectives on Global Development and Technology, 4*(1), 1–26.

Mouelhi, R. B. A. (2009). Impact of the adoption of information and communication technologies on firm efficiency in the Tunisian manufacturing sector. *Economic Modelling, 26*(5), 961–967.

Muriithi, A. G., Bett, E., & Ogaleh, S. A. (2009). Information technology for agriculture and rural development in Africa: Experiences from Kenya. In *Conference on international research on food security, natural resource management and rural development* (pp. 6–8).

Musa, N. A., Oyebisi, T. O., & Babalola, M. O. (2010). A study of the impact of information and communications technology (ICT) on the quality of quantity surveying services in Nigeria. *The Electronic Journal of Information Systems in Developing Countries, 42*(1), 1–9.

Nasab, E. H., & Aghaei, M. (2009). The effect of ICT on economic growth: Further evidence. *International Bulletin of Business Administration, 5*(2), 46–56.

Ngwenyama, O., Andoh-Baidoo, F. K., Bollou, F., & Morawczynski, O. (2006). Is there a relationship between ICT, health, education, and development? An empirical analysis of five West African countries from 1997–2003. *The Electronic Journal of Information Systems in Developing Countries, 23*(1), 1–11.

Niebel, T. (2018). ICT and economic growth–Comparing developing, emerging, and developed countries. *World Development, 104*, 197–211.

Njoh, A. J. (2018). The relationship between modern information and communications technologies (ICTs) and development in Africa. *Utilities Policy, 50*, 83–90.

Nkama, A. H. G. (2014). An analysis of the impact of ICT investment on productivity in developing countries: Evidence from Cameroon. *Africa Development/Afrique et Développement, 39*(4), 117–132.

Nurmilaakso, J. M. (2009). ICT solutions and labor productivity: Evidence from firm-level data. *Electronic Commerce Research, 9*(3), 173–181.

Olwal, T., Masonta, M., Mfupe, L., & Mzyece, M. (2013). Broadband ICT policies in Southern Africa: initiatives and dynamic spectrum regulation. In *2013 IST-Africa conference & exhibition* (pp. 1–8). IEEE.

Ossadzifo, K. (2018). Impact of telecommunications market liberalization on labor productivity in economic community of West African States. *Journal of Social Economics Research, 5*(2), 63–74.

Osunsanmi, T., Aigbavboa, C., & Oke, A. (2018). Construction 4.0: The future of the construction industry in South Africa. *World Academy of Science, Engineering and Technology, International Journal of Civil and Environmental Engineering, 12*(3), 206–212.

Piatkowski, M. (2003). The contribution of ICT investment to economic growth and labor productivity in Poland 1995–2000.

Polikanov, D., & Abramova, I. (2003). Africa and ICT: A chance for breakthrough? *Information, Communication & Society, 6*(1), 42–56.

Ponelis, S. R., & Holmner, M. A. (2015). ICT in Africa: Building a better life for all. *Information Technology for Development, 21*(2), 163–177.

Relich, M. (2017). The impact of ICT on labor productivity in the EU. *Information Technology for Development, 23*(4), 706–722.

Roztocki, N., & Weistroffer, H. R. (2016). Conceptualizing and researching the adoption of ICT and the impact on socio-economic development. *Information Technology for Development, 22*(4), 541–549.

Rybski, D., Costa, L., & Kropp, J. (2011). Correlations between human development and CO2 emissions: Projections and implications. *AGUFM, 2011*, GC51C-0981.

Salomon, R. M., & Shaver, J. M. (2005). Learning by exporting: New insights from examining firm innovation. *Journal of Economics & Management Strategy, 14*(2), 431–460.

Schelenz, L., & Schopp, K. (2018). Digitalization in Africa: Interdisciplinary perspectives on technology, development, and justice. *International Journal of Digital Society, 9*(4), 1412–1420.

Sinani, E., & Meyer, K. E. (2004). Spillovers of technology transfer from FDI: The case of Estonia. *Journal of Comparative Economics, 32*(3), 445–466.

Sousa, F., Nicolay, G., & Home, R. (2016). Information technologies as a tool for agricultural extension and farmer-to-farmer exchange: Mobile-phone video use in Mali and Burkina Faso. *International Journal of Education and Development Using Information and Communication Technology, 12*(3), 19–36.

Stanley, T. D., Doucouliagos, H., & Steel, P. (2018). Does ICT generate economic growth? A meta-regression analysis. *Journal of Economic Surveys, 32*(3), 705–726.

Summit, T. A. (2013). *The smart Africa Manifesto*. Endorsed by Heads of States and Governments in Kigali.

Taboga, M. (2017). *Lectures on probability theory and mathematical statistics*. CreateSpace Independent Publishing Platform.

UN Millennium Project. (2005). *Investing in development: A practical plan to achieve the Millennium Development Goals*. United Nations.

Wamboye, E., Adekola, A., & Sergi, B. (2016). ICTs and labor productivity growth in sub-Saharan Africa. *International Labour Review, 155*(2), 231–252.
Wamuyu, P. K., & Maharaj, M. S. (2011). Factors influencing successful use of mobile technologies to facilitate E-Commerce in small enterprises: The case of Kenya. *The African Journal of Information Systems, 3*(2), 2.
Wang, E. H. H. (1999). ICT and economic development in Taiwan: Analysis of the evidence. *Telecommunications Policy, 23*(3-4), 235–243.
Wanyoike, D. M., Mukulu, E., & Waititu, A. G. (2012). ICT attributes as determinants of e-commerce adoption by formal small enterprises in urban Kenya. *International Journal of Business and Social Science, 3*(23).
Wolf, S. (2001). Determinants and impact of ICT use for African SMEs: Implications for rural South Africa. In Center for Development Research (ZEF Bonn). Trade and Industrial Policy Strategies (TIPS), Annual Forum at Misty Hills, Mulderdrift, 10–12 September 2001 (pp. 1–24).
World Bank Group. (2019). *Ghana digital economy diagnostic*. The World Bank.
Zanello, G., & Maassen, P. (2011). Strengthening citizen agency and accountability through ICT: An extrapolation for Eastern Africa. *Public Management Review, 13*(3), 363–382.
Zhang, L. (2017). The knowledge spillover effects of FDI on the productivity and efficiency of research activities in China. *China Economic Review, 42*, 1–14.

Ipek Akad. The studies of Dr. Ipek Akad have focused on innovation economics, technological development, and economic growth and development. Her studies comprise various subjects such as the macro and micro economic impacts of R&D incentives, R&D and innovation production, general equilibrium models, and regional development. Ipek currently works as a faculty member at Bitlis Eren University and lectures on economic growth, innovation economics, regional economics, and industrial economics.

She completed her Bachelor of Economics at Gaziosmanpasa University and her Master's degree in economics at Dokuz Eylul University. Then, she started her Ph.D. studies at Ege University in 2013. Her doctoral thesis proposal was awarded an international research scholarship by (Scientific and Technological Research Council of Turkey) TUBITAK. In the same year, the Department of Management, Strategy, and Innovation (MSI) at KU Leuven granted her a research position where she worked for a year.

In her doctoral dissertation, she examined the macroeconomic impacts of R&D incentives with a general equilibrium growth model and microeconomic impacts with the micro-econometrics method. Ipek, who received her Ph.D. in Economics from Ege University in 2019, is currently working on a post-doc project to continue her education abroad. Over the coming years, she plans to work on subjects such as Technology Policies and Regional Development Dynamics of Developing Economies, R&D in Industrial Transformation, and Economic Development.

Chapter 17
Hitting the Moving Target: What Information Systems Competencies Are Required from Mid-Level Information Systems Managers by Organisations in Sub-Saharan Africa?

Mark-Oliver Kevor and Emmanuel Koree Boakye

Abstract The rapidly changing nature of digital innovations demands changing digital competencies which often lag behind the pace of digital innovations. This phenomenon has been described as aiming 'the moving target'. At the same time, these competencies differ or may have different emphasis or importance to different geographic and economic regions. Consequently, extant literature has suggested a periodic identification of information systems (IS) competencies relevant to organisations beyond the UK and USA where such research is dominant. However, extant literature focuses on current competencies of entry-level graduates with less emphasis on middle to senior managers. Again, traditional methods of identifying IS competencies by analysing job postings or through surveys have been found, not to be able to uncover certain difficult to observe competencies. Furthermore, there is less theorisation of IS competency studies in the literature. This study, therefore, explores current IS competencies, which are relevant to mid-level management IS professionals of organisations in sub-Saharan Africa (SSA), through the lens of the iceberg competency model, and using a diversified Delphi approach. The results painted a view of a strong emphasis on individual foundational competencies as compared to other competencies and contradict a stronger emphasis on IS specific competencies required for entry-level IS jobs. The implications for practice, IS education in SSA, and suggestions for future research are presented.

Keywords IS competencies · MSIS 2016 · Sub-Saharan Africa · Delphi

M.-O. Kevor (✉)
Presbyterian University College, Abetifi-Kwahu, Ghana
e-mail: kevor.markoliver@presbyuniversity.edu.gh

E. K. Boakye
University of Ghana Business School, Accra, Ghana
e-mail: ekboakye009@st.ug.edu.gh

R. Boateng et al. (eds.), *Digital Innovations, Business and Society in Africa*, Advances in Theory and Practice of Emerging Markets,
https://doi.org/10.1007/978-3-030-77987-0_17

17.1 Introduction

Information systems (IS), which is the function that plans, develops, operates, and manages an organisation's information systems (Davis, 2006), is critical for modern organisations. A report by the Association of Information Systems (AIS) and the Temple University IS job index (ISJobIndex, 2019) describes the IS job market in the USA as steady, with an estimated three million jobs relevant to IS. At the same time, the report claims that 'the recruitment, mindset, education, demographics, career paths, skills, and jobs of IS professionals are different and yet remain poorly understood' (p. 5). In addition, new technologies and emergencies, such as a global pandemic, may change the role of IS in organisations. Moreover, a move towards virtualisation, big data, and cloud-based services impacts the IS competencies required by organisations (Topi et al., 2014). For example, a roundtable discussion with nine chief information officers (CIOs) was organised by the Manufacturing Information Systems Center at the School of Business Administration at Wayne State University. They observed how, with the emergence of cloud computing, their role changed from providing and supporting technology to managing the integration of externally acquired, standardised infrastructure (Ragowsky et al., 2014). While this change may be positive, the lack of IS professionals with relevant competencies remains a problem given the dynamic nature of technology, which results in shorter lifespans for several IS skills. Furthermore, outsourcing capabilities have changed the IS competencies organisations require or must retain. According to Benamati et al. (2010), an earlier hiring model which required new hires to spend time programming while also using this period to learn about the organisation may now be outmoded. This is due to how large programming and other highly technical tasks may instead be outsourced to another country. Again, new entrepreneurial opportunities emerge as a result of changing technology and technology use, which requires new competencies to exploit such opportunities, especially in developing countries. It is therefore important for scholars and educators to '"monitor the pulse" of the industry about IS Job skills to update IS educational programs appropriately' (Cappel, 2002, p. 76).

Consequently, IS scholars periodically investigate the IS competencies which are relevant to organisations. For example, as early as the 1980s, Cheney and Lyons (1980) conducted a survey of IS managers in 32 US companies to identify the skills required for IS professionals. Subsequently, recent studies have either analysed the current IS competencies required by employers (see Aasheim et al., 2009b; Lee & Han, 2008; Osmani et al., 2016; Stefanidis et al., 2013; Stevens et al., 2011; Tan et al., 2016) or analysed how IS competencies have evolved or changed over the years through longitudinal studies (Aasheim & Shropshire, 2012; Burns et al., 2018: Todd et al., 1995). These studies normally suggest implications for hiring, training, and IS education (Bullen et al., 2009). For example, Stefanidis et al. (2013) compare the IS curriculum in the UK with career tracks defined in the undergraduate IS curriculum model, IS 2010 (Topi et al., 2010). They have found that IS programmes in the UK promote career tracks of a technological orientation, such as user interphase designer, IT operations manager, and application developer. There is less emphasis on career tracks of a strong conceptual orientation, such as business analyst, IT consultant, and e-business manager. Similarly, Burns et al. (2018) have determined the knowledge and skills required by the potential employers of students graduating from undergraduate IS programmes in the USA. They compare these results with IS information from 2010 to argue that increased soft skills and programming focus are more prominent in the IS curriculum today.

However, the existing literature on the IS competencies required by the industry has shown little or no emphasis on IS competency expectations of IS employees in mid- to senior-level management positions (Kappelman et al., 2016). Moreover, the existing literature is replete with studies done in the UK and North America but provides significantly less evidence in regions such as sub-Saharan Africa (SSA). Moreover, Bullen et al.'s (2009) study on IT workforce trends in the USA and their implications on hiring and curriculum suggests that different geographical regions with different wage levels display different IS competencies. For example, Kaiser et al. (2011) have found IS skill value differences between high-wage regions, such as the USA, Western Europe, and Australia, and low-wage regions, such as Latin America, India, China, Eastern Europe, and the Commonwealth of Independent States (formerly the Soviet Union). It may then be possible that the IS competencies required by organisations, in the UK or USA, or their importance may be different from those in SSA. As a result, the present study examines current IS competencies expected from mid-level IS managers through a Delphi study of employers and executives who are key recruitment decision-makers in SSA. In this study, mid-level IS managers are considered professionals in management positions who are below the CIO, the highest attainable IS position in an organisation (Kappelman et al., 2016). This chapter in particular seeks to identify the IS competencies expected from mid-level IS managers in SSA, determine the relative importance of these competencies, and subsequently provide implications for practice and graduate IS education.

This chapter is organised into five sections, with the first section introducing the study. The second section presents a categorisation of IS competencies and related studies. It also presents the iceberg model as the theory which guides the analysis and discussion of the results. Section 17.3 presents the Delphi research methodology, while Sect. 17.4 presents the results and a discussion of the Delphi study regarding current IS competencies in SSA. Lastly, Sect. 17.5 presents implications for practice and graduate IS education and provides suggestions for future research.

17.2 Background

17.2.1 Information Systems Competency Classifications

A number of studies have examined the IS competencies that are required by organisations and have provided different classifications. These studies are predominantly from the UK and USA. For instance, Ashenhurst's (1972) work on guidelines and recommendation for graduate IS programmes has provided a valuable initial classification of IS knowledge and skills. The author classifies IS knowledge and skills into people, models, systems, computers, organisations, and society. Based on this classification, studies such as Cheney et al. (1990) have examined past (1978–1987), current (1988), and future (1995, 5 years) trends of IS knowledge and skills through interviewing IS managers in the USA. They compared the results with the existing IS curriculum guidelines and recommendations at the time to provide further recommendations. Subsequently, different variations of Ashenhurst's (1972) classification have been developed and used by several authors (see Aasheim et al., 2009a; Cheney & Lyons, 1980; Debuse & Lawley, 2009; Havelka & Merhout, 2009; Jones et al., 2016; Lee & Han, 2008; Lee et al., 2002; Stevens et al., 2011; Trauth et al., 1993). With the exception of Ashenhurst (1972), who originally targeted the IS knowledge and skills of graduate IS programmes, the remaining studies are largely targeted at entry-level knowledge and skills of undergraduate IS programmes. The most recent model for guiding graduate IS programmes is the global competency model for graduate IS programmes, MSIS 2016 (Topi et al., 2017). The MSIS 2016 classifies IS competencies as IS specific competencies (ISSC), domain of practice competencies (DPC), and individual foundational competencies (IFC). The ISSCs are further categorised into competencies in business continuity and information assurance (BCIA), data, information and content management (DATA), enterprise architecture (EARC), ethics, impacts and sustainability (ETIS), innovation, organisational change and entrepreneurship (IOCE), IS management and operations (ISMO), IS strategy and governance (ISSG), IT infrastructure (INFR), and systems development and deployment (SDAD). IS graduates are expected to have at least a minimum proficiency in all these ISSCs. The MSIS 2016 also recognises the application of IS in other domains of practice, such as healthcare, education, law, and government for which competencies in 'any' of such domain processes are relevant. In addition, the MSIS 2016 also highlights 'relevant' IFCs, such as written and oral communication, critical thinking, ethical analysis, teamwork, and leadership. The MSIS 2016 global competency model is illustrated in Fig. 17.1.

Table 17.1 summarises the relationship between the MSIS 2016 classification and earlier classifications. This study adopts the MSIS 2016 classifications.

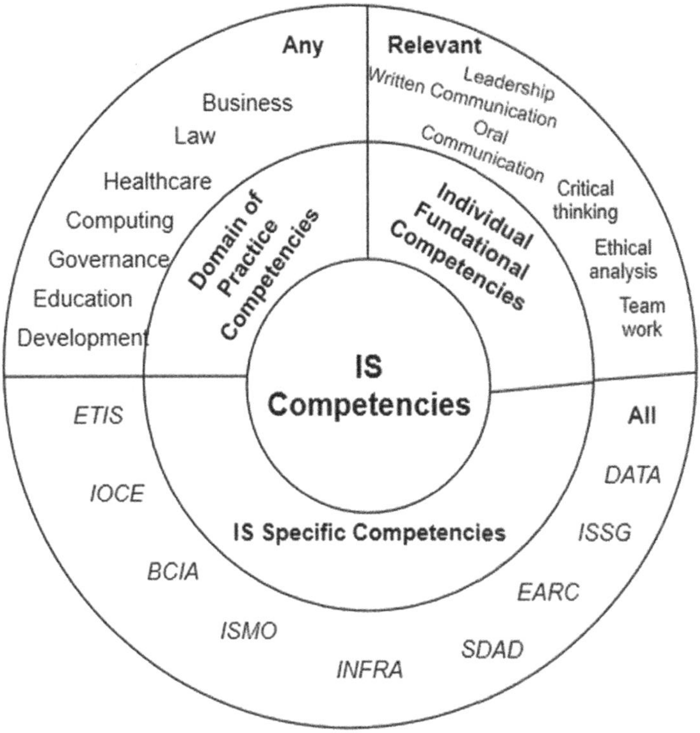

Fig. 17.1 IS competency model. (Author, adapted from MSIS 2016)

17.2.2 IS Job Competencies Studies

Studies on IS job competencies vary according to focus, region, and methodology. Studies on IS job skills focus on particular IS jobs, roles, or career tracks (Keil et al., 2013). For example, by interviewing senior IS managers in a longitudinal study (1978, 1987, 1988), Cheney et al. (1990) have identified the knowledge, skills, and abilities that were relevant to project managers, systems analysts, and programmers, which were the dominant IS entry jobs in the 1980s and early 1990s according to the authors. Moreover, Todd et al. (1995) has analysed the content of job advertisements or postings in four major newspapers over a 20-year period (1970–1990) to identify relevant knowledge and skills for programmers, systems analysts, and IS managers. These studies report a change in the skills of all IS jobs studied over the period of study. More recently, Gardiner et al. (2017), have also analysed job postings to investigate the big data knowledge and skills required by the industry. They have found that many big data jobs require competencies in developing analytical information systems and other soft skills to complement emerging hard technological skills.

Table 17.1 IS knowledge and skills classification

Earlier classifications of IS knowledge and skills	MSIS 2016 classification		
	IS specific competencies (ISSC)	Domain of practice competencies (DPC)	Individual foundation competencies (IFC)
Ashenhurst (1972)	Models, systems, computers	Organisations, society	People
Cheney and Lyons (1980)	Systems design, hardware and software, IS management, computer processing methods		Quantitative
Trauth et al. (1993)	IS tasks, technical skills		Abilities
Todd et al. (1995)	Technical knowledge, systems knowledge	Business knowledge	
Lee et al. (2002)	IS core knowledge	Organisations, society	Personal, interpersonal skills
Lee and Han (2008)	Architecture/network, hardware, software, development	Business, management, society	Problem-solving
Havelka and Merhout (2009)	Technical knowledge	Business knowledge	Personal traits, professional skills
Aasheim et al. (2009a, b)	Technical skills	Organisational/ managerial	Interpersonal, personal skills, experience, and grade point average
Debuse and Lawley (2009)	Technological skills	Business skills	People, skills, and experience
Stevens et al. (2011)	Core IS knowledge	Business expertise	Personal attributes, proficiency
Jones et al. (2016)	Technical skills	Knowledge areas	Intrapersonal/ interpersonal skills

Other studies have looked at the knowledge and skills of IS entry jobs without focusing on a particular job. For instance, Aasheim et al. (2009a, b) conducted a survey to compare the importance of IS knowledge and skills between IT managers and IS faculty. They have found that while IT managers and IS faculty disagreed on the importance of some individual knowledge and skills, they largely agreed on their order of importance when placed into broader categories. This corroborated an earlier survey by Lee et al. (2002) which compared the perceptions of IS professionals with academic works on the importance of IS knowledge and skills. The difference is that while IS professionals ranked organisational and societal competencies higher than IS technology competencies, IS academics ranked organisational competencies as less important than other competencies, especially IS technology competencies. Such misalignments inform both employers and faculty regarding how the training and curriculum should be developed. Table 17.2 presents a summary of previous IS competency studies.

Table 17.2 A summary of previous IS competency studies

Author(s)	Method/source of data	Job level	Region/country
Cheney et al. (1990)	Interview Senior IS managers	Entry-level	North America USA
Todd et al. (1995)	Job advertisements Newspapers	General	North America USA
Lu et al. (1999)	Survey IT managers	General	Pacific Asia
Lee et al. (2002)	Survey IS professionals IS faculty	Entry-level	North America USA
Noll and Wilkins (2002)	Survey IS professionals	Entry-level	North America USA
Aasheim et al. (2009a, b)	Survey IT managers IS faculty	Entry-level	North America USA
Litecky et al. (2012)	Data mining Job postings	General	North America
Harris et al. (2012)	Job advertisement Online job adverts	General	North America USA
Jones et al. (2016)	Survey IS professionals	General	North America USA
Kappelman et al. (2016)	Survey CIOs IT managers	Mid- to senior-level	North America USA
Burns et al. (2018)	Job advertisement Online job adverts	Entry-level	North America USA

Table 17.2 highlights how many previous studies have been conducted in the USA with little evidence from other regions. Given the expected IS competency differences in other regions, IS competency studies should be conducted in regions such as SSA. However, few studies on IS competency in SSA have been conducted. One example is Parker and Brown's (2019) analysis of online job postings to determine a descriptive set of skill requirements needed by cyber-security professionals in South Africa. While this study is important as one of few computing-related job competency studies in SSA, it nevertheless focuses on a specialised area of computing that is outside the scope of IS (Topi et al., 2017). The nature of IS job knowledge, skills, and attitudes in SSA is still not clear, especially at managerial levels. At the same time, existing IS job competency studies have focused on general IS competencies or entry-level competencies with little or no special focus on mid- and senior-level IS competencies. This study contributes to filling these gaps in the IS field.

17.2.3 The Iceberg Competency Model as the Analytical Lens

The iceberg metaphor has been used to explain a number of social phenomena, including competencies. According to Spencer and Spencer (1993), high-performing employees are endowed with certain underlying characteristics known as competencies. These include characteristics that are visible and easy to acquire through education and training, such as skills and knowledge and less visible, difficult to acquire through education and training such as self-concepts, traits, and motives. These competencies are illustrated with an iceberg that shows the visible competencies as the tip of the iceberg above the water and the less visible competencies as the base of the iceberg below the water (see Fig. 17.2).

Table 17.3 summarises the competency characteristics as explained by Spencer and Spencer (1993).

The majority of IS competency studies have not used the iceberg model despite its popularity in management research. However, in a study of the IT workforce, Ho and Frampton (2010) use the iceberg model to identify which competencies were critical to the work of IT architects. They confirm that while some competencies were easy to develop, others were difficult to change and presented implications both for university education and industry hiring and training. According to Litecky et al. (2012), the nature of IS competencies is such that technical skills are often advertised even though soft skills are most desirable. This dynamic regarding the visibility of IS competencies makes the iceberg model an appropriate analytical lens for studying mid-level IS competencies.

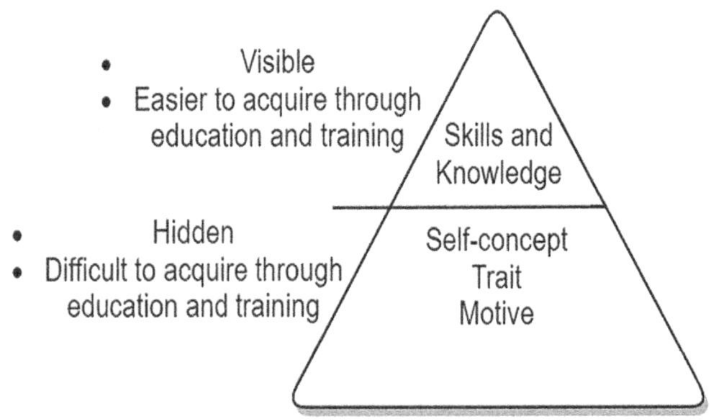

Fig. 17.2 Iceberg model of competencies (Spencer & Spencer, 1993)

Table 17.3 Competency characteristics

Competency characteristics	Meaning
Motive	The things a person consistently thinks about or the cause of action wanted (e.g. what motivates the IS manager to be successful in their role?)
Trait	Physical characteristics of a person and consistent responses to situations or information (e.g. how does the IS manager react to unpleasant situations, stress, or change?)
Self-concept	A person's attitudes, values, or self-image (e.g. do IS managers see themselves as leaders or managers?)
Knowledge	Information a person has in a specific area (e.g. knowledge of banking processes or knowledge of IS policies)
Skills	Ability to perform a certain mental or physical task (e.g. ability for an IS manager to analyse IS policies)

Source: Adapted from Spencer and Spencer (1993)

17.3 Methodology

17.3.1 Research Approach

Different methods have been used to study IS job skills. The dominant method has been content analysis of either job advertisements in paper-based newspapers (Todd et al., 1995) or job postings on online portals (Burns et al., 2018; Harris et al., 2012; Litecky et al., 2012; Parker & Brown, 2019). This analysis method has been described as unobtrusive and provides the author with a large set of data to analyse (Litecky et al., 2012), especially given the data mining tools that are available. However, this approach has also been criticised for an overemphasis on technical skills as compared with non-technical skills, as employers hardly emphasise soft skills in job advertisements (Litecky et al., 2012). IS competency researchers have suggested the need to gather job skills data directly from IT or IS managers (Gallagher et al., 2008). Consequently, some studies have used traditional questionnaire-based surveys to gather data from IS professionals or IT managers (Jones et al., 2016; S. Lee et al., 2002; Lu et al., 1999). While surveys provide a more focused approach in gathering IS job skills, it is difficult to obtain further information after the initial data has been analysed. At the same time, interviews have been used to elicit IS job skills from senior IS managers (Cheney et al., 1990). The challenge of such a method is obtaining the resources to interview a large number of IS professionals scattered across different geographical areas and from different industries.

To meet the objectives of this study, the author needs inputs from experts, with extensive IS experience, in organisations across different countries in SSA. As a result, this study adopts the Delphi technique (Dalkey & Helmer, 1963) to elicit IS job skills that are currently relevant to organisations in SSA. The approach involves the use of two or more rounds of questionnaires administered to a purposefully selected panel of experts who are anonymous to one another (Ponelis, 2019). The goal here is to achieve consensus, or an acceptable level of concordance, on a certain phenomenon of study. Current uses of the Delphi technique, especially for technology forecasting (Barnes & Mattsson, 2016; Hirschhorn, 2019), show that it is well-suited to this study. Moreover, the Delphi technique is not a new approach in IS research. Alarabiat and Ramos' (2019) recent literature review of its use in the top IS journals highlights its value in qualitative exploratory research and the identification of constructs or variables for further quantitative research. In IS research, the Delphi technique has been used to understand cloud computing issues (El-gazzar et al., 2016), identify the most important criteria for the selection of cloud providers (Lang et al., 2016, 2018), predict future blockchain applications in business and management (White, 2016), understand organisational social media risk (Gangi et al., 2017), elicit insights regarding the role of cultural values for digital transformation (Hartl & Hess, 2017), and understand current and future issues in collaborative consumption (Barnes & Mattsson, 2016). Job skills studies in different fields, such as marketing (Yeoh, 2019), have also benefitted from the Delphi technique. However, the Delphi technique has only been used in a few IS job skills studies, such as when identifying critical skills for managing IT projects from the perspective of IT project management experts (Keil et al., 2013). Another example is the investigation of the main tasks, necessary skills, the offshore coordinator's role in facilitating knowledge transfer in IS offshoring (Strasser et al., 2018). Delphi studies have also been traditionally used for forecasting or ranking the importance of identified factors (Yeoh, 2019), such as competencies. The present study is a ranking type of Delphi study, meaning that it uses the Delphi technique to identify and rank the mid-level management IS skills which are currently relevant to organisations in SSA.

17.3.2 Selection of Delphi Panel

For a successful Delphi study, it is important to collect data from experts who are personally involved and come from diverse or varying backgrounds (Yeoh, 2019). According to Hirschhorn (2019), this is done in two steps of identifying the relevant expertise and identifying individuals with that expertise. In this study, experts were required to be one of the following: an employer who employs IS professionals to fill mid- or senior-level management positions, an IS consultant, or a senior IS manager in a strategic management position of an organisations equivalent to chief information officers, who influence the hiring of IS professionals. These experts must have at least 10 years of experience in their respective positions. Furthermore, the experts are required to come from different geographical areas and industries to ensure expert diversity. There is, however, no consensus in the literature regarding the number of experts required in a Delphi study and how the size of the panel might influence the reliability or validity of the final consensus (Alarabiat & Ramos, 2019). Researchers argue that the knowledge and experiences of the experts are more relevant than the number of experts, with panel sizes ranging between 7 and

76 across different studies (Alarabiat & Ramos, 2019). The present study gathered a panel of 56 purposefully selected experts from different regions in SSA. The author arrived at this number after 14 of the initial 75 experts that were contacted dropped out of the study during different phases. The 56 participants who completed the responses across all phrases of the study represent a 74.67% participation rate. Table 17.4 summarises the characteristics of the experts used in this study.

17.3.3 Data Collection and Analysis Method

The author collected data from the experts in three rounds, using a modified seeding or brainstorming, narrowing down, and ranking process (Schmidt et al., 2001). Unlike Yeoh's (2019) study, there were no seeded lists given the paucity of studies

Table 17.4 Characteristics of Delphi panel experts

Industry			Country				Total
			Ethiopia	Ghana	Nigeria	South Africa	
Education	Position	IS/IT manager	2	2	1	1	6
		IS/IT lecturer	0	1	0	0	1
		HR manager	1	0	1	1	3
	Total		3	3	2	2	10
Telecommunication	Position	IS/IT manager	1	3	4	1	9
		CEO/owner managers	0	0	0	1	1
	Total		1	3	4	2	10
Media	Position	IS/IT manager	1	3	0	3	7
		Project manager	0	0	1	0	1
		CEO/owner managers	0	0	2	0	2
	Total		1	3	3	3	10
IT	Position	IS/IT manager	1	1	1	2	5
		IS/IT lecturer	0	0	1	0	1
		CEO/owner managers	0	1	0	0	1
		Systems analyst	1	1	0	0	2
	Total		2	3	2	2	9
Consulting	Position	CEO/owner managers	1	1	2	0	4
		Systems analyst	1	2	1	2	6
	Total		2	3	3	2	10
Banking	Position	IS/IT manager		3	2	2	7
	Total			3	2	2	7
TOTAL			9	15	14	13	56

that have identified IS competencies at mid- or senior-level management positions. To elicit current competencies required from IS professionals in mid- to senior-level management positions, the researchers instead asked experts to answer the following open-ended question: 'What are the knowledge, skills, and abilities currently expected from IS managers at a middle or senior management position?'

Experts were not expected to rank these competencies or put them in any particular order. The researchers collated the competencies from the experts and then deduplicated and categorised the same competencies to obtain a list of current competencies. The researchers validated the list with the experts to ensure that the same understanding of each item is maintained. The resulting list, together with additional competencies from the MSIS 2016, was sent to the experts. The researchers asked them to rank the competencies on a Likert scale of 1 (least important) to 10 (most important). The narrowing and ranking phases run concurrently to shorten the number of rounds and reduce participation fatigue (Okoli & Pawlowski, 2004). This data collection phase occurred between May and November 2020. The mean importance for each competency was obtained and ranked. Competencies with a mean importance less than 4.00 were dropped, and the new list of important competencies was sent back to the experts to rank again using the same Likert scale. For each round, a mean rank of the mentioned competencies is obtained. To assess the level of expert consensus on the importance of the competencies, we calculated Kendall's coefficient of concordance (W) for each round until we obtained strong consensus (W greater than 0.60) or the values levelled off in concurrent rounds (Schmidt et al., 2001). Figure 17.3 illustrates this process.

17.4 Results and Discussion

17.4.1 Brainstorming Phase

In total, the researchers obtained 195 competencies from the experts. These competencies were deduplicated and categorised to produce 38 distinct competencies. The experts validated these results to ensure a shared understanding of the various competencies. While some of these competencies were specified by the MSIS 2016, there were others in the MSIS 2016 that were not mentioned by the experts. We then included an additional 11 competencies from the MSIS 2016 to obtain an overall list of 49 items (see Table 17.5). These items include knowledge, skills, and self-concepts. At this stage, we unranked the competencies and placed them in no particular order.

In total, there were 18 individual foundational competencies, 27 IS specific competencies, 3 specialised IS competencies, and 1 suggestion regarding the need for a domain of practice competency. The researchers returned these lists to the experts for the next phase of the Delphi study ranking.

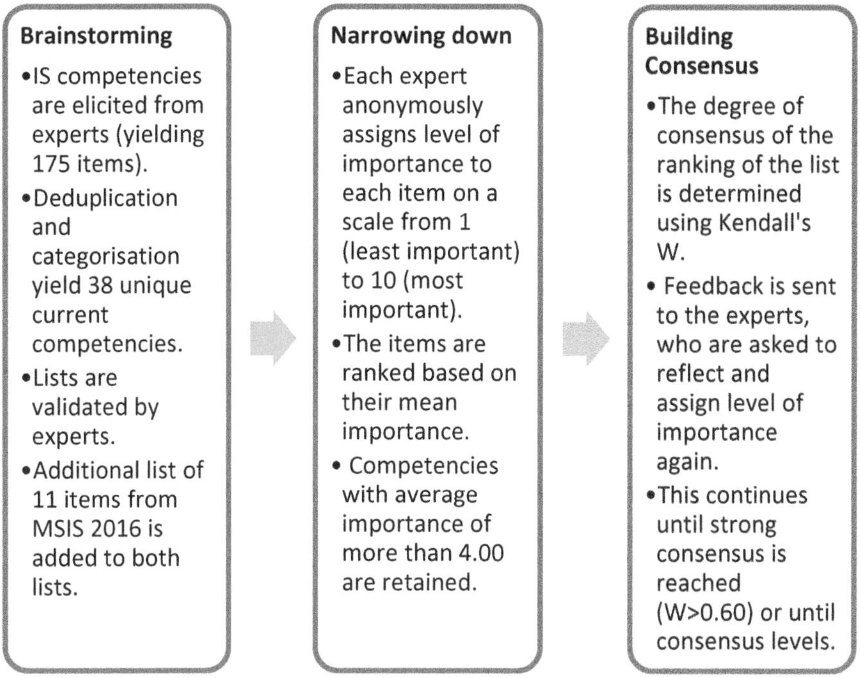

Fig. 17.3 Description of the Delphi process used in this study. (Adapted from Schmidt et al., 2001)

17.4.2 Narrowing Results Through Ranking and Building Consensus Among Experts

17.4.2.1 Current IS Competencies

The researchers asked experts to assign a value on a Likert scale of 1 (least important) to 10 (most important). Each competency item is based on how important experts feel that these competencies are to organisations. We then determined the mean importance of each competency and ranked the list based on the means. In alignment with previous studies, competencies with a mean importance less than 4.0 were rejected from the list. Table 17.5 displays the current IS competencies with their means and standard deviations.

Furthermore, we used a non-parametric test to determine the mean ranks and Kendall's coefficient of concordance (W) for this round. There was low inter-rater agreement among experts for the current IS competency rankings ($W = 0.344$). This made a second round of the ranking necessary. The researchers shared the initial first-round ranking outcomes with the experts to rethink their original ratings for the competencies. Based on the ordered competencies returned to them, the experts were required to consider their initial position regarding the importance of these competencies. This is the first opportunity for experts to observe, in aggregate, the

Table 17.5 Means and standard deviations of current IS competencies

No.	Competency	Mean	Std. deviation
1	Ability to collaborate and work with teams	9.46	0.602
2	Ability to be flexible and adapt to change	9.41	0.532
3	Monitor technology trends and innovate by exploiting an emerging method or technology	9.23	0.934
4	Ability to effectively make decisions	9.2	0.773
5	Manage IS projects and programmes and apply broadly used project management tools and techniques	9.18	0.917
6	Demonstrate an understanding of the specific business or domain processes	9.13	0.833
7	Ability to demonstrate leadership skills	9	0.953
8	Ability to demonstrate creativity	9	0.915
9	Ability to think critically	8.93	0.931
10	Manage IS development processes, including external systems development resources and contemporary practices such as DevOps	8.93	0.951
11	Ability to solve problems independently	8.91	0.959
12	Develop and implement IS/IT policies	8.88	1.129
13	Ability to negotiate with internal and external stakeholders	8.84	0.93
14	Ability to effectively manage time	8.79	1.091
15	Ability to make a financial case for IS investments	8.68	1.011
16	Conduct IS strategic analysis and planning	8.64	1.227
17	Negotiate contracts and manage infrastructure vendors	8.62	1.054
18	Engage in entrepreneurial thinking	8.57	1.024
19	Contribute to organisational development and change management	8.55	0.952
20	Implementing relevant IT governance frameworks, such as COBIT, ITIL, etc.	8.54	1.144
21	Implement and manage quality IS audit processes	8.52	1.009
22	Maintain compliance with legislation, regulations, and standards and ensure sustainability	8.5	1.009
23	Ability to demonstrate curiosity and enthusiasm for the role	8.46	0.972
24	Ability to manage business relationships	8.46	1.061
25	Manage the deployment of a new system for organisational use	8.41	1.108
26	Manage IS service production and sourcing models	8.38	1.019
27	Ability to communicate orally	8.37	1.071
28	Ability to demonstrate interpersonal skills	8.36	1.182
29	Design infrastructure solutions using external service provider(s) (cloud computing)	8.27	1.382
30	Manage the IS function and IS human capital	8.27	1.286
31	Consider the ethical implications of IS decisions	8.18	1.064
32	Ability to manage and implement IS security and risks	8.16	1.276
33	Design, build, and maintain an enterprise architecture and use it to influence organisational improvement projects	8.13	1.294
34	Ability to demonstrate written communication skills through reports	8.12	1.402

(continued)

Table 17.5 (continued)

No.	Competency	Mean	Std. deviation
35	Select and use appropriate data analytics and visualisation methods	8.11	1.186
36	Ability to resolve conflicts in a unit and the organisation	8.11	0.705
37	Ability to demonstrate intercultural competencies	8.04	1.321
38	Design data communication networks, data centre, and server solutions	7.87	1.322
39	Design and implement a data warehouse using a contemporary architectural solution	7.79	1.124
40	Ability to install, integrate, and test a new application	7.73	1.314
41	Ability to think business before technology	7.59	1.125
42	Ability to demonstrate high emotional intelligence	7.59	1.005
43	Select and implement a database management technology based on the needs of a domain	7.48	1.584
44	Plan, design, and implement a systems solution using a modern programming language	7.25	1.455
45	Ability to understand and apply artificial intelligence to specific domains for organisational benefit	7.07	1.277
46	Ability to leverage the benefits of machine learning for the organisation	6.75	1.392
47	Ability to leverage the benefits of blockchain technology for the organisation	6.64	1.407
48	Demonstrate competencies in personal productivity software skills (such as Office applications)	6.41	1.092
49	Demonstrate competencies in mathematics and statistics	5.79	1.202

Source: Author

importance other experts placed on the various competencies. Experts are then expected to reflect and use the same scale to indicate the importance of each competency. We then collected the data and prepared for analysis. We used the same non-parametric test to determine the mean rankings and Kendall's coefficient of concordance. Table 17.6 presents the results of both the first and second rankings of the IS competencies with the corresponding Kendall's coefficient of concordance. At this point, we had obtained an appreciable level of agreement among the experts ($W = 0.693$). Furthermore, we halted the ranking to avoid participation fatigue, as a number of the experts did not show interest to continue participating in the study.

With an acceptable level of agreement among experts ($W = 0.693$), the list in Table 17.7 represents, in order of importance, current IS competencies required from middle and senior IS managers in SSA. The top 10 competencies include five individual foundational competencies: ability to collaborate and work with teams, ability to be flexible and adapt to change, ability to effectively make decisions, ability to negotiate with internal and external stakeholders, and ability to demonstrate leadership. The top 10 competencies also include four specific IS competencies: monitor technology trends and innovate by exploiting an emerging method or technology, manage IS projects and programmes and apply broadly used project

Table 17.6 Initial and final ranking of mid-level management IS competencies in SSA

No.	Competency	Competency category	Round 2 mean rank	Round 1 mean rank	No.
1	Ability to collaborate and work with teams	IFC	42.84	38.72	1
2	Monitor technology trends and innovate by exploiting an emerging method or technology	ISSC	42.01	35.82	3
3	Ability to be flexible and adapt to change	IFC	40.88	37.87	2
4	Manage IS projects and programmes and apply broadly used project management tools and techniques	ISSC	40.66	34.72	5
5	Demonstrate an understanding of the specific business or domain processes	DPC	39.65	33.94	6
6	Ability to effectively make decisions	IFC	39.13	35.37	4
7	Ability to negotiate with internal and external stakeholders	IFC	39.07	31.19	13
8	Ability to demonstrate leadership skills	IFC	37.33	32.89	7
9	Develop and implement IS/IT policies	ISSC	37.14	31.89	10
10	Ability to manage and implement IS security and risks	ISSC	35.52	24.08	31
11	Engage in entrepreneurial thinking	ISSC	35.49	27.44	18
12	Ability to demonstrate creativity	IFC	34.92	32.83	8
13	Ability to solve problems independently	IFC	34.27	32.38	9
14	Ability to think critically	IFC	34.14	31.43	12
15	Ability to make a financial case for IS investments	ISSC	34.08	28.4	17
16	Manage IS development processes, including external systems development resources and contemporary practices such as DevOps	ISSC	34.07	31.63	11
17	Ability to effectively manage time	IFC	33.1	30.92	14
18	Conduct IS strategic analysis and planning	ISSC	32.09	29.03	15
19	Negotiate contracts and manage infrastructure vendors	ISSC	31.62	28.79	16
20	Implement and manage quality IS audit processes	ISSC	29.93	26.71	21
21	Ability to demonstrate curiosity and enthusiasm for the role	IFC	29.3	26.39	23
22	Ability to manage business relationships	ISSC	29.17	26.38	24
23	Implement relevant IT governance frameworks, such as COBIT, ITIL, etc.	ISSC	29.17	27.23	19
24	Maintain compliance with legislation, regulations, and standards and ensure sustainability	ISSC	29.17	26.78	20
25	Manage IS service production and sourcing models	ISSC	28.05	24.8	29
26	Contribute to organisational development and change management	ISSC	27.96	26.66	22
27	Manage the IS function and IS human capital	ISSC	25.92	24.49	30

(continued)

Table 17.6 (continued)

No.	Competency	Competency category	Round 2 mean rank	Round 1 mean rank	No.
28	Ability to communicate orally	IFC	22.55	25.79	25
29	Design infrastructure solutions using external service provider(s) (cloud computing)	ISSC	21.63	25.44	28
30	Ability to demonstrate high emotional intelligence	IFC	20.69	16.69	42
31	Manage the deployment of a new system for organisational use	ISSC	20.43	25.72	26
32	Design and implement a data warehouse using a contemporary architectural solution	ISSC	19.46	19.46	39
33	Select and use appropriate data analytics and visualisation methods	ISSC	16.27	22.72	35
34	Consider ethical implications of IS decisions	ISSC	15.25	23.24	33
35	Ability to resolve conflicts in a unit and the organisation	IFC	14.77	21.68	37
36	Select and implement a database management technology based on the needs of a domain	ISSC	14.62	17.66	41
37	Ability to install, integrate, and test a new application	ISSC	14.12	18.79	40
38	Ability to demonstrate interpersonal skills	IFC	14.04	25.54	27
39	Design data communication networks, data centre, and server solutions	ISSC	13.36	20.21	38
40	Design, build, and maintain an enterprise architecture and use it to influence organisational improvement projects	ISSC	12.82	23.11	34
41	Ability to demonstrate written communication skills through reports	IFC	12.5	23.39	32
42	Ability to demonstrate intercultural competencies	IFC	12.28	22.29	36
43	Ability to think business before technology	ISSC	12.03	16.38	43
44	Plan, design, and implement a systems solution using a modern programming language	ISSC	8.38	15.22	44
45	Ability to understand and apply artificial intelligence to specific domains for organisational benefit	SISC	8.21	11.76	45
46	Demonstrate competencies in personal productivity software skills (such as Office applications)	IFC	7.79	6.99	48
47	Ability to leverage the benefits of machine learning for the organisation	SISC	6.88	10.35	46
48	Ability to leverage the benefits of blockchain technology for the organisation	SISC	5.98	9.92	47
49	Demonstrate competencies in mathematics and statistics	IFC	4.25	3.88	49
	Kendall's W		**0.343**	**0.693**	

Source: Authors

Table 17.7 A summary of the comparison of the top 10 competencies in this study with previous studies

No	IS competency	Keil et al. (2013)	Kappelman et al. (2016)	MSIS 2016
	Individual foundational competencies			
1	Ability to collaborate and work with teams	✓	✓	✓
2	Ability to be flexible and adapt to change			
3	Ability to effectively make decisions	✓	✓	
4	Ability to negotiate with internal and external stakeholders	✓		✓
5	Ability to demonstrate leadership skills	✓		✓
6	Ability to demonstrate creativity			✓
7	Ability to solve problems independently		✓	✓
8	Ability to think critically			✓
9	**Information systems specific competencies**	✓	✓	✓
10	**Domain of practice competencies**		✓	✓

Source: Authors

management tools and techniques, develop and implement IS/IT policies, and manage and implement IS security and risks. Lastly, the top 10 competencies include the ability to demonstrate an understanding of the specific business or domain processes, which is a domain of practice competency. At the same time, specialised IS competencies, such as leveraging AI, machine learning, and blockchain technologies, were among the five lowest-rated competencies. In general, there is an emphasis on individual foundational competencies over other competencies in SSA.

17.4.3 Discussion

17.4.3.1 Important Individual Foundational Skills

Though the existing literature on IS competencies has not largely focused on the competencies of mid- and senior-level IS managers, related studies focused on similar management levels have yielded comparable results. For example, Keil et al. (2013) conducted a Delphi study to identify the most critical skills for managing IT projects. They have identified 'leadership', 'ability to motivate team members', 'good people', 'negotiation skills', and 'verbal', 'written,' and 'listening communication skills' as the top skills above technical skills. These represent individual foundational competencies. Furthermore, Kappelman et al.'s (2016) study examining what CIOs in US organisations believed were important competencies for middle IT managers has identified the following as part of the top 10 most important competencies: 'collaboration with others', 'problem-solving', 'people management', 'oral communication', 'decision-making', and 'honesty/credibility'. The MSIS 2016 also suggested the following as key individual foundational competencies: 'collaboration and teamwork', 'negotiation', 'leadership', 'written and verbal communication', and 'problem-solving'. The present study confirms similar competencies from previous studies, such as 'ability to collaborate and work with teams', 'ability to effectively make decisions', 'ability to negotiate with internal and external stakeholders', and 'ability to demonstrate leadership'. Nevertheless, this study has also identified 'ability to be flexible and adapt to change' as a new top 10 individual foundational competency that has not been reported by the existing literature. Spencer and Spencer (1993, p. 83) define flexibility or adaptability as the ability to adapt to and work effectively with a variety of situations. For example, the fast-changing technological environment of IS managers requires them to 'understand and appreciate requirements of a situation change, and to change, or easily accept changes in one's organisation or job requirements'(Spencer & Spencer, 1993, p. 84). They also have to adapt other competencies to fulfil new expectations. In contrast, this study cannot confirm 'honesty/credibility' as an important competency, and the following competencies do not appear in this study's top 10: 'communication skills', 'people (interpersonal) skills', and 'problem-solving'. From the iceberg competency model, these competencies may exist as motives, traits, self-concepts, knowledge, and skills below the iceberg. These competencies show relatively higher endurance than those between them and the very tip of the iceberg. Figure 17.4 illustrates the iceberg model based on the top 10 competencies identified in this study. Table 17.7 then summarises the results.

17.4.3.2 Domain of Practice Competencies

This study identifies the competency 'demonstrate understanding of the specific business or domain processes' among the top 10 IS competencies required from mid-level IS managers. While Keil et al. (2013) have identified this competency as important, it was relatively less important than other types of competencies and was described as a business domain skill. However, CIOs in the Kappelman et al. (2016) study rated functional area knowledge as the fifth most important competency required by mid-level IT managers. This and previous studies, confirm the MSIS 2016 classification which specifies competencies in a domain of practice such as health, education, government, business, and law as relevant. This set of competencies may exist as knowledge and skills above the IFCs but below the tip of the iceberg.

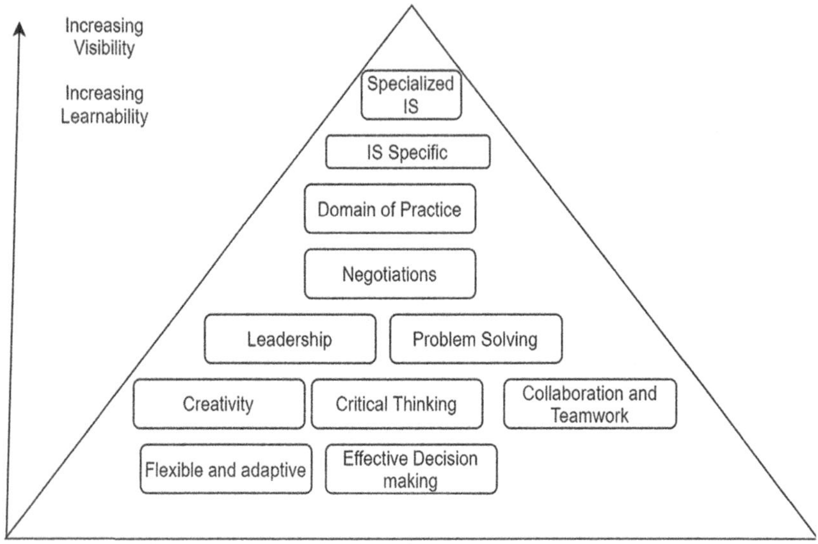

Fig. 17.4 Iceberg competency model for the top 10 competencies for mid-level IS management positions in SSA. (Based on Spencer & Spencer, 1993)

17.4.3.3 Important IS Specific Competencies

The top 10 competencies also include the following IS specific competencies: 'monitor technology trends and innovate by exploiting an emerging method or technology', 'manage IS projects and programmes and apply broadly used project management tools and techniques', 'develop and implement IS/IT policies', and 'ability to manage and implement IS security and risks'. As Keil et al. (2013) focus on competencies of IT project managers, the IS specific competencies they have identified mainly related to project management, such as 'scope management' and 'project planning'. In Kappelman et al. (2016), CIOs instead rated technical competencies among the top 10 competencies required from middle management IT professionals in the USA. All the IS specific competencies in the top 10 of this study have also been identified in the MSIS 2016. In the present study, the top IS specific competency required from middle management IS professionals is 'monitor technology trends and innovate by exploiting an emerging method or technology'. This is not unusual due to the rapidly changing nature of technology and its impact on the organisation and business processes. These competencies are mainly knowledge and skills regarding IS concepts rather than particular technologies. These competencies are above the domain of practice competencies but just below the tip of the iceberg competency model.

Table 17.7 provides a summary of the comparison of this study with previous studies. Specific competencies have been omitted to make it comparable to previous studies.

17.4.3.4 Important Specialised IS Competencies

Three (3) specialised IS competencies, though important, were ranked low among the five least important competencies. These were 'ability to understand and apply artificial intelligence to specific domains for organisational benefit', 'ability to leverage the benefits of machine learning for the organisation', and 'ability to leverage the benefits of blockchain technology for the organisation'. This phenomenon may be due to a number of reasons. First, most organisations in SSA may not have adopted information systems that depend on these technologies, which means the experts would not rank these competencies as currently important. Second, experts may be aware that these specialised technologies have shorter lifespans, may be retired in due course, or may be easily outsourced. In other words, they would rather rank relatively more enduring competencies as more important than these competencies. From the iceberg competency model, these competencies are at the very tip of the iceberg above the individual foundation and domain of practice competencies and are most influenced or shaped by environmental factors, making them susceptible to rapid change.

17.5 Implications of the Study

17.5.1 Implications for Practice

This is one of the few studies that examines IS competencies for mid-level IS managers. As a result, it provides significant implications for hiring, internal promotions, and training. Organisations in SSA may use the results (focusing on the important competencies) as a checklist of competencies they should seek out in potential hires to fill mid-level IS management positions. Similarly, this checklist may be used to determine promotions and prepare IS managers for mid-level management positions. According to Ho and Frampton (2010), competencies identified below the iceberg, which are difficult to develop through education and training, are essential to identify during the hiring process. An example from this study is the lower iceberg competency 'ability to be flexible and adapt to change', which experts identified as important for mid-level IS managers. Nevertheless, such traits may not be easily observed through traditional interviews (Spencer & Spencer, 1993). Human resource departments and hiring panels should develop creative questions or tests to determine whether prospective employees possess these competencies. Again, awareness of these competencies identified as important is critical for their acquisition through mentoring and role-playing programmes.

17.5.2 Implications for IS Education

If IS departments are to remain relevant, then the competencies students acquire from the classroom must adequately prepare them to meet industry demands (Topi et al., 2014). It is, for this reason, previous IS competency studies have gone ahead to recommend how IS curricular should be developed to meet the new competency demands by suggesting which particular courses should be taught. Most of these recommendations had been made for the undergraduate IS curriculum which prepares students for entry-level IS jobs. However, this study focused on the competencies of mid-level management IS professionals. Here, individual foundational competencies become more emphasised than IS specific and domain competencies compared to entry-level IS competencies. According to Kappelman et al. (2016), obtaining an MBA or a master's degree in IS may enhance learners preparedness to fill such mid-level management IS positions. Hence, this study may guide universities offering graduate IS programmes to provide course offerings that deliver or develops the competencies identified as highly important in this study. Though teachable IS competencies may often be at the tip of the iceberg (Ho & Frampton, 2010), making learners aware of below the iceberg competencies and also enhancing their learnability through pedagogical strategies may best prepare them for mid-level management IS positions.

17.5.3 Implications and Suggestion for Future Research

First, this study provides empirical contributions regarding the need for further research on IS competencies of mid- and top-level IS managers. This study addresses this need by eliciting IS competencies from experts from four countries in SSA using the Delphi technique. However, this study remains among a few studies in this area and requires further scholarly attention. Future research may focus on identifying competencies for different categories of IS professionals in different countries. This would enable broader comparisons to ascertain dominant and enduring competencies across a wide number of domains and contexts to inform hiring, training, and IS education. For example, a future study may focus on using statistical analysis to determine whether there is a significant difference between the mean ranks among different countries or industry expert panels. It is also important to forecast which IS competencies are likely to be relevant over time and aid in the adequate planning and preparation of the workforce.

Second, this study uses the iceberg model, which has been sparingly adopted in IS competency studies, only for analysing data. A more rigorous approach may require using the model to frame the research, develop data collection tools, and analyse IS competencies. For example, Spencer and Spencer (1993) have identified generic competencies for different organisational roles, such as salespeople, professionals, and managers, based on a competency model. This model may be extended to mid-level IS managers as in the case of this study. It is also important to examine what external factors shape these competencies beyond the rapidly changing nature of technology.

Finally, this study relies on the Delphi method to discover both visible and less visible IS competencies. This method uses the judgements of experts in the industry who have supervisory power over this employee level and understands the competency expectations. Nevertheless, this method still may not be able to fully reveal certain underlying characteristics of IS managers that make them high performers or successful in their role. Other methods, such as behavioural event interviews (Spencer & Spencer, 1993), may be used to more deeply identify both visible and less visible competencies by analysing the experiences of high-performing or successful mid-level IS managers.

References

Aasheim, C. L., Li, L., & Williams, S. (2009a). Knowledge and skill requirements for entry-level information technology workers: A comparison of industry and academia. *Journal of Information Systems Education, 20*(3), 349–357.

Aasheim, C. L., Williams, S., & Butler, E. S. (2009b). Knowledge and skill requirements for IT graduates. *Journal of Computer Information Systems, 49*(3), 48–53.

Aasheim, C., & Shropshire, J. (2012). Knowledge and skill requirements for entry-level IT workers: A longitudinal study. *Journal of Information Systems Education, 23*(2), 193–205.

Alarabiat, A., & Ramos, I. (2019). The Delphi method in information systems research (2004–2017). *Electronic Journal of Business Research Methods, 17*(2), 86–99.

Ashenhurst, R. L. (1972). Curriculum recommendations for graduate professional programs in information systems. *Communications of the ACM, 15*(5), 363–398.

Barnes, S. J., & Mattsson, J. (2016). Understanding current and future issues in collaborative consumption: A four-stage Delphi study. *Technological Forecasting & Social Change*.

Benamati, J. H., Ozdemir, Z. D., & Smith, H. J. (2010). Aligning undergraduate IS curricula with industry needs. *Communications of the ACM, 53*(3), 152–156.

Bullen, C. V., Abraham, T., Gallagher, K., Simon, J. C., & Zwieg, P. (2009). IT workforce trends: Implications for curriculum and hiring. *Communications of the Association for Information Systems, 24*(1), 129–140.

Burns, T., Gao, Y., Sherman, C., & Klein, S. (2018). Do the knowledge and skills required by employers of recent graduates of undergraduate information systems programs match the current ACM/AIS information systems curriculum guidelines? *IS Education Journal, 16*(5).

Cappel, J. J. (2002). Entry-level IS job skills: A survey of employers. *Journal of Computer Information Systems, 42*(2), 76–82.

Cheney, P. H., Hale, D. P., & Kasper, G. M. (1990). Knowledge, skills and abilities of information systems professionals: Past, present, and future. *Information and Management, 19*(4), 237–247.

Cheney, P. H., & Lyons, N. R. (1980). Information systems skill requirements: A survey. *Misq, 4*(2), 35–43. https://doi.org/10.2307/248866

Dalkey, N., & Helmer, O. (1963). An experimental application of the Delphi method to the use of experts. *Management Science, 9*(3), 458–467.

Davis, G. B. (2006). Information systems as an academic discipline. In *IFIP International Federation for Information Processing: The Past and Future of Information Systems: 1976–2006 and Beyond, 214*, 11–25.

Debuse, J., & Lawley, M. (2009). Desirable ICT graduate attributes: Theory vs. practice. *Journal of Information Systems Education*, *20*(3), 313. Retrieved from http://search.proquest.com/docview/200092949?accountid=14723

El-gazzar, R., Hustad, E., & Olsen, D. H. (2016). Understanding cloud computing adoption issues: A Delphi Study approach. *The Journal of Systems & Software*. https://doi.org/10.1016/j.jss.2016.04.061

Gallagher, K. P., Kaiser, K. M., Simon, J. C., & Beath, C. M. (2008). The requisite variety of skills for IT professionals. *Communications of the ACM*, (April).

Gangi, P. M. Di, Johnston, A. C., Worrell, J. L., & Thompson, S. C. (2017). What could possibly go wrong? A multi-panel Delphi study of organizational social media risk. *Information Systems Frontiers*. https://doi.org/10.1007/s10796-016-9714-2

Gardiner, A., Aasheim, C., Rutner, P., & Williams, S. (2017). Skill requirements in big data: A content analysis of job advertisements. *Journal of Computer Information Systems, 58*(4), 374–384.

Harris, A. H., Greer, T. H., Morris, S. A., Clark, W. J., Harris, A. H., Greer, T. H., … Greer, T. H. (2012). Information systems job market late 1970s-early 2010s information systems job market late 1970s-early 2010s. *Journal of Computer Information Systems, 53*(1), 72–79.

Hartl, E., & Hess, T. (2017). *The role of cultural values for digital transformation: Insights from a Delphi study*. In Twenty-Third Americas Conference on Information Systems, (August). Boston.

Havelka, D., & Merhout, J. (2009). Toward a theory of information technology professional competence. *Journal of Computer Information Systems, 50*(2), 106–116. https://doi.org/10.1080/08874417.2009.11645389

Hirschhorn, F. (2019). Reflections on the application of the Delphi method: Lessons from a case in public transport research from a case in public transport research. *International Journal of Social Research Methodology, 22*(3), 309–322. https://doi.org/10.1080/13645579.2018.1543841

Ho, S. Y., & Frampton, K. (2010). A competency model for the information technology workforce: Implications for training and selection. *Communications of the Association for Information Systems, 27*(1), 63–80.

Jones, K., Leonard, L. N. K., & Lang, G. (2016). Desired skills for entry level IS positions: Identification and assessment. *Journal of Computer Information Systems*, 1–7. https://doi.org/10.1080/08874417.2016.1229144

Kaiser, K. M., Goles, T., Hawk, S., Simon, J. C., & Frampton, K. (2011). Information systems skills differences between high-wage and low-wage regions: Implications for global sourcing. *Communications of the Association for Information Systems, 29*(32), 605–626.

Kappelman, L., Jones, M. C., Johnson, V., Mclean, E. R., & Boonme, K. (2016). Skills for success at different stages of an IT professional career. *Communications of the ACM, 59*(8), 64–70.

Keil, M., Lee, H. K., & Deng, T. (2013). Understanding the most critical skills for managing IT projects: A Delphi study of IT project managers. *Information and Management, 50*(7), 398–414. https://doi.org/10.1016/j.im.2013.05.005

Lang, M., Wiesche, M., & Krcmar, H. (2016). *What are the most important criteria for cloud service provider selection? A Delphi study*. In Twenty-Fourth European Conference on Information Systems. Instanbul.

Lang, M., Wiesche, M., & Krcmar, H. (2018). Criteria for selecting cloud service providers: A Delphi study of quality-of- service attributes information & management criteria for selecting cloud service providers: A Delphi study of quality-of- service attributes. *Information & Management*, (March), 1–13. https://doi.org/10.1016/j.im.2018.03.004.

Lee, C., & Han, H. (2008). Analysis of skills requirement for entry-level programmer/analysts in Fortune 500 corporations. *Journal of Information Systems Education, 19*(1), 17–27.

Lee, S., Koh, S., Yen, D., & Tang, H.-L. (2002). Perception gaps between IS academics and IS practitioners: An exploratory study. *Information and Management, 40*(1), 51–61. https://doi.org/10.1016/S0378-7206(01)00132-X

Litecky, C., Igou, A. J., & Aken, A. (2012). Skills in the management oriented IS and enterprise system job markets. *SIGMIS-CPR '12*, 35–43.

Lu, M. T., Chung, C. W., & Wang, P. (1999). Knowledge and skills of IS graduates: A Hong Kong perspective. *Journal of Computer Information Systems, 39*(2), 40–47.
Noll, C. L., & Wilkins, M. (2002). Critical skills of IS professionals: A model for curriculum development. *Journal of Information Technology Education, 1*(3).
Okoli, C., & Pawlowski, S. D. (2004). The Delphi method as a research tool: An example, design considerations and applications. *Information & Management, 42*(1), 15–29.
Osmani, M., Hindi, N., Al-Esmail, R., Weerakkody, V., Kapoor, K., & Eldabi, T. (2016). *Skills and attributes of it graduates: Evidence from employer's perspective*. In 22nd Americas Conference on Information Systems, 1–9. San Diego.
Parker, A., & Brown, I. (2019). Skills requirements for cyber security professionals: A content analysis of job descriptions in South Africa. *International Information Security Conference. Springer,2018*, 176–192.
Ponelis, S. R. (2019). *Scenarios for information and communication technology in sub-Saharan African academic libraries: A research proposal*. In Proceedings of the Fourteenth Midwest Association for Information Systems Conference, 1–3. Oshkosh, Wisconsin.
Ragowsky, A., Licker, P., Miller, J., Gefen, D., & Stern, M. (2014). Do not call me chief information officer, but chief integration officer. A summary of the 2011 Detroit CIO roundtable. *Communications of the Association for Information Systems, 34*(1), 1333–1346.
Schmidt, R., Lyytinen, K., Keil, M., & Cule, P. (2001). Identifying software project risks: An international Delphi study. *Journal of Management Information Systems, 17*(4), 5–36.
Spencer, L. M., & Spencer, S. M. (1993). *Competence at work*. Wiley.
Stefanidis, A., Fitzgerald, G., & Counsell, S. (2013). IS curriculum career tracks: A UK study. *Education + Training, 55*(3), 220–233.
Stevens, D., Totaro, M., & Zhu, Z. (2011). Assessing it critical skills and revising the MIS curriculum. *The Journal of Computer Information Systems, 51*(3), 85–95.
Strasser, A., Westner, M., & Strahringer, S. (2018). Knowledge transfer in IS offshoring: A Delphi study of the offshore coordinator role. *Journal of Systems and Information Technology, 21*(1), 36–62.
Tan, Y. L., Nakata, K., & Debra, P. (2016). Aligning IS programs with industry: Linking business analysis curricula design with the professional body. *AMCIS 2016 Proceedings*, (1995), 1–10.
Todd, P. A., McKeen, J. D., & Gallupe, R. B. (1995). The evolution of IS job skills: A content analysis of IS Job advertisements from 1970 to 1990. *MIS Quarterly, 19*(1), 1–27.
Topi, H., Conboy, K., Donnellan, B., Ramesh, V., Van Toorn, C., & Wright, R. T. (2014). Moving toward the next generation of graduate degree programs in information systems. *Communications of the Association for Information Systems, 34*(1), 693–710.
Topi, H., Karsten, H., Brown, S. A., Carvalho, João Alvaro Donnellan, B., Shen, J., Tan, B. C., & Thouin, M. F. (2017). *MSIS 2016 global competency model for graduate degree programs in information systems*. In The Joint ACM/AIS MSIS Task Force.
Topi, H., Valacich, J. S., Wright, R. T., Kaiser, K. M., Nunamaker, J. F., Jr., Sipior, J. C., & de Vreede, G.-J. (2010). IS2010: Curriculum guidelines for undergraduate degree programs in information systems. *Communications of the Association for Information Systems, 26*(1), 359–428.
Trauth, E. M., Farwell, D. W., & Lee, D. (1993). The IS expectation gap: Industry expectations versus academic preparation. *MIS Quarterly, 17*(3), 293. https://doi.org/10.2307/249773
White, G. R. T. (2016). Future applications of blockchain in business and management: A Delphi study. *Strategic Change, 26*(5), 439–451.
Yeoh, P. L. (2019). a Critical assessment of skills and knowledge for entry-level marketing jobs: A Delphi study. *Marketing Education Review, 29*(4), 242–265. https://doi.org/10.1080/10528008.2019.1661258

Mark-Oliver Kevor is a doctoral researcher in information systems. Mark-Oliver has a Masters' Degree in Information and Communications Technology and has taught a number of courses in this field at the undergraduate level. He is currently a PhD Candidate in Information Systems at the University of Ghana Business School. Mark-Oliver has research interests in information systems competencies and education and has published two book chapters and one conference paper in the area. He is currently studying for his PhD, contextualizing graduate information systems curricula for Sub-Saharan Africa.

Emmanuel Koree Boakye is an information systems doctoral researcher. He has a Masters' Degree in Information Communication Technology and is currently pursuing a Ph.D. Candidate in Information Systems at the University of Ghana Business School. Emmanuel works as a consultant for an IT firm in Ghana, in areas of information systems development and IS policy formulation. He is currently researching social media, legitimacy and microenterprise survival in his doctoral endeavour.

Index

R. Boateng et al. (eds.), *Digital Innovations, Business and Society in Africa*, Advances in Theory and Practice of Emerging Markets,
https://doi.org/10.1007/978-3-030-77987-0

The manufacturer's authorised representative in the EU is Springer Nature Customer Service Centre GmbH, Europaplatz 3, 69115 Heidelberg, Germany. If you have any concerns regarding our products, please contact ProductSafety@springernature.com

Printed and bound by CPI Group (UK) Ltd, Croydon, CR0 4YY
28/09/2026
02224061-0004